20th SIGNLL Conference on Computational Natural Language Learning (CoNLL 2016)

Berlin, Germany
11 – 12 August 2016

ISBN: 978-1-5108-2756-1

CoNLL 2016

The 20th SIGNLL Conference on Computational Natural Language Learning (CoNLL)

Proceedings of the Conference

August 11-12, 2016
Berlin, Germany

Best paper awards sponsored by Google Inc.

Google

Introduction

The 2016 Conference on Computational Natural Language Learning is the twentieth in the series of annual meetings organized by SIGNLL, the ACL special interest group on natural language learning. CoNLL 2016 will be held on August 11-12, 2016, and is co-located with the 54th annual meeting of the Association for Computational Linguistics (ACL) in Berlin, Germany.

In order to accommodate papers with extended proofs and experimental material, CoNLL 2016 accepted only long papers, allowing 9 pages of content plus unlimited pages of references and supplementary material. We received 186 submissions in total, out of which 13 had to be rejected for formal reasons, and 21 were withdrawn by the authors. Of the remaining 149 papers, 30 papers were chosen to appear in the conference program, resulting in an overall acceptance rate of 20%. All accepted papers appear here in the proceedings.

As in previous years, CoNLL 2016 features a shared task, this year on Shallow Discourse Parsing. Papers accepted for the shared task are collected in a companion volume of CoNLL 2016.

To fit the paper presentations in a 2-day program, 21 long papers were selected for oral presentation, and 9 papers were presented as posters. The papers selected for oral presentation are distributed in six main sessions. Poster presenters were given the chance to present their poster in a short oral spotlight presentation.

For the first time, CoNLL 2016 announced a special topic on statistical natural language learning beyond linear models and convex optimization. The special topic was embraced by several authors and is reflected by the invited talks given by Jürgen Schmidhuber and Fernanda Ferreira.

We would like to thank all the authors who submitted their work to CoNLL 2016, as well as the program committee for helping us select the best papers out of many high-quality submissions. We are also grateful to our invited speakers, who graciously agreed to give talks at CoNLL.

Special thanks are due to the SIGNLL board members, Xavier Carreras and Julia Hockenmaier, for their valuable advice and assistance in putting together this year's program, and to Ben Verhoeven, for maintaining the CoNLL 2016 web page. We are grateful to the ACL organization for helping us with the program, proceedings and logistics. Finally, our gratitude goes to our sponsor, Google Inc., for supporting the best paper award at CoNLL 2016.

We hope you enjoy the conference!

Yoav Goldberg and Stefan Riezler
CoNLL 2016 conference co-chairs

Organizers:

Yoav Goldberg, Bar Ilan University
Stefan Riezler, Heidelberg University

Invited Speakers:

Jürgen Schmidhuber, Institute for Artificial Intelligence (IDSIA), Lugano, Switzerland
Fernanda Ferreira, Department of Psychology, UC Davis, CA, USA

Program Committee:

Omri Abend, The Hebrew University of Jerusalem
Željko Agić, University of Copenhagen
Waleed Ammar, CMU
Yoav Artzi, Cornell University
Omid Bakhshandeh, University of Rochester
Timothy Baldwin, The University of Melbourne
Miguel Ballesteros, Pompeu Fabra University
Roy Bar-Haim, IBM Research
Yonatan Belinkov, MIT CSAIL
Jonathan Berant, Stanford University
Yonatan Bisk, ISI/USC
Michael Bloodgood, University of Maryland
Francesca Bonin, IBM Research Ireland
Chloé Braud, University of Copenhagen
Marie Candito, Univ. Paris Diderot - INRIA - Alpage
Gracinda Carvalho, Universidade Aberta
Francisco Casacuberta, Universitat Politècnica de València
Kai-Wei Chang, University of Illinois
Ming-Wei Chang, Microsoft Research
Danqi Chen, Stanford University
Colin Cherry, NRC
Christos Christodoulopoulos, University of Illinois at Urbana Champaign
Grzegorz Chrupała, Tilburg University
Volkan Cirik, Carnegie Mellon University
Alexander Clark, King's College London
Stephen Clark, University of Cambridge
Trevor Cohn, University of Melbourne
Paul Cook, University of New Brunswick
Benoit Crabbé, University Paris Diderot
Walter Daelemans, University of Antwerp, CLiPS
Dipanjan Das, Google
Georgiana Dinu, IBM Watson
Rotem Dror, Technion
Kevin Duh, Johns Hopkins University
Greg Durrett, UC Berkeley
Jacob Eisenstein, Georgia Institute of Technology
Meng Fang, The University of Melbourne

Manaal Faruqui, Carnegie Mellon University
Geli Fei, University of Illinois at Chicago
Katja Filippova, Google
George Foster, NRC
Annemarie Friedrich, Saarland University
Daniel Gildea, University of Rochester
Kevin Gimpel, Toyota Technological Institute at Chicago
Dan Goldwasser, Purdue University
Stephan Gouws, Stellenbosch University
Edward Grefenstette, Google DeepMind
Carolin Haas, Heidelberg University
Kenneth Heafield, University of Edinburgh
Felix Hieber, Amazon Research
Julian Hitschler, Heidelberg University
Julia Hockenmaier, University of Illinois Urbana-Champaign
Matthew Honnibal, Macquarie University
Andrea Horbach, Saarland University
Yufang Hou, Heidelberg University
Dirk Hovy, Center for Language Technology, University of Copenhagen
Laura Jehl, Heidelberg University
Charles Jochim, IBM Research – Dublin
Sariya Karimova, Heidelberg University
Fabio Kepler, L2F/INESC-ID and UNIPAMPA
Daniel Khashabi, University of Illinois, Urbana-Champaign
Eliyahu Kiperwasser, Bar-Ilan University
Philipp Koehn, Johns Hopkins University
Alexander Koller University of Potsdam
Mikhail Kozhevnikov, University of Saarland, Google
Julia Kreutzer, Heidelberg University
Germán Kruszewski, University of Trento
Marco Kuhlmann, Linköping University
Jonathan K. Kummerfeld, UC Berkeley
Angeliki Lazaridou, University of Trento
Richard Leibbrandt, Flinders University
Omer Levy, Bar-Ilan University
Mike Lewis, University of Washington
Wang Ling, Google DeepMind
Tal Linzen, ENS, PSL Research University
Daniel Marcu, ISI/USC
Héctor Martínez Alonso, University of Paris 7 - INRIA
Luis Marujo, Feedzai Research
Yuji Matsumoto, Nara Institute of Science and Technology
David McClosky, Google
Oren Melamud, Bar Ilan University
Marissa Milne, Flinders University of South Australia
Alessandro Moschitti, Qatar Computing Research Institute / University of Trento
Nasrin Mostafazadeh, University of Rochester
Preslav Nakov, Qatar Computing Research Institute, HBKU
Graham Neubig, Nara Institute of Science and Technology
Joakim Nivre, Uppsala University
Daniel Ortiz-Martínez, Technical University of Valencia

Miles Osborne, Bloomberg
Alexis Palmer, Heidelberg University
Denis Paperno, University of Trento
Xiaochang Peng, University of Rochester
Nghia The Pham, University of Trento
Yuval Pinter, Yahoo Labs
Barbara Plank, University of Groningen
David Powers, Flinders University
Chris Quirk, Microsoft Research
Roi Reichart, Technion - Israel Institute of Technology
Corentin Ribeyre, Univ. Paris Diderot - INRIA - ALPAGE
Brian Roark, Google
Michael Roth, University of Edinburgh
Alla Rozovskaya, Virginia Tech
Kenji Sagae, KITT.AI
Benôit Sagot, INRIA
Mark Sammons, University of Illinois at Urbana-Champaign
Shigehiko Schamoni, Heidelberg University
William Schuler, The Ohio State University
Roy Schwartz, The Hebrew University of Jerusalem
Djamé Seddah, Université Paris Sorbonne (Paris IV)
Wolfgang Seeker, spaCy GmbH
Vered Shwartz, Bar-Ilan University
Khalil Sima'an, ILLC, University of Amsterdam
Patrick Simianer, Heidelberg University
Artem Sokolov, Heidelberg University
Radu Soricut, Google
Vivek Srikumar, University of Utah
Simon Suster, University of Groningen
Anders Søgaard, University of Copenhagen
Partha Talukdar, Indian Institute of Science
Reut Tsarfaty, Open University of Israel
Oren Tsur, Harvard University
Ashish Vaswani, USC/ISI
Andreas Vlachos, University of Sheffield
Ivan Vulić, University of Cambridge
Ekaterina Vylomova, University of Melbourne
Taro Watanabe, Google
Sander Wubben, Tilburg University
Luke Zettlemoyer, University of Washington

Table of Contents

Conference Program

Thursday, August 11, 2016

9:00–9:10 **Opening**

9:10–10:30 **Session 1: Word-Level Semantics**

Generating Sentences from a Continuous Space
Samuel R. Bowman, Luke Vilnis, Oriol Vinyals, Andrew Dai, Rafal Jozefowicz and Samy Bengio

Identifying Temporal Orientation of Word Senses
Mohammed Hasanuzzaman, Gaël Dias, Stéphane Ferrari, Yann Mathet and Andy Way

Semi-supervised Clustering for Short Text via Deep Representation Learning
Zhiguo Wang, Haitao Mi and Abraham Ittycheriah

Neighborhood Mixture Model for Knowledge Base Completion
Dat Quoc Nguyen, Kairit Sirts, Lizhen Qu and Mark Johnson

10:30–11:00 **Break**

11:00–12:20   Session 2: Sentence-Level Semantics

context2vec: Learning Generic Context Embedding with Bidirectional LSTM
Oren Melamud, Jacob Goldberger and Ido Dagan

Learning to Jointly Predict Ellipsis and Comparison Structures
Omid Bakhshandeh, Alexis Cornelia Wellwood and James Allen

Event Embeddings for Semantic Script Modeling
Ashutosh Modi

Beyond Centrality and Structural Features: Learning Information Importance for Text Summarization
Markus Zopf, Eneldo Loza Mencía and Johannes Fürnkranz

12:20–12:50   SIGNLL Business Meeting

12:50–14:00   Lunch Break

14:00–15:40   Session 3: Human Language Processing

Incremental Prediction of Sentence-final Verbs: Humans versus Machines
Alvin Grissom II, Naho Orita and Jordan Boyd-Graber

A Data-driven Investigation of Corrective Feedback on Subject Omission Errors in First Language Acquisition
Sarah Hiller and Raquel Fernandez

Redefining part-of-speech classes with distributional semantic models
Andrey Kutuzov, Erik Velldal and Lilja Øvrelid

Analyzing Learner Understanding of Novel L2 Vocabulary
Rebecca Knowles, Adithya Renduchintala, Philipp Koehn and Jason Eisner

Modeling language evolution with codes that utilize context and phonetic features
Javad Nouri and Roman Yangarber

15:40–16:00   **Break**

16:00–17:15   Keynote 1: Human Processing of Disfluent Speech: Basic Findings, Theoretical
Approaches, and Implications for Natural Language Processing
Fernanda Ferreira

17:15–18:15   **Session 4: Sarcasm / Sentiment**

*Harnessing Sequence Labeling for Sarcasm Detection in Dialogue from TV Series
'Friends'*
Aditya Joshi, Vaibhav Tripathi, Pushpak Bhattacharyya and Mark J Carman

Leveraging Cognitive Features for Sentiment Analysis
Abhijit Mishra, Diptesh Kanojia, Seema Nagar, Kuntal Dey and Pushpak Bhattacharyya

Modelling Context with User Embeddings for Sarcasm Detection in Social Media
Silvio Amir, Byron C. Wallace, Hao Lyu, Paula Carvalho and Mario J. Silva

Friday, August 12, 2016

9:00–9:15 **SIGNLL Steering Committee Address**
David Powers: 20 Years Retrospect

9:15–10:30 **Keynote 2: RNNaissance**
Jürgen Schmidhuber

10:30–11:00 **Break**

11:00–12:40 **Session 5: Syntax, Named Entities, and Machine Translation**

Learning when to trust distant supervision: An application to low-resource POS tagging using cross-lingual projection
Meng Fang and Trevor Cohn

Greedy, Joint Syntactic-Semantic Parsing with Stack LSTMs
Swabha Swayamdipta, Miguel Ballesteros, Chris Dyer and Noah A. Smith

Beyond Prefix-Based Interactive Translation Prediction
Jesús González-Rubio, Daniel Ortiz Martinez, Francisco Casacuberta and Jose Miguel Benedi Ruiz

Exploring Prediction Uncertainty in Machine Translation Quality Estimation
Daniel Beck, Lucia Specia and Trevor Cohn

Cross-Lingual Named Entity Recognition via Wikification
Chen-Tse Tsai, Stephen Mayhew and Dan Roth

12:40–14:00 **Lunch Break**

14:00–15:30 **Session 6: Shared Task on Shallow Discourse Parsing**

15:30–16:00 **Break**

Friday, August 12, 2016 (continued)

16:00–16:20   **Session 7: Spotlight Presentations**

16:20–17:20   **Session 8: Posters (+ Shared Task Posters)**

Coreference in Wikipedia: Main Concept Resolution
Abbas Ghaddar and Phillippe Langlais

Event Linking with Sentential Features from Convolutional Neural Networks
Sebastian Krause, Feiyu Xu, Hans Uszkoreit and Dirk Weissenborn

Joint Learning of the Embedding of Words and Entities for Named Entity Disambiguation
Ikuya Yamada, Hiroyuki Shindo, Hideaki Takeda and Yoshiyasu Takefuji

Entity Disambiguation by Knowledge and Text Jointly Embedding
Wei Fang, Jianwen Zhang, Dilin Wang, Zheng Chen and Ming Li

Substring-based unsupervised transliteration with phonetic and contextual knowledge
Anoop Kunchukuttan, Pushpak Bhattacharyya and Mitesh M. Khapra

Abstractive Text Summarization using Sequence-to-sequence RNNs and Beyond
Ramesh Nallapati, Bowen Zhou, Cicero dos Santos, Caglar Gulcehre and Bing Xiang

Compression of Neural Machine Translation Models via Pruning
Abigail See, Minh-Thang Luong and Christopher D. Manning

Modelling the Usage of Discourse Connectives as Rational Speech Acts
Frances Yung, Kevin Duh, Taku Komura and Yuji Matsumoto

Semi-supervised Convolutional Networks for Translation Adaptation with Tiny Amount of In-domain Data
Boxing Chen and Fei Huang

17:20–18:00   **Session 9: Best Paper Awards + Closing**

Human Processing of Disfluent Speech:
Basic Findings, Theoretical Approaches, and Implications for Natural Language Processing

Fernanda Ferreira

Abstract   Disfluencies occur in human speech at the rate of about one per minute; therefore, any adequate theory of human language comprehension must explain how listeners process utterances containing them. Our theoretical approach is based on a 15-year program of research that has uncovered a number of fundamental mechanisms enabling humans to process disfluencies efficiently, including mechanisms that are backward looking (reanalysis of the input) and ones that are anticipatory or forward looking (prediction). This presentation will review the theory, the evidence that supports it, and the outstanding questions that are currently being investigated. I will also consider implications for refining NLP systems, which must be robust to speaker error and which should be capable of adapting to characteristics of particular speakers and language communities.

Biography of Speaker   Fernanda Ferreira is Professor of Psychology and Member of the Graduate Group in Linguistics at the University of California, Davis. She obtained her Ph.D. in Cognitive Psychology in 1988 from the University of Massachusetts, Amherst, and prior to moving to UC Davis in 2015, she held faculty positions at Michigan State University and the University of Edinburgh. She has published over 100 papers and her research has been funded by the NSF and the NIH in the US, and the ESRC in the UK. She served as Editor in Chief of the Journal of Experimental Psychology: General, and she is currently an Associate Editor of Cognitive Psychology and of Collabra, an Open Access journal recently launched by University of California Press. She is a Fellow of the American Psychological Society and the Royal Society of Edinburgh, and she is currently an elected member of the Psychonomic Society's Governing Board.

Keynote Talk

RNNaissance

Jürgen Schmidhuber

Abstract   Our deep learning artificial neural networks have won numerous contests in pattern recognition and machine learning. They are now widely used by the world's most valuable public companies. In particular, Long Short-Term Memory (LSTM) Recurrent Neural Networks (RNNs) are very useful not only for speech recognition but also for Computational Language Learning. I will discuss state-of-the-art results in numerous applications.

Biography of Speaker   Since age 15 or so, the main goal of professor Jürgen Schmidhuber has been to build a self-improving Artificial Intelligence (AI) smarter than himself, then retire. He has pioneered self-improving general problem solvers since 1987, and Deep Learning Neural Networks (NNs) since 1991. The recurrent NNs developed by his research groups at the Swiss AI Lab IDSIA (USI & SUPSI) & TU Munich were the first to win official international contests. They have revolutionized handwriting recognition, speech recognition, machine translation, image captioning, and are now available to over a billion users through Google, Microsoft, IBM, Baidu, and many other companies. DeepMind is heavily influenced by his lab's former students (including 2 of DeepMind's first 4 members and their first PhDs in AI, one of them co-founder, one of them first employee). His team's Deep Learners were the first to win object detection and image segmentation contests, and achieved the world's first superhuman visual classification results, winning nine international competitions in machine learning & pattern recognition (more than any other team). They also were the first to learn control policies directly from high-dimensional sensory input using reinforcement learning. His research group also established the field of mathematically rigorous universal AI and optimal universal problem solvers. His formal theory of creativity & curiosity & fun explains art, science, music, and humor. He also generalized algorithmic information theory and the many-worlds theory of physics, and introduced the concept of Low-Complexity Art, the information age's extreme form of minimal art. Since 2009 he has been member of the European Academy of Sciences and Arts. He has published 333 peer-reviewed papers, earned seven best paper/best video awards, the 2013 Helmholtz Award of the International Neural Networks Society, and the 2016 IEEE Neural Networks Pioneer Award. He is also president of NNAISENSE, which aims at building the first practical general purpose AI.

Computational Natural Language Learning:
$\pm$20years $\pm$Data $\pm$Features $\pm$Multimodal $\pm$Bioplausible

David M. W. Powers
Artificial Intelligence and Cognitive Science Group
School of Computer Science, Engineering and Mathematics
Flinders University, Adelaide, South Australia
David.Powers@flinders.edu.au

Abstract

This speech celebrates the 20th anniversary of the CoNLL conference and looks back 20 years before CoNLL and 20 years into the future in an attempt to paint a longterm roadmap of Computational Natural Language Learning. The founders of CoNLL agonized hard and long over what to call our nascent field, and how to ensure that we kept all the interdisciplinary diversity that we had in those early days, including preserving the richness of views in a field that encompassed many controversies. We will explore this diversity with a focus on new directions that are developing; we will reflect on the changing nature of our technology including the deceleration of Moore's Law and the emergence of Big Data; and we will consider the impact of and on ubiquitous technologies ranging from wearables to multimedia, from intelligent phones to driverless cars.

1 Introduction

Machine Learning has moved out of the lab and into the field, and the explosion of language-related learning-research is a massive part of this. Companies like Google, Facebook and Amazon, as well as IBM, Apple and Microsoft, have emerged as huge players in our playground, and important sponsors!

One of the most important changes we've seen over the last two decades is that we've fallen off the Moore's Law curve as far as single core processors are concerned[1] - for CoNLL's first decade SPECInt performance was a around 50%, for our second decade it was more like 20% and according to NVidia it looks like being more like 5% for the next decade. The emphasis must now be on working smart and processing in parallel, but at the same time we are introducing much higher software and data overheads with managed code and extensive markup.

20 years ago few households had a personal computer or a mobile phone, while today few western families wouldn't possess a range of equipment from phones to pads to MP-players to cars and the list goes on with microwaves, washing machines and airconditioners, averaging over 20 processing units per household. All of these can be expected to be part of the Internet of Things in the very near future. Recent developments are not focussing on doing more with our computers, but using our computers more flexibly and universally, with "the cloud" and "hands free" operation being major drivers of the technology race, with language technology "in the cloud" helping to deal with spoken or typed operations that would until recently have been regarded as office functions, with call centres being outsourced to computers, with IBM's Watson challenging the quizmasters at their own game, in their own language, and moving onto a wide range of "Cognitive Computing" applications. I will focus initially on this changing context.

The Association for Computational Linguistics reached 50 recently, starting with a strong focus on Machine Translation that was originally part of the name, and SIGNLL affiliated itself with ACL in 1993 to reflect our driving interest in language[2]: "Computational Linguistics is the scientific study of language from a computational perspective... providing computational models of various kinds of linguistic phenomena."

---

[1] http://preshing.com/20120208/a-look-back-at-single-threaded-cpu-performance

[2] http://www.aclweb.org/portal/what-is-cl

Proceedings of the 20th SIGNLL Conference on Computational Natural Language Learning (CoNLL), pages 1–9,
Berlin, Germany, August 7-12, 2016. ©2016 Association for Computational Linguistics

Artificial Intelligence is at least 60 years old, and SIGNLL adopted the "Natural Language" teminology of AI to make the connection to a rich history of AI research in NL that seldom, however, made use of Machine Learning, and rarely considered the Linguistic and Psycholinguistic problems of how human language works and how children learn language. But we didn't want NLL to be seen as just another application of Machine Learning, particularly as we (and our sister SIG-DAT) developed increasingly large and expensive resources, including tagged corpora. Thus we moved away from the name "Machine Learning of Natural Language" which was the title of the book based on my own PhD thesis (Powers and Turk, 1989) while the AAAI event I organized added "and Ontology" (Powers, 1991a).

It is worth citing the aims of SIGNLL as presented to ACL when we formalized our affiliation as a SIG, and noting that all areas of language and ontology, linguistics and psycholinguistics, are intended to be in scope for SIGNLL and CoNLL:

SIGNLL aims to promote research in:

- automated acquisition of syntax, morphology and phonology

- automated acquisition of semantic and ontological structure

- automated acquisition of inter-linguistic correspondences

- learning to recognize or produce spoken and written forms

- modelling human language acquisition theory and processes[3]

I reviewed over the last couple of days CoNLL's two full decades of proceedings, but its hard to single out some for special attention when others are equally worthy. So I will instead review from the perspective of a set of "±features", of *computation* and *language* and *learning*, that are I feel becoming increasingly important to CoNLL, and will set the stage for the next two decades. In relation to the SIGNLL aims, my feature-driven wandering will visit each of them broadly, but I see huge opportunity for crossover between these five categories and their internal subareas. So rather than separating them arbitrarily, I will draw them

together, emphasizing aspects that I think are important to the future of the field as a whole. I particularly want to encourage interdisciplinary collaboration and a Computational Cognitive Science (CoCoSci) that not only seeks to engineer better technologies, but also seeks to exploit and model and inform our understanding of human language and cognition.

From the beginning, SIGNLL and CoNLL promoted and welcomed interdisciplinary researchers and collaborations, but today most of us have a primary background in computing, and we attract mainly computing and engineering students. While the founders of CoNLL all had very interdisciplinary background, it is a daunting prospect to try to keep up with related fields when our own has grown so massive. In conclusion, I will make some suggestions as to how we can address this.

2 ±Applications

One of the new buzzwords the last two decades have brought is "Applications" or "Apps". When we set up SIGNLL we boringly referred to "software and data", and APIs were libraries, and tools and applications weren't distinguished; personal computers didn't have real user level multiprocessing capabilities, and it was only after founding SIGNLL in 1993 that the path through Windows 95/98/XP opened up the PC world, and Apple made its resurgence with the iMac and OSX, while SUN with Java started to blur the distinction between computer and network.

Software as a commodity is probably the biggest single change to the scene since CoNLL was started, and this is reflected in CoNLL through our sponsorships and the major corporate labs in this area. But the new challenge for us is mobility in a borderless world-wide cloud... Already the World Wide Web, and Google, with the web as a data resource, and information retrieval as a major application and focus for research, are putting a new complexion on our field. And now the mobile age has arrived and Apps on phones offer unprecedented ubiquitous interactivity, with new demands on language technology ranging from speech recognition to automated help desk, to instant speakable machine translation, to educational games and location-aware monitoring and advice.

The older focus on Machine Translation and Speech Recognition, which brought AI into dis-

---

[3]`http://ifarm.nl/signll/about/`

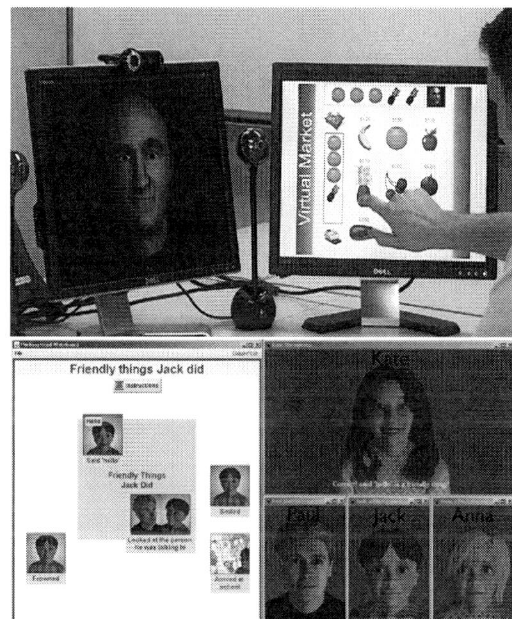

Figure 1: ECAs for teaching children in 2008 & 2010 and assisting the elderly in 2010 & 2015 (AnnaCares.com)

repute in the 1960s and 1970s with overconfident claims and predictions, has now resurged with successes due largely to the Big Data resources available (particularly to search engine companies) as well as the huge parallel computational resources available (particularly to search engine companies) and the ability to drive our statistical machine learning or artificial network tools harder and deeper (as exploited by the same companies). Now the challenge is to get these technologies into a mobile format that is interactive and dynamic, location and activity aware, and not so dependent on instant cheap access to the cloud.

We also have new and rich opportunity to collect data from these ubiquitous, multisensor devices and their increasingly intelligent Apps. We can do eyetracking, we are already developing applications that improve speech recognition and machine translation by offering choices, and a major research direction of mine is Unconscious Computer Interface where these choices and corrections are made below the level of consciousness, like our everyday articulation choices in speech and writing. This tracking and choice data is an immensely rich resource, but is also associated with ethical and privacy considerations, so it is best used for dynamic online training on device.

Traditionally, CoNLL's focus has been on *understanding* language, although Machine Translation has transferred to same-language paraphrase and summarization, and multilingual representation can be useful for monolingual *generation*. Additionally, CoNLL's focus has been on *learning* language, but from the beginning we have also interacted with the Computer Assisted Language Learning community, and there are interesting synergies as the resources and techniques developed for language learning are turned into *teaching* Apps. We've developed systems for teaching English (Powers et al., 2008; Anderson et al., 2008; Chiu et al., 2012; Anderson et al., 2012), teaching social skills to children with autism (Milne et al., 2010), as well as applications in aged care and health space[4] (Powers et al., 2010). These recent systems incorporate bots and games and simulated environments into talking/thinking/teaching heads and Embodied Conversational Agents (ECAs), while allowing us to understand the effect of different features of the system on human acceptability, understanding and

---

[4] http://annacares.com

learning (Stevens et al., 2016). An interesting 'uncanny valley' aspect of this has been our regression from human-indistinguishable disembodied heads to cartoon-like embodied agents, while at the same time controlling age, sex and ethnicity components as determined by focus groups for each application (Fig. 1).

Could we put more Mobile Apps into CoNLL?

3 ±Parallelism

Parallel computers, distributed computers, the internet and the cloud, are complemented by naturally parallel paradigms, include the Functional/Logic Programming paradigms, or the Map-Reduce paradigm that seems to have taken on a life of its own, and of course the Parallel Distributed Processing of the Artificial Neural Network. The brain is of course massively parallel, but at the same time spoken language and conscious thought are both intrinsically sequential.

When we founded SIGNLL and CoNLL, there were several competing massive custom-designed supercomputers out there, but the time and dollar cost of the custom design meant that they were seldom really that much ahead of the mainstream servers. It was actually animation, games and graphical hardware that drove parallelism to the mainstream, with the incorporation of GPUs in most modern PCs, and the development of the GPGPU and Intel's Phi, bringing enormous power to our fingertips - as well as NVidia's supercomputer (and deep learning network) in a box.[5]

Many of our *low level* operations can be performed in parallel - as elementary keyword lookups are performed in search, with AND and OR operations turning into streaming INTERSECT and UNION operations. Semantic networks and activation models are naturally parallel, as are Artificial Neural Networks. Yet the regular systolic nature of current ANNs is highly suited to GPU architectures, and there is significant challenge associated with exploiting them for more *ad hoc* network structures.

On the other hand *high level* modularity and multimodality naturally give rise to components that effectively run in parallel but need to coordinate efficiently. For example our HeadX (Luerssen et al., 2010) employs both shared memory and socket streams to coordinate speech and face synthesis while managing keyboard, mouse and speech interactivity. Although our focus on language might seems straightforward when we consider text, the natural form of language is speech, and the natural grounding of semantics in our physical, social and cultural world. Processing video for person, face, lip and eye tracking is an increasing load as NLL moves out of the lab and into a multimodal world, sensed through a phone with limited power in terms of both processing and battery capacity.

Furthermore, much of our limited power, along with the subtle features embedded in our data, is lost in repeated compression and decompression, as well as dealing with massive amounts of multiple kinds markup that must be selectively processed or skipped when embedded in a sequential stream. Conversely, access to and addition of additional streams of annotation is more efficiently achieved in a distributed parallel way,[6] and we are not only producing synchronized parallel streams for individual microphones and cameras, but for subregions and macroblocks, and image frames, and unidirectional and bidirectional prediction frames that provide information about motion and allow utilizing information about attention.

Parallelism will be increasingly key to CoNLL.

4 ±Data

The research of SIGNLL, like its sister SIGDAT, is driven by data, often Big Data. My own interest is more on unsupervised learning (Powers, 1984; Powers, 1991b; Leibbrandt and Powers, 2012), but even unsupervised systems need to be evaluated, and formal evaluation was a missing element in our early research. For supervised learning, annotated data is essential, and the Penn Treebank (Marcus et al., 1993) was a great resource in those early days and is still influential today.

In his presentation for the 10th anniversary of CoNLL, Walter Daelemans (2006) notes that there are huge costs in developing such corpora, that there are issues with annotator agreement, and that our trained systems might give high overall accuracies, or low error rates, but for key ambiguity problems error rates of 20-30% are common - and my own exploration of "problems" with my unsupervised learning using BNC2 for evaluation actually showed that BNC tags were wrong as much as

---

[5] http://www.nvidia.com/object/deep-learning-system.html

[6] http://alveo.edu.au/

60% of the time for certain specialized cases (e.g. for the PoS labeling of "work" in "going to work" the *corpus* tags have an accuracy of only 39.1%).

We need more of a focus on understanding our data, ensuring it is clean and accurate, and that the numbers that we use to characterize its accuracy are actually reflective of the hard cases rather than just the easy cases (Entwisle and Powers, 1998). Zipf's law tells us that the top 150 words of English suffice to account for half the tokens of running English text, and these and other functional words, as well as words with unambiguous or highly predictive affixes, quickly leads us to what in normal accuracy terms would be regarded as a creditable performance. This is a particular case of the 80:20 rule - the first 80% of accuracy is achieved very easily. Another sign of the problem with our tagging and parsing is limiting consideration to sentences of 40 words or less.

A further problem with corpora is that they wear out quickly! That is datasets get overused, and we treat them as an ML resource where we try to tweak every last percentage point of accuracy, using every trick in the book, but in the end with 0.05 significance testing one in twenty researchers is likely to show an improvement over their baseline system just by being different - adding noise can do the trick! As Cohen (1994) suggests, Statistical Hypothesis Inference Testing is worthy of its acronym.

We need further work on developing good corpora, including multimodal corpora where this is a richer basis for unsupervised learning, and for automated validation and correction, that is not just text corpora with syntactic or semantic annotations, but corpora involving audio-visual speech and longitudinal contextual data (Roy, 2009). One driving force of this is having the same data available for CoNLL as babies have when they are learning data, but another is the Memories4Life GrandChallenge of capturing all the important moments of our lives and exploiting the ubiquitous computing and audiovisual resources of today's mobile devices, with practical applications already being developed for alleviating dementia.

Data will continue to be pivotal to CoNLL.

5   ±Features

In the previous section, I mentioned the issue with tags for supervised training and/or evaluation of systems. Now I want to focus more on the development and evaluation of the utility of unsupervised features, and to connect back to our Apps as I propose once again an approach that allows this through the use of application-oriented evaluation Powers(1991a; 2005) - don't try to evaluate tags or features or structures directly, but comparatively in real world (or in early stages toy world) applications. Often when we talk about features we think specifically of features in visual, auditory or other signals. This is indeed what I am talking about – linguistic features derive from these modalities.

One special case is unsupervised discovery of tags, including both syntactic (PoS) and semantic tags. Much of the "unsupervised" learning we see at CoNLL already assumes a "linguistically" motivated set of tags, and often a pre-tagged corpus, for which there is no psychological, neurological or other empirical evidence other than professors/linguists have managed to formalize some kind of system and students/annotators have managed to learn the system.

If we think of the tagging and parsing with the tags as their "applications", we then have a special case of the proposal in the previous section to compare systems based on evaluation of the application, but in the end I'd still like to take it to a real world application eventually - after all nobody actually knows (yet) how we process language in our heads, and understanding this is our fifth goal. The same learning techniques applied to different sets of tags gives us a comparison - but we must be sure to use an evaluation technique that doesn't implicitly bias when we have different numbers of classes (Powers, 2008). Furthermore when we do compare techniques or parameterizations or tweak biases and thresholds, we should be wondering whether the difference are real and bioplausible, and whether they are universal or an artefact of specific data.

Tags are in fact a special kind of feature in that they are descrete and there are few enough of them to give them names (outside of Categorial Grammar). Letters of the alphabet (graphemes) also belong to this special subclass by definition, and similarly by assumption the same applies to other emic units (e.g. phonemes and morphemes, including affixes and functional words). The situation is more difficult at the level of words and sentences - I actually have my doubts as to whether those are real units psychologically in pre-literate language, as they are defined somewhat arbitrarily by the placement of punctuation: why 'out of' and not 'into' - and what is the current status of 'upto'? Is it 'today' or 'to-day' or 'to day' or 'the day'; is it 'one of' or 'one off', 'would have' or 'would of'? Do these units even have well-defined boundaries in speech? Can we tell which word a particular speech code vector actually belongs to? And all this is without descending to the etic level... There is an intrinsically fuzzy aspect to language, and it is hugely context dependent in a way that transcends the traditional phonetic, morphemic, syntactic and semantic levels implicit in CoNLL's first two aims. But it is in working towards the last two aims, in a ubiquitous, mobile, multimodal context, that we will effectively address the dynamics of language, and finally resolve all the fuzziness and ambiguity.

CoNLL will discover new vistas of features.

6 ±Multimodal

CoNLL has been very successful in relation to SIGNLL's first three "automated acquisition" aims! But what of the fourth "[hand]written and spoken" aim? And have we really got "semantics" and "ontology" under control as per the second aim? Since I first used it in the early 1980s, and incorporated it in my 1991 symposium title and the SIGNLL aims, the word "ontology" has come to mean something more like "taxonomy" rather than its traditional and etymological idea of "our understanding of the world". In the 1980s our focus was in trying to find an alternative to the word "semantics", which in practice was becoming "look it up in the dictionary" or "follow a link in a semantic net".

Feldman et al. (1990) introduced the idea of L0 as the basic bootstrap language task based on a simple toy world model, while Harnad (1987; 1990; 1991) used the term "symbol grounding" and argued strongly that even simulated worlds weren't enough, and earlier still (Hayes, 1979) had used the phrase "naive physics" to describe what he thought was needed.

Between 1984 and 1991 my students had developed and were using the Magrathea robot world extension to Prolog (Powers and Turk, 1989) but between 1995 and 1997 we built a physical humanoid baby that could crawl, feel touch to arms and legs, had omnidirectional auditory perception and stereovision, and could orient towards a touch or sound, and "feed" (charge and download) via a USB bottle/umbilical, but it was a brittle heavy system that was not suitable for a child to "mother" as originally envisaged (Powers, 2001), so that I eventually transitioned to the model of an Intelligent Room with half a dozen microphones and cameras.

Luc Steels (1995; 1997; 2003; 2015) adopted a simpler approach, transitioning from simple graphical animations, to turtle-like robots to a pair of cameras that viewed a "real world scene" that was constrained to be very simple (manipulation of cutout shapes on a board), and produced some very interesting interactions and learning.

There's another advantage to multimodal data, that is that you can use supervised techniques in a directed but unsupervised way. The 1980s idea of (holographic) autocoding of the input to self-organize features, can become a more efficient and bioplausible system where intramodal feature discovery and intermodal feature discovery are distinguished - for example visemes can be self-organized as facial/lip patterns that correlate to certain groups of phonemes. The use of multimodal autosupervision allows more bioplausible features to be self-organized, as well as facilitating a cognitive approach to learning phonology, morphology, syntax and semantics (Powers, 1997). An additional advantage is that techniques like eye-tracking and gaze-tracking can augment our user interfaces and help identify context or distinguish alternatives, boosting the accuracy of our NLL systems.

Today, Google Glass and Microsoft's Hololens (with Kinect-like 3D), are examples of the integration of multiple cameras and microphones, and a heads-up augmented-reality type display, into an efficient platform that can keep track of the 3D world in a way that will naturally complement speech capabilities as well as augment the capabilities of language learning with its richer data.

Multimodal will open a door to a new CoNLL.

7 ±Bioplausibility

So we are now up to the final "modeling human language acquisition" aim. In the end, language is a product of human biology and ecology, but Linguistics and Computational Linguistics have largely been developing without any input from Biology, Psychology or Neuroscience although there are interesting crossovers, and CoNLL has always strongly encouraged the modelling of human language acquisition theory and processes, and we do get a trickle of papers with a Psycholinguistic flavour. But I would encourage the CoNLL community to look beyond Computational Linguistics and Artificial Intelligence to the evidence being amassed in Computational Neuroscience and Cognitive Psychology, and to seek to connect to people studying language and learning from these different perspectives.

There is no compelling reason we have to make our systems bioplausible, and just because we use a neural network doesn't necessarily make it bioplausible model. But there are advantages in taking on board this aim. Indeed the introduction of neural and computational plausibility revolutionized the behavioural and cognitive sciences, with terms like neurons and agents replacing vague concepts from earlier theories of Psychology and Philosophy as they talked about demons (Selfridge, 1959) and zombies (Dennett, 1995), with the zombie argument turning up in AI in the well known guise of Mary's Room (Jackson, 1986) and the Chinese Room (Searle, 1980). Philosophers tend to shift the focus from Turing's (1950) behavioural test of indistinguishability of language performance (as a surrogate for behaviour and cognition in general), to mind, consciousness, awareness and feelings, while Computational Neuropsychology seeks to model what we find in the brain and show how that can explain and reproduce human-like language and behaviour.

Part of SIGNLL and CoNLL's charter includes the understanding and modeling of the behaviour of another, the theory of mind, as a component that is absolutely necessary for conversation, for effective communication and learning, for understanding the affective, emotional and physical states of the person we are talking to, and for understanding the human factors of the interfaces we are building.

So beyond just looking at the latest work across CoCoSci, we could be looking at our language learning systems as scientific models in their own right, or looking at interdisciplinary theories as a basis for our systems, and presenting them in a way that makes them into behaviourally, biologically and computationally plausible hypotheses and theories that are testable by their predictions about human behaviour (Popper, 1934; Popper, 1963; Lakatos, 1970).

We thus encourage collaborations with other parts of Cognitive Science who can help us improve and extend our language learning models, as well as help others keep their theories computationally realistic. CoNLL system may well give insights to other disciplines, and certainly our methodologies can and should be utilized in cognitive programs, more over our tools can help with their data collection and behavioural analysis (Stevens et al., 2016).

CoNLL is key to unlocking the human psyche.

8 ±20 Years

SIGNLL and CoNLL were born *into* an environment where Cognitive Science had brought people out of their silos and interdisciplinary research and computational modeling were recognized as essential to a proper understanding of language and cognition. Indeed Cognitive Science was born *out of* the controversies over language and learning: what was innate, what was learned, and what was biologically and computationally feasible.

This is a story for another time, and indeed one of SIGNLL's sponsored workshops, Cognitive Aspects of Natural Language Learning (CACLL) is continuing the debate as another stream during CoNLL/ACL, and there are other relevant workshops on Morphology and Phonology, and Representations and Evaluations, etc. Workshops have driven advances in the application of unsupervised and semisupervised learning, as well as covering some of the more forward thinking application areas like Companionable Dialog Systems. We don't regard them as in competition with CoNLL, but we actively sponsor workshops as additional streams that allow a focus that is not possible in the main thread of CoNLL - our sponsored workshops are just as much a part of CoNLL as of ACL, and often they capture elements that are emerging in CoNLL and will be important in the future!

While our successes with taggers and parsers and semantic models, and their applications in information retrieval and machine translation and intelligent assistants, will remain the bread and butter for CoNLL, we actively encourage people to be proactive and propose workshops and tutorials that will broaden the background of CoNLL researchers as Speech and Language become pivotal in a mobile, wearable age of ubiquitious computing and communication. It is also impressive to see how important the shared tasks have been in setting directions, and becoming a focus for future years - and we aim to improve the way in which these are made available for future use, comparison and evaluation. Your suggestions about shared tasks will also be most welcome.

In the next 20 years, I expect ubiquitous longitudinal multimodal multiangle multidirectional data, wearable processing, and cloud connectivity, will multiply both the opportunities and the challenges for CoNLL, and of course lead to further successes and new technologies to wow the world one year, and be taken for granted the next.

I hope we will make similar progress in understanding the human that wears the tech, in exploring the similarities and differences between Artificial Intelligences and Human Intelligence.

CoNLL has an exciting future ahead.

Acknowledgments

At every conference I attend, there is someone new that makes me think, that offers a challenge or provides a new direction or solution. But I would particularly like to thank Walter Daelemans and Richard Leibbrandt for being a sounding board, for keeping me honest, and for being my partners in old and new ventures - and in particlar the recent launch of the Springer Open Access journal Computational Cognitive Science[7] (see Powers (2015)) - which was designed as a venue that puts the Computational back into Cognitive Science and the Cognitive back into Computational Intelligence/CoNLL (and is currently APC-free).

CCS would be a place to expand your work into papers that seek to be both cognitively and computationally plausible - a rare animal I'm afraid! We also try to publish special themes directed at a broad audience, allowing people to explore and gain background from different perspectives.

References

Tom AF Anderson, Wu-Yuin Hwang, and Ching-Hua Hsieh. 2008. A study of a mobile collaborative learning system for chinese language learning. In *Proceedings of International Conference on Computers in Education*, pages 217–222.

Tom AF Anderson, Zhi-Hong Chen, Yean-Fu Wen, Marissa Milne, Adham Atyabi, Kenneth Treharne, Takeshi Matsumoto, Xi-Bin Jia, Martin Luerssen, Trent Lewis, Richard Leibbrandt, and David M. W. Powers. 2012. Thinking head mulsemedia. In *Multiple Sensorial Media Advances and Applications: New Developments in MulSeMedia*. IGI Global.

Yi-Hui Chiu, Tom A. F. Anderson, and David M. W. Powers. 2012. Dubbing of virtual embodied conversation agents for improving pronunciation. In *Fifteenth International CALL Conference*, pages 188–193. Taylor and Francis.

Jacob Cohen. 1994. The earth is round (p ¡ .05). *American Psychologist*, 12:997–1003.

Walter Daelemans. 2006. A mission for computational natural language learning. In *Proceedings of the Tenth Conference on Computational Natural Language Learning (CoNLL-X)*, pages 1–5, New York City, June. Association for Computational Linguistics.

Daniel Dennett. 1995. The unimagined preposterousness of zombies. *Journal of Consciousness Studies*, 2(4):322–326.

Jim Entwisle and David M. W. Powers. 1998. The present use of statistics in the evaluation of nlp parsers. In *Joint Conferences on New Methods in Language Processing and Computational Natural Language Learning (NeMLaP/CoNLL*, pages 215–224.

Jerome A. Feldman, George Lakoff, Andreas Stolcke, and Susan H. Weber. 1990. Miniature language acquisition: A touchstone for cognitive science. *Ann. Conf. of the Cog. Sci. Soc.*, pages 686–693.

Stevan Harnad, S. J. Hanson, and J. Lubin. 1991. Categorical perception and the evolution of supervised learning in neural nets. In David M. W. Powers, editor, *AAAI Spring Symposium on Machine Learning of Natural Language and Ontology*.

Stevan Harnad. 1987. *Categorical perception: The groundwork of Cognition*. Cambridge Univ. Press, New York NY.

Stevan Harnad. 1990. The symbol grounding problem. *Physica D*, 42:335–346.

Pat J. Hayes. 1979. The naive physics manifesto. *in Expert Systems in the Micro-electronics Age*, 1979:242–270.

Frank Jackson. 1986. What mary didn't know. *Journal of Philosophy*, 83:291–295.

Musgrave Lakatos, editor. 1970. *Criticism and the Growth of Knowledge*. Cambridge Univ. Press., Cambridge. ISBN 0-521-07826-1.

Richard E Leibbrandt and David M. W. Powers. 2012. Robust induction of parts-of-speech in child-directed language by co-clustering of words and contexts. In *Proceedings of the Joint Workshop on Unsupervised and Semi-Supervised Learning in NLP*, pages 44–54. Association for Computational Linguistics.

---

[7]//computationalcognitivescience.com

Martin Luerssen, Trent Lewis, and David Powers. 2010. Head x: Customizable audiovisual synthesis for a multi-purpose virtual head. In *Australasian Joint Conference on Artificial Intelligence*, pages 486–495. Springer.

Mitchell P Marcus, Mary Ann Marcinkiewicz, and Beatrice Santorini. 1993. Building a large annotated corpus of english: The penn treebank. *Computational linguistics*, 19(2):313–330.

Marissa Milne, Martin H Luerssen, Trent W Lewis, Richard E Leibbrandt, and David MW Powers. 2010. Development of a virtual agent based social tutor for children with autism spectrum disorders. In *The 2010 International Joint Conference on Neural Networks (IJCNN)*, pages 1–9. IEEE.

Karl Popper. 1934. *The Logic of Scientific Discovery*. Routledge. (1959 trans: Logik der Forschung).

Karl Popper. 1963. *Conjectures and Refutations: The Growth of Scientific Knowledge*. Harper and Row.

David M. W. Powers and Chris Turk. 1989. *Machine Learning of Natural Language*. Springer.

David Powers, Richard Leibbrandt, Martin Luerssen, Trent Lewis, and Mike Lawson. 2008. Peta: a pedagogical embodied teaching agent. In *Proceedings of the 1st international conference on PErvasive Technologies Related to Assistive Environments*, page 60. ACM.

David MW Powers, Martin H Luerssen, Trent W Lewis, Richard E Leibbrandt, Marissa Milne, John Pashalis, and Kenneth Treharne. 2010. Mana for the ageing. In *Proceedings of the 2010 Workshop on Companionable Dialogue Systems*, pages 7–12. Association for Computational Linguistics.

David M. W. Powers. 1984. Natural language the natural way. *Computer Compacts*, 2(3):100–109.

David M. W. Powers. 1991a. Goals, issues and directions in machine learning of natural language and ontology. In David M. W. Powers, editor, *AAAI Spring Symposium on Machine Learning of Natural Language and Ontology*, pages 1–22.

David M. W. Powers. 1991b. How far can self-organization go? results in unsupervised language learning. In David M. W. Powers, editor, *AAAI Spring Symposium on Machine Learning of Natural Language and Ontology*, pages 131–136.

David M. W. Powers. 1997. *Perceptual Foundations for Cognitive Linguistics*. International Cognitive Linguistics Conference.

David M. W. Powers. 2001. The robot baby meets the intelligent room. In *AAAI Spring Symposium on Learning Grounded Representations*.

David M. W. Powers. 2005. Biologically-motivated machine learning of natural language and ontology a computational cognitive model. In *Workshop on Multi-Modal User Interface*. HCSNet/NICTA.

David M. W. Powers. 2008. Evaluation evaluation: A monte carlo study. In *European Conference on Artificial Intelligence*, pages 843–844.

David MW Powers. 2015. A critical time in computational cognitive science. *Computational Cognitive Science*, 1(1):1.

Deb Roy. 2009. New horizons in the study of child language acquisition. In *Proceedings of Interspeech*.

John Searle. 1980. Minds, brains and programs. *Behavioral and Brain Sciences*, 3(3):415–457.

Oliver G. Selfridge. 1959. Pandemonium: A paradigm for learning. In D. V. Blake and A. M. Uttley, editors, *Proceedings of the Symposium on Mechanisation of Thought Processes*, pages 511–529, London.

Luc Steels. 1995. A self-organizing spatial vocabulary. *Artificial life*, 2(3):319–332.

Luc Steels. 1997. The synthetic modeling of language origins. *Evolution of communication*, 1(1):1–34.

Luc Steels. 2003. Evolving grounded communication for robots. *Trends in cognitive sciences*, 7(7):308–312.

Luc Steels. 2015. *The talking heads experiment*. Language Science Press.

Catherine J. Stevens, Bronwyn Pinchbeck, Trent Lewis, Martin Luerssen, Darius Pfitzner, David M. W. Powers, Arman Abrahamyan, Yvonne Leung, and Guillaume Gibert. 2016. Mimicry and expressiveness of an eca in human-agent interaction: familiarity breeds content! *Computational Cognitive Science*, 2(1):1–14.

Alan Turing. 1950. Computing machinery and intelligence. *Mind*, LIX(236):433–460.

Generating Sentences from a Continuous Space

Samuel R. Bowman[*]
NLP Group and Dept. of Linguistics
Stanford University
sbowman@stanford.edu

Luke Vilnis[*]
CICS
UMass Amherst
luke@cs.umass.edu

Oriol Vinyals, Andrew M. Dai, Rafal Jozefowicz & Samy Bengio
Google Brain
Google, Inc.
{vinyals, adai, bengio}@google.com, rafjoz@gmail.com

Abstract

The standard recurrent neural network language model (RNNLM) generates sentences one word at a time and does not work from an explicit global sentence representation. In this work, we introduce and study an RNN-based variational autoencoder generative model that incorporates distributed latent representations of entire sentences. This factorization allows it to explicitly model holistic properties of sentences such as style, topic, and high-level syntactic features. Samples from the prior over these sentence representations remarkably produce diverse and well-formed sentences through simple deterministic decoding. By examining paths through this latent space, we are able to generate coherent novel sentences that interpolate between known sentences. We present techniques for solving the difficult learning problem presented by this model, demonstrate its effectiveness in imputing missing words, explore many interesting properties of the model's latent sentence space, and present negative results on the use of the model in language modeling.

1 Introduction

Recurrent neural network language models (RNNLMs, Mikolov et al., 2011) represent the state of the art in unsupervised generative modeling for natural language sentences. In supervised settings, RNNLM decoders conditioned on task-specific features are the state of the art in tasks like machine translation (Sutskever et al., 2014; Bahdanau et al., 2015) and image captioning (Vinyals et al., 2015; Mao et al., 2015; Donahue et al., 2015). The RNNLM generates sentences word-by-word based on an evolving distributed state representation, which makes it a probabilistic model with no significant independence

---

i went to the store to buy some groceries .
i store to buy some groceries .
i were to buy any groceries .
horses are to buy any groceries .
horses are to buy any animal .
horses the favorite any animal .
horses the favorite favorite animal .
horses are my favorite animal .

Table 1: Sentences produced by greedily decoding from points between two sentence encodings with a conventional autoencoder. The intermediate sentences are not plausible English.

assumptions, and makes it capable of modeling complex distributions over sequences, including those with long-term dependencies. However, by breaking the model structure down into a series of next-step predictions, the RNNLM does not expose an interpretable representation of global features like topic or of high-level syntactic properties.

We propose an extension of the RNNLM that is designed to explicitly capture such global features in a continuous latent variable. Naively, maximum likelihood learning in such a model presents an intractable inference problem. Drawing inspiration from recent successes in modeling images (Gregor et al., 2015), handwriting, and natural speech (Chung et al., 2015), our model circumvents these difficulties using the architecture of a *variational autoencoder* and takes advantage of recent advances in variational inference (Kingma and Welling, 2015; Rezende et al., 2014) that introduce a practical training technique for powerful neural network generative models with latent variables.

Our contributions are as follows: We propose a variational autoencoder architecture for text and discuss some of the obstacles to training it as well as our proposed solutions. We find that on a standard language modeling evaluation where a global variable is not explicitly needed, this model yields similar performance to existing RNNLMs. We also evaluate our model using a larger corpus on the task of imputing missing words. For this task, we introduce a novel evaluation strategy using an

---

[*]First two authors contributed equally. Work was done when all authors were at Google, Inc.

Proceedings of the 20th SIGNLL Conference on Computational Natural Language Learning (CoNLL), pages 10–21,
Berlin, Germany, August 7-12, 2016. ©2016 Association for Computational Linguistics

adversarial classifier, sidestepping the issue of intractable likelihood computations by drawing inspiration from work on non-parametric two-sample tests and adversarial training. In this setting, our model's global latent variable allows it to do well where simpler models fail. We finally introduce several qualitative techniques for analyzing the ability of our model to learn high level features of sentences. We find that they can produce diverse, coherent sentences through purely deterministic decoding and that they can interpolate smoothly between sentences.

2 Background

2.1 Unsupervised sentence encoding

A standard RNN language model predicts each word of a sentence conditioned on the previous word and an evolving hidden state. While effective, it does not learn a vector representation of the full sentence. In order to incorporate a continuous latent sentence representation, we first need a method to map between sentences and distributed representations that can be trained in an unsupervised setting. While no strong generative model is available for this problem, three non-generative techniques have shown promise: sequence autoencoders, skip-thought, and paragraph vector.

Sequence autoencoders have seen some success in pre-training sequence models for supervised downstream tasks (Dai and Le, 2015) and in generating complete documents (Li et al., 2015a). An autoencoder consists of an encoder function φ_{enc} and a probabilistic decoder model $p(x|\vec{z} = \varphi_{enc}(x))$, and maximizes the likelihood of an example x conditioned on $\vec{z}$, the learned code for x. In the case of a sequence autoencoder, both encoder and decoder are RNNs and examples are token sequences.

Standard autoencoders are not effective at extracting for global semantic features. In Table 1, we present the results of computing a path or *homotopy* between the encodings for two sentences and decoding each intermediate code. The intermediate sentences are generally ungrammatical and do not transition smoothly from one to the other. This suggests that these models do not generally learn a smooth, interpretable feature system for sentence encoding. In addition, since these models do not incorporate a prior over $\vec{z}$, they cannot be used to assign probabilities to sentences or to sample novel sentences. Similarly, Iyyer et al. (2014) provide a method for generating sentences with arbitrary syntactic structure using tree-structured autoencoders, but that model only transforms existing sentences and cannot generate entirely new ones.

Two other models have shown promise in learning sentence encodings, but cannot be used in a generative setting: Skip-thought models (Kiros et al., 2015) are unsupervised learning models that take the same model structure as a sequence autoencoder, but generate text conditioned on a neighboring sentence from the target text, instead of on the target sentence itself. Finally, paragraph vector models (Le and Mikolov, 2014) are non-recurrent sentence representation models. In a paragraph vector model, the encoding of a sentence is obtained by performing gradient-based inference on a prospective encoding vector with the goal of using it to predict the words in the sentence.

2.2 The variational autoencoder

The variational autoencoder (VAE, Kingma and Welling, 2015; Rezende et al., 2014) is a generative model that is based on a regularized version of the standard autoencoder. This model imposes a prior distribution on the hidden codes $\vec{z}$ which enforces a regular geometry over codes and makes it possible to draw proper samples from the model using ancestral sampling.

The VAE modifies the autoencoder architecture by replacing the deterministic function φ_{enc} with a learned posterior *recognition model*, $q(\vec{z}|x)$. This model parametrizes an approximate posterior distribution over $\vec{z}$ (usually a diagonal Gaussian) with a neural network conditioned on x. Intuitively, the VAE learns codes not as single points, but as soft ellipsoidal *regions* in latent space, forcing the codes to fill the space rather than memorizing the training data as isolated codes.

If the VAE were trained with a standard autoencoder's reconstruction objective, it would learn to encode its inputs deterministically by making the variances in $q(\vec{z}|x)$ vanishingly small (Raiko et al., 2015). Instead, the VAE uses an objective which encourages the model to keep its posterior distributions close to a prior $p(\vec{z})$, generally a standard Gaussian ($\mu = \vec{0}$, $\sigma = \vec{1}$). Additionally, this objective is a valid lower bound on the true log likelihood of the data, making the VAE a generative model. This objective takes the following form:

$$\begin{aligned}
\mathcal{L}(\theta; x) = & -\text{KL}(q_\theta(\vec{z}|x)||p(\vec{z})) \\
& + \mathbb{E}_{q_\theta(\vec{z}|x)}[\log p_\theta(x|\vec{z})] \\
\leq & \log p(x) \ .
\end{aligned} \quad (1)$$

This forces the model to be able to decode plausible sentences from every point in the latent space that has a reasonable probability under the prior.

In the experiments presented below using VAE models, we use diagonal Gaussians for the prior and posterior distributions $p(\vec{z})$ and $q(\vec{z}|x)$, using the Gaussian reparameterization trick of Kingma and Welling (2015). We train our models with stochastic gradient descent, and at each gradient step we estimate the reconstruction cost using a

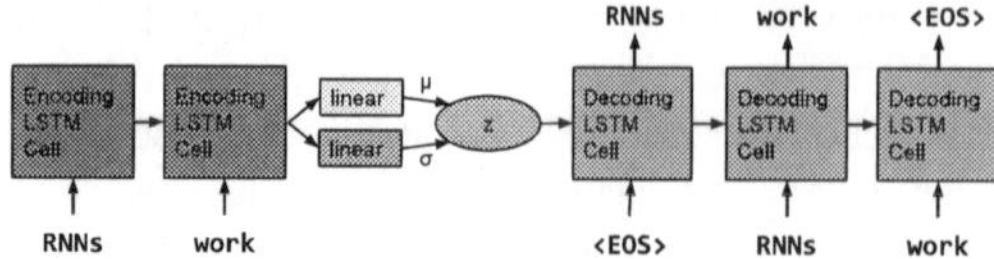

Figure 1: The core structure of our variational autoencoder language model. Words are represented using a learned randomly-initialized dictionary of embedding vectors. $\vec{z}$ is a vector-valued latent variable with a Gaussian prior and an approximate posterior parameterized by the encoder's outputs μ and σ. <EOS> marks the end of each sequence.

single sample from $q(\vec{z}|x)$, but compute the KL divergence term of the cost function in closed form, again following Kingma and Welling (2015).

3 A VAE for sentences

We adapt the variational autoencoder to text by using single-layer LSTM RNNs (Hochreiter and Schmidhuber, 1997) for both the encoder and the decoder, essentially forming a sequence autoencoder with the Gaussian prior acting as a regularizer on the hidden code. The decoder serves as a special RNN language model that is conditioned on this hidden code, and in the degenerate setting where the hidden code incorporates no useful information, this model is effectively equivalent to an RNNLM. The model is depicted in Figure 1, and is used in all of the experiments discussed below.

We explored several variations on this architecture, including concatenating the sampled $\vec{z}$ to the decoder input at every time step, using a softplus parametrization for the variance, and using deep feedforward networks between the encoder and latent variable and the decoder and latent variable. We noticed little difference in the model's performance when using any of these variations. However, when including feedforward networks between the encoder and decoder we found that it is necessary to use highway network layers (Srivastava et al., 2015) for the model to learn. We use a 4 layer highway network to parametrize the Gaussian posterior conditioned on the RNN state, and another identical network to map the Gaussian samples back to feed into the decoder RNN. We discuss hyperparameter tuning in Appendix II.

We also experimented with more sophisticated recognition models $q(\vec{z}|x)$, including a multistep sampling model styled after DRAW (Gregor et al., 2015), and a posterior approximation using normalizing flows (Rezende and Mohamed, 2015). However, we were unable to reap significant gains over our plain VAE.

While the strongest results with VAEs to date have been on continuous domains like images, there

has been some work on discrete sequences: a technique for doing this using RNN encoders and decoders, which shares the same high-level architecture as our model, was proposed under the name Variational Recurrent Autoencoder (VRAE) for the modeling of music in Fabius and van Amersfoort (2014). While there has been other work on including continuous latent variables in RNN-style models for modeling speech, handwriting, and music (Bayer and Osendorfer, 2015; Chung et al., 2015), these models include separate latent variables per timestep and are unsuitable for our goal of modeling global features.

In a recent paper with goals similar to ours, Miao et al. (2016) introduce an effective VAE-based document-level language model that models texts as bags of words, rather than as sequences. They mention briefly that they have to train the encoder and decoder portions of the network in alternation rather than simultaneously, possibly as a way of addressing some of the issues that we discuss in Section 3.1.

3.1 Optimization challenges

Our model aims to learn global latent representations of sentence content. We can quantify the degree to which our model learns global features by looking at the variational lower bound objective (1). The bound breaks into two terms: the data likelihood under the posterior (expressed as cross entropy), and the KL divergence of the posterior from the prior. A model that encodes useful information in the latent variable $\vec{z}$ will have a non-zero KL divergence term and a relatively small cross entropy term. Straightforward implementations of our VAE fail to learn this behavior: except in vanishingly rare cases, most training runs with most hyperparameters yield models that consistently set $q(\vec{z}|x)$ equal to the prior $p(\vec{z})$, bringing the KL divergence term of the cost function to zero.

When the model does this, it is essentially behaving as an RNNLM. Because of this, it can express arbitrary distributions over the output sentences (albeit with a potentially awkward left-to-right factorization) and can thereby achieve likelihoods that are close to optimal. Previous work on VAEs for image modeling (Kingma and Welling, 2015) used a much weaker independent pixel decoder model $p(x|\vec{z})$, forcing the model to use the global latent variable to achieve good likelihoods. In a related result, recent approaches to image generation that use LSTM decoders are able to do well without VAE-style global latent variables (Theis and Bethge, 2015).

This problematic tendency in learning is compounded by the LSTM decoder's sensitivity to subtle variation in the hidden states, such as that introduced by the posterior sampling process. This

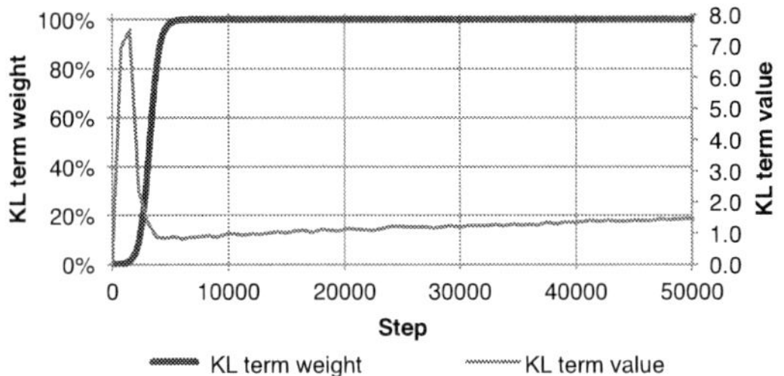

Figure 2: The weight of the KL divergence term of variational lower bound according to a typical sigmoid annealing schedule plotted alongside the (unweighted) value of the KL divergence term for our VAE on the Penn Treebank.

causes the model to initially learn to ignore $\vec{z}$ and go after low hanging fruit, explaining the data with the more easily optimized decoder. Once this has happened, the decoder ignores the encoder and little to no gradient signal passes between the two, yielding an undesirable stable equilibrium with the KL cost term at zero. We propose two techniques to mitigate this issue.

KL cost annealing In this simple approach to this problem, we add a variable weight to the KL term in the cost function at training time. At the start of training, we set that weight to zero, so that the model learns to encode as much information in $\vec{z}$ as it can. Then, as training progresses, we gradually increase this weight, forcing the model to smooth out its encodings and pack them into the region of the embedding space that is assigned a reasonably high probability by the Gaussian prior. We increase this weight until it reaches 1, at which point the weighted cost function is equivalent to the true variational lower bound. In this setting, we do not optimize the proper lower bound on the training data likelihood during the early stages of training, but we nonetheless see improvements on the value of that bound at convergence. This can be thought of as annealing from a vanilla autoencoder to a VAE. The rate of this increase is tuned as a hyperparameter.

Figure 2 shows the behavior of the KL cost term during the first 50k steps of training on Penn Treebank (Marcus et al., 1993) language modeling with KL cost annealing in place. This example reflects a pattern that we observed often: KL spikes early in training while the model can encode information in $\vec{z}$ cheaply, then drops substantially once it begins paying the full KL divergence penalty, and finally slowly rises again before converging as the model learns to condense more information into $\vec{z}$.

Word dropout and historyless decoding In addition to weakening the penalty term on the encodings, we also experiment with weakening the decoder. As in RNNLMs and sequence autoencoders, during learning our decoder predicts each word conditioned on the ground-truth previous word. A natural way to weaken the decoder is to remove some or all of this conditioning information during learning. We do this by randomly replacing some fraction of the conditioned-on word tokens with the generic unknown word token UNK. This forces the model to rely on the latent variable $\vec{z}$ to make good predictions. This technique is a variant of word dropout (Iyyer et al., 2015; Kumar et al., 2016), applied not to a feature extractor but to a decoder. We also experimented with standard dropout (Srivastava et al., 2014) applied to the input word embeddings in the decoder, but this did not help the model learn to use the latent variable.

This technique is parameterized by a keep rate $k \in [0, 1]$. We tune this parameter both for our VAE and for our baseline RNNLM. Taken to the extreme of $k = 0$, the decoder sees no input, and is thus able to condition only on the number of words produced so far, yielding a model that is extremely limited in the kinds of distributions it can model without using $\vec{z}$.

4   Results: Language modeling

In this section, we report on language modeling experiments on the Penn Treebank in an effort to discover whether the inclusion of a global latent variable is helpful for this standard task. For this reason, we restrict our VAE hyperparameter search to those models which encode a non-trivial amount in the latent variable, as measured by the KL divergence term of the variational lower bound.

Results We used the standard train–test split for the corpus, and report test set results in Table 2. The results shown reflect the training and test set performance of each model at the training step at which the model performs best on the development set. Our reported figures for the VAE reflect the variational lower bound on the test likelihood, while for the RNNLMs, which can be evaluated exactly, we report the true test likelihood. This discrepancy puts the VAE at a potential disadvantage.

In the standard setting, the VAE performs slightly worse than the RNNLM baseline, though it does succeed in using the latent space to a limited extent: it has a reconstruction cost (99) better than that of the baseline RNNLM, but makes up for this with a KL divergence cost of 2. Training a VAE in the standard setting without both word dropout and cost annealing reliably results in models with equivalent performance to the baseline RNNLM, and zero KL divergence.

To demonstrate the ability of the latent variable to encode the full content of sentences in addition

Model	Standard				Inputless Decoder			
	Train NLL	Train PPL	Test NLL	Test PPL	Train NLL	Train PPL	Test NLL	Test PPL
RNNLM	100 –	95	**100** –	**116**	135 –	600	135 –	> 600
VAE	98 (2)	100	101 (2)	119	120 (15)	300	**125** (15)	**380**

Table 2: Penn Treebank language modeling results, reported as negative log likelihoods (NLL) and as perplexities (PPL). Lower is better for both metrics. For the VAE, the KL term of the likelihood is shown in parentheses alongside the total likelihood.

to more abstract global features, we also provide numbers for an inputless decoder that does not condition on previous tokens, corresponding to a word dropout keep rate of 0. If this decoder cannot or does not take advantage of the encoder, then it is essentially equivalent to a unigram language model, with the hidden state providing information about position but noting more. In this regime we can see that the variational lower bound contains a significantly larger KL term and shows a substantial improvement over the weakened RNNLM. While it is weaker than a standard decoder, the inputless decoder has the interesting property that its sentence generating process is fully differentiable. Advances in generative models of this kind could be promising as a means of generating text while using adversarial training methods, which require differentiable generators.

Even with the techniques described in the previous section, including the inputless decoder, we were unable to train models for which the KL divergence term of the cost function dominates the reconstruction term. This suggests that it is still substantially easier to learn to factor the data distribution using simple local statistics, as in the RNNLM, such that an encoder will only learn to encode information in $\vec{z}$ when that information cannot be effectively described by these local statistics.

5   Results: Imputing missing words

We claim that the our VAE's global sentence features make it especially well suited to the task of imputing missing words in otherwise known sentences. In this section, we present a technique for imputation and a novel evaluation strategy inspired by adversarial training. Qualitatively, we find that the VAE yields more diverse and plausible imputations for the same amount of computation (see the examples given in Table 3), but precise quantitative evaluation requires intractable likelihood computations. We sidestep this by introducing a novel evaluation strategy.

While the standard RNNLM is a powerful generative model, the sequential nature of likelihood computation and decoding makes it unsuitable for performing inference over unknown words given some known words (the task of *imputation*). Except in the special case where the unknown words all ap-

pear at the end of the decoding sequence, sampling from the posterior over the missing variables is intractable for all but the smallest vocabularies. For a vocabulary of size V, it requires $O(V)$ runs of full RNN inference per step of Gibbs sampling or iterated conditional modes. Worse, because of the directional nature of the graphical model given by an RNNLM, many steps of sampling could be required to propagate information between unknown variables and the known downstream variables. The VAE, while it suffers from the same intractability problems when sampling or computing MAP imputations, can more easily propagate information between all variables, by virtue of having a global latent variable and a tractable recognition model.

For this experiment and subsequent analysis, we train our models on the Books Corpus introduced in Kiros et al. (2015). This is a collection of text from 12k e-books, mostly fiction. The dataset, after pruning, contains approximately 80m sentences. We find that this much larger amount of data produces more subjectively interesting generative models than smaller standard language modeling datasets. We use a fixed word dropout rate of 75% when training this model and all subsequent models unless otherwise specified. Our models (the VAE and RNNLM) are trained as language models, decoding right-to-left to shorten the dependencies during learning for the VAE. We use 512 hidden units.

Inference method   To generate imputations from the two models, we use beam search with beam size 15 for the RNNLM and approximate iterated conditional modes (Besag, 1986) with 3 steps of a beam size 5 search for the VAE. This allows us to compare the same amount of computation for both models. We find that breaking decoding for the VAE into several sequential steps is necessary to propagate information among the variables. Iterated conditional modes is a technique for finding the maximum joint assignment of a set of variables by alternately maximizing conditional distributions, and is a generalization of "hard-EM" algorithms like k-means (Kearns et al., 1998). For approximate iterated conditional modes, we first initialize the unknown words to the UNK token. We then alternate assigning the latent variable to its mode from the recognition model, and performing

but now , as they parked out front and owen stepped out of the car , he could see _ _ _ _ _		
True: *that the transition was complete .*	**RNNLM:** *it , " i said .*	**VAE:** *through the driver 's door .*
you kill him and his _ _		
True: *men .*	**RNNLM:** *. "*	**VAE:** *brother .*
not surprising , the mothers dont exactly see eye to eye with me _ _ _ _		
True: *on this matter .*	**RNNLM:** *, i said .*	**VAE:** *, right now .*
outside the cover , quiet _ _		
True: *fell .*	**RNNLM:** *. "*	**VAE:** *time .*
she punched the cell _ _		
True: *too .*	**RNNLM:** *again .*	**VAE:** *phone .*

Table 3: Examples of using beam search to impute missing words within sentences. Since we decode from right to left, note the stereotypical completions given by the RNNLM, compared to the VAE completions that often use topic data and more varied vocabulary.

constrained beam search to assign the unknown words. Both of our generative models are trained to decode sentences from right-to-left, which shortens the dependencies involved in learning for the VAE, and we impute the final 20% of each sentence. This lets us demonstrate the advantages of the global latent variable in the regime where the RNNLM suffers the most from its inductive bias.

Adversarial evaluation Drawing inspiration from adversarial training methods for generative models as well as non-parametric two-sample tests (Goodfellow et al., 2014; Li et al., 2015b; Denton et al., 2015; Gretton et al., 2012), we evaluate the imputed sentence completions by examining their distinguishability from the true sentence endings. While the non-differentiability of the discrete RNN decoder prevents us from easily applying the adversarial criterion at train time, we can define a very flexible test time evaluation by training a discriminant function to separate the generated and true sentences, which defines an *adversarial error*.

We train two classifiers: a bag-of-unigrams logistic regression classifier and an LSTM logistic regression classifier that reads the input sentence and produces a binary prediction after seeing the final EOS token. We train these classifiers using early stopping on a 80/10/10 train/dev/test split of 320k sentences, constructing a dataset of 50% complete sentences from the corpus (positive examples) and 50% sentences with imputed completions (negative examples). We define the *adversarial error* as the gap between the ideal accuracy of the discriminator (50%, i.e. indistinguishable samples), and the actual accuracy attained.

Results As a consequence of this experimental setup, the RNNLM cannot choose anything outside of the top 15 tokens given by the RNN's initial unconditional distribution $P(x_1|\text{Null})$ when producing the final token of the sentence, since it has not yet generated anything to condition on, and has a beam size of 15. Table 4 shows that this weakness

Model	Adv. Err. (%)		NLL
	Unigram	LSTM	RNNLM
RNNLM (15 bm.)	28.3	38.9	46.0
VAE (3x5 bm.)	**22.4**	**35.6**	46.1

Table 4: Results for adversarial evaluation of imputations. Unigram and LSTM numbers are the *adversarial error* (see text) and RNNLM numbers are the negative log-likelihood given to entire generated sentence by the RNNLM, a measure of sentence typicality. Lower is better on both metrics. The VAE is able to generate imputations that are significantly more difficult to distinguish from the true sentences.

makes the RNNLM produce far less diverse samples than the VAE and suffer accordingly versus the adversarial classifier. Additionally, we include the score given to the entire sentence with the imputed completion given a separate independently trained language model. The likelihood results are comparable, though the RNNLMs favoring of generic high-probability endings such as "he said," gives it a slightly lower negative log-likelihood. Measuring the RNNLM likelihood of sentences themselves produced by an RNNLM is not a good measure of the power of the model, but demonstrates that the RNNLM can produce what it sees as high-quality imputations by favoring typical local statistics, even though their repetitive nature produces easy failure modes for the adversarial classifier. Accordingly, under the adversarial evaluation our model substantially outperforms the baseline since it is able to efficiently propagate information bidirectionally through the latent variable.

6 Analyzing variational models

We now turn to more qualitative analysis of the model. Since our decoder model $p(x|\vec{z})$ is a sophisticated RNNLM, simply sampling from the directed

100% word keep	75% word keep
" no , " he said .	*why would i want you to look at me like this ?*
" no , " he said .	*" love you , too . "*
" thank you , " he said .	*she put her hand on his shoulder and followed him to the door .*

50% word keep	0% word keep
all this time , i could n't stay in the room .	*not , did n't be , for the time he was out in*
" maybe two or two . "	*i i hear some of of of*
she laughed again , once again , once again , and thought about it for a moment in long silence .	*i was noticed that she was holding the in in of the the in*

Table 5: Samples from a model trained with varying amounts of word dropout. We sample a vector from the Gaussian prior and apply greedy decoding to the result. Note that diverse samples can be achieved using a purely deterministic decoding procedure. Once we use reach a purely inputless decoder in the 0% setting, however, the samples cease to be plausible English sentences.

he had been unable to conceal the fact that there was a logical explanation for his inability to alter the fact that they were supposed to be on the other side of the house .
with a variety of pots strewn scattered across the vast expanse of the high ceiling , a vase of colorful flowers adorned the tops of the rose petals littered the floor and littered the floor .
atop the circular dais perched atop the gleaming marble columns began to emerge from atop the stone dais, perched atop the dais .

Table 6: Greedily decoded sentences from a model with 75% word keep probability, sampling from lower-likelihood areas of the latent space. Note the consistent topics and vocabulary usage.

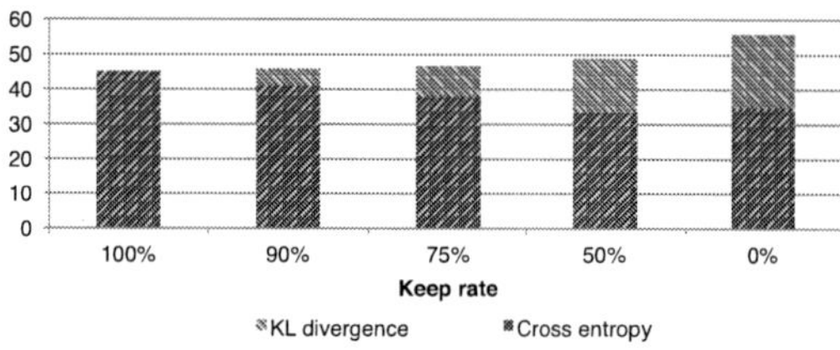

Figure 3: The values of the two terms of the cost function as word dropout increases.

6.1 Analyzing the impact of word dropout

For this experiment, we train on the Books Corpus and test on a held out 10k sentence test set from that corpus. We find that train and test set performance are very similar. In Figure 3, we examine the impact of word dropout on the variational lower bound, broken down into KL divergence and cross entropy components. We drop out words with the specified keep rate at training time, but supply all words as inputs at test time except in the 0% setting.

We do not re-tune the hyperparameters for each run, which results in the model with no dropout encoding very little information in $\vec{z}$ (i.e., the KL component is small). We can see that as we lower the keep rate for word dropout, the amount of information stored in the latent variable increases, and the overall likelihood of the model degrades somewhat. Results from the Section 4 indicate that a model with no latent variable would degrade in performance significantly more in the presence of heavy word dropout.

We also qualitatively evaluate samples, to demonstrate that the increased KL allows meaningful sentences to be generated purely from continuous sampling. Since our decoder model $p(x|\vec{z})$ is a sophisticated RNNLM, simply sampling from the directed graphical model (first $p(\vec{z})$ then $p(x|\vec{z})$)

graphical model (first $p(\vec{z})$ then $p(x|\vec{z})$) would not tell us much about how much of the data is being explained by each of the latent space and the decoder. Instead, for this part of the evaluation, we sample from the Gaussian prior, but use a greedy deterministic decoder for $p(x|\vec{z})$, the RNNLM conditioned on $\vec{z}$. This allows us to get a sense of how much of the variance in the data distribution is being captured by the distributed vector $\vec{z}$ as opposed to the decoder. Interestingly, these results qualitatively demonstrate that large amounts of variation in generated language can be achieved by following this procedure. In Appendix I, we provide some results on small text classification tasks.

INPUT	we looked out at the setting sun .	i went to the kitchen .	how are you doing ?
MEAN	*they were laughing at the same time .*	*i went to the kitchen .*	*what are you doing ?*
SAMP. 1	*ill see you in the early morning .*	*i went to my apartment .*	*" are you sure ?*
SAMP. 2	*i looked up at the blue sky .*	*i looked around the room .*	*what are you doing ?*
SAMP. 3	*it was down on the dance floor .*	*i turned back to the table .*	*what are you doing ?*

Table 7: Three sentences which were used as inputs to the VAE, presented with greedy decodes from the mean of the posterior distribution, and from three samples from that distribution.

would not tell us about how much of the data is being explained by the learned vector vs. the language model. Instead, for this part of the qualitative evaluation, we sample from the Gaussian prior, but use a greedy deterministic decoder for x, taking each token $x_t = \mathrm{argmax}_{x_t} p(x_t | x_{0,\ldots,t-1}, \vec{z})$. This allows us to get a sense of how much of the variance in the data distribution is being captured by the distributed vector $\vec{z}$ as opposed to by local language model dependencies.

These results, shown in Table 5, qualitatively demonstrate that large amounts of variation in generated language can be achieved by following this procedure. At the low end, where very little of the variance is explained by $\vec{z}$, we see that greedy decoding applied to a Gaussian sample does not produce diverse sentences. As we increase the amount of word dropout and force $\vec{z}$ to encode more information, we see the sentences become more varied, but past a certain point they begin to repeat words or show other signs of ungrammaticality. Even in the case of a fully dropped-out decoder, the model is able to capture higher-order statistics not present in the unigram distribution.

Additionally, in Table 6 we examine the effect of using lower-probability samples from the latent Gaussian space for a model with a 75% word keep rate. We find lower-probability samples by applying an approximately volume-preserving transformation to the Gaussian samples that stretches some eigenspaces by up to a factor of 4. This has the effect of creating samples that are not too improbable under the prior, but still reach into the tails of the distribution. We use a random linear transformation, with matrix elements drawn from a uniform distribution from $[-c, c]$, with c chosen to give the desired properties (0.1 in our experiments). Here we see that the sentences are far less typical, but for the most part are grammatical and maintain a clear topic, indicating that the latent variable is capturing a rich variety of global features even for rare sentences.

6.2 Sampling from the posterior

In addition to generating unconditional samples, we can also examine the sentences decoded from the posterior vectors $p(\vec{z}|x)$ for various sentences x. Because the model is regularized to produce distributions rather than deterministic codes, it does not exactly memorize and round-trip the input. Instead, we can see what the model considers to be similar sentences by examining the posterior samples in Table 7. The codes appear to capture information about the number of tokens and parts of speech for each token, as well as topic information. As the sentences get longer, the fidelity of the round-tripped sentences decreases.

6.3 Homotopies

The use of a variational autoencoder allows us to generate sentences using greedy decoding on continuous samples from the space of codes. Additionally, the volume-filling and smooth nature of the code space allows us to examine for the first time a concept of *homotopy* (linear interpolation) between sentences. In this context, a homotopy between two codes $\vec{z}_1$ and $\vec{z}_2$ is the set of points on the line between them, inclusive, $\vec{z}(t) = \vec{z}_1 * (1-t) + \vec{z}_2 * t$ for $t \in [0, 1]$. Similarly, the homotopy between two sentences decoded (greedily) from codes $\vec{z}_1$ and $\vec{z}_2$ is the set of sentences decoded from the codes on the line. Examining these homotopies allows us to get a sense of what neighborhoods in code space look like – how the autoencoder organizes information and what it regards as a continuous deformation between two sentences.

While a standard non-variational RNNLM does not have a way to perform these homotopies, a vanilla sequence autoencoder can do so. As mentioned earlier in the paper, if we examine the homotopies created by the sequence autoencoder in Table 1, though, we can see that the transition between sentences is sharp, and results in ungrammatical intermediate sentences. This gives evidence for our intuition that the VAE learns representations that are smooth and "fill up" the space.

In Table 8 (and in Table 12 in Appendix III, which shows additional homotopies) we can see that the codes mostly contain syntactic information, such as the number of words and the parts of speech of tokens, and that all intermediate sentences are grammatical. Some topic information also remains consistent in neighborhoods along the path. Additionally, sentences with similar syntax and topic but flipped sentiment valence, e.g. "the pain was unbearable" vs. "the thought made me smile", can have similar embeddings, a phenomenon which has been observed with single-

" i want to talk to you . "	
"i want to be with you . "	
"i do n't want to be with you . "	
i do n't want to be with you .	
she did n't want to be with him .	

he was silent for a long moment .
he was silent for a moment .
it was quiet for a moment .
it was dark and cold .
there was a pause .
it was my turn .

there is no one else in the world .
there is no one else in sight .
they were the only ones who mattered .
they were the only ones left .
he had to be with me .
she had to be with him .
i had to do this .
i wanted to kill him .
i started to cry .
i turned to him .

no .
he said .
" no , " he said .
" no , " i said .
" i know , " she said .
" thank you , " she said .
" come with me , " she said .
" talk to me , " she said .
" do n't worry about it , " she said .

Table 8: Paths between pairs of random points in VAE space: Note that intermediate sentences are grammatical, and that topic and syntactic structure are usually locally consistent.

word embeddings (for example the vectors for "bad" and "good" are often very similar due to their similar distributional characteristics).

7 Conclusion

This paper introduces the use of a variational autoencoder for natural language sentences. We present novel techniques that allow us to train our model successfully, and find that it can effectively impute missing words. We analyze the latent space learned by our model, and find that it is able to generate coherent and diverse sentences through purely continuous sampling and provides interpretable homotopies that smoothly interpolate between sentences.

We hope in future work to investigate factorization of the latent variable into separate style and content components, to generate sentences conditioned on extrinsic features, to learn sentence embeddings in a semi-supervised fashion for language understanding tasks like textual entailment, and to go beyond adversarial evaluation to a fully adversarial training objective.

Method	Accuracy	F1
Feats	73.2	–
RAE+DP	72.6	–
RAE+feats	74.2	–
RAE+DP+feats	76.8	83.6
ST	73.0	81.9
Bi-ST	71.2	81.2
Combine-ST	73.0	82.0
VAE	72.9	81.4
VAE+feats	75.0	82.4
VAE+combine-ST	74.8	82.3
Feats+combine-ST	75.8	83.0
VAE+combine-ST+feats	**76.9**	**83.8**

Table 9: Results for the MSR Paraphrase Corpus.

Appendix I: Text classification

In order to further examine the the structure of the representations discovered by the VAE, we conduct classification experiments on paraphrase detection and question type classification. We train a VAE with a hidden state size of 1200 hidden units on the Books Corpus, and use the posterior mean of the model as the extracted sentence vector. We train classifiers on these means using the same experimental protocol as Kiros et al. (2015).

Paraphrase detection For the task of paraphrase detection, we use the Microsoft Research Paraphrase Corpus (Dolan et al., 2004). We compute features from the sentence vectors of sentence pairs in the same way as Kiros et al. (2015), concatenating the elementwise products and the absolute value of the elementwise differences of the two vectors. We train an ℓ_2-regularized logistic regression classifier and tune the regularization strength using cross-validation.

We present results in Table 9 and compare to several previous models for this task. *Feats* is the lexicalized baseline from Socher et al. (2011). RAE uses the recursive autoencoder from that work, and DP adds their dynamic pooling step to calculate pairwise features. ST uses features from the unidirectional skip-thought model, *bi*-ST uses bidirectional skip-thought, and *combine*-ST uses the concatenation of those features. We also experimented with concatenating lexical features and the two types of distributed features.

We found that our features performed slightly worse than skip-thought features by themselves and slightly better than recursive autoencoder features, and were complementary and yielded strong performance when simply concatenated with the skip-thought features.

Question classification We also conduct experiments on the TREC Question Classification dataset of Li and Roth (2002). Following Kiros

Method	Accuracy
ST	91.4
Bi-ST	89.4
Combine-ST	**92.2**
AE	84.2
VAE	87.0
CBOW	87.3
VAE, combine-ST	92.0
RNN	90.2
CNN	**93.6**

Table 10: Results for TREC Question Classification.

	Standard		Inputless Decoder	
	RNNLM	VAE	RNNLM	VAE
D_{word}	464	353	305	499
D_{LSTM}	337	191	68	350
D_z	–	13	–	111
KR	0.66	0.62	–	–

Table 11: Automatically selected hyperparameter values used for the models used in the Penn Treebank language modeling experiments. KR is the keep rate for word dropout.

et al. (2015), we train an ℓ_2-regularized softmax classifier with 10-fold cross-validation to set the regularization. Note that using a linear classifier like this one may disadvantage our representations here, since the Gaussian distribution over hidden codes in a VAE is likely to discourage linear separability.

We present results in Table 10. Here, AE is a plain sequence autoencoder. We compare with results from a bag of word vectors (CBOW, Zhao et al., 2015) and skip-thought (ST). We also compare with an RNN classifier (Zhao et al., 2015) and a CNN classifier (Kim, 2014) both of which, unlike our model, are optimized end-to-end. We were not able to make the VAE codes perform better than CBOW in this case, but they did outperform features from the sequence autoencoder. Skip-thought performed quite well, possibly because the skip-thought training objective of next sentence prediction is well aligned to this task: it essentially trains the model to generate sentences that address implicit open questions from the narrative of the book. Combining the two representations did not give any additional performance gain over the base skip-thought model.

Appendix II: Hyperparameter tuning

We extensively tune the hyperparameters of each model using an automatic Bayesian hyperparameter tuning algorithm (based on Snoek et al., 2012)

amazing , is n't it ?
so , what is it ?
it hurts , isnt it ?
why would you do that ?
" you can do it .
" i can do it .
i ca n't do it .
" i can do it .
" do n't do it .
" i can do it .
i could n't do it .

i dont like it , he said .
i waited for what had happened .
it was almost thirty years ago .
it was over thirty years ago .
that was six years ago .
he had died two years ago .
ten , thirty years ago .
" it 's all right here .
" everything is all right here .
" it 's all right here .
it 's all right here .
we are all right here .
come here in five minutes .

this was the only way .
it was the only way .
it was her turn to blink .
it was hard to tell .
it was time to move on .
he had to do it again .
they all looked at each other .
they all turned to look back .
they both turned to face him .
they both turned and walked away .

im fine .
youre right .
" all right .
you 're right .
okay , fine .
" okay , fine .
yes , right here .
no , not right now .
" no , not right now .
" talk to me right now .
please talk to me right now .
i 'll talk to you right now .
" i 'll talk to you right now .
" you need to talk to me now .
" but you need to talk to me now .

Table 12: Selected homotopies between pairs of random points in the latent VAE space.

over development set data. We run the model with each set of hyperpameters for 10 hours, operating 12 experiments in parallel, and choose the best set of hyperparameters after 200 runs. Results for our language modeling experiments are reported in Table 11 on the next page.

Appendix III: Additional homotopies

Table 12 shows additional homotopies from our model. We observe that intermediate sentences are almost always grammatical, and often contain consistent topic, vocabulary and syntactic information in local neighborhoods as they interpolate between the endpoint sentences. Because the model is trained on fiction, including romance novels, the topics are often rather dramatic.

Acknowledgments

We thank the Google Brain team, Alireza Makhzani, Laurent Dinh, Jon Gauthier, the Stanford NLP Group, and our anonymous reviewers for their helpful contributions and feedback.

References

Dzmitry Bahdanau, Kyunghyun Cho, and Yoshua Bengio. 2015. Neural machine translation by jointly learning to align and translate. In *Proc. ICLR*.

Justin Bayer and Christian Osendorfer. 2015. Learning stochastic recurrent networks. arXiv preprint arXiv:1411.7610.

Julian Besag. 1986. On the statistical analysis of dirty pictures. *Journal of the Royal Statistical Society Series B (Methodological)* pages 48–259.

Junyoung Chung, Kyle Kastner, Laurent Dinh, Kratarth Goel, Aaron Courville, and Yoshua Bengio. 2015. A recurrent latent variable model for sequential data. In *Proc. NIPS*.

Andrew M. Dai and Quoc V. Le. 2015. Semi-supervised sequence learning. In *Proc. NIPS*.

Emily Denton, Soumith Chintala, Arthur Szlam, and Rob Fergus. 2015. Deep generative image models using a laplacian pyramid of adversarial networks. In *Proc. NIPS*.

Bill Dolan, Chris Quirk, and Chris Brockett. 2004. Unsupervised construction of large paraphrase corpora: Exploiting massively parallel news sources. In *Proc. COLING*.

Jeff Donahue, Lisa Anne Hendricks, Sergio Guadarrama, Marcus Rohrbach, Subhashini Venugopalan, Kate Saenko, and Trevor Darrell. 2015. Long-term recurrent convolutional networks for visual recognition and description. In *Proc. CVPR*.

Otto Fabius and Joost R. van Amersfoort. 2014. Variational recurrent auto-encoders. arXiv preprint arXiv:1412.6581.

Ian Goodfellow, Jean Pouget-Abadie, Mehdi Mirza, Bing Xu, David Warde-Farley, Sherjil Ozair, Aaron Courville, and Yoshua Bengio. 2014. Generative adversarial nets. In *Proc. NIPS*.

Karol Gregor, Ivo Danihelka, Alex Graves, and Daan Wierstra. 2015. DRAW: A recurrent neural network for image generation. In *Proc. ICML*.

Arthur Gretton, Karsten M Borgwardt, Malte J Rasch, Bernhard Schölkopf, and Alexander Smola. 2012. A kernel two-sample test. *JMLR* 13(1):723–773.

Sepp Hochreiter and Jürgen Schmidhuber. 1997. Long short-term memory. *Neural computation* 9(8).

Mohit Iyyer, Jordan Boyd-Graber, and Hal Daumé III. 2014. Generating sentences from semantic vector space representations. In *Proc. NIPS Workshop on Learning Semantics*.

Mohit Iyyer, Varun Manjunatha, Jordan Boyd-Graber, and Hal Daumé III. 2015. Deep unordered composition rivals syntactic methods for text classification. In *Proc. ACL*.

Michael Kearns, Yishay Mansour, and Andrew Y Ng. 1998. An information-theoretic analysis of hard and soft assignment methods for clustering. In *Learning in graphical models*, Springer, pages 495–520.

Yoon Kim. 2014. Convolutional neural networks for sentence classification. In *Proc. EMNLP*.

Diederik P. Kingma and Max Welling. 2015. Auto-encoding variational bayes. In *Proc. ICLR*.

Ryan Kiros, Yukun Zhu, Ruslan Salakhutdinov, Richard S Zemel, Antonio Torralba, Raquel Urtasun, and Sanja Fidler. 2015. Skip-thought vectors. In *Proc. NIPS*.

Ankit Kumar, Ozan Irsoy, Jonathan Su, James Bradbury, Robert English, Brian Pierce, Peter Ondruska, Ishaan Gulrajani, and Richard Socher. 2016. Ask me anything: Dynamic memory networks for natural language processing. In *Proc. ICML*.

Quoc V. Le and Tomáš Mikolov. 2014. Distributed representations of sentences and documents. In *Proc. ICML*.

Jiwei Li, Minh-Thang Luong, and Dan Jurafsky. 2015a. A hierarchical neural autoencoder for paragraphs and documents. In *Proc. ACL*.

Xin Li and Dan Roth. 2002. Learning question classifiers. In *Proc. COLING*.

Yujia Li, Kevin Swersky, and Richard Zemel. 2015b. Generative moment matching networks. In *Proc. ICML*.

Junhua Mao, Wei Xu, Yi Yang, Jiang Wang, Zhiheng Huang, and Alan Yuille. 2015. Deep captioning with multimodal recurrent neural networks (m-RNN). In *Proc. ICLR*.

Mitchell P Marcus, Mary Ann Marcinkiewicz, and Beatrice Santorini. 1993. Building a large annotated corpus of English: The Penn Treebank. *Computational linguistics* 19(2):313–330.

Yishu Miao, Lei Yu, and Phil Blunsom. 2016. Neural variational inference for text processing. In *Proc. ICML*.

Tomáš Mikolov, Stefan Kombrink, Lukáš Burget, Jan Honza Černocký, and Sanjeev Khudanpur. 2011. Extensions of recurrent neural network language model. In *Proc. ICASSP*.

Tapani Raiko, Mathias Berglund, Guillaume Alain, and Laurent Dinh. 2015. Techniques for learning binary stochastic feedforward neural networks. In *Proc. ICLR*.

Danilo J. Rezende and Shakir Mohamed. 2015. Variational inference with normalizing flows. In *Proc. ICML*.

Danilo J. Rezende, Shakir Mohamed, and Daan Wierstra. 2014. Stochastic backpropagation and approximate inference in deep generative models. In *Proc. ICML*.

Jasper Snoek, Hugo Larochelle, and Ryan P. Adams. 2012. Practical Bayesian optimization of machine learning algorithms. In *Proc. NIPS*.

Richard Socher, Eric H Huang, Jeffrey Pennin, Christopher D. Manning, and Andrew Y. Ng. 2011. Dynamic pooling and unfolding recursive autoencoders for paraphrase detection. In *Proc. NIPS*.

Nitish Srivastava, Geoffrey Hinton, Alex Krizhevsky, Ilya Sutskever, and Ruslan Salakhutdinov. 2014. Dropout: A simple way to prevent neural networks from overfitting. *JMLR* 15(1):1929–1958.

Rupesh Kumar Srivastava, Klaus Greff, and Jürgen Schmidhuber. 2015. Training very deep networks. In *Proc. NIPS*.

Ilya Sutskever, Oriol Vinyals, and Quoc V. Le. 2014. Sequence to sequence learning with neural networks. In *Proc. NIPS*.

Lucas Theis and Matthias Bethge. 2015. Generative image modeling using spatial LSTMs. In *Proc. NIPS*.

Oriol Vinyals, Alexander Toshev, Samy Bengio, and Dumitru Erhan. 2015. Show and tell: A neural image caption generator. In *Proc. CVPR*.

Han Zhao, Zhengdong Lu, and Pascal Poupart. 2015. Self-adaptive hierarchical sentence model. In *Proc. IJCAI*.

Identifying Temporality of Word Senses Based on Minimum Cuts

M. Hasanuzzaman,[1,3] **G. Dias,**[1,2] **S. Ferrari,**[1,2] **Y. Mathet,**[1,2] **and A. Way**[3]

[1]Université de Caen Normandie, Caen, France
[2]GREYC UMR 6072, Caen, France
[3]ADAPT Centre, School of Computing, Dublin City University, Dublin, Ireland

Abstract

The ability to capture time information is essential to many natural language processing and information retrieval applications. Therefore, a lexical resource associating word senses to their temporal orientation might be crucial for the computational tasks aiming at the interpretation of language of time in texts. In this paper, we propose a semi-supervised minimum cuts strategy that makes use of WordNet glosses and semantic relations to supplement WordNet entries with temporal information. Intrinsic and extrinsic evaluations show that our approach outperforms prior semi-supervised non-graph classifiers.

1 Introduction

Recognizing temporal information can significantly improve the functionality of information retrieval (Campos et al., 2014) and natural language processing (Mani et al., 2005) applications.

Most text applications have been relying on rule-based time taggers such as HeidelTime (Strötgen and Gertz, 2015) or SUTime (Chang and Manning, 2012) to identify and normalize time mentions in texts. Although interesting levels of performance have been seen (UzZaman et al., 2013), their coverage is limited to the finite number of rules they implement. Let's take the following sentence: *"Apple's iPhone is currently one of the most popular smartphone"*. When labeled by SUTime[1] or HeidelTime[2], the adverb *currently* is correctly tagged with the PRESENT_REF value. However, if we change the sentence to *"Apple's iPhone*

is one of the most popular smartphones at the present day"*, no temporal mention is found, although one may expect that within this context *currently* and *present day* share some equivalent temporal dimension. Such systems would certainly benefit from the existence of a temporal resource enumerating a large set of possible time variants (Kuzey et al., 2016).

In parallel, new trends have emerged in the context of human temporal orientation (Schwartz et al., 2015). The underlying idea is to understand how past, present, and future emphasis in text may affect people's finances, health, and happiness. For that purpose, temporal classifiers are built to detect the overall temporal dimension of a given sentence. For instance, the following Facebook post *"can't wait to get a pint tonight"* would be tagged as FUTURE. Successful features include timexes, specific temporal (past, present, future) words from a commercial dictionary, but also *n*-grams, thus indicating that temporality may be embodied by multi-word terms, whose temporal orientation is unknown.

As a consequence, discovering the temporal orientation of words is a challenging issue that may benefit many text applications. Whereas most prior studies have focused on temporal expressions and events, there has been a lack of work looking at the temporal orientation of word senses. In this paper, we focus on automatically time-tagging word senses in WordNet (Miller, 1995) as *past, present, future,* or *atemporal* based on their glosses and relational semantic structures in the line of Dias et al. (2014) and Hasanuzzaman et al. (2014b). In particular, we propose a semi-supervised graph-based strategy that relies on the max-flow min-cut theorem (Papadimitriou and Steiglitz, 1998; Blum and Chawla, 2001), that finds successive minimum cuts in a connected graph to time-tag each synset as one of the four

---

[1]`http://nlp.stanford.edu:8080/sutime/process`

[2]`http://heideltime.ifi.uni-heidelberg.de/heideltime/`

Proceedings of the 20th SIGNLL Conference on Computational Natural Language Learning (CoNLL), pages 22–30,
Berlin, Germany, August 7-12, 2016. ©2016 Association for Computational Linguistics

dimensions. Compared to previous work based on propagation strategies (Dias et al., 2014; Hasanuzzaman et al., 2014), the exploration of WordNet's graph structure with minimum cuts allows us to independently model both temporal connotation and semantic denotation. In order to evaluate our proposal, both intrinsic (inter-annotator agreement and temporal sense classification) and extrinsic (temporal sentence classification and temporal relation annotation) evaluations have been performed. In both cases, the proposed methodology outperformed state-of-the-art approaches.

2 Related Work

Dias et al. (2014) developed TempoWordNet (TWnL), an extension of WordNet, where each synset is augmented with its temporal connotation (*past*, *present*, *future*, or *atemporal*). It mainly relies on the quantitative analysis of the glosses associated to synsets, and on the use of the resulting vector space model representations for semi-supervised synset classification. In particular, temporal classifiers are learned over manually labeled synsets (seed list), and new learning synsets are chosen based on their specific semantic relation (e.g. hyponymy) with synsets from the seed list. Their class is given by the synset they have been propagated from. This process is iterated until cross-validation accuracy drops. The final classifier is used to time-tag all WordNet synsets.

While Hasanuzzaman et al. (2014) show that TWnL can be useful to time-tag web queries, less comprehensive results are shown in Filannino and Nenadic (2014), where TWnL learning features do not lead to any classification improvements. Moreover, Dias et al. (2014) mention that exclusive semantic propagation is error-prone as some semantic relations do not preserve temporal connotation. As a consequence, Hasanuzzaman et al. (2014b) defined two different propagation strategies: probabilistic and hybrid, leading to TWnP and TWnH, respectively. They follow the exact same idea of Dias et al. (2014), but for probabilistic propagation, new synsets are chosen from the most confidently classified synsets over the whole of WordNet at each iteration. In addition, for the hybrid expansion, new learning instances are included if they are highly representative of a given class but at the same time demonstrate high average semantic similarity over the seed list. Although some slight improvements were seen, no conclusive position could be reached due to the limited scope of the evaluation as well as discrepancies between human judgment, and automatic classification results.

One of the main weaknesses of the aforementioned approaches is that they mostly rely on the ability of the methodology to provide new learning instances by propagation within WordNet. However, in all cases, they do not take proper advantage of the relational structure of WordNet. Indeed, semantic coherence (for TWnL and TWnH) is only calculated between new instances and synsets from the seed list, but never between new instances themselves.[3] However, one may expect that highly correlated new instances should be treated commonly. One solution to deal with this problem is to define the classification problem as an optimization process, where both semantic coherence and temporal orientation are treated as combined objectives. For that purpose, we propose to adapt the standard s-t mincut algorithm (Blum and Chawla, 2001) to our particular semi-supervised multi-class learning problem.

3 Learning with s-t mincut

The s-t mincut algorithm is based on finding minimum cuts in a graph, and uses pairwise relationships among examples in order to learn from both labeled and unlabeled data. In particular, it outputs a classification corresponding to partitioning a graph in a way that minimizes the number of similar pairs of examples that are given different labels.

3.1 Main Principles

Let us consider n items $x_1, \ldots x_n$ to divide into two classes C_1 and C_2 based on two different types of information. The first information type – the *individual score* denoted as $ind_j(x_i)$ – measures the non-negative estimate of each x_i belonging to class C_j based on the features of x_i alone. The second information type – the *association score* denoted as $assoc(x_i, x_k)$ – represents the non-negative estimate of how important is that x_i and x_k be in the same class.

This situation can be represented as an undirected graph G with vertices $\{v_1, \ldots, v_n, s, t\}$, where s and t are respectively the *source* and *sink* vertices, which represent each class label and one vertex v_i corresponds to a given item x_i. If s

---

[3]This may occur only through a side-effect process.

(resp. t) corresponds to class C_1 (resp. C_2), we add n edges (s, v_i), each with weight $ind_1(x_i)$, and n edges (v_i, t), each with weight $ind_2(x_i)$. Finally, we add $\binom{n}{2}$ edges (v_i, v_k), each with weight $assoc(x_i, x_k)$.

The learning process corresponds to finding the minimum cut in G that minimizes some cost function, where (i) a cut (S, T) of G is a partition of its nodes into sets $S = \{s\} \cup S'$ and $T = \{t\} \cup T'$ where $s \notin S'$ and $t \notin T'$, and (ii) its cost $cost(S, T)$ is the sum of the weights of all edges crossing from S to T, as defined in equation (1):

$$\sum_{x \in C_1} ind_2(x) + \sum_{x \in C_2} ind_1(x) + \sum_{x_i \in C_1, x_k \in C_2} assoc(x_i, x_k) \quad (1)$$

3.2 Advantages and Disadvantages

Formulating the task of temporality detection on word senses in terms of graphs allows us to model item-specific and pair-wise information independently. As a consequence, machine learning algorithms representing temporal indicators can be used to derive *individual* scores for a particular sense in isolation. The edges weighted by the *individual* scores of a vertex (sense) to the source/sink can be interpreted as the probability of a sense belonging to a given temporal class without taking into account similarity to other senses.

At the same time, we can use conceptual-semantic relations from WordNet to derive the *association* scores. The edges between two senses weighted by the *association* scores can indicate how similar two senses are. If two senses are connected via a temporality-preserving relation, they are likely to both belong to a temporal class. For instance, hyponymy relation is usually a temporality-preserving relation,[4] where two hyponyms such as *present, nowadays — the period of time that is happening now* and *now — the momentary present* are both temporal.

To detect the temporal orientation of word senses, Dias et al. (2014) and Hasanuzzaman et al. (2014b) adopted a single view instead of two views on the data. The ability to combine two views on the data is precisely one of the strengths of the s-t mincut strategy.

Second, the s-t mincut algorithm is a semi-supervised framework. This is essential as the existing labeled datasets for our problem are small.

In addition, glosses are short, leading to sparse high-dimensional vectors in standard feature representations. Furthermore, WordNet connections between different parts of the WordNet hierarchy can be sparse, leading to relatively isolated senses in a graph in a supervised framework. The min-cut strategy allows us to import unlabeled data that can serve as bridges to isolated components. More importantly, the unlabeled data can be related to the labeled data (by some WordNet relation) and might help to pull unlabeled data to the right cuts.

It is also important to note that transductive methods such as the s-t mincut algorithm particularly suit our case study as all learning examples are known. However, the addition of new word senses would require the re-application of the method to the entire graph. Indeed, the model does not learn to predict unseen examples.

3.3 Methodology

The formulation of our mincut strategy for temporal classification of synsets involves the following steps.

Step I. We define two vertices s (source) and t (sink), which correspond to the *temporal* and *atemporal* categories, respectively. Vertices s and t are *classification vertices*, and all other vertices (labeled, unlabeled, and test) are *example vertices*.

Step II. The labeled examples are connected to the classification vertices they belong to via edges with high constant non-negative weight. The unlabeled examples are connected to the classification vertices via edges weighted with non-negative scores that indicate the degree of belonging to both the *temporal* and *atemporal* categories. Weights (i.e. individual scores) are calculated based on a supervised classifier learned from labeled examples (cf. Section 3.4).

Step III. For all pairs of example vertices, for which there exists a listed semantic relation in WordNet, an edge is created. This one receives a non-negative score that indicates the degree of semantic relationship between both vertices and corresponds to the association score (cf. Section 3.5).

Step IV. The max-flow theorem (Papadimitriou and Steiglitz, 1998) is applied over the built graph to find the minimum s-t cut.[5]

---

[4]Although Dias et al. (2014) show that this is not always the case.

[5]Max-flow algorithms show polynomial asymptotic running times and near-linear running times in practice.

Step V. The temporal partition is then divided into three temporal sub-partitions (*past*, *present*, and *future*) following a hierarchical strategy. First, we define two new vertices s and t, which correspond to *past* and *not_past* categories, respectively, and follow steps *II* through *IV*. This divides the subgraph into two disjoint subsets, i.e. *past* synsets, and synsets belonging either to *present* or *future*. Finally, we repeat steps *II* through *IV*, where vertices s and t correspond to *future* and *present*, respectively (cf. Section 3.6).

3.4 Individual Scores

The non-negative edge weights to s and t denote how an example vertex is related to a specific class. For the unlabeled and test examples, a supervised learning strategy is used to assign edge weights. Each synset from a labeled dataset – we use the dataset provided by Dias et al. (2014) – which contains *past*, *present*, *future* and *atemporal* senses is represented by its gloss encoded as a vector of word unigrams weighted by their frequency.[6] Then, depending on the classification task, a two-class SVM classifier is built from the Weka platform.[7] In particular, the SVM membership scores are transformed into probability estimates based on Platt calibration (Niculescu-Mizil and Caruana, 2005), which are directly mapped to edge weights. In Table 1, we present the 10-fold cross-validation results for all classifiers tested in the context of this work.

In order to ensure that the mincut procedure does not reverse the labels of the labeled examples, a high non-negative constant weight of 3 is assigned to any edge between a labeled vertex and its corresponding classification vertex, and a low non-negative constant weight of 0.001 to the edge to the other classification vertex. This is a classical implementation of $+\infty$ and $1/+\infty$ theoretical weights.

3.5 Association Scores

While formulating the graph, we connect two example vertices by an edge if they are linked by one of the 10 WordNet relations presented in Table 2. The main motivation towards using other relations in addition to the most frequently encoded relations (e.g. hypernym/hyponym) among synsets in WordNet is to achieve high graph connectivity.

---

[6]Other sentence representations could be tested but this is out of the scope of this paper.

[7]http://www.cs.waikato.ac.nz/ml/weka/

Two class problem	Accuracy	F1
temporal vs. *atemporal*	92.3	94.2
past vs. *not_past*	90.4	90.2
present vs. *not_present*	85.3	85.2
future vs. *not_future*	90.1	89.9
present vs. *future*	87.3	86.4

Table 1: SVM results for individual scores.

Wordnet Relation	#same	#different	Weight
Direct-Hyponym	73268	7246	0.91
Similar-to	6587	1914	0.77
Direct-Hypernym	61914	9600	0.76
Attribute	350	109	0.76
Also-see	1037	337	0.75
Troponym	6917	2651	0.72
Derived-from	3630	1947	0.65
Domain	2380	2895	0.45
Domain-member	2380	2895	0.45
Antonym	1905	3614	0.35

Table 2: Association scores with *DiffWt* Method.

Different weights can be assigned to different relations to reflect the degree to which they preserve temporality. Therefore, we adopt two strategies to assign weights to different WordNet relations. The first method (*ScWt*) assigns the same constant weight of 1.0 to all WordNet relations. The second method (*DiffWt*) considers several degrees of preserving temporality. In order to do this, we adopt a simple rule-based strategy to produce a large noisy set of *temporal* and *atemporal* synsets from WordNet. First, we take the list of 30 hand-crafted temporal seed synsets (equally distributed over *past*, *present*, and *future*) proposed in Dias et al. (2014) along with their direct hyponym synsets. This forms a temporal list. Then, each WordNet synset that contains a word sense from the temporal list in its gloss is 'roughly' classified as *temporal*. Otherwise, it is considered as *atemporal*. We then simply count how often two synsets connected by a given relation have the same or different temporal dimension. Finally, the weight is calculated by #same/(#same+#different) and corresponds to the association score between two example vertices. Results are reported in Table 2.

Note that the exact same strategy is used for the two hierarchical steps, for which new association scores are calculated.

3.6 Hierarchical Strategy

The order of the hierarchical process is driven by classifier accuracy over the labeled dataset provided by Dias et al. (2014) (cf. Section 4). In order to give the maximum chance of good partitioning at the second level of the hierarchy, we choose the classification problem to handle based on the SVM classifier that demonstrates highest accuracy over the following problems: *past* vs. *not_past*, *present* vs. *not_present*, and *future* vs. *not_future*. In so doing, we can rely on the best possible individual score function. As can be seen in Table 1, this is the case for *past* vs. *not_past*, which happens to be the first sub-partitioning problem. The third level is straightforward, i.e. *present* vs. *future*. We are aware that this simple strategy is prone to bias. However, as manual evaluation of the final resource is involved, producing more results was logistically hard to handle. Nonetheless, testing all combinations remains work that needs to be conducted in the future.

4 Datasets

Labeled Dataset. We used a list that consists of 632 *temporal* synsets and an equal number of *atemporal* synsets provided by Dias et al. (2014) as labeled data for our experiments. Temporal synsets are distributed as follows: 210 synsets marked as *past*, 291 as *present*, and 131 as *future*.

Test Dataset. As the labeled dataset is small, we created an annotation task using the Crowd-Flower platform[8] in order to produce a testset. For the annotation task, 398 synsets equally distributed over nouns, verbs, adjectives, and adverbs along with their lemmas and glosses were randomly selected from WordNet[9] as representative of the whole WordNet. Note that this number is a statistically significant representative sample of all WordNet synsets calculated as defined in Israel (1992).

The annotators were expected to answer two questions for a given synset (lemmas and gloss were also provided). While the first question is related to the decision as to whether a synset is *temporal* or *atemporal*, the motivation behind the second question is to collect a more fine-grained (*past*, *present*, *future*) gold-standard.[10] The reliability of the annotators was evaluated on 60 control synsets from the labeled dataset, and 10

---

[8] http://www.crowdflower.com/

[9] WordNet version 3.0 was used and all sysnsets were selected outside the labeled dataset.

[10] Details of the annotation guidelines are out of the scope of this paper.

ambiguous synsets associated to more than one temporal dimension. Similary to Tekiroglu et al. (2014), raters who scored at least 70% accuracy on average on both sets were considered to be reliable. Finally, each synset was annotated by at least 10 reliable raters.

To have a concrete idea about the agreement between annotators, we calculated the majority class for each synset in our dataset. A synset belongs to a majority class k if the most frequent annotation for the synset was selected by at least k annotators. As a consequence, a large percentage of synsets belonging to high majority classes are symptomatic of good inter-annotator agreement. Table 3 shows the observed agreement. Similarly to Özbal et al. (2011), we consider all annotations with a majority class greater than 5 as reliable. In this case, for the *temporal* vs. *atemporal* annotation scheme, 84.83% of the synsets were annotated identically by the majority of annotators, while for *past*, *present*, and *future*, 72.36% of the annotations fell into this case. As such, we can be confident that the annotation process was successful and the dataset is reliable.

5 Intrinsic and Extrinsic Evaluations

Different intrinsic and extrinsic evaluations have been proposed in prior studies. We compare our work to the same tasks as proposed by Dias et al. (2014) and Hasanuzzaman et al. (2014b), and introduce an extra experiment on temporal relation annotation.

5.1 Inter-Annotator Agreement

In order to compare our approach to prior works, we adopted a similar evaluation strategy as proposed in Dias et al. (2014) and Hasanuzzaman et al. (2014b). To assess human judgment regarding the temporal parts, inter-rater agreement with multiple raters (i.e. 3 human annotators with the 4th annotator being the classifier) was performed over a set of 398 randomly selected synsets. The free-marginal multirater kappa (Randolph, 2005) and the fixed-marginal multirater kappa (Siegel and Castellan, 1988) values are reported in Table 4 and assess moderate agreement for previous versions of TempoWordNet (TWnL, TWnP and TWnH), while good agreement is obtained for the resources constructed by mincuts with both *ScWt* (MC1) and *DiffWt* (MC2) weighting schemes. Note that slightly different results than the ones reported by

Majority Class	3	4	5	6	7	8	9	10
Synset as *temporal* or *atemporal*	0.20	1.21	4.32	10.69	14.56	29.34	19.23	11.01
Temporal synset into *past*, *present*, or *future*	1.23	3.01	10.45	20.22	16.56	12.34	14.23	9.01

Table 3: Percentage of synsets in each majority class.

Hasanuzzaman et al. (2014b) are seen as the number of annotated synsets is much bigger in our experiment (398 instead of 50). These agreement values provide a first and promising estimate of the improvement over the previous versions of TempoWordNet. We plan to confirm that in the future by comparing the systems to a true reference instead of observing the agreement between the systems and a multi-reference as we currently do.

Metric	TWnL	TWnP	TWnH	MC1	MC2
Fixed-marginal κ	0.51	0.46	0.54	0.71	0.78
Free-marginal κ	0.52	0.55	0.59	0.85	0.86

Table 4: Inter-annotator agreement.

5.2 Word Sense Classification

In order to compare our semi-supervised mincut approach to a reasonable baseline, we use a rule-based approach to classify test data into *past*, *present*, *future*, or *atemporal* categories. First, time expressions in glosses are identified and resolved via SUTime tagger (Chang and Manning, 2012). Then, for each synset, its time tags (e.g. FUTURE_REF) are considered as the temporal class for that particular synset. In cases where more than one temporal expression was observed (which occurred in less than 1% of the cases), the majority class is selected. If no time expression is identified by the time tagger, the list composed of 30 hand-crafted temporal seeds proposed in Dias et al. (2014) along with their direct hyponyms and a given list of standard temporal adverbials, prepositions and adjectives are used to classify synsets with one *temporal* dimension or *atemporal*. The performance of this simple rule-based approach is measured for the test data and presented in Table 5 as the baseline configuration. Note that to figure out the contribution of word sense disambiguation, the classical Lesk algorithm (Lesk, 1986) was used to choose the right sense for a given word instead of the most frequent sense. We found that this contribution is negligible ($< 0.4\%$ improvement in accuracy).

Comparative results are also presented against prior works: TWnL, TWnP, and TWnH. Table 5

shows that our configurations (MC1, MC2) perform significantly better than previous approaches. In particular, they achieve highest accuracies for *temporal* vs. *atemporal* and *past*, *present*, *future* classifications with improvements of 11.3% and 10.3%, respectively, over the second-best strategy, namely TWnH. Note that this enhancement is mainly due to higher precision overall.

Different training data sizes. In order to better understand the importance of the size of labeled data in the context of semi-supervised classification strategies, we propose the following experiments.

We randomly generate equally distributed subsets of training data L_i (from a set of 632 *temporal* and 632 *atemporal* synsets) such that $L_1 \subset L_2 \subset L_3 \ldots \subset L_n$. For each labeled dataset, we run the mincut strategy with *DiffWt* (i.e. MC2) and compare it to the hybrid propagation proposed by Hasanuzzaman et al. (2014b) (i.e. TWnH). Accuracies of both approaches over the test data are presented in Table 6.

The s-t mincut approach performs consistently better than the propagation strategy. In particular, we show that with 400 labeled examples better results can be obtained than relying on 1264 training items within a propagation paradigm.

Considering the above findings, we selected the MC2 configuration obtained with maximum labeled data for the extrinsic experiments, which includes 110,002 atemporal synsets, 1733 past synsets, 4193 present synsets, and 1730 future synsets.

5.3 Temporal Sentence Classification

Temporal sentence classification has traditionally been used as the baseline extrinsic evaluation and consists of labeling a given sentence as *past*, *present* or *future*. In order to produce comparative results with prior works, we test our methodology on the balanced dataset produced in Dias et al. (2014), which consists of 1038 sentences equally distributed as *past*, *present* and *future*.

Moreover, we propose to extend these experiments with a corpus of 300 temporal posts from

Method	Baseline	TWnL	TWnP	TWnH	MC1	MC2
Accuracy	48.8	65.6	62.0	68.4	74.4	**79.7**
temporal (p, r, f1)	(52.0, 56.3, 54.0)	(63.5, 82.1, 71.6)	(55.8, 84.2, 67.1)	(67.4, 81.9, 73.9)	(84.5, 79.8, 82.0)	(89.1, 79.3, 83.9)
atemporal (p, r, f1)	(58.2, 54.2, 56.1)	(68.3, 79.2, 73.3)	(58.9, 75.6, 66.2)	(69.3, 82.6, 75.3)	(81.3, 86.6, 83.8)	(87.4, 90.8, 89.1)
Accuracy	45.6	62.0	59.6	65.7	72.7	**76.0**
past (p, r, f1)	(49.3, 46.7, 47.9)	(61.2, 73.0, 66.5)	(59.3, 79.1, 67.7)	(63.1, 75.0, 68.0)	(71.1, 79.5, 75.0)	(81.2, 78.5, 79.8)
present (p, r, f1)	(55.3, 48.2, 51.5)	(63.0, 75.2, 68.5)	(58.0, 78.2 66.0)	(77.4, 69.2, 73.0)	(73.0, 71.5, 72.2)	(85.1, 74.7, 79.0)
future (p, r, f1)	(48.5, 49.0, 48.7)	(62.1, 71.9, 66.6)	(57.0, 83.1, 67.6)	(60.0, 75.6, 66.8)	(79.4, 69.5, 74.0)	(86.1, 70.0, 77.2)

Table 5: Accuracy for *temporal vs. atemporal* and *past, present, future* classifications using different methods measured over test data. Results are broken down by precision (p), recall (r), and f1-measure (f1) scores.

Twitter. This corpus contains 100 tweets for each temporal class, which have been time-tagged using the CrowdFlower platform footnote Annotation details are out of the scope of this paper. For both experiments, each sentence/tweet is represented as a semantic vector space model in the exact same way as proposed in Dias et al. (2014). Thus, a given learning example is a feature vector, where each attribute is either a unigram or a synonym of any temporal word contained in the sentence/tweet and its value is the tf.idf. Note that word sense disambiguation is performed using the Lesk algorithm (Lesk, 1986).

Amount of labeled data	TWnH	MC2
100	59.8	64.3
200	62.6	67.5
400	65.5	73.7
600	67.4	77.6
800	67.9	79.2
1000	68.0	79.0
1264 (all)	68.4	79.7

Table 6: Accuracy results with different sizes of labeled data for *temporal* vs. *atemporal* classification.

Comparative classification results are reported in Table 7 and show small improvements in the mincut strategy, when compared to propagation strategies. In particular, for tweet classification, TWnP shows similar results mainly due to its large coverage of temporal senses (counterbalanced by low precision as confirmed by Table 5). Indeed, TWnP contains 53,001 temporal synsets while MC2 only has 7656 temporal synsets. Note that the semantic enhancement is limited only to the synonymy relation, which drastically restricts the benefit of the semantic vector space model and due to the limited number of analyzed sentences/tweets, huge improvements were not expected.

5.4 Temporal Relation Annotation

Finally, we focus on the problem of classifying temporal relations as proposed in TempEval-3, assuming that the identification of events and timexes is already performed.

In order to produce comparative results with the best-performing system at TempEval-3, namely UTTime (Laokulrat et al., 2013) for the above task, we follow the guidelines and use the same datasets provided by the organizers (UzZaman et al., 2013).

In particular, we restrict our experiment to a subset of relations, namely BEFORE (*past*), AFTER (*future*), and INCLUDES (*present*), with all other relations mapped to the NA−RELATION for the following two subtasks: *event to document creation time* and *event to same sentence event*. This choice is motivated by the complexity of mapping the 14 relations of TempEval-3 into three temporal classes (*past, present, future*). As such, we test a simpler configuration of the original problem, but we do expect to draw conclusive remarks as minimum bias is introduced.

Note that the underlying idea of this evaluation is to measure the intuition expressed by (Kuzey et al., 2016) that temporal information extraction systems may benefit from the existence of temporal resources. If this is confirmed, deeper research should be conducted to adequately use such a proposed temporal resource for the whole task.

To solve this classification problem, we adopt a simple supervised learning strategy based on state-of-the-art characteristics, plus features from a time-augmented version of WordNet. In particular, each pair of entities to be classified as BEFORE, AFTER, INCLUDES or NA-RELATION is encoded with the following features:

- **String features:** the tokens and lemmas of each entity pair;

- **Grammatical features:** the part-of-speech tags

Method	TWnL	TWnP	TWnH	MC2
Sentence classification (p,r,f1)	(69.7,66.1,66.7)	(68.2,70.5,69.3)	(69.8,67.6,68.6)	(73.3,70.1 **71.4**)
Tweet classification (p,r,f1)	(51.4,47.1,49.1)	(50.4,52.8,51.5)	(51.8,48.2,49.8)	(52.8,50.6,**51.6**)

Table 7: Results for temporal sentence and tweet classification performed on 10-fold cross validation with SVM with Weka default parameters.

of the entity pair (only for event-event pairs), and a binary feature indicating whether the entity pair has the same PoS tag;

- **Entity attributes:** the entity pair attributes as provided in the dataset. These include class, tense, aspect, and polarity for events, while the attributes of time expressions are its type, value, and dct (indicating whether a time expression is the document creation time or not);

- **Dependency relation:** the type of dependency and the dependency order between entities;

- **Textual context:** the textual order of the entity pair;

- **Temporal lexicon:** the relative frequency of each temporal category (*past*, *present*, *future*) appearing in the context of an entity pair; the context is considered as (i) the text appearing between entities, (ii) the text of all tokens in a time expression, and (iii) 5 tokens around time expressions or events. The features are encoded as the frequency with which a word from a temporal category appeared in the text divided by the total number of tokens in the text.

Approaches	Precision	Recall	F1
UTTime	57.5	58.7	58.1
TRMC2	**66.9**	**68.7**	**67.7**
TRTWnH	61.2	62.5	61.8

Table 8: Temporal relation classification results.

Based on this feature representation, the two best classifiers for *event to document creation time* and *event to same sentence event* subtasks are selected via a grid search over parameter settings. The grid is evaluated with a 5-fold cross validation on the training data and SVM classifiers are chosen with default parameters of the Weka platform. This produces two systems, namely TRMC2 and TRTWnH depending on the temporal lexicon used: MC2 or TWnH. Note that we also measure the performance of UTTime for the settings stated above.

Table 8 presents comparative evaluations. Re-sults show that TRMC2 outperforms all other approaches and achieves highest performance in terms of precision, recall, and F1-measure. However, more important still is the fact that a simple learning strategy with some temporal lexicon (MC2 or TWnH) leads to improved results, when compared to some solution that does not take advantage of such a resource (UTTime, here).

Features	F1	Features	F1
mfc baseline	33.55	all features	**67.7**
string alone	45.06	w/o *string*	65.70
grammatical alone	46.96	w/o *grammatical*	64.85
entity alone	52.23	w/o *entity*	62.08
dependency alone	48.65	w/o *dependency*	65.06
textual alone	46.82	w/o *textual*	64.96
temporal alone	51.62	w/o *temporal*	62.76

Table 9: Feature ablation analysis. The most frequent class baseline (mfc).

In order to measure the real impact of the temporal lexicon features, we present feature ablation analyses in Table 9. Results clearly show the importance of the features based on the temporal lexicon, being the second best-performing feature set. As a consequence, we may conclude that improvements in temporal analysis may be obtained by the correct use of some temporal lexical resource.

6 Conclusions

In this paper, we proposed a semi-supervised min-cut strategy to address the relatively unexplored problem of associating word senses with their underlying temporal dimensions. We produce a reliable temporal lexical resource by automatically time-tagging WordNet synsets into *past*, *present*, *future* or *atemporal* categories. The underlying idea is that instead of using a single view on the data (as done in prior work), multiple views result in better temporal classification accuracy. In particular, both intrinsic and extrinsic experimental results confirm the soundness of the proposed approach and support our initial hypotheses. Note that the all resources created within this work are publicly available.

Acknowledgments

The ADAPT Centre for Digital Content Technology is funded under the SFI Research Centres Programme (Grant 13/RC/2106) and is co-funded under the European Regional Development Fund.

References

Avrim Blum and Shuchi Chawla. 2001. Learning from labeled and unlabeled data using graph mincuts. In *Proceedings of the Eighteenth International Conference on Machine Learning (ICML)*, pages 19–26, Massachusetts, USA.

Ricardo Campos, Gaël Dias, Alípio M. Jorge, and Adam Jatowt. 2014. Survey of temporal information retrieval and related applications. *ACM Computing Survey*, 47(2):15:1–15:41.

Angel X. Chang and Christopher Manning. 2012. Sutime: A library for recognizing and normalizing time expressions. In *Proceedings of the Eight International Conference on Language Resources and Evaluation (LREC)*, pages 3735–3740, Istanbul, Turkey.

Gaël Dias, Mohammed Hasanuzzaman, Stéphane Ferrari, and Yann Mathet. 2014. Tempowordnet for sentence time tagging. In *Proceedings of the Companion Publication of the 23rd International Conference on World Wide Web Companion (WWW)*, pages 833–838, Seoul, South Korea.

Mohammed Hasanuzzaman, Gaël Dias, Stéphane Ferrari, and Yann Mathet. 2014. Propagation strategies for building temporal ontologies. In *Proceedings of the 14th Conference of the European Chapter of the Association for Computational Linguistics (EACL)*, pages 6–11, Gothenburg, Sweden.

Erdal Kuzey, Jannik Strötgen, Vinay Setty, and Gerhard Weikum. 2016. Temponym tagging: Temporal scopes for textual phrases. In *Proceedings of the 25th International Conference Companion on World Wide Web (WWW)*, pages 841–842, Montreal, Canada.

Natsuda Laokulrat, Makoto Miwa, Yoshimasa Tsuruoka, and Takashi Chikayama. 2013. Uttime: Temporal relation classification using deep syntactic features. In *Proceedings of the Second Joint Conference on Lexical and Computational Semantics (*SEM)*, pages 88–92, Atlanta GA, USA.

Michael Lesk. 1986. Automatic sense disambiguation using machine readable dictionaries: How to tell a pine cone from an ice cream cone. In *Proceedings of the 5th Annual International Conference on Systems Documentation*, SIGDOC '86, pages 24–26, New York, NY, USA. ACM.

Inderjeet Mani, James Pustejovsky, and Robert Gaizauskas. 2005. *The language of time: a reader*, volume 126. Oxford University Press.

Georges A. Miller. 1995. Wordnet: a lexical database for English. *Communications of the ACM*, 38(11):39–41.

Alexandru Niculescu-Mizil and Rich Caruana. 2005. Predicting good probabilities with supervised learning. In *Proceedings of the 22Nd International Conference on Machine Learning*, ICML '05, pages 625–632, New York, NY, USA. ACM.

Christos H. Papadimitriou and Kenneth Steiglitz. 1998. *Combinatorial optimization: algorithms and complexity*. Courier Corporation.

Justus J. Randolph. 2005. Free-marginal multirater kappa (multirater κfree): an alternative to fleiss' fixed-marginal multirater kappa. *Joensuu Learning and Instruction Symposium*.

H. Andrew Schwartz, Greg Park, Maarten Sap, Evan Weingarten, Johannes Eichstaedt, Margaret Kern, Jonah Berger, Martin Seligman, and Lyle Ungar. 2015. Extracting human temporal orientation in facebook language. In *Proceedings of The 2015 Conference of the North American Chapter of the Association for Computational Linguistics-Human Language Technologies (NAACL)*, Denver, Colorado, USA.

Sydney Siegel and John Castellan. 1988. *Nonparametric Statistics for the Social Sciences*. Mcgraw-hill edition.

Jannik Strötgen and Michael Gertz. 2015. A baseline temporal tagger for all languages. In *Proceedings of the 2015 Conference on Empirical Methods in Natural Language Processing (EMNLP)*, pages 541–547, Lisbon, Portugal.

Naushad UzZaman, Hector Llorens, Leon Derczynski, James Allen, Marc Verhagen, and James Pustejovsky. 2013. Semeval-2013 task 1: Tempeval-3: Evaluating time expressions, events, and temporal relations. In *Proceedings of 2nd Joint Conference on Lexical and Computational Semantics (*SEM)*, pages 1–9, Atlanta, Georgia, USA.

Semi-supervised Clustering for Short Text via Deep Representation Learning

Zhiguo Wang and **Haitao Mi** and **Abraham Ittycheriah**
IBM T.J. Watson Research Center
Yorktown Heights, NY, USA
{zhigwang, hmi, abei}@us.ibm.com

Abstract

In this work, we propose a semi-supervised method for short text clustering, where we represent texts as distributed vectors with neural networks, and use a small amount of labeled data to specify our intention for clustering. We design a novel objective to combine the representation learning process and the k-means clustering process together, and optimize the objective with both labeled data and unlabeled data iteratively until convergence through three steps: (1) assign each short text to its nearest centroid based on its representation from the current neural networks; (2) re-estimate the cluster centroids based on cluster assignments from step (1); (3) update neural networks according to the objective by keeping centroids and cluster assignments fixed. Experimental results on four datasets show that our method works significantly better than several other text clustering methods.

1 Introduction

Text clustering is a fundamental problem in text mining and information retrieval. Its task is to group similar texts together such that texts within a cluster are more similar to texts in other clusters. Usually, a text is represented as a bag-of-words or term frequency-inverse document frequency (TF-IDF) vector, and then the k-means algorithm (MacQueen, 1967) is performed to partition a set of texts into homogeneous groups.

However, when dealing with short texts, the characteristics of short text and clustering task raise several issues for the conventional unsupervised clustering algorithms. First, the number of uniqe words in each short text is small, as a re-

(a) What's the color of apples?
(b) When will this apple be ripe?
(c) Do you like apples?
(d) What's the color of oranges?
(e) When will this orange be ripe?
(f) Do you like oranges?

Table 1: Examples for short text clustering.

sult, the lexcical sparsity issue usually leads to poor clustering quality (Dhillon and Guan, 2003). Second, for a specific short text clustering task, we have prior knowledge or particular intentions before clustering, while fully unsupervised approaches may learn some classes the other way around. Take the sentences in Table 1 for example, those sentences can be clustered into different partitions based on different intentions: *apple* {a, b, c} and *orange* {d, e, f} with a fruit type intention, or *what-question* {a, d}, *when-question* {b, e}, and *yes/no-question* cluster {c, f} with a question type intension.

To address the lexical sparity issue, one direction is to enrich text representations by extracting features and relations from Wikipedia (Banerjee et al., 2007) or an ontology (Fodeh et al., 2011). But this approach requires the annotated knowledge, which is also language dependent. So the other direction, which directly encode texts into distributed vectors with neural networks (Hinton and Salakhutdinov, 2006; Xu et al., 2015), becomes more interesting. To tackle the second problem, semi-supervised approaches (e.g. (Bilenko et al., 2004; Davidson and Basu, 2007; Bair, 2013)) have gained significant popularity in the past decades. Our question is can we have a unified model to integrate neural networks into the semi-supervised framework?

In this paper, we propose a unified framework for the short text clustering task. We employ a

Proceedings of the 20th SIGNLL Conference on Computational Natural Language Learning (CoNLL), pages 31–39,
Berlin, Germany, August 7-12, 2016. ©2016 Association for Computational Linguistics

deep neural network model to represent short sentences, and integrate it into a semi-supervised algorithm. Concretely, we extend the objective in the classical unsupervised k-means algorithm by adding a penalty term from labeled data. Thus, the new objective covers three key groups of parameters: centroids of clusters, the cluster assignment for each text, and the parameters within deep neural networks. In the training procedure, we start from random initialization of centroids and neural networks, and then optimize the objective iteratively through three steps until converge:

(1) assign each short text to its nearest centroid based on its representation from the current neural networks;

(2) re-estimate cluster centroids based on cluster assignments from step (1);

(3) update neural networks according to the objective by keeping centroids and cluster assignments fixed.

Experimental results on four different datasets show that our method achieves significant improvements over several other text clustering methods.

In following parts, we first describe our neural network models for text representation (Section 2). Then we introduce our semi-supervised clustering method and the learning algorithm (Section 3). Finally, we evaluate our method on four different datasets (Section 4).

2 Representation Learning for Short Texts

We represent each word with a dense vector w, so that a short text s is first represented as a matrix $S = [w_1, ..., w_{|s|}]$, which is a concatenation of all vectors of w in s, $|s|$ is the length of s. Then we design two different types of neural networks to ingest the word vector sequence S: the convolutional neural networks (CNN) and the long short-term memory (LSTM). More formally, we define the presentation function as $x = f(s)$, where x represents the vector of the text s. We test two encoding functions (CNN and LSTM) in our experiments.

Inspired from Kim (2014), our CNN model views the sequence of word vectors as a matrix, and applies two sequential operations: *convolution* and *max-pooling*. Then, a fully connected layer is

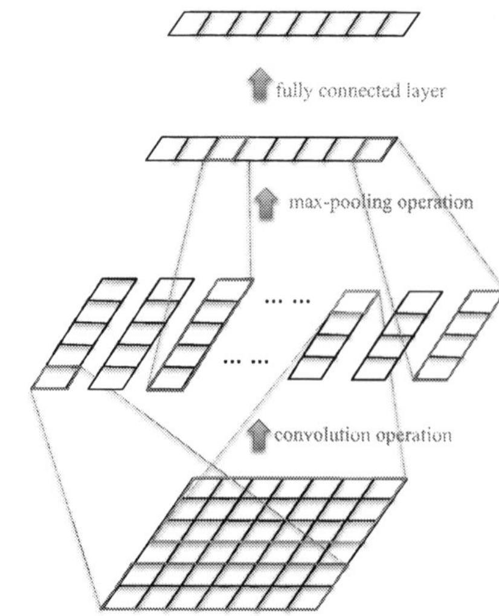

Figure 1: CNN for text representation learning.

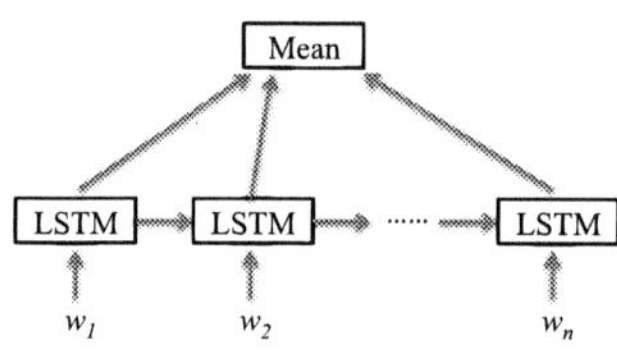

Figure 2: LSTM for text representation learning.

employed to convert the final representation vector into a fixed size. Figure 1 gives the diagram of the CNN model. In the *convolution* operation, we define a list of filters $\{w_o\}$, where the shape of each filter is $d \times h$, d is the dimension of word vectors and h is the window size. Each filter is applied to a patch (a window size h of vectors) of S, and generates a feature. We apply this filter to all possible patches in S, and produce a series of features. The number of features depends on the shape of the filter w_o and the length of the input short text. To deal with variable feature size, we perform a *max-pooling* operation over all the features to select the maximum value. Therefore, after the two operations, each filter generates only one feature. We define several filters by varying the window size and the initial values. Thus, a vector of features is captured after the *max-pooling* operation, and the feature dimension is equal to the number of filters.

Figure 2 gives the diagram of our LSTM model. We implement the standard LSTM block described in Graves (2012). Each word vector is fed into the LSTM model sequentially, and the mean of the hidden states over the entire sentence is taken as the final representation vector.

3 Semi-supervised Clustering for Short Texts

3.1 Revisiting K-means Clustering

Given a set of texts $\{s_1, s_2, ..., s_N\}$, we represent them as a set of data points $\{x_1, x_2, ..., x_N\}$, where x_i can be a bag-of-words or TF-IDF vector in traditional approaches, or a dense vector in Section 2. The task of text clustering is to partition the data set into some number K of clusters, such that the sum of the squared distance of each data point to its closest cluster centroid is minimized. For each data point x_n, we define a set of binary variables $r_{nk} \in \{0, 1\}$, where $k \in \{1, ..., K\}$ describing which of the K clusters x_n is assigned to. So that if x_n is assigned to cluster k, then $r_{nk} = 1$, and $r_{nj} = 0$ for $j \neq k$. Let's define μ_k as the centroid of the k-th cluster. We can then formulate the objective function as

$$J_{unsup} = \sum_{n=1}^{N} \sum_{k=1}^{K} r_{nk} \|x_n - \mu_k\|^2 \qquad (1)$$

Our goal is the find the values of $\{r_{nk}\}$ and $\{\mu_k\}$ so as to minimize J_{unsup}.

The k-means algorithm optimizes J_{unsup} through the gradient descent approach, and results in an iterative procedure (Bishop, 2006). Each iteration involves two steps: *E-step* and *M-step*. In the *E-step*, the algorithm minimizes J_{unsup} with respect to $\{r_{nk}\}$ by keeping $\{\mu_k\}$ fixed. J_{unsup} is a linear function for $\{r_{nk}\}$, so we can optimize for each data point separately by simply assigning the n-th data point to the closest cluster centroid. In the *M-step*, the algorithm minimizes J_{unsup} with respect to $\{\mu_k\}$ by keeping $\{r_{nk}\}$ fixed. J_{unsup} is a quadratic function of $\{\mu_k\}$, and it can be minimized by setting its derivative with respect to $\{\mu_k\}$ to zero.

$$\frac{\partial J_{unsup}}{\partial \mu_k} = 2 \sum_{n=1}^{N} r_{nk}(x_n - \mu_k) = 0 \qquad (2)$$

Then, we can easily solve $\{\mu_k\}$ as

$$\mu_k = \frac{\sum_{n=1}^{N} r_{nk} x_n}{\sum_{n=1}^{N} r_{nk}} \qquad (3)$$

In other words, μ_k is equal to the mean of all the data points assigned to cluster k.

3.2 Semi-supervised K-means with Neural Networks

The classical k-means algorithm only uses unlabeled data, and solves the clustering problem under the unsupervised learning framework. As already mentioned, the clustering results may not be consistent to our intention. In order to acquire useful clustering results, some supervised information should be introduced into the learning procedure. To this end, we employ a small amount of labeled data to guide the clustering process.

Following Section 2, we represent each text s as a dense vector x via neural networks $f(s)$. Instead of training the text representation model separately, we integrate the training process into the k-means algorithm, so that both the labeled data and the unlabeled data can be used for representation learning and text clustering. Let us denote the labeled data set as $\{(s_1, y_1), (s_2, y_2), ..., (s_L, y_L)\}$, and the unlabeled data set as $\{s_{L+1}, s_{L+2}, ..., s_N\}$, where y_i is the given label for s_i. We then define the objective function as:

$$J_{semi} = \alpha \sum_{n=1}^{N} \sum_{k=1}^{K} r_{nk} \|f(s_n) - \mu_k\|^2$$

$$+ (1 - \alpha) \sum_{n=1}^{L} \{\|f(s_n) - \mu_{g_n}\|^2 +$$

$$\sum_{j \neq g_n} [l + \|f(s_n) - \mu_{g_n}\|^2 - \|f(s_n) - \mu_j\|^2]_+ \}$$

$$(4)$$

The objective function contains two terms. The first term is adapted from the unsupervised k-means algorithm in Eq. (1), and the second term is defined to encourage labeled data being clustered in correlation with the given labels. $\alpha \in [0, 1]$ is used to tune the importance of unlabeled data. The second term contains two parts. The first part penalizes large distance between each labeled instance and its correct cluster centroid, where $g_n = G(y_n)$ is the cluster ID mapped from the given label y_n, and the mapping function $G(\cdot)$ is implemented with the Hungarian algorithm (Munkres, 1957). The second part is denoted as a hinge loss with a margin l, where $[x]_+ = max(x, 0)$. This part incurs some loss if the distance to the correct centroid is not shorter (by the margin l) than distances to any of incorrect cluster centroids.

There are three groups of parameters in J_{semi}: the cluster assignment of each text $\{r_{nk}\}$, the clus-

> 1. Initialize $\{\mu_k\}$ and $f(\cdot)$.
> 2. *assign_cluster*: Assign each text to its nearest cluster centroid.
> 3. *estimate_centroid*: Estimate the cluster centroids based on the cluster assignments from step 2.
> 4. *update_parameter*: Update parameters in neural networks.
> 5. Repeat step 2 to 4 until convergence.

Table 2: Pseudocode for semi-supervised clustering

ter centroids $\{\mu_k\}$, and the parameters within the neural network model $f(\cdot)$. Our goal is to find the values of $\{r_{nk}\}$, $\{\mu_k\}$ and parameters in $f(\cdot)$, so as to minimize J_{semi}. Inspired from the k-means algorithm, we design an algorithm to successively minimize J_{semi} with respect to $\{r_{nk}\}$, $\{\mu_k\}$, and parameters in $f(\cdot)$. Table 2 gives the corresponding pseudocode. First, we initialize the cluster centroids $\{\mu_k\}$ with the `k-means++` strategy (Arthur and Vassilvitskii, 2007), and randomly initialize all the parameters in the neural network model. Then, the algorithm iteratively goes through three steps (*assign_cluster*, *estimate_centroid*, and *update_parameter*) until J_{semi} converges.

The *assign_cluster* step minimizes J_{semi} with respect to $\{r_{nk}\}$ by keeping $f(\cdot)$ and $\{\mu_k\}$ fixed. Its goal is to assign a cluster ID for each data point. We can see that the second term in Eq. (4) has no relation with $\{r_{nk}\}$. Thus, we only need to minimize the first term by assigning each text to its nearest cluster centroid, which is identical to the *E-step* in the k-means algorithm. In this step, we also calculate the mappings between the given labels $\{y_i\}$ and the cluster IDs (with the Hungarian algorithm) based on cluster assignments of all labeled data.

The *estimate_centroid* step minimizes J_{semi} with respect to $\{\mu_k\}$ by keeping $\{r_{nk}\}$ and $f(\cdot)$ fixed, which corresponds to the *M-step* in the k-means algorithm. It aims to estimate the cluster centroids $\{\mu_k\}$ based on the cluster assignments $\{r_{nk}\}$ from the *assign_cluster* step. The second term in Eq. (4) makes each labeled instance involved in the estimating process of cluster centroids. By solving $\partial J_{semi}/\partial \mu_k = 0$, we get

$$\mu_k = \frac{\sum_{n=1}^{N} \alpha r_{nk} f(s_n) + \sum_{n=1}^{L} w_{nk} f(s_n)}{\sum_{n=1}^{N} \alpha r_{nk} + \sum_{n=1}^{L} w_{nk}} \quad (5)$$

$$w_{nk} = (1-\alpha)(I'_{nk} + \sum_{j \neq g_n} I''_{nkj} - \sum_{j \neq g_n} I'''_{nkj})$$
$$I'_{nk} = \delta(k, g_n)$$
$$I''_{nkj} = \delta(k, j) \cdot \delta'_{nj}$$
$$I'''_{nkj} = (1 - \delta(k, j)) \cdot \delta'_{nj}$$
$$\delta'_{nj} = \delta(l + \|f(s_n) - \mu_{g_n}\|^2 - \|f(s_n) - \mu_j\|^2 > 0)$$
$$(6)$$

where $\delta(x_1, x_2)$=1 if x_1 is equal to x_2, otherwise $\delta(x_1, x_2)$=0, and $\delta(x)$=1 if x is true, otherwise $\delta(x)$=0. The first term in the numerator of Eq. (5) is the contributions from all data points, and αr_{nk} is the weight of s_n for μ_k. The second term is acquired from labeled data, and w_{nk} is the weight of a labeled instance s_n for μ_k.

The *update_parameter* step minimizes J_{semi} with respect to $f(\cdot)$ by keeping $\{r_{nk}\}$ and $\{\mu_k\}$ fixed, which has no counterpart in the k-means algorithm. The main goal is to update parameters for the text representation model. We take J_{semi} as the loss function, and train neural networks with the *Adam* algorithm (Kingma and Ba, 2014).

4 Experiment

4.1 Experimental Setting

We evaluate our method on four short text datasets. (1) *question_type* is the TREC question dataset (Li and Roth, 2002), where all the questions are classified into 6 categories: abbreviation, description, entity, human, location and numeric. (2) *ag_news* dataset contains short texts extracted from the AG's news corpus, where all the texts are classified into 4 categories: World, Sports, Business, and Sci/Tech (Zhang and Le-Cun, 2015). (3) *dbpedia* is the DBpedia ontology dataset, which is constructed by picking 14 non-overlapping classes from DBpedia 2014 (Lehmann et al., 2014). (4) *yahoo_answer* is the 10 topics classification dataset extracted from Yahoo! Answers Comprehensive Questions and Answers version 1.0 dataset by Zhang and LeCun

34

dataset	class#	total#	labeled#
question_type	6	5,953	595
ag_news	4	4,000	400
dbpedia	14	14,000	1,400
yahoo_answer	10	10,000	1,000

Table 3: Statistics for the short text datasets

(2015). We use all the 5,952 questions for the *question_type* dataset. But the other three datasets contain too many instances (e.g. 1,400,000 instances in yahoo_answer). Running clustering experiments on such a large dataset is quite inefficient. Following the same solution in (Xu et al., 2015), we randomly choose 1,000 samples for each classes individually for the other three datasets. Within each dataset, we randomly sample 10% of the instances as labeled data, and evaluate the performance on the remaining 90% instances [1]. Table 3 summarizes the statistics of these datasets.

In all experiments, we set the size of word vector dimension as $d=300$ [2], and pre-train the word vectors with the *word2vec* toolkit (Mikolov et al., 2013) on the English Gigaword (LDC2011T07). The number of clusters is set to be the same number of labels in the dataset. The clustering performance is evaluated with two metrics: Adjusted Mutual Information (AMI) (Vinh et al., 2009) and accuracy (ACC) (Amigó et al., 2009). In order to show the statistical significance, the performance of each experiment is the average of 10 trials.

4.2 Model Properties

There are several hyper-parameters in our model, e.g., the output dimension of the text representation models, and the α in Eq. (4). The choice of these hyper-parameters may affect the final performance. In this subsection, we present some experiments to demonstrate the properties of our model, and find a good configuration that we use to evaluate our final model. All the experiments in this

---

[1] We didn't split dataset into train/dev/test portions which is commonly used for classification tasks, because it is not the convention for clustering task. First, the goal of clustering is to group given instances into clusters, instead of applying the trained model to new instances. Second, the evaluation process requires the clustering result of the whole set to map the clustering labels to the annotated labels.

[2] We tuned different dimensions for word vectors. When the size is small (50 or 100), performance drops significantly. When the size is larger (300, 500 or 1000), the curve flattens out. To make our model more efficient, we fixed it as 300.

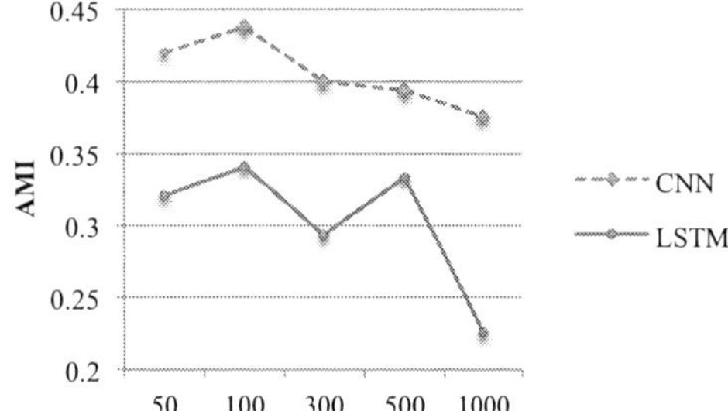

Figure 3: Influence of the short text representation model, where the x-axis is the output dimension of the text representation models.

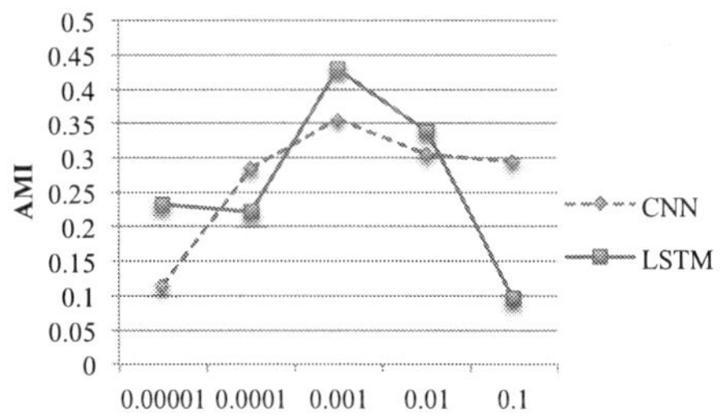

Figure 4: Influence of unlabeled data, where the x-axis is α in Eq. (4).

subsection were performed on the *question_type* dataset.

First, we evaluated the effectiveness of the output dimension in text representation models. We switched the dimension size among {50, 100, 300, 500, 1000}, and fixed the other options as: $\alpha = 0.5$, the filter types in the CNN model including {unigram, bigram, trigram} and 500 filters for each type. Figure 3 presents the AMIs from both CNN and LSTM models. We found that 100 is the best output dimension for both CNN and LSTM models. Therefore, we set the output dimension as 100 in the following experiments.

Second, we studied the effect of α in Eq. (4), which tunes the importance of unlabeled data. We varied α among {0.00001, 0.0001, 0.001, 0.01, 0.1}, and remain the other options as the last experiment. Figure 4 shows the AMIs from both CNN and LSTM models. We found that the clustering performance is not good when using a very small α. By increasing the value of α, we acquired progressive improvements, and reached to the peak point at $\alpha=0.01$. After that, the performance dropped. Therefore, we choose $\alpha=0.01$ in

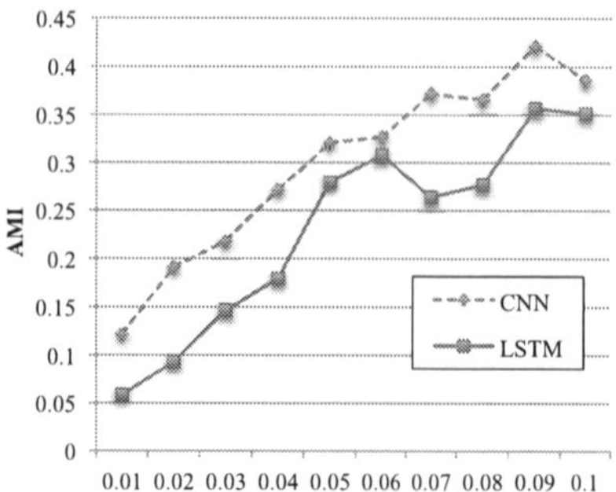

Figure 5: Influence of labeled data, where the x-axis is the ratio of data with given labels.

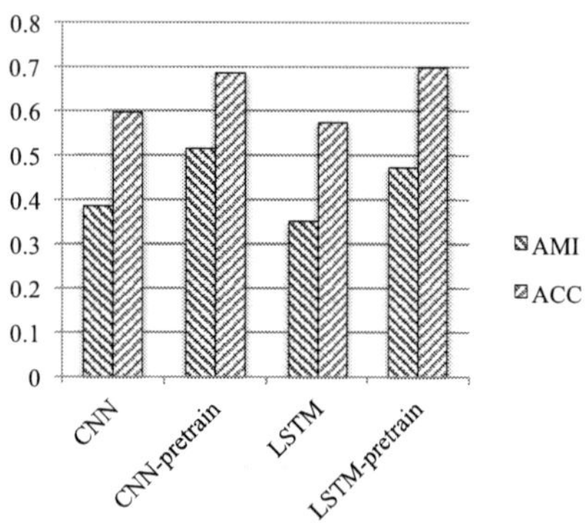

Figure 6: Influence of the pre-training strategy.

the following experiments. This results also indicate that the unlabeled data are useful for the text representation learning process.

Third, we tested the influence of the size of labeled data. We tuned the ratio of labeled instances from the whole dataset among [1%, 10%], and kept the other configurations as the previous experiment. The AMIs are shown in Figure 5. We can see that the more labeled data we use, the better performance we get. Therefore, the labeled data are quite useful for the clustering process.

Fourth, we checked the effect of the pre-training strategy for our models. We added a softmax layer on top of our CNN and LSTM models, where the size of the output layer is equal to the number of labels in the dataset. We then trained the model through the classification task using all labeled data. After this process, we removed the top layer, and used the remaining parameters to initialize our CNN and LSTM models. The performance for our models with and without pre-training strategy are given in Figure 6. We can see that the pre-training

strategy is quite effective for our models. Therefore, we use the pre-training strategy in the following experiments.

4.3 Comparing with other Models

In this subsection, we compared our method with some representative systems. We implemented a series of clustering systems. All of these systems are based on the k-means algorithm, but they represent short texts differently:

bow represents each text as a bag-of-words vector.

tf-idf represents each text as a TF-IDF vector.

average-vec represents each text with the average of all word vectors within the text.

metric-learn-bow employs the metric learning method proposed by Weinberger et al. (2005), and learns to project a bag-of-words vector into a 300-dimensional vector based on labeled data.

metric-learn-idf uses the same metric learning method, and learns to map a TF-IDF vector into a 300-dimensional vector based on labeled data.

metric-learn-ave-vec also uses the metric learning method, and learns to project an averaged word vector into a 100-dimensional vector based on labeled data.

We designed two classifiers (cnn-classifier and lstm-classifier) by adding a softmax layer on top of our CNN and LSTM models. We trained these two classifiers with labeled data, and utilized them to predict labels for unlabeled data. We also built two text representation models ("cnn-represent." and "lstm-represent.") by setting parameters of our CNN and LSTM models with the corresponding parameters in cnn-classifier and lstm-classifier. Then, we used them to represent short texts into vectors, and applied the k-means algorithm for clustering.

Table 4 summarizes the results of all systems on each dataset, where "semi-cnn" is our semi-supervised clustering algorithm with the CNN model, and "semi-lstm" is our semi-supervised clustering algorithm with the LSTM model. We

		question_type		ag_news		dbpedia		yahoo_answer	
		AMI	ACC	AMI	ACC	AMI	ACC	AMI	ACC
Unsup.	bow	0.028	0.257	0.029	0.311	0.578	0.546	0.019	0.140
	tf-idf	0.031	0.259	0.168	0.449	0.558	0.527	0.023	0.145
	average-vec	0.135	0.356	0.457	0.737	0.610	0.619	0.077	0.222
Sup.	metric-learn-bow	0.104	0.380	0.459	0.776	0.808	0.854	0.125	0.329
	metric-learn-idf	0.114	0.379	0.443	0.765	0.821	0.876	0.150	0.368
	metric-learn-ave-vec	0.304	0.553	0.606	0.851	0.829	0.879	0.221	0.400
	cnn-classifier	0.511	**0.771**	0.554	0.771	0.879	0.938	0.285	0.501
	cnn-represent.	0.442	0.618	0.604	0.833	0.864	0.899	0.210	0.334
	lstm-classifier	0.482	0.741	0.524	0.763	0.862	0.928	0.283	0.512
	lstm-represent.	0.421	0.618	0.535	0.771	0.667	0.706	0.152	0.272
Semisup.	semi-cnn	**0.529**	0.739	**0.662**	**0.876**	**0.894**	**0.945**	**0.338**	**0.554**
	semi-lstm	0.492	0.712	0.599	0.830	0.788	0.802	0.187	0.337

Table 4: Performance of all systems on each dataset.

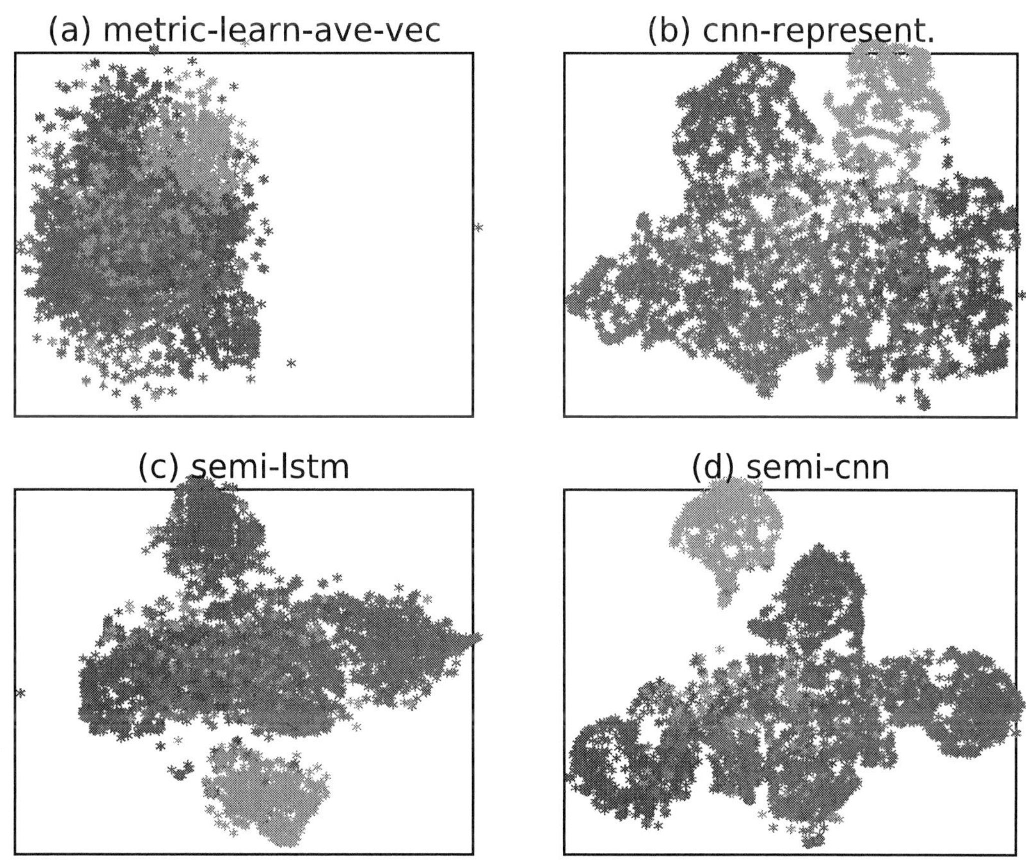

Figure 7: t-SNE visualizations of clustering results.

grouped all the systems into three categories: un-supervised (Unsup.), supervised (Sup.), and semi-supervised (Semisup.) [3]. We found that the supervised systems worked much better than the unsupervised counterparts, which implies that the small amount of labeled data is necessary for better performance. We also noticed that within the supervised systems, the systems using deep learning (CNN or LSTM) models worked better than the systems using metric learning method, which shows the power of deep learning models for short text modeling. Our "semi-cnn" system got the best performance on almost all the datasets.

Figure 7 visualizes clustering results on the *question_type* dataset from four representative systems. In Figure 7(a), clusters severely overlap with each other. When using the CNN sentence representation model, we can clearly identify all clusters in Figure 7(b), but the boundaries between clusters are still obscure. The clustering results from our semi-supervised clustering algorithm are given in Figure 7(c) and Figure 7(d). We can see that the boundaries between clusters become much clearer. Therefore, our algorithm is very effective for short text clustering.

5 Related Work

Existing semi-supervised clustering methods fall into two categories: *constraint-based* and *representation-based*. In *constraint-based* methods (Davidson and Basu, 2007), some labeled information is used to constrain the clustering process. In *representation-based* methods (Bair, 2013), a representation model is first trained to satisfy the labeled information, and all data points are clustered based on representations from the representation model. Bilenko et al. (2004) proposed to integrate there two methods into a unified framework, which shares the same idea of our proposed method. However, they only employed the metric learning model for representation learning, which is a linear projection. Whereas, our method utilized deep learning models to learn representations in a more flexible non-linear space. Xu et al. (2015) also employed deep learning models for short text clustering. However, their method separated the representation learning

process from the clustering process, so it belongs to the *representation-based* method. Whereas, our method combined the representation learning process and the clustering process together, and utilized both labeled data and unlabeled data for representation learning and clustering.

6 Conclusion

In this paper, we proposed a semi-supervised clustering algorithm for short texts. We utilized deep learning models to learn representations for short texts, and employed a small amount of labeled data to specify our intention for clustering. We integrated the representation learning process and the clustering process into a unified framework, so that both of the two processes get some benefits from labeled data and unlabeled data. Experimental results on four datasets show that our method is more effective than other competitors.

References

Enrique Amigó, Julio Gonzalo, Javier Artiles, and Felisa Verdejo. 2009. A comparison of extrinsic clustering evaluation metrics based on formal constraints. *Information retrieval*, 12(4):461–486.

David Arthur and Sergei Vassilvitskii. 2007. k-means++: The advantages of careful seeding. In *Proceedings of the eighteenth annual ACM-SIAM symposium on Discrete algorithms*, pages 1027–1035.

Eric Bair. 2013. Semi-supervised clustering methods. *Wiley Interdisciplinary Reviews: Computational Statistics*, 5(5):349–361.

Somnath Banerjee, Krishnan Ramanathan, and Ajay Gupta. 2007. Clustering short texts using wikipedia. In *Proceedings of the 30th annual international ACM SIGIR conference on Research and development in information retrieval*, pages 787–788.

Mikhail Bilenko, Sugato Basu, and Raymond J Mooney. 2004. Integrating constraints and metric learning in semi-supervised clustering. In *Proceedings of the twenty-first international conference on Machine learning*, page 11. ACM.

Christopher M Bishop. 2006. *Pattern recognition and machine learning*. springer.

Ian Davidson and Sugato Basu. 2007. A survey of clustering with instance level constraints. *ACM Transactions on Knowledge Discovery from Data*, 1:1–41.

---

[3]All clustering systems are based on the same number of instances (total# in Table 3). For the semi-supervised and supervised systems, the labels for 1% of the instances are given (labeled# in Table 3). And the evaluation was conducted only on the unlabeled portion.

Inderjit S. Dhillon and Yuqiang Guan. 2003. Information theoretic clustering of sparse co-occurrence data. pages 517–520. IEEE Computer Society.

Samah Fodeh, Bill Punch, and Pang-Ning Tan. 2011. On ontology-driven document clustering using core semantic features. *Knowledge and information systems*, 28(2):395–421.

Alex Graves. 2012. *Supervised sequence labelling with recurrent neural networks*, volume 385.

Geoffrey E Hinton and Ruslan R Salakhutdinov. 2006. Reducing the dimensionality of data with neural networks. *Science*, 313(5786):504–507.

Yoon Kim. 2014. Convolutional neural networks for sentence classification. In *Proceedings of the 2014 Conference on Empirical Methods in Natural Language Processing*, pages 1746–1751.

Diederik Kingma and Jimmy Ba. 2014. Adam: A method for stochastic optimization. *arXiv preprint arXiv:1412.6980*.

Jens Lehmann, Robert Isele, Max Jakob, Anja Jentzsch, Dimitris Kontokostas, Pablo N Mendes, Sebastian Hellmann, Mohamed Morsey, Patrick van Kleef, Sören Auer, et al. 2014. Dbpedia-a large-scale, multilingual knowledge base extracted from wikipedia. *Semantic Web Journal*, 5:1–29.

Xin Li and Dan Roth. 2002. Learning question classifiers. In *Proceedings of the 19th international conference on Computational linguistics-Volume 1*, pages 1–7.

James MacQueen. 1967. Some methods for classification and analysis of multivariate observations. In *Proceedings of the fifth Berkeley symposium on mathematical statistics and probability*, volume 1, pages 281–297. Oakland, CA, USA.

Tomas Mikolov, Kai Chen, Greg Corrado, and Jeffrey Dean. 2013. Efficient estimation of word representations in vector space. *arXiv preprint arXiv:1301.3781*.

James Munkres. 1957. Algorithms for the assignment and transportation problems. *Journal of the Society for Industrial and Applied Mathematics*, 5(1):32–38.

Nguyen Xuan Vinh, Julien Epps, and James Bailey. 2009. Information theoretic measures for clusterings comparison: is a correction for chance necessary? In *Proceedings of the 26th Annual International Conference on Machine Learning*, pages 1073–1080.

Kilian Q Weinberger, John Blitzer, and Lawrence K Saul. 2005. Distance metric learning for large margin nearest neighbor classification. In *Advances in neural information processing systems*, pages 1473–1480.

Jiaming Xu, Peng Wang, Guanhua Tian, Bo Xu, Jun Zhao, Fangyuan Wang, and Hongwei Hao. 2015. Short text clustering via convolutional neural networks. In *Proceedings of NAACL-HLT*, pages 62–69.

Xiang Zhang and Yann LeCun. 2015. Text understanding from scratch. *arXiv preprint arXiv:1502.01710*.

Neighborhood Mixture Model for Knowledge Base Completion

Dat Quoc Nguyen[1], **Kairit Sirts**[1], **Lizhen Qu**[2] and **Mark Johnson**[1]

[1] Department of Computing, Macquarie University, Sydney, Australia
dat.nguyen@students.mq.edu.au, {kairit.sirts, mark.johnson}@mq.edu.au
[2] Data61 & Australian National University
lizhen.qu@data61.csiro.au

Abstract

Knowledge bases are useful resources for many natural language processing tasks, however, they are far from complete. In this paper, we define a novel entity representation as a mixture of its neighborhood in the knowledge base and apply this technique on TransE—a well-known embedding model for knowledge base completion. Experimental results show that the neighborhood information significantly helps to improve the results of the TransE, leading to better performance than obtained by other state-of-the-art embedding models on three benchmark datasets for triple classification, entity prediction and relation prediction tasks.

Keywords: Knowledge base completion, embedding model, mixture model, link prediction, triple classification, entity prediction, relation prediction.

1 Introduction

Knowledge bases (KBs), such as WordNet (Miller, 1995), YAGO (Suchanek et al., 2007), Freebase (Bollacker et al., 2008) and DBpedia (Lehmann et al., 2015), represent relationships between entities as triples $(\text{head entity}, \text{relation}, \text{tail entity})$. Even very large knowledge bases are still far from complete (Socher et al., 2013; West et al., 2014). *Knowledge base completion* or *link prediction* systems (Nickel et al., 2015) predict which triples not in a knowledge base are likely to be true (Taskar et al., 2004; Bordes et al., 2011).

Embedding models for KB completion associate entities and/or relations with dense feature vectors or matrices. Such models obtain state-of-the-art performance (Bordes et al., 2012; Bordes et al., 2013; Socher et al., 2013; Wang et al., 2014; Guu

et al., 2015; Nguyen et al., 2016) and generalize to large KBs (Krompa et al., 2015).

Most embedding models for KB completion learn only from triples and by doing so, ignore lots of information implicitly provided by the structure of the knowledge graph. Recently, several authors have addressed this issue by incorporating relation path information into model learning (García-Durán et al., 2015; Lin et al., 2015a; Guu et al., 2015; Toutanova et al., 2016) and have shown that the relation paths between entities in KBs provide useful information and improve knowledge base completion. For instance, a three-relation path

$$(\text{head}, \text{born\_in\_hospital}/r_1, e_1)$$
$$\Rightarrow (e_1, \text{hospital\_located\_in\_city}/r_2, e_2)$$
$$\Rightarrow (e_2, \text{city\_in\_country}/r_3, \text{tail})$$

is likely to indicate that the fact $(\text{head}, \text{nationality}, \text{tail})$ could be true, so the relation path here $p = \{r_1, r_2, r_3\}$ is useful for predicting the relationship "nationality" between the head and tail entities.

Besides the relation paths, there could be other useful information implicitly presented in the knowledge base that could be exploited for better KB completion. For instance, the whole neighborhood of entities could provide lots of useful information for predicting the relationship between two entities. Consider for example a KB fragment given in Figure 1. If we know that Ben Affleck has won an Oscar award and Ben Affleck lives in Los Angeles, then this can help us to predict that Ben Affleck is an actor or a film maker, rather than a lecturer or a doctor. If we additionally know that Ben Affleck's gender is male then there is a higher chance for him to be a film maker. This intuition can be formalized by representing an entity vector as a relation-specific mixture of its neighborhood as follows:

40

Proceedings of the 20th SIGNLL Conference on Computational Natural Language Learning (CoNLL), pages 40–50,
Berlin, Germany, August 7-12, 2016. ©2016 Association for Computational Linguistics

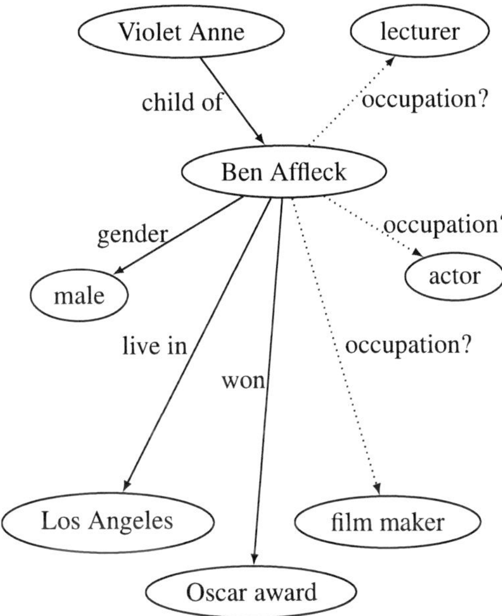

Figure 1: An example fragment of a KB.

$$
\begin{aligned}
\text{Ben\_Affleck} = \ &\omega_{r,1}(\text{Violet\_Anne}, \text{child\_of}) \\
&+ \omega_{r,2}(\text{male}, \text{gender}^{-1}) \\
&+ \omega_{r,3}(\text{Los\_Angeles}, \text{lives\_in}^{-1}) \\
&+ \omega_{r,4}(\text{Oscar\_award}, \text{won}^{-1}),
\end{aligned}
$$

where $\omega_{r,i}$ are the mixing weights that indicate how important each neighboring relation is for predicting the relation r. For example, for predicting the occupation relationship, the knowledge about the child_of relationship might not be that informative and thus the corresponding mixing coefficient can be close to zero, whereas it could be relevant for predicting some other relationship, such as parent or spouse, in which case the relation-specific mixing coefficient for the child_of relationship could be high.

The primary contribution of this paper is introducing and formalizing the neighborhood mixture model. We demonstrate its usefulness by applying it to the well-known TransE model (Bordes et al., 2013). However, it could be applied to other embedding models as well, such as Bilinear models (Bordes et al., 2012; Yang et al., 2015) and STransE (Nguyen et al., 2016). While relation path models exploit extra information using longer paths existing in the KB, the neighborhood mixture model effectively incorporates information about many paths simultaneously. Our extensive experiments on three benchmark datasets show that it achieves superior performance over competitive baselines in three KB completion tasks: triple classification, entity prediction and relation prediction.

2 Neighborhood mixture modeling

In this section, we start by explaining how to formally construct the neighbor-based entity representations in section 2.1, and then describe the Neighborhood Mixture Model applied to the TransE model (Bordes et al., 2013) in section 2.2. Section 2.3 explains how we train our model.

2.1 Neighbor-based entity representation

Let $\mathcal{E}$ denote the set of entities and $\mathcal{R}$ the set of relation types. Denote by $\mathcal{R}^{-1}$ the set of inverse relations r^{-1}. Denote by $\mathcal{G}$ the knowledge graph consisting of a set of correct tiples (h, r, t), such that $h, t \in \mathcal{E}$ and $r \in \mathcal{R}$. Let $\mathcal{K}$ denote the symmetric closure of $\mathcal{G}$, i.e. if a triple $(h, r, t) \in \mathcal{G}$, then both (h, r, t) and $(t, r^{-1}, h) \in \mathcal{K}$.

Define:

$$
\mathcal{N}_{e,r} = \{e' | (e', r, e) \in \mathcal{K}\}
$$

as a set of neighboring entities connected to entity e with relation r. Then

$$
\mathcal{N}_e = \{(e', r) | r \in \mathcal{R} \cup \mathcal{R}^{-1}, e' \in \mathcal{N}_{e,r}\}
$$

is the set of all entity and relation pairs that are neighbors for entity e.

Each entity e is associated with a k-dimensional vector $\boldsymbol{v}_e \in \mathbb{R}^k$ and relation-dependent vectors $\boldsymbol{u}_{e,r} \in \mathbb{R}^k, r \in \mathcal{R} \cup \mathcal{R}^{-1}$. Now we can define the neighborhood-based entity representation $\boldsymbol{\vartheta}_{e,r}$ for an entity $e \in \mathcal{E}$ for predicting the relation $r \in \mathcal{R}$ as follows:

$$
\boldsymbol{\vartheta}_{e,r} = a_e \boldsymbol{v}_e + \sum_{(e',r') \in \mathcal{N}_e} b_{r,r'} \boldsymbol{u}_{e',r'}, \quad (1)
$$

a_e and $b_{r,r'}$ are the mixture weights that are constrained to sum to 1 for each neighborhood.

$$
a_e \propto \delta + \exp \alpha_e \quad (2)
$$
$$
b_{r,r'} \propto \exp \beta_{r,r'} \quad (3)
$$

where $\delta \geqslant 0$ is a hyper-parameter that controls the contribution of the entity vector $\boldsymbol{v}_e$ to the neighbor-based mixture, α_e and $\beta_{r,r'}$ are the learnable exponential mixture parameters.

In real-world factual KBs, e.g. Freebase (Bollacker et al., 2008), some entities, such as "male", can have thousands or millions neighboring entities sharing the same relation "gender." For such entities, computing the neighbor-based vectors can be computationally very expensive. To overcome this problem, we introduce in our implementation a filtering threshold τ and consider in the neighbor-based entity representation construction only those relation-specific neighboring entity sets for which $|\mathcal{N}_{e,r}| \leq \tau$.

2.2 TransE-NMM: applying neighborhood mixtures to TransE

Embedding models define for each triple $(h, r, t) \in \mathcal{G}$, a *score function* $f(h, r, t)$ that measures its implausibility. The goal is to choose f such that the score $f(h, r, t)$ of a plausible triple (h, r, t) is smaller than the score $f(h', r', t')$ of an implausible triple (h', r', t').

TransE (Bordes et al., 2013) is a simple embedding model for knowledge base completion, which, despite of its simplicity, obtains very competitive results (García-Durán et al., 2016; Nickel et al., 2016). In TransE, both entities e and relations r are represented with k-dimensional vectors $v_e \in \mathbb{R}^k$ and $v_r \in \mathbb{R}^k$, respectively. These vectors are chosen such that for each triple $(h, r, t) \in \mathcal{G}$:

$$v_h + v_r \approx v_t \qquad (4)$$

The score function of the TransE model is the norm of this translation:

$$f(h, r, t)_{\text{TransE}} = \|v_h + v_r - v_t\|_{\ell_{1/2}} \qquad (5)$$

We define the score function of our new model TransE-NMM in terms of the neighbor-based entity vectors as follows:

$$f(h, r, t) = \|\vartheta_{h,r} + v_r - \vartheta_{t,r^{-1}}\|_{\ell_{1/2}}, \qquad (6)$$

using either the ℓ_1 or the ℓ_2-norm, and $\vartheta_{h,r}$ and $\vartheta_{t,r^{-1}}$ are defined following the Equation 1. The relation-specific entity vectors $u_{e,r}$ used to construct the neighbor-based entity vectors $\vartheta_{e,r}$ are defined based on the TransE translation operator:

$$u_{e,r} = v_e + v_r \qquad (7)$$

in which $v_{r^{-1}} = -v_r$. For each correct triple (h, r, t), the sets of neighboring entities $\mathcal{N}_{h,r}$ and $\mathcal{N}_{t,r^{-1}}$ exclude the entities t and h, respectively.

If we set the filtering threshold $\tau = 0$ then $\vartheta_{h,r} = v_h$ and $\vartheta_{t,r^{-1}} = v_t$ for all triples. In this case, TransE-NMM reduces to the plain TransE model. In all our experiments presented in section 4, the baseline TransE results are obtained with the TransE-NMM with $\tau = 0$.

2.3 Parameter optimization

The TransE-NMM model parameters include the vectors v_e, v_r for entities and relation types, the entity-specific weights $\alpha = \{\alpha_e | e \in \mathcal{E}\}$ and relation-specific weights $\beta = \{\beta_{r,r'} | r, r' \in \mathcal{R} \cup \mathcal{R}^{-1}\}$. To learn these parameters, we minimize the L_2-regularized margin-based objective function:

$$\mathcal{L} = \sum_{\substack{(h,r,t)\in\mathcal{G} \\ (h',r',t')\in\mathcal{G}'_{(h,r,t)}}} [\gamma + f(h, r, t) - f(h', r, t')]_+$$
$$+ \frac{\lambda}{2}\Big(\|\alpha\|_2^2 + \|\beta\|_2^2\Big), \qquad (8)$$

where $[x]_+ = \max(0, x)$, γ is the margin hyper-parameter, λ is the L_2 regularization parameter and

$$\mathcal{G}'_{(h,r,t)} = \{(h', r, t) \mid h' \in \mathcal{E}, (h', r, t) \notin \mathcal{G}\}$$
$$\cup \{(h, r, t') \mid t' \in \mathcal{E}, (h, r, t') \notin \mathcal{G}\}$$

is the set of incorrect triples generated by corrupting the correct triple $(h, r, t) \in \mathcal{G}$. We applied the "*Bernoulli*" trick to choose whether to generate the head or tail entity when sampling an incorrect triple (Wang et al., 2014; Lin et al., 2015b; He et al., 2015; Ji et al., 2015; Ji et al., 2016).

We use Stochastic Gradient Descent (SGD) with RMSProp adaptive learning rate to minimize $\mathcal{L}$, and impose the following hard constraints during training; $\|v_e\|_2 \leqslant 1$ and $\|v_r\|_2 \leqslant 1$. We employ alternating optimization to minimize $\mathcal{L}$. We first initialize the entity and relation-specific mixing parameters α and β to zero and only learn the randomly initialized entity and relation vectors v_e and v_r. Then we fix the learned vectors and only optimize the mixing parameters. In the final step, we fix again the mixing parameters and fine-tune the vectors. In all experiments presented in section 4, we train for 200 epochs during each three optimization step.

3 Related work

Table 1 summarizes related embedding models for link prediction and KB completion. The models

Model	Score function $f(h, r, t)$	Opt.
STransE	$\|\mathbf{W}_{r,1}v_h + v_r - \mathbf{W}_{r,2}v_t\|_{\ell_{1/2}}$; $\mathbf{W}_{r,1}, \mathbf{W}_{r,2} \in \mathbb{R}^{k \times k}$; $v_r \in \mathbb{R}^k$	SGD
SE	$\|\mathbf{W}_{r,1}v_h - \mathbf{W}_{r,2}v_t\|_{\ell_{1/2}}$; $\mathbf{W}_{r,1}, \mathbf{W}_{r,2} \in \mathbb{R}^{k \times k}$	SGD
Unstructured	$\|v_h - v_t\|_{\ell_{1/2}}$	SGD
TransE	$\|v_h + v_r - v_t\|_{\ell_{1/2}}$; $v_r \in \mathbb{R}^k$	SGD
TransH	$\|(\mathbf{I} - r_p r_p^\top)v_h + v_r - (\mathbf{I} - r_p r_p^\top)v_t\|_{\ell_{1/2}}$ $r_p, v_r \in \mathbb{R}^k$; $\mathbf{I}$: Identity matrix size $k \times k$	SGD
TransD	$\|(\mathbf{I} + r_p h_p^\top)v_h + v_r - (\mathbf{I} + r_p t_p^\top)v_t\|_{\ell_{1/2}}$ $r_p, v_r \in \mathbb{R}^n$; $h_p, t_p \in \mathbb{R}^k$; $\mathbf{I}$: Identity matrix size $n \times k$	AdaDelta
TransR	$\|\mathbf{W}_r v_h + v_r - \mathbf{W}_r v_t\|_{\ell_{1/2}}$; $\mathbf{W}_r \in \mathbb{R}^{n \times k}$; $v_r \in \mathbb{R}^n$	SGD
TranSparse	$\|\mathbf{W}_r^h(\theta_r^h)v_h + v_r - \mathbf{W}_r^t(\theta_r^t)v_t\|_{\ell_{1/2}}$; $\mathbf{W}_r^h, \mathbf{W}_r^t \in \mathbb{R}^{n \times k}$; $\theta_r^h, \theta_r^t \in \mathbb{R}$; $v_r \in \mathbb{R}^n$	SGD
SME	$(\mathbf{W}_{1,1}v_h + \mathbf{W}_{1,2}v_r + \mathbf{b}_1)^\top (\mathbf{W}_{2,1}v_t + \mathbf{W}_{2,2}v_r + \mathbf{b}_2)$ $\mathbf{b}_1, \mathbf{b}_2 \in \mathbb{R}^n$; $\mathbf{W}_{1,1}, \mathbf{W}_{1,2}, \mathbf{W}_{2,1}, \mathbf{W}_{2,2} \in \mathbb{R}^{n \times k}$	SGD
DISTMULT	$v_h^\top \mathbf{W}_r v_t$; $\mathbf{W}_r$ is a diagonal matrix $\in \mathbb{R}^{k \times k}$	AdaGrad
NTN	$v_r^\top tanh(v_h^\top \mathbf{M}_r v_t + \mathbf{W}_{r,1}v_h + \mathbf{W}_{r,2}v_t + \mathbf{b}_r)$ $v_r, \mathbf{b}_r \in \mathbb{R}^n$; $\mathbf{M}_r \in \mathbb{R}^{k \times k \times n}$; $\mathbf{W}_{r,1}, \mathbf{W}_{r,2} \in \mathbb{R}^{n \times k}$	L-BFGS
Bilinear-COMP	$v_h^\top \mathbf{W}_{r_1} \mathbf{W}_{r_2} ... \mathbf{W}_{r_m} v_t$; $\mathbf{W}_{r_1}, \mathbf{W}_{r_2}, ..., \mathbf{W}_{r_m} \in \mathbb{R}^{k \times k}$	AdaGrad
TransE-COMP	$\|v_h + v_{r_1} + v_{r_2} + ... + v_{r_m} - v_t\|_{\ell_{1/2}}$; $v_{r_1}, v_{r_2}, ..., v_{r_m} \in \mathbb{R}^k$	AdaGrad

Table 1: The score functions $f(h, r, t)$ and the optimization methods (Opt.) of several prominent embedding models for KB completion. In all of these models, the entities h and t are represented by vectors v_h and $v_t \in \mathbb{R}^k$ respectively.

differ in their score function $f(h, r, t)$ and the algorithm used to optimize their margin-based objective function, e.g., SGD, AdaGrad (Duchi et al., 2011), AdaDelta (Zeiler, 2012) or L-BFGS (Liu and Nocedal, 1989).

The *Unstructured* model (Bordes et al., 2012) assumes that the head and tail entity vectors are similar. As the Unstructured model does not take the relationship into account, it cannot distinguish different relation types. The *Structured Embedding* (SE) model (Bordes et al., 2011) extends the Unstructured model by assuming that the head and tail entities are similar only in a relation-dependent subspace, where each relation is represented by two different matrices. Futhermore, the SME model (Bordes et al., 2012) uses four different matrices to project entity and relation vectors into a subspace. The TransH model (Wang et al., 2014) associates each relation with a relation-specific hyperplane and uses a projection vector to project entity vectors onto that hyperplane. TransD (Ji et al., 2015) and TransR/CTransR (Lin et al., 2015b) extend the TransH model by using two projection vectors and a matrix to project entity vectors into a relation-specific space, respectively. STransE

(Nguyen et al., 2016) and TranSparse (Ji et al., 2016) are extensions of the TransR model, where head and tail entities are associated with their own projection matrices.

The DISTMULT model (Yang et al., 2015) is based on the *Bilinear* model (Nickel et al., 2011; Bordes et al., 2012; Jenatton et al., 2012) where each relation is represented by a diagonal rather than a full matrix. The neural tensor network (NTN) model (Socher et al., 2013) uses a bilinear tensor operator to represent each relation. Similar quadratic forms are used to model entities and relations in KG2E (He et al., 2015) and TATEC (García-Durán et al., 2016).

Recently, Neelakantan et al. (2015), Gardner and Mitchell (2015), Luo et al. (2015), Lin et al. (2015a), García-Durán et al. (2015), Guu et al. (2015) and Toutanova et al. (2016) showed that relation paths between entities in KBs provide richer information and improve the relationship prediction. In fact, our new TransE-NMM model can be also viewed as a three-relation path model as it takes into account the neighborhood entity and relation information of both head and tail entities in each triple.

Luo et al. (2015) constructed relation paths between entities and viewing entities and relations in the path as pseudo-words applied Word2Vec algorithms (Mikolov et al., 2013) to produce pre-trained vectors for these pseudo-words. Luo et al. (2015) showed that using these pre-trained vectors for initialization helps to improve the performance of the TransE, SME and SE models. RTransE (García-Durán et al., 2015), PTransE (Lin et al., 2015a) and TransE-COMP (Guu et al., 2015) are extensions of the TransE model. These models similarly represent a relation path by a vector which is the sum of the vectors of all relations in the path, whereas in the Bilinear-COMP model (Guu et al., 2015), each relation is a matrix and so it represents the relation path by matrix multiplication. Our neighborhood mixture model can be adapted to both relation path models Bilinear-COMP and TransE-COMP, by replacing head and tail entity vectors by the neighbor-based vector representations, thus combining advantages of both path and neighborhood information. Nickel et al. (2015) reviews other approaches for learning from KBs and multi-relational data.

4   Experiments

To investigate the usefulness of the neighbor mixtures, we compare the performance of the TransE-NMM against the results of the baseline TransE and other state-of-the-art embedding models on the triple classification, entity prediction and relation prediction tasks.

4.1   Datasets

Dataset:	WN11	FB13	NELL186
#R	11	13	186
#E	38,696	75,043	14,463
#Train	112,581	316,232	31,134
#Valid	2,609	5,908	5,000
#Test	10,544	23,733	5,000

Table 2: Statistics of the experimental datasets used in this study (and *previous works*). #E is the number of entities, #R is the number of relation types, and #Train, #Valid and #Test are the numbers of correct triples in the training, validation and test sets, respectively. Each validation and test set also contains the same number of incorrect triples as the number of correct triples.

We conduct experiments using three publicly available datasets WN11, FB13 and NELL186. For all of them, the validation and test sets containing both correct and incorrect triples have already been constructed. Statistical information about these datasets is given in Table 2.

The two benchmark datasets[1], WN11 and FB13, were produced by Socher et al. (2013) for triple classification. WN11 is derived from the large lexical KB WordNet (Miller, 1995) involving 11 relation types. FB13 is derived from the large real-world fact KB FreeBase (Bollacker et al., 2008) covering 13 relation types. The NELL186 dataset[2] was introduced by Guo et al. (2015) for both triple classification and entity prediction tasks, containing 186 most frequent relations in the KB of the CMU Never Ending Language Learning project (Carlson et al., 2010).

4.2   Evaluation tasks

We evaluate our model on three commonly used benchmark tasks: triple classification, entity prediction and relation prediction. This subsection describes those tasks in detail.

Triple classification: The triple classification task was first introduced by Socher et al. (2013), and since then it has been used to evaluate various embedding models. The aim of the task is to predict whether a triple (h, r, t) is correct or not.

For classification, we set a relation-specific threshold θ_r for each relation type r. If the implausibility score of an unseen test triple (h, r, t) is smaller than θ_r then the triple will be classified as correct, otherwise incorrect. Following Socher et al. (2013), the relation-specific thresholds are determined by maximizing the micro-averaged accuracy, which is a per-triple average, on the validation set. We also report the macro-averaged accuracy, which is a per-relation average.

Entity prediction: The entity prediction task (Bordes et al., 2013) predicts the head or the tail entity given the relation type and the other entity, i.e. predicting h given $(?, r, t)$ or predicting t given $(h, r, ?)$ where ? denotes the missing element. The results are evaluated using a ranking induced by the function $f(h, r, t)$ on test triples. Note that the incorrect triples in the validation and test sets are not used for evaluating the entity prediction task nor the relation prediction task.

[1] http://cs.stanford.edu/people/danqi/data/nips13-dataset.tar.bz2
[2] http://aclweb.org/anthology/attachments/P/P15/P15-1009.Datasets.zip

Each correct test triple (h, r, t) is corrupted by replacing either its head or tail entity by each of the possible entities in turn, and then we rank these candidates in ascending order of their implausibility score. This is called as the "Raw" setting protocol. For the "Filtered" setting protocol described in Bordes et al. (2013), we also filter out before ranking any corrupted triples that appear in the KB. Ranking a corrupted triple appearing in the KB (i.e. a correct triple) higher than the original test triple is also correct, but is penalized by the "Raw" score, thus the "Filtered" setting provides a clearer view on the ranking performance.

In addition to the mean rank and the Hits@10 (i.e., the proportion of test triples for which the target entity was ranked in the top 10 predictions), which were originally used in the entity prediction task (Bordes et al., 2013), we also report the mean reciprocal rank (**MRR**), which is commonly used in information retrieval. In both "Raw" and "Filtered" settings, mean rank is always greater or equal to 1 and lower mean rank indicates better entity prediction performance. The MRR and Hits@10 scores always range from 0.0 to 1.0, and higher score reflects better prediction result.

Relation prediction: The relation prediction task (Lin et al., 2015a) predicts the relation type given the head and tail entities, i.e. predicting r given $(h, ?, t)$ where ? denotes the missing element. We corrupt each correct test triple (h, r, t) by replacing its relation r by each possible relation type in turn, and then rank these candidates in ascending order of their implausibility score. Just as in the entity prediction task, we use two setting protocols, "Raw" and "Filtered", and evaluate on mean rank, MRR and Hits@10.

4.3 Hyper-parameter tuning

For all evaluation tasks, results for TransE are obtained with TransE-NMM with the filtering threshold $\tau = 0$, while we set $\tau = 10$ for TransE-NMM.

For triple classification, we first performed a grid search to choose the optimal hyper-parameters for TransE by monitoring the micro-averaged triple classification accuracy after each training epoch on the validation set. For all datasets, we chose either the ℓ_1 or ℓ_2 norm in the score function f and the initial RMSProp learning rate $\eta \in \{0.001, 0.01\}$. Following the previous work (Wang et al., 2014; Lin et al., 2015b; Ji et al., 2015; He et al., 2015; Ji et al., 2016), we selected

the margin hyper-parameter $\gamma \in \{1, 2, 4\}$ and the number of vector dimensions $k \in \{20, 50, 100\}$ on WN11 and FB13. On NELL186, we set $\gamma = 1$ and $k = 50$ (Guo et al., 2015; Luo et al., 2015). The highest accuracy on the validation set was obtained when using $\eta = 0.01$ for all three datasets, and when using ℓ_2 norm for NELL186, $\gamma = 4$, $k = 20$ and ℓ_1 norm for WN11, and $\gamma = 1$, $k = 100$ and ℓ_2 norm for FB13.

We set the hyper-parameters η, γ, k, and the ℓ_1 or the ℓ_2-norm in our TransE-NMM model to the same optimal hyper-parameters searched for TransE. We then used a grid search to select the hyper-parameter $\delta \in \{0, 1, 5, 10\}$ and L_2 regularizer $\lambda \in \{0.005, 0.01, 0.05\}$ for TransE-NMM. By monitoring the micro-averaged accuracy after each training epoch, we obtained the highest accuracy on validation set when using $\delta = 1$ and $\lambda = 0.05$ for both WN11 and FB13, and $\delta = 0$ and $\lambda = 0.01$ for NELL186.

For both entity prediction and relation prediction tasks, we set the hyper-parameters η, γ, k, and the ℓ_1 or the ℓ_2-norm for both TransE and TransE-NMM to be the same as the optimal parameters found for the triple classification task. We then monitored on TransE the filtered MRR on validation set after each training epoch. We chose the model with highest validation MRR, which was then used to evaluate the test set. For TransE-NMM, we searched the hyper-parameter $\delta \in \{0, 1, 5, 10\}$ and L_2 regularizer $\lambda \in \{0.005, 0.01, 0.05\}$. By monitoring the filtered MRR after each training epoch, we selected the best model with the highest filtered MRR on the validation set. Specifically, for the entity prediction task, we selected $\delta = 10$ and $\lambda = 0.005$ for WN11, $\delta = 5$ and $\lambda = 0.01$ for FB13, and $\delta = 5$ and $\lambda = 0.005$ for NELL186. For the relation prediction task, we selected $\delta = 10$ and $\lambda = 0.005$ for WN11, $\delta = 10$ and $\lambda = 0.05$ for FB13, and $\delta = 1$ and $\lambda = 0.05$ for NELL186.

5 Results

5.1 Quantitative results

Table 3 presents the results of TransE and TransE-NMM on triple classification, entity prediction and relation prediction tasks on all experimental datasets. The results show that TransE-NMM generally performs better than TransE in all three evaluation tasks.

Specifically, TransE-NMM obtains higher triple

Data		Method	Triple class.		Entity prediction			Relation prediction		
			Mic.	Mac.	MR	MRR	H@10	MR	MRR	H@10
WN11	R	TransE	85.21	82.53	4324	**0.102**	**19.21**	2.37	0.679	**99.93**
		TransE-NMM	**86.82**	**84.37**	**3687**	0.094	17.98	**2.14**	**0.687**	99.92
	F	TransE			4304	**0.122**	**21.86**	2.37	0.679	**99.93**
		TransE-NMM			**3668**	0.109	20.12	**2.14**	**0.687**	99.92
FB13	R	TransE	87.57	86.66	9037	0.204	35.39	1.01	0.996	99.99
		TransE-NMM	**88.58**	**87.99**	**8289**	0.258	35.53	1.01	0.996	**100.0**
	F	TransE			5600	0.213	36.28	1.01	0.996	99.99
		TransE-NMM			**5018**	0.267	36.36	1.01	0.996	**100.0**
NELL186	R	TransE	92.13	88.96	309	0.192	36.55	8.43	0.580	77.18
		TransE-NMM	**94.57**	**90.95**	**238**	**0.221**	**37.55**	**6.15**	**0.677**	**82.16**
	F	TransE			279	0.268	47.13	8.32	0.602	77.26
		TransE-NMM			**214**	**0.292**	**47.82**	**6.08**	**0.690**	**82.20**

Table 3: Experimental results of TransE (i.e. TransE-NMM with $\tau = 0$) and TransE-NMM with $\tau = 10$. Micro-averaged (labeled as **Mic.**) and Macro-averaged (labeled as **Mac.**) accuracy results are for the triple classification task. MR, MRR and H@10 abbreviate the mean rank, the mean reciprocal rank and Hits@10 (in %), respectively. "R" and "F" denote the "Raw" and "Filtered" settings used in the entity prediction and relation prediction tasks, respectively.

Method	W11	F13
TransR (Lin et al., 2015b)	85.9	82.5
CTransR (Lin et al., 2015b)	85.7	-
TransD (Ji et al., 2015)	<u>86.4</u>	**89.1**
TranSparse-S (Ji et al., 2016)	<u>86.4</u>	88.2
TranSparse-US (Ji et al., 2016)	**86.8**	87.5
NTN (Socher et al., 2013)	70.6	87.2
TransH (Wang et al., 2014)	78.8	83.3
SLogAn (Liang and Forbus, 2015)	75.3	85.3
KG2E (He et al., 2015)	85.4	85.3
Bilinear-COMP (Guu et al., 2015)	77.6	86.1
TransE-COMP (Guu et al., 2015)	80.3	87.6
TransE	85.2	87.6
TransE-NMM	**86.8**	<u>88.6</u>

Table 4: Micro-averaged accuracy results (in %) for triple classification on WN11 (labeled as **W11**) and FB13 (labeled as **F13**) test sets. Scores in **bold** and <u>underline</u> are the best and second best scores, respectively.

Method	Triple class.		Entity pred.	
	Mic.	Mac.	MR	H@10
TransE-LLE	90.08	84.50	535	20.02
SME-LLE	93.64	89.39	<u>253</u>	37.14
SE-LLE	<u>93.95</u>	88.54	447	31.55
TransE-SkipG	85.33	80.06	385	30.52
SME-SkipG	92.86	<u>89.65</u>	293	**39.70**
SE-SkipG	93.07	87.98	412	31.12
TransE	92.13	88.96	309	36.55
TransE-NMM	**94.57**	**90.95**	**238**	<u>37.55</u>

Table 5: Results on on the NELL186 test set. Results for the entity prediction task are in the "Raw" setting. "-SkipG" abbreviates "-Skip-gram".

classification results than TransE in all three experimental datasets, for example, with 2.44% absolute improvement in the micro-averaged accuracy on the NELL186 dataset (i.e. 31% reduction in error). In terms of entity prediction, TransE-NMM obtains better mean rank, MRR and

Hits@10 scores than TransE on both FB13 and NELL186 datasets. Specifically, on NELL186 TransE-NMM gains a significant improvement of $279 - 214 = 65$ in the filtered mean rank (which is about 23% relative improvement), while on the FB13 dataset, TransE-NMM improves with $0.267 - 0.213 = 0.054$ in the filtered MRR (which is about 25% relative improvement). On the WN11 dataset, TransE-NMM only achieves better mean rank for entity prediction. The relation prediction results of TransE-NMM and TransE are relatively similar on both WN11 and FB13 because the number of relation types is small in these two datasets. On NELL186, however, TransE-NMM does significantly better than TransE.

In Table 4, we compare the micro-averaged triple classification accuracy of our TransE-NMM model with the previously reported results on the WN11 and FB13 datasets. The first five rows report the performance of models that use TransE to initialize the entity and relation vectors. The last eight rows present the accuracy of models with randomly initialized parameters.

Table 4 shows that our TransE-NMM model obtains the highest accuracy on WN11 and achieves the second highest result on FB13. Note that there are higher results reported for NTN (Socher et al., 2013), Bilinear-COMP (Guu et al., 2015) and TransE-COMP when entity vectors are initialized by averaging the pre-trained word vectors (Mikolov et al., 2013; Pennington et al., 2014). It is not surprising as many entity names in Word-Net and FreeBase are lexically meaningful. It is possible for all other embedding models to utilize the pre-trained word vectors as well. However, as pointed out by Wang et al. (2014) and Guu et al. (2015), averaging the pre-trained word vectors for initializing entity vectors is an open problem and it is not always useful since entity names in many domain-specific KBs are not lexically meaningful.

Table 5 compares the accuracy for triple classification, the raw mean rank and raw Hits@10 scores for entity prediction on the NELL186 dataset. The first three rows present the best results reported in Guo et al. (2015), while the next three rows present the best results reported in Luo et al. (2015). TransE-NMM obtains the highest triple classification accuracy, the best raw mean rank and the second highest raw Hits@10 on the entity prediction task in this comparison.

5.2 Qualitative results

Table 6 presents some examples to illustrate the useful information modeled by the neighbors. We took the relation-specific mixture weights from the learned TransE-NMM model optimized on the entity prediction task, and then extracted three neighbor relations with the largest mixture weights given a relation.

Table 6 shows that those relations are semantically coherent. For example, if we know the place of birth and/or the place of death of a person and/or the location where the person is living, it is likely

Relation	Top 3-neighbor relations
has_instance (WN11)	type_of subordinate_instance_of domain_topic
synset_domain_topic (WN11)	domain_region member_holonym member_meronym
nationality (FB13)	place_of_birth place_of_death location
spouse (FB13)	children, spouse, parents
CEOof (NELL186)	WorksFor TopMemberOfOrganization PersonLeadsOrganization
AnimalDevelopDisease (NELL186)	AnimalSuchAsInsect AnimalThatFeedOnInsect AnimalDevelopDisease

Table 6: Qualitative examples.

that we can predict the person's nationality. On the other hand, if we know that a person works for an organization and that this person is also the top member of that organization, then it is possible that this person is the CEO of that organization.

5.3 Discussion

Despite of the lower triple classification scores of TransE reported in Wang et al. (2014), Table 4 shows that TransE in fact obtains a very competitive accuracy. Particularly, compared to the relation path model TransE-COMP (Guu et al., 2015), when model parameters were randomly initialized, TransE obtains $85.2 - 80.3 = 4.9\%$ absolute accuracy improvement on the WN11 dataset while achieving similar score on the FB13 dataset. Our high results of the TransE model are probably due to a careful grid search and using the "Bernoulli" trick. Note that Lin et al. (2015b), Ji et al. (2015) and Ji et al. (2016) did not report the TransE results used for initializing TransR, TransD and TranSparse, respectively. They directly copied the TransE results previously reported in Wang et al. (2014). So it is difficult to determine exactly how much TransR, TransD and TranSparse gain over TransE. These models might obtain better results than previously reported when the TransE used for initalization performs as well as reported in this paper. Furthermore, García-Durán et al. (2015), Lin et al. (2015a), García-Durán et al. (2016) and Nickel et al. (2016) also showed that for entity prediction TransE obtains very competitive results which are much higher than the TransE results

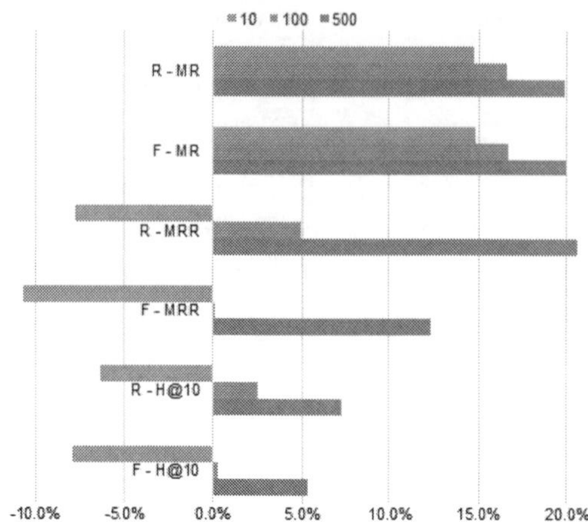

Figure 2: Relative improvement of TransE-NMM against TransE for entity prediction task in WN11 when the filtering threshold $\tau = \{10, 100, 500\}$ (with other hyper-parameters being the same as selected in Section 4.3). Prefixes "R-" and "F-" denote the "Raw" and "Filtered" settings, respectively. Suffixes "-MR", "-MRR" and "-H@10" abbreviate the mean rank, the mean reciprocal rank and Hits@10, respectively.

originally published in Bordes et al. (2013).[3]

As presented in Table 3, for entity prediction using WN11, TransE-NMM with the filtering threshold $\tau = 10$ only obtains better mean rank than TransE (about 15% relative improvement) but lower Hits@10 and mean reciprocal rank. The reason might be that in semantic lexical KBs such as WordNet where relationships between words or word groups are manually constructed, whole neighborhood information might be useful. So when using a small filtering threshold, the model ignores a lot of potential information that could help predicting relationships. Figure 2 presents relative improvements in entity prediction of TransE-NMM over TransE on WN11 when varying the filtering threshold τ. Figure 2 shows that TransE-NMM gains better scores with higher τ value. Specifically, when $\tau = 500$ TransE-NMM does significantly better than TransE in all entity prediction metrics.

6 Conclusion and future work

We introduced a neighborhood mixture model for knowledge base completion by constructing neighbor-based vector representations for entities. We demonstrated its effect by extending TransE (Bordes et al., 2013) with our neighborhood mixture model. On three different datasets, experimental results show that our model significantly improves TransE and obtains better results than the other state-of-the-art embedding models on triple classification, entity prediction and relation prediction tasks. In future work, we plan to apply the neighborhood mixture model to other embedding models, especially to relation path models such as TransE-COMP, to combine the useful information from both relation paths and entity neighborhoods.

Acknowledgments

This research was supported by a Google award through the Natural Language Understanding Focused Program, and under the Australian Research Council's *Discovery Projects* funding scheme (project number DP160102156). This research was also supported by NICTA, funded by the Australian Government through the Department of Communications and the Australian Research Council through the ICT Centre of Excellence Program. The first author was supported by an International Postgraduate Research Scholarship and a NICTA NRPA Top-Up Scholarship.

References

Kurt Bollacker, Colin Evans, Praveen Paritosh, Tim Sturge, and Jamie Taylor. 2008. Freebase: A Collaboratively Created Graph Database for Structuring Human Knowledge. In *Proceedings of the 2008 ACM SIGMOD International Conference on Management of Data*, pages 1247–1250.

Antoine Bordes, Jason Weston, Ronan Collobert, and Yoshua Bengio. 2011. Learning Structured Embeddings of Knowledge Bases. In *Proceedings of the Twenty-Fifth AAAI Conference on Artificial Intelligence*, pages 301–306.

Antoine Bordes, Xavier Glorot, Jason Weston, and Yoshua Bengio. 2012. A Semantic Matching Energy Function for Learning with Multi-relational Data. *Machine Learning*, 94(2):233–259.

Antoine Bordes, Nicolas Usunier, Alberto Garcia-Duran, Jason Weston, and Oksana Yakhnenko. 2013. Translating Embeddings for Modeling Multi-relational Data. In *Advances in Neural Information Processing Systems 26*, pages 2787–2795.

Andrew Carlson, Justin Betteridge, Bryan Kisiel, Burr Settles, Estevam R. Hruschka, Jr., and Tom M.

---

[3]They did not report the results on WN11 and FB13 datasets, which are used in this paper, though.

Mitchell. 2010. Toward an Architecture for Never-ending Language Learning. In *Proceedings of the Twenty-Fourth AAAI Conference on Artificial Intelligence*, pages 1306–1313.

John Duchi, Elad Hazan, and Yoram Singer. 2011. Adaptive Subgradient Methods for Online Learning and Stochastic Optimization. *The Journal of Machine Learning Research*, 12:2121–2159.

Alberto García-Durán, Antoine Bordes, and Nicolas Usunier. 2015. Composing Relationships with Translations. In *Proceedings of the 2015 Conference on Empirical Methods in Natural Language Processing*, pages 286–290.

Alberto García-Durán, Antoine Bordes, Nicolas Usunier, and Yves Grandvalet. 2016. Combining Two and Three-Way Embedding Models for Link Prediction in Knowledge Bases. *Journal of Artificial Intelligence Research*, 55:715–742.

Matt Gardner and Tom Mitchell. 2015. Efficient and Expressive Knowledge Base Completion Using Subgraph Feature Extraction. In *Proceedings of the 2015 Conference on Empirical Methods in Natural Language Processing*, pages 1488–1498.

Shu Guo, Quan Wang, Bin Wang, Lihong Wang, and Li Guo. 2015. Semantically Smooth Knowledge Graph Embedding. In *Proceedings of the 53rd Annual Meeting of the Association for Computational Linguistics and the 7th International Joint Conference on Natural Language Processing (Volume 1: Long Papers)*, pages 84–94.

Kelvin Guu, John Miller, and Percy Liang. 2015. Traversing Knowledge Graphs in Vector Space. In *Proceedings of the 2015 Conference on Empirical Methods in Natural Language Processing*, pages 318–327.

Shizhu He, Kang Liu, Guoliang Ji, and Jun Zhao. 2015. Learning to Represent Knowledge Graphs with Gaussian Embedding. In *Proceedings of the 24th ACM International on Conference on Information and Knowledge Management*, pages 623–632.

Rodolphe Jenatton, Nicolas L. Roux, Antoine Bordes, and Guillaume R Obozinski. 2012. A latent factor model for highly multi-relational data. In *Advances in Neural Information Processing Systems 25*, pages 3167–3175.

Guoliang Ji, Shizhu He, Liheng Xu, Kang Liu, and Jun Zhao. 2015. Knowledge Graph Embedding via Dynamic Mapping Matrix. In *Proceedings of the 53rd Annual Meeting of the Association for Computational Linguistics and the 7th International Joint Conference on Natural Language Processing (Volume 1: Long Papers)*, pages 687–696.

Guoliang Ji, Kang Liu, Shizhu He, and Jun Zhao. 2016. Knowledge Graph Completion with Adaptive Sparse Transfer Matrix. In *Proceedings of the Thirtieth AAAI Conference on Artificial Intelligence*, pages 985–991.

Denis Krompa, Stephan Baier, and Volker Tresp. 2015. Type-Constrained Representation Learning in Knowledge Graphs. In *Proceedings of the 14th International Semantic Web Conference*, pages 640–655.

Jens Lehmann, Robert Isele, Max Jakob, Anja Jentzsch, Dimitris Kontokostas, Pablo N. Mendes, Sebastian Hellmann, Mohamed Morsey, Patrick van Kleef, Sören Auer, and Christian Bizer. 2015. DBpedia - A Large-scale, Multilingual Knowledge Base Extracted from Wikipedia. *Semantic Web*, 6(2):167–195.

Chen Liang and Kenneth D. Forbus. 2015. Learning Plausible Inferences from Semantic Web Knowledge by Combining Analogical Generalization with Structured Logistic Regression. In *Proceedings of the Twenty-Ninth AAAI Conference on Artificial Intelligence*, pages 551–557.

Yankai Lin, Zhiyuan Liu, Huanbo Luan, Maosong Sun, Siwei Rao, and Song Liu. 2015a. Modeling Relation Paths for Representation Learning of Knowledge Bases. In *Proceedings of the 2015 Conference on Empirical Methods in Natural Language Processing*, pages 705–714.

Yankai Lin, Zhiyuan Liu, Maosong Sun, Yang Liu, and Xuan Zhu. 2015b. Learning Entity and Relation Embeddings for Knowledge Graph Completion. In *Proceedings of the Twenty-Ninth AAAI Conference on Artificial Intelligence Learning*, pages 2181–2187.

D. C. Liu and J. Nocedal. 1989. On the Limited Memory BFGS Method for Large Scale Optimization. *Mathematical Programming*, 45(3):503–528.

Yuanfei Luo, Quan Wang, Bin Wang, and Li Guo. 2015. Context-Dependent Knowledge Graph Embedding. In *Proceedings of the 2015 Conference on Empirical Methods in Natural Language Processing*, pages 1656–1661.

Tomas Mikolov, Wen-tau Yih, and Geoffrey Zweig. 2013. Linguistic Regularities in Continuous Space Word Representations. In *Proceedings of the 2013 Conference of the North American Chapter of the Association for Computational Linguistics: Human Language Technologies*, pages 746–751.

George A. Miller. 1995. WordNet: A Lexical Database for English. *Communications of the ACM*, 38(11):39–41.

Arvind Neelakantan, Benjamin Roth, and Andrew McCallum. 2015. Compositional Vector Space Models for Knowledge Base Completion. In *Proceedings of the 53rd Annual Meeting of the Association for Computational Linguistics and the 7th International Joint Conference on Natural Language Processing (Volume 1: Long Papers)*, pages 156–166.

Dat Quoc Nguyen, Kairit Sirts, Lizhen Qu, and Mark Johnson. 2016. STransE: a novel embedding model of entities and relationships in knowledge bases. In *Proceedings of the 2016 Conference of the North American Chapter of the Association for Computational Linguistics: Human Language Technologies*, pages 460–466.

Maximilian Nickel, Volker Tresp, and Hans-Peter Kriegel. 2011. A Three-Way Model for Collective Learning on Multi-Relational Data. In *Proceedings of the 28th International Conference on Machine Learning*, pages 809–816.

Maximilian Nickel, Kevin Murphy, Volker Tresp, and Evgeniy Gabrilovich. 2015. A Review of Relational Machine Learning for Knowledge Graphs. *Proceedings of the IEEE, to appear*.

Maximilian Nickel, Lorenzo Rosasco, and Tomaso A. Poggio. 2016. Holographic Embeddings of Knowledge Graphs. In *Proceedings of the Thirtieth AAAI Conference on Artificial Intelligence*, pages 1955–1961.

Jeffrey Pennington, Richard Socher, and Christopher Manning. 2014. Glove: Global Vectors for Word Representation. In *Proceedings of the 2014 Conference on Empirical Methods in Natural Language Processing*, pages 1532–1543.

Richard Socher, Danqi Chen, Christopher D Manning, and Andrew Ng. 2013. Reasoning With Neural Tensor Networks for Knowledge Base Completion. In *Advances in Neural Information Processing Systems 26*, pages 926–934.

Fabian M. Suchanek, Gjergji Kasneci, and Gerhard Weikum. 2007. YAGO: A Core of Semantic Knowledge. In *Proceedings of the 16th International Conference on World Wide Web*, pages 697–706.

Ben Taskar, Ming fai Wong, Pieter Abbeel, and Daphne Koller. 2004. Link Prediction in Relational Data. In *Advances in Neural Information Processing Systems 16*, pages 659–666.

Kristina Toutanova, Xi Victoria Lin, Wen tau Yih, Hoifung Poon, and Chris Quirk. 2016. Compositional Learning of Embeddings for Relation Paths in Knowledge Bases and Text. In *Proceedings of the 54th Annual Meeting of the Association for Computational Linguistics*, June.

Zhen Wang, Jianwen Zhang, Jianlin Feng, and Zheng Chen. 2014. Knowledge Graph Embedding by Translating on Hyperplanes. In *Proceedings of the Twenty-Eighth AAAI Conference on Artificial Intelligence*, pages 1112–1119.

Robert West, Evgeniy Gabrilovich, Kevin Murphy, Shaohua Sun, Rahul Gupta, and Dekang Lin. 2014. Knowledge Base Completion via Search-based Question Answering. In *Proceedings of the 23rd International Conference on World Wide Web*, pages 515–526.

Bishan Yang, Wen-tau Yih, Xiaodong He, Jianfeng Gao, and Li Deng. 2015. Embedding Entities and Relations for Learning and Inference in Knowledge Bases. In *Proceedings of the International Conference on Learning Representations*.

Matthew D. Zeiler. 2012. ADADELTA: An Adaptive Learning Rate Method. *CoRR*, abs/1212.5701.

context2vec:
Learning Generic Context Embedding
with Bidirectional LSTM

Oren Melamud	**Jacob Goldberger**	**Ido Dagan**
Computer Science Dept.	Faculty of Engineering	Computer Science Dept.
Bar-Ilan University	Bar-Ilan University	Bar-Ilan University
`melamuo@cs.biu.ac.il`	`goldbej@eng.biu.ac.il`	`dagan@cs.biu.ac.il`

Abstract

Context representations are central to various NLP tasks, such as word sense disambiguation, named entity recognition, co-reference resolution, and many more. In this work we present a neural model for efficiently learning a generic context embedding function from large corpora, using bidirectional LSTM. With a very simple application of our context representations, we manage to surpass or nearly reach state-of-the-art results on sentence completion, lexical substitution and word sense disambiguation tasks, while substantially outperforming the popular context representation of averaged word embeddings. We release our code and pre-trained models, suggesting they could be useful in a wide variety of NLP tasks.

1 Introduction

Generic word embeddings capture semantic and syntactic information about individual words in a compact low-dimensional representation. While they are trained to optimize a generic task-independent objective function, word embeddings were found useful in a broad range of NLP tasks, making an overall huge impact in recent years. A major advancement in this field was the introduction of highly efficient models, such as *word2vec* (Mikolov et al., 2013a) and *GloVe* (Pennington et al., 2014), for learning generic word embeddings from very large corpora. Capturing information from such corpora substantially increased the value of word embeddings to both un-supervised and semi-supervised NLP tasks.

To make inferences regarding a concrete target word instance, good representations of both the target word type and the given context are helpful. For example, in the sentence *"I can't find [April]"*, we need to consider both the target word *April* and its context *"I can't find [ ]"* to infer that *April* probably refers to a person. This principle applies to various tasks, including word sense disambiguation, co-reference resolution and named entity recognition (NER).

Like target words, contexts are commonly represented via word embeddings. In an unsupervised setting, such representations were found useful for measuring context-sensitive similarity (Huang et al., 2012), word sense disambiguation (Chen et al., 2014), word sense induction (Kågebäck et al., 2015), lexical substitution (Melamud et al., 2015b), sentence completion (Liu et al., 2015) and more. The context representations used in such tasks are commonly just a simple collection of the individual embeddings of the neighboring words in a window around the target word, or a (sometimes weighted) average of these embeddings. We note that such approaches do not include any mechanism for optimizing the representation of the entire sentential context as a whole.

In supervised settings, various NLP systems use labeled data to learn how to consider context word representations in a more optimized task-specific way. This was done in tasks, such as chunking, NER, semantic role labeling, and co-reference resolution (Turian et al., 2010; Collobert et al., 2011; Melamud et al., 2016), mostly by considering the embeddings of words in a window around the target of interest. More recently, bidirectional recurrent neural networks, and specifically bidirectional LSTMs, were used in such tasks to learn

51

Proceedings of the 20th SIGNLL Conference on Computational Natural Language Learning (CoNLL), pages 51–61,
Berlin, Germany, August 7-12, 2016. ©2016 Association for Computational Linguistics

internal representations of wider sentential contexts (Zhou and Xu, 2015; Lample et al., 2016). Since supervised data is usually limited in size, it has been shown that training such systems, using word embeddings that were pre-trained on large corpora, improves performance significantly. Yet, pre-trained word embeddings carry limited information regarding the inter-dependencies between target words and their sentential context as a whole. To model this (and more), the supervised systems still need to rely heavily on their albeit limited supervised data.

In this work we present *context2vec*, an unsupervised model and toolkit[1] for efficiently learning *generic* context embedding of wide sentential contexts, using bidirectional LSTM. Essentially, we use large plain text corpora to learn a neural model that embeds entire sentential contexts and target words in the same low-dimensional space, which is optimized to reflect inter-dependencies between targets and their entire sentential context as a whole. To demonstrate their high quality, we show that with a very simple application of our context representations, we are able to surpass or nearly reach state-of-the-art results on sentence completion, lexical substitution and word sense disambiguation tasks, while substantially outperforming the common average-of-word-embeddings representation (denoted *AWE*). We further hypothesize that both unsupervised and semi-supervised systems may benefit from using our pre-trained models, instead or in addition to individual pre-trained word embeddings.

2 *Context2vec*'s Neural Model

2.1 Model Overview

The main goal of our model is to learn a generic task-independent embedding function for variable-length sentential contexts around target words. To do this, we propose a neural network architecture, which is based on *word2vec*'s *CBOW* architecture (Mikolov et al., 2013a), but replaces its naive context modeling of averaged word embeddings in a fixed window, with a much more powerful neural model, using bidirectional LSTM. Our proposed architecture is illustrated in Figure 1, together with the analogical *word2vec* architecture. Both models learn context and target

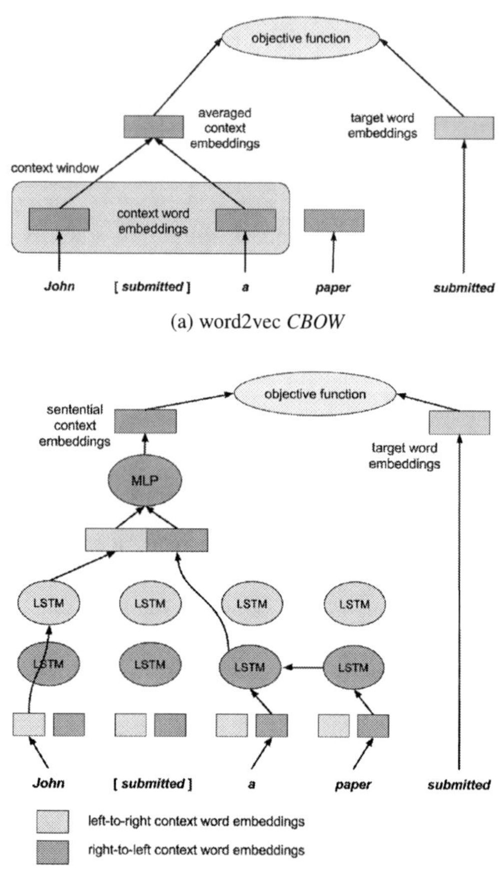

(a) word2vec *CBOW*

(b) *context2vec*

Figure 1: *word2vec* and *context2vec* architectures.

word representations at the same time, by embedding them into the same low-dimensional space, with the objective of having the context predict the target word via a log linear model. However, we utilize a much more powerful parametric model to capture the essence of sentential context.

The left-hand side of Figure 1b illustrates how *context2vec* represents sentential context. We use a bidirectional LSTM recurrent neural network, feeding one LSTM network with the sentence words from left to right, and another from right to left. The parameters of these two networks are completely separate, including two separate sets of left-to-right and right-to-left context word embeddings. To represent the context of a target word in a sentence (e.g. for "*John [submitted] a paper*"), we first concatenate the LSTM output vector representing its left-to-right context ("*John*") with the one representing its right-to-left context ("*a paper*"). With this, we aim to capture the relevant

---

[1]Source code and pre-trained models are available at: http://www.cs.biu.ac.il/nlp/resources/downloads/context2vec/

information in the sentential context, even when it is remote from the target word. Next, we feed this concatenated vector into a multi-layer perceptron to be capable of representing non-trivial dependencies between the two sides of the context. We consider the output of this layer as the embedding of the entire joint sentential context around the target word. At the same time, the target word itself (right-hand side of Figure 1b) is represented with its own embedding, equal in dimensionality to that of the sentential context. We note that the only (yet crucial) difference between our model and *word2vec*'s *CBOW* (Figure 1a) is that *CBOW* represents the context around a target word as a simple average of the embeddings of the context words in a window around it, while *context2vec* utilizes a full-sentence neural representation of context.

Finally, to learn the parameters of our network, we use *word2vec*'s negative sampling objective function, with a positive pair being a target word and its entire sentential context, and respective k negative pairs as random target words, sampled from a (smoothed) unigram distribution over the vocabulary, paired with the same context. With this, we learn both the context embedding network parameters and the target word embeddings.

In contrast to *word2vec* and similar word embedding models that use context modeling mostly internally and consider the target word embeddings as their main output, our primary focus is the context representation. Our model achieves its objective by assigning similar embeddings to sentential contexts and their associated target words. Further, similar to the case in *word2vec* models, this indirectly results in assigning similar embeddings to target words that are associated with similar sentential contexts, and conversely to sentential contexts that are associated with similar target words. We will show in the following sections how these properties make our model useful.

2.2 Formal Specification and Analysis

We use a bidirectional LSTM recurrent neural network to obtain a sentence-level context representation. Let lLS be an LSTM reading the words of a given sentence from left to right, and let rLS be a reverse one reading the words from right to left. Given a sentence $w_{1:n}$, our 'shallow' bidirectional LSTM context representation for the target w_i is

defined as the following vector concatenation:

$$\text{biLS}(w_{1:n}, i) = \text{lLS}(l_{1:i-1}) \oplus \text{rLS}(r_{n:i+1})$$

where l/r represent distinct left-to-right/right-to-left word embeddings of the sentence words.[2] This definition is a bit different than standard bidirectional LSTM, as we do not feed the LSTMs with the target word itself (i.e. the word in position i). Next, we apply the following non-linear function on the concatenation of the left and right context representations:

$$\text{MLP}(x) = L_2(\text{ReLU}(L_1(x)))$$

where MLP stands for Multi Layer Perceptron, ReLU is the Rectified Linear Unit activation function, and $L_i(x) = W_i x + b_i$ is a fully connected linear operation. Let $c = (w_1, ..., w_{i-1}, -, w_{i+1}, ..., w_n)$ be the sentential context of the word in position i. We define *context2vec*'s representation of c as:

$$\vec{c} = \text{MLP}(\text{biLS}(w_{1:n}, i)).$$

Next, we denote the embedding of a target word t as $\vec{t}$. We use the same embedding dimensionality for target and sentential context representations. To learn target word and context representations, we use the *word2vec* negative sampling objective function (Mikolov et al., 2013b):

$$S = \sum_{t,c} \left(\log \sigma(\vec{t} \cdot \vec{c}) + \sum_{i-1}^{k} \log \sigma(-\vec{t_i} \cdot \vec{c}) \right) \quad (1)$$

where the summation goes over each word token t in the training corpus and its corresponding (single) sentential context c, and σ is the sigmoid function. $t_1, ..., t_k$ are the negative samples, independently sampled from a smoothed version of the target words unigram distribution: $p_\alpha(t) \propto (\#t)^\alpha$, such that $0 \leq \alpha < 1$ is a smoothing factor, which increases the probability of rare words.

Levy and Goldberg (2014b) proved that when the objective function in Equation (1) is applied to single-word contexts, it is optimized when:

$$\vec{t} \cdot \vec{c} = \text{PMI}_\alpha(t, c) - \log(k) \quad (2)$$

where $\text{PMI}(t, c) = \log \frac{p(t,c)}{p_\alpha(t)p(c)}$ is the pointwise mutual information between the target word t and

---

[2] We pad every input sentence with special BOS and EOS words in positions 0 and $n + 1$, respectively.

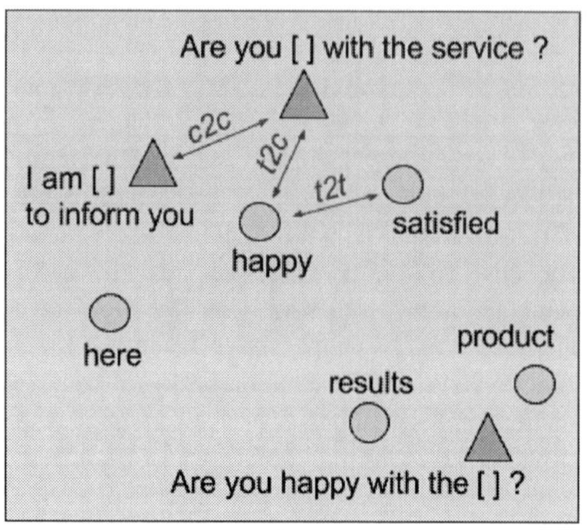

Figure 2: A 2D illustration of *context2vec*'s embedded space and similarity metrics. Triangles and circles denote sentential context embeddings and target word embeddings, respectively.

the context word c. The analysis presented in Levy and Goldberg (2014b) is valid for every co-occurrence matrix that describes the joint distribution of two random variables. Specifically, it can be applied to our case, where the context is not just a single word but an entire sentential context of a target word. Accordingly, we can view the target-context embedding obtained by our algorithm as a factorization of the PMI matrix between all possible target words and all possible different sentential contexts. Unlike the case of single-word contexts, it is not feasible to explicitly compute here this PMI matrix due to the exponential number of possible sentential contexts. However, the objective function that we optimize still aims to best approximate it. Based on the above analysis, we can expect the inner-product of our target and context embeddings to approximate $\text{PMI}_\alpha(c, t)$. We note that accordingly, with larger values of α, there will be more bias towards placing rare words closer to their associated contexts in this space.

2.3 Model Illustration

To demonstrate the qualities of the embedded space learned by *context2vec*, we illustrate three types of similarity metrics in that space: target-to-context (*t2c*), context-to-context (*c2c*) and target-to-target (*t2t*). All these are measured by the vector cosine value between the respective embedding representations. Only the latter target-to-target metric is the one typically used when illustrating

and evaluating word embedding models, such as *word2vec*. Figure 2 provides a 2D illustration of such a space and respective metrics.

In Table 1 we show sentential contexts and the target words that are closest to them, using the target-to-context similarity metric with *context2vec* embeddings. As can be seen, the bidirectional LSTM modeling of *context2vec* is indeed capable in this case to capture long range dependencies, as well as to take both sides of the context into account. In Table 2 we show the closest target words to given contexts, using different *context2vec* models, each learned with a different negative sampling smoothing parameter α. This illustrates the bias that high α values introduce towards rare words, as predicted with the analysis in section 2.2.

Next, to illustrate the context-to-context similarity metric, we took the set of contexts for the target lemma *add* from the training set of Senseval-3 (Mihalcea et al., 2004). In Table 3 we show an example for a 'query' context from that set and the other two most similar contexts to it, based on *context2vec* and *AWE* (average of Skip-gram word embeddings) context representations. Melamud et al. (2015a) argues that since contexts induce meanings (or senses) for target words, a good context similarity measure should assign high similarity values to contexts that induce similar senses for the same target word. As can be seen in this example, *AWE*'s similarity measure seems to be influenced by the presence of the location names in the contexts, even though they have little effect on the perceived meaning of *add* in the sentences. Indeed, the sense of *add* in the closest contexts retrieved by *AWE* is different than that in the 'query' context. In this case, *context2vec*'s similarity measure was robust to this problem.

Finally, in Table 4, we show the closest target words to a few given target words, based on the target-to-target similarity metric. We compare *context2vec*'s target word embeddings to Skip-gram *word2vec* embeddings, trained with 2-word and 10-word windows. As can be seen, our model seems to better preserve the function of the given target words including part-of-speech and even tense, in comparison to the 2-word window model, and even more so compared to the 10-word window one. The intuition for this behavior is that Skip-gram literally skips words in the context

Sentential Context	Closest target words
This [ ] is due	item, fact-sheet, offer, pack, card
This [ ] is due not just to mere luck	offer, suggestion, announcement, item, prize
This [ ] is due not just to mere luck, but to outstanding work and dedication	award, prize, turnabout, offer, gift
[ ] is due not just to mere luck, but to outstanding work and dedication	it, success, this, victory, prize-money

Table 1: Closest target words to various sentential contexts, illustrating *context2vec*'s sensitivity to long range dependencies, and both sides of the target word.

α	John was [ ] last year
0.25	born, late, married, out, back
0.50	born, back, married, released, elected
0.75	born, interviewed, re-elected
1.00	starstruck, goal-less, unwed

Table 2: Closest target words to a given sentential context using different α values in *context2vec*.

around the target word and therefore may find, for instance, the contexts of *san* and *francisco* to be very similar. In contrast, our model considers only entire sentential contexts, taking context word order and position into consideration. Melamud et al. (2016) showed that target word embeddings, learned from context representations that are generated using n-gram language models, also exhibit function-preserving similarities, which is consistent with our observations.

2.4 Relation to Language Models

Our model is closely related to language models, as can be seen in section 2.2 and tables 1 and 2. In particular, it has a lot in common with LSTM-based language models, as both train LSTM neural networks with the objective to predict target words based on their (short and long range) context, and both use techniques, such as negative sampling, to address large vocabulary computational challenges during training (Jozefowicz et al., 2016). The main difference is that LSTM language models are mainly concerned with optimizing predictions of conditional probabilities for target words given their history, while our model is focused on deriving generally useful representations to whole history-and-future contexts of target words. We follow *word2vec*'s learning framework as it is known to produce high-quality representations for single words. It does so by having $\vec{t} \cdot \vec{c}$ approximate $\text{PMI}(t, c)$ rather than $\log p(t|c)$.

3 Evaluation Settings

We intend *context2vec*'s generic context embedding function to be integrated into various more optimized task-specific systems. However, to demonstrate its qualities independently, we address three different types of tasks by the simple means of measuring cosine distances between its embedded representations. Yet, we compare our performance against the state-of-the-art results of highly competitive task-optimized systems on each task. In addition we use *AWE* as a baseline representing a commonly used generic context representation, which like ours, can represent variable-length contexts with a fixed-size vector. Our evaluation includes the following tasks: sentence completion, lexical substitution and supervised word sense disambiguation (WSD).

3.1 Learning corpus

With the exception of the sentence completion task (MSCC), which comes with its own learning corpus, we used the two billion word ukWaC (Ferraresi et al., 2008) as our learning corpus. To speed-up the training of *context2vec*, we discarded all sentences that are longer than 64 words, reducing the size of the corpus by ∼10%. However, we train the embeddings used in the *AWE* baseline on the full corpus to not penalize it on account of our model. We lower-cased all text and considered any token with fewer than 100 occurrences as an unknown word. This yielded a vocabulary of a little over 180K words for the full corpus, and 160K words for the trimmed version.

3.2 Compared Methods

context2vec We implemented our model using the Chainer toolkit (Tokui et al., 2015), and Adam (Kingma and Ba, 2014) for optimization. To speed-up the learning time we used mini-batch training, where only sentences of equal length are

Query	Furthermore our work in Uganda and Romania [adds] a wider perspective.
context2vec closest	... themes in art have a fascination , since they [add] a subject interest to a viewer's enjoyment of artistic qualities.
	Richard is joining us every month to pass on tips , ideas and news from the world of horticulture , and [add] a touch of humour too
AWE closest	... the foreign ministers said political and economic reforms in Poland and Hungary had made considerable progress but [added] : the process remains fragile ...
	... Germany had announced the solution as a humanitarian act by the government, [adding] that it hoped Bonn in future would run its embassies in normal manner...

Table 3: An example for a given 'query' context and the two closest contexts to it, as 'retrieved' by *context2vec* similarity and *AWE* similarity.

context2vec	*word2vec*-w2	*word2vec*-w10	*context2vec*	*word2vec*-w2	*word2vec*-w10
	flying			*syntactically*	
gliding	flew	flew	semantically	grammatically	semantically
sailing	fly	fly	lexically	phonologically	grammatically
diving	aerobatics	aeroplane	grammatically	semantically	syntax
flown	low-flying	flown	phonologically	ungrammatical	syntactic
travelling	flown	bi-plane	topologically	lexically	lexically
	san			*prize*	
agios	francisco	francisco	prizes	prizes	prizes
aghios	diego	diego	award	prize-winner	winner
los	fransisco	fransisco	trophy	prizewinner	winners
tanjung	los	bernardino	medal	prize	prizewinner
puerto	obispo	los	prizewinner	prizewinners	prize.

Table 4: Top-5 closest target words to a few given target words.

assigned to the same batch. We discuss the hyperparameters tuning of our model in section 4.1.

AWE We learned word embeddings with the popular *word2vec* Skip-gram model using standard hyperparameters: 600 dimensions, 10 negative samples, window-size 10 and 3/5 iterations for the ukWaC/MSCC learning corpora, respectively. Then we used a simple average of these embeddings as our *AWE* context representation.[3] In addition, we experimented with the following variations: (1) ignoring stopwords (2) performing a weighted average of the words in the context using tf-idf weights (3) considering just the 5-word window around the target word instead of the whole sentence. Specifically, in the WSD experiment the context provided for the target words is a full paragraph. Though it could be extended, *context2vec* is currently not designed to take advantage of such large context and therefore ignores all context out-

side of the sentence of the target word. However, for *AWE* we also experimented with the option of generating the context representation based on the entire paragraph. In all cases, the size (dimensionality) of the *AWE* context representation was equal to that of *context2vec*, and the context-to-target and context-to-context similarities were computed using vector cosine between the respective embedding representations, as with *context2vec*.

3.3 Sentence Completion Challenge

The Microsoft Sentence Completion Challenge (MSCC) (Zweig and Burges, 2011) includes 1,040 items. Each item is a sentence with one word replaced by a gap, and the challenge is to identify the word, out of five choices, that is most meaningful and coherent as the gap-filler. While there is no official dev/test split for this dataset, we followed previous work (Mirowski and Vlachos, 2015) and used the first 520 sentences for parameter tuning and the rest as the test set.[4]

---

[3]We made some preliminary experiments using word embeddings learned with *word2vec*'s *CBOW* model, instead of Skip-gram, but this yielded worse results.

[4]Mikolov et al. (2013a) did not specify their dev/test split and all other works reported results only on the entire dataset.

The MSCC includes a learning corpus of 50 million words. To use this corpus for training our models, we first discarded all sentences longer than 128 words, which resulted in a negligible reduction of $\sim 1\%$ in the size of the corpus. Then, we converted all text to lowercase and considered all words with frequency less than 3 as unknown, yielding a vocabulary of about 100K word types.

Finally, as the gap-filler, we simply choose the word whose target word embedding is the most similar to the embedding of the given context using the target-to-context similarity metric. We report the accuracy achieved in this task.

3.4 Lexical Substitution Task

The lexical substitution task requires finding a substitute word for a given target word in sentential context. The difference between this and the sentence completion task is that the substitute word needs not only to be coherent with the sentential context, but also preserve the meaning of the original word in that context. Most recent works evaluated their performance on a ranking variant of the lexical substitution task, which uses predefined candidate lists provided with the gold standard, and requires to rank them considering the sentential context. Performance in this task is reported with generalized average precision (GAP).[5] As in MSCC, in this evaluation we rank lexical substitutes according to the measured similarity between their target word embeddings and the embedding of the given sentential context.

We used two lexical substitution datasets in our experiments. The first is the dataset introduced in the lexical substitution task of SemEval 2007 (McCarthy and Navigli, 2007), denoted LST-07, split into 300 dev sentences and 1,710 test sentences. The second is a more recent 'all-words ' dataset (Kremer et al., 2014), denoted LST-14, with over 15K target word instances. It comes with a predefined 35%/65% split. We used the smaller set as the dev set for parameter tuning and the larger one as our test set.

3.5 Supervised WSD

In supervised WSD tasks, the goal is to determine the correct sense of words in context, based on a manually tagged training set. To classify a test word instance in context, we consider all of the

---

context word units	300
LSTM hidden/output units	600
MLP input units	1200
MLP hidden units	1200
sentential context units	600
target word units	600
negative samples	10

Table 5: *context2vec* hyperparameters

tagged instances of the same word lemma in the training set, and find the instance whose context embedding is the most similar to the context embedding of the test instance using the context-to-context similarity metric. Then, we use the tagged senses[6] of that instance. We note that this is essentially the simplest form of a k-nearest-neighbor algorithm, with $k = 1$.

As our supervised WSD dataset we used the Senseval-3 lexical sample dataset (Mihalcea et al., 2004), denoted SE-3, which includes 7,860 train and 3,944 test instances. We used the training set for parameter tuning and report accuracy results on the test set.

4 Results

4.1 Development Experiments

The hyperparameters used in our reported experiments with *context2vec* are summarized in Table 5. In preliminary development experiments, we used only 200 units for representing sentential contexts, and then saw significant improvement in results, when moving to 600 units. Increasing the representation size to 1,000 units did not seem to further improve results.

With mini-batches of 1,000 sentences at a time, we started by training our models with a single iteration over the 2-billion-word ukWaC corpus. This took $\sim$30 hours, using a single Tesla K80 GPU. For the smaller 50-million-word MSCC learning corpus, a full iteration with a batch size of 100 took only about 3 hours. For this corpus, we started with 5 training iterations.

To explore the rare-word bias effect of the vocabulary smoothing factor α, we varied its value in our development experiments. The results appear in Table 6 on the left hand side. Since we preferred to keep our model as simple as possible, based on these results, we chose the single

---

	context2vec				iters+	AWE			
	neg sampling parameter α				0.75	best	best	worst	worst
	0.25	0.50	0.75	1.00		config	result	config	result
MSCC-dev	52.5	56.5	**60.0**	52.7	**66.2**	sent+stop	**51.0**	W5	36.5
LST-07-dev	50.1	52.9	53.6	**54.3**	**55.4**	W5+stop	**45.8**	sent	40.0
LST-14-dev	48.2	**48.9**	48.0	46.1	48.3	sent+stop	**40.4**	sent	39.2
SE-3-dev	72.1	**72.4**	71.6	**72.5**	72.6	W5+tf-idf	**62.4**	sent	57.3

Table 6: Development set results. *iters+* denotes the best model found when running more training iterations with $\alpha = 0.75$. *AWE* config: *W5*/sent denotes using a 5-word-window/full-sentence, and *stop*/tf-idf denotes ignoring stop words or using tf-idf weights, respectively.

value $\alpha = 0.75$ for all of our test sets experiments. With this choice, we also tried training our models with more iterations and found that with 3 iterations over the ukWaC corpus and 10 iterations over the MSCC corpus we can obtain some further improvement in results, see *iters+* in Table 6.

The results of our experiments with all of the *AWE* variants, described in section 3.2, appear on the right hand side of Table 6. For brevity, we report only the best and worst configuration for each benchmark. As can be seen, in two out of four benchmarks, a window of 5 words yields better performance than a full sentential context, suggesting that the *AWE* representation is not very successful in leveraging effectively long range information. Removing stop words or using tf-idf weights improves performance significantly. However, the results are still much lower than the ones achieved with *context2vec*. To raise the bar, in each test-set experiment we used the best *AWE* configuration found for the corresponding development-set experiment.

4.2 Test Sets Results

The test set results are summarized in Table 7. First, we see that *context2vec* substantially outperforms *AWE* across all benchmarks. This suggests that our context representations are much better optimized for capturing sentential context information than *AWE*, at least for these tasks. Further, we see that with *context2vec* we either surpass or almost reach the state-of-the-art on all benchmarks. This is quite impressive, considering that all we did was measure cosine distances between *context2vec*'s representations to compete with more complex and task-optimized systems.

More specifically, in the sentence completion task (MSCC) the prior state-of-the-art result is due to Mikolov et al. (2013a) and was achieved by a

	c2v iters+	c2v	AWE	S-1	S-2
	MCSS				
test	**64.0**	62.7	48.4	-	-
all	**65.1**	61.3	49.7	58.9	56.2
	LST-07				
test	**56.1**	54.8	41.9	55.2	-
all	**56.0**	54.6	42.5	55.1	53.6
	LST-14				
test	47.7	47.3	38.1	**50.0**	-
all	47.9	47.5	38.9	**50.2**	48.3
	SE-3				
test	72.8	71.2	61.4	**74.1**	73.6

Table 7: Results on test sets. *c2v* is *context2vec* and *iters+* denotes the model that was trained with more iterations. S-1/S-2 stand for the best/second-best prior result reported for the benchmark.

weighted combination of scores from two different models: a recurrent neural network language model, and a Skip-gram model. The second-best result is due to Liu et al. (2015) and is based on word embeddings that are learned based on both corpora and structured knowledge resources, such as WordNet. *context2vec* outperforms both of them. In the lexical substitution tasks, the best prior results are due to Melamud et al. (2015a).[7] They employ an exemplar-based approach that requires keeping thousands of exemplar contexts for every target word type. The second-best is due to Melamud et al. (2015b). They propose a simple approach, but it requires dependency-parsed text as input. *context2vec* achieves comparable results with these works, using the same learning corpus. In the Senseval-3 supervised WSD task, the best result is due to Ando (2006) and the second-best to

---

[7]Szarvas et al. (2013) achieved almost the same result, but with a supervised model, not directly compared to ours.

Rothe and Schütze (2015). *context2vec* is almost on par with these results, which were achieved with dedicated feature engineering and supervised machine learning models.

5   Related Work

Substitute vectors (Yuret, 2012) represent contexts as a probabilistic distribution over the potential gap-filler words for the target slot, pruned to its top-k most probable words. While using this representation showed interesting potential (Yatbaz et al., 2012; Melamud et al., 2015a), it can currently be generated efficiently only with n-gram language models and hence is limited to fixed-size context windows. It is also high dimensional and sparse, in contrast to our proposed representations.

Syntactic dependency context embeddings have been proposed recently (Levy and Goldberg, 2014a; Bansal et al., 2014). They depend on the availability of a high-quality dependency parser, and can be viewed as a 'bag-of-dependencies' rather than a single representation for the entire sentential context. However, we believe that incorporating such dependency-based information in our model is an interesting future direction.

A couple of recent works extended *word2vec*'s *CBOW* by replacing its internal context representation. Ling et al. (2015b) proposed a *continuous window*, which is a simple linear projection of the context window embeddings into a low dimensional vector. Ling et al. (2015a) proposed '*CBOW with attention*', which is used for finding the relevant features in a context window. In contrast to our model, both approaches confine the context to a fixed-size window. Furthermore, they limit their scope to using these context representations only internally to improve the learning of target words embeddings, rather than evaluate the benefit of using them directly in NLP tasks, as we do.

Kawakami and Dyer (2016) represent words in context using bidirectional LSTMs and multilingual supervision. In contrast, our model is focused on representing the context alone. Yet, as shown in our lexical substitution and word sense disambiguation evaluations, it can easily be used for modeling the meaning of words in context as well.

Finally, there is considerable work on using recurrent neural networks to represent word sequences, such as phrases or sentences (Socher et al., 2011; Kiros et al., 2015). We note that the techniques used for learning sentence representations have much in common with those we use for sentential context representations. Yet, sentential context representations aim to reflect the information in the sentence only inasmuch as it is relevant to the target slot. Specifically, different target positions in the same sentence can yield completely different context representations. In contrast, sentence representations aim to reflect the entire contents of the sentence.

6   Conclusions and Future Potential

We presented *context2vec*, a neural model that learns a generic embedding function for variable-length contexts of target words. We demonstrated that it can be trained in a reasonable time over billions of words and generate high quality context representations, which substantially outperform the traditional average-of-word-embeddings approach on three different tasks. As such, we hypothesize that it could contribute to various NLP systems that model context. Specifically, semi-supervised systems may benefit from using our model, as it may carry more useful information learned from large corpora, than individual pre-trained word embeddings do.

Acknowledgments

We thank our anonymous reviewers for their useful comments. This work was partially supported by the Israel Science Foundation grant 880/12 and the German Research Foundation through the German-Israeli Project Cooperation (DIP, grant DA 1600/1-1).

References

Rie Kubota Ando. 2006. Applying alternating structure optimization to word sense disambiguation. In *Proceedings of the Tenth Conference on Computational Natural Language Learning*, pages 77–84. Association for Computational Linguistics.

Mohit Bansal, Kevin Gimpel, and Karen Livescu. 2014. Tailoring continuous word representations for dependency parsing. In *Proceedings of the Annual Meeting of the Association for Computational Linguistics*.

Xinxiong Chen, Zhiyuan Liu, and Maosong Sun. 2014. A unified model for word sense representation and disambiguation. In *Proceedings of EMNLP*.

Ronan Collobert, Jason Weston, Léon Bottou, Michael Karlen, Koray Kavukcuoglu, and Pavel Kuksa.

2011. Natural language processing (almost) from scratch. *The Journal of Machine Learning Research*, 12:2493–2537.

Adriano Ferraresi, Eros Zanchetta, Marco Baroni, and Silvia Bernardini. 2008. Introducing and evaluating ukwac, a very large web-derived corpus of English. In *Proceedings of the 4th Web as Corpus Workshop (WAC-4)*.

Eric H. Huang, Richard Socher, Christopher D. Manning, and Andrew Y. Ng. 2012. Improving word representations via global context and multiple word prototypes. In *Proceedings of ACL*.

Rafal Jozefowicz, Oriol Vinyals, Mike Schuster, Noam Shazeer, and Yonghui Wu. 2016. Exploring the limits of language modeling. *arXiv preprint arXiv:1602.02410*.

Mikael Kågebäck, Fredrik Johansson, Richard Johansson, and Devdatt Dubhashi. 2015. Neural context embeddings for automatic discovery of word senses. In *Proceedings of NAACL*.

Kazuya Kawakami and Chris Dyer. 2016. Learning to represent words in context with multilingual supervision. In *Workshop in ICLR*.

Diederik Kingma and Jimmy Ba. 2014. Adam: A method for stochastic optimization. *arXiv preprint arXiv:1412.6980*.

Ryan Kiros, Yukun Zhu, Ruslan R Salakhutdinov, Richard Zemel, Raquel Urtasun, Antonio Torralba, and Sanja Fidler. 2015. Skip-thought vectors. In *Proceedings of NIPS*.

Gerhard Kremer, Katrin Erk, Sebastian Padó, and Stefan Thater. 2014. What substitutes tell us-analysis of an all-words lexical substitution corpus. In *Proceedings of EACL*.

Guillaume Lample, Miguel Ballesteros, Sandeep Subramanian, Kazuya Kawakami, and Chris Dyer. 2016. Neural architectures for named entity recognition. *arXiv preprint arXiv:1603.01360*.

Omer Levy and Yoav Goldberg. 2014a. Dependency-based word embeddings. In *Proceedings of ACL*.

Omer Levy and Yoav Goldberg. 2014b. Neural word embeddings as implicit matrix factorization. In *Proceedings of NIPS*.

Wang Ling, Lin Chu-Cheng, Yulia Tsvetkov, and Silvio Amir. 2015a. Not all contexts are created equal: Better word representations with variable attention. In *Proceedings of EMNLP*.

Wang Ling, Chris Dyer, Alan Black, and Isabel Trancoso. 2015b. Two/too simple adaptations of word2vec for syntax problems. In *Proceedings of NAACL*.

Quan Liu, Hui Jiang, Si Wei, Zhen-Hua Ling, and Yu Hu. 2015. Learning semantic word embeddings based on ordinal knowledge constraints. *Proceedings of ACL*.

Diana McCarthy and Roberto Navigli. 2007. Semeval-2007 task 10: English lexical substitution task. In *Proceedings of SemEval*.

Oren Melamud, Ido Dagan, and Jacob Goldberger. 2015a. Modeling word meaning in context with substitute vectors. In *Proceedings of ACL*.

Oren Melamud, Omer Levy, and Ido Dagan. 2015b. A simple word embedding model for lexical substitution. In *Proceedings of Workshop on Vector Space Modeling for NLP (VSM)*.

Oren Melamud, David McClosky, Siddharth Patwardhan, and Mohit Bansal. 2016. The role of context types and dimensionality in learning word embeddings. In *Proceedings of NAACL*.

Rada Mihalcea, Timothy Anatolievich Chklovski, and Adam Kilgarriff. 2004. The senseval-3 english lexical sample task. ACL.

Tomas Mikolov, Kai Chen, Greg Corrado, and Jeffrey Dean. 2013a. Efficient estimation of word representations in vector space. *arXiv preprint arXiv:1301.3781*.

Tomas Mikolov, Ilya Sutskever, Kai Chen, Greg S Corrado, and Jeff Dean. 2013b. Distributed representations of words and phrases and their compositionality. In *Proceedings of NIPS*.

Piotr Mirowski and Andreas Vlachos. 2015. Dependency recurrent neural language models for sentence completion. *arXiv preprint arXiv:1507.01193*.

Jeffrey Pennington, Richard Socher, and Christopher D Manning. 2014. Glove: Global vectors for word representation. In *Proceedings EMNLP*.

Sascha Rothe and Hinrich Schütze. 2015. Autoextend: Extending word embeddings to embeddings for synsets and lexemes. *Proceedings of ACL*.

Richard Socher, Jeffrey Pennington, Eric H Huang, Andrew Y Ng, and Christopher D Manning. 2011. Semi-supervised recursive autoencoders for predicting sentiment distributions. In *Proceedings of EMNLP*.

György Szarvas, Róbert Busa-Fekete, and Eyke Hüllermeier. 2013. Learning to rank lexical substitutions. In *Proceedings of EMNLP*.

Seiya Tokui, Kenta Oono, Shohei Hido, and Justin Clayton. 2015. Chainer: a next-generation open source framework for deep learning. In *Proceedings of Workshop on Machine Learning Systems (LearningSys) in NIPS*.

Joseph Turian, Lev Ratinov, and Yoshua Bengio. 2010.
Word representations: A simple and general method
for semisupervised learning. In *Proceedings of ACL*.

Mehmet Ali Yatbaz, Enis Sert, and Deniz Yuret. 2012.
Learning syntactic categories using paradigmatic
representations of word context. In *Proceedings
EMNLP*.

Deniz Yuret. 2012. FASTSUBS: An efficient and exact procedure for finding the most likely lexical substitutes based on an n-gram language model. *Signal
Processing Letters, IEEE*, 19(11):725–728.

Jie Zhou and Wei Xu. 2015. End-to-end learning of
semantic role labeling using recurrent neural networks. In *Proceedings of ACL*.

Geoffrey Zweig and Christopher JC Burges. 2011. The
microsoft research sentence completion challenge.
Technical report, Technical Report MSR-TR-2011-
129, Microsoft.

Learning to Jointly Predict Ellipsis and Comparison Structures

Omid Bakhshandeh[1], Alexis Wellwood[2], James Allen[1,3]

1 University of Rochester, 2 Northwestern University, 3 Florida Institute for Human and Machine Cognition

{omidb,james}@cs.rochester.edu, wellwood@northwestern.edu

Abstract

Domain-independent meaning representation of text has received a renewed interest in the NLP community. Comparison plays a crucial role in shaping objective and subjective opinion and measurement in natural language, and is often expressed in complex constructions including ellipsis. In this paper, we introduce a novel framework for jointly capturing the semantic structure of comparison and ellipsis constructions. Our framework models ellipsis and comparison as interconnected predicate-argument structures, which enables automatic ellipsis resolution. We show that a structured prediction model trained on our dataset of 2,800 gold annotated review sentences yields promising results. Together with this paper we release the dataset and an annotation tool which enables two-stage expert annotation on top of tree structures.

1 Introduction

Representing the underlying meaning of text has been a long-standing topic of interest in computational linguistics. Recently there has been a renewed interest in representation of meaning for various tasks such as semantic parsing, where the task is to map a natural language sentence into its corresponding formal meaning representation (Zelle and Mooney, 1996; Berant and Liang, 2014). Open-domain and broad-coverage semantic representation of text (Banarescu et al., 2013; Bos, 2008; Allen et al., 2008) is crucial for many language understanding tasks such as reading comprehension tests and question answering.

With the rise of continuous-space models there is even more interest in capturing deeper generic semantics of text as opposed to surface word representations.

One of the most common ways for expressing evaluative sentiment towards different entities is using comparison. A simple natural language example of comparison is *Their pizza is the best*. Capturing the underlying meaning of comparison structures, as opposed to their surface wording, is required for accurate evaluation of qualities and quantities. For instance, given a more complex comparison example, *The pizza was great, but it was not as awesome as the sandwich*, the state-of-the-art sentiment analysis system (Manning et al., 2014) assigns an overall 'neutral' sentiment value, which clearly lacks deeper understanding of the comparison happening in the sentence.

Consider the generic meaning representation depicted in in Figure 1 according to frame semantic parsing [1] (Das et al., 2014) for the following sentence:

(1)   My Mazda drove faster than his Hyundai.

It is evident that this meaning representation does not fully capture how the semantics of the adjective *fast* relates to the *driving* event, and what it actually means for a car to drive *faster than* another car. More importantly, there is an ellipsis in this sentence, the resolution of which results in complete understood reading of *My Mazda drove faster than his Hyundai $_{drove\ fast}$*, which is in no way captured in Figure 1[2]. Having a comprehensive meaning representation of comparison struc-

---

[1] We used Semafor tool: http://demo.ark.cs.cmu.edu/parse

[2] The same shortcomings are shared among other generic meaning representations such as LinGO English Resource Grammar (ERG) (Flickinger, 2011), Boxer (Bos, 2008), or AMR (Banarescu et al., 2013), among others.

Proceedings of the 20th SIGNLL Conference on Computational Natural Language Learning (CoNLL), pages 62–74,
Berlin, Germany, August 7-12, 2016. ©2016 Association for Computational Linguistics

$$
\frac{\text{My Mazda}}{\text{Self\_mover}} \quad \frac{\text{drove}}{\textbf{Self\_motion}} \quad \frac{\text{faster than his Hyundai}}{\text{Manner}}
$$

Figure 1: The frame-semantic parsing of the sentence *My Mazda drove faster than his Hyundai.*

tures which can capture the mentioned phenomena can enable the development of computational semantic models which are suitable for various reasoning tasks.

In this paper we introduce a joint theoretical model for comprehensive semantic representation of the structure of comparison and ellipsis in natural language. We jointly model comparison and ellipsis as inter-connected predicate-argument structures, which enables automatic ellipsis resolution. The main contributions of this paper can be summarized as follows: (1) introducing a novel framework for jointly representing the semantics of comparison and ellipsis on top of syntactic trees, (2) releasing a dataset of 2,800 expert annotated user review comparison instances[3], which significantly increases the size of the available resources on comparison structures in the community, (3) presenting a new structured prediction model for automatic extraction of semantic structures of comparison text together with ellipsis resolution, (4) releasing an interactive tool for tree-based human annotation of corpora, which can be helpful for many other annotation tasks in NLP.

To our knowledge, this paper presents the first comprehensive computational framework of its kind for ellipsis and comparison constructions. Our semantic model can be incorporated as a part of any broad-coverage semantic parser (Banarescu et al., 2013; Allen et al., 2008; Bos, 2008) for augmenting their meaning representation.

2   Background and Related Work

Broadly, elliptical constructions involve the omission of one or more phrases from a clause (such as 'drove fast' phrase at the end of example (1)) whose content can still be fully recovered from the unelided words of the sentence (Kennedy, 2003; Merchant, 2013). Resolving ellipsis is crucial for deep language understanding. Although ellipsis has been studied in great depth in linguistics, there only have been a few computational studies of el-

lipsis, most of which have focused on Verb Phrase Ellipsis (VPE) (Nielsen, 2004; Schiehlen, 2002; Hardt, 1997) such as *Larry is not telling the truth, neither is Jim* $\triangle$. where $\triangle$ is a verb phrase ellipsis site, which can be resolved to 'telling the truth'.

In 2010, a SemEval task was organized with the goals of (1) automatically detecting VPE in text, and (2) resolving the antecedent of each VPE (Bos and Spenader, 2011). For this task, they manually annotated a portion of OntoNotes corpus, consisting of Wall Street Journal (WSJ) articles. Throughout all the 25 sections of WSJ, they found 487 instances of VPE (ranging from predicative ellipsis, deletion, and comparative constructions, to pseudo-gapping) in about 53,600 sentences. Among 487 ellipsis items, there were 96 comparative constructions. They show that simply searching the parse trees for empty VPs achieves a high precision (0.95) but low recall (0.58). Our work presents the first attempt on comparison ellipsis resolution of various types, within a semantically rich framework of comparisons.

The syntax and semantics of comparison structures in natural language have been the subject of extensive systematic research in linguistics for a long time (Bresnan, 1973; Cresswell, 1976; Von Stechow, 1984). Measurement in language is mainly expressed by using comparative morphemes such as *more, less, -er, as, too, enough, -est, etc*[4]. The main component of the sentence carrying out the measurement can have either of adjective (JJ), adverb (RB), noun (NN), or verb (VB) parts of speech. The earliest efforts on the computational modeling of comparatives have been in the context of sentiment analysis, ranging from works on identifying sentences containing comparisons (Jindal and Liu, 2006b) to identifying the components of the comparisons in the form of triplets or other templatic patterns (Jindal and Liu, 2006a; Xu et al., 2011; Kessler and Kuhn, 2014). These works provide a basis for computational analysis of comparatives, however, they lack depth and broader coverage as they are limited to only a few comparison patterns.

The most recent work on the computational semantics of comparison (Bakhshandeh and Allen, 2015) sets the stage for a deeper semantic representation of comparisons. Bakshandeh and Allen introduce the first computational semantic frame-

---

[3]Throughout this paper we refer to any statement comparing two or more entities as a comparison instance.

[4]These morphemes are often referred to as the comparison operators.

work for representing the meaning of comparatives in natural language. This framework models comparisons as predicate-argument pairs interconnected via semantic role links. Our framework differs in the following crucial aspects:

— **Joint Ellipsis and Comparison Modeling**: Effective modeling and reasoning on comparison structures requires addressing ellipsis as well. While Bakhshandeh and Allen only model comparisons, we provide a novel semantic framework for comprehensive annotation of ellipsis structures within comparison structures (details in Section 3.2).

— **Tree-based Structure Modeling**: Bakhshandeh and Allen use span-based predicate-argument treatment, which is often prone to errors and lower inter-annotator agreement. We base our framework on top of constituency syntactic parse trees, which leads to more accurate[5] capture of semantic structures.

— **Reviews Dataset**: While Bakhshandeh and Allen use newswire text, we shift our focus to the actual user reviews, which contain more comparison structures (Section 4.2). Furthermore, while their dataset included 531 sentences, we collect gold annotations for 2,800 sentences, which significantly increases the size of the available data for the community.

3 A Comprehensive Semantic Framework for Comparison

In this Section we introduce a novel semantic framework of comparison structures which incorporates ellipsis. Our framework extends and improves the state-of-the-art semantic framework for comparison structures in various ways (outlined in Section 2). We follow the model of interconnected predicate-argument structures. In this model the predicates are either comparison or ellipsis operators, and each predicate takes a set of arguments called its *semantic frame*. For instance, in *[Sam] is the tallest [student] [in the gym]*, the morpheme *-est* expresses a comparison operator and the brackets delimit its various arguments. In this Section we provide details about our semantic framework.

3.1 Comparison Structures

Comparison structures are modeled as sets of inter-connected predicate-arguments. We base our comparison framework on Bakhshandeh and Allen (Bakhshandeh and Allen, 2015), however, we extend and improve on the set of predicate types and arguments to capture more diverse structures which results in a different semantic framework.

3.1.1 Predicates

We consider two main categories of comparison predicates, each of which can grade any of the four parts of speech including adjectives, adverbs, nouns, and verbs.

1. **Ordering**: Indicates how two or more entities are ordered along a scale. The subtypes of this predicate are the following:

— <u>Comparatives</u> with '$>$', '$<$' indicate that one degree is greater or lesser than another; expressed by the morphemes *more/-er* and *less*.

   (2)   The steak is tastier than the potatoes.

   (3)   Tom ate more soup.

— <u>Equatives</u> involving '$\geq$' indicate that one degree meets or exceeds another; expressed by *as* in constructions such as *as tall* or *as much*.

   (4)   The Mazda drives as fast as the Nissan.

— <u>Superlatives</u> indicate an entity or event has the 'highest' or 'lowest' degree on a scale; expressed by *most/-est* and *least*.

   (5)   That chef made the best soup.

2. **Extreme**: Indicates having too much or enough of a quality or quantity. The subtypes of this predicate are the following:

— <u>Excessive</u> indicate that an entity or event is 'too high' on a scale; expressed by *too*.

— <u>Assetive</u> indicate that an entity or event has 'enough' of a degree; expressed by *enough*.

3.1.2 Arguments

Each predicate takes a set of arguments that we refer to as the predicate's 'semantic frame'. Following are the arguments included in our framework:

— <u>Figure</u> (Fig) is the main role which is being compared.

— <u>Ground</u> is the main role Figure is compared to.

— <u>Scale</u> (-/neutral/+) is the scale for the comparison, such as size, beauty, temperature. We assign the generic sentiment values positive (+), neutral, and negative (-) to the underlying scales.

---

[5]This is crucial, given the fact that the syntactic structure of many comparison instances are complex, e.g., *The server was the rudest ever and made me feel as I was wasting her time.*

– <u>Standard</u> (Std) is the reason a degree is 'too much' (excessive predicates) or 'enough' (assetive predicates). An individual j may be 'too tall *to reach the top shelf*' but 'tall enough *to get on this ride*'.

– <u>Differential</u> (Diff) is an explicit phrase indicating the 'size' of a difference between degrees. For instance, '*2 inches* taller' or '*6 degrees* warmer'.

– <u>Domain</u> (Dom) is an explicit expression of the type of domain in which the comparison takes place (superlatives). An individual m may be 'the tallest *girl*' but not 'the tallest *student*'.

– <u>Domain Specifier</u> (D-Spec) is the specification of the domain argument, further narrowing the scope of the domain. An individual m may be 'the tallest girl *in the class*' but not 'the tallest girl *in the country*'.

The Case of Copulas: A copula is a form of the verb *to be* that links the subject of a sentence with a predicate, such as *was* in the sentence *She <u>was</u> a doctor*. Comparison structures are often formed on the basis of copular constructions, for example (6a). Compare this with (6b), and their corresponding comparison structures.

(6) a. This was the best pizza in town.
     b. I ate the best pizza in town.

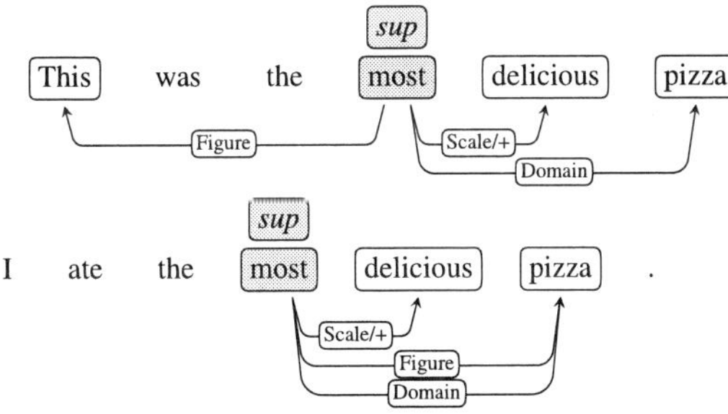

As you can see, in (6a) *was* links *this* to *pizza*. In this sentence the argument Figure is *this*. On the other hand, in (6b), the word *pizza* takes the role of both Figure and Domain.

3.2 Ellipsis Structures

Perhaps the most common type of comparison structure is the comparative construction, with (13) as an example, where Δ marks an ellipsis site. Roughly, (13) is interpreted as a greater-than relation between 'how appetizingly the steak sizzles' and 'how appetizingly the hamburger sizzles', which might be formalized as in (14) with e_1 and e_2 representing the two sizzling events.

(7) The steak sizzled more appetizingly than the hamburger Δ.

(8) $appetizingness(e_1) > appetizingness(e_2)$

On the surface, the sentence in (13) does not relate *sizzle* or *appetizingly* to the hamburger; these must be filled in for Δ by a process called *ellipsis resolution*—finding the *antecedent* of an ellipsis. Speakers of English are readily able to infer from the surface material in (13) that the dependent clause is interpreted as in (9), where the resolved ellipsis is written in subscript.

(9) than the hamburger$_{\text{sizzled appetizingly}}$

It is clear that resolving ellipsis in comparison structures is crucial for language understanding and failure to do so would deliver an incorrect meaning representation. Numerous subtypes of elliptical constructions are distinguished in linguistics (Kennedy, 2003; Merchant, 2013; Yoshida et al., 2016). In our framework we mainly include six types that can be detected in comparison structures: 'VP-deletion', 'Stripping'[6], 'Pseudogapping', 'Gapping', 'Sluicing', and 'Subdeletion'. Ellipsis more often occurs in comparative and equative constructions (applicable to any of the four parts of speech) as follows.

- **Comparatives**: Ellipsis takes place in the dependent clause headed by *than*. We indicate the three ellipsis possibilities for these clauses resuming (10), a nominal comparative. The elided materials are written in subscript.

(10) **Mary ate more rice** ...

- VP-deletion (aka 'Comparative Deletion'):
  ... than John did $_{\text{eat rice}}$.
- Stripping (aka 'Phrasal Comparative'):
  ... than John $_{\text{ate rice}}$.
- Gapping:
  ... than John, $_{\text{ate how-much}}$ soup.
- Pseudogapping:
  ... than John did $_{\text{eat}}$ soup.
- Sluicing:
  ... than someone, but I don't remember than who $_{\text{ate how-much rice}}$.
- Subdeletion:
  ... than John ate $_{\text{how-much}}$ soup.

- **Equatives**: Ellipsis takes place in the dependent clause headed by *as*. We indicate the possibilities for these clauses resuming (11), a nominal equative.

(11) **Mary ate as much rice** ...

- VP-deletion:
  ... as John did $_{\text{eat how-much rice}}$.

---

[6]VP-deletion and stripping are the more frequent types.

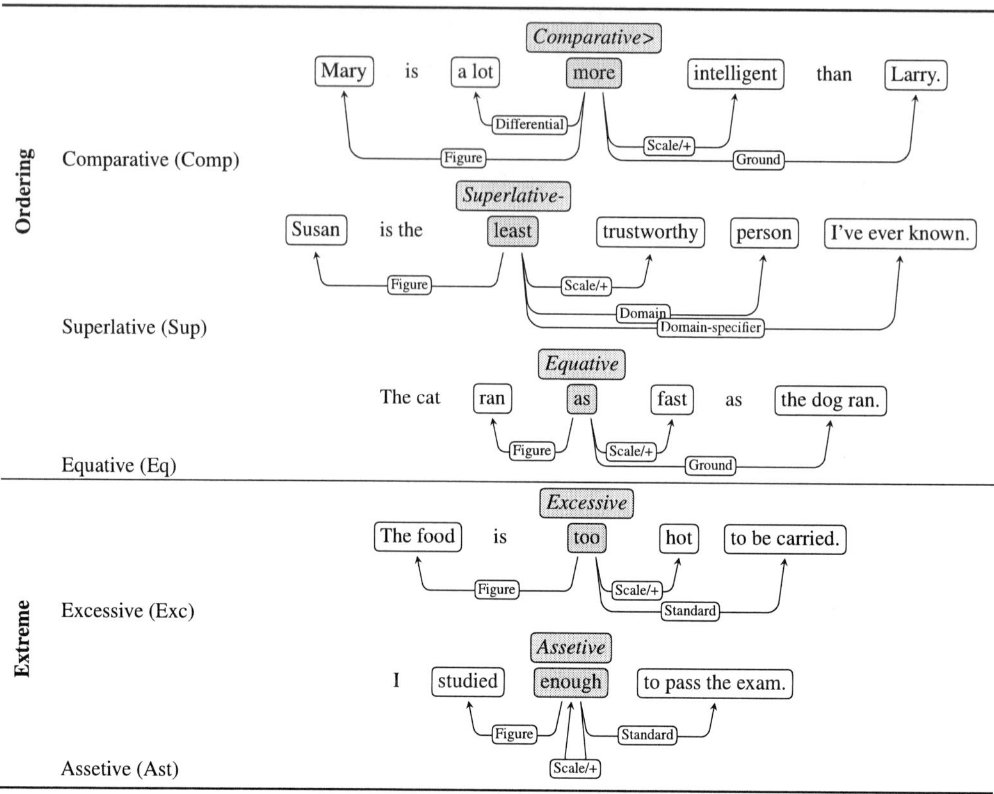

Table 1: Predicates together with their semantic frames shown in example sentences.

- Stripping:
  ... as John $_{eat}$ $_{how\text{-}much}$ rice.
- Gapping:
  ... as John, $_{ate\ how\text{-}much}$ soup.
- Pseudogapping:
  ... as John did $_{ate\ how\text{-}much}$ soup.
- Sluicing:
  ... as someone, but I don't remember as who $_{ate\ how\text{-}much\ rice}$.[7]
- Subdeletion:
  ... as John ate $_{how\text{-}much}$ soup.

Now that we have the ellipsis predicate types, we want to empirically model ellipsis constructions as predicate-argument structures with reference to an antecedent, where each ellipsis predicate is associated with its corresponding comparative predicate. The question is how to represent the ellipsis construction in a sentence. Consider the example of VP-deletion in the following adverbial comparative:

(12) The steak was cooked more carefully than the burger Δ.

where Δ should be resolved to *was cooked how-carefully*. *How* is called the null operator, which

serves as the placeholder for the measurement of a degree.

In order to represent the resolution of the elided material such as Δ, we first annotate the predicate of an ellipsis construction as an 'attachment' site in the syntactic tree, right next to the node that the elided material should follow. Hence, in (12), the token *the burger* will be annotated as the ellipsis predicate, which signifies the start of an ellipsis construction.

Defining the arguments for ellipsis predicates can be complicated. Here the goal is to thoroughly construct the antecedent of the elided material by annotating the existing words of the context sentence. In order to address this, we define the following three argument types for ellipsis:

– <u>Reference</u> is the constituency node which is the base of an antecedent.

– <u>EXclude</u> (Ex) is the constituency node which should be excluded from the Reference.

– <u>How-much</u> (?) is the constituency node which should be replaced by a null operator such as *how* or *how-much*; this is always the argument matching *more/-er* or *as (much)* in the context sentence.

---

[7]Whether this construction is grammatical is controversial.

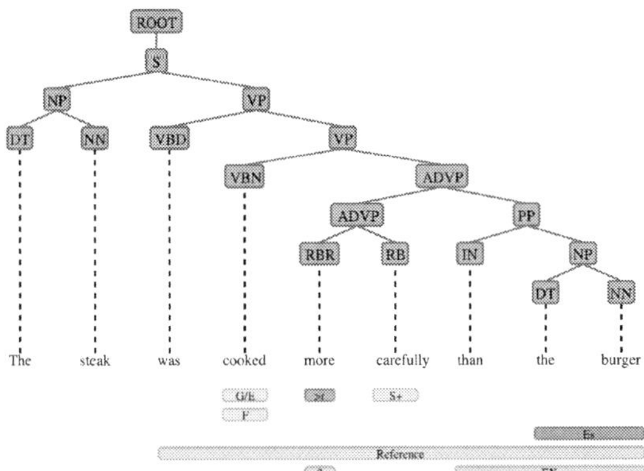

Figure 2: Full tree-based annotation of comparison and ellipsis structures for the sentence presented in example 12. The tag 'Es' refers to the Stripping predicate type.

Following the above annotation schema the ellipsis site in (12) will be annotated as shown in red in Figure 2. This shows how to do automatic ellipsis resolution given our representation: one should start *after* the node 'the burger', and perform the following: [was cooked ~~more~~$_{How?}$ carefully than the burger]$_{Reference}$ − [than the burger]$_{EXclude}$ = *was cooked how carefully*. Another important thing to note in Figure 2 is our treatment of the comparison structure (in green) jointly with ellipsis: The argument F (Figure) of the comparison predicate *more* is *cooked*. The G argument (Ground), is the second elided 'cooked' event, which should come from the ellipsis construction. We thus annotate the explicit node *cooked* as the Ground-Ellipsis (G/E) which also links the comparison construction to the ellipsis predicate.

4 Data Collection Methodology

4.1 Comparison Instance Sampling

The sentences used for annotation play a significant role in the diversity and comprehensiveness of the comparison structures represented in our dataset. Earlier work (Bakhshandeh and Allen, 2015) experimented with annotating semantic structures on OntoNotes dataset. We shift our focus to actual product and restaurant reviews, which inherently include many natural comparison instances. For this purpose we mainly use Google English Web Treebank[8]. This corpus contains more than 250,000 words in about 10,000

sentences of English weblogs, newsgroups, email, reviews (product, restaurant, etc.) and question-answers, annotated with gold syntactic trees. This corpus is suitable for our task since it provides a good coverage of web domain text, mainly reviews.

In order to augment the volume of review content, we also use the Movie Reviews dataset (Pang and Lee, 2005). This dataset consists of 11,855 sentences extracted from movie reviews. Given that these Movie reviews do not come with the syntactic trees, we used the Berkeley parser (Petrov et al., 2006), which outperformed the other off-the-shelf parsers on comparison syntactic structure. Of course it is not efficient to include any arbitrary sentence of a corpus for manual annotation. We employ various linguistic filters to filter the sentences which potentially contain comparison. The details of this process can be found in the supplementary material.

4.2 Tree-based Annotation

We trained six linguists to do the semantic annotation for comparison and ellipsis structures for the sampled comparison instances according to the framework presented in Section 3. The annotations were done via our interactive two-stage tree-based annotation tool. In this tool, each annotator can be assigned with a set of tree-based annotation assignments, where pairing annotators to do the same task for inter-annotator analysis is also feasible. For this task, the annotations were done on top of constituency parse trees, and the annotators were instructed to choose the top-most constituency node when choosing the predicate or arguments.[9] Annotating on gold-standard syntactic trees helps with resolving ambiguous instances which have multiple interpretations. Furthermore, it gives annotators syntactic signals for choosing the types of predicates (e.g., adverbial vs adjectival comparatives), all of which increase the accuracy of our annotation.

Our annotation tool sets up the data collection as a two stage expert annotation process: (1) for each sentence, one expert annotates and submits the annotation, (2) another expert reviews the submission and either returns the submission with feedback or marks it as a gold. This recursive

---

[8]https://catalog.ldc.upenn.edu/ LDC2012T13

[9]This enables accurate capturing of arguments, e.g., in *I am the tallest [in our school]*, the constituency node corresponding to the entire phrase in brackets is annotated as Domain-specifier.

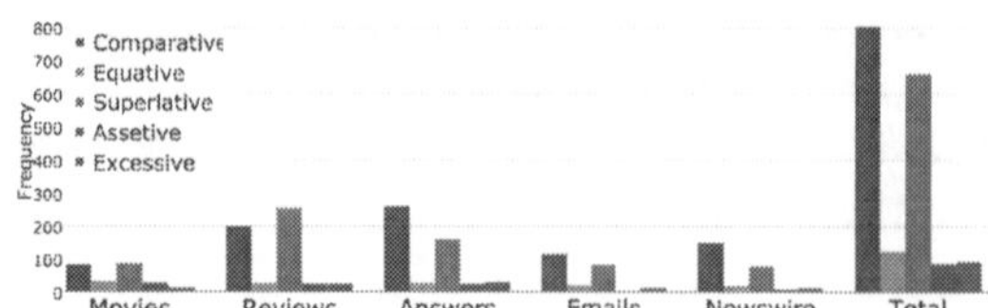

Figure 3: The number of various predicate types across different resources.

Table 2: The percentage of each argument type.

Scale	Fig	Ground	Dom	D-Spec	Diff	Std
38.8	31.5	6.33	9.31	7.01	4.09	2.98

process ensures higher annotation quality. We iterate over the sentences until getting 100% inter-annotator agreement. On average, annotating every sentence takes about one minute and revising controversial sentences (12% of the time) takes about 4 minutes of expert annotation time.

This process yields a total of 2,800 annotated sentences with 100% agreement. Figure 3 visualizes the distribution of various predicate types from the various resources. In order, these resources each include 11,855, 3,813, 3,488, 4,900, and 2,391 sentences. As this Figure depicts, reviews are indeed the richest resource for comparisons, with more comparison instances than any other resource of even a bigger size. There are a total of 5,564 comparison arguments in our dataset, with the distribution summarized in Table 2. The total number of ellipsis predicates is 240, with 197 Stripping, 31 VP-deletion and 12 Pseudo-gapping.

5 Predicting Semantic Structures

In this Section we describe our methodology for joint prediction of comparison and ellipsis structure for a given sentence.

5.1 Modeling

We model the problem as a joint predicate-argument prediction of comparison and ellipsis structures. It is important to note that our predicate-argument semantic structure itself looks similar to a dependency parse tree, however, as explained earlier, we base this representation on top of constituency parse trees. For each training sentence, we denote the underlying constituency tree as T. The set of all constituency nodes in T is V_T. Each $v \in V_T$ can be tagged as a comparison predicate $c \in C = \{Comp, Sup, Eq, Exc,$

$Ast\}$[10], a comparison argument $a_c \in A_C = all$-$comparison$-$arguments$, an ellipsis predicate $e =$ 'Ellipsis', an ellipsis argument $a_e \in A_E = \{Reference, Ex, '?'\}$, or $NONE$.

In Equation 1, we define a globally normalized model for the probability distribution of comparison labels over all $v \in V_T$ if $CompFilter(T) =$ True. We define $CompFilter$ to filter the following:

– Any sentence containing a word with POS tag equal to *JJR, RBR, JJS,* or *RBS*.

– Any sentence containing a comparison morpheme such as *more, most, less, enough, too.*

The next step is to define the probability distribution in Equation 2 for ellipsis labels, conditioning on the comparison label. This is motivated by the fact that the Ellipsis predicate is dependent on its corresponding comparison predicate. Given the comparison and ellipsis predicate labels, for each comparison and ellipsis argument type we define a binomial probability distribution as defined in Equations 3 and 4.

$$p_C(c|v, T, \theta_C) \propto exp(\boldsymbol{f}_C(c, T)^T \boldsymbol{\theta_C}) \quad (1)$$

$$p_E(e|c, v, T, \theta_E) \propto exp(\boldsymbol{f}_E(e, c, T)^T \boldsymbol{\theta_E}) \quad (2)$$

$$p_{A_c}(a_c|c, e, v, T, \theta_{a_c}) \propto exp(\boldsymbol{f}_{A_C}(c, e, T)^T \boldsymbol{\theta_{a_c}}) \quad (3)$$

$$p_{A_e}(a_e|c, e, v, T, \theta_{a_e}) \propto exp(\boldsymbol{f}_{A_E}(e, c, T)^T \boldsymbol{\theta_{a_e}}) \quad (4)$$

In each of the above equations, f is the corresponding feature function. For predicates the main features are lexical features, bigram features, node's constituency position, node's minimum distance from leaves, and node's parent constituency label. For the arguments, we use the same feature-set as for the predicates, but also including the leftmost verb (for the case of copulas), the constituency path between argument and the predicate, and the predicate type. θ_C, θ_E, θ_{a_c} and θ_{a_e} are the parameters of the log-linear model. We calculate these parameters using Stochastic Gradient Descent algorithm.

5.2 Joint Inference of Ellipsis and Comparison

For inference we model the problem as a structured prediction task. Given the syntactic tree of a given sentence, for each node we first select the predicate type with the highest p_C. Then for each

---

[10]*Each predicate should be further tagged with one of the four possible POS tags (JJ, RB, NN, VB), resulting in a total of 20 predicate types.*

selected comparison predicate, we find the corresponding ellipsis predicate that has the highest p_E probability. Define $\langle tc, te \rangle \in R$, where R is the set of all tuples of corresponding comparison and ellipsis predicates, tc is the index of the comparison predicate and te is the index of the ellipsis predicate.

We tackle the problem of argument assignment by using Integer Linear Programming, where one can pose domain-specific knowledge as constraints. We define a binary variable b_{ij} and b'_{ik} where i is the a node in tree, j is a comparison argument label and k is a ellipsis argument label. For each $\langle tc, te \rangle$, we maximize the linear Equation 5, subject to a few linguistically-motivated constraints.

$$\max_{b_{ij}, b'_{jk} \in \{0,1\}} \sum_{i \in V_T, j \in A_C, k \in A_E} \Big(b_{ij} p_{A_c}(tc, te, i, j) + b'_{ik} p_{A_e}(tc, te, i, k) \Big) \quad (5)$$

ILP Constraints: Any specific comparison label calls for a unique set of constraints in the ILP formulation, which ensures the validity of predictions. For instance, the *Superlative* predicate type never takes any *Ground* arguments, or the argument *Standard* is only applicable to the excessive predicate type. We implement the semantic frame (as listed in Table 1) of each predicate type using hard ILP constraints. For example, in order to encode the semantic frame for predicate type *Excessive*, we employ the ILP constraints in Equation 6, which simply enforce this predicate to have 0 Ground arguments and maximum 1 Figure arguments.

$$\sum_{i \in V_T, j = Ground} b_{ij} = 0, \quad \sum_{i \in V_T, j = Figure} b_{ij} \leq 1 \quad (6)$$

We incorporate a few other ILP constraints for encoding our knowledge regarding ellipsis structures as well as comparison. For more details of these knowledge-driven constraints please refer to the supplementary material.

6 Experimental Result

We divide our dataset into train and train-dev (70%), and test (30%) sets. For evaluation of a given system prediction against the reference gold annotation, for each constituency node in the reference, we give the system a point in two ways:

	ILP Model		
	P	**R**	**F1**
Excessive	0.68/0.68	1.00/1.00	0.81/0.81
Assetive	0.97/0.97	1.00/1.00	0.98/0.98
Comparative	0.95/0.95	0.99/0.99	0.97/0.97
Superlative	0.97/0.98	0.98/0.99	0.98/0.98
Equative	0.57/0.58	0.95/0.98	0.71/0.73
Stripping	0.75/0.96	0.75/0.96	0.75/0.96
Deletion	0.20/0.41	0.72/0.89	0.31/0.13
Average	0.72/0.78	0.91/0.97	0.76/0.80
	Baseline		
Excessive	0.65/0.65	1.00/1.00	0.79/0.79
Assetive	0.97/0.97	1.00/1.00	0.98/0.98
Comparative	0.95/0.97	0.96/0.97	0.95/0.97
Superlative	0.98/0.98	0.98/0.98	0.98/0.98
Equative	0.13/0.13	1.00/1.00	0.23/0.23
Stripping	0.05/0.14	0.31/0.91	0.08/0.25
Deletion	0.00/0.00	0.00/0.00	0.00/0.00
Average	0.62/0.64	0.87/0.97	0.66/0.69

Table 3: Predicate prediction results on test set. Each cell contains scores according to Exact/Head measurement.

(1) <u>Exact</u>: the label assigned to the node by the system exactly matches the gold label; (2) <u>Head</u>: the reference label matches the label of the head word of the node in system's prediction. We report on Precision (P), Recall (R) and F1 score. We test three models: our comprehensive ILP model (detailed in Section 5), our model without the ILP constraints, and a rule-based baseline. The baseline encodes the same linguistically motivated ILP constraints via rules. It further uses a few pattern extraction functions for pinpointing comparison morphemes which detect comparison and ellipsis predicates. More details about the baseline can be found in the supplementary material.

The results on predicate prediction is shown in Table 3. Given that our ILP constraints only encode argument structures, in this Table we only compare the baseline with our full ILP model. As the results show, overall, the scores are high for predicting the predicates, with ellipsis predicates being the most challenging. The baseline has a near perfect prediction on Assetive and Superlative types, which shows that the linguistic patterns can capture these types well. Our model performs the poorest on *Equatives*. If we look at the specific cases it misses, it is often regarding the morpheme 'as', which takes part in many various linguistics constructions, many of which are not comparatives. For example, for the test sentence *We will let them manage our other investment properties as well as us getting older.*, our system wrongly classifies 'as' as an equative

	ILP Model (Exact/Head)			ILP No Constraints (Exact/Head)			Baseline (Exact/Head)		
	P	**R**	**F1**	**P**	**R**	**F1**	**P**	**R**	**F1**
Standard	0.40/0.80	0.42/0.84	0.41/0.82	0.00/0.00	0.71/1.00	0.00/0.00	0.00/0.00	0.00/0.00	0.00/0.00
Scale	0.58/0.64	0.89/0.99	0.70/0.78	0.02/0.02	0.94/1.00	0.04/0.04	0.47/0.69	0.67/0.98	0.55/0.81
Ground	0.27/0.48	0.46/0.84	0.34/0.61	0.00/0.00	0.98/1.00	0.01/0.01	0.06/0.18	0.24/0.71	0.10/0.29
Figure	0.38/0.81	0.44/0.94	0.41/0.87	0.02/0.02	0.94/1.00	0.03/0.03	0.09/0.43	0.17/0.80	0.12/0.56
D-Specifier	0.41/0.63	0.57/0.87	0.48/0.73	0.00/0.00	1.00/1.00	0.01/0.01	0.00/0.00	0.00/0.00	0.00/0.00
Domain	0.56/0.76	0.66/0.91	0.61/0.83	0.01/0.01	0.99/1.00	0.01/0.01	0.00/0.39	0.00/0.55	0.00/0.46
Exclude	0.33/0.56	0.49/0.84	0.39/0.67	0.01/0.01	0.63/1.00	0.02/0.02	0.00/0.00	0.00/0.00	0.00/0.00
Ref	0.18/0.53	0.28/0.80	0.22/0.63	0.01/0.01	0.61/1.00	0.01/0.02	0.00/0.00	0.00/0.00	0.00/0.00
How-much	0.27/0.36	0.65/0.88	0.38/0.51	0.01/0.01	0.96/1.00	0.01/0.01	0.00/0.00	0.00/0.00	0.00/0.00
Average	0.37/0.61	0.54/0.87	0.43/0.71	0.01/0.01	0.86/1.00	0.10/0.10	0.20/0.42	0.36/0.73	0.25/0.52

Table 4: Results of argument prediction on test set. The average for the models only takes into account non-zero results.

predicate, which is clearly an ambiguous and challenging test sentence. Analysis shows that the errors are often due to inaccuracies in automatically generated parse trees, e.g., challenging long sentences (average length > 12 tokens) with informal language which are generally hard to parse.

The task of predicting arguments is a more demanding task. As you can see in Table 4, the baseline model often fails at predicting the arguments. Our comprehensive ILP model consistently outperforms the *No Constraints* model, showing the effectiveness of our linguistically motivated ILP constraints. Our ILP model performs the best on Scale and Domain argument types, which is partly due to the frequency of these types in our dataset. We are planning on annotating more data to improve the argument prediction in future.

7 Conclusion

Systems that can understand comparison and make inferences about how entities and events compare in natural language are crucial for various NLP applications, ranging from question answering to product review analysis. Having a comprehensive semantic framework which can represent the underlying meaning of comparison structures is the first step toward enabling such an inference. In this paper we introduced a novel semantic framework for jointly capturing the meaning of comparison and ellipsis constructions. We modeled the problem as inter-connected predicate-argument prediction. Based on this framework, we trained experts to annotate a dataset of ellipsis and comparison structures, which we are making publicly available[11]. Furthermore, we introduced

a structured prediction model which can automatically extract comparison structures and perform ellipsis resolution for a given text, which performs reasonably well for major predicate and argument types.

In future, we are planning on improving our joint prediction models for further improving the performance. Moreover, we plan on using our semantic framework for text comprehension applications.

Acknowledgment

We thank the anonymous reviewers for their invaluable comments and Brian Rinehart and other annotators for their great work on the annotations. This work was supported in part by Grant W911NF-15-1-0542 with the US Defense Advanced Research Projects Agency (DARPA) and the Army Research Office (ARO).

---

[11]In order to access the dataset and our interactive two-stage tree-based annotation tool please refer to `http://cs.rochester.edu/~omidb`.

Background on Ellipsis

Elliptical constructions involve the omission of one or more phrases from a clause, while the content can still be understood from the rest of the sentence (Kennedy, 2003; Merchant, 2013). Resolving ellipsis in comparison structures is crucial for language understanding. Failure to do so for (13) as an example, would deliver an incorrect representation, something like 'how appetizingly the steak sizzled is greater than the hamburger'. To arrive at an interpretation equivalent to (14) in a way that systematically relates to the syntax of (13) requires a semantics for comparatives based on 'events' and 'degrees'.

(13)   The steak sizzled more appetizingly than the hamburger Δ.

(14) $appetizingness(e_1) > appetizingness(e_2)$

In event semantics, sentences like (15) and (16) are interpreted as existential statements about events (Davidson, 1967). For example, (15) is interpreted as 'there is an event e whose Theme (Th) is the steak, and e is a sizzling event' (Parsons, 1990).

(15)   The steak sizzled. $\rightsquigarrow$
$\exists e_1[Th(e_1)(steak)\ \&\ \textbf{sizzle}(e_1)]$

(16)   The hamburger sizzled. $\rightsquigarrow$
$\exists e_2[Th(e_2)(hamburger)\ \&\ \textbf{sizzle}(e_2)]$

A comparative like (13) is built on top of two clauses much like (15) and (16) (Bresnan, 1973). In concert with *appetizingly* in (13), *more* introduces a greater-than relation between the degrees to which the two events are appetizing (Wellwood, 2015). 'Degrees' represent points on a scale, said to be the output of a 'measure function' like **appetizing** (Cresswell, 1976; Kennedy, 1999). In what follows, we first introduce this framework in the simpler case where no dependent clause appears in the sentence.

In the 'implicit' comparison (17), what is compared to must be recovered from the use context; this is indicated by the free variable δ, standing for some degree. The interpretation of this sentence is read, 'there is an event e in which the steak sizzles, and e is appetizing to a degree greater than δ'.

(17)   The steak sizzled more appetizingly. $\rightsquigarrow$
$\exists e[Th(e)(s)\ \&\ \textbf{sizzle}(e)\ \&\ \textbf{appetizing}(e) > \delta]$

When the dependent clause is present, the combination of ellipsis resolution and semantic composition delivers a degree that takes the place of δ

in a representation like that in (17). (18) is read as, 'the maximal degree d to which there is an event e of the hamburger sizzling, and e is appetizing to at least degree d'. Semantically, the maximal degree ($max\ d$) is introduced by a null operator that we will call *how* (Kennedy, 2002) throughout this paper.

(18)   ...than the hamburger did. $\overset{resolve\ ellipsis}{\rightsquigarrow}$

(19)   ...the hamburger did$_{\text{sizzle how-appetizingly}}$ $\rightsquigarrow$
$max\ d.\exists e[Th(e)(h)\ \&\ \textbf{sizzle}(e)\ \&\ \textbf{appetiz}(e) \geq d]$

Putting the pieces together, (13) in fact has the richer and more accurate meaning representation in (20).

(20) $\exists e_1[Th(e_1)(s)\ \&\ \textbf{sizz}(e_1)\ \&\ \textbf{appetiz}(e_1) > max\ d.]$
$\exists e_2[Th(e_2)(h)\ \&\ \textbf{sizz}(e_2)\ \&\ \textbf{appetiz}(e_2) \geq d]$

In comparatives with *more/-er*, and equatives with *as*, how the 'scale' is introduced in the dependent clause differs according to the major part of speech of the comparison structure. For adjectival and adverbial comparisons (*taller*, *as quickly*), the scale is provided by those categories (height, appetizingness) and the null operator is simply *how*. For nominal and verbal comparisons (*more rice*, *sizzle as much*), *much* introduces a variable scale (μ), and the null operator is called *how-much*.

Related Work

In addition to the major characteristics pointed out in the paper, our framework improves on the following issues as compared with Bakhshandeh and Allen (Bakhshandeh and Allen, 2015):

– While we also model comparison structures as predicate-argument pairs, we do not use additional semantic role links. We retain all semantic information on predicate and argument types, which results in better semantic generalization across all predicates (Section 3).

– We categorize arguments into semantic frames associated with each predicate type. This enables addressing complex cases such as 'copulas' (Section 3.1.2) which play a crucial role in asserting properties about entities. Furthermore, we introduce a more comprehensive set of argument types which more accurately capture the syntactic and semantic properties of various predicate types.

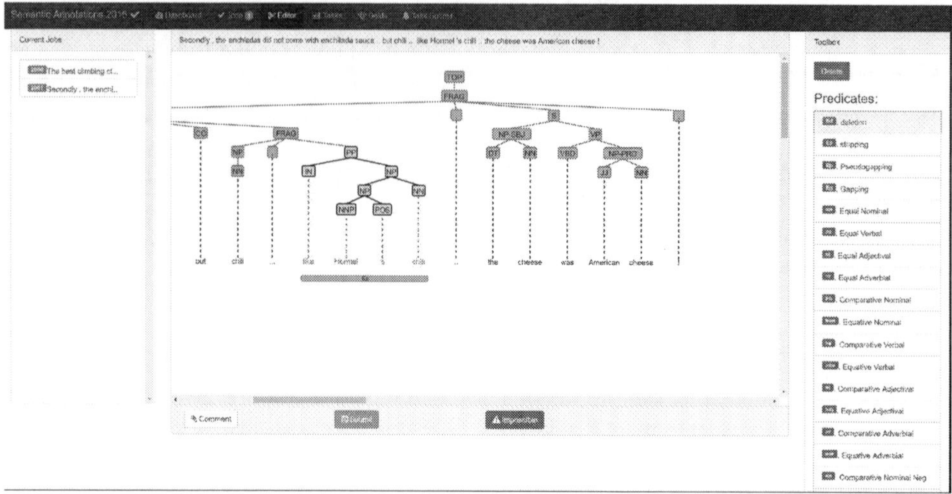

Figure 4: A screen-shot of our two-stage tree-based annotation tool.

Integer Linear Programming Constraints

Overall, our ILP constraints (which encode restrictions on the arguments of predicates) are either applied in general (to any predicate type) or are tailored to encode the semantic frame of a specific predicate. Following are our generic constraints:

1. The maximum number of arguments per node is 3.
2. The maximum number of arguments in the entire syntactic tree is 10.

We incorporate the following ILP constraints for encoding knowledge regarding Ellipsis predicates:

1. The constituency span of comparison predicate's *Figure* and *Ground* should overlap with the *Reference* argument of ellipsis predicate, if any.
2. The constituency node of *Exclude* argument should be a child of the *Reference*.
3. One node can only have more than one comparison argument type if those types are *Figure* and *Ground*.

The constraints for encoding the semantic frame of the other comparison predicate types follows straightforwardly from the semantic frames presented in the paper.

Data Collection Methodology

One approach for extracting sentences containing comparisons is to mine the text for some (automatically or manually created) patterns, then train a classifier for labeling comparison and non-comparison sentences (Jindal and Liu, 2006b).

However, the variety of comparison structures is so vast that being limited to some specific patterns or syntactic structures will not result in good coverage of comparisons. Instead, we use the following filter ($CompFilter$) with a set of basic comparison structure linguistic markers for extracting potential comparison instances:

– Any sentence containing a word with POS tag equal to *JJR*, *RBR*, *JJS*, or *RBS*.

– Any sentence containing a comparison morpheme such as *more*, *most*, *less*, *enough*, *too*.

This filter is guaranteed not to have any false negatives since it is exhaustive enough to capture any possible comparison sentence. We applied this filter to the English Web Corpus and the Movie Reviews dataset and extracted a pool of 2,800 sentences for final annotation in the next step. It is important to note that this filter will capture some cases which look like comparison instances at the surface level, but which are not so semantically (e.g., (21)-(22), extracted from the Google Web Treebank). Such negative examples help the quality of the final prediction models.

(21) Very nice ambiance and friendly staff *too*.

(22) We had sesame chicken and kung pao chicken *as well as* cheese puffs.

Baseline Model

We implemented a rule-based baseline for predicate-argument structure prediction. This model mainly uses POS and lexical wording rules for predicate prediction. For example, we have the following rule for predicate prediction: Any JJS POS tag can be tagged as a superlative predicate.

For argument prediction, we mainly implement our knowledge-driven ILP constraints as rules. Furthermore, this baseline uses rules such as the following: in any *than-clause*, the first NP should be tagged as Ground argument. Also, the subject (if any) should be tagged as Figure argument, and the closest adjective to the comparison morpheme is the Scale indicator.

Two-stage Tree-based Annotation Tool

We are releasing our interactive two-stage tree-based annotation tool with this paper. In this tool each annotator can be assigned with a set of tree-based annotation assignments, where pairing annotators to do the same task for inter-annotator analysis is also feasible. This annotation tool sets up the data collection as a two-stage expert annotation process: (1) for each sentence, one expert annotates and submits the annotation, (2) another expert reviews the submission and either returns the submission with feedback or marks it as a gold. Figure 4 shows a screen-shot of this tool.

References

James F. Allen, Mary Swift, and Will de Beaumont. 2008. Deep semantic analysis of text. In *Proceedings of the 2008 Conference on Semantics in Text Processing*, STEP '08, pages 343–354, Stroudsburg, PA, USA. Association for Computational Linguistics.

Omid Bakhshandeh and James Allen. 2015. Semantic framework for comparison structures in natural language. In *Proceedings of the 2015 Conference on Empirical Methods in Natural Language Processing*, pages 993–1002, Lisbon, Portugal, September. Association for Computational Linguistics.

Laura Banarescu, Claire Bonial, Shu Cai, Madalina Georgescu, Kira Griffitt, Ulf Hermjakob, Kevin Knight, Philipp Koehn, Martha Palmer, and Nathan Schneider. 2013. Abstract meaning representation for sembanking. In *Proceedings of the 7th Linguistic Annotation Workshop and Interoperability with Discourse*, pages 178–186, Sofia, Bulgaria, August. Association for Computational Linguistics.

Jonathan Berant and Percy Liang. 2014. Semantic parsing via paraphrasing. In *Association for Computational Linguistics (ACL)*.

Johan Bos and Jennifer Spenader. 2011. An annotated corpus for the analysis of vp ellipsis. *Language Resources and Evaluation*, 45(4):463–494.

Johan Bos. 2008. Wide-coverage semantic analysis with boxer. In Johan Bos and Rodolfo Delmonte, editors, *Semantics in Text Processing. STEP 2008 Conference Proceedings*, Research in Computational Semantics, pages 277–286. College Publications.

Joan Bresnan. 1973. Syntax of the comparative clause construction in English. *Linguistic Inquiry*, 4(3):275–343.

Max Cresswell. 1976. The semantics of degree. *Barbara Hall Partee (ed.)*, pages 261–292.

Dipanjan Das, Desai Chen, AndrÃl' F. T. Martins, Nathan Schneider, and Noah A. Smith. 2014. Frame-semantic parsing. *Computational Linguistics*, 40:1:9–56.

Donald Davidson. 1967. The logical form of action sentences. In Nicholas Rescher, editor, *The Logic of Decision and Action*, pages 81–95. Pittsburgh University Press, Pittsburgh.

Dan Flickinger. 2011. Accuracy vs. robustness in grammar engineering. In Emily M. Bender and Jennifer E. Arnold, editors, *Language from a Cognitive Perspective: Grammar, Usage and Processing*, number 201, pages 31–50. CSLI Publications, Stanford.

Daniel Hardt. 1997. An empirical approach to vp ellipsis. *Comput. Linguist.*, 23(4):525–541, December.

Nitin Jindal and Bing Liu. 2006a. Identifying comparative sentences in text documents. In *Proceedings of the 29th Annual International ACM SIGIR Conference on Research and Development in Information Retrieval*, SIGIR '06, pages 244–251, New York, NY, USA. ACM.

Nitin Jindal and Bing Liu. 2006b. Mining comparative sentences and relations. In *Proceedings of the 21st National Conference on Artificial Intelligence - Volume 2*, AAAI'06, pages 1331–1336. AAAI Press.

Chris Kennedy. 1999. *Projecting the Adjective: The Syntax and Semantics of Gradability and Comparison*. Garland, New York.

Chris Kennedy. 2002. Comparative deletion and optimality in syntax. *Natural Language and Linguistic Theory*, 20(3):553–621.

Christopher Kennedy. 2003. Ellipsis and syntactic representation. In Kerstin Schwabe and Susanne Winkler, editors, *The Interfaces: Deriving and Interpreting Omitted Structures*, number 61 in Linguistics Aktuell, pages 29–54. John Benjamins.

Wiltrud Kessler and Jonas Kuhn. 2014. Detecting comparative sentiment expressions – a case study in annotation design decisions. In *Proceedings of KONVENS*, Hildesheim, Germany.

Christopher D. Manning, Mihai Surdeanu, John Bauer, Jenny Finkel, Steven J. Bethard, and David Mc-Closky. 2014. The Stanford CoreNLP natural language processing toolkit. In *Proceedings of 52nd Annual Meeting of the Association for Computational Linguistics: System Demonstrations*, pages 55–60.

Jason Merchant. 2013. Voice and ellipsis. *Linguistic Inquiry*, 44(1):77–108.

Leif Arda Nielsen. 2004. Verb phrase ellipsis detection using automatically parsed text. In *Proceedings of the 20th International Conference on Computational Linguistics*, COLING '04, Stroudsburg, PA, USA. Association for Computational Linguistics.

Bo Pang and Lillian Lee. 2005. Seeing stars: Exploiting class relationships for sentiment categorization with respect to rating scales. In *Proceedings of ACL*, pages 115–124.

Terence Parsons. 1990. Events in the semantics of English: A study in subatomic semantics. In *Current Studies in Linguistics Series no. 19*, page 334. MIT Press, Cambridge, Massachusetts.

Slav Petrov, Leon Barrett, Romain Thibaux, and Dan Klein. 2006. Learning accurate, compact, and interpretable tree annotation. In *Proceedings of the 21st International Conference on Computational Linguistics and the 44th Annual Meeting of the Association for Computational Linguistics*, ACL-44, pages 433–440, Stroudsburg, PA, USA. Association for Computational Linguistics.

Michael Schiehlen. 2002. Ellipsis resolution with underspecified scope. In *Proceedings of the 40th Annual Meeting on Association for Computational Linguistics*, ACL '02, pages 72–79, Stroudsburg, PA, USA. Association for Computational Linguistics.

Arnim Von Stechow. 1984. Comparing semantic theories of comparison. *Journal of Semantics*, 3(1):1–77.

Alexis Wellwood. 2015. On the semantics of comparison across categories. *Linguistics and Philosophy*, 38(1):67–101.

Kaiquan Xu, Stephen Shaoyi Liao, Jiexun Li, and Yuxia Song. 2011. Mining comparative opinions from customer reviews for competitive intelligence. *Decision Support Systems*, 50(4):743–754.

Masaya Yoshida, Chizuru Nakao, and IvÃąn Ortega-Santos. 2016. *Ellipsis*. Routledge Handbook of Syntax, London, UK.

John M. Zelle and Raymond J. Mooney. 1996. Learning to parse database queries using inductive logic programming. In *Proceedings of the Thirteenth National Conference on Artificial Intelligence - Volume 2*, AAAI'96, pages 1050–1055. AAAI Press.

Event Embeddings for Semantic Script Modeling

Ashutosh Modi
Saarland University,
Germany
`ashutosh@coli.uni-sb.de`

Abstract

Semantic scripts is a conceptual representation which defines how events are organized into higher level activities. Practically all the previous approaches to inducing script knowledge from text relied on count-based techniques (e.g., generative models) and have not attempted to compositionally model events. In this work, we introduce a neural network model which relies on distributed compositional representations of events. The model captures statistical dependencies between events in a scenario, overcomes some of the shortcomings of previous approaches (e.g., by more effectively dealing with data sparsity) and outperforms count-based counterparts on the narrative cloze task.

1 Introduction

It is generally believed that the lack of knowledge on how individual events are organized into higher-level scenarios is one of the major obstacles for natural language understanding. Texts often do not provide a detailed specification of underlying events as writers rely on the ability of humans to read between the lines or, more specifically, on their common sense knowledge of underlying scenarios. For example, going to a restaurant involves entering the restaurant, getting seated, making an order and so on. Consequently, when describing a visit to a restaurant, a writer will not specify all the events, as they are obvious to the reader. This kind of knowledge is typically refereed to as semantic scripts (Schank and Abelson, 1977), and, in this work, will aim to capture some aspects of this knowledge within our probabilistic model.

Early work on scripts focused on manual construction of knowledge bases and rule-based systems for inference using these knowledge bases (Schank and Abelson, 1977). More recent approaches relied on automatically learning script knowledge either from crowd-sourced or naturally-occurring texts (Chambers and Jurafsky, 2008; Regneri et al., 2010; Modi and Titov, 2014; Frermann et al., 2014; Jans et al., 2012; Pichotta and Mooney, 2014; Rudinger et al., 2015a).

Most of these methods represent events as verbal predicates along with tuples of their immediate arguments (i.e. syntactic dependents of the predicate). These approaches model statistical dependencies between events (or, more formally, mentions of events) in a document, often restricting their model to capturing dependencies only between events sharing at least one entity (a common protagonist). We generally follow this tradition in our approach.

Much of this previous work has focused on count-based techniques using, for example, either the generative framework (Frermann et al., 2014) or relying on information-theoretic measures such as pointwise mutual information (PMI) (Chambers and Jurafsky, 2008). Some of these techniques treat predicate-argument structures as an atomic whole (e.g., Pichotta and Mooney (2014)), in other words their probability estimates are based on co-occurrences of entire (predicate, arguments) tuples. Clearly such methods fail to adequately take into account compositional nature of expressions used to refer to events and suffer from data sparsity.

In this work our goal is to overcome the shortcomings of the count-based methods described above by representing events as real-valued vectors (*event embeddings*), with the embeddings computed in a compositional way relying on the predicate and its arguments. These embeddings capture semantic properties of events: events which differ in surface forms of their constituents

Proceedings of the 20th SIGNLL Conference on Computational Natural Language Learning (CoNLL), pages 75–83,
Berlin, Germany, August 7-12, 2016. ©2016 Association for Computational Linguistics

but are semantically similar will get similar embeddings. The event embeddings are used and estimated within our probabilistic model of semantic scripts. We evaluate our model on predicting left-out events (the *narrative cloze task*) where it outperforms existing count-based methods.

2 Background

The general idea in the previous count based methods is to collect events sequences for an entity from the corpus (referred as a script). An *entity* is typically a noun/pronoun describing a person, location or temporal construct mentioned in a document. A document is parsed using a statistical dependency parser. Then, the document is processed with a coreference resolution system, linking all the mentions of an entity in the document. Information from the parser and the coreference system is used to collect all the events corresponding to an entity. Different systems differ on how they represent an event. We later explain in detail these event representation differences. The process described above is repeated for all the documents in the corpus to collect event chains for each of the entities. The collected event sequences are used to build different statistical script models. These script models are typically evaluated using a narrative cloze test as explained in section 3. In the cloze test, an event is removed from an event chain and the task is to predict the missing event.

As described above different script models differ in, how they represent an event. Chambers and Jurafsky (2008), Jans et al. (2012) and Rudinger et al. (2015a) represent an event as verb dependency type (for example subject, object etc) pair. Using dependency parser and coreference system, they collect verbs governing entity mentions, this chain of verbs along with corresponding dependency, forms the event chain. Recently, Pichotta and Mooney (2014) extended the concept of an event to include multiple arguments. In their model, an event is a tuple $v(e_s, e_o, e_p)$, where, entities e_s, e_o and e_p are arguments with subject, object and prepositional relation with the governing verb v. A multi-argument event model encodes a richer representation of events. They have empirically show the advantages of having multiple arguments in an event. In our work, we follow the event definition of Pichotta and Mooney (2014) and include multiple arguments in an event.

One of the disadvantage of the count based models described above is poor event representations. Due to these impoverished representations, these models fail to take into account compositional nature of an event and suffer from sparsity issues. These models treat verb-argument pair as one unit and collect chains of verb-arguments pair observed during training. Verb-arguments combinations never observed during training are assigned zero (or very small, if model is smoothed) probability, even if these are semantically similar to the ones in training. These models fail to account for semantic similarity between individual components (verbs and arguments) of an event. For example, events *cook(John,spaghetti,dinner)* and *prepared(Mary,pasta,dinner)* are semantically very similar but count based models would not take this into account unless both events occur in similar context. Due to sparsity issues, these models can fail. This can be exemplified as follows. Suppose the following text is observed during model training :

John cooked spaghetti for dinner. Later, John ate dinner with his girlfriend. After dinner, John took a dog for a walk. After 30 minutes, John came home. After a while, John slept on the bed.

Event sequence (script) corresponding to the above story is:

cook(john,spaghetti,dinner)→eat(john,dinner,girlfriend)→take(john,dog,walk)→come(john,home)→sleep(john,bed)

Suppose during testing the following event sequence is observed :

prepared(mary,pasta,dinner)→eat(mary,dinner,boyfriend)→take(mary,cat,walk)→ ? →sleep(mary, couch)

The model is required to guess the missing event marked with '?'. A count-based model would fail if it never encountered the same events during training. It would fail to take into account the semantic similarity between words prepared and cook, dog and cat.

A related disadvantage of a count based script models is that they suffer from the curse of dimensionality (Bengio et al., 2001). Since these methods are based on co-occurrence counts of events, the number of instances required to model the joint probability distribution of events grows exponentially. For example, if event vocabulary size is 10 and number of events occurring in a chain are 5, then number of instances required to model the joint distribution of events is $5^{10} - 1$. This is so because the number of instances required are directly proportional to number of free parameters in the model.

To counter the shortcomings of count based script models, we propose a script model based on distributed representations (Bengio et al., 2001; Turian et al., 2010; Collobert et al., 2011). Our model tries to overcome the curse of dimensionality and sparsity by representing events as vector of real values. Both verbs and arguments are represented as a vector of real values (a.k.a *embeddings*). Verb and argument embeddings are composed to get event vector (event embedding). The model automatically learns these embeddings from the data itself and in the process encodes semantic properties in the event representations.

3 Tasks Definition

One of the standard tasks used for evaluating script models is Narrative Cloze (Chambers and Jurafsky, 2008; Jans et al., 2012; Pichotta and Mooney, 2014; Rudinger et al., 2015a). Origins of narrative cloze lie in psychology where it was used to assess child's ability to fill in missing word in a sentence (Taylor, 1953). In our setting the cloze task is described as follows : given a sequence of events with an event removed from the sequence, guess the missing event. For example, given the sequence cook(john,spaghetti,dinner)→eat(john,dinner,girlfriend)→ take(john,dog,walk)→?→sleep(john,bed) , predict the event that should come at position marked by ?

Narrative cloze task evaluates models for exact correctness of the prediction. It penalizes predictions even if they are semantically plausible. It would be more realistic to evaluate script models on a task that gives credit for predicting semantically plausible alternatives as well. We propose adversarial narrative cloze task. In this task, the model is shown two event sequences, one is the correct event sequence and another is same sequence but with one event replaced by a random event. The task is to guess which of the two, is the correct event sequence. For example, given two sequences below, the model should be able to distinguish the correct event sequence from the incorrect one. Interestingly, Manshadi et al. (2008) also propose a similar task for evaluating event based language model and they refer to it as event ordering task. As explained in section 5, we evaluate our model on both the tasks: narrative cloze and adversarial narrative cloze.

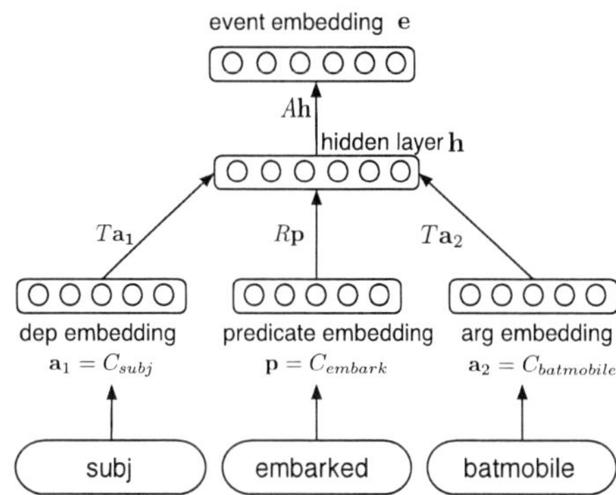

Figure 1: Computation of an event representation for a predicate with dependency and an argument (*subj (batman) embarked batmobile*), an arbitrary number of arguments is supported by our approach.

Correct:

cook(john,spaghetti,dinner)→eat(john,dinner,girlfriend) →take(john,dog,walk)→**come(john,home)**→sleep(john,bed)

Incorrect:

cook(john,spaghetti,dinner)→eat(john,dinner,girlfriend) →take(john,dog,walk)→**play(john,tennis)**→sleep(john,bed)

4 Script Model

We propose a probabilistic model for learning a sequence of events corresponding to a script. The proposed model predicts the event incrementally. It first predicts a verbal predicate, followed by protagonist position (since the protagonist argument is already known) and followed by remaining arguments. We believe this is more natural way of predicting the event as opposed to predicting the complete event, treating it as an atomic unit. The information about the predicate influences the possible arguments that could come next due to selectional preferences of the verb.

As done in previous work, (Chambers and Jurafsky, 2008; Jans et al., 2012; Pichotta and Mooney, 2014; Rudinger et al., 2015a) each event in a sequence of events has a common entity (protagonist) as one of the argument. We represent an event as a tuple $v(d, a^{(1)}, a^{(2)})$ where v is the verbal predicate, d is the position (subj, obj or prep) of the protagonist, $a^{(1)}$ and $a^{(2)}$ are the other dependent arguments of the verb. We marked absent argument as 'NULL'.

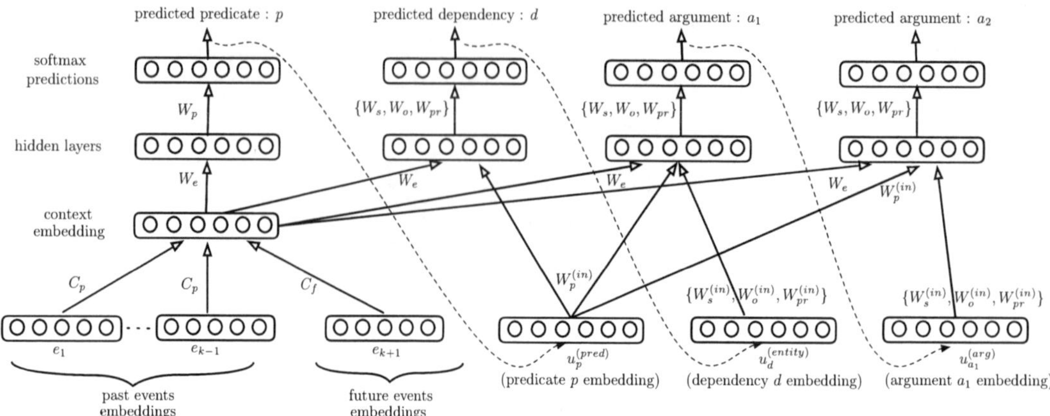

Figure 2: Model for learning event sequence. Here, we are given sequence of events $e_1, e_2, ..., e_{k-1}, e_k, e_{k+1}$. Event e_k is removed from the sequence and it is predicted incrementally.

4.1 Event Representation

For event representation, one could use a sophisticated compositional model based on recursive neural networks (Socher et al., 2012) , we take a simpler approach and choose a feedforward network based compositional model as this is easier to train and more robust to choice of hyperparameters. Our event representations model is inspired from the event ordering model of Modi and Titov (2014). Their model uses distributed word representations for representing verb and argument lemmas constituting the event. Distributed word representations (also known as word embeddings) encode semantic and syntactic properties of a word in a vector of real values (Bengio et al., 2001; Turian et al., 2010; Collobert et al., 2011). Word embeddings have been shown to be beneficial in many NLP applications Turian et al. (2010); Collobert et al. (2011).

The event model is a simple compositional model representing an event. The model is shown in Figure 1. Given an event, $e = (v, d, a_1, a_2)$, (here v is the predicate lemma, d the dependency and a_1, a_2 are corresponding argument lemmas), each lemma (and dependency) is mapped to a vector using a lookup matrix C. For example, a particular row number of C, corresponding to index of a predicate in the vocabulary, gives the embedding for the predicate. These constituent embeddings are projected into same space by multiplying with respective projection matrices R (for predicates) and T (for arguments). Hidden layer h is obtained by applying a nonlinear activation function ($tanh$ in our case). Final event representation

e is obtained by projecting the hidden layer using a matrix A. Formally, event representation is given by $e = A*tanh(T*C_{a_1,:} + R*C_{v,:} + T*C_{a_2,:}) + b$. All the projection matrices (R, T, A) and lookup matrix C are learned during training. We also experimented with different matrices T for subject and object positions, in order to take into account the positional information. Empirically, this had negligible effect on the final results.

4.2 Event Sequence Model

A good script model should capture the meaning as well as the statistical dependencies between events in an event sequence. More importantly, the model should be able to learn these representations from unlabeled script sequences available in abundance.

We propose a neural network based probabilistic model for event sequences, for learning event sequence as well as the event representations. The model is shown in Figure 2. The model is trained by predicting a missing event in an event sequence. During training, a window (size = 5 = 3*2 + 1) is moved over all events in each event sequence corresponding to each entity. The event in window's center is the event to be predicted and events on the left and right of the window are the context events. As explained earlier, the missing event is predicted incrementally, beginning with a predicate, followed by the protagonist position, followed by other participants in the event.

In order to get an intuition how our model predicts an event, consider the following event sequence in a script, with a missing event : $(e_1 \rightarrow e_2 \cdots \rightarrow e_{k-1} \rightarrow ? \rightarrow e_{k+1} \rightarrow \ldots e_n)$. We would like to predict the missing event, say e_k. The event model is used to obtain event representations for each event in the context. These event representations are then composed into context representation by summing the representation for each of the event in the context. We sum the representations, as this formulation works well in practice. The desired event e_k is predicted incrementally, beginning with the predicate p for e_k. The context embedding is used to predict the verbal predicate via a hidden layer followed by a multiclass logistic regression (softmax) classification. Next, the protagonist position d (subject, object etc) is predicted. For predicting d, the context embedding and the predicate embedding (corresponding to the predicate predicted in previous step) are linearly combined to be given as input to a hidden layer. This is followed by regular softmax prediction. Similarly, arguments are predicted. For each of the argument, predicate embedding and the previous prediction (position or argument) are linearly combined with the context embedding. If at each prediction stage we used gold predicate/position/argument embedding for linearly combining with context embedding, our model would not be robust to wrong predictions during testing. Using the embeddings corresponding to predicted unit would make the model robust against noise and would help the model to partially recover from wrong predictions during testing.

We train the model by minimizing the negative likelihood function for the event prediction. Formally, we minimize the objective function $-J(\Theta)$ as shown in equation 1 and 2. As shown in equation 3, we factorize the event distribution into constituents, making appropriate independence assumptions as explained earlier. Each of the factor is a multiclass logistic regression (softmax) function. Equation 4 illustrates the probability distribution for the predicate given the context. Here, u_{v_i} is the word embedding for the predicate v_i, E is the context embedding and b_{v_i} is the bias. Probability distributions for arguments has similar form and are not shown here due to space constraints.

$\Theta = \{C, T, R, A, C_p, C_f, W_e, W_p, W_s, W_o,$
$W_{pr}, W_p^{(in)}, W_s^{(in)}, W_o^{(in)}, W_{pr}^{(in)}, B\}$ is the parameter vector to be learned. Parameters are learned using mini-batch (size=1000) stochastic gradient descent with adagrad (Duchi et al., 2011) learning schedule. During training, the error in-

curred during predictions at each stage are back-propagated to update the parameters for the model including the embeddings for predicates and arguments (matrix C).

We regularize the parameters of the model using L2 regularization (regularization parameter = 0.01). All the hidden layers have a dropout factor of 0.5. We trained a word2vec model on train set documents to learn word embeddings. Predicate and arguments vectors are initialized using the learned word embeddings. Predicate and argument embeddings have dimensionality of 50 and hidden layers have dimensionality of 50. All the hyper-parameters were tuned using a dev set.

$$\Theta^* = argmin_\Theta - J(\Theta) \tag{1}$$

$$J(\Theta) = \prod_{i=1}^{N} \underbrace{p(e_i \mid e_1, ..., e_{i-1}, e_{i+1}, e_k, \Theta)}_{prob.\ of\ an\ event\ given\ context} \tag{2}$$

$$= \prod_{i=1}^{N} p(e_i \mid \underbrace{\mathbf{e}}_{\substack{context \\ events}}, \Theta)$$

$$p(e_i \mid \mathbf{e}, \Theta) = p(v_i, d_i, a_i^{(1)}, a_i^{(2)} \mid \mathbf{e}, \Theta)$$
$$= \underbrace{p(v_i \mid \mathbf{e}, \Theta)}_{verb\ prob.} * \underbrace{p(d_i \mid v_i, \mathbf{e}, \Theta)}_{dependency\ prob.} *$$
$$\underbrace{p(a_i^{(1)} \mid v_i, d_i, \mathbf{e}, \Theta)}_{first\ arg\ prob.} *$$
$$\underbrace{p(a_i^{(2)} \mid v_i, a_i^{(1)}, \mathbf{e}, \Theta)}_{second\ arg\ prob.} \tag{3}$$

$$p(v_i \mid \mathbf{e}, \Theta) = \frac{exp(u_{v_i}^T (W_p \tanh(W_e E)) + b_{v_i})}{\sum_k exp(u_k^T (W_p \tanh(W_e E)) + b_k)} \tag{4}$$

5 Experiments and Analysis

5.1 Data

There is no standard dataset for evaluating script models. We experimented with movies summary corpus[1] (Bamman et al., 2014). The corpus is created by extracting 42,306 movie summaries from November, 2012 dump of Wikipedia[2]. Each document in the corpus concisely describes a movie plot along with descriptions of various characters involved in the plot. Average length of a document in the corpus is 176 words. But more popular movies have much more elaborate descriptions going up to length of 1,000 words. The corpus has been processed by the Stanford Corenlp pipeline (Manning et al., 2014). The texts in the corpus were tokenized and annotated with POS

---

[1] http://www.cs.cmu.edu/~ark/personas/
[2] http://dumps.wikimedia.org/enwiki/

Data Set	No. of Scripts	No. of Unique Events
Train Set	104,041	856,823
Dev Set	15,169	119,302
Test Set	29,943	231,539

Table 1: Data statistics

tags, dependencies, NER and coreference (coref) information. Since, each of the document in the corpus is about a movie, the scripts in this corpus involve interesting interactions between different entities (actors/objects). In order to study and explore the above mentioned rich script structure, we selected this corpus for our experiments. Nevertheless, our model is domain agnostic, the experiments performed on this corpus are generalizable to any other corpus as well.

As mentioned in section 2, we extract scripts corresponding to each of the entities using the dependency annotations and coref information. The corpus documents are divided randomly into three parts: train (~70%), development (~10%) and test (~20%). Data statistics about the data set are given in Table 1. As a preprocessing step, low frequency (<100) predicates and arguments are mapped to a special UNK (unknown) symbol. Similarly, arguments consisting of only digits are mapped to a NUMB (number) symbol. There are 703 unique predicate lemmas and $46,644$ unique argument lemmas in the train set. Average length of a script is 10 events. During testing, predicate and arguments not observed during training are mapped to the same UNK symbol.

5.2 Baselines Systems

We compare our model against two baseline models: **Unigram** model and **MultiProtagonist** model.

A unigram model is a simple but competitive script model. This model predicts an event by sampling from unigram event frequency distribution of the train set. The events are predicted independent of the context.

MultiProtagonist (M-Pr) is the model proposed by Pichotta and Mooney (2014) and described as *joint* model in Pichotta and Mooney (2014). The model calculates conditional probability of an event given another context event ($P(e_2 \mid e_1)$) by counting the co-occurrence counts of the events in the corpus. The model predicts the missing event

given the context events by maximizing the sum of log conditional probabilities of an event w.r.t each of the context events i.e.

$$e^* = \text{argmax}_e \sum_{i=1}^{k-1} log\, P(e \mid e_i) + \sum_{i=k+1}^{K} log\, P(e_i \mid e)$$

For evaluation and comparison purposes, we reimplemented both baselines on our dataset. In the experiments described next, we refer our model as NNSM (Neural Network based Script Model).

5.3 Evaluation Metrics

We evaluated models for narrative cloze task with three metrics **Recall@50** and **Accuracy** and **Event Perplexity**. Recall@50 is the standard metric used for evaluating script models (Jans et al., 2012; Pichotta and Mooney, 2014). The idea here is to evaluate top 50 predictions of a script model on a test script with a missing event. The metric is calculated as fraction of the predictions containing the gold held-out event. Its value lies in the range 0 (worst) and 1(best). Accuracy is a new metric introduced by Pichotta and Mooney (2014). This metric evaluates the event prediction, taking into account prediction of each constituent. Specifically, it is defined as average of the accuracy of the predicate, the dependency, the first argument and the second argument predictions. This is a more robust metric as it does not treat an event as an atomic unit. This is in contrast to Recall@50 which penalizes semantically correct guesses and awards only events which have exactly the same surface form.

The baseline models and our model are probabilistic by nature. Taking inspiration from language modeling community, we propose a new metric Event Perplexity. We define event perplexity as $2^{-\frac{1}{N}\sum_i log_2 p(e_i|e_{(\text{context},i)})}$. The perplexity measure, like the accuracy takes into account the constituents of an event and is a good indicator of the model predictions.

5.4 Narrative Cloze Evaluation

Narrative Cloze task was tested on 29,943 test set scripts. The results are shown in Table 2 and 3. We evaluated with two versions of the cloze task. In the first version, events are the predicate argument tuple as defined before. Second version, evaluates on predicates only i.e. an event is not a tuple but only a predicate. Our model, NNSM outperforms both the unigram and M-Pr models on both the versions of the task with all the metrics. This further strengthens our hypothesis of

Model	R@50	Accuracy	Event Perplexity
Unigram	0.32	34.26%	298.45
M-Pr	0.31	35.67%	276.54
NNSM$_{full}$	0.37	44.36%	256.41

Table 2: Model evaluation on test set for narrative cloze task against the baselines

Model	R@50	Accuracy	Event Perplexity
Unigram$_{pred}$	0.27	23.79%	264.16
M-Pr$_{pred}$	0.27	24.04%	260.34
NNSM$_{pred}$	0.49	33.40%	247.64

Table 3: Model evaluation on predicate only event test set for narrative cloze task against the baselines

Model	Accuracy
Unigram	50.07%
M-Pr	53.04%
NNSM$_{full}$	55.32%

Table 4: Model evaluation on test set for adversarial narrative cloze task against the baselines

Model	Accuracy
Unigram$_{pred}$	49.97%
M-Pr$_{pred}$	55.09%
NNSM$_{pred}$	57.94%

Table 5: Model evaluation on predicate only test set for adversarial narrative cloze task against the baselines

having distributed representation for events rather than atomic representations. Unigram, although a simple model, is competitive with the M-Pr model.

We performed an interesting experiment. We evaluated another simplistic baseline model, most frequent event. This baseline model predicts by sampling from top-5 most frequent predicate/argument in the full event narrative cloze task. Surprisingly, the accuracy reported by this simple baseline is 45.04% which is slightly more than our best performing NNSM model and much more than the M-Pr baseline. This simple looking baseline is hard to beat by both count-based methods and NNSM. None of the previous methods have been evaluated against this baseline. We propose using this baseline for evaluation of script models. We think this outperformance is due to skewed distribution of the predicate and arguments in the corpus. As we found empirically, these distributions have a very long tail and this makes it hard for the models to beat the most frequent baseline.

5.5 Adversarial Narrative Cloze Evaluation

Similar to narrative cloze, adversarial narrative cloze task was evaluated on 29,943 test set scripts. In each of the event sequence an event was replaced by a random event. The results for the adversarial narrative cloze task are shown in Table 4 and 5. As evident from the results Unigram model is as good as random. In this task as well, our model outperforms the count based M-Pr model by 2.3% and 2.9% for full and pred model respec-

tively.

6 Related Work

Work on scripts dates back to 70's beginning with introduction of Frames by Minsky (1974), schemas by Rumelhart (1975) and scripts by Schank and Abelson (1977). These early formulations were not statistical in nature and used hand-crafted complex rules for modeling relations between events. These formulations were limited to few scenarios and did not generalize well.

Miikkulainen (1990) proposed DISCERN system for learning script knowledge. Their neural network based model read event sequences and stored them in episodic memory. The model was capable of generating expanded paraphrases of narratives and was able to answer simple questions. Similarly, Lee et al. (1992) proposed DYNASTY (DYNAmic STory understanding sYstem). This system was also based on distributed representations. It predicted missing events in event sequences and performed script based information retrieval. Their system was limited to only few scenarios and did not generalize well.

As mentioned previously, in past few years a number of count based systems for script learning have been proposed for learning script knowledge in unsupervised fashion. (Chambers and Jurafsky, 2008; Jans et al., 2012; Pichotta and Mooney, 2014; Rudinger et al., 2015a). Recently, Regneri et al. (2010), Modi et al. (2016) and Wanzare et al. (2016) used crowd-sourcing methods for acquiring script knowledge. They in the process created script databases which are used to develop automatic script learning systems. McIntyre and Lapata (2009) developed a system for generating stories, they learned an object based script model on fairy tales.

Orr et al. (2014) proposed hidden markov model (HMM) approach to learn scripts. The model clusters event descriptions into different event types and then learns an HMM over the sequence of event types. Again this model treats an event as an atomic unit and the inference algorithm may not generalize well, as the number of event types increases. Similarly, Frermann et al. (2014) proposed non-parametric Bayesian model for learning script ordering. The inference procedure may not scale well, as number of event chains increases.

Manshadi et al. (2008) proposed language model based approach to learning event sequences, in their approach as well, events are treated as atomic units (a predicate-argument tuple). Recently, Rudinger et al. (2015b) have proposed a neural network approach to learn scripts by learning a bilinear distributed representation based language model over events. Their model is non-compositional in nature and they also consider events as an atomic unit and directly learn distributed representation for events. Granroth-Wilding and Clark (2015) also propose a compositional neural network based model for events. Our model is more general than their model. They learn event representations by modeling pair wise event scores for calculating compatibility between two events. This score is then used to predict the missing event by selecting an event that maximizes the average score between the event and the context events.

7 Conclusion and Future Work

In this paper we proposed a probabilistic compositional model for scripts. As shown in experiments, our model outperforms the existing co-occurrence count based methods. This further reinforces our hypothesis of having more richer compositional representations for events. Current tasks to evaluate script models are crude, in the sense that they penalize semantically plausible events. In the future, we propose to create a standard data set of event sequence pairs (correct sequence vs incorrect sequence). The replaced event in the incorrect sequence should not be a random event but rather a semantically close but incorrect event. Models evaluated on this data set would give a better in-

dication of script learning capability of the model. Another area which needs further investigation is related to developing models which can learn long tail event distributions. Current models do not capture this well and hence do not perform better than most frequent event baseline on accuracy task.

In this paper, we proposed a very simple compositional feed forward neural network model. In the future we plan to explore more sophisticated recurrent neural network (RNN) based models. Recently, RNN based models have shown success in variety of applications (Graves, 2012).

Acknowledgments

We would like to thank anonymous reviewers for their helpful comments. This research was funded by the German Research Foundation (DFG) as part of SFB 1102 'Information Density and Linguistic Encoding'.

References

David Bamman, Brendan O'Connor, and Noah A Smith. 2014. Learning latent personas of film characters. In *Proceedings of the Annual Meeting of the Association for Computational Linguistics (ACL)*. page 352.

Yoshua Bengio, Réjean Ducharme, and Pascal Vincent. 2001. A neural probabilistic language model. In *Proceedings of NIPS*.

Nathanael Chambers and Daniel Jurafsky. 2008. Unsupervised learning of narrative event chains. In *Proceedings of ACL*.

R. Collobert, J. Weston, L. Bottou, M. Karlen, K. Kavukcuoglu, and P. Kuksa. 2011. Natural language processing (almost) from scratch. *Journal of Machine Learning Research* 12:2493–2537.

John Duchi, Elad Hazan, and Yoram Singer. 2011. Adaptive subgradient methods for online learning and stochastic optimization. *The Journal of Machine Learning Research* 12:2121–2159.

Lea Frermann, Ivan Titov, and Manfred Pinkal. 2014. A hierarchical bayesian model for unsupervised induction of script knowledge. In *EACL, Gothenberg, Sweden*.

Mark Granroth-Wilding and Stephen Clark. 2015. What happens next? event prediction using a compositional neural network model. In *Proceedings of AAAI*.

Alex Graves. 2012. *Supervised sequence labelling*. Springer.

Bram Jans, Steven Bethard, Ivan Vulić, and Marie Francine Moens. 2012. Skip n-grams and ranking functions for predicting script events. In *Proceedings of the 13th Conference of the European Chapter of the Association for Computational Linguistics*. Association for Computational Linguistics, Stroudsburg, PA, USA, EACL '12, pages 336–344.

Geunbae Lee, Margot Flowers, and Michael G Dyer. 1992. Learning distributed representations of conceptual knowledge and their application to script-based story processing. In *Connectionist Natural Language Processing*, Springer, pages 215–247.

Christopher D Manning, Mihai Surdeanu, John Bauer, Jenny Rose Finkel, Steven Bethard, and David McClosky. 2014. The stanford corenlp natural language processing toolkit. In *ACL (System Demonstrations)*. pages 55–60.

Mehdi Manshadi, Reid Swanson, and Andrew S Gordon. 2008. Learning a probabilistic model of event sequences from internet weblog stories. In *FLAIRS Conference*. pages 159–164.

Neil McIntyre and Mirella Lapata. 2009. Learning to tell tales: A data-driven approach to story generation. In *Proceedings of the Joint Conference of the 47th Annual Meeting of the ACL and the 4th International Joint Conference on Natural Language Processing of the AFNLP: Volume 1-Volume 1*. Association for Computational Linguistics, pages 217–225.

Risto Miikkulainen. 1990. *DISCERN: A Distributed Artificial Neural Network Model Of Script Processing And Memory*. Ph.D. thesis, University of California.

Risto Miikkulainen. 1995. Script-based inference and memory retrieval in subsymbolic story processing. *Applied Intelligence* 5(2):137–163.

Marvin Minsky. 1974. A framework for representing knowledge .

Ashutosh Modi, Tatjana Anikina, and Manfred Pinkal. 2016. Inscript: Narrative texts annotated with script information. In *Proceedings of the 10th International Conference on Language Resources and Evaluation (LREC 16), Portorož, Slovenia.*.

Ashutosh Modi and Ivan Titov. 2014. Inducing neural models of script knowledge. In *CoNLL*. volume 14, pages 49–57.

John Walker Orr, Prasad Tadepalli, Janardhan Rao Doppa, Xiaoli Fern, and Thomas G Dietterich. 2014. Learning scripts as hidden markov models. In *AAAI*. pages 1565–1571.

Karl Pichotta and Raymond J Mooney. 2014. Statistical script learning with multi-argument events. In *EACL*. volume 14, pages 220–229.

Michaela Regneri, Alexander Koller, and Manfred Pinkal. 2010. Learning script knowledge with web experiments. In *Proceedings of ACL*.

Rachel Rudinger, Vera Demberg, Ashutosh Modi, Benjamin Van Durme, and Manfred Pinkal. 2015a. Learning to predict script events from domain-specific text. *Lexical and Computational Semantics (* SEM 2015)* page 205.

Rachel Rudinger, Pushpendre Rastogi, Francis Ferraro, and Benjamin Van Durme. 2015b. Script induction as language modeling. In *Proceedings of the 2015 Conference on Empirical Methods in Natural Language Processing (EMNLP-15)*.

David E Rumelhart. 1975. Notes on a schema for stories. *Representation and understanding: Studies in cognitive science* 211(236):45.

R. C Schank and R. P Abelson. 1977. *Scripts, Plans, Goals, and Understanding*. Lawrence Erlbaum Associates, Potomac, Maryland.

Richard Socher, Brody Huval, Christopher D. Manning, and Andrew Y. Ng. 2012. Semantic compositionality through recursive matrix-vector spaces. In *Proceedings of EMNLP*.

Wilson L Taylor. 1953. Cloze procedure: a new tool for measuring readability. *Journalism and Mass Communication Quarterly* 30(4):415.

Joseph Turian, Lev Ratinov, and Yoshua Bengio. 2010. Word representations: A simple and general method for semi-supervised learning. In *Proceedings of ACL*.

Lilian Wanzare, Alessandra Zarcone, Stefan Thater, and Manfred Pinkal. 2016. Descript: A crowdsourced database for the acquisition of high-quality script knowledge. In *Proceedings of the 10th International Conference on Language Resources and Evaluation (LREC 16), Portorož, Slovenia.*.

Beyond Centrality and Structural Features: Learning Information Importance for Text Summarization

Markus Zopf, Eneldo Loza Mencía, and Johannes Fürnkranz
Research Training Group AIPHES / Knowledge Engineering Group
Department of Computer Science, Technische Universität Darmstadt
Hochschulstraße 10, 64289 Darmstadt, Germany
{zopf@aiphes, eneldo@ke, juffi@ke}.tu-darmstadt.de

Abstract

Most automatic text summarization systems proposed to date rely on centrality and structural features as indicators for information importance. In this paper, we argue that these features cannot reliably detect important information in heterogeneous document collections. Instead, we propose *CPSum*, a summarizer that learns the importance of information objects from a background source. Our hypothesis is tested on a multi-document corpus where we remove centrality and structural features. *CPSum* proves to be able to perform well in this challenging scenario whereas reference systems fail.

1 Introduction

The goal of text summarization is to *take an information source, extract content from it, and present the most important content to the user [...]* (Mani, 2001). Identifying important information in source documents is therefore a major goal in summarization. Most methods to date rely on structural features such as sentence position, number of upper-case words, or title words, and a wide range of measures of sentence centrality as signals for what is important in source documents.

In particular in news articles, such as those used for the DUC2002 single-document summarization and the DUC2004 multi-document summarization tasks,[1] it is quite common that the most important information is repeated most frequently. Indeed, Nenkova et al. (2006) showed that information which appears frequently in the input documents is likely to appear in a human-generated summary. Similar conclusions can be drawn for single-document news corpora, where, for example, important information is likely to be found at the beginning of the document (for impatient readers), and repeated and expanded later in the article.

Even though most research in text summarization to date focused on newswire documents, this special kind of text genre is not the only one to be considered for summarization. Recently, about 400 journalists organized by the International Consortium of Investigative Journalists (ICIJ) [2] spent more than a year to analyze 11.5 million documents in the Panama Papers repository,[3] which consists of emails, PDFs, and other text documents not belonging to the newswire genre. In such a heterogeneous collection of raw and unprocessed source documents we cannot assume that frequency information correlates with importance, and therefore cannot rely on (in)frequency as (un)importance signal.

Nevertheless, journalists are able to cope with such situations because they bring along their background knowledge about the world, which allows them to estimate what information is important and what is not. We therefore propose to incorporate world knowledge to handle more challenging summarization scenarios where centrality cannot be used as a signal for importance. Our assumption is that summarization systems which are aware of the importance of information without analyzing the structure of the source documents are able to summarize heterogeneous documents properly. The key question of the paper is whether a knowledge-based summarization system is still able to detect important information even when structural and centrality-based features cannot be used as signals for importance.

We first review well-known summarization sys-

---

[1] http://duc.nist.gov/

[2] https://www.icij.org/
[3] https://panamapapers.icij.org/

Proceedings of the 20th SIGNLL Conference on Computational Natural Language Learning (CoNLL), pages 84–94,
Berlin, Germany, August 7-12, 2016. ©2016 Association for Computational Linguistics

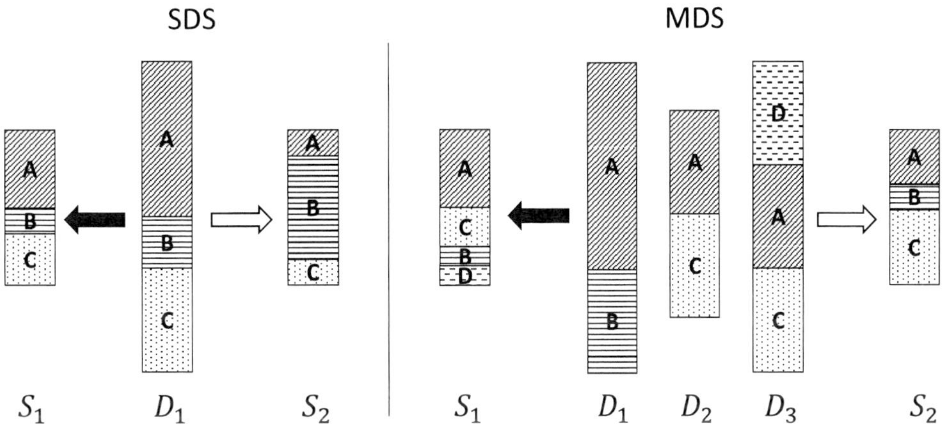

Figure 1: Differences between centrality-based summarization (black arrow) and importance-aware summarization (white arrow) in single- (left) and multi-document summarization (right).

tems for single- and multi-document summarization in Section 2. Particular emphasis is put on the methodologies used to identify important information and avoid redundancy since this is the main innovation of our knowledge-based system described in Section 3.

CPSum learns about importance by analyzing an independent background corpus of document-summary pairs and applies this knowledge in the summarization task. A major difference to previous systems is that we do not use similarity measures to compute centrality, neither for detecting importance nor for avoiding redundancy.

In order to verify our assumptions, we compare our approach on a commonly used evaluation corpus, both in its original version and in various version in which we remove redundancy and sentence order. We describe the corpus modification in Section 4. Expectedly, our experiments described in Section 5 and 6 show a substantial performance decrease for all tested reference systems, whereas the performance of *CPSum* remains essentially unchanged. The conclusions we draw from this study are summarized in Section 7.

2 Related Work

In this section, we review prior work in single- and multi-document summarization. The essential differences between these approaches and our approach are illustrated in Figure 1. On the left, a centrality-based SDS system summarizes a document D to a summary S_1. The result is a text with a similar topic distribution as in the source document. A system with a differ-

ent notion of importance is able to produce a summary S_2 with a varied distribution of topics. On the right, we observe a similar situation, where a centrality-based MDS system summarizes a document collection $D_1, \ldots, D_3$ to a summary S_1 and a importance-aware summarization system produces the summary S_2 with a different topic distribution. Centrality-bases methods produce a smaller version of the source document(s) whereas an importance-aware summarization system is able to emphasis on important parts even if they are not frequent.

2.1 Single-Document Summarization

Early work in single-document summarization (SDS) by Luhn (1958) and Edmundson (1969) tries to identify salient information in documents. Luhn (1958) identifies words which are frequent in the source documents and infrequent in a background corpus. Edmundson (1969) extends this approach by using cue words and structural features such as title words and sentence position.

Several more recent methods are inspired by algorithms such as HITS (Kleinberg, 1999) and PageRank (Brin and Page, 1998) and model the source documents as graphs. TextRank (Mihalcea and Tarau, 2004) models sentences as nodes in a graph, where the strength of the connections between the nodes is determined by the similarity of the sentences measured by means of syntactic word overlap. Since Mihalcea and Tarau (2004) assume the absence of redundancy in single-document summarization there is no need for a re-ranking after selecting sentences. They also rely on sentence order by always including the first sentences in the summary.

Parveen and Strube (2015) use a bipartite graph to represent a document. This so-called topic graph has two sets of nodes, one containing sentences and one containing topics. To rank the sentences, they apply HITS . Since they deal with very long texts which may contain repetitive information they also apply a redundancy avoidance strategy by maximizing topic coverage in the summary and therefore minimizing redundancy.

All these approaches have in common that they focus on selecting the most central information from a document. However, in a noisy document with a significant amount of unimportant text, extracting the most central text may not be a good strategy. Summaries produced by these approaches will rather contain noise than important information, since the noise might be quite central (c.f. Figure 1). Most of the approaches assume that there is no redundancy in the source document and do not apply a redundancy avoidance strategy.

2.2 Multi-Document Summarization

In comparison to SDS the task in extractive multi-document summarization (MDS) is to summarize not one but a set of documents. The additional challenge in comparison to extractive SDS is that the document set may contain the same information redundantly in different documents. Therefore, in addition to detect important information, a second challenge is to avoid redundancy in the generated summary.

McKeown and Radev (1995) introduce the task of summarizing multiple news documents. Their system, called SUMMONS (SUMMarizing Online NewS articles), extends already existing template-driven message understanding systems.

Carbonell and Goldstein (1998) introduce Maximal Marginal Relevance (MMR) to reward centrality and penalize redundancy jointly with a linear combination of both attributes. In a query-based setup, sentences are greedily selected according to their similarity to the query and similarity according to already selected sentences. The similarity measure is based on the Cosine similarity between sentences.

Radev et al. (2000) use a clustering method to find a centroid. Clusters are built based on a topic detection system. For redundancy avoidance, they apply a redundancy penalty similar to the nega-

tive factor proposed by Carbonell and Goldstein (1998) and re-rank the sentences iteratively until re-ranking does not change the resulting summary.

LexRank (Erkan and Radev, 2004) is a graph-based MDS method inspired by social networks which uses intra-sentences cosine similarity to compute an adjacency matrix to represent the sentences as a graph similar to the graph-based methods in SDS. The most central sentence is considered to be the most important sentence. LexRank itself does not apply redundancy avoidance but only ranks sentences according to importance. As redundancy avoidance strategy, cross-sentence informational subsumption (CSIS) (Radev, 2000) is applied as a re-ranking strategy.

The best performing system at the DUC 2004 shared task in MDS, CLASSY (Conroy et al., 2004), uses TF-IDF scores to calculate the importance of sentences. ICSI Summ (Gillick et al., 2009), a well-performing system at TAC 2009, applies a global linear optimization to search for a set of sentences that covers relevant concepts in the source documents as well as possible. As concepts they use word bi-grams weighted by their frequency, thereby deriving importance from frequency. Since they search for a set of sentences which maximizes the sum of unique concept values, their system is able to avoid redundancy implicitly.

Lin and Bilmes (2011) treat MDS as a submodular maximization problem. By rewarding diversity rather than penalizing redundancy they created a monotone nondecreasing submodular utility function (in comparison to Carbonell and Goldstein (1998)) which has a constant factor guarantee of optimality. In contract to ICSI Summ, Yogatama et al. (2015) seek to not maximize bi-gram coverage but to maximize the semantic volume. They use embeddings to represent sentences and choose the subset of sentences that maximizes the size of the convex hull in the generated embedding space as summary.

We summarize that systems for MDS use (similar to systems for SDS) various centrality measures to detect important information. Furthermore, they apply redundancy avoidance strategies based on sentence similarity. *CPSum*, on the other hand, does not apply any similarity measure but learns from contextual preferences if something is important in the context of other information/sentences.

3 The *CPSum* Algorithm

In this section, we first define the summarization task formally. We then present the novel preference-based summarization system *CPSum* in detail. In particular, we explain our training procedure and (contextual) sentence ranking methodology.

3.1 Problem Definition

The task of a generic extractive summarization system is to create sequences of sentences (the summaries) from given sequences of sentences (the source documents) for different topics. The objective is that the selected sentences form a good summary of the source documents.

To formalize the task, we define a *sentence* $\mathbf{s}$ of length n as a sequence of n words $(s_1, \ldots, s_n)$. For convenience we use the term *word* for all elements of a sentence identified by a sentence segmentation method. Therefore, numbers, punctuation marks, and similar elements are all considered to be words. A *document* D of length m is a sequence of m sentences $(\mathbf{s}_1, \ldots, \mathbf{s}_m)$, and consequently also a sequence of words. $|X|$ denotes the length of the sequence X.

A *topic* is a pair $(\mathcal{D} = \{D_1, \ldots, D_o\}, \mathcal{R} = \{R_1, \ldots, R_p\})$ of input documents $\mathcal{D}$ and reference summaries $\mathcal{R}$. $|\mathcal{D}| = 1$ in single-document summarization and $|\mathcal{D}| > 1$ in multi-document summarization where $|\mathcal{D}|$ denotes the size of $\mathcal{D}$. Since we do not distinguish between different source documents we introduce $\dot{D} = D_1 \circ \cdots \circ D_o$ as the concatenation of all sentences of all source documents in $\mathcal{D}$.

The task of extractive document summarization is to find a sequence of sentences $\hat{S} \in \mathfrak{P}_{l_{max}}(\dot{D})$ that maximizes a utility function u where $\mathfrak{P}_{l_{max}}(\dot{D})$ denotes the set of all sequences of elements in $\dot{D}$ with $\sum_{\mathbf{s} \in \dot{D}} |\mathbf{s}| \leq l_{max}$. Formally, the task is to search for S_{max} with

$$S_{max} = \operatorname*{arg\,max}_{S \in \mathfrak{P}_{l_{max}}(\dot{D})} u(S). \qquad (1)$$

A proper utility function u is supposed to measure the quality of the summary. Approaches are usually evaluated by a comparison with given reference summaries. We refer to Section 5 where we introduce ROUGE as the utility function which is used to grade the produced summaries. The difficulty when developing summarization systems is

to find an approximation of u without having access to the reference summaries.

3.2 Object Importance

The key idea of our approach is to learn the importance of objects from external sources. This assessment of importance should then be used in order to select the most relevant sentences independently of features derived directly from the source documents, such as structural information or redundancy and centrality. Hence, we believe that our system is more suitable for handling heterogeneous summarization scenarios where such features may not helpful for detecting important information.

As a proof-of-concept, we study a simple approach which learns the importance of objects from a large background corpus of document-summary pairs. Note that this corpus does not have to consist of document-summary pairs. The system could also learn from very diverse sources such as stock market prices to judge the importance of a company, the length of Wikipedia articles for learning about the importance of people, or the number of inhabitants as a signal of importance for cities. In a way this corresponds to the way humans use fast and frugal heuristics for problem solving (Gigerenzer and Todd, 1999).

We model object importance in the form of pairwise preferences (Fürnkranz and Hüllermeier, 2011). A preference $a \succ b$ models the situation that object a is preferred to object b. In this paper, we take a simple approach and model object importance in the form of pairwise preferences between bi-grams of stemmed words that occur in the documents. Preferences may be probabilistic, i.e., the probability that $a \succ b$ rather than $b \succ a$ is $\Pr(a \succ b) \in [0, 1]$, and it holds that $\Pr(a \succ b) + \Pr(b \succ a) = 1$. Due to the large number of observed preferences, each preference only provides a weak signal about the importance of an object, and object importance will be determined by aggregating probabilistic preferences (cf. Section 3.4).

Furthermore, we model the situation that an object a is preferred to object b in a *context* C with *contextual preferences* $a \succ b \mid C$. The intuition is that the preference relation between two objects may depend on a context. In summarization, this context models the information need of a reader, which depends e.g. on personal interests and already observed information. Since object preferences are context-aware they can be used to adapt to difference users and summarization situations. We use the context to model already observed information of a user. Since we select summary sentences iteratively, we model with the context knowledge which is already contained in a partial summary. Since we measure importance in a context and model the context with the partial summary we do not need an additional redundancy avoidance mechanism like most other approaches for multi-document summarization.

The fact, that object importance is learned from an external corpus, also increases the adaptiveness of our system. Since all people may have a different notion of importance, the system can be trained easily on different sources which reflect these different notions. For example, a summary generated for an engineer may look differently than a summary created for a business administration employee. Systems which do not have an adaptive notion of importance are not able to create different summaries for different information needs.

3.3 Learning of Object Importance

To learn the importance of an object we use a background corpus denoted by $\mathbb{B} = \bigcup(D_i, R_i)$ which provides a set of document-summary pairs. For the i-th topic in the corpus we observe the document D_i as well as the summary R_i. We use the same notation for the occurrence of objects in sentences and documents as for words, hence $a \in \mathbf{s}$ or $a \in D_i$ denotes that object a can be observed in $\mathbf{s}$ or D_i, respectively.

For each object pair a, b, for which it holds that a occurs in the summary as well as in the source document, and b occurs in the source document but not in the summary, we observe a preference $a \succ b$, since a was selected to be included in the summary whereas b was not. To formalize this, we first define two sets P_i and N_i for topic i. P_i contains all elements which were selected from the source document to be included in the summary and N_i contains all elements which are not included in the summary. To define the sets P_i and N_i we introduce first the notation $\sigma(D_i)$ and $\sigma(R_i)$ to reduce the sequences D_i and R_i to sets which contain each element at most once. We then define $P_i = \sigma(D_i) \cap \sigma(R_i)$ and $N_i = \sigma(D_i) \setminus P_i$. With P_i and N_i we define the number of observations for $a \succ b$ in the background corpus $\mathbb{B}$ as

$$n_{\mathbb{B}}(a \succ b) = \sum_{(D_i, R_i) \in \mathbb{B}} \mathbb{1}_{P_i}(a) \cdot \mathbb{1}_{N_i}(b) \qquad (2)$$

where $\mathbb{1}_X(x)$ is 1 if $x \in X$ and 0 otherwise.

To define the number of observations $a \succ b$ for a context C we extend the definitions for $\sigma(P_i)$ and $\sigma(N_i)$. First, we define $A \setminus\!\setminus B$ for two sequences A and B similarly to the set difference, i.e., the result is a sequence of elements where we remove elements from the first sequence which appear in the second sequence. If an element x occurs n-times in A and m-times in B, $A \setminus\!\setminus B$ contains the element x exactly $max(0, n - m)$-times (e.g. $(a, a, b, c) \setminus\!\setminus (a, b, d) = (a, c)$). We then define the set $P_i \mid C = \sigma(D_i) \cap \sigma(R_i \setminus\!\setminus C)$ and the set $N_i \mid C = \sigma(D_i) \setminus \sigma(R_i \setminus\!\setminus C)$. $P_i \mid C$ contains, similarly to P_i, all elements which are contained in the source document as well as in the reference documents without the context elements. The intuition is that these elements are important in the context of C whereas the elements in $N_i \mid C$ are not important given C.

The number of contextual preferences for the elements a and b and the sequence of context elements C in the background corpus $\mathbb{B}$ is defined as

$$n_{\mathbb{B}}(a \succ b \mid C) =$$
$$\sum_{(D_i, R_i) \in \mathbb{B}} \mathbb{1}_{P_i \mid C}(a) \cdot \mathbb{1}_{N_i \mid C}(b). \qquad (3)$$

The context C models the objects which are already in a partial summary. Since our approach selects sentences sequentially, we have to detect the importance of objects according to already selected objects.

We can estimate the prior probability of observing $a \succ b$ as

$$\Pr(a \succ b) = \frac{n(a \succ b)}{n(a \succ b) + n(b \succ a)} \qquad (4)$$

and analogously for $\Pr(a \succ b \mid C)$.

3.4 Sentence Ranking

In this section, we propose a ranking methodology for all available sentences $\dot{D}$ in a multi-document summarization topic from a sentence-level utility function u. To rank the sentences, we iteratively search for the sentence $\hat{\mathbf{s}}$ with

$$\hat{\mathbf{s}} = \arg\max_{\mathbf{s} \in \dot{D}} u(\mathbf{s} \mid C) \qquad (5)$$

where $u(\mathbf{s} \mid C)$ is a utility function that encodes the importance of sentence $\mathbf{s}$ in a context C. The intuition is that the value of a sentence depends on already selected sentences which are modeled by the context C. Hence, we greedily set

$$\hat{S} \leftarrow \hat{S} \circ \arg\max_{\mathbf{s} \in \dot{D}} u(\mathbf{s} \mid \hat{S}) \qquad (6)$$

as long as $\hat{S} \in \mathfrak{P}_{l_{max}}(\dot{D})$ and starting with $\hat{S} = \emptyset$.

Since we do not have access to the reference summaries when generating summaries, we use the learned knowledge from the training phase to estimate the utility of each sentence in order to find the sentence with the highest utility value. To do so, we propose a utility function u in the next section, which assigns a utility score to each individual sentence.

It is important to note at this point that we neither use any form of similarity measure between sentences nor any structural features such as sentence positions to determine the importance of a sentence, which is a crucial difference to previous works.

3.5 Individual Sentence Scoring

We obtain individual sentence scores, which means that each sentence is assigned a score independently from the other available sentences. Removing or adding sentences to the source documents will therefore not change the value of the sentences. The intuition of the score is, that we want to find the sentence which has the highest average probability that the objects in the sentence occur in the reference summary. The desired sentence $\hat{\mathbf{s}}$ is therefore selected by the utility function

$$u(\mathbf{s} \mid C) = \frac{\sum_{x \in \mathbf{s}} v(x \mid C)}{n} \qquad (7)$$

where v is an object-level utility function which measures the importance of an object a in a context C. We define v for element x and a corpus $\mathbb{B}$ as

$$v(a \mid C) = \frac{1}{|V|} \sum_{x \in V} \Pr(a \succ x \mid C) \qquad (8)$$

where $V = \bigcup_{(D_i, R_i) \in \mathbb{B}} \{x : x \in D_i\}$ is the set of all considered objects in the background corpus $\mathbb{B}$ (i.e. the vocabulary) and $\Pr(a \succ b)$ if $C = \emptyset$ and $\Pr(a \succ b \mid C)$ are estimated as in (4).

Note that it may happen that an object a or a preference $a \succ b \mid C$ might not have been observed in the background corpus. These cases are ignored in the computation.

4 Evaluation Corpora

The fundamental hypothesis of centrality-based summarization systems is that frequency within the source documents implies importance of information. All information which is frequent in the source documents is considered to be important and therefore extracted for the summary. While this may be a suitable assumption for some document collections (such as newswire documents), we do not believe that it is suitable for the task of summarizing heterogeneous document collections.

Since most of the work in summarization has been done for newswire data, there is a lack of evaluation data where structural and centrality signals do not provide a strong indicator for importance. We therefore modify the DUC2004 multi-document summarization corpus by *shuffling* and *oversampling* to remove the commonly used indicators for importance. By doing so, we intend to demonstrate that centrality-based document summarization algorithms break down, whereas *PLSum* will maintain its performance.

Shuffling: In order to remove order-dependency, we randomly shuffle the sentences to hide the very strong sentence position signal, which is commonly used to detect importance in news documents.

Oversampling: With oversampling we aim for hiding the important information in the corpus by increasing the frequency of unimportant information. In particular, we iteratively search for a sentence $\hat{\mathbf{s}}$ with

$$\hat{\mathbf{s}} = \arg\min_{\mathbf{s} \in \dot{D}} \sum_{\mathbf{s}_x \in \dot{D}} sim(\mathbf{s}, \mathbf{s}_x), \qquad (9)$$

where sim is a similarity measure for two sentences, and add $\hat{\mathbf{s}}$ to a random document in topic $\mathcal{D}$. Since we duplicate the sentences we make sure that we do not introduce new, important information to the corpus which is not reflected in the summary. For the similarity measure we use

$$sim(\mathbf{s}_1, \mathbf{s}_2) = \frac{cos(\mathbf{s}_1, \mathbf{s}_2) + jacc(\mathbf{s}_1, \mathbf{s}_2)}{2} \qquad (10)$$

in our experiments, where cos is a cosine similarity implemented in the DKPro Similarity framework (Bär et al., 2013) with TF-IDF values based on English Wikipedia articles, and $jacc$ denotes to the well-known Jaccard measure. This simple

Dataset	∅ Similarity
DUC2004	0.0877
DUC2004	0.0880
DUC2004 200%	0.0692
DUC2004 500%	0.0620
DUC2004 1000%	0.0607

Table 1: Average similarities of the sentences contained in the test corpora.

combination lead to reasonably good results on the English subtask of the SemEval2014 Semantic Textual Similarity dataset.[4]

With this methodology, we create four new corpora with 100%, 200%, 500%, and 1000% of the size of DUC2004. The bigger the corpora is, the more unimportant information has been added to it. In the 100% corpus sentences are only shuffled without duplicating sentences. With increasing size we hide the originally frequent information better and make it therefore harder to detect important information. An analysis of the result of the oversampling is displayed in Table 1. The average similarity decreases which means that we hide dense regions by adding sentences to less dense regions.

5 Evaluation

Since the DUC data provides manually written reference summaries, we can compare these gold standard summaries to the newly generated summaries of the automatic summarization systems. We provide in the evaluation ROUGE-1 (R1) and ROUGE-2 (R2) based recall scores according to Owczarzak et al. (2012) who showed that R2 provides the best agreement with manual evaluations when using stemming and without removing stopwords. As Rankel et al. (2013) showed that there is no clear winner between R1 and R2, we provide R1 as well, which is well suited to identify the better summary in a pair of summaries. Furthermore, all automatically generated summaries are truncated at a length of 100 words by the ROUGE system (Hong et al., 2014). Summarized, we use `ROUGE-1.5.5` with parameters `-a -m -n 2 -x -c 95 -r 1000 -f A -p 0.5 -t 0 -l 100 -d`.

5.1 Reference Systems

We will compare our algorithm, *CPSum*, to two baselines and to two well-known summarization algorithms.

[4] http://alt.qcri.org/semeval2014/

Baselines: The first baseline *Optimal* has access to the reference summaries and is therefore no fair competitor for the remaining systems. Nevertheless, it provides useful information about the maximal reachable score for each dataset. Since computing the true optimal score is computational expensive, we only provide a pseudo-optimal value computed by a greedy search. The second baseline system, *Random*, selects sentences from the source documents randomly. It does not have access to the reference systems and is therefore the first system which can be compared with the other systems. Since most important information in news are often contained in the first sentences, just selecting the first few sentences as a summary is a strong baseline. We use *Lead* to provide evaluation scores for a system, which selects the first sentences of each document.

Summarization Systems: We use *Centroid* (Radev et al., 2000) as a representative system for centroid-based systems. To generate the summaries for this approach we apply the widely used MEAD system (Radev et al., 2004), in which *Centroid* is implemented. For *Centroid* we used the default linear feature combination, length cutoff and re-ranker. As a competitive state-of-the-art representative for graph-based approaches (Hong and Nenkova, 2014) we apply *LexRank* (Erkan and Radev, 2004), which is also implemented in the MEAD system. For *LexRank* we used the LexRank feature, standard length cutoff and the default re-ranker.

5.2 CPSum

Since *CPSum* learns about importance of objects from a background corpus, we need first a concrete instantiation for the abstract objects and second a background corpus to learn from. As instances for the objects for which we learn contextual preferences of the form $a \succ b \mid C$ we use bi-grams of stemmed words, which means that *CPSum* will learn about the importance of bi-grams. The contexts C is therefore a sequence of bi-grams. As mentioned above, any other linguistic entity like named-entities, opinions, or events would also be possible choices. Furthermore, vector representations for sentences could be applied as well. We decided to use bi-grams of stemmed words since they do not need any sophisticated pre-processing. Furthermore, showing that our approach is able to handle difficult summarization scenarios without a

System / Dataset	ROUGE-1 Recall					ROUGE-2 Recall				
	D04	D04-1	D04-2	D04-5	D04-10	D04	D04-1	D04-2	D04-5	D04-10
Optimal	0.4043	0.4043	0.4046	0.4043	0.4044	0.0940	0.0941	0.0943	0.0940	0.0942
Random	0.2955	0.3095	0.2863	0.2736	0.2633	0.0435	0.0463	0.0360	0.0313	0.0322
Lead	0.3424	0.3138	0.2786	0.2636	0.2548	0.0766	0.0524	0.0382	0.0313	0.0282
Centroid	**0.3542**	0.3158	0.3082	0.2690	0.2474	**0.0867**	0.0605	0.0576	0.0396	0.0331
LexRank	0.3231	0.3219	0.3186	0.3052	0.2990	0.0659	**0.0645**	**0.0631**	0.0542	0.0522
CPSum	0.3267	**0.3247**	**0.3264**	**0.3264**	**0.3264**	0.0603	0.0604	0.0617	**0.0617**	**0.0617**

Table 2: ROUGE-1 and ROUGE-2 scores on the original and the modified DUC 2004 corpora.

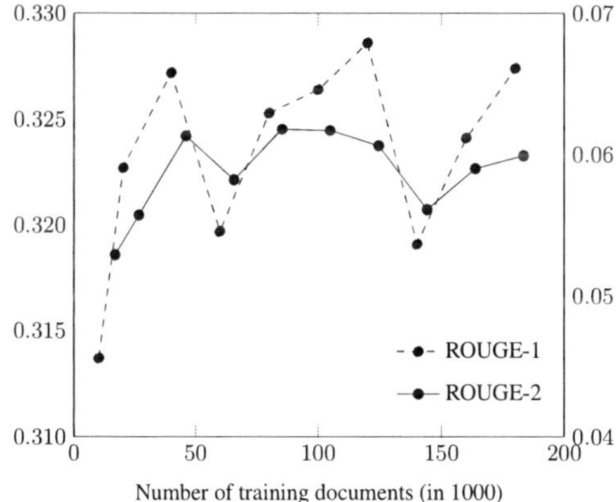

Figure 2: Learning curve of CPSum on DUC2004 for different background corpus sizes. ROUGE-1 scores (left scale) are displayed in blue and ROUGE-2 (right scale) in red.

sophisticated linguistic analysis of the data and re-lying solely on simple elements is an even stronger argument for the strength of *CPSum*.

For learning the importance of bi-grams we use a background corpus originally created by Hermann et al. (2015) for question answering tasks. Although this corpus does not provide well-written summaries for each article but only sentence-length bullet points summarizing the content of the article, we can use this informa-tion to derive the necessary training signals for learning object importance. The corpus con-tains about 100k CNN document-summary pairs crawled from CNN and about 197k pairs crawled from DailyMail. For training, we use a subset of 100k randomly selected documents in total.

Since we will not observe most of the bi-grams from the training corpus in the test data, we apply a lazy learning strategy to only learn about ele-ments which appear in the test data. Furthermore, we only learn preferences for contexts which we actually observe during summarization. This de-creases the learning effort significantly.

6 Results

Table 2 shows the ROUGE evaluation scores of the tested systems on the test datasets. First, we see that the evaluation scores for both, ROUGE-1 and ROUGE-2 recall stays nearly constant for the oracle system *Optimal*. From this result we con-clude that our modifications did neither remove from nor add important information to the corpus. After the modifications, it is still possible to gen-erate summaries with a ROUGE-1 value of at least 0.40 and a ROUGE-2 value of at least 0.09. The performance of *Random* decreases when we add more irrelevant information to the corpus. This behavior is expected since the probability of pick-ing an irrelevant sentences increases when more irrelevant sentences are in the corpus. The base-line *Lead*, which simply uses the first sentences of each article, but is considered to be a strong base-line in newswire documents, is able to summa-rize the original DUC 2004 data reasonably well. However, in the modified corpora with random-ized sentence order, its performance is obviously not better than *Random*.

As expected, the two state-of-the-art reference systems work well on the original DUC 2004 cor-pus, where *Centroid* achieves the best results. This behavior is also expected, since it uses positional and centrality features, which provide very good signals for importance in the corpus. When these signals are more and more removed in D04-1 – D04-10, we observe a big performance decrease in both, ROUGE-1 and ROUGE-2. *LexRank* behaves similarly to *Centroid* but with a less fast decrease of performance.

CPSum performs only moderately at the orig-inal DUC 2004 dataset. This is again expected, since it does not use the strong importance sig-nals sentence position and sentence centrality. The strength of *CPSum* can be observed in the modi-fied corpora, where the performance stays compa-rable to the performance at the original corpus and does not decrease as it can be observed for all other

Saudi exile Osama bin Laden , the alleged mastermind of a conspiracy to attack U.S. targets around the world, and Muhammad *Atef,* the alleged military commander of bin Laden's terrorist organization, Al-Qaeda, were charged in a separate *238-page* indictment with murder and conspiracy in the bombings.
Saudi exile Osama bin Laden , the alleged mastermind of a conspiracy to attack U.S. targets around the world, *and* Muhammad *Atef,* the alleged military commander of bin Laden's terrorist organization, Al-Qaeda, were charged in a separate *238-page* indictment with murder and conspiracy in the bombings.

Figure 3: Example of the importance of the elements in a sentence before (top) and after (bottom) adding the sentence to the summary. The darker the font color the more important the element. Elements with less than 100 gathered preferences are displayed in italics. The importance scores are estimated by v as defined in Equation 8.

approaches. In terms of ROUGE-1 scores, *CPSum* has the best performance on the four modified corpora. In terms of ROUGE-2, its original performance is similar to the performance of *LexRank*, but lower that *Centroid*. The performance of *Centroid* drops significantly after shuffling the sentences. If we add more and more irrelevant sentences, the performance of *Centroid* drops again faster than the performance of *LexRank*. *CPSum* outperforms all systems when we increase the amount of noise in the corpora D04-5 and D04-10.

We show an example of the sentences scoring in Figure 3. We display the same sentence twice. In the top, we display the context-free scores of the elements of the sentence by using a darker font for more important information. In the bottom, we show the contextual scores of the same sentence after adding this particular sentence to the summary. We observe that the importance scores of elements such as *Osama bin Laden* are estimated properly. After adding the sentence to the summary we can see how *PLSum* discounts the scores for different elements differently.

7   Conclusions

In this paper we introduced *CPSum*, a text summarization system that learns the importance of entities from an independent background corpus of document summary pairs. *CPSum* is able to cope with summarization scenarios where neither centrality nor structural features help to detect important information. We showed that the performance of conventional text summarization systems decreases in such a setting. Previous approaches can be confused easily by adding more and more irrelevant information whereas the performance of *CPSum* stays constant. We would argue that by

relying on learned prior knowledge about what information is important for a summary, *CPSum* is able to detect important information similar to the way human experts address a summarization task.

CPSum is also different in the way it copes with redundancy. Instead of measuring the similarity to already selected sentences such as the majority of the previous systems, we estimate the score of the elements with contextual preferences. This enables *CPSum* not only to detect redundancy, but also to use synergy effects between sentences. Adding one sentence to the summary can therefore also increase the utility of other sentences. Furthermore, our system can be adapted easily to different user interest by learning from other source documents.

We intend to investigate other basis elements for the preferences as well as alternatives for modeling world knowledge in future work. Similarly, we are also working on a corpus with which we can further investigate summarization scenarios where centrality and structural features are no good signals for importance. The results of this first study make us confident that a knowledge-based approach towards importance information is necessary in order to enable summarization systems to handle difficult summarization scenarios where signals for importance cannot be inferred from the source documents.

Acknowledgments

This work has been supported by the German Research Foundation (DFG) as part of the Research Training Group Adaptive Preparation of Information from Heterogeneous Sources (AIPHES) under grant No. GRK 1994/1.

References

D. Bär, T. Zesch, and I. Gurevych. 2013. DKPro Similarity: An open source framework for text similarity. In *Proc. 51st Annual Meeting of the Association for Computational Linguistics: System Demonstrations*, pp. 121–126, Sofia, Bulgaria. ACL.

S. Brin and L. Page. 1998. The anatomy of a large-scale hypertextual web search engine. *Computer networks*, 30(1-7):107–117.

J. Carbonell and J. Goldstein. 1998. The use of MMR, diversity-based reranking for reordering documents and producing summaries. In *Proc. 21st Annual International ACM SIGIR Conference on Research and Development in Information Retrieval*, pp. 335–336. ACM.

J.M. Conroy, J.D. Schlesinger, J. Goldstein, and D.P. O'Leary. 2004. Left-brain/right-brain multi-document summarization. In *Proceedings of the Document Understanding Conference (DUC 2004)*.

H.P. Edmundson. 1969. New methods in automatic extracting. *Journal of the ACM*, 16(2):264–285.

G. Erkan and D.R. Radev. 2004. LexRank: Graph-based lexical centrality as salience in text summarization. *Journal of Artificial Intelligence Research* 22:457–479.

J. Fürnkranz and E. Hüllermeier (eds.) 2011. *Preference learning*. Springer.

G. Gigerenzer and P.M. Todd. 1999. *Simple heuristics that make us smart*. Oxford University Press, USA.

D. Gillick, B. Favre, D. Hakkani-Tur, B. Bohnet, Y. Liu, and S. Xie. 2009. The ICSI/UTD summarization system at TAC 2009. In *Proc. 2nd Text Analysis Conference (TAC-09)*, Gaithersburg, MD (USA).

K.M. Hermann, T. Kocisky, E. Grefenstette, L. Espeholt, W. Kay, M. Suleyman, and P. Blunsom. 2015. Teaching machines to read and comprehend. In *Advances in Neural Information Processing Systems 28 (NIPS-15)*, pp. 1684–1692.

K. Hong and A. Nenkova. 2014. Improving the estimation of word importance for news multi-document summarization. In *Proc. 14th Conference of the European Chapter of the Association for Computational Linguistics (EACL-14)*, Gothenburg, Sweden, pp. 712–721.

K. Hong, J.M. Conroy, B. Favre, A. Kulesza, H. Lin, and A. Nenkova. 2014. A repository of state of the art and competitive baseline summaries for generic news summarization. In *Proc. 9th International Conference on Language Resources and Evaluation (LREC-14)*, Reykjavik, Iceland, pp. 1608–1616.

J.M. Kleinberg. 1999. Authoritative sources in a hyperlinked environment. *Journal of the ACM*, 46(5):604–632.

H. Lin and J. Bilmes. 2011. A class of submodular functions for document summarization. In *Proc. 49th Annual Meeting of the Association for Computational Linguistics: Human Language Technologies, Vol. 1*, pp. 510–520. ACL.

C.-Y. Lin. 2004. Rouge: A package for automatic evaluation of summaries. In *Proceedings of the ACL-04 Text Summarization Workshop*, pages 74–81.

H.P. Luhn. 1958. The automatic creation of literature abstracts. *IBM Journal of Research and Development*, 2(2):159–165.

I. Mani. 2001. *Automatic summarization*, Vol. 3. John Benjamins Publishing.

K. McKeown and D.R. Radev. 1995. Generating summaries of multiple news articles. In *Proc. 18th annual international ACM SIGIR Conference on Research and Development in Information Retrieval*, pp. 74–82. ACM.

R. Mihalcea and P. Tarau. 2004. TextRank: Bringing order into texts. In *Proc. 2004 Conference on Empirical Methods in Natural Language Processing (EMNLP-04)*, pp. 404–411. ACL.

A. Nenkova, L. Vanderwende, and K. McKeown. 2006. A compositional context sensitive multi-document summarizer: exploring the factors that influence summarization. In *Proc. 29th Annual International ACM SIGIR Conference on Research and Development in Information Retrieval*, pp. 573–580. ACM.

K. Owczarzak, J.M. Conroy, H. Trang Dang, and A. Nenkova. 2012. An assessment of the accuracy of automatic evaluation in summarization. In *Proc. Workshop on Evaluation Metrics and System Comparison for Automatic Summarization*, pp. 1–9. ACL.

D. Parveen and M. Strube. 2015. Integrating importance, non-redundancy and coherence in graph-based extractive summarization. In *Proc. 24th International Conference on Artificial Intelligence (AAAI-15)*, pp. 1298–1304. AAAI Press.

D.R. Radev. 2000. A common theory of information fusion from multiple text sources—Step one: cross-document structure. In *Proceedings of the 1st SIGdial workshop on Discourse and dialogue (SIGDIAL-00), Vol. 10*, pp. 74–83. ACL.

D.R. Radev, T. Allison, S. Blair-Goldensohn, J. Blitzer, A. Celebi, S. Dimitrov, E. Drabek, A. Hakim, W. Lam, D. Liu, J. Otterbacher, H. Qi, H. Saggion, S. Teufel, M. Topper, A. Winkel, and Z. Zhang. 2004. MEAD-a platform for multidocument multilingual text summarization. In *Proc. 4th International Conference on Language Resources and Evaluation (LREC-04)*. European Language Resources Association.

D.R. Radev, H. Jing, and M. Budzikowska. 2000. Centroid-based summarization of multiple documents: sentence extraction, utility-based evaluation, and user studies. In *Proceedings of the 2000 NAACL-ANLP Workshop on Automatic Summarization*, pp. 21–30. ACL.

P.A. Rankel, J.M. Conroy, E.V. Slud, and D.P. O'Leary. 2011. Ranking human and machine summarization systems. In *Proc. 2011 Conference on Empirical Methods in Natural Language Processing (EMNLP-11)*, pp. 467–473. ACL.

P.A. Rankel, J.M. Conroy, H. Trang Dang, and A. Nenkova. 2013. A decade of automatic content evaluation of news summaries: Reassessing the state of the art. In *Proc. 51st Annual Meeting of the Association for Computational Linguistics (ACL-13)*, Sofia, Bulgaria, pp. 131–136.

J. Sjöbergh. 2007. Older versions of the rougeeval summarization evaluation system were easier to fool. *Information Processing & Management*, 43(6):1500–1505.

X. Wan. 2010. Towards a unified approach to simultaneous single-document and multi-document summarizations. In *Proc. 23rd International Conference on Computational Linguistics (ACL-10)*, pp. 1137–1145. ACL.

D. Yogatama, F. Liu, and N.A. Smith. 2015. Extractive summarization by maximizing semantic volume. In *Proc. Conference on Empirical Methods in Natural Language Processing (EMNLP-15)*, pp. 961–1966, Lisbon, Portugal. ACL.

Incremental Prediction of Sentence-final Verbs: Humans versus Machines

Alvin C. Grissom II[1], Naho Orita[2], and Jordan Boyd-Graber[1]

[1]University of Colorado Boulder, Department of Computer Science
[2]Tohoku University, Graduate School of Information Sciences
{Alvin.Grissom,Jordan.Boyd.Graber}@colorado.edu
naho@ecei.tohoku.ac.jp

Abstract

Verb prediction is important in human sentence processing and, practically, in simultaneous machine translation. In verb-final languages, speakers select the final verb before it is uttered, and listeners predict it before it is uttered. Simultaneous interpreters must do the same to translate in real-time. Motivated by the problem of SOV-SVO simultaneous machine translation, we provide a study of incremental verb prediction in verb-final languages. As a basis of comparison, we examine incremental verb prediction with human participants in a multiple choice setting using crowdsourcing to gain insight into incremental human performance in a constrained setting. We then examine a computational approach to incremental verb prediction using discriminative classification with shallow features. Both humans and machines predict verbs more accurately as more of a sentence becomes available, and case markers—when available—help humans and sometimes machines predict final verbs.

1 The Importance of Verb Prediction

Humans predict future linguistic input before it is observed (Kutas et al., 2011). This predictability has been formalized in information theory (Shannon, 1948)—the more predictable a word is, the lower the entropy—and has explained various linguistic phenomena, such as garden path ambiguity (Den and Inoue, 1997; Hale, 2001). Such instances of linguistic prediction are fundamental to statistical NLP. Auto-complete from search engines has made next-word prediction one of best known NLP applications.

Long-distance word prediction, such as verb prediction in SOV languages (Levy and Keller, 2013; Momma et al., 2015; Chow et al., 2015), is important in simultaneous machine translation from subject-object-verb (SOV) languages to subject-verb-object (SVO) languages. In SVO languages such as English, for example, the main verb phrase usually comes after the first noun phrase—the main subject—in a sentence, while in verb-final languages such as Japanese or German, it comes very last. Human simultaneous translators must make predictions about the unspoken final verb to incrementally translate the sentence. Minimizing interpretation delay thus requires making constant predictions and deciding when to trust those predictions and commit to translating in real-time.

Such prediction can also aid machines. Matsubara et al. (2000) use pattern-matching rules; Grissom II et al. (2014) use a statistical n-gram approach; and Oda et al. (2015) extend the idea of using prediction by predicting entire syntactic constituents for English-Japanese translation. These systems require fast, accurate verb prediction to further improve simultaneous translation systems. We focus on verb prediction in verb-final languages such as Japanese with this motivation in mind.

In Section 2, we present what is, to our knowledge, the first study of humans' ability to incrementally predict the verbs in Japanese. We use these human data as a yardstick to which to compare computational incremental verb prediction. Incorporating some of the key insights from our human study into a discriminative model—namely, the importance of case markers— Section 3 presents a better incremental verb classifier than existing verb prediction schemes. Having established both human and computer performance on this challenging and interesting task, Section 4 reviews our work's relationship to other studies in NLP and linguistics.

Proceedings of the 20th SIGNLL Conference on Computational Natural Language Learning (CoNLL), pages 95–104,
Berlin, Germany, August 7-12, 2016. ©2016 Association for Computational Linguistics

2 Human Verb Prediction

We first examine human verb selection in a constrained setting to better understand what performance we should demand of computational approaches. While we know that humans make incremental predictions across sentences, we do not know how skilled they are in doing so. While it's possible that machines—with unbounded memory and access to Internet-sized data—could do better than humans, this study allows us to appropriately gauge our expectations for computational systems.

We use crowdsourcing to measure how well novice humans can predict the final verb phrase of incomplete Japanese sentences in a multiple choice setting. We use Japanese text of the Kyoto Free Translation Task corpus (Neubig, 2011, KFT), a collection of Wikipedia articles in English and Japanese, representing standard, grammatical text and readily usable for future SOV-SVO machine translation experiments.

2.1 Extracting Verbs and Sentences

This section describes the data sources, preparation, and methodology for crowdsourced verb prediction. Given an incomplete sentence, participants select a sentence-final verb phrase containing a verb from a list of four choices to complete the sentence, one of which is the original completion.

We randomly select 200 sentences from the development set of the KFT corpus (Neubig, 2011). We use these data because the sentences are from Wikipedia articles and thus represent widely-read, grammatical sentences. These data are directly comparable to our computational experiments and readily usable for future SOV-SVO machine translation experiments.

We ask participants to predict a "verb chunk" that would be natural for humans. More technically, this is a sentence-final *bunsetsu*.[1] We identify verb *bunsetsu* with a dependency parser (Kurohashi and Nagao, 1994). Of interest are *bunsetsu* at the end of a sentence that contain a verb. We also use *bunsetsu* for segmenting the incomplete sentences we show to humans, only segmenting between *bunsetsu* to ensure each segment is a meaningful unit.

---

[1] A *bunsetsu* is a commonly used linguistic unit in Japanese, roughly equivalent to an English phrase: a collection of content words and zero or more functional words. Japanese verb *bunsetsu* often encompass complex conjugation. For example, a verb phrase 読みたくなかった (read-DESI-NEG-PAST), meaning 'didn't want to read', has multiple tokens capturing tense, negation, etc. necessary for translation.

Answer Choice Selection   We display the correct verb *bunsetsu* and three incorrect *bunsetsu* completions as choices that occur in the data with frequency close to the correct answer in the overall corpus. We manually inspect the incorrect answers to ensure that these choices are semantically distant, i.e., excluding synonyms or troponyms.

Sentence Presentation   We create two test sets of truncated sentences from the KFT corpus: The first, the **full context set**, includes all but the final *bunsetsu*—i.e., the verb phrase—to guess. The second set, the **random length set**, contains the same sentences truncated at predetermined, random *bunsetsu* boundaries. The average sentence length is nine *bunsetsu*, with a maximum of fourteen and minimum of three. We display sentences in the original Japanese script.

Participants view the task as a game of guessing the final verb. Each fragment has four concurrently displayed completion options, as in the prompt (2) and answers (3). Users receive no feedback from the interface.

We use CrowdFlower[2] to collect participants' answers, at a total cost of approximately USD$300. From an initial pool of fifty-six participants, we remove twenty via a Japanese fluency screening. We verify the efficacy of this test with non-native but highly proficient Japanese learners; none passed. We collect five judgments per sentence from each participant.

(2) 谷崎潤一郎は
   Junichiro Tanizaki-TOP
   数寄屋を
   tea-ceremony house-OBJ

(3) (a) 好んだ
       like PAST

   (b) 変えられた
       change-PASS CAP-PAST

   (c) 始まったとされている
       begin-PAST-COMP-suppose-AUX.PRES

   (d) 増やしていた
       increase-AUX.PAST

2.2 Presenting Partial and Complete Sentences

The first task, on the **full context set**, shows how humans predict the sentence-final verb chunk with all context available. The second task, on the

---

[2] http://www.crowdflower.com/

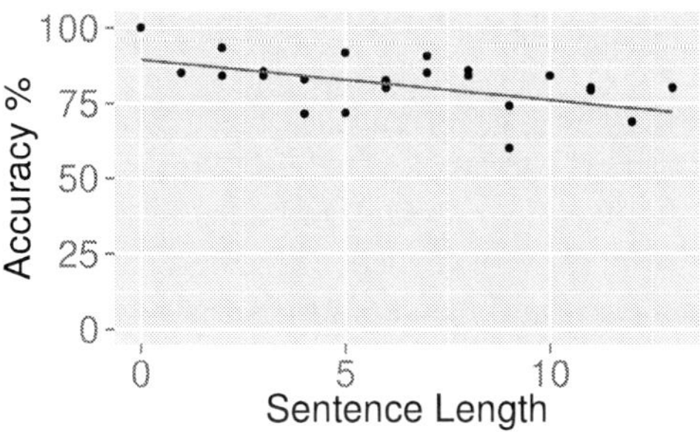

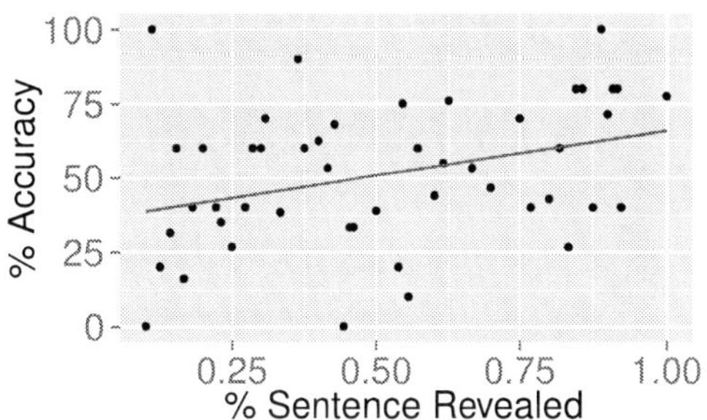

Figure 1: Full context set: Accuracy is generally high, but slightly decreases on longer, more complicated sentences, averaging 81.1%.

Figure 2: Random length set: The accuracy of human verb predictions reliably increases as more of the sentence is revealed.

random length set, shows how the amount of revealed data affects the predictability of the final verb chunk. We examine a correlation between the length of the pre-verb sentence fragment and participants' accuracy (Figure 1).

Psycholinguistic experiments using lexical decision tasks suggest Japanese speakers start syntactic processing by using case—the type and number of case-marked arguments—before the verb's availability (Yamashita, 2000). We also examine the correlation between the number of case markers[3] and accuracy. It is likely that the number of case markers and the length of the sentence fragment are confounded; so, we create a measure, the proportion of case markers to the overall sentence information (the number of case markers in the fragment divided by the number of *bunsetsu* chunks). We call this **case density**.

2.3 Results of Human Experiments

In the **full context set**, average accuracy over 200 sentences is 81.1%, significantly better than chance ($p < 2.2 \cdot 10^{-16}$). Figure 1 shows the accuracy per sentence length as defined by the *bunsetsu* unit. A one-way ANOVA reveals a significant effect of the sentence length ($F(1, 998) = 7.512, p < 0.00624$), but not the case density ($F(1, 998) = 1.2, p = 0.274$).

In the **random length set**, average accuracy over 200 sentences is 54.2%, significantly better than chance ($t(199) = 11.8205, p < 2.2 \cdot 10^{-16}$). Figure 2 shows the accuracy per percentage of length

of the presented sentence fragment. A one-way ANOVA reveals a significant effect of the sentence length ($F(1, 998) = 57.44, p < 7.94 \cdot 10^{-14}$). We also find a significant effect of the case density ($F(1, 998) = 5.884, p = 0.0155$).

2.4 Discussion

Predictability increases with the percent of the sentence available in all of our experiments. By the end of the sentence, the verb chunks are highly predictable by humans in the multiple choice setting. Participants choose the final verb more accurately as they gain access to more case markers in the **random length set** but not in the **full context set**.

Case density is a significant factor in predictive accuracy on the **random length set** for humans, suggesting that case is more helpful in predicting a sentence-final verb when the preceding contextual information is insufficient. The following example illustrates how case helps in prediction. The nominative and accusative markers greatly narrow the choices, as shown in (4).[4] Our results further support the proposition case markers modulate predictability in SOV verb-final processing.

(4) 江戸幕府区-が　　　　　成立すると
    Edo shogunate-**NOM**　　establish-do-**CONJ**
    寺院法度-に-より　　　　　　—
    temple-prohibition etc. ACC-for

---

[3] In this study, we counted case markers that mark nominative (*-ga*), accusative (*-wo*), ablative (*-kara*), and dative (*-ni*).

[4] A recent psycholinguistics study on incremental Japanese verb-final processing (Momma et al., 2015) argues that native Japanese speakers plan verbs in advance, before the articulation of object nouns, but not subject nouns. Since case markers assign the roles of subject and object in Japanese, we expect that a high ratio of case markers to words will increase predictability of verbs. In addition, Yamashita (1997) argues that the *variety* of case markers increases predictability just before the verb.

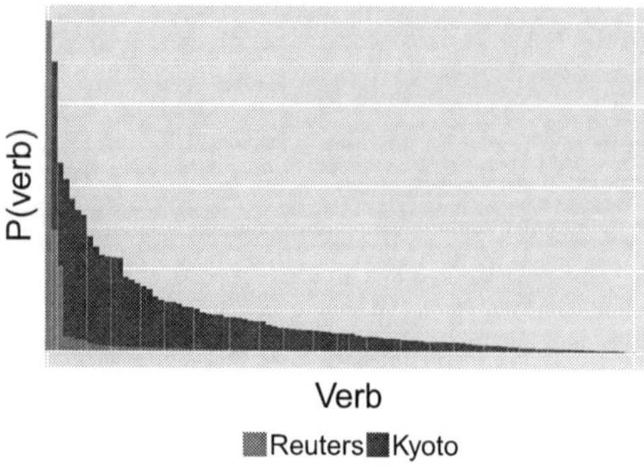

Figure 3: Distribution of the top 100 content verbs in the Kyoto corpus and the Reuters Japanese news corpus. Both are Zipfian, but the Reuters corpus is even more skewed, even with the common special cases excluded.

'After Edo shogunate has established, due to the temple prohibition etc. —'

In other cases, there exist choices, which, while incorrect, could naturally complete the sentence. These questions are frequently missed. For instance, in one 90% revealed sentence, the participant has the choices: (i) 収める (put-PRES), (ii) 厳しくなる (strict-become), (iii) 収録されている (record-do.PASS-AUX.PRES), and (iv) 務める (work-PRES). Choice (i) is the correct answer, but choice (iii) is a reasonable choice for a Japanese speaker. All participants missed this question, and all chose the same wrong answer (iii). We leave a cloze task where participants can freely fill in the sentence-final to future work.

These results provide a basis of comparison for automatic prediction. In the next section, we examine whether computational models can predict final verbs and compare the models' performance to that of humans.

3 Machine Verb Prediction

Now that we have the results of the previous section, we have baselines against which we can compare computational verb prediction approaches. In this section, we introduce incremental verb classification with a linear classifier.[5] For our investigation of computational verb classification, we use two

very different languages that both have verb-final syntax—Japanese, which is agglutinative, and German, which is not—and show that discriminative classifiers can predict final verbs with increasing accuracy as more context of sentences is revealed.

A simple verb prediction scheme applied to German (Grissom II et al., 2014) achieves poor accuracy. Their approach creates a Kneser-Ney n-gram language model for the prior context associated with each verb in the corpus; i.e., 50 n-gram models for 50 verbs. Given pre-verb n-gram context c in a sentence S_t, and verb prediction $v^{(t)} \in V$, the verb selection is defined by the following equation:

$$v^{(t)} \equiv \arg \max_v \prod_{c \in S_t} p(c \mid v)p(v). \qquad (1)$$

It chooses the verb that maximizes the probability of the observed context, scaled by the prior probability of the verb in the overall corpus. Unsurprisingly, given the distribution of verbs in real data (Figure 3), this n-gram-based approach has low accuracy and tends to predict the most common verb. For a translation system, this often degenerates into the less interesting problem of whether to trust whether the final verb is indeed a common one. While this improves translation delay, better predictions will lead to more significant improvements. We instead opt for a one-vs-all discriminative classification approach.[6]

3.1 Classification on Human Data

We first incrementally classify verbs on the same 200 sentences from Section 2. Since the answer choices are often complex verb *bunsetsu* and since many of these verb phrase answer choices do not appear among the most common verbs, lemmatizing the verbs and performing one-vs-all classification yields extremely low accuracy. Thus, we use binary classification with a single linear classifier to produce a probability for each candidate answer, encoding the verb phrase itself into the feature vector.

3.1.1 Training a Morphological Model

The processing is as follows: We train on 463,716 verb-final sentences extracted from the training data. We use both **context features** and **final verb features**. Our context features, i.e., those preceding the final verb, are represented as follows: the context **unigrams** and **bigrams** take a value of 1

---

[5]While we use logistic regression, using hinge loss achieves similar accuracy.

[6]One-vs-all classification builds a classifier for each class versus the aggregate all other classes.

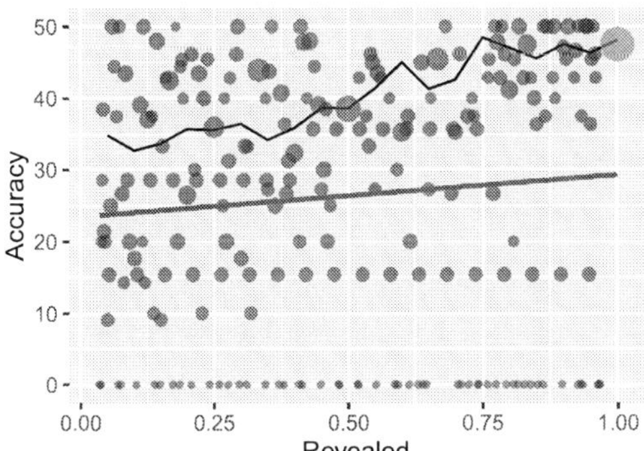

Figure 4: Verb classification results on crowd-sourced sentences. Despite many out-of-vocabulary items and significant noise, the average accuracy, shown in the non-monotonic line in the plot, increases over the course of the sentence. Larger, darker circles indicate more examples for a given position. Accuracy was calculated by aggregating the guesses at 5% intervals.

if they are present and 0 otherwise; **case markers** observed in the sentence context are represented as unigrams and bigrams in the order that they appear; and we reserve a distinct feature for the **last observed case marker** in the sentence. Our **verb features** consist of the final verb's tokens given by the morphological analyzer, which, in addition to the verb stem itself, typically include tense and aspect information. These are represented as unigrams and bigrams in the feature vector.

To allow the classifier to learn, we must encode the interactions between the verb features and the context features. Thus, we use the Cartesian product of sentence and verb features to encode interactions between them: for each training sentence we generate both a positive and a negative example. The example with the correct verb phrase is labeled as a positive example $(+1)$, and we uniformly select a random verb phrase from one of the 500 most common verb phrases and label it as negative (-1) example for the same sentence context,[7] yielding 927,432 training examples and 267,037,571 features.

For clarity, we describe this feature representation more formally. Given sentence S_t with a pre-

verb context consisting of unigrams, bigrams, and case marker tokens, $C = \{c_0, ..., c_n\}$, and *bunsetsu* verb phrase tokens $A = \{a_0, ..., a_k\}$, the feature vector consists of $C \times A = \{c_0 \wedge a_0, c_0 \wedge a_1, ..., c_n \wedge a_k\}$, where $\wedge$ concatenates the two context and answer strings. During learning, the weights learned for the concatenated tokens are thus based on the relationship between a context token and a *bunsetsu* token and mapped to $\{+1, -1\}$. More concretely, individual morphemes of the Japanese verb phrase are combined with the pre-verb unigrams, bigrams, and uniquely identified case marker tokens. Accuracy improves when the morphemes used in the negative examples and positive examples are disjoint; so, we enforce this constraint when selecting negative examples. For example, if the positive example includes the past tense morpheme, た, the negative example is altogether disallowed from having this morpheme as a verb feature.

3.1.2 Choosing an Answer

At test time, we test progressively longer fragments of each sentence, extracting the aforementioned features online until the entire pre-verb context is available. For every sentence fragment, the classifier determines the probability of each of the four possible verbs by adding their verb features to the feature vector of the example. The answer choice with the highest probability of $+1$ (or the lowest probability of -1) is chosen as the answer. By taking this approach, we can model complex verbs and their context jointly. Intuitively, the probability of a $(+1)$ is the model's prediction of how well the *bunsetsu* verb phrase fits with the sentence context (represented by the feature vector).

Some verbs are absent from the training data, forcing the classifier to rely on morphemes to distinguish between them. The alternative—e.g., in a typical one-vs-all classification approach—is that the classifier could reason from nothing whatsoever when a fully-inflected verb is absent from the training data. Given the complexity of *bunsetsu*, this happens often even in large corpora for a language such as Japanese.

3.1.3 Multiple Choice Results

Despite only choosing among four choices, this task is in many ways more difficult than the 50-label classification problem described in the next section because of the added complexity inherent modeling the effect of morphemes and missing examples. These limitations notwithstanding, the

---

[7]We experimented with several numbers of weighted negative examples and found that one negative example with of equal weight to the positive gave the best results of the configurations we tried.

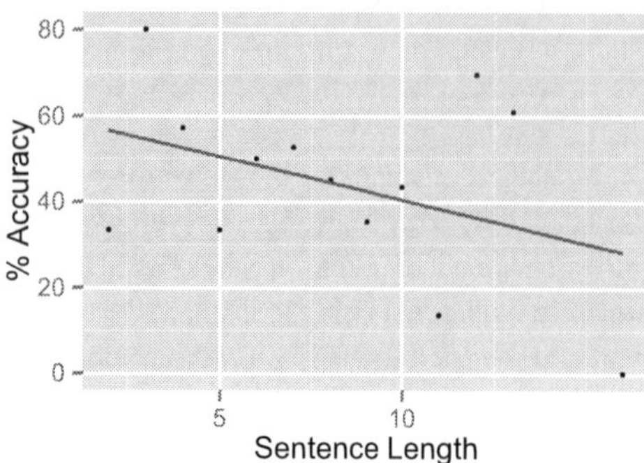

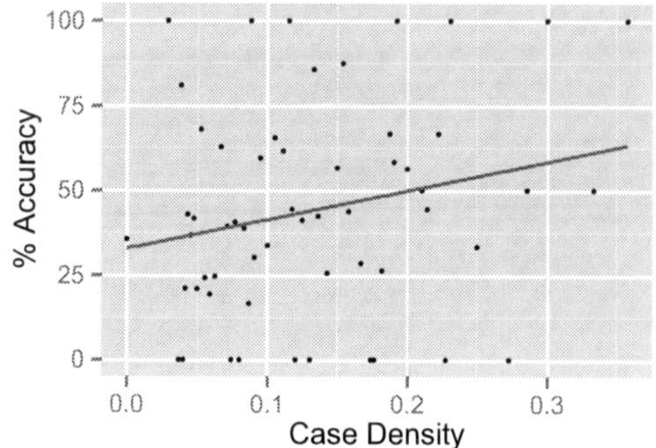

Figure 5: Classification accuracy as a function of sentence length on the full context set. While there is a clear correlation between sentence length and accuracy, there are several outliers. Compare to Figure 1.

Figure 6: Classification accuracy as a function of case density on the incremental sentences. The accuracy is correlated with case density, but the data are extremely noisy. Full-context accuracy has a similar trend (not shown).

accuracy does improve as more of the sentence is revealed (Figure 4), indicating that the algorithm learns to use these features to rank verbs, though the performance significantly lags that of both the human participants and our later experiments. Additionally, on the **full context set**, sentence length is negatively correlated with accuracy (Figure 5), as in the much more convincing results of our human experiments (Figure 1), though the trend is not entirely consistent, making it difficult to draw firm conclusions. Case density is again positively correlated with accuracy on both the random (Figure 6) and full context sets.

An Illustrative Example   To gain some insight into how features can influence the classifier, we here examine an example of the classifier's behavior on the multiple choice data.

(5) 少年時代-は　　　　　熊本藩-の
childhood days-TOP Kumamoto domain-GEN

藩校-で　　　　　　儒学-を
clan school-LOC   Confucianism-ACC

学び、　　　　　　後-に
study:MED   subsequently-LOC

西本願寺-において　　修行-に
Nishihongan Temple-LOC discipline-ALL

(6) (a) 励ん-だ
strive-PAST

(b) 創刊-さ-れ-る
issue-do-PASS-NPST

(c) 加え-られ-てい-る
add-PASS-CONT-NPST

(d) 勤め-る
serve-NPST

In Example (5), the classifier incorrectly chooses "issue" as the verb until observing the accusative case marker attached to "Confucianism". At this point, the classifier's confidence in the correct answer rises to 0.74—and correctly chooses "strive". This answer goes unchanged for the remainder of the sentence, though "study" attaches to "Confucianism", not the final verb. The combined evidence, however, is enough for the classifier to select correctly, and indeed, most of the following tokens only increase the classifier's confidence. Adding "subsequently" increases confidence to 0.84, an intuitive increase given the likely tense information contained in such a word. The somewhat redundant case marker here only increases confidence to 0.86. Adding the reference to the temple decreases confidence again to 0.79. But adding the **final case marker**, which also forms a new bigram with the previous word, results in a huge increase in confidence, to 0.90.

3.2 Multiclass Verb Prediction

While the multiple choice experiment was more open-ended (predicting random verbs), we now focus on a more constrained task: how well can we predict the most frequent verbs. This is the central conceit of Grissom II et al. (2014): if you can do a good job of this, you can improve simultaneous translation. They show a slight improvement in simultaneous translation by using n-gram language model-based verb prediction. We show a large improvement over their approach to verb prediction using a discriminative multiclass logistic classifier (Langford et al., 2007).

Data Preparation Our classes for multiclass classification are the fifty most common verbs in the KFT (Japanese, as in the human study) and Wortschatz corpora (Biemann et al., 2007, German).

We use data from the training and test sets of the KFT Japanese corpus of Wikipedia articles and a random split of the German Wortschatz web corpus, from which we extract the verb-final sentences. Grissom II et al. (2014) use an n-gram model to distinguish between the fifty most common German verbs for SOV-SVO simultaneous machine translation, which we replicate as our baseline. Following this study, we train a model on the fifty most common verbs in the training set.

In Japanese, due to the small size of the standard test set, we split the data randomly, training on 60,926 verb-final sentences ending in the top fifty verbs and testing on 1,932. Our total feature count is 4,649,055. We use the MeCab (Kudo, 2005) morphological analyzer for segmentation and verb identification. We consider only verb-final sentences. We skip semantically vacuous post-verbal copulas when identifying final verbs.

Finding Verbs We identify verbs in the German text with a part-of-speech tagger (Toutanova et al., 2003) and select from the top fifty verbs. We consider the sentence-ending set of verbs to be the final verbs. We train on 76,209 verb-final sentences ending in the top fifty verbs and test on 9,386. In German, to approximate the case information that we extract in Japanese, we test the inclusion of equivalent unigram and bigram features for German **articles**, the surface forms of which determine the case of the next noun phrase.

In Japanese, we omit some special cases of light verbs that combine with other verbs, as well as ambiguous surface forms and copulas.[8]

Features All features are encoded as binary features indicating their presence or absence. For Japanese, we again include **case unigrams**, and **case bigrams**, which encode as distinct features the for case markers observed thus far.[9] We also include a feature for the **last observed case marker**. For both Japanese and German, we normalize the verbs to the non-past, plain form, both providing more training data for each verb and simplifying the job of our classifier.

German case is conveyed primarily through articles and pronouns, so we include special features for articles. For example, for the sentence "Es wurde ihnen von einem alten Freund geholfen", we add the features ART_es_ihnen and ART_ihnen_einem to convey case information beyond individual words and bigrams.

Individual tokens are also used as binary features, as well as token bigrams.

An Example for Every Word In a simultaneous interpretation, a person or algorithm receives a constant stream of words, and each new word provides new information that can aid in prediction. Previous predictive approaches to simultaneous machine interpretation have taken this approach, and we also use it here: as each new word is observed, we make a prediction. This is a generalization of *random* presentation of prefixes in the human study.

3.3 Classification Results and Discussion

Better at the End A discriminative classifier does better than an n-gram classifier, which has a tendency to over-predict frequent verbs. By the end of the sentence, accuracy reaches 39.9% for German (Figure 7) and 29.9% Japanese (Figure 8), greatly exceeding choosing the most frequent class baseline of 3.7% (German) and 6.05% (Japanese). The n-gram language model also outperforms this baseline, but not by much. It also improves over the course of the sentence, but the model cannot reliably predict more than a handful of verbs in either language.

---

copula *de aru*. Distinguishing between all of these cases is beyond the scope of this study; so, they are excluded. We also omit duplicates that are spelled differently (i.e., the same word but spelled without Chinese (*kanji*) characters and slightly different forms of the same root).

We also omit the light verb *naru* ("to become" or "to make up") for similar reasons to *suru*. The increasing trend shown in the results does not change with their inclusion.

[9]For instance, given a sentence fragment X-に Y-を, representing X-DAT Y-ACC, the case bigram would be に∧を.

[8]In Japanese, we omit some ambiguous cases and variants of "is" and "do": excluded are variants of *suru* ("to do"), which combines with nouns to form new verbs, *aru* ("is", inanimate case), and *iru* ("is", animate case). The tokens *aru* and *iru* also combine with other verbs to change tense and aspect, in which case they are not verbs, and can form the

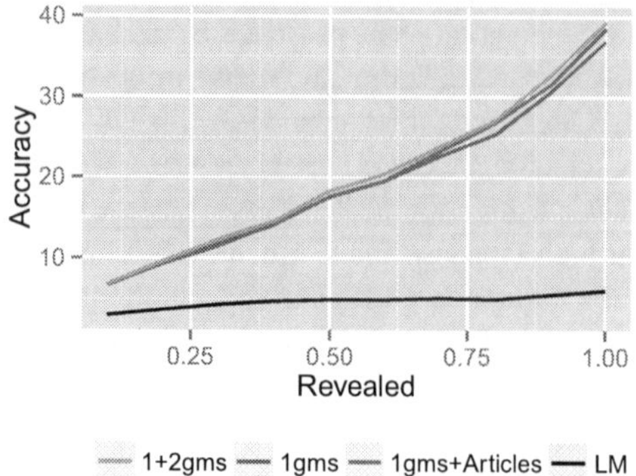

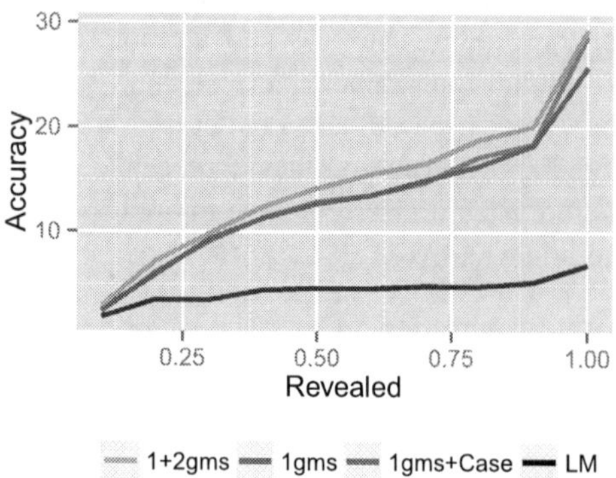

Figure 7: German average prediction accuracy over the course of sentences. Bigrams help slightly in the second half of the sentence. Adding special features for case-assigning articles to unigrams nearly matches the performance of adding all bigrams in the final 10%. All handily outperform the trigram language model.

Figure 8: Japanese average prediction accuracy over the course of sentences. Adding bigrams consistently outperforms unigrams alone in Japanese, possibly due to the agglutinative nature of the language. The accuracies diverge the most toward the end of the sentences: Adding only explicit case markers to unigrams nearly matches performance of adding all bigrams toward the end. All outperform the trigram language model.

Richer Features Help (Mostly at the End)   Bigram features help both languages, but Japanese more than German; beyond bigrams, however, trigrams and longer features overfit the training data and hurt performance. The better performance for Japanese bigrams is likely because word boundaries are not well-defined in Japanese, and individual morphemes can combine in ways that significantly add information. German word boundaries are more precise and words (particularly nouns) can carry substantial information themselves.

Richer features matter more toward the end of the sentence. In Japanese, adding bigrams consistently outperforms unigrams alone, but in both languages, adding special features for tokens with case information helps almost as much as adding the full set of bigrams. In Japanese, case markings always immediately follow the words marked, and in German the articles precede the nouns to which they assign case; thus, rather than relying on isolated unigrams, using bigrams provides opportunities to encode case-marked words that more narrowly select for verbs. In Japanese, the differences are more pronounced toward the very end of the sentences (and less so in German).

Richer features help more at the end, but not merely because the last words of the sentence represent the densest feature vectors. In Japanese, the last word is usually a case-marked noun phrase or adverb that matches the main predicate. The final word is therefore immune to subclause interference and must modify the final verb, boosting the classifier performance in these final positions and amplifying the predictive discrepancies between the various feature sets. Accuracy spikes at the end of Japanese sentences, where case information helps nearly as much as adding the entire set of bigrams, further supporting case information's importance. Deeper processing—e.g., separating case-marked words in subclauses from those in the main clause—would likely be more useful. Features and feature-selection strategies that we tried which did not help included the following: adding only case marker unigrams (instead of bigrams); filtering the features by using only case-marked words; only allowing one word per case marker in the feature vector (the most recent); using decaying weights on features further in the past; adding part-of-speech tag n-grams; and adding the word nearest to the centroid of the observed context in a word embedding space. While these features may have potential, they did not lead to meaningful increases in accuracy in our experiments.

4   Related Work

While to our knowledge our work is the first in-depth study of incremental verb prediction, it is not the first study of verb prediction in humans or machines. This section reviews that related work.

Human Verb Prediction   Prediction is easier with more context and explicit case markings. Teramura (1987) shows that *next word prediction* in Japanese improves as more words are incrementally revealed. While only looking at verb prediction given the *complete* preceding context, Yamashita (1997) finds that scrambling word order in Japanese—a case rich language that allows such scrambling—does not harm final verb prediction, but that explicit case marking helps final verb prediction. Our results show that this is true even for incremental verb prediction. Levy and Keller (2013) also find that dative markers aid German verb prediction.

Neurolinguistic measurements by Friederici and Frisch (2000) suggest processing verb-final clauses in German use both semantic and syntactic information, but that they are processed differently. In Japanese, Koso et al. (2011) measure the effect of case markings on predicting verbs with strong case preferences. This is consistent with our use of case-based features and suggests that further gains are possible using richer syntactic representations. Chow et al. (2015) use N400 measurements to investigate two competing hypotheses for the initial prediction of an upcoming verb: whether predictions are dependent on all words equally (the Bag-of-words hypothesis), or alternatively, whether prediction is selectively modulated by the final verb's arguments (the Bag-of-arguments hypothesis). They argue for the latter.

The literature on incremental verb prediction is sparse. A key finding of Matsubara et al. (2002) is that Japanese-English simultaneous interpreters, when given access to lecture slides, would refer to them to predict the next phrase.

Prediction for Simultaneous Machine Translation   The Verbmobil simultaneous translation system (Kay et al., 1992) uses deleted interpolation (Jelinek, 1990) to create a weighted n-gram models to predict dialogue acts—almost identical to predicting the next word (Reithinger et al., 1996). Konieczny and Döring (2003) predict verbs with a recurrent neural network, but Matsubara et al. (2000) was the first to use verb predictions as part of a simultaneous interpretation system. They use pattern matching-based predictions of English verbs. In contrast, Grissom II et al. (2014) use a statistical approach, using n-gram models to predict German verbs and particles (in Section 3 we show that this model predicts verbs poorly). However, their simultaneous translation system is able to learn when to trust these predictions. Oda et al. (2015) extend the idea of using prediction by predicting entire syntactic constituents for English-Japanese simultaneous machine translation. Both systems will likely benefit from our improved verb prediction presented here.

5   Conclusion

Verb prediction is hard for both machines and humans but impossible for neither. Verbs become more predictable in discriminative settings as more of the sentence is revealed, and when all of the prior context is available, the verbs are highly predictable by humans when a limited number of choices is available, though even then not perfectly so. While we make no claims concerning upper or lower bounds of predictability in different settings, our dataset provides benchmarks for future verb prediction research on publicly available corpora: cognitive scientists can validate prediction, confusion, and anticipation; engineers have a human benchmark for their systems; and linguists can conduct future experiments on predictability. Shallow features can be used to predict verbs more accurately with more context. Improving verb prediction can benefit simultaneous translations systems that have already shown to benefit from verb predictions, as well as enable new applications that involve predicting future linguistic input.

6   Acknowledgments

We would like to thank the anonymous reviewers for their comments. We thank Yusuke Miyao for his helpful support. We would also like to thank James H. Martin, Martha Palmer, Hal Daumé III, Mans Hulden, Mohit Iyyer, John Morgan, Shota Momma, Graham Neubig, and Shu Hoshino for their invaluable discussions and input. This work was supported by NSF grant IIS-1320538. Boyd-Graber is also partially supported by NSF grants CCF-1409287 and NCSE-1422492. Any opinions, findings, conclusions, or recommendations expressed here are those of the authors and do not necessarily reflect the view of the sponsor.

References

Chris Biemann, Gerhard Heyer, Uwe Quasthoff, and Matthias Richter. 2007. The Leipzig corpora collection-monolingual corpora of standard size. *Proceedings of Corpus Linguistics*.

Wing-Yee Chow, Cybelle Smith, Ellen Lau, and Colin Phillips. 2015. A "bag-of-arguments" mechanism for initial verb predictions. *Language, Cognition and Neuroscience*, pages 1–20.

Yasuhara Den and Masakatsu Inoue. 1997. Disambiguation with verb-predictability: Evidence from Japanese garden-path phenomena. In *Proceedings of the Cognitive Science Society*, pages 179–184. Lawrence Erlbaum.

Angela D Friederici and Stefan Frisch. 2000. Verb argument structure processing: The role of verb-specific and argument-specific information. *Journal of Memory and Language*, 43(3):476–507.

Alvin C. Grissom II, He He, Jordan Boyd-Graber, John Morgan, and Hal Daumé III. 2014. Don't until the final verb wait: Reinforcement learning for simultaneous machine translation. In *Empirical Methods in Natural Language Processing*.

John Hale. 2001. A probabilistic earley parser as a psycholinguistic model. In *Conference of the North American Chapter of the Association for Computational Linguistics*.

Fred Jelinek. 1990. Self-organized language modeling for speech recognition. *Readings in speech recognition*, pages 450–506.

Martin Kay, Peter Norvig, and Mark Gawron. 1992. *Verbmobil: A translation system for face-to-face dialog*. University of Chicago Press.

Lars Konieczny and Philipp Döring. 2003. Anticipation of clause-final heads: Evidence from eye-tracking and srns. In *Proceedings of iccs/ascs*.

Ayumi Koso, Shiro Ojima, and Hiroko Hagiwara. 2011. An event-related potential investigation of lexical pitch-accent processing in auditory Japanese. *Brain research*, 1385:217–228.

Taku Kudo. 2005. Mecab: Yet another part-of-speech and morphological analyzer. *http://mecab. source-forge. net/*.

Sadao Kurohashi and Makoto Nagao. 1994. Kn parser: Japanese dependency/case structure analyzer. In *Proceedings of the Workshop on Sharable Natural Language Resources*.

Marta Kutas, Katherine A DeLong, and Nathaniel J Smith. 2011. A look around at what lies ahead: prediction and predictability in language processing. *Predictions in the brain: Using our past to generate a future*, pages 190–207.

John Langford, Lihong Li, and Alex Strehl. 2007. Vowpal wabbit online learning project.

Roger P Levy and Frank Keller. 2013. Expectation and locality effects in german verb-final structures. *Journal of memory and language*, 68(2):199–222.

Shigeki Matsubara, Keiichi Iwashima, Nobuo Kawaguchi, Katsuhiko Toyama, and Yasuyoshi Inagaki. 2000. Simultaneous Japanese-English interpretation based on early predition of English verb. In *Symposium on Natural Language Processing*.

Shigeki Matsubara, Akira Takagi, Nobuo Kawaguchi, and Yasuyoshi Inagaki. 2002. Bilingual spoken monologue corpus for simultaneous machine interpretation research. In *LREC*.

Shota Momma, L Robert Slevc, and Colin Phillips. 2015. The timing of verb selection in japanese sentence production. *Journal of experimental psychology. Learning, memory, and cognition*.

Graham Neubig. 2011. The Kyoto free translation task. *Available online at http://www. phontron. com/kftt*.

Yusuke Oda, Graham Neubig, Sakriani Sakti, Tomoki Toda, and Satoshi Nakamura. 2015. Syntax-based simultaneous translation through prediction of unseen syntactic constituents. *Proceedings of the Association for Computational Linguistics*, June.

Norbert Reithinger, Ralf Engel, Michael Kipp, and Martin Klesen. 1996. Predicting dialogue acts for a speech-to-speech translation system. volume 2, pages 654–657. IEEE.

Claude Elwood Shannon. 1948. A mathematical theory of communication. *Bell Systems Technical Journal*, 27:379–423, 623–656.

Hideo Teramura. 1987. Kikitori ni okeru yosoku nouryoku to bunpouteki tisiki. *Nihongogaku*, 3;6:56–68.

Kristina Toutanova, Dan Klein, Christopher D Manning, and Yoram Singer. 2003. Feature-rich part-of-speech tagging with a cyclic dependency network. In *Conference of the North American Chapter of the Association for Computational Linguistics*, pages 173–180.

Hiroko Yamashita. 1997. The effects of word-order and case marking information on the processing of Japanese. *Journal of Psycholinguistic Research*, 26(2):163–188.

Hiroko Yamashita. 2000. Structural computation and the role of morphological markings in the processing of japanese. *Language and speech*, 43(4):429–455.

A Data-driven Investigation of Corrective Feedback on Subject Omission Errors in First Language Acquisition

Sarah Hiller and **Raquel Fernández**
Institute for Logic, Language & Computation
University of Amsterdam
sarah.hiller@posteo.de | raquel.fernandez@uva.nl

Abstract

We investigate implicit corrections in the form of contrastive discourse in child-adult interaction, which have been argued to contribute to language learning. In contrast to previous work in psycholinguistics, we adopt a data-driven methodology, using comparably large amounts of data and leveraging computational methods. We conduct a corpus study on the use of parental corrective feedback and show that its presence in child directed speech is associated with a reduction of child subject omission errors in English.

1 Introduction

It is widely agreed that children learn how to use language through interaction with their caregivers and peers. There is, however, a long-standing discussion concerning the exact nature of the learning mechanism enabling this. For example, while there is no doubt that children are exposed to *positive input* (i.e., grammatically correct utterances in context), it is an open question whether they also receive *negative input*—evidence about the inadequacy of their erroneous utterances.

What seems clear is that explicit disapprovals are very rarely used to correct grammatical mistakes, as already shown by Brown and Hanlon (1970). However, certain contrastive constructions may provide negative input in an implicit way. For instance, in the following exchange between 2-year-old Lara and her father, from the corpus by Rowland and Fletcher (2006), the father picks up the child's erroneous utterance in the following turn and presents a form with the appropriate preposition:

(1) CHI: I climb up daddy .
    DAD: you did climb over daddy .

The contrast between the two forms is particularly noticeable and could potentially lead the child to recognise and correct their own error. It has thus been argued that this type of construction presents children with negative evidence and, unlike explicit corrections, it does so in the course of conversation, without disrupting the dialogue flow.

Researchers have used different terms to refer to this phenomenon, including *recast* (Brown, 1973), *reformulation* (Chouinard and Clark, 2003), *embedded correction* (Clark, 2003), and *corrective input* (Saxton, 2000). In this paper, we adopt the term *corrective feedback* (CF), which we will define precisely in Section 3, and analyse its effect on first language learning—in particular on retreating from subject omission errors in English. In contrast to previous work in psycholinguistics, we investigate these questions in a data-driven manner, using comparably large amounts of data from the CHILDES Database (MacWhinney, 2000a) and developing computational methods to support linguistically motivated studies. More concretely, we make the following contributions:

- We present a taxonomy of child error types that can receive CF and an annotation scheme for coding instances of CF.

- We report the results of a corpus study showing that subject omission errors make up the largest proportion of errors met with CF.

- We develop classifiers to automatically detect subject omission errors and CF on those errors, training on the manually annotated data.

- Using automatically processed data, we investigate the impact of CF on learning subject inclusion in English with a series of linear regression models, showing that CF has predictive power over a variety of control factors. Our results indicate that the effects of CF are most noticeable after a period of about 9 months.

Proceedings of the 20th SIGNLL Conference on Computational Natural Language Learning (CoNLL), pages 105–114,
Berlin, Germany, August 7-12, 2016. ©2016 Association for Computational Linguistics

2 Related Work

Adult repetitions of child speech with different degrees of variation are a hallmark of child-adult dialogue. As mentioned before, this kind of phenomenon is often referred to as *recast*, and was first studied by Brown and Bellugi (1964). Brown and Hanlon (1970) were the first to suggest that recasts had corrective potential and thus "could be instructive". Since then, several studies have pointed out that contrastive discourse of this kind is very common (e.g., Demetras et al. (1986), Strapp (1999), Chouinard and Clark (2003), Saxton et al. (2005)). There is however no full agreement regarding what motivates the production of corrective feedback. According to Chouinard and Clark (2003), reformulations follow from general cooperative principles: Since children's contributions are often difficult to comprehend due to their limited linguistic abilities, adults explicitly check up on their intended meaning by rephrasing the child's utterance. In contrast, for Saxton et al. (2005), most often corrective feedback does not arise from semantic uncertainty but rather "it is only the linguistic *form* that the adult might take issue with". In any case, researchers generally agree that it is unlikely that adults consciously recast child speech, despite doing it very frequently.

The fact that negative input is available, however, does not immediately mean that it contributes to language development. Some small-scale studies have indeed found an association between corrective feedback and language growth (e.g., Newport et al. (1977), Nelson et al. (1984), Eadie et al. (2002), i.a.). Chouinard and Clark (2003) investigated children's immediate responses to parental reformulations for 5 children and found that acknowledgements and repeats by the child were very frequent. This indicates that children attend to their parent's corrective input and can immediately revert to the correct form. However, it is less clear whether this has a long-term effect. In this respect, Saxton et al. (2005) recorded interactions between 12 mother-child pairs at two time periods with a lag of 12 weeks and found that reformulations had a positive effect on the correct use of 3 out of 13 investigated grammatical structures after this time lag.

Despite the existing evidence, teasing apart the effect of corrective feedback from all other sources of input available to the child is not an easy matter empirically, which explains why the influence of corrective feedback on learning remains controversial (Tomasello, 2009). Here we aim to shed some light on this debate by investigating this phenomenon using much more data than ever before, taking advantage of NLP techniques.

3 Corrective Feedback

We start by defining what we mean by corrective feedback (CF) and by providing a taxonomy of errors in child language that CF can target.

3.1 Definition of corrective feedback

An utterance by the child followed by an utterance by an adult constitutes an instance of corrective feedback if all the following constraints are met:

(C1) The child's utterance contains a grammatical anomaly.

(C2) There is some degree of overlap between the adult and child utterances: the adult's response is anchored to the child utterance through at least one exactly matching word.

(C3) The adult utterance is not a mere repetition of the child's, i.e., there is some contrast.

(C4) This contrast offers a correct counterpart of the child's erroneous form.

While this definition does not make any claims regarding the intentions of the adult nor the possible uptake by the child, which may be considered a simplification, arguably it can be operationalised in a corpus study, which is our main goal here.

3.2 Taxonomy of errors

Now that we have a general definition of the phenomenon, we can proceed towards a more fine-grained classification of types of CF. Mainly, the exchanges can be discriminated via the kind of error in the child utterance and via the kind of correction employed by the adult. Here we focus on the type of error observable in the child utterance, restricting ourselves to grammatical errors, i.e., syntactic and morphological.[1] We differentiate between the linguistic *level* at which the error occurs and the *type* of error observed. For *level*, we follow Saxton et al. (2005) in distinguishing four main classes sub-divided into a total of 13 categories. Regarding *type*, inspired by Sokolov (1993) we distinguish between *omissions, additions,* and *substitutions*:[2]

---

[1] We do not consider phonological and lexical errors as they are not easily identifiable in a transcribed corpus.

[2] Note that Sokolov (1993) uses these terms to characterise the way in which parental utterances diverge from child utter-

- Error Level:
  - *Syntactic:* subject, object, verb[3]
  - *Noun morphology:* possessive, regular plural, irregular plural
  - *Verb morphology:* 3rd person singular, regular past, irregular past
  - *Unbound morphology:* determiner, preposition, auxiliary, present progressive
- Error Type:
  - *Omission, Addition, Substitution*

The following examples illustrate some of the categories above:

(2) a. *synt: subject, omission*
    CHI: don't want to .
    MOT: you don't want to ?

   b. *v. morph: irregular past, substitution*
    CHI: he falled out and bumped his head .
    MOT: he fell out and bumped his head .

   c. *u. morph: auxiliary, addition*
    CHI: I'm read it .
    DAD: you read it to mummy .

4 Dataset

Selection. Our dataset consists of a selection of files from the English language section of the CHILDES Database (MacWhinney, 2000a) including all transcripts of conversations between adults and unimpaired, naturally developing children that contain a minimum of 50 utterances by the child and 100 utterances in total, and where the mean length of utterance (MLU; in words) of the child is at least 2. This ensures that the child is already at a stage where grammatical constructions are starting to be used. Finally, since we are conducting a longitudinal study, in order to make sure there is enough data per child we consider only transcripts of children for which there is data over at least one year, with a file density of at least 5 transcripts per year and a minimum of 10 transcripts overall per child.

The resulting dataset contains a total number of 1,683 transcripts from 25 different children, with 1,598,838 utterances overall. The average child age at the time of the first transcribed conversation lays around 2 years, with very little variation. The mean difference between the child's age in the first and the last gathered transcript varies considerably

	Total	Avg. per child
transcripts	1,683	67.32
utterances	1,598,838	63,953.52
candidate CF pairs	136,152	5,446.08

Table 1: Overview of our dataset containing longitudinal data from 25 different children.

more across children, but overall also lies around 2 years.[4]

Preprocessing. Most of the transcripts in the dataset already include part-of-speech tagging, morphological analysis, and dependency parsing. We used the CLAN toolbox (MacWhinney, 2000b) and the MEGRASP dependency parser (Sagae et al., 2007) to add POS tags and to morphologically and syntactically parse the transcripts where this information was not available. We also automatically coded each adult response to a child utterance with information on overlap using the CHIP programme (Sokolov and MacWhinney, 1990), also part of the CLAN toolbox. CHIP provides information on added ($ADD), deleted ($DEL), and exactly matching ($EXA) morphemes in the source and response utterances, as well as the proportion of morphemes in the response utterance which match exactly morphemes in the source ($REP). Figure 1 shows a sample child-adult exchange with all the layers of information computed during the preprocessing stage.[5]

Selection of candidate CF utterance pairs. In order to investigate the effect of CF on language learning, we need to quantify the CF exchanges present in the corpus. That is, we need to find mechanisms for automatically detecting these. We use the overlap information to extract candidate instances of CF. In line with constraints (C2) and (C3) in our definition, we consider candidate instances all child-adult utterance pairs with a percentage of repetition $0 < \$REP < 1$, where the overlap is not exclusively due to stopwords.[6] We also require that the child's utterance contains a minimum of two distinct words so that there is scope for a grammatical anomaly (C1).

An overview of the dataset in shown in Table 1.

---

ances, while we use them to characterise the type of error in a child utterance.

[3]We deviate from Saxton et al. (2005) slightly here by considering any main verb including copulas, rather than only copulative verbs as they do.

[4]Further details are given in the supplementary material available at http://tinyurl.com/cf-conll2016.

[5]The **manual annotation** layer in Figure 1 is discussed in the next section.

[6]The list of stopwords was empirically derived by taking the function words amongst the 100 most frequent words in the dataset. See the supplementary material for the full list.

CHI: I climb up daddy .

– POS & morph	`%mor: pro.sub|I v|climb prep|up n|daddy`
– dependency	`%gra: 1|2|SUBJ 2|0|ROOT 3|2|JCT 4|3|POBJ`

DAD: you did climb over daddy .

– POS & morph	`%mor: pro|you v|do.PAST v|climb prep|over n|daddy`
– dependency	`%gra: 1|2|SUBJ 2|0|ROOT 3|2|OBJ 4|3|JCT 5|4|POBJ`
– overlap	`%adu: $EXA:climb $EXA:daddy $ADD:you did $ADD:over $DEL:i $DEL:up $REP=0.40`
manual annotation	`%cof: $CF $ERR=umorph:prep; $TYP=subst`

Figure 1: Sample child-adult utterance pair with information layers automatically added during preprocessing, plus a Corrective Feedback layer manually annotated with the decision tree in Figure 2.

5   Corpus Study

The simple heuristic used to extract candidate instances of CF fares very well on recall, but it is of course not very precise: a large quantity of candidate utterance pairs are not instances of CF since (C1) and (C4) in our definition (Section 3.1) are not fully accounted for. We therefore manually annotated a subset of the data to have a reliable basis for analysis and to use as training data for an automatic classifier. For this annotation task, we selected a subset of data that was representative of the entire dataset. We randomly picked four children in the dataset and selected between four and six files per child that covered a minimum period of one year and did not diverge by more than 20 utterances from the average transcript length in the overall dataset. This makes up 25,191 utterances in total (of which 9,783 are child utterances).[7]

We run our heuristic for extracting candidate CF utterance pairs, which resulted in a total of 2,627 pairs of child-adult utterances to be annotated. Of these, 350 instances were annotated by two coders to test the reliability of the annotation. The annotation scheme used distinguishes between CF and non-CF pairs. It subsequently uses the taxonomy of corrective feedback presented in Section 3.2 to indicate the kind of error picked up by the parent in those pairs coded as CF. If several child errors are implicitly corrected in a single CF response, all of them are included in the annotation. Figure 2 shows a simplified version of the decision tree used by the annotators. Inter-annotator agreement was measured with Cohen's *kappa* and was reasonably high ($\kappa = 0.77$). The annotators discussed cases of disagreement and arrived at a consensus label for the fi-

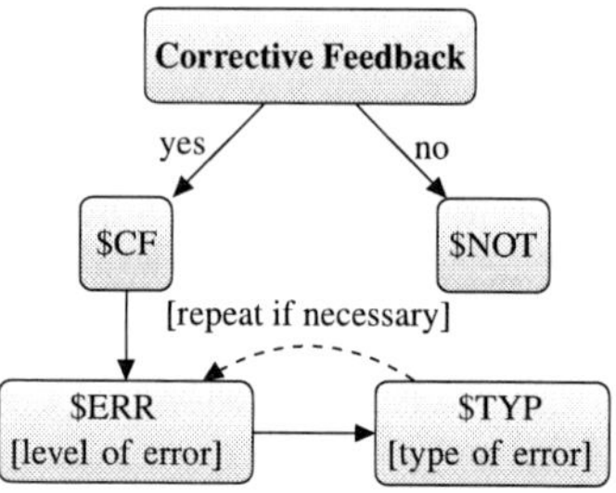

Figure 2: Decision tree for the annotation task.

nal annotation. The annotated dataset as well as the complete annotation guidelines are available at `http://tinyurl.com/cf-conll2016`.

Table 2 shows the results of the corpus study. Out of 2,627 candidate utterance pairs, 580 where coded as instances of CF. Most of the errors that receive corrective feedback are omissions. This should not necessarily be interpreted as omissions receiving a higher proportion of CF over other error types, but rather as a consequence of omission errors being predominant at this stage of development (Saxton et al., 2005). In particular, most instances of CF (30.8%) occur as a response to subject omission errors (SOEs); an example can be found in excerpt (2a), Section 3.2. In the remainder of the paper we thus focus on this type of error.

Figure 3 shows how the amount of CF received by the children (averaging over all types of errors) changes over time. Not surprisingly, corrective feedback has a clear tendency to decrease as children develop and make fewer errors. An exception amongst the four children targeted for the corpus study is the case of Emily, who has considerably higher MLU than the other three children at 2.5 years of age (MLU of 5 words vs. 4 for Lara and Trevor and 3 for Thomas) and is therefore more proficient, thus offering fewer opportunities for corrections.

---

[7]See the supplementary material for more details on the selected files.

	Om	*Add*	*Sub*	**Total**
Syntax				
subject	171	–	1	172
verb	90	1	–	91
object	13	–	–	13
N morph				
poss -'s	4	1	–	5
regular pl	–	3	–	3
irregular pl	–	–	3	3
V morph				
3rd person	4	–	–	4
regular past	10	1	–	11
irregular past	1	–	4	5
Unb. morph				
det	79	–	6	85
prep	21	1	12	34
aux verb	114	5	1	120
progressive	9	0	0	9
Other	4	2	19	25
Total	520	14	46	580

Table 2: Types of errors in exchanges coded as CF.

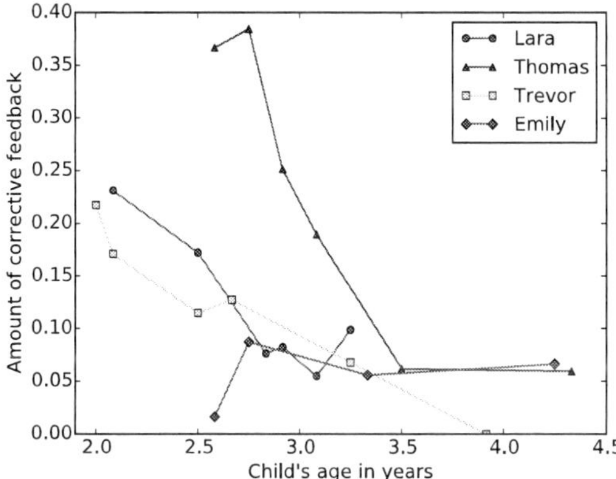

Figure 3: Amount of CF exchanges against child's age. Pearson's $r=-0.90$ (Lara), $r=-0.88$ (Thomas), $r=-0.97$ (Trevor), and $r-\ +0.32$ (Emily)

6 Automatic Detection

Our corpus study has provided insight on the types of errors that are met with CF, showing that subject omission errors (SOEs) make up the largest proportion. Our aim is to investigate the extent to which CF on SOEs plays a part in overcoming such errors during language acquisition. A large-scale data-driven investigation, however, requires the development of methods for the automatic extraction of these phenomena. We therefore use the manually annotated data to develop automatic extraction procedures to detect SOEs and CF on SOEs in order to extend our analysis to the entire dataset, beyond the manually annotated data.

For extracting SOEs, a rule-based algorithm was used, while for the more complex task of de-tecting CF on SOEs we trained a Support Vector Machine. Overall, we are interested in high-precision classifiers: Given our aims, it is preferable to have a conservative but reasonably accurate estimate of amount of error and of presence of corrective feedback in order to avoid unreliable boosting of the possible effect of CF on learning.

6.1 Subject omission errors

To construct a base set for developing a SOE classifier, we coded part of the annotated subset for the presence or absence of subject omission errors (recall that the original annotation only indicated the error type when this was present and received corrective feedback). The resulting base set contains 453 utterances, of which 206 are positive instances and 247 are negative instances of SOEs. This data was randomly split into a training set and a test set, roughly corresponding to 90% and 10% of the data, respectively.

We used the training set to derive a set of simple features that were combined in a non-probabilistic rule-based algorithm classifying utterances as SOE or non-SOE. Feature tuning was done by qualitative analysis of classification errors in a 5-fold cross-validation setting. Our baseline consisted in classifying all child utterances with no SUBJ node in the dependency parse tree as positive instances of SOE. This already achieves an F1-score of 0.82, with 0.74 precision and 0.93 recall. To improve precision while not lowering recall too dramatically, we experimented with additional features aimed at accounting for parsing errors. The algorithm that produced the highest precision results first considers utterances with no SUBJ node (baseline feature) or erroneously parsed utterances where the SUBJ tag is assigned to an implausible word such as a negation particle. It assigns them the positive class (SOE) if additionally the first word in the utterance is not a noun and the subject is not overlooked in the dependency parse due to a missing verb (captured by checking whether the ROOT node is assigned to a proper name). All instances that do not meet these constraints are classified as non-SOE.[8]

This classifier resulted in a precision of 0.83 on both training and test sets, and a recall of 0.86 on the training set and of 0.8 on the test set.

---

[8]The algorithm is spelled out in pseudocode in the supplementary material.

6.2 CF on subject omission errors

Given a child utterance with a SOE, the CF-SOE classifier is intended to detect whether or not the parental response contains corrective feedback for this type of error. Using the SOE detector described above, we extracted 514 utterance pairs where the child utterance exhibits a SOE. Manual inspection showed that this base set contains 250 positive instances and 264 negative instances of CF on SOEs. Again, we randomly split off the data into a training and a test set, corresponding to approx. 90% and 10% of the data, respectively.

To capture the interaction between the child and adult utterance needed for this classification proved to be harder than extracting the simple features representative of a SOE. For this task, we used the SVM implementation provided with the Python scikit-learn module (Pedregosa et al., 2011). Again, features were selected via qualitative analysis of wrongly classified instances in a 5-fold cross-validation setting over the training set. The final set of features used includes the presence of a SUBJ node in the dependency parse of the adult utterance, and exact matches in ROOT nodes (typically verbs) or OBJ nodes in the child and adult utterances.[9] In order to boost precision, we tuned the parameters of the SVM by giving a higher error-score to misclassifications of non-CF instances, while making sure the F-score did not fall below 0.5. The final class weights were 3:1 for the non-CF vs. CF class.

Overall, precision of the selected classifier reached 0.89 and recall 0.36 on the test set, compared to a majority class baseline of 0.49 for both values. Given the importance of precision for our aims, this classifier was preferred over a more balanced one.

7 CF and Language Learning

In this section, we investigate whether the presence of corrective feedback on subject omission errors contributes to the reduction of such errors in children's speech and thus has an impact on language acquisition.

7.1 Overview of the experimental design

Our experiments are designed as follows: We estimate the amount of SOEs at a particular period

of time (defined in terms of child age in months) as the proportion of child utterances that contain a SOE. We compute the amount of SOEs at two different time periods, t_0 and a later time t_1. We then calculate the *relative error reduction* (rer) as the proportion of SOEs at t_0 that has been overcome at t_1:

$$\texttt{rer}(t_0, t_1) = \frac{SOE_{t_0} - SOE_{t_1}}{SOE_{t_0}} \qquad [1]$$

Our aim is to investigate the relationship between *relative error reduction* (rer) of SOEs at t_1 and the presence of corrective feedback on SOEs at t_0. The latter is calculated as the number of instances of CF on SOE at t_0 divided by the total number of child SOEs at t_0. We consider all possible instantiations of t_0 and t_1 per child in the corpus, with a minimum time distance of one month between the two. This allows us to investigate at what age CF seems more effective (different t_0 values) and how much time is needed for its effect to be noticeable on learning (distance between t_0 and t_1).

We construct several linear regression models, where $\texttt{rer}(t_0, t_1)$ is always the dependent variable we are interested in predicting and CF at t_0 is the independent variable whose predictive power we are investigating, while controlling for several other factors characterising child directed speech and children's own speech.

7.2 Setup details

Data. We apply the SOE and the CF-SOE high-precision detectors presented in Section 5 and trained on manually annotated data to the entire dataset (summarised in Table 1). This allows us to quantify the amount of SOE and CF on SOE a child receives at a given age. Overall, we detected 287,309 cases of child SOEs and 31,080 cases of CF on a SOE.

Control variables. To study the effects of CF we control for other features that may also contribute to predicting relative error reduction. We consider factors representative of the general language development exhibited by the child as well as of the quality and quantity of the input. To be precise, we consider the following factors:

(a) child age in months (age);

(b) mean length of utterance of child speech and of child directed speech (chi.mlu/cds.mlu);

(c) vocabulary size of child speech and of child directed speech (chi.vocab/cds.vocab);

---

[9]The complete list of features passed to the SVM, together with an explanation of what they represent, can be found in the supplementary material.

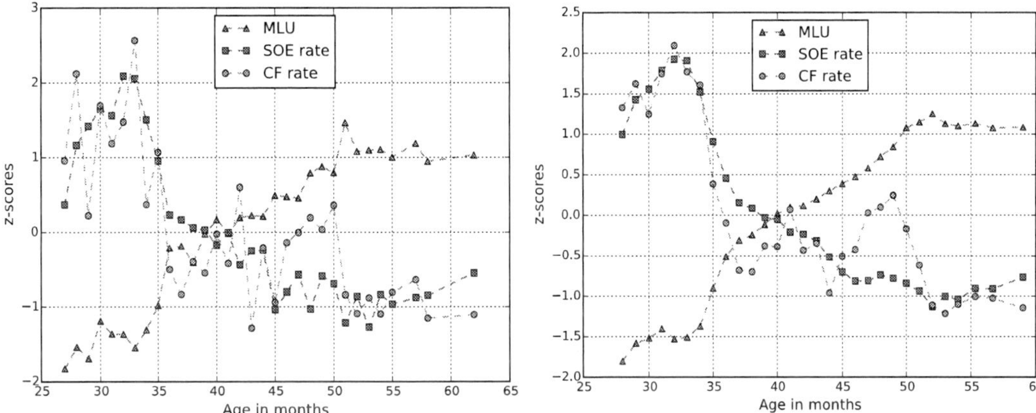

Figure 4: Development of child MLU, proportion of SOE and CF frequency (in standardised z scores) for Adam in the Brown corpus, when measured by month (left) and after smoothing (right).

(d) proportion of child SOEs (`chi.soe`);

(e) proportion of child directed utterances with subject omissions (`cds.so`);

(f) proportion of words uttered by the child over all words uttered in the child-adult interactions (`chi.speech`).[10]

All factors are computed at t_0, except for vocabulary size, which corresponds to the vocabulary of all transcripts available for a given child up to t_0. Note that we also encode how often adults produce utterances without an explicit subject (e), which does of course happen relatively often in spontaneous conversation (Fernández and Ginzburg, 2002). All of these features are expected to influence the degree to which a child learns subject inclusion in English. Our goal is to test to what extent (if at all) CF on SOEs has a positive influence on learning independently of these factors.

Feature computation. There is substantial variation amongst children in the corpus regarding the density and the length of transcripts. Therefore, to estimate the values of the variables above as well as amount of CF and `rer` at a given age, in months, t_i, we employ an averaging procedure over possibly several transcripts. This procedure consists first of all in averaging over all available transcripts in the same month. The resulting estimate for relatively steady measures such as MLU still shows a considerable fluctuation. We thus employ

a smoothing procedure by averaging again over three consecutive available months t_{i-1}, t_i, t_{i+1}. Figure 4 illustrates the effect of such smoothing procedure for some of the variables.

7.3 Analysis and results

We first consider the entire dataset as a whole, taking all possible pairs (t_0, t_1) for the 25 children in the corpus (N= 2613). We observe that CF correlates positively with $\text{rer}(t_0, t_1)$ (Pearson's r=0.29, p<0.001); that is, the more corrective feedback at any given time t_0, the more error reduction at later times in development. A linear regression model controlling for the additional factors listed above shows that CF explains a significant proportion of the variance in relative error reduction of SOEs independently from all other factors.

Table 3 shows the standardised regression coefficients for the predictors considered, representing the change in $\text{rer}(t_0, t_1)$ associated with a change of 1 in the given predictor when all other factors are held constant. Note that since in this setting neither t_0 nor t_1 are fixed, we can include age at these two time periods as independent predictors in the model.

While this analysis shows that CF on SOEs contributes to predicting error reduction, it does not provide any information regarding the developmental period at which corrective feedback may be more effective or the time lapse required for learning to take place. The following analyses aim at offering insight on these aspects.

To investigate the time lag required for CF to have an impact on `rer`, we fix the distance be-

---

[10]Given the nature of the CHILDES corpus (with unequal frequency and length of transcripts per child), it is not possible to properly estimate the amount of input received; we can only quantify the proportion of child speech vs. child directed speech.

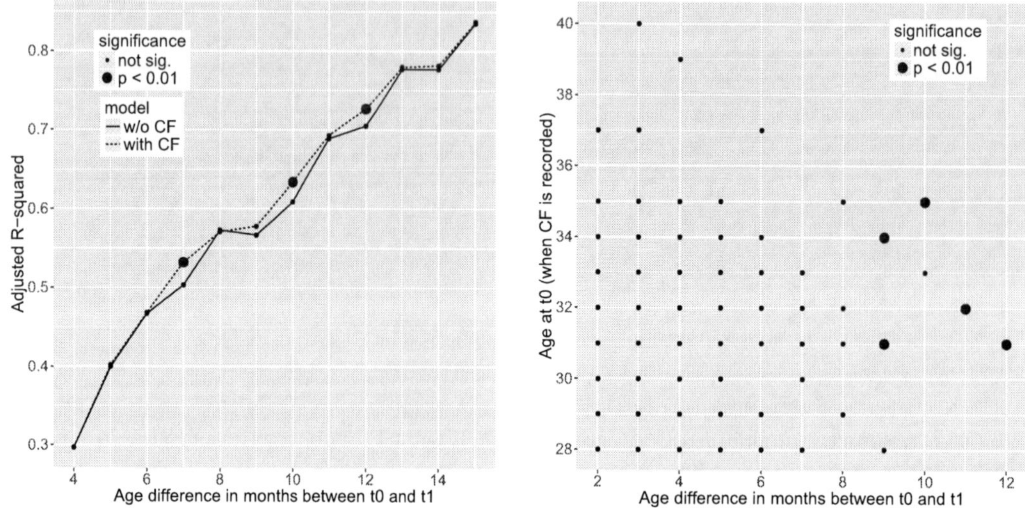

Figure 5: Impact of CF on SOE reduction after different time lags (left) and after different time lags for a fixed age at t_0 (right).

age.t0	-0.586 ***	age.t1	0.474 ***
chi.soe	0.843 ***	cds.so	0.101 **
chi.mlu	0.365 ***	cds.mlu	0.217 ***
chi.vocab	0.479 ***	cds.vocab	-0.450 ***
chi.speech	0.853 ***	cf.soe	0.123 ***

Table 3: Beta coefficients for linear regression model; *** $p<0.001$, ** $p<0.01$. Overall variance in `rer` captured by the model (adjusted R^2): 0.53.

tween t_0 and t_1 and construct two different linear regression models for each distance value, a model with all control factors without CF (and without age at t_1 as it is dependent on age at t_0 in this setting) and a model where CF is included. This allows us to test whether CF makes a significant contribution in accounting for the variance in `rer`, independently of the control factors. We should note that for each distance value (and thus for each pair of models) there are fewer datapoints than in the previous analysis, as not all distance values are available for all children in the corpus. The average number of datapoints per model is N=186.6 (sd=57.3). Figure 5 (left) shows the adjusted R^2 values for the pairs of models for a range of time spans between t_0 and t_1. As can be seen, CF has a significant effect after a time lapse of 7 to 12 months.

Finally, to investigate not only the time lapse but also the age at which CF may be more effective, we construct linear regression models with fix values for both (i) the difference between t_0 and t_1

and (ii) age at t_0. Again, the number of available datapoints drops substantially with this additional constraint; we consider only settings for which there are at least 10 datapoints (t_0 from 28 to 35 months). The results are shown in Figure 5 (right), where the larger dots indicate that the model that incorporates CF on top of the control factors has significantly more predictive power to explain the variance in `rer`.[11] We can see that the effect of CF is noticeable after a time lapse of 9 months (consistently with the previous analysis) and that this holds for any starting age t_0 for which there is available data. This is consistent with the results of Saxton et al. (2005), who did not find an effect of CF on this error type after a lag of only 3 months (the only time lag studied by these authors). Our results show that indeed, for SOEs, the learning effects are cumulative and can only be statistically appreciated at a later stage.

The results plotted in Figure 5 (left) may seem to indicate that after a lag of over 12 months this learning effect disappears, since we observe no significant difference between the two models (with and without CF). However, we believe that this is an artefact of the dataset. In our dataset a larger time lag between t_0 and t_1 coincides with a relatively advanced age at t_1: on average, children are 47 to 49 months old at t_1 for differences of 13 to 15 months between t_0 and t_1. The fre-

<hr>

[11] Since the experiments reported in Figure 5 involve multiple statistical comparisons (thus increasing the chance of Type I errors), we use a stricter significance threshold (0.01) than the standard 0.05.

quency of subject omissions observed in the child speech converges towards a non-zero limit with increasing child age (a limit akin to the amount of subject omissions in child directed speech). Thus, predicting the relative error reduction when given the frequency of SOE at t_0 becomes easy at advanced child ages, with or without including CF as a predictor. The observed increase of adjusted R^2 scores as age distance becomes larger seems to support this hypothesis.

8 Conclusions

We have investigated the impact of corrective feedback on first language acquisition, in particular on the reduction of subject omission errors in English—a type of error which we found to be the most commonly met with CF in our corpus study. In contrast to previous small-scale studies in psycholinguistics, we have addressed this problem using a comparatively large data-driven setting. We have used machine learning methods trained on manually annotated data and then applied statistical modelling to the automatically extracted instances of CF on SOEs. The annotated dataset is publicly available at `http://tinyurl.com/cf-conll2016`.

Our results have shown that CF contributes to predict learning independently of other factors characterising the input received by the child and the child level of development. In our dataset, this is noticeable after a time lag of approximately 9 months. This suggests that CF does have an impact on long-term learning and not only on immediate responses by the child, as observed in other analyses with a few children (e.g., Chouinard and Clark (2003)). Of course, our results need to be interpreted with prudence, since the automatic classifiers for detecting SOEs and CF on SOEs in the whole dataset are far from perfect. Nevertheless, since we opted for high-precision classifiers, the results may in fact be a low estimate of the effect of CF on learning grammar.

Acknowledgments

We are grateful to the anonymous reviewers for their comments, as well as to Stella Frank and Willem Zuidema, who provided useful feedback on an earlier version of this work. This research has received funding from the Netherlands Organisation for Scientific Research (NWO) under VIDI grant nr. 276-89-008, *Asymmetry in Conversation*.

References

Roger Brown and Ursula Bellugi. 1964. Three processes in the child's acquisition of syntax. *Harvard educational review*, 34(2):133–151.

Roger Brown and Camille Hanlon. 1970. Derivational complexity and order of acquisition in child speech. In John R. Hayes, editor, *Cognition and the Development of Language*. John Wiley & Sons, Inc.

Roger Brown. 1973. *A first language: The early stages*. Harvard U. Press.

Michelle M. Chouinard and Eve V. Clark. 2003. Adult reformulations of child errors as negative evidence. *Journal of Child Language*, 30(3):637–670.

Eve V. Clark. 2003. *First language acquisition*. CUP.

Marty J. Demetras, K. Nolan Post, and C. E. Snow. 1986. Feedback to first language learners: The role of repetitions and clarification questions. *Journal of Child Language*, 13(02):275–292.

Patricia A. Eadie, M. E. Fey, J. M. Douglas, and C. L. Parsons. 2002. Profiles of grammatical morphology and sentence imitation in children with specific language impairment and down syndrome. *Journal of Speech, Language, and Hearing Research*, 45(4):720–732.

Raquel Fernández and Jonathan Ginzburg. 2002. Non-sentential utterances in dialogue: A corpus study. In *Proceedings of the Third SIGdial Workshop on Discourse and Dialogue*, pages 15–26, Philadelphia, USA. Association for Computational Linguistics.

Brian MacWhinney. 2000a. *The CHILDES Project: Tools for analyzing talk.*, volume 2: The Database. Lawrence Erlbaum Associates, 3 edition.

Brian MacWhinney. 2000b. *The CHILDES Project: Tools for analyzing talk.*, volume 1, Part 2. the CLAN Programs. Lawrence Erlbaum Associates, 3 edition.

Keith E. Nelson, M. M. Denninger, J. D. Bonvillian, B. J. Kaplan, and N. D. Baker. 1984. Maternal input adjustments and non-adjustments as related to children's linguistic advances and to language acquisition theories. In *The development of oral and written language in social contexts*, volume 13, pages 31–56. Ablex Norwood, NJ.

Elissa L. Newport, H. Gleitman, and L. R. Gleitman. 1977. Mother, I'd rather do it myself: Some effects and noneffects of maternal speech style. In *Talking to children*, pages 109–49. Cambridge U. Press.

Fabian Pedregosa, G. Varoquaux, A. Gramfort, V. Michel, B. Thirion, O. Grisel, M. Blondel, P. Prettenhofer, R. Weiss, V. Dubourg, J. Vanderplas, A. Passos, D. Cournapeau, M. Brucher, M. Perrot, and E. Duchesnay. 2011. Scikit-learn: Machine learning in Python. *Journal of Machine Learning Research*, 12:2825–2830.

Caroline F. Rowland and Sarah L. Fletcher. 2006. The effect of sampling on estimates of lexical specificity and error rates. *Journal of Child Language*, 33(4):859–877, November.

Kenji Sagae, E. Davis, A. Lavie, B. MacWhinney, and S. Wintner. 2007. High-accuracy annotation and parsing of CHILDES transcripts. In *Proceedings of the ACL-2007 Workshop on Cognitive Aspects of Computational Language Acquisition*, Prague, Czech Republic.

Matthew Saxton, P. Backley, and C. Gallaway. 2005. Negative input for grammatical errors: Effects after a lag of 12 weeks. *Journal of Child Language*, 32(03):643 – 672.

Matthew Saxton. 2000. Negative evidence and negative feedback: Immediate effects on the grammaticality of child speech. *First Language*, 20(60):221.

Jeffrey L. Sokolov and Brian MacWhinney. 1990. The CHIP framework: Automatic coding and analysis of parent-child conversational interaction. *Behaviour Research Methods, Instruments and Computers*, 22(2):151 – 161.

Jeffrey L. Sokolov. 1993. A local contingency analysis of the fine-tuning hypothesis. *Developmental Psychology*, 29(6):1008 – 1023.

Chehalis M. Strapp. 1999. Mothers', fathers', and siblings' responses to children's language errors: Comparing sources of negative evidence. *Journal of Child Language*, 26(02):373–391.

Michael Tomasello. 2009. The usage-based theory of language acquisition. In *The Cambridge handbook of child language*, pages 69–87. Cambridge Univ. Press.

Redefining part-of-speech classes with distributional semantic models

Andrey Kutuzov
Department of Informatics
University of Oslo
andreku@ifi.uio.no

Erik Velldal
Department of Informatics
University of Oslo
erikve@ifi.uio.no

Lilja Øvrelid
Department of Informatics
University of Oslo
liljao@ifi.uio.no

Abstract

This paper studies how word embeddings trained on the British National Corpus interact with part of speech boundaries. Our work targets the Universal PoS tag set, which is currently actively being used for annotation of a range of languages. We experiment with training classifiers for predicting PoS tags for words based on their embeddings. The results show that the information about PoS affiliation contained in the distributional vectors allows us to discover groups of words with distributional patterns that differ from other words of the same part of speech.

This data often reveals hidden inconsistencies of the annotation process or guidelines. At the same time, it supports the notion of 'soft' or 'graded' part of speech affiliations. Finally, we show that information about PoS is distributed among dozens of vector components, not limited to only one or two features.

1 Introduction

Parts of speech (PoS) are useful abstractions, but still abstractions. Boundaries between them in natural languages are flexible. Sometimes, large open classes of words are situated on the verge between several parts of speech: for example, participles in English are in many respects both verbs and adjectives. In other cases, closed word classes 'intersect', e.g., it is often difficult to tell a determiner from a possessive pronoun. As Houston (1985) puts it, '*Grammatical categories exist along a continuum which does not exhibit sharp boundaries between the categories*'.

When annotating natural language texts for parts of speech, the choice of a PoS tag in many ways depends on the human annotators themselves, but also on the quality of linguistic conventions behind the division into different word classes. That is why there have been several attempts to refine the definitions of parts of speech and to make them more empirically grounded, based on corpora of real texts: see, among others, the seminal work of Biber et al. (1999). The aim of such attempts is to identify clusters of words occurring naturally and corresponding to what we usually call 'parts of speech'. One of the main distance metrics that can be used in detecting such clusters is a distance between distributional features of words (their contexts in a reference training corpus).

In this paper, we test this approach using predictive models developed in the field of distributional semantics. Recent achievements in training distributional models of language using machine learning allow for robust representations of natural language semantics created in a completely unsupervised way, using only large corpora of raw text. Relations between dense word vectors (embeddings) in the resulting vector space are as a rule used for semantic purposes. But can they be employed to discover something new about grammar and syntax, particularly parts of speech? Do learned embeddings help here? Below we show that such models do contain a lot of interesting data related to PoS classes.

The rest of the paper is organized as follows. In Section 2 we briefly cover the previous work on the subject of parts of speech and distributional models. Section 3 describes data processing and the training of a PoS predictor based on word embeddings. In Section 4 errors of this predictor are analyzed and insights gained from them described. Section 5 introduces an attempt to build a full-fledged PoS tagger within the same approach. It also analyzes the correspondence between partic-

115

Proceedings of the 20th SIGNLL Conference on Computational Natural Language Learning (CoNLL), pages 115–125,
Berlin, Germany, August 7-12, 2016. ©2016 Association for Computational Linguistics

ular word embedding components and PoS affiliation, before we conclude in Section 6.

2   Related work

Traditionally, 3 types of criteria are used to distinguish different parts of speech: *formal* (or morphological), *syntactic* (or distributional) and *semantic* (Aarts and McMahon, 2008). Arguably,
syntactic and semantic criteria are not very different from each other, if one follows the famous distributional hypothesis stating that meaning is determined by context (Firth, 1957). Below we show
that unsupervised distributional semantic models
contain data related to parts of speech.

For several years already it has been known
that some information about morphological word
classes is indeed stored in distributional models.
Words belonging to different parts of speech possess different contexts: in English, articles are typically followed by nouns, verbs are typically accompanied by adverbs and so on. It means that
during the training stage, words of one PoS should
theoretically cluster together or at least their embeddings should retain some similarity allowing
for their separation from words belonging to other
parts of speech. Recently, among others, Tsuboi
(2014) and Plank et al. (2016) have demonstrated
how word embeddings can improve supervised
PoS-tagging.

Mikolov et al. (2013b) showed that there also
exist regular relations between words from different classes: the vector of '*Brazil*' is related to
'*Brazilian*' in the same way as '*England*' is related to '*English*' and so on. Later, Liu et al.
(2016) demonstrated how words of the same part
of speech cluster into distinct groups in a distributional model, and Tsvetkov et al. (2015) proved
that dimensions of distributional models are correlated with different linguistic features, releasing
an evaluation dataset based on this.

Various types of distributional information has
also played an important role in previous work
done on the related problem of unsupervised PoS
acquisition. As discussed in Christodoulopoulos et al. (2010), we can separate at least three
main directions within this line of work: *Disambiguation* approaches (Merialdo, 1994; Toutanova
and Johnson, 2007; Ravi and Knight, 2009) that
start out from a dictionary providing possible tags
for different words; *prototype-driven* approaches
(Haghighi and Klein, 2006; Christodoulopoulos

et al., 2010) based on a small number of prototypical examples for each PoS; *induction* approaches that are completely unsupervised and
make no use of prior knowledge. This is also the
main focus of the comparative survey provided by
(Christodoulopoulos et al., 2010).

Work on PoS induction has a long history – including the use of distributional methods – going
back at least to Schütze (1995), and recent work
has demonstrated that word embeddings can be
useful for this task as well (Yatbaz et al., 2012;
Lin et al., 2015; Ling et al., 2015a).

In terms of positioning this study relative to previous work, it falls somewhere in between the distinctions made above. It is perhaps closest to disambiguation approaches, but it is not unsupervised
given that we make use of existing tag annotations
when training our embeddings and predictors. The
goal is also different; rather than performing PoS
acquisition or tagging for its own sake, the main
focus here is on analyzing the boundaries of different PoS classes. In Section 5, this analysis is
complemented by experiments with using word
embeddings for PoS prediction on unlabeled data,
and here our approach can perhaps be seen as related to previous so-called prototype-driven approaches, but in these experiments we also make
use of labeled data when defining our prototypes.

It seems clear that one can infer data about
PoS classes of words from distributional models in
general, including embedding models. As a next
step then, these models could also prove useful
for deeper analysis of part of speech boundaries,
leading to discovery of separate words or whole
classes that tend to behave in non-typical ways.
Discovering such cases is one possible way to improve the performance of existing automatic PoS
taggers (Manning, 2011). These 'outliers' may
signal the necessity to revise the annotation strategy or classification system in general. Section 3
describes the process of constructing typical PoS
clusters and detecting words that belong to a cluster different from their traditional annotation.

3   PoS clusters in distributional models

Our hypothesis is that for the majority of words
their parts of speech can be inferred from their embeddings in a distributional model. This inference
can be considered a classification problem: we are
to train an algorithm that takes a word vector as input and outputs its part of speech. If the word em-

beddings do contain PoS-related data, the properly trained classifier will correctly predict PoS tags for the majority of words: it means that these lexical entities conform to a dominant distributional pattern of their part of speech class. At the same time, the words for which the classifier outputs *incorrect* predictions, are expected to be 'outliers', with distributional patterns different from other words in the same class. These cases are the points of linguistic interest, and in the rest of the paper we mostly concentrate on them.

To test the initial hypothesis, we used the XML Edition of British National Corpus (BNC), a balanced and representative corpus of English language of about 98 million word tokens in size. As stated in the corpus documentation, *'it was [PoS-]tagged automatically, using the CLAWS4 automatic tagger developed by Roger Garside at Lancaster, and a second program, known as Template Tagger, developed by Mike Pacey and Steve Fligelstone'* (Burnard, 2007). The corpus authors report a precision of 0.96 and recall of 0.99 for their tools, based on a manually checked sample. For this research, it is important that BNC is an established and well-studied corpus of English with PoS-tags and lemmas assigned to all words.

We produced a version of BNC where all the words were replaced with their lemmas and PoS-tags converted into the Universal Part-of-Speech Tagset (Petrov et al., 2012)[1]. Thus, each token was represented as a concatenation of its lemma and PoS tag (for example, *'love_VERB'* and *'love_NOUN'* yield different word types). The mappings between BNC tags and Universal tags were created by us and released online[2].

The main motivation for the use of the Universal PoS tag set was that this is a newly emerging standard which is actively being used for annotation of a range of different languages through the community-driven Universal Dependencies effort (Nivre et al., 2016). Additionally, this tag set is coarser than the original BNC one: it simplifies the workflow and eliminates the necessity to merge 'inflectional' tags into one (e.g., singular and plural nouns into one 'noun' class). This conforms with our interest in parts of speech proper, not inflectional forms within one PoS. We worked with the following 16 Universal tags: **ADJ, ADP, ADV, AUX, CONJ, DET, INTJ, NOUN, NUM,**

PART, PRON, PROPN, SCONJ, SYM, VERB, X (punctuation tokens marked with the PUNCT tag were excluded).

Then, a *Continuous Skipgram* embedding model (Mikolov et al., 2013a) was trained on this corpus, using a vector size of 300, 10 negative samples, a symmetric window of 2 words, no down-sampling, and 5 iterations over the training data. Words with corpus frequency less than 5 were ignored. This model represents the semantics of the words it contains. But at the same time, for each word, a PoS tag is known (from the BNC annotation). It means that is is possible to test how good the word embeddings are in grouping words according to their parts of speech.

To this end, we extracted vectors for the 10 000 most frequent words from the resulting model (roughly, these are the words with corpus frequency more than 500). Then, these vectors were used to train a simple logistic regression multinomial classifier aimed to predict the word's part of speech.

It is important that we applied classification, not clustering here. Naive *K-Means* clustering of word embeddings in our model into 16 groups showed very poor performance (adjusted Rand index of 0.52 and adjusted Mutual Information score of 0.61 in comparison to the original BNC tags). This is because PoS-related features form only a part of embeddings, and in the fully unsupervised setting, the words tend to cluster into semantic groups rather than 'syntactic' ones. But when we train a classifier, it locates exactly the features (or combinations of features) that correspond to parts of speech, and uses them subsequently.

Note that during training (and subsequent testing), each word's vector was used several times, proportional to frequency of the word in the corpus, so the classifier was trained on 177 343 (sometimes repeating) instances, instead of the original 10 000. This was done to alleviate classification bias due to class imbalance: There are much fewer word types in the closed PoS classes (pronouns, conjunctions, etc.) than in the open ones (nouns, verbs, etc.), so without considering word frequency, the model does not have a chance to learn good predictors for 'small' classes and ends up never predicting them. At the same time, words from closed classes occur very frequently in the running text, so after 'weighting' training instances by corpus frequency, the balance is re-

---

[1]We used the latest version of the tagset available at http://universaldependencies.org

[2]http://bit.ly/291BlpZ

stored and the classifier model has enough training instances to learn to predict closed PoS classes as well. As an additional benefit, by this modification we make frequent words from all classes more 'influential' in training the classifier.

The resulting classifier showed a weighted macro-averaged F-score (over all PoS classes) and accuracy equal to 0.98, with 10-fold cross-validation on the training set.

This is a significant improvement over the *one-feature* baseline classifier (classify using only one vector dimension with maximum F-value in relation to class tags), with F-score equal to only 0.22. Thus, the results support the hypothesis that word embeddings contain information that allows us to group words together based on their parts of speech. At the same time, we see that this information is not restricted to some particular vector component: rather, it is distributed among several axis of the vector space. After training the classifier, we were able to use it to detect 'outlying' words in the BNC (judging by the distributional model). So as not to experiment on the same data we had trained our classifier on, we compiled another test set of 17 000 vectors for words with the BNC frequencies between 100 and 500. They were weighted by word frequencies in the same way as the training set, and the resulting test set contained 30 710 instances. Compared to the training error reported above we naturally observe a drop in performance when predicting PoS for this unseen data, but the classifier still appears quite robust, yielding an F-score of 0.91. However, some of the drop is also due to the fact that we are applying the classifier to words with lower frequency, and hence we have somewhat less training data for the input embeddings.

Furthermore, to make sure that the results can potentially be extended to other texts, we applied the trained classifier to all lemmas from the human-annotated Universal Dependencies English Treebank (Silveira et al., 2014). The words not present in the distributional model were omitted (they sum to 27% of word types and 10% of word tokens). The classifier showed an F-Score equal to 0.99, further demonstrating the robustness of the classifier. Note, however, that part of this performance is because the UD Treebank contains many words from the classifier training set. Essentially, it means that the decisions of the UD human annotators are highly consistent with the dis-

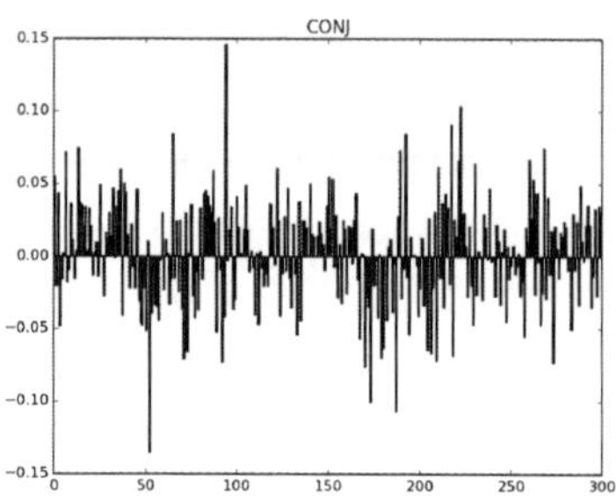

Figure 1. Centroid embedding for coordinating conjunctions

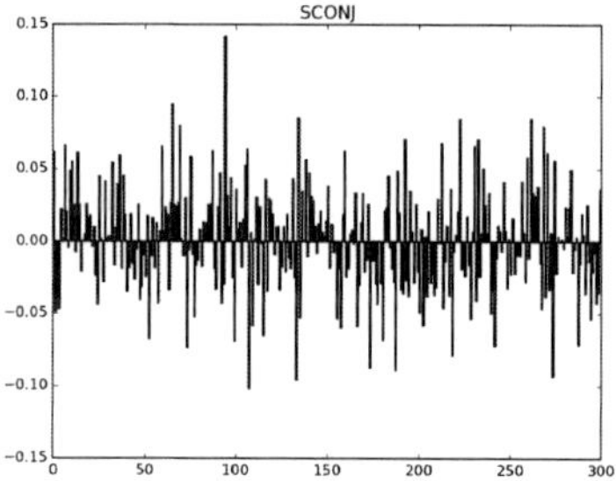

Figure 2. Centroid embedding for subordinating conjunctions

tributional patterns of words in the BNC. In sum, the vast majority of words are classified correctly, which means that their embeddings enable the detection of their parts of speech. In fact, one can visualize 'centroid' vectors for each PoS by simply averaging vectors of words belonging to this part of speech. We did this for 10 000 words from our training set.

Plots for centroid vectors of coordinating and subordinating conjunctions are shown in Figures 1 and 2 respectively. Even visually one can notice a very strongly expressed feature near the '100' mark in the horizontal axis (component number 94). In fact, this is indeed an idiosyncratic feature of conjunctions: none of the other parts of speech shows such a property. More details about what vector components are relevant to part of speech affiliation are given in Section 5.

Additionally, with centroid PoS vectors we can find out how similar different parts of speech are to each other, by simply measuring cosine similarity between them. If we rank PoS pairs according to their similarity (Table 1), what we see is that nominative parts of speech are close to each other, determiners and pronouns are also similar, as well as

Table 1. Distributional similarity between parts of speech (fragment)

Cosine similarity	PoS pair
0.81	NOUN ADJ
0.77	ADV PRON
0.73	DET PRON
0.73	ADV ADJ
...	...
...	...
0.37	INTJ NUM
0.36	AUX NUM

Table 2. Most frequent PoS misclassifications of the distributional predictor. The # column lists the number of word types.

#	Actual PoS	Predicted PoS
347	PROPN	NOUN
313	ADJ	NOUN
190	NOUN	ADJ
91	NOUN	PROPN
87	PROPN	ADJ
57	VERB	ADJ
55	NOUN	NUM
52	NUM	NOUN
45	NUM	PROPN
28	ADV	PROPN
25	ADV	NOUN
25	ADJ	PROPN
20	ADV	ADJ

prepositions and subordinating conjunctions; quite in accordance with linguistic intuition. Proper nouns are not very similar to common nouns, with cosine similarity between them only 0.67 (even adverbs are closer). Arguably, this is explained by co-occurrences together with the definite article, and as we show below, this helps the model to successfully separate the former from the latter.

Despite generally good performance of the classifier, if we look at our BNC test set, 1741 word types (about 10% of the whole test set vocabulary) were still classified incorrectly. Thus, they are somehow dissimilar to 'prototypical' words of their parts of speech. These are the 'outliers' we were after. We analyze the patterns found among them in the next section.

4 Not from this crowd: analyzing outliers

First, we filtered out misclassified word types with 'X' BNC annotation (they are mostly foreign words or typos). This leaves us with 1558 words for which the classifier assigned part of speech tags different from the ones in the BNC. It probably means that these words' distributional patterns differ somehow from what is more typically observed, and that they tend to exhibit behavior similar to another part of speech. Table 2 shows the most frequent misclassification cases, together accounting for more than 85% of errors.

Additionally, we ranked misclassification cases by 'part of speech coverage', that is by the ratio of the words belonging to a particular PoS for which our classifier outputs this particular type of misclassification. For example, proper nouns misclassified as common nouns constitute the most numerous error type in Table 2, but in fact only 9% of all proper nouns in the test set were misclassified in this way. There are parts of speech with a much larger portion of word-types predicted erroneously: e.g., 22% of subordinate conjunctions were classified as adverbs. Table 3 lists error types with the highest coverage (we excluded error types with absolute frequency equal to 1, as it is impossible to speculate on solitary cases).

We now describe some of the interesting cases. Almost 30% of error types (judging by absolute amount of misclassified words) consist of proper nouns predicted to be common ones and vice versa. These cases do not tell us anything new, as it is obvious that distributionally these two classes of words are very similar, take the same syntactic contexts and hardly can be considered different parts of speech at all. At the same time, it is interesting that the majority of proper nouns in the test set (88%) was correctly predicted as such. It means that in spite of contextual similarity, the distributional model has managed to extract features typical for proper names. Errors mostly cover comparatively rare names, such as 'luftwaffe', 'stasi', 'stonehenge', or 'himalayas'. Our guess is that the model was just not presented with enough contexts for these words to learn meaningful representations. Also, they are mostly not personal names but toponyms or organization names, probably occurring together with the definite article *the*, unlike personal names.

Another 30% of errors are due to vague boundaries between nominal and adjectival distribution patterns in English: nouns can be modified by both (it seems that cases where a proper noun is mistaken for an adjective are often caused by the same factor). Words like '*materialist_NOUN*', '*starboard_NOUN*' or '*hypertext_NOUN*' are tagged as nouns in the BNC, but they often modify other nouns, and their contexts are so 'adjectival' that the distributional model actually assigned them semantic features highly similar to those of adjectives. Vice versa, '*white-collar_ADJ*' (an adjective in BNC) is regarded as a noun from the point of view of our model. Indeed, there can be contradicting views on the correct part of speech for this word in phrases like '*and all the other white-collar workers*'. Thus, in this case the distributional model highlights the already known similarity between two word classes.

The cases of verbs mistaken for adjectives seem to be caused mostly by passive participles ('*was overgrown*', '*is indented*', ''), which intuitively are indeed very adjective-like. So, this gives us a set of verbs dominantly (or almost exclusively, like '*to intertwine*' or '*to disillusion*') used in passive. Of course, we will hardly announce such verbs to be adjectives based on that evidence, but at least we can be sure that this sub-class of verbs is clearly semantically and distributionally different from other verbs.

The next numerous type of errors consists of common nouns predicted to be numerals. A quick glance at the data reveals that 90% of these 'nouns' are in fact currency amounts and percentages ('*£70*', '*33%*', '*$1*', etc). It seems reasonable to classify these as numerals, even though they contain some kind of nominative entities inside. Judging by the decisions of the classifier, their contexts do not differ much from those of simple numbers, and their semantics is similar. The Universal Dependencies Treebank is more consistent in this respect: it separates entities like '*1$*' into two tokens: a numeral (NUM) and a symbol (SYM). Consequently, when our classifier was tested on the words from the UD Treebank, there was only one occurrence of this type of error.

Related to this is the inverse case of numerals predicted to be common or proper nouns. It is interesting that this error type also ranks quite high in terms of coverage: If we combine numerals predicted to be common and proper nouns, we will see that 17% of all numerals in the test set were subject to this error. The majority of these

Table 3. Coverage of misclassifications with distributional predictor, i.e., ratio of errors over all word types of a given PoS. The absolute type count is given by #.

Coverage	Actual PoS	Predicted PoS	#
0.22	SCONJ	ADV	2
0.17	INTJ	PROPN	8
0.11	ADP	ADJ	3
0.09	ADJ	NOUN	313
0.09	PROPN	NOUN	347
0.09	NUM	NOUN	52
0.08	NUM	PROPN	45

'numerals' are years ('*1804*', '*1776*', '*1822*') and decades ('*1820s*', '*60s*' and even '*twelfths*'). Intuitively, such entities do indeed function as nouns ('*I'd like to return to the sixties*'). Anyway, it is difficult to invent a persuasive reason for why '*fifty pounds*' should be tagged as a noun, but '*the year 1776*' as a numeral. So, this points to possible (minor) inconsistencies in the annotation strategy of the BNC. Note that a similar problem exists in the Penn Treebank as well (Manning, 2011).

Adverbs classified as nouns (53 words in total for both common and proper nouns) are possibly the ones often followed by verbs or appearing in company of adjectives (examples are '*ultra*' and '*kinda*'). This made the model treat them as close to the nominative classes. Interestingly, most 'adverbs' predicted to be proper nouns are time indicators ('*7pm*', '*11am*'); this also raises questions about what adverbial features are really present in these entities. Once again, unlike the BNC, the UD Treebank does not tag them as adverbs.

The cases we described above revealed some inconsistencies in the BNC annotation. However, it seems that with adverbs mistaken for adjectives, we actually found a systematic error in the BNC tagging: these cases are mostly connected to adjectives like '*plain*', '*clear*' or '*sharp*' (including comparative and superlative forms) erroneously tagged in the corpus as adverbs. These cases are not rare: just the three adjectives we mentioned alone appear in the BNC about 600 times with an adverb tag, mostly in clauses of the kind '*the author makes it plain that...*', so-called small clauses (Aarts, 2012). Sometimes these tokens are tagged as ambiguous, and the adjective tag is there as a second variant; however, the corpus documentation states that in such cases the first variant is always more likely. Thus, distributional models can actually detect outright errors in PoS-tagged corpora, when incorrectly tagged words strongly tend to cluster with another part of speech. In the UD treebank such examples can also be observed, but they are much fewer and more 'adverbial', like '*it goes **clear** through*'.

Turning to Table 3, most of the entries were already covered above, except the first 3 cases. These relate to closed word classes (functional words), which is why the absolute number of influenced word types is low, but the coverage (ratio of all words of this PoS) is quite high.

First, out of 9 distinct subordinate conjunctions in the test set, 2 were predicted to be adverbs. This is not surprising, as these words are '*seeing*' and '*immediately*'. For '*seeing*' the prediction seems to be just a random guess (the prediction confidence was as low as 0.3), but with '*immediately*' the classifier was actually more correct than the BNC tagger (the prediction confidence was about 0.5). In BNC, these words are mostly tagged as subordinate conjunctions in cases when they occur sentence-initially ('***Immediately**, she lowered the gun*'). The other words marked as SCONJ in the test set are really such, and the classifier made correct predictions matching the BNC tags.

Interjections mistaken for proper names do not seem very interpretable (examples are '*gee*', '*oy*' and '*farewell*'). At the same time, 3 prepositions predicted to be adjectives clearly form a separate group: they are '*cross*', '*pre*' and '*pro*'. They are not often used as separate words, but when they are ('*Did anyone encounter any trouble from Hibs fans in Edinburgh **pre** season?*'), they are very close to adjectives or adverbs, so the predictions of the distributional classifier once again suggest shifting parts of speech boundaries a bit.

Error analysis on the vocabulary from the Universal Dependencies Treebank showed pretty much the same results, except for some differences already mentioned above.

There exists another way to retrieve this kind of data: to process tagged data with a conventional PoS tagger and analyze the resulting confusion matrix. We tested this approach by processing the whole BNC with the Stanford PoS Tagger (Toutanova et al., 2003). Note that as an input to the tagger we used not the whole sentences from the corpora, but separate tokens, to mimic our

Table 4. Most frequent PoS misclassifications with the Stanford tagger (counting word types).

#	Actual	Predicted
172675	NNP	NN
47202	VB	NN
40218	JJ	NN
24075	NN	JJ
9723	JJ	VB

workflow with the distributional predictor. Prior to this, BNC tags were converted to the Penn Treebank tagset[3] to match the output of the tagger. As we are interested in coarse, 'overarching' word classes, inflectional forms were merged into one tag. That was easy to accomplish by dropping all characters of the tags after the first two (excluding proper noun tags, which were all converted to NNP).

Analysis of the confusion matrix (cases where the tag predicted by the Stanford tagger was different from the BNC tag) revealed the most frequent error types shown in Table 4. Despite similar top positions of errors types '*proper noun predicted as common noun*' and '*nouns and adjectives mistaken for each other*', there are also very frequent errors of types '*verb to noun*' and '*adjective to verb*', not observed in the distributional confusion matrix (Table 2). We would not be able to draw the same insights that we did from the distributional confusion matrix: the case with verbs mistaken for adjective is ranked only 12th, adverbs mistaken for nouns - 13th, etc.

Table 5 shows top misclassification types by their word type coverage. Once again, interesting cases we discovered with the distributional confusion matrix (like subordinating conjunctions mistaken for adverbs and prepositions mistaken for adjectives) did not show up. Obviously, a lot of other insights can be extracted from the Stanford Tagger errors (as has been shown in previous work), but it seems that employing a distributional predictor reveals different error cases and thus is useful in evaluating the sanity of tag sets.

To sum up, the analysis of 'boundary cases' detected by a classifier trained on distributional vectors, indeed reveals sub-classes of words lying on the verge between different parts of speech. It also allows for quickly discovering systematic errors or

---

[3] https://www.cis.upenn.edu/~treebank/

Table 5. Coverage of misclassifications (from all word types of this PoS) with the Stanford tagger.

Coverage	Actual	Predicted	#
0.91	NNP	NN	172675
0.8	UH	NN	576
0.79	DT	NN	217
0.78	EX	JJ	11
0.78	PR	NN	517

inconsistencies in PoS annotations, whether they be automatic or manual. Thus, discussions about PoS boundaries would benefit from taking this kind of data into consideration.

5 Embeddings as PoS predictors

In the experiment described in the previous section, we used a model trained on words concatenated with their PoS tags. Thus, our 'classifier' was a bit artificial in that it required a word plus a tag as an input, and then its output is a judgment about what tag is most applicable to this combination from the point of view of the BNC distributional patterns. This was not a problem for us, as our aim was exactly to discover lexical outliers.

But is it possible to construct a proper predictor in the same way, which is able to predict a PoS tag for a word without any pre-existing tags as hints? Preliminary experiments seem to indicate that it is.

We trained a *Continuous Skipgram* distributional model on the BNC lemmas without PoS tags. After that, we constructed a vocabulary of all unambiguous lemmas from the UD Treebank training set. 'Unambiguous' here means that the lemma either was always tagged with one and the same PoS tag in the Treebank, or has one 'dominant' tag, with frequencies of other PoS assignments not exceeding 1/2 of the dominant assignment frequency. Our hypothesis was that these words are prototypical examples of their PoS classes, with corresponding prototypical features most pronounced; this approach is conceptually similar to (Haghighi and Klein, 2006). We also removed words with frequency less than 10 in the Treebank. This left us with 1564 words from all Universal Tag classes (excluding PUNCT, X and SYM, as we hardly want to predict punctuation or symbol tag).

Then the same simple logistic regression classifier was trained on the distributional vectors from the model for these 1564 words only, using UD Treebank tags as class labels (the training instances were again weighted proportionally to the words' frequencies in the Treebank). The resulting classifier showed an accuracy of 0.938 after 10-fold cross-validation on the training set.

We then evaluated the classifier on tokens from the UD Treebank test set. Now the input to the classifier consisted of these tokens' lemmas only. Lemmas which were missing from the model's vocabulary were omitted (860 of a total of 21759 tokens in the test set). The model reached an accuracy of 0.84 (weighted precision 0.85, weighted recall 0.84).

These numbers may not seem very impressive in comparison with the performance of current state-of-the-art PoS taggers. However, one should remember that this classifier knows absolutely nothing about a word's context in the current sentence. It assigns PoS tags based solely on the proximity of the word's distributional vector in an unsupervised model to those of prototypical PoS examples. The classifier was in fact based only on knowledge of what words occurred in the BNC near other words within a symmetric window of 2 words to the left and to the right. It did not even have access to the information about exact word order within this sliding window, which makes its performance even more impressive.

It is also interesting that one needs as few as a thousand example words to train a decent classifier. Thus, it seems that PoS affiliation is expressed quite strongly and robustly in word embeddings. It can be employed, for example, in preliminary tagging of large corpora of resource-poor languages. Only a handful of non-ambiguous words need to be manually PoS-tagged, and the rest is done by a distributional model trained on the corpus.

Note that applying a *K-neighbors* classifier instead of logistic regression returned somewhat lower results, with 0.913 accuracy on 10-fold cross-validation with the training set, and 0.81 accuracy on the test set. This seems to support our hypothesis that several particular embedding components correspond to part of speech affiliation, but not all of them. As a result, *K-neighbors* classifier fails to separate these important features from all the others and predicts word class based on its nearest neighbors with all dimensions of the semantic space equally important. At the same time, logistic regression learns to pay more atten-

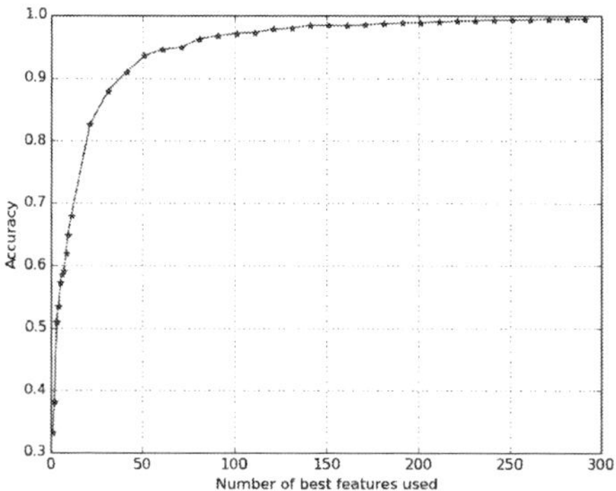

Figure 3. Classifier accuracy depending on the number of used vector components (k)

tion to the relevant features, neglecting unimportant ones.

To find out how many features are important for the classifier, we used the same training and test set, and ranked all embedding components (features, vector dimensions) by their ANOVA F-value related to PoS class. Then we successively trained the classifier on increasing amounts of top-ranked features (top k best) and measured the training set accuracy.

The results are shown in Figure 3. One can see that the accuracy smoothly grows with the number of used features, eventually reaching almost ideal performance on the training set. It is difficult to define the point where the influence of adding features reaches a plateau; it may lie somewhere near $k = 100$. It means that the knowledge about PoS affiliation is distributed among at least one hundred components of the word embeddings, quite consistent with the underlying idea of embedding models.

One might argue that the largest gap in performance is between $k = 2$ and $k = 3$ (from 0.38 to 0.51) and thus most PoS-related information is contained in the 3 components with the largest F-value (in our case, these 3 features were components 31, 51 and 11). But an accuracy of 0.51 is certainly not an adequate result, so even if important, these components are not sufficient to robustly predict part of speech affiliation for a word. Further research is needed to study the effects of adding features to the classifier training.

Regardless, an interesting finding is that part of speech affiliation is distributed among many components of the word embeddings, not concentrated in one or two specific features. Thus, the strongly expressed component 94 in the average vector of conjunctions (Figures 1 and 2) seems to be a solitary case.

6 Conclusion

Distributional semantic vectors trained on word contexts from large text corpora can learn knowledge about part of speech clusters. Arguably, they are good at this precisely because part of speech boundaries are not strict, and even sometimes considered to be a non-categorical linguistic phenomenon (Manning, 2015).

In this paper we have demonstrated that semantic features derived in the process of training a PoS prediction model on word embeddings can be employed both in supporting linguistic hypotheses about part of speech class changes and in detecting and fixing possible annotation errors in corpora. The prediction model is based on simple logistic regression and the word embeddings are trained using *Continuous Skip-Gram* model over PoS-tagged lemmas. We show that the word embeddings contain robust data about the PoS classes of the corresponding words, and that this knowledge seems to be distributed among several components (at least a hundred in our case of 300-dimensional model). We also report preliminary results for predicting PoS tags using a classifier trained on a small number of prototypical members (words with a dominant PoS class) and applying it to embeddings estimated from unlabeled data. A detailed error analysis and experimental results are reported for both the BNC and the UD Treebank.

The reported experiment form part of ongoing research, and we plan to extend it, particularly conducting similar experiments with other languages typologically different from English. We also plan to continue studying the issue of correspondence between particular embedding components and part of speech affiliation. Another direction of future work is finding out how different hyperparameters for training distributional models (including training corpus pre-processing) influence their performance in PoS discrimination, and also comparing the results to using structured embedding models like those of Ling et al. (2015b).

References

Bas Aarts and April McMahon. 2008. *The handbook of English linguistics*. John Wiley & Sons.

Bas Aarts. 2012. *Small Clauses in English. The Nonverbal Types*. De Gruyter Mouton, Boston.

Douglas Biber, Stig Johansson, Geoffrey Leech, Susan Conrad, Edward Finegan, and Randolph Quirk. 1999. *Longman grammar of spoken and written English*, volume 2. MIT Press.

Lou Burnard. 2007. *Users Reference Guide for British National Corpus (XML Edition)*. Oxford University Computing Services, UK.

Christos Christodoulopoulos, Sharon Goldwater, and Mark Steedman. 2010. Two decades of unsupervised POS induction: How far have we come? In *Proceedings of the 2010 Conference on Empirical Methods in Natural Language Processing*, pages 575–584. Association for Computational Linguistics.

John Firth. 1957. *A synopsis of linguistic theory, 1930-1955*. Blackwell.

Aria Haghighi and Dan Klein. 2006. Prototype-driven learning for sequence models. In *Proceedings of the main conference on Human Language Technology Conference of the North American Chapter of the Association of Computational Linguistics*, pages 320–327. Association for Computational Linguistics.

Ann Celeste Houston. 1985. *Continuity and change in English morphology: The variable (ING)*. Ph.D. thesis, University of Pennsylvania.

Chu-Cheng Lin, Waleed Ammar, Chris Dyer, and Lori Levin. 2015. Unsupervised POS induction with word embeddings. *arXiv preprint arXiv:1503.06760*.

Wang Ling, Lin Chu-Cheng, Yulia Tsvetkov, and Silvio Amir. 2015a. Not all contexts are created equal: Better word representations with variable attention. In *Proceedings of the 2015 Conference on Empirical Methods in Natural Language Processing*.

Wang Ling, Chris Dyer, Alan W. Black, and Isabel Trancoso. 2015b. Two/too simple adaptations of word2vec for syntax problems. In *Proceedings of the 2015 Conference of the North American Chapter of the Association for Computational Linguistics – Human Language Technologies*, pages 1299–1304, Denver, Colorado.

Quan Liu, Zhen-Hua Ling, Hui Jiang, and Yu Hu. 2016. Part-of-speech relevance weights for learning word embeddings. *arXiv preprint arXiv:1603.07695*.

Christopher D Manning. 2011. Part-of-speech tagging from 97% to 100%: is it time for some linguistics? In *Computational Linguistics and Intelligent Text Processing*, pages 171–189. Springer.

Christopher D Manning. 2015. Computational linguistics and deep learning. *Computational Linguistics*, 41:701–707.

Bernard Merialdo. 1994. Tagging english text with a probabilistic model. *Computational Linguistics*, 20(2):155–172.

Tomas Mikolov, Ilya Sutskever, Kai Chen, Greg S Corrado, and Jeff Dean. 2013a. Distributed representations of words and phrases and their compositionality. In *Advances in neural information processing systems*, pages 3111–3119.

Tomas Mikolov, Wen-tau Yih, and Geoffrey Zweig. 2013b. Linguistic regularities in continuous space word representations. In *Proceedings of NAACL-HLT 2013*, pages 746–751.

Joakim Nivre, Marie-Catherine de Marneffe, Filip Ginter, Yoav Goldberg, Jan Hajič, Christopher D. Manning, Ryan McDonald, Slav Petrov, Sampo Pyysalo, Natalia Silveira, Reut Tsarfaty, and Daniel Zeman. 2016. Universal Dependencies v1: A multilingual treebank collection. In *Proceedings of the International Conference on Language Resources and Evaluation (LREC)*.

Slav Petrov, Dipanjan Das, and Ryan McDonald. 2012. A universal part-of-speech tagset. In *LREC 2012*.

Barbara Plank, Anders Søgaard, and Yoav Goldberg. 2016. Multilingual part-of-speech tagging with bidirectional long short-term memory models and auxiliary loss. *arXiv preprint arXiv:1604.05529*.

Sujith Ravi and Kevin Knight. 2009. Minimized models for unsupervised part-of-speech tagging. In *Proceedings of ACL-IJCNLP 2009*, pages 504–512, Singapore.

Hinrich Schütze. 1995. Distributional part-of-speech tagging. In *Proceedings of the seventh conference on European chapter of the Association for Computational Linguistics*, pages 141–148. Morgan Kaufmann Publishers Inc.

Natalia Silveira, Timothy Dozat, Marie-Catherine de Marneffe, Samuel Bowman, Miriam Connor, John Bauer, and Christopher D. Manning. 2014. A gold standard dependency corpus for English. In *Proceedings of the Ninth International Conference on Language Resources and Evaluation (LREC-2014)*.

Kristina Toutanova and Mark Johnson. 2007. A Bayesian LDA-based model for semi-supervised part-of-speech tagging. In *Proceedings of the Neural Information Processing Systems Conference (NIPS)*.

Kristina Toutanova, Dan Klein, Christopher D Manning, and Yoram Singer. 2003. Feature-rich part-of-speech tagging with a cyclic dependency network. In *Proceedings of the 2003 NAACL-HLT Conference-Volume 1*, pages 173–180. Association for Computational Linguistics.

Yuta Tsuboi. 2014. Neural networks leverage corpus-wide information for part-of-speech tagging. In *Proceedings of the 2014 Conference on Empirical Methods in Natural Language Processing (EMNLP)*, pages 938–950.

Yulia Tsvetkov, Manaal Faruqui, Wang Ling, Guillaume Lample, and Chris Dyer. 2015. Evaluation of word vector representations by subspace alignment. In *Proceedings of the 2015 Conference on Empirical Methods in Natural Language Processing, Lisbon, Portugal, 17-21 September 2015*, pages 2049–2054.

Mehmet Ali Yatbaz, Enis Sert, and Deniz Yuret. 2012. Learning syntactic categories using paradigmatic representations of word context. In *Proceedings of the 2012 Joint Conference on Empirical Methods in Natural Language Processing and Computational Natural Language Learning*, pages 940–951. Association for Computational Linguistics.

Analyzing Learner Understanding of Novel L2 Vocabulary

Rebecca Knowles and **Adithya Renduchintala** and **Philipp Koehn** and **Jason Eisner**
Department of Computer Science
Johns Hopkins University
{rknowles,adi.r,phi,eisner}@jhu.edu

Abstract

In this work, we explore how learners can infer second-language noun meanings in the context of their native language. Motivated by an interest in building interactive tools for language learning, we collect data on three word-guessing tasks, analyze their difficulty, and explore the types of errors that novice learners make. We train a log-linear model for predicting our subjects' guesses of word meanings in varying kinds of contexts. The model's predictions correlate well with subject performance, and we provide quantitative and qualitative analyses of both human and model performance.

1 Introduction

Second language (L2) instruction includes an emphasis on vocabulary, as reflected in curricular materials and educational technology. Learners acquire new vocabulary in several ways, including direct instruction, memorization, and incidental acquisition. In this work, we seek a predictive model of the circumstances in which incidental acquisition is possible. That is, when can a learner *guess* the meaning of a novel word?

We present novice learners with new L2 words inserted in sentences otherwise written in their native language (L1). This experimental design allows us to assume that all subjects understand the full context, rather than needing to assess how much of an L2 context each subject understood.

We also present novice learners with the same novel words out of context. This allows us to study how cognateness and context interact, in a well-controlled setting. Cognates and very common words may be easy to translate without context, while contextual clues may be needed to make other words guessable.

In the initial experiments we present here, we focus on the language pair of English L1 and German L2, selecting subjects who self-identify as fluent English speakers with minimal exposure to German. We confine ourselves to novel nouns, as we expect that their relative lack of morphological inflection in both languages[1] will produce less noisy results than verbs, for example. (For verbs, naive learners would be required to attend to tense and mood in addition to the lemma.)

The goal of this work is to develop intuitions that may transfer to less artificial learning settings. Even experienced L2 readers will encounter novel words when reading L2 text. Their ability to decipher a novel word is known to depend on both their understanding of the surrounding context words (to understand a text, a reader needs to understand at least 95% of its words (Huckin and Coady, 1999)) and the cognateness of the novel word. We seek to evaluate this quantitatively and qualitatively in "extreme" cases where the context is either completely comprehensible or absent, and where the cognateness information is either present or absent. In doing so, we are able to see how learners react differently to novel words in different contexts. Our controlled experiments can serve as a proxy for incidental learning in other settings: encountering novel words in isolation (e.g. vocabulary lists), while reading in a familiar language, or while using a language-learning interface such as our own mixed-language reading system (Renduchintala et al., 2016a).

We train a log-linear model to predict the translations that our novice learners will guess, given what we show them and their L1 knowledge. Within this setup, we evaluate the usefulness of a

---

[1]Both languages mark for number and German occasionally marks for case.

126

Proceedings of the 20th SIGNLL Conference on Computational Natural Language Learning (CoNLL), pages 126–135,
Berlin, Germany, August 7-12, 2016. ©2016 Association for Computational Linguistics

variety of features—that is, we try to identify cues that our learners might plausibly use.

2 Motivation and Related Work

In Renduchintala et al. (2016a) we presented a user interface that allows learners to read "macaronic" (mixed L1/L2) texts, and thus to pick up L2 words and constructions by experiencing them in context. Our interface allows users to click on tokens to translate or reorder words (to make the text more L1-like when they find it too difficult to understand). In the future, we hope to adapt the L1/L2 mix to the individual learner's competence. That is, we wish to present learners with interesting macaronic text that they are able to read with minimal assistance, but which still challenges them: text within the learner's "zone of proximal development" (Vygotsky, 1978).

In order to do this, we must be able to predict when learners will be able to understand a novel L2 vocabulary item. In a previous study (Renduchintala et al., 2016b), we used a small set of simple features to build user-specific models of lexical understanding in macaronic sentences. The present paper evaluates a larger set of features under a more tightly controlled experimental setup. In particular, in the present paper, our model does not have to predict which context words the learner understands, because there is only one L2 word per trial: any context words are always in L1.

A similar project by Labutov and Lipson (2014) likewise considers the effect of context on guessing the L2 word. However, it does not consider the effect of the L2 word's spelling, which we show is also important.

Our experimental setup, particularly the cloze task, is closely related to research in the L2 education and computer-assisted language learning (CALL) domains. Educators often use cloze tasks to evaluate learner vocabulary (though these generally use L2 context). Beinborn et al. (2014a) look at automatically predicting the difficulty of C-tests (a cloze-like task where blanks are introduced at the character level, rather than at the whole-word level). They find features similar to ours to be useful even at the character level, including cognateness, n-gram probabilities, and word length and frequency.

In this work, we focus on predicting the understanding of single words, but this must be ex-

tended into larger models of sentence understanding. Vajjala and Meurers (2012) classify the difficulty level of longer L2 texts. Beinborn et al. (2014b) provide an overview of ways that readability measures and user background may be modeled specifically in the context of L2 learners, including through the use of cognateness features. They include a 17-word pilot study of German L1 speakers' ability to guess the meanings of Czech cognates with no context, and hypothesize that observing the words in an understandable context would improve guessability (which we confirm in the English-German case in this work).

3 Data and Methodology

3.1 Textual Data

We use data from `NachrichtenLeicht.de` (Deutschlandfunk, 2016), a source of news articles in Simple German (Leichte Sprache, "easy language"). Simple German is intended for readers with cognitive impairments and/or less than native fluency in German. It follows several guidelines, such as short sentences, simple sentence structure, active voice, hyphenation of compound nouns (which are common in German), and use of prepositions instead of the genitive case (Wikipedia, 2016).

We chose 188 German sentences and manually translated them into English. In each sentence, we selected a single German noun whose translation is a single English noun. This yields a triple of (German noun, English noun, English translation of the context). Each German noun/English noun pair appears only once,[2] for a total of 188 triples. Sentences ranged in length from 5 tokens to 28 tokens, with a mean of 11.47 tokens (median 11). Due to the short length of the sentences, there was often only one possible pair of aligned German and English nouns. In the cases where there were multiple, the translator chose one that had not yet been chosen, and attempted to ensure a wide range of clear cognates to non-cognates, as well as a range of how easy the word was to guess from context.

3.2 Collecting Learner Guesses

Our main goal is to examine learners' ability to understand novel L2 words. To better separate the

---

[2] The English word may appear in other sentences, but never in the sentence in which its German counterpart appears. In one case, two tuples with different German nouns share the same English noun translation.

Task	Text Presented to Learner	Correct Answer
cloze	The next important _____ conference is in December.	climate
word	*Klima*	climate
combined	The next important *Klima* conference is in December.	climate

Table 1: Three tasks derived from the same German sentence.

effects of context and cognate cues (and general familiarity with the nouns), we assess subjects on the three tasks illustrated in Table 1:

cloze A single noun is deleted from an English sentence, and subjects are asked to fill in the blank.

word Subjects are presented with a single German word out of context, and are asked to provide their best guess for the translation.

combined Subjects are asked to provide their best-guess translation for a single German noun in the context of an English sentence. This is identical to the cloze task, except that the German noun replaces the blank.

We used Amazon Mechanical Turk (henceforth MTurk), a crowdsourcing platform, to recruit subjects and collect their responses to our tasks. Tasks on MTurk are referred to as HITs (Human Intelligence Tasks). In order to qualify for our tasks, subjects completed short surveys on their language skills. They were asked to rate their language proficiency in four languages (English, Spanish, German, and French) on a scale from "None" to "Fluent." The intermediate options were "Up to 1 year of study (or equivalent)" and "More than 1 year of study (or equivalent)".[3] Only subjects who indicated that they were fluent in English but indicated "None" for German experience were permitted to complete the tasks.

Additional stratification of subjects into groups is described in the subsection below. The HITs were presented to subjects in a somewhat randomized order (as per MTurk standard setup).

3.3 Data Collection Protocol

Each triple gives rise to one cloze, one word, and one combined task. For each of those tasks, 9 subjects make guesses, for a total of 27 guesses per triple.

In this setup, each subject may be asked to complete instances of all three tasks. However, the subject is shown at most one task instance derived from a given data triple (for example, at most one line from Table 1). Subjects were paid between \$0.05 and \$0.08 per HIT, where a HIT consists of 5 instances of the same task. Each HIT was completed by 9 unique subjects. Subjects voluntarily completed from 5 to 90 task instances (1–18 hits), with a median of 25 instances (5 HITs). HITs took subjects a median of 80.5 seconds according to the MTurk output timing.

Data was preprocessed to lowercase all guesses and to correct obvious typos.[4] The $188 \times 27 = 5076$ guesses included 1863 unique strings. Of these, 142 were determined to be errors of some sort: 79 were correctable spelling errors, 54 were multiple-word phrases rather than single words, 8 were German words, and 1 was an ambiguous spelling error. In our experiments, we correct obvious typos and then treat all of the other errors as uncorrectable, replacing them with a special out-of-vocabulary token.

3.4 Data Splits

After collecting data on all triples from our subjects, we split the dataset for purposes of predictive modeling. We randomly partitioned the triples into a training set (112 triples), a development set (38 triples), and a test set (38 triples).

Note that the same partition by triples was used across all tasks. As a result, a German noun/English noun pair that appears in test data is genuinely unseen—it did not appear in the training data for *any* task.

4 Modeling Subject Guesses

When developing educational technology, such as a tool for learning vocabulary, we would like a way to compute the difficulty of examples automatically, in order to present learners with an appropri-

---

[3]Subjects were instructed to list themselves as having experience equivalent to language instruction if they had been exposed to the language by living in a place that it was spoken, playing online language-learning games, or other such experiences, even if they had not studied it in a classroom.

[4]All guesses that were flagged by spell-check were manually checked to see if they constituted typos (e.g., "langauges" for "languages") or spelling errors (e.g., "speach" for "speech") with clear corrections.

ate balance of challenge and guessability. For such an application, it would be useful to know not only whether the learner is likely to correctly guess the vocabulary item, but also whether their incorrect guesses are "close enough" to allow the subject to understand the sentence and proceed with reading. We seek to build models that can predict a subject's likely guesses and their probabilities, given the context with which they have been presented.

We use various features (described below) to characterize and predict subjects' guesses. Feature functions can jointly evaluate a subject's guess with the task instance seen by the subject.

4.1 Guessability and Guess Quality

We train a log-linear model to predict the words that our subjects guess on training data, and we will check its success at this on test data. However, from an engineering perspective, we do not actually need to predict the user's *specific* good or bad answers, but only *whether* they are good or bad. A language-learning interface should display an L2 word only when the user has a good chance of guessing its L1 translation.

Thus we also assess our features and model on the easier task of predicting the *guessability* of a task instance x—that is, the average empirical accuracy of our subjects on this instance, meaning the fraction of the 9 subjects whose guess $\hat{y}$ exactly matched the reference English translation y^*.

Finally, relaxing the exact-match criterion, we evaluate our model's ability to predict the *guess quality*—the average value over subjects of $\text{sim}(\hat{y}, y^*) \in [0, 1]$. Here "sim" denotes Wu-Palmer similarity (Fellbaum, 1998),[5] which is 1 for exact matches, morphological variants (plural/singular), and synonyms; ≈ 0 for antonyms and unrelated words; and intermediate values for words in the same WordNet lexical neighborhood.

4.2 Features

The subject observes a task instance x (consisting of a German word and/or an English context), and guesses an English word $\hat{y}$. We use features of a "candidate" English word y to evaluate whether it is likely to be that guess ($\hat{y} = y$). Our features are functions whose arguments are x and y, and sometimes the true English word y^*. Note that x and y^* are both derived from the triple.

The features are divided into three categories according to which properties of x they consider. When a particular feature had several reasonable definitions (e.g., which phonetic representation to use, or whether or not to normalize), we chose—and describe below—the version that correlated most strongly with guessability on training data.

As an outside resource for training language models and other resources consulted by our features, we used Simple English Wikipedia (Wikimedia Foundation, 2016). It contains 767,826 sentences, covers a similar set of topics to the `NachrichtenLeicht.de` data, and uses simple sentence structure. The sentence lengths are also comparable, with a mean of 17.6 tokens and a median of 16 tokens. This makes it well-matched for our task. We also use pre-trained vector representations of words; for these we chose to use the 300-dimensional GloVe vectors trained on a 6B-token dataset by Pennington et al. (2014).

4.2.1 Generic Features

These features ignore x, and hence can be computed in all three tasks.

Log Unigram Frequency of candidate y in the Simple English Wikipedia corpus. A positive weight means that subjects tend to guess more frequent words.

Candidate=Correct Answer This binary feature fires when $y = y^*$. A positive weight on this feature means that subjects are able to guess the correct answer more often than our other features would predict. This may occur because subjects use better features than we do (e.g., their language model analyzes the semantics of the context more deeply than ours) or because they have some outside knowledge of some of the German words, despite not having formally studied German.

Candidate=OOV This binary feature fires when y is not a valid English word (for example, multiple words or an incomprehensible typo), in which case all other features (generic or otherwise) are set to 0.

The following features are "soft" versions of the "Candidate=Correct Answer" feature:

Embedding $1 - \frac{e(y) \cdot e(y^*)}{\|e(y)\|_2 \|e(y^*)\|_2}$ between GloVe embedding of the candidate $e(y)$ and of the correct answer $e(y^*)$.

Levenshtein Distance Unweighted edit distance between y and y^*.

Sound Edit Distance Unweighted edit distance between phonetic representations of y and y^*, as given by Metaphone (Philips, 1990).

LCS Length of longest common substring between y and y^*, normalized by the length of the shorter of the two strings.

Normalized Trigram Overlap count of character trigram types that match between the candidate and correct answer, normalized by the number of trigram types in either the candidate or the correct answer (whichever is smaller).

4.2.2 Word Features

We measure cognateness between the candidate guess y and the German word (which is part of x) using the same 4 string similarity measures used in the final 4 features of the previous section. Note that sound edit distance obtains a pronunciation of the German word using Metaphone, which is designed for English words; this corresponds to the hypothesis that our novice learners may be applying English pronunciation rules to German.

These features depend on the German word, so when used in our models we set them to 0 in the cloze task (where the German word is unobserved).[6]

4.2.3 Cloze Features

The following features depend on the surrounding English context, so they are set 0 in the word task (where the context is unobserved) when used in our models.

Language Model Scores of candidate in context, using a 5-gram language model (LM) built using KenLM (Heafield et al., 2013) and a neural RNN-LM (Mikolov et al., 2011).[7] We compute three different features for each language model: a raw LM score, a sentence-length-normalized LM score, and the difference between the LM score with the correct answer in the sentence and the LM score with the candidate in its place.

PMI Maximum pointwise mutual information between any word in the context and the candidate. This is estimated within a sentence using Simple English Wikipedia and is unsmoothed.

Left Bigram Collocations These are the bigram association measures defined in Church and Hanks (1990) between the candidate's neighbor(s) to the left and the candidate. We train a version that just examines the neighbor directly to the left (which we'd expect to do well in collocations like "San Francisco") as well as one that returns the maximum score over a window of the five previous words.

Context Embeddings The minimum embedding score (defined in 4.2.1) between the candidate and any word in the context.

4.3 Which English Words are Guessable?

Intuitively, we expect it to be hardest to guess the correct English word from the German word alone, followed by guessing it in context, followed by guessing from both cues.[8] As shown in Figure 1, this is borne out in our data.

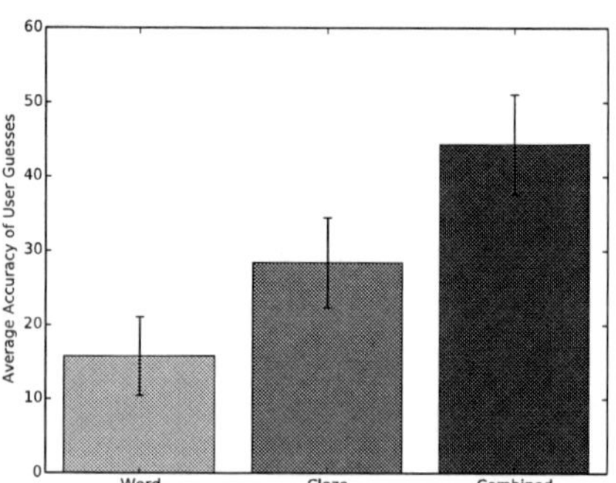

Figure 1: Average guessability (section 4.1) of the 112 training triples, according to which parts of the triple were shown. Error bars show 95%-confidence intervals for the mean, under bootstrap resampling of the 112 triples (we use BCa intervals). Mean accuracy increases significantly from each task to the next (same test on difference of means, $p < 0.01$).

In Table 2 we show Spearman correlations between several features and the guessability of the word (given a word, cloze, or combined context). The first feature in Table 2 (log unigram probability) belongs to the generic category of features. We expect that learners may have an easier time guessing short or common words (for instance, it

---

[6] In theory, any unavailable features could be indirectly correlated with guessability, but in fact their correlation with guessability is low (absolute value < 0.15) and not statistically significant even at the $p < 0.05$ level.

[7] We use the Faster-RNNLM toolkit available at `https://github.com/yandex/faster-rnnlm`.

[8] All plots/values in the remainder of this section are computed only over the training data unless otherwise noted.

Feature	Correlation w/ Guessability			
	Word	*Cloze*	*Combined*	*All*
Log Unigram Frequency	0.310*	0.262*	0.279*	0.255*
Sound Edit Distance (German + Answer)	-0.633*	n/a	-0.575*	-0.409*
Levenshtein Distance (German + Answer)	-0.606*	n/a	-0.560*	-0.395*
Max PMI (Answer + Context)	n/a	0.480*	0.376*	0.306*
Max Left Bigram Collocations (Answer + Window=5)	n/a	0.474*	0.186	0.238*
Max Right Bigram Collocations (Answer + Window=5)	n/a	0.119	0.064	0.038

Table 2: Spearman's rho correlations between selected feature values and answer guessability, computed on training data (starred correlations significant at $p < 0.01$). Unavailable features are represented by "n/a" (for example, since the German word is not observed in the cloze task, its edit distance to the correct solution is unavailable to the subject).

may be easier to guess *cat* than *trilobite*) and we do observe such correlations.

The middle section focuses on cognateness, which in cases like *Gitarrist* (*guitarist*) can enable all or nearly all subjects to succeed at the challenging word-only task. The correlation between guessability and Sound Edit Distance as well Levenshtein Distance demonstrate their usefulness as proxies for cognateness. The other word features described earlier also show strong correlation with guessability in the word and combined tasks.

Similarly, in some cloze tasks, strong collocations or context clues, as in the case of "His plane landed at the ______." make it easy to guess the correct solution (*airport*). We would expect, for instance, a high PMI between *plane* and *airport*, and we see this reflected in the correlation between high PMI and guessability. The final two lines of the table examine an interesting quirk of bigram association measures. We see that Left Bigram Collocations with a window of 5 (that is, where the feature returns the maximum collocation score between a word in the window to the left of the word to be guessed) shows reasonable correlation with guessability. The reverse, Right Bigram Collocations, however, do not appear to correlate. This suggests that the subjects focus more on the words preceding the blank when formulating their guess (which makes sense as they read left-to-right). Due to its poor performance, we do not include Right Bigram Collocations in our later experiments.

4.4 What English Words are Guessed?

We now move from modeling guessability (via features of the correct answer y^*) to modeling subjects' actual guesses (via features of the guess $\hat{y}$).

We expect that learners who see only the word will make guesses that lean heavily on cognateness (for example, incorrectly guessing *Austria* for *Ausland*), while learners who see the cloze task will choose words that make sense semantically (e.g. incorrectly guessing *tornado* in the sentence "The ______ destroyed many houses and uprooted many trees.").

In Figure 2, we see this holds true; incorrect guesses in the word task have higher average Normalized Character Trigram Overlap than guesses in the cloze task, with the combined task in between. This pattern of the combined task falling between the word and combined task is consistent across most features examined. For example, the difference between the language model scores with the guesses and correct answer is low for the cloze and combined tasks (meaning that users are making guesses that the language model finds about equally plausible to the correct answer), while it is high for the word task (meaning that the users are guessing words that are nonsensical in the context, which they didn't observe). This reinforces that the subjects are making plausible guesses given the cues they observe.

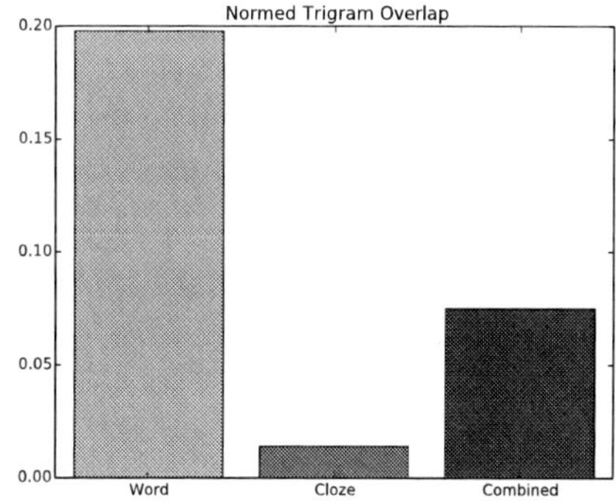

Figure 2: Average Normalized Character Trigram Overlap between incorrect guesses and the German word.

5 Model

The correlations in the previous section support our intuitions about how to model subject behavior in terms of cognateness and context. Section 4.4 suggests that subjects are performing cue combination, balancing cognate and context clues when both are available.

We now build a simple model of cue combination, namely a log-linear model of subjects' guesses:

$$p(y \mid x) = \frac{\exp(\vec{w} \cdot \vec{f}(x, y))}{\sum_{y' \in V} \exp(\vec{w} \cdot \vec{f}(x, y'))} \qquad (1)$$

where $\vec{w}$ is a weight vector and $\vec{f}(x, y)$ is a feature vector.

In practice we set V in the denominator to be a 5000-word vocabulary. It contains the complete English vocabulary from the triples (reference translations *and* their context words) as well as all subject guesses. These account for 2238 types (including the special out-of-vocabulary token). To reach 5000 words, we then pad the vocabulary with the most frequent words from the Simple English Wikipedia dataset.

Given the context x that the subject was shown (word, cloze, or combined), $p(y \mid x)$ represents the probability that a subject would guess the vocabulary item $y \in V$. We train the model to maximize the total conditional log-likelihood $\sum_i \log p(\hat{y}_i \mid x_i)$ of all subject guesses $\hat{y}_i$ on all training instances x_i of all three tasks, plus an L2 regularization term.[9]

In order to best leverage the cloze features (shared across the cloze and combined tasks), the word features (shared across the word and combined task) and the generic features (shared across all tasks), we take the domain adaptation approach used in (Daumé III, 2007). In this approach, instead of a single feature for Levenshtein distance between a German word and a candidate guess, we have three copies of this feature, one that fires only when the subject is presented with the word task, one that fires when the subject is presented with the combined task, and a "shared" version that fires in either of those situations. (Note that since a subject who sees the cloze task does not see the German word, we omit such a version of the feature.) This allows us to learn different weights for different tasks. For example, the model can learn that Levenshtein distance is weighted highly in general but especially highly in the word task. The "shared" features mean that the training examples from one task help to set some weights that are used on other tasks (i.e., generalization from limited data), while the task-specific features allow task-specific weights when motivated by the evidence.

5.1 Evaluating the Model

We evaluate the model in several ways: using conditional cross-entropy, by computing mean reciprocal rank, and by examining its ability to predict guessability and guess quality as defined in section 4.1.

The *conditional cross-entropy* is defined to be the mean negative log probability over all test task instances (pairs of subject guesses $\hat{y}$ and contexts x), $\frac{1}{N} \sum_{i=0}^{N} -\log_2 p(\hat{y}_i \mid x_i)$.

The *mean reciprocal rank* is computed after ranking all vocabulary words (in each context) by the probability assigned to them by the model, calculating the reciprocal rank of the each subject guess $\hat{y}_i$, and then averaging this across all contexts x in the set X of all contexts, as shown in Equation 2.

$$MRR = \frac{1}{N} \sum_{i=1}^{N} \frac{1}{\text{rank}(\hat{y}_i | x_i)} \qquad (2)$$

The model predicts the guessability of x_i to be $p(y_i^* \mid x_i)$, the predicted probability that a user will guess the truth. It predicts the guess quality of x_i, in expectation, to be $\sum_{y \in V} p(y \mid x_i) \text{sim}(y, y_i^*)$. We measure how well the *predicted* guessability and guess quality correlate with their *actual* empirical values, using Spearman's rho.[10]

6 Results and Analysis

In Table 3 we show the performance of our full model (last line), as well as several ablated models that use only a subset of the features. The full model performs best. Indeed, an ablated model that uses only generic features, word features, or cloze features cannot reasonably be expected to perform well on the full test set, which contains instances of all three tasks. Using domain adaptation improves performance.

---

[9] We used MegaM (Daumé III, 2004) via the NLTK interface, with default settings.

[10] In our previous study (Renduchintala et al., 2016b), we measured similar correlations using Pearson's r.

Features	Cross-Entropy	MRR	Guessability Correlation
LCS (Candidate + Answer)	10.72	0.067	0.346*
All Generic Features	8.643	0.309	0.168
Sound Edit Dist. (Cand. + German Word)	10.847	0.081	0.494*
All Word Features	10.018	0.187	0.570*
LM Difference	11.214	0.051	0.398*
All Cloze Features	10.008	0.105	0.351*
Generic + Word	7.651	0.369	0.585*
Generic + Cloze	8.075	0.320	0.264*
Word + Cloze	8.369	0.227	0.706*
All Features (No Domain Adapt.)	7.344	0.338	0.702*
All Features + Domain Adapt.	**7.134**	**0.382**	**0.725***

Table 3: Feature ablation. The single highest-correlating feature (on dev set) from each feature group is shown, followed by the entire feature group. All versions with more than one feature include a feature for the OOV guess. In the correlation column, p-values < 0.01 are marked with an asterisk.

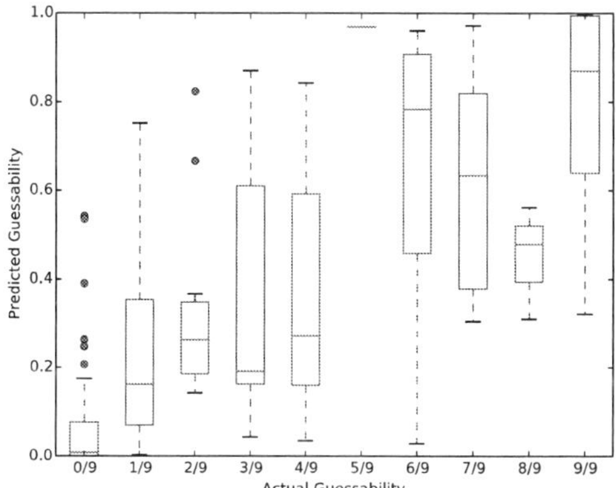

Figure 3: Correlation between actual guessability and the model's prediction of it, across all tasks in the test set. Each point is a task instance, with actual guessability being average equal$(\hat{y}, y^*) \in \{0, 1\}$ over 9 subjects. Spearman's rank correlation of 0.725.

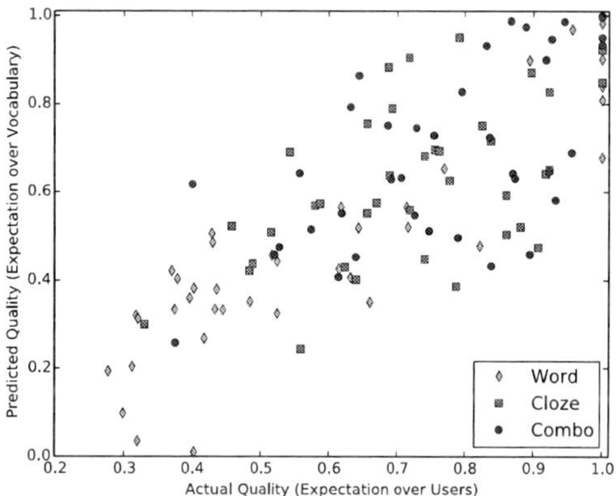

Figure 4: Correlation between actual guess quality and the model's prediction of it. Each point is a task instance, with actual guess quality being average $\text{sim}(\hat{y}, y^*) \in [0, 1]$ over 9 subjects. Spearman's rank correlation of 0.769.

Figure 3 visualizes the correlation shown in our full model (last row of Table 3). This figure illustrates that a single model works well for all three tasks. As the empirical guessability increases, so does the median model probability assigned to the correct answer. However, in our applications, we are less interested in only the 1-best prediction; we'd like to know whether users can understand the novel vocabulary, so we'd prefer to allow WordNet synonyms to also be counted as correct. In Figure 4 we show that the model's prediction of guess quality (see section 4.1) correlates strongly with the actual empirical guess quality.

This means that our model makes predictions that look plausibly like those made by the hu-

man subjects. For example, given the context "In _________, the AKP now has the most representatives." the model ranks the correct answer (*parliament*) first, followed by *undersecretary*, *elections*, and *congress*, all of which are thematically appropriate, and most of which fit contextually into the sentence. For the German word *Spieler*, the top ranking predictions made by the model are *spider*, *smaller*, and *spill*, while one of the actual subject guesses, *speaker*, is ranked as 10th most likely (out of a vocabulary of 5000 items).

6.1 Annotated Guesses

To take a fine-grained look at guesses, we broke down subject guesses into several categories.

We had 4 annotators (fluent English speakers,

Context Observed	Guess	Truth	Hypothesized Explanation
Helfer	cow	helpers	False Friend: Helfer → Heifer → Cow
Journalisten	reporter	journalists	Synonym and incorrect number.
The *Lage* is too dangerous.	lake	location	Influenced by spelling and context.

Table 4: Examples of incorrect guesses and potential sources of confusion.

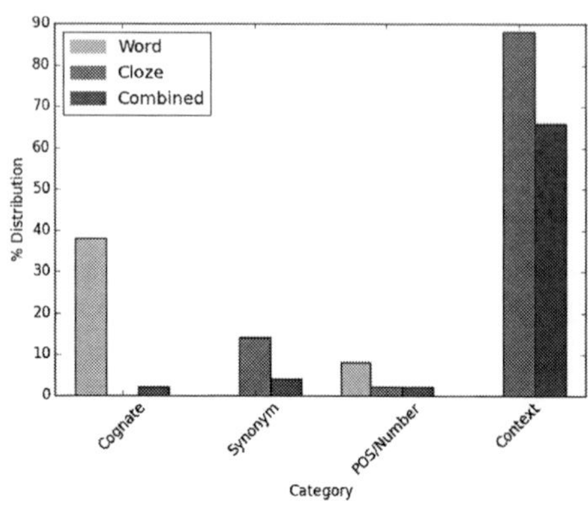

Figure 5: Percent of examples labeled with each label by a majority of annotators (may sum to more than 100%, as multiple labels were allowed).

but non-experts) label 50 incorrect subject guesses from each task, sampled randomly from the spell-corrected incorrect guesses in the training data, with the following labels indicating why the annotator thought the subject made the (incorrect) guess they did, given the context that the subject saw: **false friend/cognate/spelling bias** (learner appears to have been influenced by the spelling of the German word), **synonym** (learner guess is a synonym or near-synonym to the correct answer), **incorrect number/POS** (correct noun with incorrect number or incorrect POS), and **context influence** (a word that makes sense in the cloze/combo context but is not correct). Examples of the range of ways in which errors can manifest are shown in Table 4. Annotators made a binary judgment for each of these labels. Inter-annotator agreement was substantial, with Fleiss's kappa of 0.654. Guesses were given a label only if the majority of annotators agreed.

In Figure 5, we can make several observations about subject behavior. First, the labels for the combined and cloze tasks tend to be more similar to one another, and quite different from the word task labels. In particular, in the majority of cases, subjects completing cloze and combo tasks choose words that fit the context they've observed,

while spelling influence in the word task doesn't appear to be quite as strong. Even if the subjects in the cloze and combined tasks make errors, they choose words that still make sense in context more than 50% of the time, while spelling doesn't exert an equally strong influence in the word task.

7 Conclusions

We have shown that by cue combination of various cognate and context features, we can model the behavior of subjects guessing the meanings of novel L2 vocabulary items. Not only does our model correlate well with the guessability of novel words in a variety of contexts, it also produces reasonable predictions for the range of incorrect guesses that subjects make. Such predictions can be used in downstream tasks, such as personalized language learning software, or evaluating the difficulty level of texts.

Acknowledgments

This material is based upon work supported by a National Science Foundation Graduate Research Fellowship (Grant No. DGE-1232825) to the first author and by a seed grant from the Science of Learning Institute at Johns Hopkins University. We thank Chadia Abras for useful discussions, and Nancy Fink, Biman Gujral, Huda Khayrallah and Nitisha Rastogi for volunteering to assist with annotation. We thank the reviewers for their comments and suggestions.

References

Lisa Beinborn, Torsten Zesch, and Iryna Gurevych. 2014a. Predicting the difficulty of language proficiency tests. *Transactions of the ACL*, 2:517–529.

Lisa Beinborn, Torsten Zesch, and Iryna Gurevych. 2014b. Readability for foreign language learning: The importance of cognates. *ITL-International Journal of Applied Linguistics*, 165(2):136–162.

Kenneth Ward Church and Patrick Hanks. 1990. Word association norms, mutual information, and lexicography. *Computational Linguistics*, 16(1):22–29, March.

Hal Daumé III. 2004. Notes on CG and LM-BFGS optimization of logistic regression. August.

Hal Daumé III. 2007. Frustratingly easy domain adaptation. In *Proceedings of ACL*, Prague, Czech Republic.

Deutschlandfunk. 2016. Nachrichtenleicht. [Online; accessed 16-March-2016].

Christiane Fellbaum, editor. 1998. *WordNet: An Electronic Lexical Database*. MIT Press.

Kenneth Heafield, Ivan Pouzyrevsky, Jonathan H. Clark, and Philipp Koehn. 2013. Scalable modified Kneser-Ney language model estimation. In *Proceedings of ACL*, pages 690–696, Sofia, Bulgaria, August.

Thomas Huckin and James Coady. 1999. Incidental vocabulary acquisition in a second language. *Studies in Second Language Acquisition*, 21(02):181–193.

Igor Labutov and Hod Lipson. 2014. Generating code-switched text for lexical learning. In *Proceeding of ACL*, pages 562–571.

Tomas Mikolov, Stefan Kombrink, Anoop Deoras, Lukar Burget, and Jan Cernocky. 2011. RNNLM—Recurrent neural network language modeling toolkit. In *Proc. of the 2011 ASRU Workshop*, pages 196–201.

Jeffrey Pennington, Richard Socher, and Christopher D. Manning. 2014. GloVe: Global vectors for word representation. In *Empirical Methods in Natural Language Processing (EMNLP)*, pages 1532–1543.

Lawrence Philips. 1990. Hanging on the metaphone. *Computer Language*, 7(12).

Adithya Renduchintala, Rebecca Knowles, Philipp Koehn, and Jason Eisner. 2016a. Creating interactive macaronic interfaces for language learning. In *Proceedings of ACL (System Demonstrations)*.

Adithya Renduchintala, Rebecca Knowles, Philipp Koehn, and Jason Eisner. 2016b. User modeling in language learning with macaronic texts. In *Proceedings of ACL*.

Sowmya Vajjala and Detmar Meurers. 2012. On improving the accuracy of readability classification using insights from second language acquisition. In *Proceedings of the Seventh Workshop on Building Educational Applications Using NLP*, pages 163–173. ACL.

Lev Vygotsky. 1978. *Mind in Society: The development of higher psychological processes*. Harvard University Press.

Wikimedia Foundation. 2016. Simple English Wikipedia. Retrieved from `https://dumps.wikimedia.org/simplewiki/20160407/` 8-April-2016.

Wikipedia. 2016. Leichte sprache — Wikipedia, die freie enzyklopädie. [Online; accessed 16-March-2016].

Modeling language evolution
with codes that utilize context and phonetic features

Javad Nouri and **Roman Yangarber**
Department of Computer Science
University of Helsinki, Finland
first.last@cs.helsinki.fi

Abstract

We present methods for investigating processes of evolution in a language family by modeling relationships among the observed languages. The models aim to find regularities—regular correspondences in lexical data. We present an algorithm which codes the data using phonetic features of sounds, and learns long-range contextual rules that condition recurrent sound correspondences between languages. This gives us a measure of model quality: better models find more regularity in the data. We also present a procedure for imputing unseen data, which provides another method of model comparison. Our experiments demonstrate improvements in performance compared to prior work.

1 Introduction

We present work on modeling evolution within language families, by discovering regularity in data from observed languages.

The study of evolution of language families covers several problems, including: a. discovering *cognates*—"genetically related" words, i.e., words that derive from a common ancestor word in an ancestral proto-language; b. determining genetic relationships among languages in the given language family based on observed data; c. discovering patterns of sound correspondence across languages; and d. reconstruction of forms in proto-languages. In this paper, we treat a. (sets of cognates) as given, and focus on problems b. and c.[1]

Given a corpus of cognate sets,[2] we first aim to

find as much regularity as possible in the data at the sound (or symbol) level.[3] An important goal is that our methods be data-driven—we aim to use all data available, and to learn the patterns of regular correspondence directly from the data. We allow only the data to determine which rules underlie it—correspondences that are *inherently encoded* in the corpus itself—rather than relying on externally supplied (and possibly biased) rules or "priors." We try to refrain from *a priori* assumptions or "universal" principles—e.g., no preference to align consonants with consonants, to align a symbol with itself, etc.

We claim that alignment may not be the best way to address the problem of regularity. Finding alignments is indeed finding a kind of regularity, but not all regularity is expressed as alignment.

The paper is organized as follows. In section 2 we review the data used in our experiments and recent approaches to modeling language evolution. We formalize the problem and present our models in section 3. The models treat sounds as vectors of phonetic *features*, and utilize the *context* of the sounds to discover patterns of regular correspondence. Once we have obtained the regularity, the question arises how we can evaluate it effectively. In section 4, we present a procedure for imputation—prediction of unseen data—to evaluate the strength of the learned rules of correspondence, by how well they predict words in one language given corresponding words in another language. We further evaluate the models by using them for building phylogenies—family trees, and comparing them to gold standards, in section 4.2. We conclude with a discussion in section 5.

We have experimented with several language families: Uralic, Turkic and Indo-European; the paper focuses on results from the Uralic family.

---

[1] Extending the methods to problem d. is future work.

[2] The members of a cognate set are posited (by linguists) to derive from a common, shared origin: a word-form in the (typically unobserved) ancestral proto-language.

[3] NB: we use *sounds* and *symbols* interchangeably, as we assume that input data is rendered in a phonetic transcription.

Proceedings of the 20th SIGNLL Conference on Computational Natural Language Learning (CoNLL), pages 136–145,
Berlin, Germany, August 7-12, 2016. ©2016 Association for Computational Linguistics

We use large-scale digital etymological resources/dictionaries. For Uralic, the StarLing database, (Starostin, 2005), contains 2586 Uralic cognate sets, based on (Rédei, 1991). The etymological dictionary *Suomen Sanojen Alkuperä* (SSA), "The Origin of Finnish Words," (Itkonen and Kulonen, 2000), has over 5000 cognate sets.

2 Related work and motivation

One traditional arrangement of the Uralic languages is shown in Figure 1; several alternative arrangements appear in the literature.

The last 15 years have seen a surge in computational modeling of language relationships, change and evolution. We provide a detailed discussion of related prior work in (Nouri et al., 2016).

In earlier work, e.g., (Wettig et al., 2011), we presented two perspectives on the problem of finding regularity. It can be seen as a problem of aligning the data. From an information-theoretic perspective, finding regularity is a problem of compression: the more regularity we find in data, the more we can compress it. In (Wettig et al., 2011), we presented baseline models, which focus on alignment of symbols, in a 1-1 fashion. We showed that aligning more than one symbol at a time—e.g., 2-2—gives better performance. Alignment is a natural way to think of comparing languages. E.g., in Figure 2, obtained by the 1-1 model, we can observe[4] that most of the time Finnish k corresponds to Estonian k (we write Fin. $k \sim$ Est. k). However, models that focus on alignments have certain shortcomings. For example, substantial probability mass is assigned to Fin. $k \sim$ Est. g, yet the model cannot explain why. Fin. $k \sim$ Est. g in certain environments—in non-first syllables, between vowels or after a voiced consonant—but the model cannot capture this regularity, because it has no notion of *context*. In fact, the regularity is much deeper: not only Fin. k, but all Finnish voiceless stops become voiced in Estonian in this environment: $p \sim b$, $t \sim d$. This type of regularity cannot be captured by the baseline model because it treats symbols as atoms, and does not know about their shared phonetic features.

We claim that alignment may always not be the best way to think about the problem of finding regularity. Figure 2 shows a prominent "diagonal,"

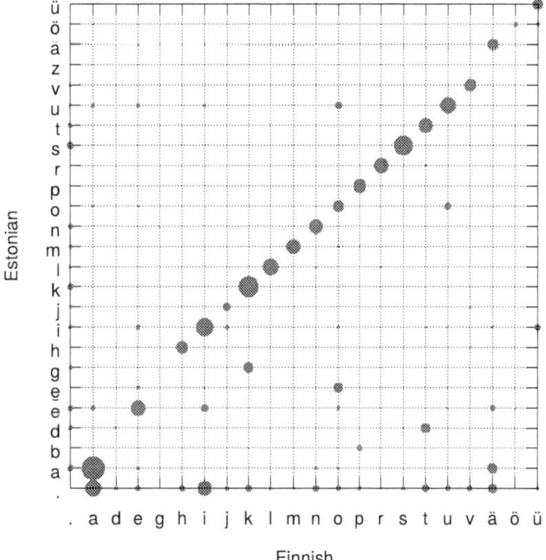

Figure 2: 1-1 alignment for Finnish and Estonian

many sounds correspond—they "align with themselves." However, as languages diverge further, this correspondence becomes blurry; e.g., when we try to align Finnish and Hungarian, the probability distribution of aligned symbols has much higher entropy, Figure 3. The reason is that the regularity lies on a much deeper level: predicting which sound occurs in a given position in a word requires knowledge of a wider context, in both Finnish and Hungarian. Hence we will prefer to think in terms of *coding*, rather than alignment.

Methods in (Kondrak, 2002), learn one-to-one sound correspondences between words in pairs of languages. Kondrak (2003), Wettig et al. (2011) find more complex—many-to-many—correspondences. These methods focus on alignment, and model *context* of the sound changes in a limited way, while it is known that most evolutionary changes are conditioned on the context of the evolving sound. Bouchard-Côté et al. (2007) use MCMC-based methods to model context, and operate on more than a pair of languages.[5]

Our models, similarly to other work, operate at the phonetic level only, leaving semantic judgements to the creators of the database. Some prior work attempts to approach semantics by computational means as well, e.g., (Kondrak, 2004; Kessler, 2001). We begin with a set of etymological data for a language family as given, and treat each cognate set as a fundamental unit of in-

---

[4]The size of the circle is proportional to the probability of aligning the corresponding symbols on the X and Y axes. The *dot* coordinates "." correspond to deletions/insertions.

[5]The running time did not scale well when the number of languages was above three.

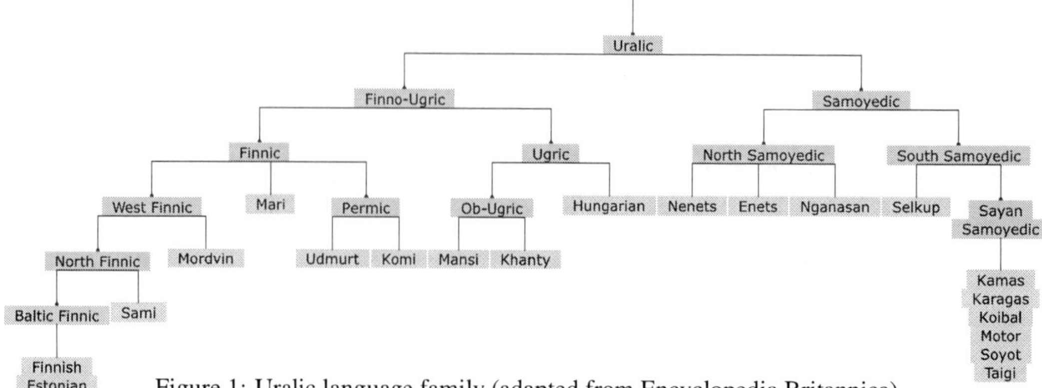

Figure 1: Uralic language family (adapted from Encyclopedia Britannica)

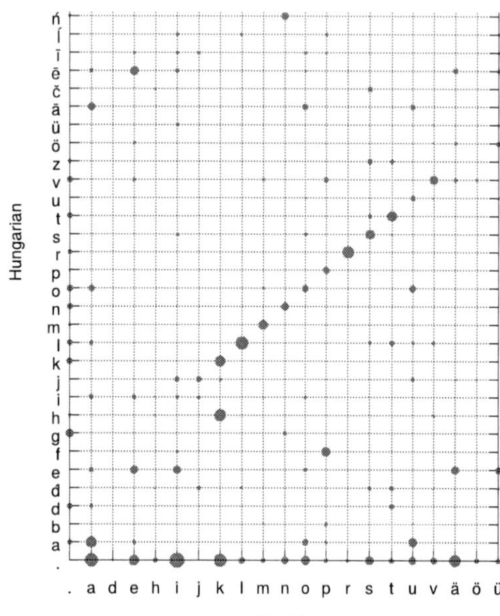

Figure 3: 1-1 alignment for Finnish and Hungarian

put. We use the principle of *recurrent sound correspondence*, as in much of the literature.

Alignment can be evaluated by measuring relationships among entire languages within the family. Construction of phylogenies is studied, e.g., in (Nakhleh et al., 2005; Ringe et al., 2002; Barbançon et al., 2009).

Our work is related to the generative "Berkeley" models, (Bouchard-Côté et al., 2007), (Hall and Klein, 2011), in the following respects.

Context: in (Wettig et al., 2011) we capture *some* context by coding *pairs* of symbols, as in (Kondrak, 2003). Berkeley models handle context by conditioning the symbol being generated upon the immediately preceding and following symbols. Our method uses broader context by

building decision trees, so that non-relevant context information does not grow model complexity.

Phonetic features: in (Wettig et al., 2011) we treated sounds/symbols as atomic—not analyzed in terms of their phonetic makeup. Berkeley models use "natural classes" to define the context of a sound change, but not to generate the symbols themselves; (Bouchard-Côté et al., 2009) encode as a prior which sounds are "similar" to each other. We code symbols in terms of phonetic features. Our models are based on information-theoretic Minimum Description Length principle (MDL), e.g., (Grünwald, 2007)—unlike Berkeley. MDL brings some theoretical benefits, since models chosen in this way are guided by data with no free parameters or hand-picked "priors." The data analyst chooses the model class and structure, and the coding scheme, i.e., a decodable way to encode model and data. This determines the learning strategy—we optimize the cost function, which is the code length determined by these choices.

Objective function: we use NML—the normalized maximum likelihood, not reported previously in this setting. It is preferable for theoretical and practical reasons, e.g., to prequential coding used in (Wettig et al., 2011), as explained in section 3.1.

Models that utilize more than the immediate adjacent environment of a sound to build a complete alignment of a language family have not been reported previously, to the best of our knowledge.

3 Coding pairs of words

We begin with baseline algorithms for pairwise coding: in (Wettig et al., 2011; Wettig et al., 2012) we code pairs of words, from two related languages in our corpus of cognates. For each word pair, the task of alignment is finding which symbols correspond best; the task of coding is achieving more compression. The simplest form of symbol alignment is a pair $(\sigma : \tau) \in \Sigma \times T$, a single symbol σ from the *source alphabet* Σ with a symbol τ from the *target alphabet* T.

To model *insertions* and *deletions*, we augment both alphabets with a special "empty" symbol—denoted by a dot—and write the augmented alphabets as $\Sigma^{\cdot}$ and $T^{\cdot}$. We can then align word pairs, such as *hiiri—löŋkər* (meaning "mouse" in Finnish and Khanty) in many different ways; putting Finnish (source level, above) and Khanty (target level, below), for example:

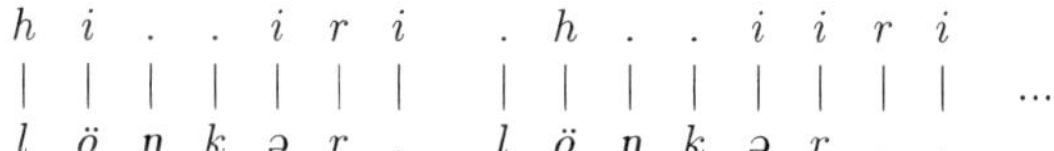

A final note about alignments: we find no satisfactory way to *evaluate* alignments. Which of the above alignments is "better"? It may be satisfying to prefer the left one, observing that Fin. h corresponds well to Khn. l (since they both go back to Proto-Uralic š); Fin. $r \sim$ Khn. r, etc. However, if a model achieves better compression by preferring the alignment on the right, then it is difficult to argue that that alignment is "not correct."

3.1 Context model with phonetic features

Our coding method is based on MDL. The most refined form of MDL, NML—Normalized Maximum Likelihood, (Rissanen, 1996)—cannot be efficiently computed for our model. Therefore, we resort to a classic two-part coding scheme. The first part of the two-part code is responsible for splitting the data into subsets corresponding to certain contexts. However, given the contexts, we *can* use NML to encode these subsets.[6]

We begin with a raw set of observed data—word pairs in two languages. We search for a way to code the data, by capturing regular correspondences. The goodness of the code is defined formally below. MDL says that the more regularity we can find in the data, the fewer bits we will need to encode (or compress) it. More regularity means lower entropy in the distribution that describes the data, and lower entropy lets us construct a more economical code.

Features: Rather than coding symbols (sounds) as atomic, we code them in terms of their pho-

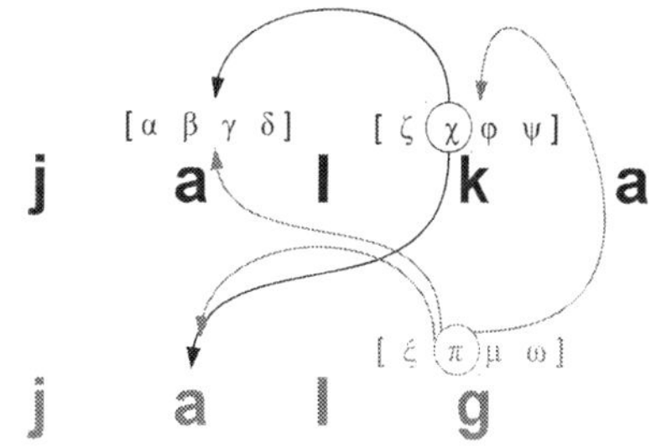
Figure 4: Fin. *jalka* (source) $\sim$ Est. *jalg* (target)

netic features. For example, figure 4 shows how a model might code Finnish *jalka* and Estonian *jalg* (meaning "leg"). We code the symbols in a fixed order: top to bottom, left to right. Each symbol is coded as a vector of its phonetic features, e.g., $k = [\xi \, \chi \, \phi \, \psi]$.

For each symbol, first we code a special **Type** feature, with values: K (consonant), V (vowel), dot (insertion / deletion), or # (*word boundary*).[7] Consonants and vowels have different sets of features; each feature has 2–8 values, listed in Figure 5A. Features are coded in a fixed order.

Contexts: While coding each *feature* of the symbol, the model is allowed to query a fixed and finite a set of *candidate contexts*. The idea is that the model can query its "history"—information that has already been coded previously. When coding k, e.g., the model may query features of blue a (β, γ, etc.), as well as features of red a, etc. When coding g the model may query those, and in addition also the features of k (χ, ϕ, etc.)

Formally, a context is a triplet (L, P, F): L is the level—source (σ) or target (τ); P is one of the positions that the model may query—relative to the position currently being coded; for example, we may query positions shown in Figure 5B. F is one of the possible features found at that position. Thus, we have in total about 2 levels $\times$ 8 positions $\times$ 5 features $\approx$ 80 candidate contexts that can be queried, as explained in detail below.

3.2 Two-part code

We code the complete (i.e., aligned) data using a two-part code, following MDL. We first code which model instance we select from our model *class*, and then code the data given the model. Our model class is defined as follows: a set of decision trees (forest)—one tree per feature per level (*separately* for source and for target). A model *instance*

---

[6] Theoretical benefits of NML over other coding schemes include freedom from priors, invariance to reparametrization, and other optimality properties, which are outside the scope of this paper, (Rissanen, 1996).

[7] Type feature and word end (#) not shown in figure.

Consonant articulation		
M	**Manner**	plosive, fricative, glide, ...
P	**Place**	labial, dental, ..., velar, uvular
X	**Voiced**	$-$, +
S	**Secondary**	$-$, affricate, aspirate, ...
Vowel articulation		
V	**Vertical**	high—mid—low
H	**Horizontal**	front—center—back
R	**Rounding**	$-$, +
L	**Length**	1—5

Contexts	
I	itself, possibly dot
–P	previous position, possibly dot
–S	previous non-dot symbol
–K	previous consonant
–V	previous vowel
+S	previous or self non-dot symbol
+K	previous or self consonant
+V	previous or self vowel
...	*(other contexts possible)*

Figure 5: (A: left) Phonetic features and (B: right) phonetic contexts / environments.

will define a particular structure for each tree.

Cost of coding the structure: Thus, the forest consists of 18 decision trees—one for each feature on the source and the target level: the type feature, 4 vowel and 4 consonant features, times 2 levels. Each node in a tree will either be a leaf, or will be split—by querying one of the candidate contexts defined above. The cost of a tree is one bit for every node n_i—to encode whether n_i is internal (was split) or a leaf—plus the number of internal nodes $\times \approx \log 80$—to encode *which* particular context was chosen to split each n_i. We explain how the model chooses the best candidate context on which to split a node in section 3.3.

Each feature and level define a tree, e.g., the "voiced" (**X**) feature of the source symbols—corresponds to the σ-**X** tree. A node N in this tree holds a distribution over the values of feature **X** of only those symbol instances in the complete data that have reached node N, by following the context queries from the root downward. The tree structure tells us precisely which path to follow—completely determined by the context. When coding a symbol α based on another symbol found in the context C of α—for example, $C = (\tau, -K, \mathbf{M})$: at level τ, position –K, and one of the features **M**—the next edge down the tree is determined by that feature's value; and so on, down to a leaf.[8]

Cost of the data given the model: is computed by taking into account only the distributions at *the leaves*. The code will assign a cost (code-length) to every possible alignment of the data. The total code-length is the *objective* function that the learning algorithm will optimize.

Coding scheme: we use Normalized Maximum Likelihood (NML), and prequential coding as in (Wettig et al., 2011). We code the distribution at

---

[8]Model code to construct trees from data, and examples of decision trees learned by the model are made publicly available on the Project Web site: *etymon.cs.helsinki.fi/*.

each leaf node separately; the sum of the costs of all leaves gives the total cost of the complete data—the value of the objective function.

Suppose n instances reach a leaf node N, of the tree for feature F on level λ, and F has k values: e.g., n consonants satisfying N's context constraints in the σ-**X** tree, with $k = 2$ values: $\{-, +\}$. Suppose also that the values are distributed so that n_i instances have value i, with $i \in \{1, \ldots, k\}$. Then this requires an NML code-length of:

$$L_{NML}(\lambda; F; N) = -\log P_{NML}(\lambda; F; N)$$

$$= -\log \frac{\prod_i \left(\frac{n_i}{n}\right)^{n_i}}{C(n, k)} \qquad (1)$$

Here $\prod_i \left(\frac{n_i}{n}\right)^{n_i}$ is the maximum likelihood of the multinomial data at node N, and the term

$$C(n, k) = \sum_{n_1' + \ldots + n_k' = n} \prod_i \left(\frac{n_i'}{n}\right)^{n_i'} \qquad (2)$$

is a normalizing constant to make P_{NML} a probability distribution. In MDL literature, (Grünwald, 2007), the term $-\log C(n, k)$ is called the *parametric complexity* or the *(minimax) regret* of the model—in this case, the multinomial model.

The NML distribution is the unique solution to the mini-max problem posed in (Shtarkov, 1987),

$$\min_{\hat{P}} \max_{\mathbf{x^n}} \log \frac{P(\mathbf{x^n} | \hat{\Theta}(\mathbf{x^n}))}{\hat{P}(\mathbf{x^n})} \qquad (3)$$

where $\hat{\Theta}(\mathbf{x^n}) = \arg \max_{\Theta} \mathbf{P}(\mathbf{x^n})$ are the *maximum likelihood parameters* for the data $\mathbf{x^n}$. Thus, P_{NML} minimizes the worst-case regret, i.e., the number of excess bits in the code as compared to the best model in the model class, with hind-sight. Details on the computation of this code length are given in (Kontkanen and Myllymäki, 2007).

Learning the model from the observed data now means aligning word pairs and building decision trees so as to minimize the two-part code length: the sum of the model's code length—encoding the structure of the trees,—and the code length of the data given the model—encoding the aligned word pairs using these trees.

Summary of the algorithm: We start with an initial *random* alignment for each pair of words in the corpus. We then alternate between two steps: **A.** re-build the decision trees for all features on source and target levels, and **B.** re-align all word pairs in the corpus, using dynamic programming. Both of these operations monotonically decrease the two-part cost function and thus compress the data. We continue until we reach convergence.

Simulated annealing with a slow cooling schedule is used to avoid getting trapped in local optima.

3.3 Building decision trees

Given a complete alignment of the data, we need to build a decision tree, for each feature on both levels, yielding the lowest two-part cost. The term "decision tree" is meant in a probabilistic sense: at each node we store a *distribution* over the respective feature values, for all instances that reach this node. The distribution at a given leaf is then used to code an instance when it reaches the leaf. We code the features in a fixed, pre-set order, and source level (σ-level) before target (τ-level).

We now describe in detail the process of building the tree—using as example a tree for the σ-level feature **X**. (We will need do the same for all other features, on both levels, as well.) First, we collect all instances of consonants on σ-level, gather the the counts for feature **X**, and build an initial count vector; suppose it is:

value of $\mathbf{X} \rightarrow$	+	−
	1001	1002

This vector is stored at the *root* of the tree; the cost of this node is computed using NML, eq. 1. Note that this vector / distribution has rather high entropy.

Next, we try to split this node, by finding such a context that if we query the values of the feature in that context, it will help us reduce the entropy in this count vector. We check in turn all possible candidate contexts (L, P, F), and choose the best one. Each candidate refers to some symbol found on σ-level or τ-level, at some relative position P, and to one of that symbol's features F. We will condition the split on the possible values of F. For each candidate, we try to split on its feature's

values, and collect the resulting alignment counts.

Suppose one such candidate is $(\sigma, -V, \mathbf{H})$, i.e., (σ-level, previous vowel, Horizontal feature), and suppose that the **H**-feature has two values: *front / back*. Suppose also that the vector at the root node (recall, this tree is for the **X**-feature) would then split into two vectors, for example:

value of $\mathbf{X} \rightarrow$	+	−
$\mathbf{X} \mid \mathbf{H}$=*front*	1000	1
$\mathbf{X} \mid \mathbf{H}$=*back*	1	1001

This would likely be a very good split, since it reduces the entropy of the distribution in each row to near zero. The criterion that guides the choice of the best candidate context to use for splitting a node is the *sum* of the code lengths of the resulting split vectors, and the code length is proportional to the entropy.

We go through all candidates exhaustively,[9] and greedily choose the one that yields the greatest reduction in entropy, and drop in cost. We proceed recursively down the tree, trying to split nodes, and stop when the total tree cost stops decreasing.

This completes the tree for feature **X** on level σ. We build all remaining trees—for all features and all levels similarly—based on the current alignment of the complete data.

3.4 Variations of context-based models

The context models enable us to discover more regularities in the data by querying the context of sounds. However building decision trees repeatedly in the process of searching for the optimal alignments is very time consuming. We have explored several variations of context-based models in an attempt to make the search converge more quickly, without sacrificing quality.

3.4.1 Zero-depth context model

In this variant of the model, during the simulated annealing phase (i.e., when there is some randomness in the search algorithm), the trees are not expanded to their full depth. Instead, for source-level trees, only the root node is calculated and the target level trees are allowed to query only the *itself* position on the source level. Once the simulated annealing reaches the greedy phase, the trees are

---

[9] We augment the set of possible feature values at every node with two additional special branches: $\neq$ means that the symbol at the queried position is of the wrong **type** and hence does not have the queried feature; # means the query ran past the beginning of the word.

grown in the same way as they would have been normally, without any restrictions.

This model results in reasonable alignments and relatively low costs and lower running time.

3.4.2 Infinite-depth context model

This is another restrictive variation of the context model, which is more permissive than the zero-depth model. In this variation during the simulated annealing phase of the algorithm, the candidates that can be queried to expand the root nodes of the trees are limited to already encoded features of the *itself* position.

4 Evaluation

We discuss two views on evaluation—*strict* evaluations vs. *intuitive* evaluations.

4.1 Comparing context models to each other

From a strictly information-theoretic point of view, a sufficient condition to claim that model M_1 is better than M_2, is that M_1 assigns a higher probability (equivalently—lower cost) to the observed data. Figure 7A shows the absolute costs, *in bits*, for all language pairs—for the baseline 1-1 model and six context models. The six context models are: the "normal" model, zero-depth and infinite-depth—and for each, the objective function uses either NML or prequential coding.

Here is how we interpret the points in these scatter plots. Each box in the triangular plot compares one model, M_x—whose scores are plotted on the X-axis—against another model, M_y (on the Y-axis). For example, the leftmost column compares the baseline 1-1 model as M_x against each of the six context models in turn; etc. In every plot box, each of the 10×9 points is a comparison of the two models M_x and M_y on one language pair (L_1, L_2). Therefore, for each point (L_1, L_2), the X-coordinate gives the score of model M_x, and the Y-coordinate gives the score of the other model, M_y. If the point (L_1, L_2) is below the diagonal, M_x has higher cost on (L_1, L_2) than M_y. The further away the point is from the "break-even" diagonal line $x = y$, the greater the advantage of one model over the other.

The left column of figure 7A shows that all context models always produce much lower cost compared to the basic context-free 1-1 model defined in (Wettig et al., 2011).

The remaining five columns compare the context models among themselves. Here we see that

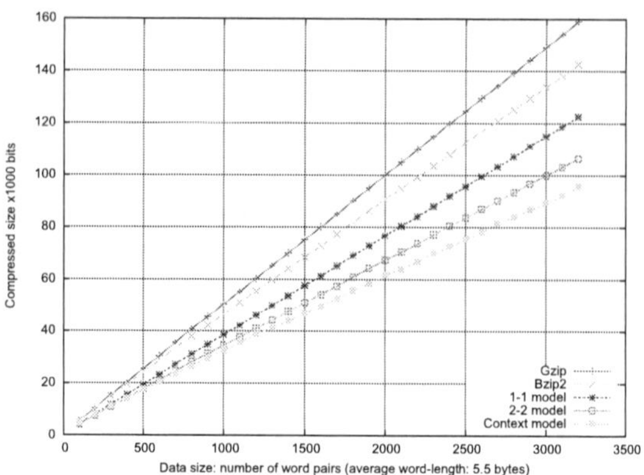

Figure 6: Comparison of compression power

no model variant is a clear winner. Since the variants do not show a clear preference for the "best" context model among this set, we will use *all* of them, to vote as an ensemble.

In figure 6, we compare the context model against standard data compressors, Gzip and Bzip, as well as the baseline models in (Wettig et al., 2011), tested on 3200 Finnish–Estonian data from SSA. Gzip/Bzip compress data by finding regularities—which are frequent sub-strings.

These comparisons confirm that the context model finds more regularity in the data than the off-the-shelf data compressors—which have no knowledge that the words in the data are genetically related—as well as the 1-1 and 2-2 models.

4.2 Imputation

Strictly, the improvement in the compression cost is adequate proof that the presented model outperforms the baselines. For a more intuitive evaluation of improvement in model quality, we can compare models by using them to *impute* unseen data. This is done as follows.

For a given model M, and a language pair (L_1, L_2)—e.g., (Finnish, Estonian)—we hold out one word pair, and train the model on all remaining word pairs. Then we show the model the held out Finnish word and let it impute—i.e., guess—the corresponding Estonian word. Imputation can be done for all models with a dynamic programming algorithm, similar to the Viterbi-like search used during model training. Formally, given the held-out Finnish string, the imputation procedure selects—from *all* possible Estonian strings—the most probable Estonian string, given the model.

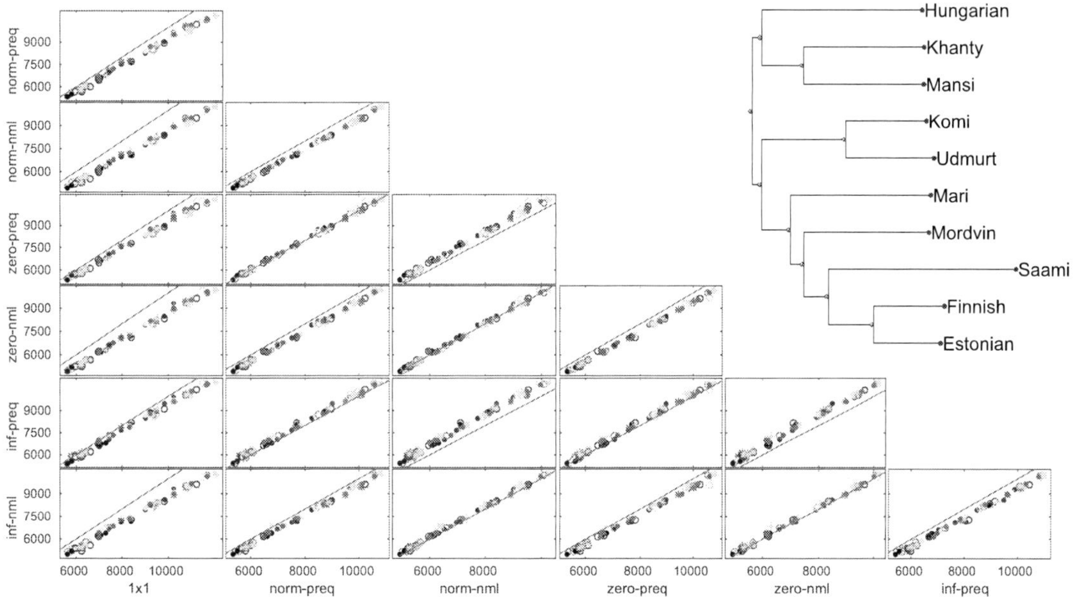

Figure 7: *(A: left) Comparison of costs of context models and the baseline 1-1;*
(B: upper right) Finno-Ugric tree induced by imputation and normalized edit distances, via NeighborJoin

We then compute an edit distance (e.g., the Levenshtein edit distance) between the imputed Estonian string and the correct withheld word.

We repeat this procedure for all word pairs in the (L_1, L_2) data set, sum the edit distances, and normalize by the total size of the correct L_2 data—giving the *Normalized Edit Distance*: $NED(L_2|L_1, M)$ from L_1 to L_2, under M.

NED indicates how much regularity the model has learned about the language pair (L_1, L_2) Finally, we used NED to compare models across all language pairs. The context models always have lower cost than the baseline, and lower NED in $\approx 88\%$ of the language pairs. This is encouraging indication that optimizing the code length is a good approach: the models *do not* optimize NED directly, and yet the cost correlates with NED—a simple and intuitive measure of model quality.

A similar kind of imputation was used in (Bouchard-Côté et al., 2007) for cross-validation.

4.3 Voting for phylogenies

Each context model assigns its own MDL cost to every language pair. These raw MDL costs are not directly comparable, since different language pairs have different amounts of data—different number of shared cognate words. We can make these costs comparable by normalizing them, using *NCD*—Normalized Compression Distance, (Cilibrasi and Vitanyi, 2005), as in (Wettig et al., 2011). Then, each model produces its own pairwise distance matrix for *all* language pairs—where the distance is NCD. A pairwise distance matrix can be used to construct a phylogeny for the language family.

NED, introduced above, provides yet another *distance measure* between any pair of languages, similarly to NCD. Thus, the NED scores can also be used to make inferences about how far the languages are from each other, and used as in put to algorithms for creating phylogenetic trees. For example, applying the *NeighborJoin* algorithm, (Saitou and Nei, 1987), to the pairwise NED matrix produced by the normal context model, yields the phylogeny in Figure 7B.

To compute how far a given phylogeny is from a gold-standard tree, we can use a distance measure for unrooted, leaf-labeled (URLL) trees. One such URLL distance measure is given in (Robinson and Foulds, 1981). The URLL distance between this tree and the gold standard in Figure 1 is 0.12.[10]

However, the MDL costs do not allow us to prefer any one of the context models over the others.

---

[10]This URLL distance of 0.12 is also quite small. We computed the *expected* URLL distance from a *random* tree with this leaf set over a sample of 1000 randomly generated trees—which is over 0.8. The number of leaf-labeled trees with n nodes is $(2n - 3)!!$ (see, e.g., (Ford, 2010)).

Model	Brit.	Ant.	Volga
normal-nml-avg.NCD	0.14	0	0.14
normal-nml-avg.NED	0.14	0	0.14
normal-nml-min.NCD	0.14	0	0.14
normal-nml-min.NED	0.28	0.14	0.28
normal-prequential-avg.NCD	0.14	0	0.14
normal-prequential-avg.NED	0.14	0.28	0.42
normal-prequential-min.NCD	0.14	0	0.14
normal-prequential-min.NED	0.14	0.28	0.42
∞-nml-avg.NCD	0.28	0.14	0.28
∞-nml-avg.NED	0.42	0.28	0.42
∞-nml-min.NCD	0.28	0.14	0.28
∞-nml-min.NED	0.28	0.14	0.28
∞-prequential-avg.NCD	0.14	0	0.14
∞-prequential-avg.NED	0.28	0.14	0.28
∞-prequential-min.NCD	0.14	0.28	0.42
∞-prequential-min.NED	0.28	0.14	0.28
zero-nml-avg.NCD	0.42	0.42	0.57
zero-nml-avg.NED	0	0.14	0.28
zero-nml-min.NCD	0.14	0	0.14
zero-nml-min.NED	0.28	0.28	0.42
zero-prequential-avg.NCD	0.14	0	0.14
zero-prequential-avg.NED	0.28	0.14	0.28
zero-prequential-min.NCD	0.14	0	0.14
zero-prequential-min.NED	0.28	0.28	0.42
Total vote	5.14	**3.28**	6.71

Table 1: Context models voting for Britannica, Anttila and Volga gold standards

Therefore, we use all models as an ensemble.

Gold-standard trees: Different linguists advocate different, conflicting theories about the structure of the Uralic family tree, and Finno-Ugric in particular. Figure 1 shows one such phylogeny, we call "Britannica." Another phylogeny, isomorphic to the tree in Figure 7B, we call "Anttila." A third tree in the literature pairs Mari and Mordvin together into a "Volgaic" branch of Finno-Ugric.

In Table 1, we compare trees generated by the context models to these three gold-standard trees, using the URLL distance defined above.

The context models induce phylogenetic trees as follows. Each model can use prequential coding or NML. Each model yields one NCD matrix and one NED matrix. Finally, for any pair of languages L_1 and L_2, the model in general produces different distances for (L_1, L_2) vs. (L_2, L_1), depending on which language is the source and which is the target (since some languages preserve more information than others). Therefore, each of the three context models produces 8 trees, 24 in total. The distance from each tree to the three gold-standard phylogenies is in Table 1.

The measures show which gold-standard tree is favored by all models taken together. The models strongly prefer "Anttila"—which happens to be the phylogeny favored by a majority of Uralic scholars at present, (Anttila, 1989).

5 Discussion and future work

We have presented an approach to modeling evolutionary processes within a language family by coding data from all languages pair-wise. To our knowledge, these models represent the first attempt to capture *longer-range* context in evolutionary modeling, where prior work allowed small neighboring context to condition the correspondences. We present a feature-based context-aware MDL coding scheme, and compare it against our earlier models, in terms of compression cost and imputation power. Language distances induced by compression cost and by imputation for all pairs of languages, enable us to build complete phylogenies. The model takes a set of lexical data as input, and makes no further assumptions. In this regard, it is as objective as possible given the data.[11]

Finally, we note that our experiments with the context models confirm that the notion of alignment is secondary in modeling evolution. In the old approach, we aligned symbols *jointly*, and hoped to find symbol pairs that align to each other frequently. In the new approach, we code symbols separately one by one on the source and target level, and A. we code the symbols one feature at a time, and B. while coding each feature, we allow the model to use information from any feature of any symbol that has been coded previously.

These models do better, with no alignment.

The objectivity of models given the data opens new possibilities for comparing entire data sets. For example, we can begin to compare the Finnish/Estonian data in StarLing vs. other datasets—and the comparison will be impartial, relying solely on the given data. The models also enable us to quantify the uncertainty of individual entries in the corpus of etymological data. For example, for a given entry x in language L_1, we can compute the probability that x would be imputed by any of the models, trained on all the remaining data from L_1 plus any other set of languages in the family. This can be applied in particular to entries marked as dubious by the database creators.

---

[11]The data set itself, of course, may be highly subjective. Refining the data set is in itself an important challenge, as presented in problem a. in the Introduction, to be addressed in future work.

Acknowledgments

This research was supported in part by the Uralink Project and the FinUgRevita Project of the Academy of Finland, and by the National Centre of Excellence "ALGODAN: Algorithmic Data Analysis" of the Academy of Finland. We thank Teemu Roos for his assistance. We are grateful to the anonymous reviewers for their comments and suggestions.

References

Raimo Anttila. 1989. *Historical and comparative linguistics*. John Benjamins.

François G. Barbançon, Tandy Warnow, Don Ringe, Steven N. Evans, and Luay Nakhleh. 2009. An experimental study comparing linguistic phylogenetic reconstruction methods. In *Proceedings of the Conference on Languages and Genes*, UC Santa Barbara. Cambridge University Press.

Alexandre Bouchard-Côté, Percy Liang, Thomas Griffiths, and Dan Klein. 2007. A probabilistic approach to diachronic phonology. In *Proceedings of the Joint Conference on Empirical Methods in Natural Language Processing and Computational Natural Language Learning (EMNLP-CoNLL:2007)*, pages 887–896, Prague, Czech Republic.

Alexandre Bouchard-Côté, Thomas L. Griffiths, and Dan Klein. 2009. Improved reconstruction of protolanguage word forms. In *Proceedings of the North American Chapter of the Association for Computational Linguistics (NAACL09)*.

Rudi Cilibrasi and Paul M.B. Vitanyi. 2005. Clustering by compression. *IEEE Transactions on Information Theory*, 51(4):1523–1545.

Daniel J. Ford. 2010. Encodings of cladograms and labeled trees. *Electronic Journal of Combinatorics*, 17:1556–1558.

Peter Grünwald. 2007. *The Minimum Description Length Principle*. MIT Press.

David Hall and Dan Klein. 2011. Large-scale cognate recovery. In *Empirical Methods in Natural Language Processing (EMNLP)*.

Erkki Itkonen and Ulla-Maija Kulonen. 2000. *Suomen Sanojen Alkuperä (The Origin of Finnish Words)*. Suomalaisen Kirjallisuuden Seura, Helsinki, Finland.

Brett Kessler. 2001. *The Significance of Word Lists: Statistical Tests for Investigating Historical Connections Between Languages*. The University of Chicago Press, Stanford, CA.

Grzegorz Kondrak. 2002. Determining recurrent sound correspondences by inducing translation models. In *Proceedings of COLING 2002: 19th International Conference on Computational Linguistics*, pages 488–494, Taipei.

Grzegorz Kondrak. 2003. Identifying complex sound correspondences in bilingual wordlists. In A. Gelbukh, editor, *Computational Linguistics and Intelligent Text Processing (CICLing-2003)*, pages 432–443, Mexico City. Springer-Verlag Lecture Notes in Computer Science, No. 2588.

Grzegorz Kondrak. 2004. Combining evidence in cognate identification. In *Proceedings of the Seventeenth Canadian Conference on Artificial Intelligence (Canadian AI 2004)*, pages 44–59, London, Ontario. Lecture Notes in Computer Science 3060, Springer-Verlag.

Petri Kontkanen and Petri Myllymäki. 2007. A linear-time algorithm for computing the multinomial stochastic complexity. *Information Processing Letters*, 103(6):227–233.

Luay Nakhleh, Don Ringe, and Tandy Warnow. 2005. Perfect phylogenetic networks: A new methodology for reconstructing the evolutionary history of natural languages. *Language (Journal of the Linguistic Society of America)*, 81(2):382–420.

Javad Nouri, Jukka Sirén, Jukka Corander, and Roman Yangarber. 2016. From alignment of etymological data to phylogenetic inference via population genetics. In *Proceedings of CogACLL: the 7th Workshop on Cognitive aspects of Computational Language Learning, at ACL-2016*, Berlin, Germany, August. Association for Computational Linguistics.

Károly Rédei. 1991. *Uralisches etymologisches Wörterbuch*. Harrassowitz, Wiesbaden.

Don Ringe, Tandy Warnow, and A. Taylor. 2002. Indo-European and computational cladistics. *Transactions of the Philological Society*, 100(1):59–129.

Jorma Rissanen. 1996. Fisher information and stochastic complexity. *IEEE Transactions on Information Theory*, 42(1):40–47.

D.F. Robinson and L.R. Foulds. 1981. Comparison of phylogenetic trees. *Mathematical Biosciences*, 53(1–2):131–147.

Naruya Saitou and Masatoshi Nei. 1987. The Neighbor-Joining method: a new method for reconstructing phylogenetic trees. *Molecular biology and evolution*, 4(4):406–425.

Yuri M. Shtarkov. 1987. Universal sequential coding of single messages. *Problems of Information Transmission*, 23:3–17.

Sergei A. Starostin. 2005. Tower of Babel: StarLing etymological databases. http://newstar.rinet.ru/.

Hannes Wettig, Suvi Hiltunen, and Roman Yangarber. 2011. MDL-based Models for Alignment of Etymological Data. In *Proceedings of RANLP: the 8th Conference on Recent Advances in Natural Language Processing*, Hissar, Bulgaria.

Hannes Wettig, Kirill Reshetnikov, and Roman Yangarber. 2012. Using context and phonetic features in models of etymological sound change. In *Proc. EACL Workshop on Visualization of Linguistic Patterns and Uncovering Language History from Multilingual Resources*, pages 37–44, Avignon, France.

Harnessing Sequence Labeling for Sarcasm Detection in Dialogue from TV Series 'Friends'

Aditya Joshi[1,2,3]   **Vaibhav Tripathi**[1]
Pushpak Bhattacharyya[1]   **Mark Carman**[2]
[1]Indian Institute of Technology Bombay, India
[2]Monash University, Australia
[3]IITB-Monash Research Academy, India
{adityaj, vtripathi,pb}@cse.iitb.ac.in, mark.carman@monash.edu

Abstract

This paper is a novel study that views sarcasm detection in dialogue as a sequence labeling task, where a dialogue is made up of a sequence of utterances. We create a manually-labeled dataset of dialogue from TV series 'Friends' annotated with sarcasm. Our goal is to predict sarcasm in each utterance, using sequential nature of a scene. We show performance gain using sequence labeling as compared to classification-based approaches.

Our experiments are based on three sets of features, one is derived from information in our dataset, the other two are from past works. Two sequence labeling algorithms (SVM-HMM and SEARN) outperform three classification algorithms (SVM, Naive Bayes) for all these feature sets, with an increase in F-score of around 4%. Our observations highlight the viability of sequence labeling techniques for sarcasm detection of dialogue.

1 Introduction

Sarcasm is defined as 'the use of irony to mock or convey contempt'[1]. An example of a sarcastic sentence is *'Being stranded in traffic is the best way to start the week'*. In this case, the positive word *'best'* together with the undesirable situation *'being stranded in traffic'* conveys the sarcasm. Because sarcasm has an implied sentiment (negative) that is different from surface sentiment (positive due to presence of 'best'), it poses a challenge to sentiment analysis systems that aim to determine polarity in text (Pang and Lee, 2008).

Some sarcastic expressions may be more difficult to detect. Consider the possibly sarcastic statement *'I absolutely love this restaurant'*. Unlike in the traffic example above, sarcasm in this sentence, if any, can be understood using context which is 'external' to the sentence *i.e.,* beyond common world knowledge. [2]. This external context may be available in the conversation

that this sentence is a part of. For example, the conversational context may be situational: the speaker discovers a fly in her soup, then looks at her date and says, *'I absolutely love this restaurant'*. The conversational context may also be verbal: her date says, *'They've taken 40 minutes to bring our appetizers'* to which the speaker responds *'I absolutely love this restaurant'*. Both these examples point to the intuition that for dialogue (*i.e.,* data where more than one speaker participates in a discourse), conversational context is often a clue for sarcasm.

For such dialogue, prior work in sarcasm detection (determining whether a text is sarcastic or not) captures context in the form of classifier features such as the topic's probability of evoking sarcasm, or the author's tendency to use sarcasm (Rajadesingan et al., 2015; Wallace, 2015). In this paper, we present an alternative hypothesis: **sarcasm detection of dialogue is better formulated as a sequence labeling task, instead of classification task.**

The central message of our work is the efficacy of using sequence labeling as a learning mechanism for sarcasm detection in dialogue, and not in the set of features that we propose for sarcasm detection - although we experiment with three feature sets. For our experiments, we create a manually labeled dataset of dialogues from TV series 'Friends'. Each dialogue is considered to be a sequence of utterances, and every utterance is annotated as sarcastic or non-sarcastic (Details in Section 3). It may be argued that a TV series episode is dramatized and hence does not reflect real-world conversations. However, although the script of 'Friends' is dramatized to suit the situational comedy genre, it takes away nothing from its relevance to real-life conversations except for the volume of sarcastic sentences. Therefore, our findings from this work can, in theory, be reliably extended to work for any real-life utterances. Also, such datasets that are not based on real-world conversations have been used in prior work: emotion detection of children stories in Zhang et al. (2014) and speech transcripts of a MTV show in Rakov and Rosenberg (2013). As a first step in the direction of using sequence labeling, our dataset is a good 'controlled experiment' environment (The details are discussed in Section 2). In fact, use of a dataset in a new

---

[1]As defined by the Oxford Dictionary.

[2]Common world knowledge here refers to a general sentiment map of situations to sentiment. For example, being stranded in traffic is a negative situation to most.

Proceedings of the 20th SIGNLL Conference on Computational Natural Language Learning (CoNLL), pages 146–155,
Berlin, Germany, August 7-12, 2016. ©2016 Association for Computational Linguistics

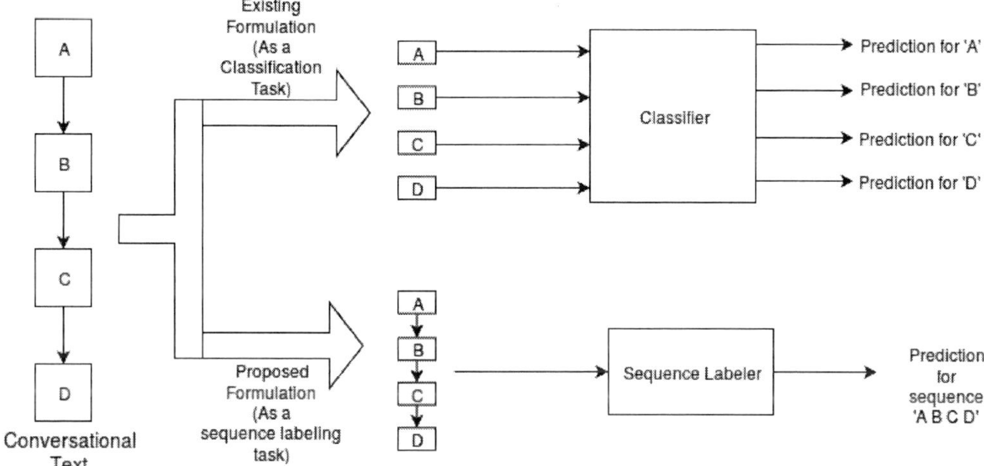

Figure 1: Illustration of our hypothesis for sarcasm detection of conversational text (such as dialogue); A, B, C, D indicate four utterances

genre (TV series transcripts, specifically) has potential for future work in sarcasm detection. Our dataset without the actual dialogues from the show (owing to copyright restrictions) may be available on request.

Based on information available in our dataset (names of speakers, etc.), we present new features. We then compare two sequence labelers (SEARN and SVM-HMM) with three classifiers (SVM with oversampled and undersampled data, and Naïve Bayes), for this set of features and also for features from two prior works. In case of our novel features as well as features reported in prior work, sequence labeling algorithms outperform classification algorithms. There is an improvement of 3-4% in F-score when sequence labelers are used, as compared to classifiers, for sarcasm detection in our dialogue dataset. Since many datasets such as tweet conversations, chat transcripts, etc. are currently available, our findings will be useful to obtain additional contexts in future work.

The rest of the paper is organized as follows. Section 2 motivates the approach and presents our hypothesis. Section 3 describes our dataset, while Section 4 presents the features we use (this includes three configurations: novel features based on our dataset, and features from past work). Experiment setup is in Section 5 and results are given in Section 6. We present a discussion on which types of sarcasm are handled better by sequence labeling and an error analysis in Section 7, and describe related work in Section 8. Finally, we conclude in Section 9.

2 Motivation & Hypothesis

In dialogue, multiple participants take turns to speak. Consider the following snippet from 'Friends' involving two of the lead characters, Ross and Chandler.

[Chandler is at the table. Ross walks in, looking very tanned.]
Chandler: *Hold on! There is something different.*
Ross: *I went to that tanning place your wife suggested.*
Chandler: *Was that place... The Sun?*

Chandler's statement '*Was that place... The Sun?*' is sarcastic. The sarcasm can be understood based on two kinds of contextual information: (a) general knowledge (that sun is indeed hot) (b) Conversational context (In the previous utterance, Ross states that he went to a tanning place). Without information (b), the sarcasm cannot be understood. Thus, dialogue presents a peculiar opportunity: using sequential nature of text for the task at hand.

We hypothesize that '*for sarcasm detection of dialogue, sequence labeling performs better than classification*'. To validate our hypothesis, we consider two feature configurations: (a) novel features designed for our dataset, (b) features as given in two prior works. To further understand where exactly sequence labeling techniques do better, we also present a discussion on which linguistic types of sarcasm benefit the most from sequence labeling in place of classification.

Figure 1 summarizes the scope of this paper. We consider two formulations for sarcasm detection of conversational text. In the first option (i.e. classification), a sequence is broken down into individual instances. One instance as an input to a classification algorithm returns an output for that instance. In the second option (i.e. sequence labeling), a sequence as input to a sequence labeling algorithm returns a sequence of labels as an output. In rest of the paper, we use the following terms:

# Utterances	17338
# Scenes	913
Vocabulary	9345 unigrams
Average Length of Utterance	15.08 words
Average Length of Scene	18.6 utterances

Table 1: Dataset Statistics

1. **Utterance**: An utterance is a contiguous set of sentences spoken by an individual without interruption (from another individual). Every utterance has a speaker, and may be characterized by additional information (such as speaker's expressions and intonation) in the transcript.

2. **Scene/Sequence**: A scene is a sequence of utterances, in which different speakers take turns to speak. We use the terms *'scene'* and *'sequence'* interchangeably.

3 *'Friends'* Dataset

Datasets based on literary/creative works have been explored in the past. One such example is emotion classification of children's stories by Zhang Z (2014). Similarly, we create a sarcasm-labeled dataset that consists of transcripts of a comedy TV show, 'Friends[3]' (by Bright/Kauffman/Crane Productions, and Warner Bros. Entertainment Inc.). We download these transcripts from OpenSubtitles[4] as given by Lison and Tiedemann (2016), with additional pre-processing from a fan-contributed website called `http://www.friendstranscripts.tk`. Each scene begins with a description of the location/situation followed by a series of utterances spoken by characters. Figure 2 shows an illustration of our dataset. This is (obviously) a dummy example that has been anonymized.

The reason behind choosing a TV show transcript as our dataset was to restrict to a small set of characters (so as to leverage on speaker-specific features) that use a lot of humor. These characters are often sarcastic towards each other because of their inter-personal relationships. In fact, past linguistic studies also show how sarcasm is more common between familiar speakers, and often friends (Gibbs, 2000). A typical snippet is:

[Scene: Chandler and Monica's room. Chandler is packing when Ross knocks on the door and enters...]
Ross: Hey!
Chandler: Hey!
Ross: You guys ready to go?
Chandler: Not quite. Monica's still at the salon, and I'm just finishing packing.

Our annotators are linguists with an experience of more than 8k hours of annotation, and are not authors

---

[3] http://www.imdb.com/title/tt0108778/
[4] http://www.opensubtitles.org

	Label
[Scene: Dummy Location. Characters present, etc.]	No label
Joey: Joey's first utterance, sentence 1. Joey's first utterance, sentence 2.	Non-sarcastic
Ross: Ross' utterance, sentence 1. Ross' utterance, sentence 2.	Sarcastic
Chandler: (action Chandler does while speaking this) Chandler's utterance, sentence 1.Chandler's utterance, sentence 2. Chandler's utterance, sentence 3.	Sarcastic

Action words:(action Chandler does while speaking this)
Spoken words: Chandler's utterance, sentence 1....
Speaker: Chandler
Speaker-Listener: Chandler-Ross

Figure 2: Example from our Dataset: Part of a Scene

of this paper. A complete scene is visible to the annotators at a time, so that they understand complete context of the scene. They perform the task of annotating every utterance in this scene with two labels: sarcastic and non-sarcastic. The two annotators separately perform this annotation over multiple sessions. To minimize bias beyond the scope of this annotation, we selected annotators who had never watched Friends before this annotation task.

The annotations [5] may be available on request, subject to copyright restrictions. Every utterance is annotated with a label while description of a scene is not annotated.

The inter-annotator agreement for a subset of 105 scenes[6] (around 1600 utterances) is 0.44. This is comparable with other manually annotated datasets in sarcasm detection (Tsur et al., 2010). Table 1 shows the relevant statistics of the complete dataset (in addition to 105 scenes as mentioned above). There are 17338 utterances in 913 scenes. Out of these, 1888 utterances are labeled as sarcastic. Average length of a scene is 18.6 utterances.

Table 2 shows additional statistics. Table 2(a) shows that Chandler is the character with highest proportion of sarcastic utterances (22.24%). Table 2(b) shows that sarcastic utterances have higher surface positive word score[7] (1.55) than non-sarcastic (0.97) or overall utterances (1.03). This validates the past observation that sarcasm is often expressed through positive words (and sometimes contrasted with negation)(Joshi et al., 2015). Finally, Table 2(c) shows that sarcastic utterances also have higher proportion of non-verbal indicators (action words) (28.23%) than non-sarcastic or overall utterances.

---

[5] without textual content, keeping in view copyright restrictions.

[6] For these scenes, the annotators later discussed and arrived at a consensus- they were then added to the dataset. The remaining scenes are done by either of the two annotators.

[7] This is computed using a simple lexicon lookup, as in case of conversational context features below.

Character	% sarcastic
Phoebe	9.70
Joey	11.05
Rachel	9.74
Monica	8.87
Chandler	22.24
Ross	8.42

	Surface Positive Sentiment Score	Surface Negative Sentiment Score
Sarcastic	1.55	1.20
Non-sarcastic	0.97	0.75
All	1.03	0.79

	Actions (%)
Sarcastic	28.23
Non-sarcastic	23.95
All	24.43

Table 2: Dataset statistics related to: (a) percentage of sarcastic utterances for six lead characters, (b) average surface positive and negative scores for the two classes, (c) percentage of sarcastic and non-sarcastic utterances with actions

Feature	Description
Lexical Features	
Spoken words	Unigrams of spoken words
Conversational Context Features	
Actions	Unigrams of action words
Sentiment Score	Positive & Negative score of utterance
Previous Sentiment Score	Positive & Negative score of previous utterance in the sequence
Speaker Context Features	
Speaker	Speaker of this utterance
Speaker-Listener	Pair of speaker of this utterance and speaker of the previous utterance

Table 3: Our Dataset-Derived Features

4 Features

To ensure that our hypothesis is not dependent on choice of features, we show our results on two configurations: (a) when dataset-derived features (*i.e.*, novel features designed based on our dataset) are used, and (b) when features reported in prior work are used. We describe these in forthcoming subsections.

4.1 Dataset-derived Features

We design our dataset-derived features based on information available in our dataset. An utterance consists of three parts:

1. **Speaker**: The name of the speaker is the first word of an utterance, and is followed by a colon. In case of the second utterance in Figure 2, the speaker is '*Ross*' while in the third, the speaker is '*Chandler*'.

2. **Spoken words**: This is the textual portion of what the speaker says. In the second utterance in Figure 2, the spoken words are '*Chandler's utterance, sentence 1..*'.

3. **Action words**: Actions that a speaker performs while speaking the utterance are indicated in parentheses. These are useful clues that form additional context. Unlike speaker and spoken words, action words may or may not be present. In the second utterance in Figure 2, there are no action words while in the third utterance, '*action Chandler does while reading this*' are action words.

Based on this information, we design three categories of features (listed in Table 3). These are:

1. **Lexical Features**: These are unigrams in the spoken words. We experimented with both count and boolean representations, and the results are comparable. We report values for boolean representation.

2. **Conversational Context Features**: In order to capture conversational context, we use three kinds of features. *Action words* are unigrams indicated within parentheses. The intuition is that a character 'raising her eyebrows' (action) is different from saying "raising her eyebrows". As the next feature, we use *sentiment score* of this utterance. These are two values: positive and negative scores. These scores are the positive and negative words present in an utterance. The third kind of conversational context features is the *sentiment score of the previous utterance*. This captures phenomena such as a negative remark from one character eliciting sarcasm from another. This is similar to the situation described in Joshi et al. (2015). Thus, for the third utterance in Figure 2, the sentiment score of Chandler's utterance forms the *Sentiment score* feature, while that of Ross's utterance forms *Sentiment score of previous utterance*.

3. **Speaker Context Features**: We use name of the speaker and name of the speaker-listener pair as features. The listener is assumed to be the speaker of the previous utterance in the sequence[8]. The speaker feature aims to capture the sarcastic nature of each of these characters, while

[8]The first utterance in a sequence has a null value for previous speaker.

the speaker-listener feature aims to capture inter-personal interactions between different characters. In the context of third utterance in Figure 2, the speaker is '*Chandler*' while speaker-listener pair is '*Chandler-Ross*'.

4.2 Features from Prior Work

We also compare our results with features presented in two prior works[9]:

1. **Features given in González-Ibánez et al. (2011)**: These features are: (a) Interjections, (b) Punctuations, (c) Pragmatic features (where we include action words as well), (d) Sentiment lexicon-based features from LIWC (Pennebaker et al., 2001) (where they include counts of linguistic process words, positive/negative emotion words, etc.).

2. **Features given in Buschmeier et al. (2014)**: In addition to unigrams, the features used by them are: (a) Hyperbole (captured by three positive or negative words in a row), (b) Quotation marks and ellipsis, (c) Positive/Negative Sentiment Scores followed by punctuation (this includes more than one positive or negative words with an exclamation mark or question mark at the end), (d) Positive/Negative Sentiment Scores followed by ellipsis (this includes more than one positive or negative words with a '...' at the end, (e) Punctuation, (f) Interjections, and (g) Laughter expressions (such as 'haha').

5 Experiment Setup

We experiment with three classification techniques and two sequence labeling techniques:

1. **Classification Techniques**: We use Naïve Bayes and SVM as classification techniques. Naïve Bayes implementation provided in Scikit (Pedregosa et al., 2011) is used. For SVM, we use SVM-Light (Joachims, 1999). Since SVM does not do well for datasets with a large class imbalance (Akbani et al., 2004)[10], we use sampling to deal with this skew as done in Kotsiantis et al. (2006). We experiment with two configurations:

   - SVM (Oversampled) *i.e.*, **SVM (O)**: Sarcastic utterances are duplicated to match the count of non-sarcastic utterances.
   - SVM (Undersampled) *i.e.*, **SVM (U)**: Random non-sarcastic utterances are dropped to match the count of sarcastic utterances.

2. **Sequence Labeling Techniques**: We use **SVM-HMM** by Altun et al. (2003) and **SEARN** by Daumé III et al. (2009). SVM-HMM is a sequence labeling algorithm that combines Support Vector Machines and Hidden Markov Models. SEARN is a sequence labeling algorithm that integrates search and learning to solve prediction problems. The implementation of SEARN that we use relies on perceptron as the base classifier. Daumé III et al. (2009) show that SEARN outperforms other sequence labeling techniques (such as CRF) for tasks like character recognition and named entity class identification.

Thus, we wish to validate our hypothesis in case of:

1. Our data-derived features as given in Section 4.1.

2. Past features from González-Ibánez et al. (2011) and Buschmeier et al. (2014) as given in Section 4.2.

Algorithm	Precision (%)	Recall (%)	F-Score (%)
Formulation as Classification			
SVM (U)	83.6	48.6	57.2
SVM (O)	**84.4**	76.8	79.8
Naïve Bayes	77.2	33.8	42
Formulation as Sequence Labeling			
SVM-HMM	83.8	**88.2**	**84.2**
SEARN	82.6	83.4	82.8

Table 4: Comparison of sequence labeling techniques with classification techniques, for features reported in dataset-derived features

We report **weighted average values of precision, recall and F-score** computed using five-fold cross-validation for all experiments, and class-wise precision, recall, F-score wherever necessary. The folds are created on the basis of sequences and not utterances. This means that a sequence does not get split across different folds.

6 Results

Section 6.1 describes performance of traditional models that use dataset-derived features (as given in Section 4.1), while Section 6.2 does so for features from prior work (as given in Section 4.2).

6.1 Performance on Dataset-derived Features

Table 4 compares the performance of the two formulations: classification and sequence labeling, for our dataset-derived features. When classification techniques are used, we obtain the best F-score of 79.8% with SVM (O). However, when sequence labeling techniques are used, the best F-score is 84.2%. In terms of

---

[9]The two prior works are chosen based on what information was available in our dataset for the purpose of re-implementation. For example, approaches that use the Twitter profile information or the follower/friends structure in the Twitter, cannot be computed for our dataset.

[10]We also observe the same.

	Sarcastic			Non-Sarcastic		
	Precision	**Recall**	**F-Score**	**Precision**	**Recall**	**F-Score**
SVM (U)	14	**68.8**	23	**92.2**	46.2	61.6
SVM (O)	22.4	44	**29**	91.8	81	86
Naive Bayes	9.8	59.8	16.8	85.8	30.6	45
SVM-HMM	**35.8**	7.6	12.6	89.4	**98.2**	**93.6**
SEARN	22.2	19.4	20	90	91.6	90.4

Table 5: Class-wise precision/recall values for all techniques using our dataset-derived features

F-score, **our two sequence labeling techniques perform better than all three classification techniques.** The increase in recall is high - the best value for classification techniques is (SVM (O)) 76.8%, while that for sequence labeling techniques (SVM-HMM) is 88.2%. It must be noted that sentiment of previous utterance is one of the features of both the classification and sequence labeling techniques. Despite that, sequence labeling techniques perform better.

Alg.	Feature (Best)	P (%)	R (%)	F (%)
	Formulation as Classification			
SVM (U)	Unigram+ Spkr-Listnr+ Action+ Senti. Score	**84.8**	49.4	57.4
SVM (O)	Unigram+ Speaker+ Spkr-Listnr+Senti. Score	84	79	81.2
Naïve Bayes	All features	77.2	33.8	42
	Formulation as Sequence Labeling			
SVM-HMM	Unigram+ Speaker+ Spkr-Listnr+ Prev. Senti. Score + Action	83.2	**87.8**	**84.4**
SEARN	All features	82.6	83.4	82.8

Table 6: Feature Combinations for which different techniques exhibit their best performance for dataset-derived features

Table 5 shows class-wise precision/recall values for these techniques. The best value of precision for sarcastic class is obtained in case of SVM-HMM, *i.e.*, 35.8%. The best F-score for the sarcastic class is in the case of SVM (O) (29%) whereas that for the non-sarcastic class is in the case of SVM-HMM (93.6%). Tables 4 and 5 show that it is due to a high recall, sequence labeling techniques perform better than classification techniques.

It may be argued that the benefit in case of sequence labeling is due to our features, and is not a benefit of the sequence labeling formulation itself. Hence, we ran these five techniques with all possible combinations of features. Table 6 shows the best performance obtained by each of the classifiers, and the corresponding (best) feature combinations. The table can be read as: SVM (O) obtains a F-score of 81.2% when spoken words, speaker, speaker-listener and sentiment score are used as features. The table shows that **even if we consider the best performance of each of the techniques (with different feature sets), classifiers are not able to perform as well as sequence labeling**. The best sequence labeling algorithm (SVM-HMM) gives a F-score of 84.4% while the best classifier (SVM(O)) has an F-score of 81.2%. We emphasize that both SVM-HMM and SEARN have higher recall values than the three classification techniques.

These findings show that **for our novel set of dataset-derived features, sequence labeling works better than classification.**

6.2 Performance on Features Reported in Prior Work

We now show our evaluation on two sets of features reported in prior work. These sets of features as given in two prior works by Buschmeier et al. (2014) and González-Ibánez et al. (2011).

Table 7 compares classification techniques with sequence labeling techniques for features given in González-Ibánez et al. (2011)[11]. Table 8 shows corresponding values for features given in Buschmeier et al. (2014)[12]. For features by González-Ibánez et al. (2011), SVM (O) gives the best F-score for classification techniques (79%), whereas SVM-HMM shows an improvement of 4% over that value. Recall **increases by 11.8%** when sequence labeling techniques are used instead of classification.

In case of features by Buschmeier et al. (2014), the improvement in performance achieved by using sequence labeling as against classification is 2.8%. The best recall for classification techniques is 77.8% (for SVM (O)). In this case as well, the recall increases by 10% for sequence labeling.

These findings show that **for two feature sets reported in prior work, sequence labeling works bet-**

---

[11]The paper reports best accuracy of 65.44% for their dataset. This shows that our implementation is competent.

[12]The paper reports best F-score of 67.8% for their dataset. This shows that our implementation is competent.

ter than classification.

Algorithm	P (%)	R (%)	F (%)
Features from Gonzalez-Ibanez et al. (2011)			
Formulation as Classification			
SVM (U)	**86.4**	26	27
SVM (O)	84.6	75.6	79
Naive Bayes	77.2	43.8	48.4
Formulation as Sequence Labeling			
SVM-HMM	83.4	**87.4**	**83**
SEARN	82	82.4	81.8

Table 7: Comparison of sequence labeling techniques with classification techniques, for features reported in Gonzalez-Ibanez et al. (2011)

Algorithm	P (%)	R (%)	F (%)
Features from Buschmeier et al. (2014)			
Formulation as Classification			
SVM (U)	**85.4**	40.6	46.8
SVM (O)	84.6	77.8	80.4
Naïve Bayes	76.6	27.2	32.8
Formulation as Sequence Labeling			
SVM-HMM	84.2	**87.8**	**83.2**
SEARN	82.4	83.8	82.4

Table 8: Comparison of sequence labeling techniques with classification techniques, for features reported in Buschmeier et al. (2014)

7 Discussion

In previous sections, we show that quantitatively, sequence labeling techniques perform better than classification techniques. In this section, we delve into the question: '*What does this improved performance mean, in terms of forms of sarcasm that sequence labeling techniques are able to handle better than classification?*' To understand the implication of using sequence labeling, we randomly select 100 examples that were correctly labeled by sequence labeling techniques but incorrectly labeled by classification techniques. Our annotators manually annotated them into one among four categories of sarcasm as given in Camp (2012). Table 9 shows the proportion of these utterances. Like-prefixed and illocutionary sarcasm types are the ones that require context for understanding sarcasm. We observe that around 71% of our examples belong to these two types of sarcasm. This means that **our intuition that sequence labeling will better capture conversational context reflects in the forms of sarcasm for which sequence labeling improves over classification.**

On the other hand, examples where our system makes errors can be grouped as:

- **Topic Drift**: Eisterhold et al. (2006) state that topic change/drift is a peculiarity of sarcasm. For example, when Phoebe gets irritated with another character talking for a long time, she says,"See? Vegetarianism benefits everyone". This was misclassified by our system.

- **Short expressions**: Short expressions occurring in the context of a conversation may express sarcasm. Expressions such as *"Oh God, is it"* and *"Me too"* were misclassified as non-sarcastic. However, in the context of the scene, these were sarcastic utterances.

- **Dry humor**: In the context of a conversation, sarcasm may be expressed in response to a long serious description. Our system was unable to capture such sarcasm in some cases. When a character gives long description of advantages of a particular piece of clothing, Chandler asks sarcastically, *"Are you aware that you're still talking?"*.

- **Implications in popular culture**: The utterance *"Ok, I smell smoke. Maybe that's cause someone's pants are on fire"* was misclassified by our system. The popular saying 'Liar, liar, pants on fire[13]' was the context that was missing in our case.

- **Background knowledge**: When a petite girl walks in, Rachel says *"She is so cute! You could fit her right in your little pocket"*.

- **Long-range connection**: In comedy shows like Friends, humor is often created by introducing a concept in the initial part and then repeating it as an impactful, sarcastic remark. For example, in beginning of an episode, Ross says that he has never grabbed a spoon before - and at the end of the episode, he says with a sarcastic tone *"I grabbed a spoon"*.

- **Incongruity with situation in the scenes**: Utterances that were incongruent with non-verbal situations could not be adequately identified. For example, Ross enters an office wearing a piece of steel bandaged to his nose. In response, the receptionist says, "Oh, that's attractive".

- **Sarcasm as a part of a longer sentence**: In several utterances, sarcasm is a subset of a longer sentence, and hence, the non-sarcastic portion may dominate the rest of the sentence.

These errors point to future directions in which sequence labeling algorithms may be optimized to improve their impact on sarcasm detection.

---

[13]http://www.urbandictionary.com/define.php?term=Liar%20Liar%20Pants%20On%20Fire

Type	Examples (%)
Propositional	14.28
Embedded	4.08
Illocutionary	**40.81**
Like-prefixed	**31.63**
Other	9.18

Table 9: Proportion of utterances of different types of sarcasm that were correctly labeled by sequence labeling but incorrectly labeled by classification techniques

8   Related Work

Sarcasm detection approaches using different features have been reported (Tepperman et al., 2006; Kreuz and Caucci, 2007; Tsur et al., 2010; Davidov et al., 2010; Veale and Hao, 2010; González-Ibánez et al., 2011; Reyes et al., 2012; Joshi et al., 2015; Buschmeier et al., 2014). However, Wallace et al. (2014) show how context beyond the target text (*i.e.*, extra-textual context) is necessary for humans as well as machines, in order to identify sarcasm. Following this, the new trend in sarcasm detection is to explore the use of such extra-textual context (Khattri et al., 2015; Rajadesingan et al., 2015; Bamman and Smith, 2015; Wallace, 2015). (Wallace, 2015) uses meta-data about reddits to predict sarcasm in a reddit[14] comment. (Rajadesingan et al., 2015) present a suite of classifier features that capture different kinds of context: context related to the author, conversation, etc. The new trend in sarcasm detection is, thus, to look at additional context beyond the text where sarcasm is to be predicted.

The work closest to ours is by Wang et al. (2015). They use a labeled dataset of 1500 tweets, the labels for which are obtained **automatically**. Due to their automatically labeled gold dataset and their lack of focus on labeling utterances in a sequence, our analysis seems to be more rigorous. Our work substantially differs from theirs: (a) They do not deal with dialogue, (b) Their goal is to predict sarcasm of a tweet, using series of past tweets as the context *i.e.*, only the last tweet in the sequence. Our goal is to predict sarcasm in *every* element of the sequence: a lot more rigorous task. **Note that the two differ in the way precision/recall values will be computed. (c) Their 'gold' standard dataset is annotated by an automatic classifier. On the other hand, every textual unit (utterance) in our gold standard dataset is manually labeled - making our dataset and hence, findings lot more reliable.** (c) They consider three types of sequences: conversational, historical and topic-based. Historical context is series of tweets by this author, while topic-based context is series of tweets containing a hashtag in the tweet to be classified. We do not use the two because they do not seem suitable for our dataset. They show that a sequence labeling algorithm works well to detect sarcasm of a tweet with a pseudo-sequence generated using such additional context. They attempt to obtain correct prediction only for a single target tweet with no consideration to other elements in the context, which is completely different from our goal. They do not bother about other elements in the sequence but only *use* an algorithm to perform sarcasm detection of a tweet.

Several approaches for sequence labeling in sentiment classification have been studied. Zhao et al. (2008) perform sentiment classification using conditional random fields. Zhang et al. (2014) deal with emotion classification. Using a dataset of children's stories manually annotated at the sentence level, they employ HMM to identify sequential structure and a classifier to predict emotion in a particular sentence. Mao and Lebanon (2006) present a isotonic CRF that predicts global and local sentiment of documents, with additional mechanism for author-specific distributions and smoothing sentiment curves. Yessenalina et al. (2010) present a joint learning algorithm for sentence-level subjectivity labeling and document-level sentiment labeling. Choi and Cardie (2010) deal with sequence learning to jointly identify scope of opinion polarity expressions, and polarity labels. Taking inspiration from use of sequence labeling for sarcasm detection, our work takes the first step to show if sequence labeling techniques are helpful at all. They experiment with MPQA corpus that is labeled at the sentence level for polarity as well as intensity. Specialized sequence labeling techniques like these are the next step to our first step: showing if sequence labeling techniques are helpful at all, for sarcasm detection of dialogue.

9   Conclusion & Future Work

We explored how sequence labeling can be used for sarcasm detection of dialogue. We formulated sarcasm detection of dialogue as a task of labeling each utterance in a sequence, with one among two labels: sarcastic and non-sarcastic. For our experiments, we created a manually annotated dataset of transcripts from a popular TV show 'Friends'. Our dataset consisted of 913 scenes where every utterance was annotated as sarcastic or not.

We experiment with: (a) a novel set of features derived from our dataset, (b) sets of features from two prior works. Our dataset-derived features are: (a) lexical features, (b) conversational context features, and (c) author context features. Using these features, we compared two classes of learning techniques: classifiers (SVM (undersampled), SVM (oversampled) and Naïve Bayes) and sequence labeling techniques (SVM-HMM and SEARN). For our classifiers, the best F-score was obtained with SVM (O) (i.e. 79.8%) while the best F-score for sequence labeling techniques was obtained using SVM-HMM (i.e. 84.2%). Even in case of the **best combinations** of our features for each algorithm, both sequence labeling techniques outperformed the classifiers. In addition, we also experimented with

---

[14]`www.reddit.com`

features introduced in two prior works. We observed an improvement of 2.8% for features in Buschmeier et al. (2014) and 4% for features in González-Ibánez et al. (2011) when sequence labeling techniques were used as against classifiers. In all cases, **sequence labeling techniques had a substantially high recall as compared to classification techniques (10% in case of Buschmeier et al. (2014), 12% in case of González-Ibánez et al. (2011))**. To understand which forms of sarcasm get correctly labeled by sequence labeling (and not by classification), we manually evaluated 100 examples. 71% of these examples consisted of sarcasm that could be understood only with conversational context. Our error analysis points to interesting future work for sarcasm detection of dialogue such as long-range connection, lack of conversational clues, and sarcasm a part of long utterances.

Thus, we observe that for sarcasm detection of our dataset, in case of different feature configurations, sequence labeling performs better than classification. **Our observations establish the efficacy of sequence labeling techniques for sarcasm detection of dialogue.**

Future work on repeating these experiments for other forms of dialogue (such as twitter conversations, chat transcripts, etc.) is imperative. Also, a combination of unified sarcasm and emotion detection using sequence labeling is another promising line of work. It would be interesting to see if deep learning-based models that perform sequence labeling perform better than those that perform classification.

Acknowledgment

We express our gratitude towards our annotators, Rajita Shukla and Jaya Saraswati. We also thank Prerana Singhal for her support. Aditya's PhD is funded by TCS Research Scholar Fellowship.

References

Rehan Akbani, Stephen Kwek, and Nathalie Japkowicz. 2004. Applying support vector machines to imbalanced datasets. In *Machine learning: ECML 2004*, pages 39–50. Springer.

Yasemin Altun, Ioannis Tsochantaridis, Thomas Hofmann, et al. 2003. Hidden markov support vector machines. In *ICML*, volume 3, pages 3–10.

David Bamman and Noah A Smith. 2015. Contextualized sarcasm detection on twitter. In *Ninth International AAAI Conference on Web and Social Media*.

Konstantin Buschmeier, Philipp Cimiano, and Roman Klinger. 2014. An impact analysis of features in a classification approach to irony detection in product reviews. In *Proceedings of the 5th Workshop on Computational Approaches to Subjectivity, Sentiment and Social Media Analysis*, pages 42–49.

Elisabeth Camp. 2012. Sarcasm, pretense, and the semantics/pragmatics distinction*. *Noûs*, 46(4):587–634.

Yejin Choi and Claire Cardie. 2010. Hierarchical sequential learning for extracting opinions and their attributes. In *Proceedings of the ACL 2010 conference short papers*, pages 269–274. Association for Computational Linguistics.

Hal Daumé III, John Langford, and Daniel Marcu. 2009. Search-based structured prediction.

Dmitry Davidov, Oren Tsur, and Ari Rappoport. 2010. Semi-supervised recognition of sarcastic sentences in twitter and amazon. In *Proceedings of the Fourteenth Conference on Computational Natural Language Learning*, pages 107–116. Association for Computational Linguistics.

Jodi Eisterhold, Salvatore Attardo, and Diana Boxer. 2006. Reactions to irony in discourse: Evidence for the least disruption principle. *Journal of Pragmatics*, 38(8):1239–1256.

Raymond W Gibbs. 2000. Irony in talk among friends. *Metaphor and symbol*, 15(1-2):5–27.

Roberto González-Ibánez, Smaranda Muresan, and Nina Wacholder. 2011. Identifying sarcasm in twitter: a closer look. In *Proceedings of the 49th Annual Meeting of the Association for Computational Linguistics: Human Language Technologies: short papers-Volume 2*, pages 581–586. Association for Computational Linguistics.

T. Joachims. 1999. Making large-scale SVM learning practical. In B. Schölkopf, C. Burges, and A. Smola, editors, *Advances in Kernel Methods - Support Vector Learning*, chapter 11, pages 169–184. MIT Press, Cambridge, MA.

Aditya Joshi, Vinita Sharma, and Pushpak Bhattacharyya. 2015. Harnessing context incongruity for sarcasm detection. In *Proceedings of the 53rd Annual Meeting of the Association for Computational Linguistics and the 7th International Joint Conference on Natural Language Processing*, volume 2, pages 757–762.

Anupam Khattri, Aditya Joshi, Pushpak Bhattacharyya, and Mark James Carman. 2015. Your sentiment precedes you: Using an authors historical tweets to predict sarcasm. In *6th Workshop on Computational Approaches to Subjectivity, Sentiment and Social Media Analysis (WASSA)*, page 25.

Sotiris Kotsiantis, Dimitris Kanellopoulos, Panayiotis Pintelas, et al. 2006. Handling imbalanced datasets: A review. *GESTS International Transactions on Computer Science and Engineering*, 30(1):25–36.

Roger J Kreuz and Gina M Caucci. 2007. Lexical influences on the perception of sarcasm. In *Proceedings of the Workshop on computational approaches to Figurative Language*, pages 1–4. Association for Computational Linguistics.

Pierre Lison and Jörg Tiedemann. 2016. Opensubtitles2016: Extracting large parallel corpora from movie and tv subtitles. In *Proceedings of LREC 2016*.

Yi Mao and Guy Lebanon. 2006. Isotonic conditional random fields and local sentiment flow. In *Advances in neural information processing systems*, pages 961–968.

Bo Pang and Lillian Lee. 2008. Opinion mining and sentiment analysis. *Foundations and trends in information retrieval*, 2(1-2):1–135.

Fabian Pedregosa, Gaël Varoquaux, Alexandre Gramfort, Vincent Michel, Bertrand Thirion, Olivier Grisel, Mathieu Blondel, Peter Prettenhofer, Ron Weiss, Vincent Dubourg, et al. 2011. Scikit-learn: Machine learning in python. *The Journal of Machine Learning Research*, 12:2825–2830.

James W Pennebaker, Martha E Francis, and Roger J Booth. 2001. Linguistic inquiry and word count: Liwc 2001. *Mahway: Lawrence Erlbaum Associates*, 71:2001.

Ashwin Rajadesingan, Reza Zafarani, and Huan Liu. 2015. Sarcasm detection on twitter: A behavioral modeling approach. In *Proceedings of the Eighth ACM International Conference on Web Search and Data Mining*, pages 97–106. ACM.

Rachel Rakov and Andrew Rosenberg. 2013. " sure, i did the right thing": a system for sarcasm detection in speech. In *INTERSPEECH*, pages 842–846.

Antonio Reyes, Paolo Rosso, and Davide Buscaldi. 2012. From humor recognition to irony detection: The figurative language of social media. *Data & Knowledge Engineering*, 74:1–12.

Joseph Tepperman, David R Traum, and Shrikanth Narayanan. 2006. " yeah right": sarcasm recognition for spoken dialogue systems. In *INTERSPEECH*. Citeseer.

Oren Tsur, Dmitry Davidov, and Ari Rappoport. 2010. Icwsm-a great catchy name: Semi-supervised recognition of sarcastic sentences in online product reviews. In *ICWSM*.

Tony Veale and Yanfen Hao. 2010. Detecting ironic intent in creative comparisons. In *ECAI*, volume 215, pages 765–770.

Byron C Wallace, Laura Kertz Do Kook Choe, and Eugene Charniak. 2014. Humans require context to infer ironic intent (so computers probably do, too). In *Proceedings of the Annual Meeting of the Association for Computational Linguistics (ACL)*, pages 512–516.

Byron C Wallace. 2015. Sparse, contextually informed models for irony detection: Exploiting user communities,entities and sentiment. In *ACL*.

Zelin Wang, Zhijian Wu, Ruimin Wang, and Yafeng Ren. 2015. Twitter sarcasm detection exploiting a context-based model. In *Web Information Systems Engineering–WISE 2015*, pages 77–91. Springer.

Ainur Yessenalina, Yisong Yue, and Claire Cardie. 2010. Multi-level structured models for document-level sentiment classification. In *Proceedings of the 2010 Conference on Empirical Methods in Natural Language Processing*, pages 1046–1056. Association for Computational Linguistics.

Zhengchen Zhang, Minghui Dong, and Shuzhi Sam Ge. 2014. Emotion analysis of children's stories with context information. In *Asia-Pacific Signal and Information Processing Association, 2014 Annual Summit and Conference (APSIPA)*, pages 1–7. IEEE.

Ge S S Zhang Z, Dong M. 2014. Emotion analysis of children's stories with context information. In *Asia-Pacific Signal and Information Processing Association*, volume 38, pages 1–7. IEEE.

Jun Zhao, Kang Liu, and Gen Wang. 2008. Adding redundant features for crfs-based sentence sentiment classification. In *Proceedings of the conference on empirical methods in natural language processing*, pages 117–126. Association for Computational Linguistics.

Leveraging Cognitive Features for Sentiment Analysis

**Abhijit Mishra[†], Diptesh Kanojia[†,♣], Seema Nagar [⋆], Kuntal Dey[⋆],
Pushpak Bhattacharyya[†]**
[†]Indian Institute of Technology Bombay, India
[♣]IITB-Monash Research Academy, India
[⋆]IBM Research, India
[†]{abhijitmishra, diptesh, pb}@cse.iitb.ac.in
[⋆]{senagar3, kuntadey}@in.ibm.com

Abstract

Sentiments expressed in user-generated short text and sentences are nuanced by subtleties at lexical, syntactic, semantic and pragmatic levels. To address this, we propose to augment traditional features used for sentiment analysis and sarcasm detection, with cognitive features derived from the eye-movement patterns of readers. Statistical classification using our enhanced feature set improves the performance (F-score) of polarity detection by a maximum of 3.7% and 9.3% on two datasets, over the systems that use only traditional features. We perform feature significance analysis, and experiment on a held-out dataset, showing that cognitive features indeed empower sentiment analyzers to handle complex constructs.

1 Introduction

This paper addresses the task of Sentiment Analysis (SA) - automatic detection of the sentiment polarity as positive versus negative - of user-generated short texts and sentences. Several sentiment analyzers exist in literature today (Liu and Zhang, 2012). Recent works, such as Kouloumpis et al. (2011), Agarwal et al. (2011) and Barbosa and Feng (2010), attempt to conduct such analyses on user-generated content. Sentiment analysis remains a hard problem, due to the challenges it poses at the various levels, as summarized below.

1.1 Lexical Challenges

Sentiment analyzers face the following three challenges at the lexical level: (1) **Data Sparsity**, *i.e.,* handling the presence of unseen words/phrases. (*e.g., The movie is messy, uncouth, incomprehensible, vicious and absurd*) (2) **Lexical Ambiguity**,

e.g., finding appropriate senses of a word given the context (e.g., *His face fell when he was dropped from the team* vs *The boy fell from the bicycle,* where the verb "fell" has to be disambiguated) (3) **Domain Dependency**, tackling words that change polarity across domains. (*e.g.,* the word *unpredictable* being positive in case of *unpredictable movie* in movie domain and negative in case of *unpredictable steering* in car domain). Several methods have been proposed to address the different lexical level difficulties by - (a) using WordNet synsets and word cluster information to tackle lexical ambiguity and data sparsity (Akkaya et al., 2009; Balamurali et al., 2011; Go et al., 2009; Maas et al., 2011; Popat et al., 2013; Saif et al., 2012) and (b) mining domain dependent words (Sharma and Bhattacharyya, 2013; Wiebe and Mihalcea, 2006).

1.2 Syntactic Challenges

Difficulty at the syntax level arises when the given text follows a complex phrasal structure and, *phrase attachments* are expected to be resolved before performing SA. For instance, the sentence *A somewhat crudely constructed but gripping, questing look at a person so racked with self-loathing, he becomes an enemy to his own race.* requires processing at the syntactic level, before analyzing the sentiment. Approaches leveraging syntactic properties of text include generating dependency based rules for SA (Poria et al., 2014) and leveraging local dependency (Li et al., 2010).

1.3 Semantic and Pragmatic Challenges

This corresponds to the difficulties arising in the higher layers of NLP, *i.e.,* semantic and pragmatic layers. Challenges in these layers include handling: (a) Sentiment expressed implicitly (*e.g., Guy gets girl, guy loses girl, audience falls asleep.*) (b) Presence of sarcasm and other

Proceedings of the 20th SIGNLL Conference on Computational Natural Language Learning (CoNLL), pages 156–166,
Berlin, Germany, August 7-12, 2016. ©2016 Association for Computational Linguistics

forms of irony (*e.g., This is the kind of movie you go because the theater has air-conditioning.*) and (c) Thwarted expectations (*e.g., The acting is fine. Action sequences are top-notch. Still, I consider it as a below average movie due to its poor story-line.*).

Such challenges are extremely hard to tackle with traditional NLP tools, as these need both linguistic and pragmatic knowledge. Most attempts towards handling *thwarting* (Ramteke et al., 2013) and *sarcasm and irony* (Carvalho et al., 2009; Riloff et al., 2013; Liebrecht et al., 2013; Maynard and Greenwood, 2014; Barbieri et al., 2014; Joshi et al., 2015), rely on distant supervision based techniques (*e.g.,* leveraging hashtags) and/or stylistic/pragmatic features (emoticons, laughter expressions such as "lol" *etc*). Addressing difficulties for linguistically well-formed texts, in absence of explicit cues (like emoticons), proves to be difficult using textual/stylistic features alone.

1.4 Introducing Cognitive Features

We empower our systems by augmenting cognitive features along with traditional linguistic features used for general sentiment analysis, thwarting and sarcasm detection. Cognitive features are derived from the eye-movement patterns of human annotators recorded while they annotate short-text with sentiment labels. Our hypothesis is that cognitive processes in the brain are related to eye-movement activities (Parasuraman and Rizzo, 2006). Hence, considering readers' eye-movement patterns while they read sentiment bearing texts may help tackle linguistic nuances better. We perform statistical classification using various classifiers and different feature combinations. With our augmented feature-set, we observe a significant improvement of accuracy across all classifiers for two different datasets. Experiments on a carefully curated held-out dataset indicate a significant improvement in sentiment polarity detection over the state of the art, specifically text with complex constructs like irony and sarcasm. Through feature significance analysis, we show that cognitive features indeed empower sentiment analyzers to handle complex constructs like irony and sarcasm. Our approach is the first of its kind to the best of our knowledge. We share various resources and data related to this work at http://www.cfilt.iitb.ac.in/cognitive-nlp

The rest of the paper is organized as follows. Section 2 presents a summary of past work done in traditional SA and SA from a psycholinguistic point of view. Section 3 describes the available datasets we have taken for our analysis. Section 4 presents our features that comprise both traditional textual features, used for sentiment analysis and cognitive features derived from annotators' eye-movement patterns. In section 5, we discuss the results for various sentiment classification techniques under different combinations of textual and cognitive features, showing the effectiveness of cognitive features. In section 6, we discuss on the feasibility of our approach before concluding the paper in section 7.

2 Related Work

Sentiment classification has been a long standing NLP problem with both supervised (Pang et al., 2002; Benamara et al., 2007; Martineau and Finin, 2009) and unsupervised (Mei et al., 2007; Lin and He, 2009) machine learning based approaches existing for the task.

Supervised approaches are popular because of their superior classification accuracy (Mullen and Collier, 2004; Pang and Lee, 2008) and in such approaches, feature engineering plays an important role. Apart from the commonly used bag-of-words features based on unigrams, bigrams etc. (Dave et al., 2003; Ng et al., 2006), syntactic properties (Martineau and Finin, 2009; Nakagawa et al., 2010), semantic properties (Balamurali et al., 2011) and effect of negators. Ikeda et al. (2008) are also used as features for the task of sentiment classification. The fact that sentiment expression may be complex to be handled by traditional features is evident from a study of comparative sentences by Ganapathibhotla and Liu (2008). This, however has not been addressed by feature based approaches.

Eye-tracking technology has been used recently for sentiment analysis and annotation related research (apart from the huge amount of work in psycholinguistics that we find hard to enlist here due to space limitations). Joshi et al. (2014) develop a method to measure the sentiment annotation complexity using cognitive evidence from eye-tracking. Mishra et al. (2014) study sentiment detection, and subjectivity extraction through anticipation and homing, with the use of eye tracking. Regarding other NLP tasks, Joshi et al.

	NB			SVM			RB		
	P	**R**	**F**	**P**	**R**	**F**	**P**	**R**	**F**
D1	66.15	66	**66.15**	64.5	65.3	**64.9**	56.8	60.9	**53.5**
D2	74.5	74.2	**74.3**	77.1	76.5	**76.8**	75.9	53.9	**63.02**

Table 1: Classification results for different SA systems for dataset 1 (D1) and dataset 2 (D2). P→ Precision, R→ Recall, F→ F score

(2013) propose a studied the cognitive aspects if Word Sense Disambiguation (WSD) through eye-tracking. Earlier, Mishra et al. (2013) measure translation annotation difficulty of a given sentence based on gaze input of translators used to label training data. Klerke et al. (2016) present a novel multi-task learning approach for sentence compression using labelled data, while, Barrett and Søgaard (2015) discriminate between grammatical functions using gaze features. The recent advancements in the literature discussed above, motivate us to explore gaze-based cognition for sentiment analysis.

We acknowledge that some of the well performing sentiment analyzers use Deep Learning techniques (like Convolutional Neural Network based approach by Maas et al. (2011) and Recursive Neural Network based approach by dos Santos and Gatti (2014)). In these, the features are automatically learned from the input text. Since our approach is feature based, we do not consider these approaches for our current experimentation. Taking inputs from gaze data and using them in a deep learning setting sounds intriguing, though, it is beyond the scope of this work.

3 Eye-tracking and Sentiment Analysis Datasets

We use two publicly available datasets for our experiments. Dataset 1 has been released by Mishra et al. (2016) which they use for the task of *sarcasm understandability* prediction. Dataset 2 has been used by Joshi et al. (2014) for the task of sentiment annotation complexity prediction. These datasets contain many instances with higher level nuances like presence of implicit sentiment, sarcasm and thwarting. We describe the datasets below.

3.1 Dataset 1

It contains 994 text snippets with 383 positive and 611 negative examples. Out of this, 350 are sarcastic or have other forms of irony. The snippets are a collection of reviews, normalized-tweets and

quotes. Each snippet is annotated by seven participants with binary positive/negative polarity labels. Their eye-movement patterns are recorded with a high quality *SR-Research Eyelink*-1000 *eye-tracker* (sampling rate 500Hz). The annotation accuracy varies from $70\% - 90\%$ with a Fleiss kappa inter-rater agreement of 0.62.

3.2 Dataset 2

This dataset consists of 1059 snippets comprising movie reviews and normalized tweets. Each snippet is annotated by five participants with positive, negative and objective labels. Eye-tracking is done using a low quality Tobii T120 eye-tracker (sampling rate 120Hz). The annotation accuracy varies from $75\% - 85\%$ with a Fleiss kappa inter-rater agreement of 0.68. We rule out the objective ones and consider 843 snippets out of which 443 are positive and 400 are negative.

3.3 Performance of Existing SA Systems Considering Dataset -1 and 2 as Test Data

It is essential to check whether our selected datasets really pose challenges to existing sentiment analyzers or not. For this, we implement two statistical classifiers and a rule based classifier to check the test accuracy of Dataset 1 and Dataset 2. The statistical classifiers are based on Support Vector Machine (SVM) and Näive Bayes (NB) implemented using Weka (Hall et al., 2009) and Lib-SVM (Chang and Lin, 2011) APIs. These are on trained on 10662 snippets comprising movie reviews and tweets, randomly collected from standard datasets released by Pang and Lee (2004) and Sentiment 140 (http://www.sentiment140.com/). The feature-set comprises traditional features for SA reported in a number of papers. They are discussed in section 4 under the category of *Sentiment Features*. The *in-house* rule based (RB) classifier decides the sentiment labels based on the counts of positive and negative words present in the snippet, computed using MPQA lexicon (Wilson et al., 2005). It also considers negators as explained by Jia et al. (2009) and intensifiers as explained by Dragut and Fellbaum (2014).

Table 1 presents the accuracy of the three systems. The F-scores are not very high for all the systems (especially for dataset 1 that contains more sarcastic/ironic texts), possibly indicating that the snippets in our dataset pose challenges for existing sentiment analyzers. Hence, the selected datasets are ideal for our current experimentation that involves cognitive features.

4 Enhanced feature set for SA

Our feature-set into four categories *viz.* (1) Sentiment features (2) Sarcasm, Irony and Thwarting related Features (3) Cognitive features from eye-movement (4) Textual features related to reading difficulty. We describe our feature-set below.

4.1 Sentiment Features

We consider a series of textual features that have been extensively used in sentiment literature (Liu and Zhang, 2012). The features are described below. Each feature is represented by a unique abbreviated form, which are used in the subsequent discussions.

1. **Presence of Unigrams (NGRAM˙PCA) *i.e.*** Presence of unigrams appearing in each sentence that also appear in the vocabulary obtained from the training corpus. To avoid overfitting (since our training data size is less), we reduce the dimension to 500 using Principal Component Analysis.

2. **Subjective words (Positive_words, Negative_words) *i.e.*** Presence of positive and negative words computed against MPQA lexicon (Wilson et al., 2005), a popular lexicon used for sentiment analysis.

3. **Subjective scores (PosScore, NegScore) *i.e.*** Scores of positive subjectivity and negative subjectivity using SentiWordNet (Esuli and Sebastiani, 2006).

4. **Sentiment flip count (FLIP) *i.e.*** Number of times words polarity changes in the text. Word polarity is determined using MPQA lexicon.

5. **Part of Speech ratios (VERB, NOUN, ADJ, ADV) *i.e.*** Ratios (proportions) of verbs, nouns, adjectives and adverbs in the text. This is computed using NLTK[1].

6. **Count of Named Entities (NE) *i.e.*** Number of named entity mentions in the text. This is computed using NLTK.

7. **Discourse connectors (DC) *i.e.*** Number of discourse connectors in the text computed using an in-house list of discourse connectors (like *however*, *although* etc.)

4.2 Sarcasm, Irony and Thwarting related Features

To handle complex texts containing constructs irony, sarcasm and thwarted expectations as explained earlier, we consider the following features. The features are taken from Riloff et al. (2013), Ramteke et al. (2013) and Joshi et al. (2015).

1. **Implicit incongruity (IMPLICIT_PCA) *i.e.*** Presence of positive phrases followed by negative situational phrase (computed using bootstrapping technique suggested by Riloff et al. (2013)). We consider the top 500 principal components of these phrases to reduce dimension, in order to avoid overfitting.

2. **Punctuation marks (PUNC) *i.e.*** Count of punctuation marks in the text.

3. **Largest pos/neg subsequence (LAR) *i.e.*** Length of the largest series of words with polarities unchanged. Word polarity is determined using MPQA lexicon.

4. **Lexical polarity (LP) *i.e.*** Sentence polarity found by supervised logistic regression using the dataset used by Joshi et al. (2015).

4.3 Cognitive features from eye-movement

Eye-movement patterns are characterized by two basic attributes: (1) Fixations, corresponding to a longer stay of gaze on a visual object (like characters, words *etc.* in text) (2) Saccades, corresponding to the transition of eyes between two fixations. Moreover, a saccade is called a *Regressive Saccade* or simply, *Regression* if it represents a phenomenon of going back to a pre-visited segment. A portion of a text is said to be *skipped* if it does not have any fixation. Figure 1 shows eye-movement behavior during annotation of the given sentence in dataset-1. The circles represent

---

[1] http://www.nltk.org/

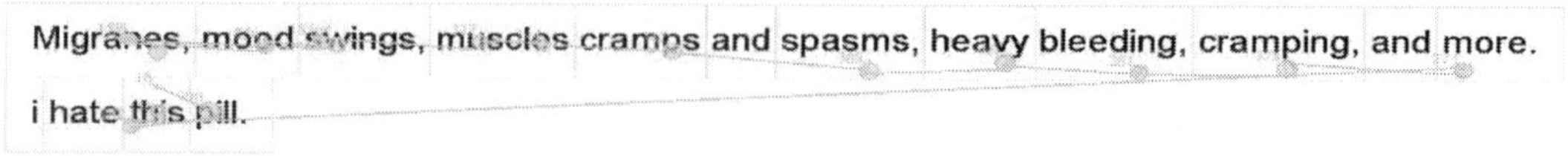

Figure 1: Snapshot of eye-movement behavior during annotation of an opinionated text. The circles represent fixations and lines connecting the circles represent saccades. Boxes represent Areas of Interest (AoI) which are words of the sentence in our case.

fixation and the line connecting the circles represent saccades. Our cognition driven features are derived from these basic eye-movement attributes. We divide our features in two sets as explained ahead.

4.4 Basic gaze features

Readers' eye-movement behavior, characterized by fixations, forward saccades, skips and regressions, can be directly quantified by simple statistical aggregation (*i.e.,* computing features for individual participants and then averaging). Since these behaviors intuitively relate to the cognitive process of the readers (Rayner and Sereno, 1994), we consider simple statistical properties of these factors as features to our model. Some of these features have been reported by Mishra et al. (2016) for modeling sarcasm understandability of readers. However, as far as we know, these features are being introduced in NLP tasks like sentiment analysis for the first time.

1. **Average First-Fixation Duration per word (FDUR)** *i.e.* Sum of *first-fixation duration* divided by word count. First fixations are fixations occurring during the first pass reading. Intuitively, an increased first fixation duration is associated to more time spent on the words, which accounts for lexical complexity. This is motivated by Rayner and Duffy (1986).

2. **Average Fixation Count (FC)** *i.e.* Sum of fixation counts divided by word count. If the reader reads fast, the first fixation duration may not be high even if the lexical complexity is more. But the number of fixations may increase on the text. So, fixation count may help capture lexical complexity in such cases.

3. **Average Saccade Length (SL)** *i.e.* Sum of saccade lengths (measured by number of words) divided by word count. Intuitively, lengthy saccades represent the text being structurally/syntactically complex. This is

also supported by von der Malsburg and Vasishth (2011).

4. **Regression Count (REG)** *i.e.* Total number of gaze regressions. Regressions correspond to both lexical and syntactic reanalysis (Malsburg et al., 2015). Intuitively, regression count should be useful in capturing both syntactic and semantic difficulties.

5. **Skip count (SKIP)** *i.e.* Number of words skipped divided by total word count. Intuitively, higher skip count should correspond lesser semantic processing requirement (assuming that skipping is not done intentionally).

6. **Count of regressions from second half to first half of the sentence (RSF)** *i.e.* Number of regressions from second half of the sentence to the first half of the sentence (given the sentence is divided into two equal half of words). Constructs like sarcasm, irony often have phrases that are incongruous (*e.g. "The book is so great that it can be used as a paperweight"- the incongruous phrases are "book is so great" and "used as a paperweight"..* Intuitively, when a reader encounters such incongruous phrases, the second phrases often cause a surprisal resulting in a long regression to the first part of the text. Hence, this feature is considered.

7. **Largest Regression Position (LREG)** *i.e.* Ratio of the absolute position of the word from which a regression with the largest amplitude (in terms of number of characters) is observed, to the total word count of sentence. This is chosen under the assumption that regression with the maximum amplitude may occur from the portion of the text which causes maximum surprisal (in order to get more information about the portion causing maximum surprisal). The relative starting position of such portion, captured by LREG,

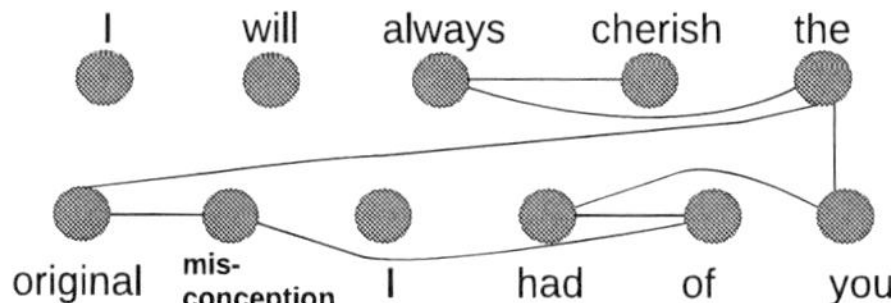

Figure 2: Saliency graph of a human annotator for the sentence *I will always cherish the original misconception I had of you.*

may help distinguish between sentences with different linguistic subtleties.

4.5 Complex gaze features

We propose a graph structure constructed from the gaze data to derive more complex gaze features. We term the graph as *gaze-saliency graphs.*

A gaze-saliency graph for a sentence S for a reader R, represented as $G = (V, E)$, is a graph with vertices (V) and edges (E) where each vertex $v \in V$ corresponds to a word in S (may not be unique) and there exists an edge $e \in E$ between vertices v_1 and v_2 if R performs at least one saccade between the words corresponding to $v1$ and $v2$. Figure 2 shows an example of such a graph.

1. **Edge density of the saliency gaze graph (ED) *i.e.*** Ratio of number of edges in the gaze saliency graph and total number of possible links $((|V| \times |V| - 1|)/2)$ in the saliency graph. As, *Edge Density* of a saliency graph increases with the number of distinct saccades, it is supposed to increase if the text is semantically more difficult.

2. **Fixation Duration at Left/Source as Edge Weight (F1H, F1S) *i.e.*** Largest weighted degree (F1H) and second largest weighted degree (F1S) of the saliency graph considering the fixation duration on the word of node i of edge E_{ij} as edge weight.

3. **Fixation Duration at Right/Target as Edge Weight (F2H, F2S) *i.e.*** Largest weighted degree (F2H) and second largest weighted degree (F2S) of the saliency graph considering the fixation duration of the word of node i of edge E_{ij} as edge weight.

4. **Forward Saccade Count as Edge Weight (FSH, FSS) *i.e.*** Largest weighted degree (FSH) and second largest weighted degree (FSS) of the saliency graph considering the number of forward saccades between nodes i and j of an edge E_{ij} as edge weight..

5. **Forward Saccade Distance as Edge Weight (FSDH, FSDS) *i.e.*** Largest weighted degree (FSDH) and second largest weighted degree (FSDS) of the saliency graph considering the total distance (word count) of forward saccades between nodes i and j of an edge E_{ij} as edge weight.

6. **Regressive Saccade Count as Edge Weight (RSH, RSS) *i.e.*** Largest weighted degree (RSH) and second largest weighted degree (RSS) of the saliency graph considering the number of regressive saccades between nodes i and j of an edge E_{ij} as edge weight.

7. **Regressive Saccade Distance as Edge Weight (RSDH, RSDS) *i.e.*** Largest weighted degree (RSDH) and second largest weighted degree (RSDS) of the saliency graph considering the number of regressive saccades between nodes i and j of an edge E_{ij} as edge weight.

The "highest and second highest degree" based gaze features derived from saliency graphs are motivated by our qualitative observations from the gaze data. Intuitively, the highest weighted degree of a graph is expected to be higher if some phrases have complex semantic relationships with others.

4.6 Features Related to Reading Difficulty

Eye-movement during reading text with sentiment related nuances (like sarcasm) can be similar to text with other forms of difficulties. To address the effect of sentence length, word length and syllable count that affect reading behavior, we consider the following features.

1. **Readability Ease (RED) *i.e.*** Flesch Readability Ease score of the text (Kincaid et al., 1975). Higher the score, easier is the text to comprehend.

2. **Sentence Length (LEN) *i.e.*** Number of words in the sentence.

We now explain our experimental setup and results.

5 Experiments and results

We test the effectiveness of the enhanced feature-set by implementing three classifiers *viz.,* SVM (with linear kernel), NB and Multi-layered Neural Network. These systems are implemented using

Classifier	Näive Bayes			SVM			Multi-layer NN		
	Dataset 1								
	P	**R**	**F**	**P**	**R**	**F**	**P**	**R**	**F**
Uni	58.5	57.3	57.9	67.8	68.5	68.14	65.4	65.3	65.34
Sn	58.7	57.4	58.0	69.6	70.2	69.8	67.5	67.4	67.5
Sn + Sr	63.0	59.4	61.14	72.8	73.2	72.6	69.0	69.2	69.1
Gz	61.8	58.4	60.05	54.3	52.6	53.4	59.1	60.8	60
Sn+Gz	60.2	58.8	59.2	69.5	70.1	69.6	70.3	70.5	70.4
Sn+ Sr+Gz	**63.4**	**59.6**	**61.4**	**73.3**	**73.6**	**73.5**	**70.5**	**70.7**	**70.6**
	Dataset 2								
Uni	**51.2**	**50.3**	**50.74**	57.8	57.9	57.8	53.8	53.9	53.8
Sn	51.1	50.3	50.7	62.5	62.5	62.5	58.0	58.1	58.0
Sn+Sr	50.7	50.1	50.39	70.3	70.3	70.3	66.8	66.8	66.8
Gz	49.9	50.9	50.39	48.9	48.9	48.9	53.6	54.0	53.3
Sn+Gz	51	50.3	50.6	62.4	62.3	62.3	59.7	59.8	59.8
Sn+ Sr+Gz	50.2	49.7	50	**71.9**	**71.8**	**71.8**	**69.1**	**69.2**	**69.1**

Table 2: Results for different feature combinations. (P,R,F)→ Precision, Recall, F-score. Feature labels Uni→Unigram features, Sn→Sentiment features, Sr→Sarcasm features and Gz→Gaze features along with features related to reading difficulty

the Weka (Hall et al., 2009) and LibSVM (Chang and Lin, 2011) APIs. Several classifier hyperparameters are kept to the default values given in Weka. We separately perform a 10-fold cross validation on both Dataset 1 and 2 using different sets of feature combinations. The average F-scores for the class-frequency based random classifier are 33% and 46.93% for dataset 1 and dataset 2 respectively.

The classification accuracy is reported in Table 2. We observe the maximum accuracy with the complete feature-set comprising Sentiment, Sarcasm and Thwarting, and Cognitive features derived from gaze data. For this combination, SVM outperforms the other classifiers. The novelty of our feature design lies in (a) First augmenting sarcasm and thwarting based features (Sr) with sentiment features (Sn), which shoots up the accuracy by 3.1% for Dataset1 and 7.8% for Dataset2 (b) Augmenting gaze features with $Sn+Sr$, which further increases the accuracy by 0.6% and 1.5% for Dataset 1 and 2 respectively, amounting to an overall improvement of 3.7% and 9.3% respectively. It may be noted that the addition of gaze features may seem to bring meager improvements in the classification accuracy but the improvements are consistent across datasets and several classifiers. Still, we speculate that aggregating various eye-tracking parameters to extract the cognitive features may have caused loss of information, there by limiting the improvements. For example, the graph based features are computed for each participant and eventually averaged to get the graph features for a sentence, thereby not leveraging the power of individual eye-movement patterns. We intend to address this issue in future.

Since the best ($Sn + Sr + Gz$) and the second best feature ($Sn + Sr$) combinations are close in terms of accuracy (difference of 0.6% for dataset 1 and 1.5% for dataset 2), we perform a statistical significance test using McNemar test ($\alpha = 0.05$). The difference in the F-scores turns out to be strongly significant with $p = 0.0060$ (The odds ratio is 0.489, with a 95% confidence interval). However, the difference in the F-scores is not statistically significant ($p = 0.21$) for dataset 2 for the best and second best feature combinations.

5.1 Importance of cognitive features

We perform a *chi-squared test* based feature significance analysis, shown in Table 3. For dataset 1, 10 out of the top 20 ranked features are gaze-based features and for dataset 2, 7 out of top 20 features are gaze-based, as shown in bold letters. Moreover, if we consider gaze features alone for feature ranking using chi-squared test, features *FC*, *SL*, *FSDH*, *FSDS*, *RSDH* and *RSDS* turn out to be insignificant.

To study whether the cognitive features actually help in classifying complex output as hypoth-

Rank	Dataset 1	Dataset 2
1	PosScore	LP
2	LP	Negative_Words
3	NGRAM_PCA_1	Positive_Words
4	**FDUR**	NegCount
5	**F1H**	PosCount
6	**F2H**	NGRAM_PCA_1
7	NGRAM_PCA_2	IMPLICIT_PCA_1
8	**F1S**	**FC**
9	ADJ	**FDUR**
10	**F2S**	NGRAM_PCA_2
11	NGRAM_PCA_3	**SL**
12	NGRAM_PCA_4	**LREG**
13	**RSS**	**SKIP**
14	**FSDH**	**RSF**
15	**FSDS**	**F1H**
16	IMPLICIT_PCA_1	RED
17	**LREG**	LEN
18	**SKIP**	PUNC
19	IMPLICIT_PCA_2	IMPLICIT_PCA_2

Table 3: Features as per their ranking for both Dataset 1 and Dataset 2. Integer values N in NGRAM_PCA_N and IMPLICIT_PCA_N represent the Nth principal component.

	Irony	Non-Irony
Sn	58.2	75.5
Sn+Sr	60.1	75.9
Gz+Sn+Sr	64.3	77.6

Table 4: F-scores on held-out dataset for Complex Constructs (Irony), Simple Constructs (Non-irony)

esized earlier, we repeat the experiment on a held-out dataset, randomly derived from Dataset 1. It has 294 text snippets out of which 131 contain complex constructs like irony/sarcasm and rest of the snippets are relatively simpler. We choose SVM, our best performing classifier, with similar configuration as explained in section 5. As seen in Table 4, the relative improvement of F-score, when gaze features are included, is 6.1% for complex texts and is 2.1% for simple texts (all the values are statistically significant with $p < 0.05$ for McNemar test, except Sn and $Sn + Sr$ for Nonirony case.). This demonstrates the efficacy of the gaze based features.

Table 5 shows a few example cases (obtained from test folds) showing the effectiveness of our enhanced feature set.

6 Feasibility of our approach

Since our method requires gaze data from human readers to be available, the methods practicability becomes questionable. We present our views on this below.

6.1 Availability of Mobile Eye-trackers

Availability of inexpensive embedded eye-trackers on hand-held devices has come close to reality now. This opens avenues to get eye-tracking data from inexpensive mobile devices from a huge population of online readers non-intrusively, and derive cognitive features to be used in predictive frameworks like ours. For instance, *Cogisen: (http://www.sencogi.com)* has a patent (ID: EP2833308-A1) on "eye-tracking using inexpensive mobile web-cams". Wood and Bulling (2014) have introduced *EyeTab*, a model-based approach for binocular gaze estimation that runs entirely on tablets.

6.2 Applicability Scenario

We believe, mobile eye-tracking modules could be a part of mobile applications built for e-commerce, online learning, gaming *etc.* where automatic analysis of online reviews calls for better solutions to detect and handle linguistic nuances in sentiment analysis setting. To give an example, let's say a book gets different reviews on Amazon. Our system could watch how readers read the review using mobile eye-trackers, and thereby, decide the polarity of opinion, especially when sentiment is not expressed explicitly (*e.g.,* using strong polar words) in the text. Such an application can horizontally scale across the web, helping to improve automatic classification of online reviews.

6.3 Getting Users' Consent for Eye-tracking

Eye-tracking technology has already been utilized by leading mobile technology developers (like Samsung) to facilitate richer user experiences through services like *Smart-scroll* (where a user's eye movement determines whether a page has to be scrolled or not) and *Smart-lock* (where user's gaze position decided whether to lock the screen or not). The growing interest of users in using such services takes us to a promising situation where getting users' consent to record eye-movement patterns will not be difficult, though it is yet not the current state of affairs.

7 Conclusion

We combined traditional sentiment features with (a) different textual features used for sarcasm and

Sentence	Gold	SVM_Ex.	NB_Ex.	RB_Ex.	Sn	Sn+Sr	Sn+Sr+Gz
1. I find television very educating. Every time somebody turns on the set, I go into the other room and read a book	-1	1	1	0	1	-1	-1
2. I love when you do not have two minutes to text me back.	-1	1	-1	1	1	1	-1

Table 5: Example test-cases from the heldout dataset. Labels Ex→Existing classifier, Sn→Sentiment features, Sr→Sarcasm features and Gz→Gaze features. Values (-1,1,0)→ (negative,positive,undefined)

thwarting detection, and (b) cognitive features derived from readers' eye movement behavior. The combined feature set improves the overall accuracy over the traditional feature set based SA by a margin of 3.6% and 9.3% respectively for Datasets 1 and 2. It is significantly effective for text with complex constructs, leading to an improvement of 6.1% on our held-out data. In future, we propose to explore (a) devising deeper gaze-based features and (b) *multi-view* classification using independent learning from linguistics and cognitive data. We also plan to explore deeper graph and gaze features, and models to learn complex gaze feature representation. Our general approach may be useful in other problems like emotion analysis, text summarization and question answering, where textual clues alone do not prove to be sufficient.

Acknowledgments

We thank the members of CFILT Lab, especially Jaya Jha and Meghna Singh, and the students of IIT Bombay for their help and support.

References

Apoorv Agarwal, Boyi Xie, Ilia Vovsha, Owen Rambow, and Rebecca Passonneau. 2011. Sentiment analysis of twitter data. In *Proceedings of the Workshop on Languages in Social Media*, pages 30–38. ACL.

Cem Akkaya, Janyce Wiebe, and Rada Mihalcea. 2009. Subjectivity word sense disambiguation. In *Proceedings of the 2009 Conference on Empirical Methods in Natural Language Processing: Volume 1-Volume 1*, pages 190–199. ACL.

AR Balamurali, Aditya Joshi, and Pushpak Bhattacharyya. 2011. Harnessing wordnet senses for supervised sentiment classification. In *Proceedings of the Conference on Empirical Methods in Natural Language Processing*, pages 1081–1091.

Francesco Barbieri, Horacio Saggion, and Francesco Ronzano. 2014. Modelling sarcasm in twitter, a novel approach. *ACL 2014*, page 50.

Luciano Barbosa and Junlan Feng. 2010. Robust sentiment detection on twitter from biased and noisy data. In *Proceedings of the 23rd International Conference on Computational Linguistics: Posters*, pages 36–44. ACL.

Maria Barrett and Anders Søgaard. 2015. Using reading behavior to predict grammatical functions. In *Proceedings of the Sixth Workshop on Cognitive Aspects of Computational Language Learning*, pages 1–5, Lisbon, Portugal, September. Association for Computational Linguistics.

Farah Benamara, Carmine Cesarano, Antonio Picariello, and Venkatramana S Subrahmanian. 2007. Sentiment analysis: Adjectives and adverbs are better than adjectives alone. In *ICWSM*.

Paula Carvalho, Luís Sarmento, Mário J Silva, and Eugénio De Oliveira. 2009. Clues for detecting irony in user-generated contents: oh...!! it's so easy;-). In *Proceedings of the 1st international CIKM workshop on Topic-sentiment analysis for mass opinion*, pages 53–56. ACM.

Chih-Chung Chang and Chih-Jen Lin. 2011. LIBSVM: A library for support vector machines. *ACM Transactions on Intelligent Systems and Technology*, 2:27:1–27:27. Software available at http://www.csie.ntu.edu.tw/~cjlin/libsvm.

Kushal Dave, Steve Lawrence, and David M Pennock. 2003. Mining the peanut gallery: Opinion extraction and semantic classification of product reviews. In *Proceedings of the 12th international conference on World Wide Web*, pages 519–528. ACM.

Cícero Nogueira dos Santos and Maira Gatti. 2014. Deep convolutional neural networks for sentiment analysis of short texts. In *Proceedings of COLING*.

Eduard C Dragut and Christiane Fellbaum. 2014. The role of adverbs in sentiment analysis. *ACL 2014*, 1929:38–41.

Andrea Esuli and Fabrizio Sebastiani. 2006. Sentiwordnet: A publicly available lexical resource for opinion mining. In *Proceedings of LREC*, volume 6, pages 417–422. Citeseer.

Murthy Ganapathibhotla and Bing Liu. 2008. Mining opinions in comparative sentences. In *Proceedings of the 22nd International Conference on Computational Linguistics-Volume 1*, pages 241–248. Association for Computational Linguistics.

Alec Go, Richa Bhayani, and Lei Huang. 2009. Twitter sentiment classification using distant supervision. *CS224N Project Report, Stanford*, 1:12.

Mark Hall, Eibe Frank, Geoffrey Holmes, Bernhard Pfahringer, Peter Reutemann, and Ian H Witten. 2009. The weka data mining software: an update. *ACM SIGKDD explorations newsletter*, 11(1):10–18.

Daisuke Ikeda, Hiroya Takamura, Lev-Arie Ratinov, and Manabu Okumura. 2008. Learning to shift the polarity of words for sentiment classification. In *IJCNLP*, pages 296–303.

Lifeng Jia, Clement Yu, and Weiyi Meng. 2009. The effect of negation on sentiment analysis and retrieval effectiveness. In *Proceedings of the 18th ACM Conference on Information and Knowledge Management*, CIKM '09, pages 1827–1830, New York, NY, USA. ACM.

Salil Joshi, Diptesh Kanojia, and Pushpak Bhattacharyya. 2013. More than meets the eye: Study of human cognition in sense annotation. In *HLT-NAACL*, pages 733–738.

Aditya Joshi, Abhijit Mishra, Nivvedan Senthamilselvan, and Pushpak Bhattacharyya. 2014. Measuring sentiment annotation complexity of text. In *ACL (2)*, pages 36–41.

Aditya Joshi, Vinita Sharma, and Pushpak Bhattacharyya. 2015. Harnessing context incongruity for sarcasm detection. *Proceedings of 53rd Annual Meeting of the ACL, Beijing, China*, page 757.

J Peter Kincaid, Robert P Fishburne Jr, Richard L Rogers, and Brad S Chissom. 1975. Derivation of new readability formulas (automated readability index, fog count and flesch reading ease formula) for navy enlisted personnel. Technical report, DTIC Document.

Sigrid Klerke, Yoav Goldberg, and Anders Søgaard. 2016. Improving sentence compression by learning to predict gaze. In *Proceedings of the 15th Annual Conference of the North American Chapter of the ACL: HLT*. ACL.

Efthymios Kouloumpis, Theresa Wilson, and Johanna Moore. 2011. Twitter sentiment analysis: The good the bad and the omg! *ICWSM*, 11:538–541.

Fangtao Li, Minlie Huang, and Xiaoyan Zhu. 2010. Sentiment analysis with global topics and local dependency. In *AAAI*, volume 10, pages 1371–1376.

Christine Liebrecht, Florian Kunneman, and Antal van den Bosch. 2013. The perfect solution for detecting sarcasm in tweets# not. *WASSA 2013*, page 29.

Chenghua Lin and Yulan He. 2009. Joint sentiment/topic model for sentiment analysis. In *Proceedings of the 18th ACM conference on Information and knowledge management*, pages 375–384. ACM.

Bing Liu and Lei Zhang. 2012. A survey of opinion mining and sentiment analysis. In *Mining text data*, pages 415–463. Springer.

Andrew L Maas, Raymond E Daly, Peter T Pham, Dan Huang, Andrew Y Ng, and Christopher Potts. 2011. Learning word vectors for sentiment analysis. In *Proceedings of the 49th Annual Meeting of the ACL: Human Language Technologies-Volume 1*, pages 142–150. ACL.

Titus Malsburg, Reinhold Kliegl, and Shravan Vasishth. 2015. Determinants of scanpath regularity in reading. *Cognitive science*, 39(7):1675–1703.

Justin Martineau and Tim Finin. 2009. Delta tfidf: An improved feature space for sentiment analysis. *ICWSM*, 9:106.

Diana Maynard and Mark A Greenwood. 2014. Who cares about sarcastic tweets? investigating the impact of sarcasm on sentiment analysis. In *Proceedings of LREC*.

Qiaozhu Mei, Xu Ling, Matthew Wondra, Hang Su, and ChengXiang Zhai. 2007. Topic sentiment mixture: modeling facets and opinions in weblogs. In *Proceedings of the 16th international conference on World Wide Web*, pages 171–180. ACM.

Abhijit Mishra, Pushpak Bhattacharyya, Michael Carl, and IBC CRITT. 2013. Automatically predicting sentence translation difficulty. In *ACL (2)*, pages 346–351.

Abhijit Mishra, Aditya Joshi, and Pushpak Bhattacharyya. 2014. A cognitive study of subjectivity extraction in sentiment annotation. *ACL 2014*, page 142.

Abhijit Mishra, Diptesh Kanojia, and Pushpak Bhattacharyya. 2016. Predicting readers' sarcasm understandability by modeling gaze behavior. In *Proceedings of AAAI*.

Tony Mullen and Nigel Collier. 2004. Sentiment analysis using support vector machines with diverse information sources. In *EMNLP*, volume 4, pages 412–418.

Tetsuji Nakagawa, Kentaro Inui, and Sadao Kurohashi. 2010. Dependency tree-based sentiment classification using crfs with hidden variables. In *NAACL-HLT*, pages 786–794. Association for Computational Linguistics.

Vincent Ng, Sajib Dasgupta, and SM Arifin. 2006. Examining the role of linguistic knowledge sources in the automatic identification and classification of reviews. In *Proceedings of the COLING/ACL on Main conference poster sessions*, pages 611–618. Association for Computational Linguistics.

Bo Pang and Lillian Lee. 2004. A sentimental education: Sentiment analysis using subjectivity summarization based on minimum cuts. In *Proceedings of the 42nd annual meeting on ACL*, page 271. ACL.

Bo Pang and Lillian Lee. 2008. Opinion mining and sentiment analysis. *Foundations and trends in information retrieval*, 2(1-2):1–135.

Bo Pang, Lillian Lee, and Shivakumar Vaithyanathan. 2002. Thumbs up?: sentiment classification using machine learning techniques. In *ACL-02 conference on Empirical methods in natural language processing-Volume 10*, pages 79–86. ACL.

Raja Parasuraman and Matthew Rizzo. 2006. *Neuroergonomics: The brain at work*. Oxford University Press.

Kashyap Popat, Balamurali Andiyakkal Rajendran, Pushpak Bhattacharyya, and Gholamreza Haffari. 2013. The haves and the have-nots: Leveraging unlabelled corpora for sentiment analysis. In *ACL 2013 (Hinrich Schuetze 04 August 2013 to 09 August 2013)*, pages 412–422. ACL.

Soujanya Poria, Erik Cambria, Gregoire Winterstein, and Guang-Bin Huang. 2014. Sentic patterns: Dependency-based rules for concept-level sentiment analysis. *Knowledge-Based Systems*, 69:45–63.

Ankit Ramteke, Akshat Malu, Pushpak Bhattacharyya, and J Saketha Nath. 2013. Detecting turnarounds in sentiment analysis: Thwarting. In *ACL (2)*, pages 860–865.

Keith Rayner and Susan A Duffy. 1986. Lexical complexity and fixation times in reading: Effects of word frequency, verb complexity, and lexical ambiguity. *Memory & Cognition*, 14(3):191–201.

Keith Rayner and Sara C Sereno. 1994. Eye movements in reading: Psycholinguistic studies.

Ellen Riloff, Ashequl Qadir, Prafulla Surve, Lalindra De Silva, Nathan Gilbert, and Ruihong Huang. 2013. Sarcasm as contrast between a positive sentiment and negative situation. In *EMNLP*, pages 704–714.

Hassan Saif, Yulan He, and Harith Alani. 2012. Alleviating data sparsity for twitter sentiment analysis. CEUR Workshop Proceedings (CEUR-WS. org).

Raksha Sharma and Pushpak Bhattacharyya. 2013. Detecting domain dedicated polar words. In *Proceedings of the International Joint Conference on Natural Language Processing*.

Titus von der Malsburg and Shravan Vasishth. 2011. What is the scanpath signature of syntactic reanalysis? *Journal of Memory and Language*, 65(2):109–127.

Janyce Wiebe and Rada Mihalcea. 2006. Word sense and subjectivity. In *International Conference on Computational Linguistics and the 44th annual meeting of the ACL*, pages 1065–1072. ACL.

Theresa Wilson, Janyce Wiebe, and Paul Hoffmann. 2005. Recognizing contextual polarity in phrase-level sentiment analysis. In *EMNLP-HLT*, pages 347–354. Association for Computational Linguistics.

Erroll Wood and Andreas Bulling. 2014. Eyetab: Model-based gaze estimation on unmodified tablet computers. In *Proceedings of the Symposium on Eye Tracking Research and Applications*, pages 207–210. ACM.

Modelling Context with User Embeddings
for Sarcasm Detection in Social Media

Silvio Amir **Byron C. Wallace**[†] **Hao Lyu**[†] **Paula Carvalho** **Mário J. Silva**

INESC-ID Lisboa, Instituto Superior Técnico, Universidade de Lisboa
[†]iSchool, University of Texas at Austin

samir@inesc-id.pt byron.wallace@utexas.edu xalh8083@gmail.com
pcc@inesc-id.pt mjs@inesc-id.pt

Abstract

We introduce a deep neural network for automated sarcasm detection. Recent work has emphasized the need for models to capitalize on *contextual* features, beyond lexical and syntactic cues present in utterances. For example, different speakers will tend to employ sarcasm regarding different subjects and, thus, sarcasm detection models ought to encode such speaker information. Current methods have achieved this by way of laborious feature engineering. By contrast, we propose to automatically learn and then exploit *user embeddings*, to be used in concert with lexical signals to recognize sarcasm. Our approach does not require elaborate feature engineering (and concomitant data scraping); fitting user embeddings requires only the text from their previous posts. The experimental results show that the our model outperforms a state-of-the-art approach leveraging an extensive set of carefully crafted features.

1 Introduction

Existing social media analysis systems are hampered by their inability to accurately detect and interpret figurative language. This is particularly relevant in domains like the social sciences and politics, in which the use of figurative communication devices such as verbal irony (roughly, sarcasm) is common. Sarcasm is often used by individuals to express opinions on complex matters and regarding specific targets (Carvalho et al., 2009).

Early computational models for verbal irony and sarcasm detection tended to rely on shallow methods exploiting conditional token count regularities. But lexical clues alone are insufficient

Figure 1: An illustrative tweet.

to discern ironic intent. Appreciating the *context* of utterances is critical for this; even for humans (Wallace et al., 2014). Indeed, the exact same sentence can be interpreted as literal or sarcastic, *depending on the speaker*. Consider the sarcastic tweet in Figure 1 (ignoring for the moment the attached #sarcasm hashtag). Without knowing the author's political leanings, it would be difficult to conclude with certainty whether the remark was intended sarcastically or in earnest.

Recent work in sarcasm detection on social media has tried to incorporate contextual information by exploiting the preceding messages of a user, to e.g., detect contrasts in sentiments expressed towards named entities (Khattri et al., 2015), infer behavioural traits (Rajadesingan et al., 2015) and capture the relationship between authors and the audience (Bamman and Smith, 2015). However, all of these approaches require the design and implementation of complex features that explicitly encode the content and (relevant) context of messages to be classified. This feature engineering is labor intensive, and depends on external tools and resources. Therefore, deploying such systems in practice is expensive, time-consuming and unwieldy.

We propose a novel approach to sarcasm detection on social media that does not require extensive manual feature engineering. Instead, we develop a neural model that learns to represent and exploit embeddings of both *content* and *context*. For the former, we induce vector lexical repre-

167

Proceedings of the 20th SIGNLL Conference on Computational Natural Language Learning (CoNLL), pages 167–177,
Berlin, Germany, August 7-12, 2016. ©2016 Association for Computational Linguistics

sentations via a convolutional layer; for the latter, our model learns *user embeddings*. Inference concerning whether an utterance (tweet) was intended ironically (or not) is then modelled as a joint function of lexical representations and corresponding author embeddings.

The main contributions of this paper are as follows. (i) We propose a novel convolutional neural network based model that explicitly learns and exploits user embeddings in conjunction with features derived from utterances. (ii) We show that this model outperforms the strong baseline recently proposed by Bamman and Smith (2015) by more than 2% in absolute accuracy, while obviating the need to manually engineer features. (iii) We show that the learned user embeddings can capture relevant user attributes.

2   Related Work

Verbal irony is a rhetorical device in which speakers say something other than, and often opposite to, what they actually mean.[1] Sarcasm may be viewed as a special case of irony, where the positive literal meaning is perceived as an indirect insult (Dews et al., 1995).

Most of the previously proposed computational models to detect irony and sarcasm have used features similar to those used in sentiment analysis. Carvalho et al. (2009) analyzed comments posted by users on a Portuguese online newspaper and found that oral and gestural cues indicate irony. These included: emoticons, onomatopoeic expressions for laughter, heavy punctuation, quotation marks and positive interjections. Others have used text classifiers with features based on word and character n-grams, sentiment lexicons, surface patterns and textual markers (Davidov et al., 2010; González-Ibánez et al., 2011; Reyes et al., 2013; Lukin and Walker, 2013). Elsewhere, Barbieri and Saggion (2014) derived new word-frequency based features to detect irony, e.g., combinations of frequent and rare words, ambiguous words, 'spoken style' words combined with 'written style' words and intensity of adjectives. Riloff et al. (2013) demonstrated that one may exploit the apparent expression of contrasting sentiment in the same utterance as a marker of verbal irony.

The aforementioned approaches rely predominantly on features *intrinsic* to texts, but these will often be insufficient to infer figurative meaning: context is needed. There have been some recent attempts to exploit contextual information, e.g. Khattri et al. (2015) extended the notion of *contrasting sentiments* beyond the textual content at hand. In particular, they analyzed previous posts to estimate the author's prior sentiment towards specific *targets* (i.e., entities). A tweet is then predicted to be sarcastic if it expresses a sentiment about an entity that contradicts the author's (estimated) prior sentiment regarding the same.

Rajadesingan et al. (2015) built a system based on theories of sarcasm expression from psychology and behavioral sciences. To operationalize such theories, they used several linguistic tools and resources (e.g. lexicons, sentiment classifiers and a PoS tagger), in addition to user profile information and previous posts, to model a range of behavioural aspects (e.g., mood, writing style). Wallace et al. (2015) developed an approach for classifying posts on *reddit*[2] as sarcastic or literal, based in part on the interaction between the specific sub-reddit to which a post was made, the entities mentioned, and the (apparent) sentiment expressed. For example, if a post in the (politically) conservative sub-reddit mentions Obama, it is more likely to have been intended ironically than posts mentioning Obama in the progressive sub-reddit. But this approach is limited because it relies on the unique sub-reddit structure. Bamman and Smith (2015) proposed an approach that relied on an extensive, rich set of features capturing various contextual information about authors of tweets and the audience (in addition to lexical cues). We review these at length in Section 5.1.

A major downside of these and related approaches, however, is the amount of manual effort required to derive these feature sets. A primary goal of this work is to explore whether neural models can effectively learn these rich contextualizing features, thus obviating the need to manually craft them. In particular, the model we propose similarly aims to combine lexical clues with extra-linguistic information. Unlike prior work, however, our model attempts to automatically induce representations for the content and the author of a message that are predictive of sarcasm.

---

[1] Like other forms of subjective expression, irony and sarcasm are difficult to define precisely.

---

[2] http://reddit.com is a social news aggregation site comprising specific topical *sub-reddits*.

3   Learning User Embeddings

Our goal is to learn representations (vectors) that encode latent aspects of users and capture homophily, by projecting similar users into nearby regions of the embedding space. We hypothesize that such representations will naturally capture some of the signals that have been described in the literature as important indicators of sarcasm, such as contrasts between what someone believes and what they have ostensibly expressed (Campbell and Katz, 2012) or Kreuz (1996) principle of *inferability*, stating that sarcasm requires a common ground between parties to be understood.

To induce the user embeddings, we adopt an approach similar to that described in the preliminary work of Li et al. (2015). In particular, we capture relations between users and the content they produce by optimizing the conditional probability of texts, given their authors (or, more precisely, given the vector representations of their authors). This method is akin to Le and Mikolov (2014)'s *Paragraph Vector* model, which jointly estimates embeddings for words and paragraphs by learning to predict the occurrence of a word w within a paragraph p conditioned on the (learned) representation for p.

Given a sentence $S = \{w_1, \ldots, w_N\}$ where w_i denotes a word drawn from a vocabulary $\mathcal{V}$, we aim to maximize the following probability:

$$
P(S|\text{user}_j) = \sum_{w_i \in S} \log P(w_i|\mathbf{u}_j)
$$
$$
+ \sum_{w_i \in S} \sum_{w_k \in C(w_i)} \log P(w_i|\mathbf{e}_k) \quad (1)
$$

Where $C(w_i)$ denotes the set of words in a prespecified window around word w_i, $\mathbf{e}_k \in \mathbb{R}^d$ and $\mathbf{u}_j \in \mathbb{R}^d$ denote the embeddings of word k and user j, respectively. This objective function encodes the notion that the occurrence of a word w, depends both on the author of S and it's neighbouring words.

The conditional probabilities in Equation 1 can be estimated with log-linear models of the form:

$$
P(w_i|\mathbf{x}) = \frac{\exp(\mathbf{W}_i \cdot \mathbf{x} + \mathbf{b}_i)}{\sum_{k=1}^{Y} \exp(\mathbf{W}_k \cdot \mathbf{x} + \mathbf{b}_k)} \quad (2)
$$

Where $\mathbf{x}$ denotes a feature vector, $\mathbf{W}_k$ and $\mathbf{b}_k$ are the weight vectors and bias for class k. In our case, we treat words as classes to be predicted.

Calculating the denominator thus requires summing over all of the words in the (large) vocabulary, an expensive operation. To avoid this computational bottleneck, we approximate the term $P(w_i|\mathbf{e}_k)$ with Morin and Bengio (2005) Hierarchical Softmax.[3]

To learn meaningful user embeddings, we seek representations that are predictive of individual word-usage patterns. In light of this motivation, we approximate $P(w_i|\mathbf{u}_j)$ via the following hinge-loss objective which we aim to minimize:

$$
\mathcal{L}(w_i, \text{user}_j) =
$$
$$
\sum_{w_l \in V, w_l \notin S} \max(0, 1 - \mathbf{e}_i \cdot \mathbf{u_j} + \mathbf{e}_l \cdot \mathbf{u_j})
$$
$$
(3)
$$

Here, each w_l (and corresponding embedding, $\mathbf{e}_l$) is a *negative example*, i.e., a word not in the sentence under consideration, which was authored by user j. The intuition is that in the aggregate, such words are less likely to be employed by user j than words observed in sentences she has authored. Thus minimizing this objective attempts to induce a representation that is discriminative with respect to word usage.

In practice, V will be very large and hence we approximate the objective via *negative sampling*, a variant of Noise Contrastive Estimation. The idea is to approximate the objective function in a binary classification task by learning to discriminate between observed positive examples (sampled from the true distribution) and *pseudo*-negative examples (sampled from a large space of predominantly negative instances). Intuitively, this shifts probability mass to plausible observations. See Dyer (2014) for notes on Negative Sampling and Noise Contrastive Estimation.

Previous work by Collobert et al. (2011) showed that this approach works well in representation learning tasks when a sufficient amount of training data is available . However, we have access to only a limited amount of text for each user (see Section 5). We hypothesize that this problem can be alleviated by carefully selecting the negative samples that mostly contribute to 'push' the vectors into the appropriate region of the embedding space (i.e., closer to the words commonly employed by a given user and far from other words).

---

[3]As implemented in `Gensim` (Řehůřek and Sojka, 2010).

This requires designing a strategy for selectively sampling negative examples. One straightforward approach would be to sample from a user-specific unigram model, informing which words are less likely to be utilized by that user. But estimating the parameters of such model with scarce data would be prone to overfitting. Instead, we sample from a unigram distribution estimated from the posts authored by all the users. The goal is to select the most commonly used words as the negative samples, thereby forcing the representations to capture the differences between the words a given individual employs and the words that everyone commonly uses.

4 Proposed Model

We now present the details of our proposed sarcasm detection model. Given a message S authored by user u, we wish to capture both the relevant aspects of the *content* and the relevant *contextual* information about the author. To represent the content, we use pre-trained word embeddings as the input to a convolutional layer that extracts high-level features. More formally, let $\mathbf{E} \in \mathbb{R}^{d \times |\mathcal{V}|}$ be a pre-trained word embedding matrix, where each column represents a word from the vocabulary $\mathcal{V}$ as a d dimensional vector. By selecting the columns of $\mathbf{E}$ corresponding to the words in S, we form the sentence matrix:

$$\mathbf{S} = \begin{bmatrix} - & \mathbf{e}_1 & - \\ & \vdots & \\ - & \mathbf{e}_m & - \end{bmatrix} \qquad (4)$$

A convolutional layer is composed of a set of filters $\mathbf{F} \in \mathbb{R}^{d \times h}$ where h is the *height* of the filter. Filters *slide* across the input, extracting h-gram features that constitute a feature map $\mathbf{m} \in \mathbb{R}^{|S|-h+1}$, where each entry is obtained as

$$\mathbf{m}_i = \alpha(\mathbf{F} \cdot \mathbf{S}_{[i:i-h+1]} + b) \qquad (5)$$

with $i = 1, \ldots i - h + 1$. Here, $\mathbf{S}_{[i:j]}$ denotes a sub-matrix of $\mathbf{S}$ (from row i to row j), $b \in \mathbb{R}$ is an additive bias and $\alpha(\cdot)$ denotes a non-linear activation function, applied element-wise. We transform the resultant feature map into a scalar using *max-pooling*, i.e., we extract the largest value in the map. We use 3 filters (with varying heights) each of which generates M feature maps that are reduced to a vector $\mathbf{f}^k = [max(\mathbf{m}^1) \oplus max(\mathbf{m}^2) \ldots \oplus max(\mathbf{m}^M)]$,

where $\oplus$ denotes concatenation. We set $\alpha(\cdot)$ to be the *Rectified Linear Unit* activation function (Nair and Hinton, 2010). The output of all the filters is then combined to form the final representation $\mathbf{c} = [\mathbf{f}^1 \oplus \mathbf{f}^2 \oplus \mathbf{f}^3]$. We will denote this feature vector of a specific sentence S by $\mathbf{c}_S$.

To represent the context, we assume there is a user embedding matrix $\mathbf{U} \in \mathbb{R}^{d \times N}$, where each column represents one of N users with a d dimensional vector. The parameters of this embedding matrix can be initialized randomly or using the approach described in Section 3. Then, we simply map the author of the message into the user embedding space by selecting the corresponding column of $\mathbf{U}$. Letting $\mathbf{U}_u$ denote the user embedding of author u, we formulate our sarcasm detection model as follows:

$$P(y = k|s, u; \theta) \propto \mathbf{Y}_k \cdot g(\mathbf{c}_S \oplus \mathbf{U}_u) + \mathbf{b}_k$$
$$g(\mathbf{x}) = \alpha(\mathbf{H} \cdot \mathbf{x} + \mathbf{h}) \qquad (6)$$

where $g(\cdot)$ denote the activations of a hidden layer, capturing the relations between the content and context representations, and $\theta = \{\mathbf{Y}, \mathbf{b}, \mathbf{H}, \mathbf{h}, \mathbf{F}^1, \mathbf{F}^2, \mathbf{F}^3, \mathbf{E}, \mathbf{U}\}$ are parameters to be estimated during training. Here, $\mathbf{Y} \in \mathbb{R}^{2 \times z}$ and $\mathbf{b} \in \mathbb{R}^2$ are the weights and bias of the output layer; $\mathbf{H} \in \mathbb{R}^{z \times 3M+d}$ and $\mathbf{h} \in \mathbb{R}^z$ are the weights and bias of the hidden layer; and $\mathbf{F}^i$ are the weights of the convolutional filters. Henceforth, we will refer to this approach as *Content and User Embedding Convolutional Neural Network* (CUE-CNN). Figure 2 provides an illustrative schematic depicting this model.

5 Experimental Setup

We replicated Bamman and Smith (2015) experimental setup using (a subset of) the same Twitter corpus. The labels were inferred from self-declarations of sarcasm, i.e., a tweet is considered sarcastic if it contains the hashtag #sarcasm or #sarcastic and deemed non-sarcastic otherwise.[4] To comply with Twitter terms of service, we were given only the tweet ids along with the corresponding labels and had to retrieve the messages ourselves. By the time we tried to retrieve the messages, some of them were not available. We also did not have access to the historical user tweets used by Bamman and Smith, hence, for

---

[4]Note that this is a form of noisy supervision, as of course all sarcastic tweets will not be explicitly flagged as such.

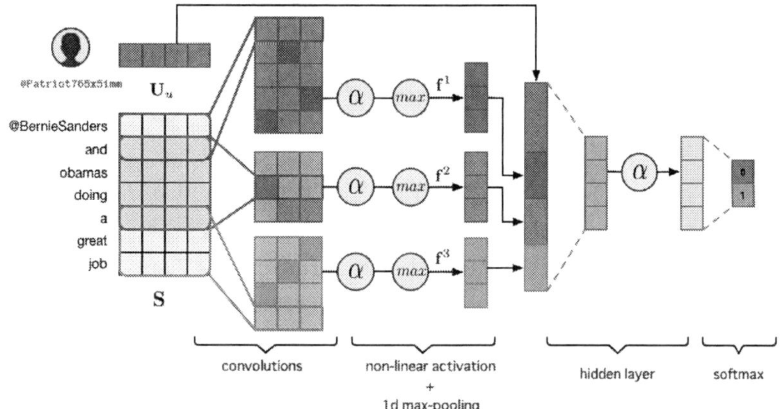

Figure 2: Illustration of the CUE-CNN model for sarcasm detection. The model learns to represent and exploit embeddings of both *content* and *users* in social media.

each author and mentioned user, we scraped additional tweets from their Twitter feed. Due to restrictions in the Twitter API, we were only able to crawl at most 1000 *historical tweets* per user.[5] Furthermore, we were unable to collect historical tweets for a significant proportion of the users, thus, we discarded messages for which no contextual information was available, resulting in a corpus of $11,541$ tweets involving $12,500$ unique users (authors and mentioned users). It should also be noted that our historical tweets were posted *after* the ones in the corpus used for the experiments.

5.1 Baselines

We reimplemented Bamman and Smith (2015)'s sarcasm detection model. This a simple, logistic-regression based classifier that exploits rich feature sets to achieve strong performance. These are detailed at length in the original paper, but we briefly summarize them here:

- **tweet-features**, encoding attributes of the target tweet text, including: uni- and bigram bag of words (BoW) features; Brown et al. (1992) word clusters indicators; unlabeled dependency bigrams (both BoW and with Brown cluster representations); part-of-speech, spelling and abbreviation features; inferred sentiment, at both the tweet and word level; and 'intensifier' indicators.

- **author-features**, aimed at encoding attributes of the author, including: historically

'salient' terms used by the author; the inferred distribution over topics[6] historically tweeted about by the user; inferred sentiment historically expressed by the user; and author profile information (e.g., profile BoW features).

- **audience-features**, capturing properties of the *addressee* of tweets, in those cases that a tweet is directed at someone (via the @ symbol). A subset of these, duplicate the aforementioned author features for the addressee. Additionally, author/audience interaction features are introduced, which capture similarity between the author and addressee, w.r.t. inferred topic distributions. Finally, this sct includes a feature capturing the frequency of past communication between the author and addressee.

- **response-features**, for tweets written in response to another tweet. This set of features captures information relating the two, with BoW features of the original tweet and pairwise cluster indicator features, which the encode Brown clusters observed in both the original and response tweet.

We emphasize that implementing this rich set of features took considerable time and effort. This motivates our approach, which aims to effectively induce and exploit contextually-aware representations without manual feature engineering.

---

[5]The original study (Bamman and Smith, 2015) was done with at most $3,200$ historical tweets.

[6]The topics were extracted from Latent Dirichlet Allocation (Blei et al., 2003).

To assess the importance of modelling contextual information in sarcasm detection, we considered two groups of models as baselines: the first only takes into account the content of a target tweet. The second, combines lexical cues with contextual information. The first group includes the following models:

- UNIGRAMS: ℓ_2-regularized logistic regression classifier with binary unigrams as features.

- TWEET ONLY: ℓ_2-regularized logistic regression classifier with binary unigrams and **tweet-features**.

- NBOW: Logistic regression with neural word embeddings as features. Given a sentence matrix $\mathbf{S}$ (Eq. 4) as input, a d-dimensional feature vector is computed by summing the individual word embeddings.

- NLSE: The Non-linear subspace embedding model due to Astudillo et al. (2015). The NLSE model adapts pre-trained word embeddings for specific tasks by learning a projection into a small subspace. The idea is that this subspace captures the most discriminative latent aspects encoded in the word embeddings. Given a sentence matrix $\mathbf{S}$, each word vector is first projected into the subspace and then transformed through an element-wise sigmoid function. The final sentence representation is obtained by summing the (adapted) word embeddings and passed into a softmax layer that outputs the predictions.

- CNN: The CNN model for text classification proposed by Kim (2014), using only features extracted from the convolutional layer acting on the lexical content. The input layer was initialized with pre-trained word embeddings.

The second group of baselines consists of the following models:

- TWEET+*: ℓ_2-regularized logistic regression classifier with a combination of **tweet-features** and each of the aforementioned Bamman and Smith (2015) feature sets.

- SHALLOW CUE-CNN: A simplified version of our neural model for sarcasm detection, without the hidden layer. We evaluated two variants: initializing the user embeddings at random, and initializing the user embeddings with the approach described in Section 3 (SHALLOW CUE-CNN+USER2VEC). In both cases, the (word and user) embeddings weights were updated during training.

- CUE-CNN+*: Our proposed neural network for sarcasm detection. We also evaluated the two aforementioned variants: randomly initialized user embeddings and pre-trained user embeddings. But here we compared two different approaches for the negative sampling procedure, namely, sampling from a unigram distribution (CUE-CNN+USER2VEC) and sampling uniformly at random from the vocabulary (CUE-CNN+USER2VEC-UNIFRAND).

5.2 Pre-Training Word and User Embeddings

We first trained Mikolov et al. (2013)'s *skip-gram* model variant to induce word embeddings using the union of: Owoputi et al. (2013)'s dataset of 52 Million unlabeled tweets, Bamman and Smith (2015) sarcasm dataset and 5 Million historical tweets collected from users.

To induce user embeddings, we estimated a unigram distribution with maximum likelihood estimation. Then, for each word in a tweet, we extracted 15 negative samples (for the first term in Eq.1) and used the skip-gram model to pre-compute the conditional probabilities of words occurring in a window of size 5 (for the second term in Eq.1). Finally, Equation 1 was minimized via Stochastic Gradient Descent on 90% of the historical data, holding out the remainder for validation and using the $P(\text{tweet text}|\text{user})$ as early stopping criteria.

Note that the parameters for each user only depend on their own tweets; this allowed us to perform these computations in parallel to speed-up the training.

m

5.3 Model Training and Evaluation

Evaluation was performed via 10-fold cross-validation. For each split, we fit models to 80% of the data, tuned them on 10% and tested on the remaining, held-out 10%. These data splits were kept fixed in all the experiments. For the linear classifiers, in each split, the regularization constant was selected with a linear search over the

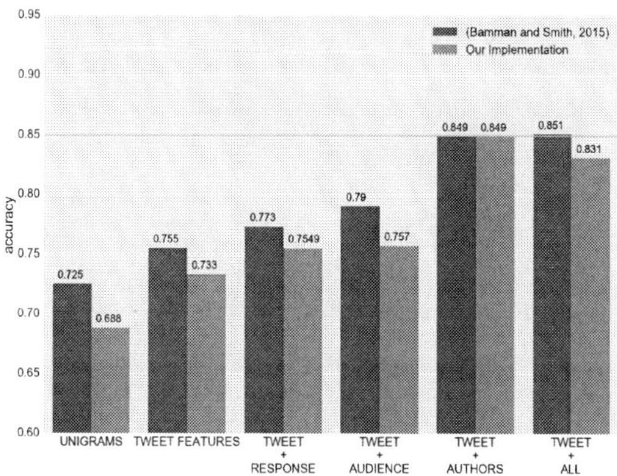

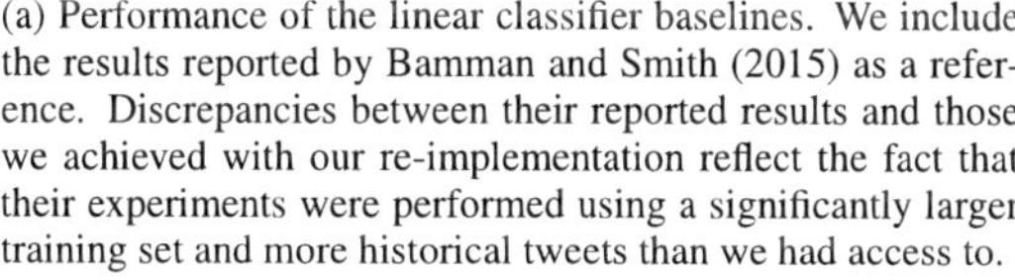

(a) Performance of the linear classifier baselines. We include the results reported by Bamman and Smith (2015) as a reference. Discrepancies between their reported results and those we achieved with our re-implementation reflect the fact that their experiments were performed using a significantly larger training set and more historical tweets than we had access to.

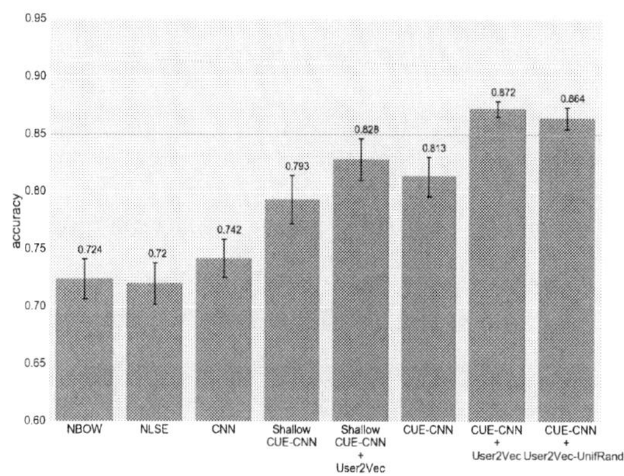

(b) Performance of the proposed neural models. We compare simple neural models that only consider the lexical content of a message (first 3 bars) with architectures that explicitly model the context. Bars 4 and 5 show the gains obtained by pre-training the user embeddings. The last 2 bars compare different negative sampling procedures for the user embedding pre-training.

Figure 3: Comparison of different models. The left sub-plot shows linear model performance; the right shows the performance of neural variants. The horizontal line corresponds to the best performance achieved via linear models with rich feature sets. Performance was measured in terms of average accuracy over 10-fold cross-validation; error bars depict the variance.

range $C = [1e^{-4}, 1e^{-3}, 1e^{-2}, 1e^{-1}, 1, 10]$ using the training set to fit the model and evaluating on the tuning set. After selecting the best regularization constant, the model was re-trained on the union of the train and tune sets, and evaluated on the test set.

To train our neural model, we first had to choose a suitable architecture and hyperparameter set. However, selecting the optimal network parametrization would require an extensive search over a large configuration space. Therefore, in these experiments, we followed the recommendations in Zhang and Wallace (2015), focusing our search over combinations of dropout rates $D = [0.0, 0.1, 0.3, 0.5]$, filter heights $H = [(1, 3, 5), (2, 4, 6), (3, 5, 7), (4, 6, 8), (5, 7, 9)]$, number of feature maps $M = [100, 200, 400, 600]$ and size of the hidden layer $Z = [25, 50, 75, 100]$.

We performed random search by sampling without replacement over half of the possible configurations. For each data split, 20% of the training set was reserved for early stopping. We compared the sampled configurations by fitting the model on the remaining training data and testing on the tune set. After choosing the best configuration, we re-trained the model on the union of the train and tune set (again reserving 20% of the data for early stopping) and evaluated on the test set.

The model was trained by minimizing the cross-entropy error between the predictions and true labels, the gradients w.r.t to the network parameters were computed with backpropagation (Rumelhart et al., 1988) and the model weights were updated with the AdaDelta rule (Zeiler, 2012).

6 Results

6.1 Classification Results

Figure 3 presents the main experimental results. In Figure 3a, we show the performance of linear classifiers with the manually engineered feature sets proposed by Bamman and Smith (2015). Our results differ slightly from those originally reported. Nonetheless, we observe the same general trends: namely, that including contextual features significantly improves the performance, and that the biggest gains are attributable to features encoding information about the authors of tweets.

The results of neural model variants are shown in Figure 3b. Once again, we find that modelling the context (i.e., the author) of a tweet yields significant gains in accuracy. The difference is that here the network jointly *learns* appropriate user representations, lexical feature extractors and, finally, the classification model. Further improvements are realized by pre-training the user embed-

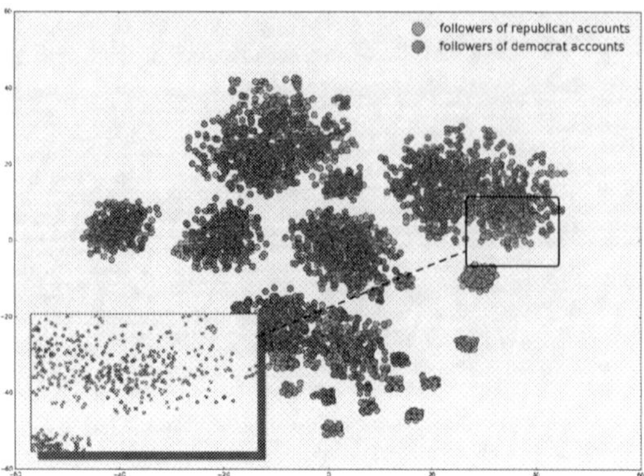
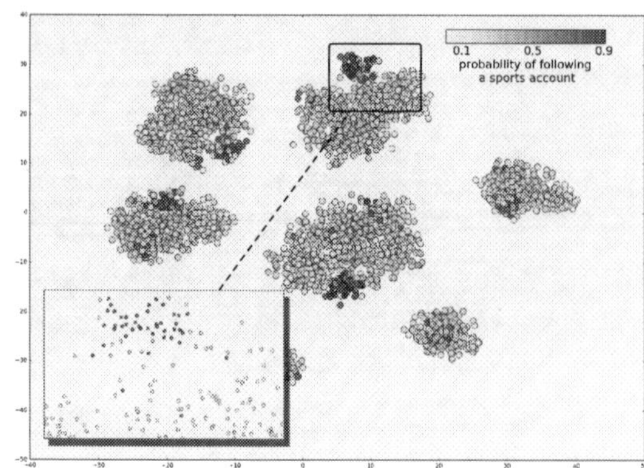
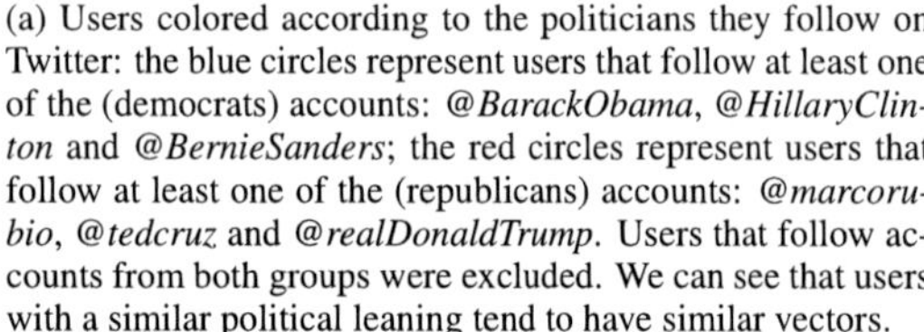

(a) Users colored according to the politicians they follow on Twitter: the blue circles represent users that follow at least one of the (democrats) accounts: *@BarackObama*, *@HillaryClinton* and *@BernieSanders*; the red circles represent users that follow at least one of the (republicans) accounts: *@marcorubio*, *@tedcruz* and *@realDonaldTrump*. Users that follow accounts from both groups were excluded. We can see that users with a similar political leaning tend to have similar vectors.

(b) Users colored with respect to the likelihood of following a sports account. The 500 most popular accounts (according to the authors in our training data) were manually inspected and 100 sports related accounts were selected, e.g., *@SkySports*, *@NBA* and *@cristiano*. We should note that users for which the probabilities lied in the range between $0.3 - 0.7$ were discarded to emphasize the extremes.

Figure 4: T-SNE projection of the user embeddings into 2-dimensions. The users are color coded according to their political preferences and interest in sports. The visualization suggests that the learned embeddings capture some notion of homophily.

dings (we elaborate on this in the following section). We see additional gains when we introduce a hidden layer capturing the *interactions* between the context (i.e., user vectors) and the content (lexical vectors). This is intuitively agreeable: the recognition of sarcasm is possible when we jointly consider the speaker and the utterance at hand. Interestingly, we observed that our proposed model not only outperforms all the other baselines, but also shows less variance over the cross-validation experiments.

Finally, we compared the effect of obtaining negative samples uniformly at random with sampling from a unigram distribution. The experimental results show that the latter improves the accuracy of the model by 0.8%. We believe the reason is that considering the most likely words (under the model) as negative samples, helps by pushing the user vectors away from non-informative words and simultaneously closer to the most discriminative words for that user.

6.2 User Embedding Analysis

We now investigate the user embeddings in more detail. In particular, we are interested in two questions: first, what aspects are being captured in these representations; and second, how they contribute to the improved performance of our model.

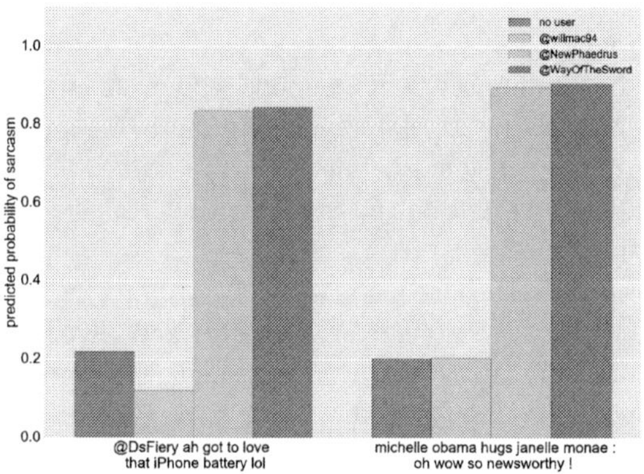

Figure 5: Two sarcastic examples that were misclassified by a simple CNN (`no user`). Using the CUE-CNN with contextual information drastically changes the model's predictions on the same examples.

To investigate the first question, we plotted a T-SNE projection (Maaten and Hinton, 2008) of the high-dimensional vector space where the users are represented into two-dimensions. We then colored each point (representing a user) according to their apparent political leaning (Figure 4a), and according to their interest in sports (Figure 4b). These attributes were inferred using the Twitter accounts that a user follows, as a proxy. The plots suggest that the user vectors are indeed able to capture latent aspects, such as political preferences and personal interests. Moreover, the embeddings seem to uncover a notion of homophily, i.e. similar users tend to occupy neighbouring regions of the embedding space. Regarding the second question, we examined the influence of the contextual information on the model's predictions. To this end, we measured the response of our model to the same textual content with different hypothetical contexts (authors). We selected two examples that were misclassified by a simple CNN and ran them trough the CUE-CNN model with three different user embeddings. In Figure 5, we show these examples along with the predicted probabilities of being a sarcastic post, when no user information is considered and when the author is taken into account. We can see that the predictions drastically change when contextual information is available and that two of the authors trigger similar responses on both examples. This example provides evidence that our model captures the intuition that the same utterance can be interpreted as sarcastic or not, depending on the speaker.

7 Conclusions

We have introduced CUE-CNN, a novel, deep neural network for automatically recognizing sarcastic utterances on social media. Our model jointly learns and exploits embeddings for the content and users, thus integrating information about the speaker and what he or she has said. This is accomplished without manual feature engineering. Nonetheless, our model *outperforms* (by over 2% in absolute accuracy) a recently proposed state-of-the-art model that exploits an extensive, hand-crafted set of features encoding user attributes and other contextual information. Unlike other approaches that explicitly exploit the structure of particular social media services, such as the forum where a message was posted or metadata about the users, learning user embeddings only requires their preceding messages. Yet, the obtained vectors are able to capture relevant user attributes and a soft notion of homophily. This, we believe, makes our model easier to deploy over different social media environments.

Our implementation of the proposed method and the datasets used in this paper have been made publicly available[7]. As future work, we intended to further explore the user embeddings for context representation, namely by also incorporating the interaction between the author and the audience into the model.

Acknowledgments

This work was supported in part by the Army Research Office (grant W911NF-14-1-0442) and by The Foundation for Science and Technology, Portugal (FCT), through contracts UID/CEC/50021/2013, EXCL/EEI-ESS/0257/2012 (DataStorm), grant UTAP-EXPL/EEIESS/0031/2014 and Ph.D. scholarship SFRH/BD/89020/2012. This work was also made possible by the support of the Texas Advanced Computer Center (TACC) at UT Austin.

References

Ramón Astudillo, Silvio Amir, Wang Ling, Mario Silva, and Isabel Trancoso. 2015. Learning word representations from scarce and noisy data with embedding subspaces. In *Proceedings of the 53rd Annual Meeting of the Association for Computational Linguistics and the 7th International Joint Conference on Natural Language Processing (Volume 1: Long Papers)*, pages 1074–1084, Beijing, China, July.

David Bamman and Noah A Smith. 2015. Contextualized sarcasm detection on twitter. In *Proceedings of the 9th International Conference on Web and Social Media*, pages 574–77. AAAI Menlo Park, CA.

Francesco Barbieri and Horacio Saggion. 2014. Modelling irony in twitter. In *EACL*, pages 56–64.

David M Blei, Andrew Y Ng, and Michael I Jordan. 2003. Latent dirichlet allocation. *the Journal of machine Learning research*, 3:993–1022.

Peter F Brown, Peter V Desouza, Robert L Mercer, Vincent J Della Pietra, and Jenifer C Lai. 1992. Class-based n-gram models of natural language. *Computational linguistics*, 18(4):467–479.

John D Campbell and Albert N Katz. 2012. Are there necessary conditions for inducing a sense of sarcastic irony? *Discourse Processes*, 49(6):459–480.

Paula Carvalho, Luís Sarmento, Mário J Silva, and Eugénio De Oliveira. 2009. Clues for detecting irony in user-generated contents: oh...!! it's so easy;-). In *Proceedings of the 1st international CIKM workshop on Topic-sentiment analysis for mass opinion*, pages 53–56. ACM.

Ronan Collobert, Jason Weston, Léon Bottou, Michael Karlen, Koray Kavukcuoglu, and Pavel Kuksa. 2011. Natural language processing (almost) from scratch. *The Journal of Machine Learning Research*, 12:2493–2537.

---

[7] https://github.com/samiroid/CUE-CNN

Dmitry Davidov, Oren Tsur, and Ari Rappoport. 2010. Semi-supervised recognition of sarcastic sentences in twitter and amazon. In *Proceedings of the Fourteenth Conference on Computational Natural Language Learning*, pages 107–116. Association for Computational Linguistics.

Shelly Dews, Joan Kaplan, and Ellen Winner. 1995. Why not say it directly? the social functions of irony. *Discourse processes*, 19(3):347–367.

Chris Dyer. 2014. Notes on noise contrastive estimation and negative sampling. *arXiv preprint arXiv:1410.8251*.

Roberto González-Ibánez, Smaranda Muresan, and Nina Wacholder. 2011. Identifying sarcasm in twitter: a closer look. In *Proceedings of the 49th Annual Meeting of the Association for Computational Linguistics: Human Language Technologies: short papers-Volume 2*, pages 581–586. Association for Computational Linguistics.

Anupam Khattri, Aditya Joshi, Pushpak Bhattacharyya, and Mark James Carman. 2015. Your sentiment precedes you: Using an author's historical tweets to predict sarcasm. In *6th Workshop on Computational Approaches To Subjectivity, Sentiment And Social Media Analysis WASSA 2015*, page 25.

Yoon Kim. 2014. Convolutional neural networks for sentence classification. In *Proceedings of the 2014 Conference on Empirical Methods in Natural Language Processing (EMNLP)*, pages 1746–1751, Doha, Qatar, October. Association for Computational Linguistics.

Roger J Kreuz. 1996. The use of verbal irony: Cues and constraints. *Metaphor: Implications and applications*, pages 23–38.

Quoc V Le and Tomas Mikolov. 2014. Distributed representations of sentences and documents. *arXiv preprint arXiv:1405.4053*.

Jiwei Li, Alan Ritter, and Dan Jurafsky. 2015. Learning multi-faceted representations of individuals from heterogeneous evidence using neural networks. *arXiv preprint arXiv:1510.05198*.

Stephanie Lukin and Marilyn Walker. 2013. Really? well. apparently bootstrapping improves the performance of sarcasm and nastiness classifiers for online dialogue. In *Proceedings of the Workshop on Language Analysis in Social Media*, pages 30–40.

Laurens van der Maaten and Geoffrey Hinton. 2008. Visualizing data using t-sne. *Journal of Machine Learning Research*, 9(Nov):2579–2605.

Tomas Mikolov, Ilya Sutskever, Kai Chen, Greg S Corrado, and Jeff Dean. 2013. Distributed representations of words and phrases and their compositionality. In *Advances in neural information processing systems*, pages 3111–3119.

Frederic Morin and Yoshua Bengio. 2005. Hierarchical probabilistic neural network language model. In *Aistats*, volume 5, pages 246–252. Citeseer.

Vinod Nair and Geoffrey E Hinton. 2010. Rectified linear units improve restricted boltzmann machines. In *Proceedings of the 27th International Conference on Machine Learning (ICML-10)*, pages 807–814.

Olutobi Owoputi, Brendan O'Connor, Chris Dyer, Kevin Gimpel, Nathan Schneider, and Noah A Smith. 2013. Improved part-of-speech tagging for online conversational text with word clusters. Association for Computational Linguistics.

Ashwin Rajadesingan, Reza Zafarani, and Huan Liu. 2015. Sarcasm detection on twitter: A behavioral modeling approach. In *Proceedings of the Eighth ACM International Conference on Web Search and Data Mining*, pages 97–106. ACM.

Radim Řehůřek and Petr Sojka. 2010. Software Framework for Topic Modelling with Large Corpora. In *Proceedings of the LREC 2010 Workshop on New Challenges for NLP Frameworks*, pages 45–50, Valletta, Malta, May. ELRA. http://is.muni.cz/publication/884893/en.

Antonio Reyes, Paolo Rosso, and Tony Veale. 2013. A multidimensional approach for detecting irony in twitter. *Language resources and evaluation*, 47(1):239–268.

Ellen Riloff, Ashequl Qadir, Prafulla Surve, Lalindra De Silva, Nathan Gilbert, and Ruihong Huang. 2013. Sarcasm as contrast between a positive sentiment and negative situation. In *EMNLP*, pages 704–714.

David E Rumelhart, Geoffrey E Hinton, and Ronald J Williams. 1988. Learning representations by back-propagating errors. *Cognitive modeling*, 5(3):1.

Byron C. Wallace, Do Kook Choe, Laura Kertz, and Eugene Charniak. 2014. Humans require context to infer ironic intent (so computers probably do, too). In *Proceedings of the 52nd Annual Meeting of the Association for Computational Linguistics (Volume 2: Short Papers)*, pages 512–516, Baltimore, Maryland, June. Association for Computational Linguistics.

Byron C. Wallace, Do Kook Choe, and Eugene Charniak. 2015. Sparse, contextually informed models for irony detection: Exploiting user communities, entities and sentiment. In *Proceedings of the 53rd Annual Meeting of the Association for Computational Linguistics and the 7th International Joint Conference on Natural Language Processing (Volume 1: Long Papers)*, pages 1035–1044, Beijing, China, July. Association for Computational Linguistics.

Matthew D Zeiler. 2012. Adadelta: an adaptive learning rate method. *arXiv preprint arXiv:1212.5701*.

Ye Zhang and Byron Wallace. 2015. A sensitivity analysis of (and practitioners' guide to) convolutional neural networks for sentence classification. *arXiv preprint arXiv:1510.03820.*

Learning when to trust distant supervision: An application to low-resource POS tagging using cross-lingual projection

Meng Fang and **Trevor Cohn**
Department of Computing and Information Systems, The University of Melbourne
meng.fang@unimelb.edu.au, t.cohn@unimelb.edu.au

Abstract

Cross lingual projection of linguistic annotation suffers from many sources of bias and noise, leading to unreliable annotations that cannot be used directly. In this paper, we introduce a novel approach to sequence tagging that learns to correct the errors from cross-lingual projection using an explicit debiasing layer. This is framed as joint learning over two corpora, one tagged with gold standard and the other with projected tags. We evaluated with only 1,000 tokens tagged with gold standard tags, along with more plentiful parallel data. Our system equals or exceeds the state-of-the-art on eight simulated low-resource settings, as well as two real low-resource languages, Malagasy and Kinyarwanda.

1 Introduction

Part-of-speech (POS) tagging is a critical task for natural language processing (NLP) applications, providing lexical syntactic information. Automatic POS tagging has been extremely successful for many rich resource languages through the use of supervised learning over large training corpora (McCallum et al., 2000; Lafferty et al., 2001; Ammar et al., 2016). However, learning POS taggers for low-resource languages from small amounts of annotated data is very challenging (Garrette and Baldridge, 2013; Duong et al., 2014). For such problems, distant supervision via heuristic methods can provide cheap but inaccurately labelled data (Mintz et al., 2009; Takamatsu et al., 2012; Ritter et al., 2013; Plank et al., 2014). A compromise, considered here, is to use a mixture of both resources: a small collection of clean annotated data and noisy "distant" data.

A popular method for distant supervision is to use parallel data between a low-resource language and a rich-resource language. Although annotated data in low-resource languages is difficult to obtain, bilingual resources are more plentiful. For example parallel translations into English are often available, in the form of news reports, novels or the Bible. Parallel data allows annotation from a high-resource language to be projected across alignments to the low-resource language, which has been shown to be effective for several language processing tasks including POS tagging (Yarowsky and Ngai, 2001; Das and Petrov, 2011), named entity recognition (Wang and Manning, 2014) and dependency parsing (McDonald et al., 2013).

Although cross-lingual POS projection is popular it has several problems, including errors from poor word alignments and cross-lingual syntactic divergence (Täckström et al., 2013; Das and Petrov, 2011). Previous work has proposed heuristics or constraints to clean the projected tag before or during learning. In contrast, we consider compensating for these problems explicitly, by learning a bias transformation to encode the mapping between 'clean' tags and the kinds of tags produced from projection.

We propose a new neural network model for sequence tagging in a low-resource language, suitable for training with both a tiny gold standard annotated corpus, as well as distant supervision using cross-lingual tag projection. Our model uses a bidirectional Long Short-Term Memory (BiLSTM), which produces two types of output: gold tags generated directly from the hidden states of a neural network, and uncertain projected tags generated after applying a further linear transformation. This transformation, encodes the mapping between the projected tags from the high-resource language, and the gold tags in the target low-

Proceedings of the 20th SIGNLL Conference on Computational Natural Language Learning (CoNLL), pages 178–186,
Berlin, Germany, August 7-12, 2016. ©2016 Association for Computational Linguistics

resource language, and learns when and how much to trust the projected data. For example, for languages without determiners, the model can learn to map projected determiner tags to nouns, or if verbs are often poorly aligned, the model can learn to effectively ignore the projected verb tag, by associating all tags with verbs. Our model is trained jointly on gold and distant projected annotations, and can be trained end-to-end with backpropagation.

Our approach captures the relations among tokens, noisy projected POS tags and ground truth POS tags. Our work differs in the use of projection, in that we explicitly model the transformation between tagsets as part of a more expressive deep learning neural network. We make three main contributions. First, we study the noise of projected data in word alignments and describe it with an additional transformation layer in the model. Second, we integrate the model into a deep neural network and jointly train the model on both annotated and projected data to make the model learn from better supervision. Finally, evaluating on eight simulated and two real-world low-resource languages, experimental results demonstrate that our approach uniformly equals or exceeds existing methods on simulated languages, and achieves 86.7% accuracy for Malagasy and 82.6% on Kinyarwanda, exceeding the state-of-the-art results of Duong et al. (2014).

2 Related Work

For most natural language processing tasks, the conventional approach to developing a system is to use supervised learning algorithms trained on a set of annotated data. However, this approach is inappropriate for low-resource languages due to the lack of annotated data. An alternative approach is to harness different source of information aside from annotated text. Knowledge-bases such as dictionaries are one such source, which can be used to inform or constrain models, such as limiting the search space for POS tagging (Banko and Moore, 2004; Goldberg et al., 2008; Li et al., 2012).

Parallel bilingual corpora provide another important source of information. These corpora are often plentiful even for many low-resource languages in the form of multilingual government documents, book translations, multilingual websites, etc. Word alignments can provide a bridge to project information from a resource-rich source language to a resource-poor target language. For example, parallel data has been used for named entity recognition (Wang and Manning, 2014) based on the observation that named entities are most often preserved in translation and also in syntactic tasks such as POS tagging (Yarowsky and Ngai, 2001; Das and Petrov, 2011) and dependency parsing (McDonald et al., 2013). Clues from related languages can also compensate for the lack of annotated data, as we expect there to be information shared between closely related languages in terms of the lexical items, morphology and syntactic structure. Some successful applications using language relatedness information are dependency parsing (McDonald et al., 2011) and POS tagging (Hana et al., 2004). However, these approaches are limited to closely related languages such as Czech and Russian, or Telugu and Kannada, and it is unclear whether these techniques will work well in situations where parallel data only exists for less-related languages, as is often the case in practice.

To summarize, for all these mentioned tasks, lexical resources are valuable sources of knowledge, but are also costly to build. Language relatedness information is applicable for closely related languages, but it is often the case that a given low-resource language does not have a closely-related, resource-rich language. Parallel data therefore appears to be the most realistic additional source of information for developing NLP systems for low-resource languages (Yarowsky and Ngai, 2001; Duong et al., 2014; Guo et al., 2015), and here we primarily investigate methods to exploit parallel texts.

Yarowsky and Ngai (2001) pioneered the use of parallel data for projecting POS tag information from a resource-rich language to a resource-poor language. Duong et al. (2014) proposed an approach using a maximum entropy classifier trained on 1000 tagged tokens, and used projected tags as auxiliary outputs. Das and Petrov (2011) used parallel data and exploited graph-based label propagation to expand the coverage of labelled tokens. Our work is closest to Duong et al. (2014), and we share the same evaluation setting, which we believe is well suited to the low-resource applications. Our approach differs from theirs in two ways: first we propose a deep learning model based on a long short-term memory recurrent structure versus their maximum entropy classifier, and secondly we model the projection tag explicitly as a biased variant of the classification output, while they attempt to capture the correlations between tagsets only implicitly through a joint feature set over both tags. We believe that our work is the first to explicitly model the bias affecting cross-lingual projected annotations, thereby allowing this rich data resource to be better exploited for learning NLP models in low-resource languages.

3 Framework

In this work, we consider the POS tagging problem for a low-resource language using both the gold annotated and distant projected corpora. For a low-resource language, we assume two sets of data. First, there is a small conventional corpus for the low-resource language, annotated with gold tags. Second, there is a parallel corpus between the language and English, where we can reliably tag the English side and project these annotations across the word alignments. Then based on the annotated and the projected data, we learn a deep neural model for the POS tagging. The goal of learning here is to improve the POS tagging accuracy on the low-resource language.

3.1 POS projection via word alignments

Parallel data is often available for low-resource languages. For example, for Malagasy we can obtain bilingual documents with English directly from the web. This provides ample opportunity for projecting annotations from English into the low-resource language. Although the POS tags can be projected, given sentence and word-alignments, direct projection has several issues and results in noisy, biased and often unreliable annotations (Yarowsky and Ngai, 2001; Duong et al., 2014). One source of error are the word alignments. These errors arise from words in the source language that are not aligned to any words in the target language, which might be due to them not being translated well enough, errors in alignments, or translation phenomena that do not fit the assumptions underlying the word based alignment models (e.g., many-to-many translations cannot be captured).

An example of POS projection via word alignments between Malagasy and English is shown in Figure 1. A word in Malagasy is connected to a

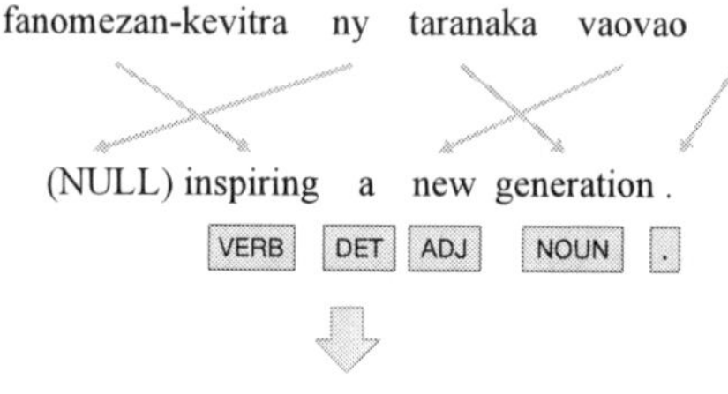

Figure 1: An example of POS projection via word alignments. * indicates unknown POS tag, which we treat as having a tag distribution over all tokens in the source sentence (in the example, a uniform mix of VERB, DET, ADJ, NOUN and '.').

word in English or the NULL word. Thus there exist words in the target language which are not aligned to a word in the source language, for example *ny* in Figure 1. Previous work has either used the majority projected POS tag for a token or used a default value to represent the token (Duong et al., 2014; Täckström et al., 2013). Another problem are errors in the projected tags: for example, in this sentence, *fanomezan-kevitra* is labelled as VERB incorrectly, but should be NOUN, a consequence of a non-literal translation.

We now turn to the labelling of the projected data. For the parallel data, we consider each token in the low-resource language. Where this token is aligned to a single token in English, we assign the tag for that English token. For tokens that are aligned to many English words or none at all (NULL), we assign a distribution over tags according to the tag frequency distribution over the whole English sentence.

A natural question is whether this projected labelling might be suitable for use directly in supervised learning of a POS tagger. To test this, we compare training a bidirectional Long Short-Term Memory (BiLSTM) tagger on this data, a small 1000 token dataset with gold-standard tags, and the union of the two.[1] Evaluating the tagging accuracy against gold standard tags, we observe in Tables 1 and 2 (top section, rows labelled

---

[1] See §3.2 for the model details, and §4.1 for a description of the datasets and evaluation.

BiLSTM) that the use of the gold-standard (Annotated) data is considerably superior to training on the directly Projected data, despite the smaller amount of Annotated data, while using the union of the two datasets results in mild improvements in a few languages, but worsens performance for others.

These sobering results raise the question of how we might use the bilingual resources in a more effective manner than direct projection. Clearly projections contain useful information, as the tagging accuracy is well above chance. However, they are riddled with noise and biases, which need to be accounted for to improve performance.

3.2 BiLSTM with bias layer

To address this problem, we propose a model that jointly models the clean annotated data and the projected data. For this we use a bidirectional LSTM tagger, as illustrated on the left in Figure 2, although other classifiers could be easily used in its place. The BiLSTM offers access to both the left and right lexical contexts around a given word (Graves et al., 2013), which are likely be of considerable use in POS tagging where context of central importance.

Let x_t indicate a word in a sentence and y_t indicate its corresponding POS tag, and K denotes the size of the tagset.[2] The recurrent layer is designed to store contextual information, while the values in the hidden and output layers are computed as follows:

$$
\begin{aligned}
\overrightarrow{h}_t &= \texttt{lstm}(\overrightarrow{h}_{t-1}, x_t) \\
\overleftarrow{h}_t &= \texttt{lstm}(\overleftarrow{h}_{t+1}, x_t) \\
o_t &= \text{softmax}(W_{\rightarrow}\overrightarrow{h}_t + W_{\leftarrow}\overleftarrow{h}_t + b) \quad (1) \\
y_t &\sim \text{Multinomial}(o_t).
\end{aligned}
$$

This supervised model is trained on annotated gold data in the standard manner using a cross-entropy objective with stochastic gradient descent through the use of gradient backpropagation.

The projected data, however, needs to be treated differently to the annotated data: the tagging is often uncertain, as tokens may have been aligned to words with different parts of speech, or multiply aligned, or left as an unaligned word. These tags are not to be trusted in the same way as the gold

annotated data. Our work accounts for bias explicitly in the training objective, by modelling the correspondence between the true tags and the errorful projected tags. The projected data consists of pairs, $(x_t, \tilde{y})$, where $\tilde{y}$ denotes the projected POS tag or tag distribution. In this setting, we assume that the true label, y_t, is latent variable and both $\tilde{y}$ and y are K-dimensional binary random variables: $\tilde{y}_t$ is a vector representation of a projected tag, and y_t is a one-hot representation of a gold tag.

We augment the deep neural network model to include a bias transformation such that its prediction matches the distribution of the projected tags, as follows:

$$
p(\tilde{Y}_t = j | x_t, \theta, A) = \text{softmax}\left(\sum_i a_{i,j} o_{t,i}\right),
$$
$$(2)$$

where $o_{t,i} = p(Y_t = i | x_t, \theta)$ is the probability of tag i in position t according to (1). This equation is parameterized by a $K \times K$ matrix A.[3] Each cell $a_{i,j}$ denotes the confusion score between classes i and j, with negative values quashing the correspondance, and positive values rewarding a pairing; in the situations where the projected tags closely match the supervised tagging, we expect that $A \propto I$.

Joint modelling of the gold supervision and projected data gives rise to a training objective combining two cross-entropy terms,

$$
\begin{aligned}
\mathcal{L}(\theta, A) = &-\frac{1}{|T^p|}\sum_{t \in T^p} \langle \tilde{y}_t, \log \text{softmax}\,(A o_t)\rangle \\
&-\frac{1}{|T^t|}\sum_{t \in T^t} \langle y_t, \log o_t\rangle,
\end{aligned}
$$

where T^p indexes all the token positions in the projected dataset, and T^t does similarly for the annotated training set.

We illustrate the combined model in Figure 2, showing on the left the gold supervised model and on the right the distant supervised components. The distant model builds on the base part by feeding the output through a bias layer, which is finally used in a softmax to produce the biased output layer. The matrix A parameterizes the final layer, to adjust the tag probabilities from the supervised model into a distribution that better matches the projected POS tags. However, the ultimate goal is

---

[2] We use the universal tagset from Petrov et al. (2011), enabling easier comparison with related work, although this is not a requirement of our work.

[3] Our approach also supports mismatching tagsets, in which case A would be rectangular with dimensions based on the sizes of the two tag sets.

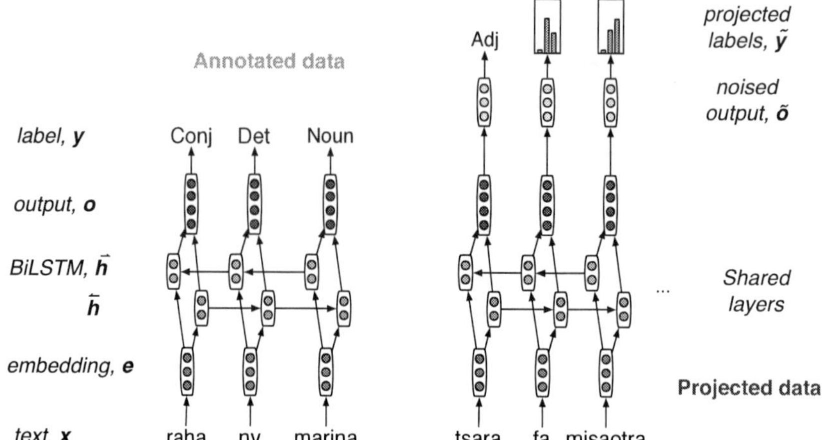

Figure 2: Illustration of the model architecture, which uses a bidirectional LSTM recurrent network, with a tag classification output. The left part illustrates the supervised training scenario and test setting, where each word x is assigned a tag y; the right part shows the projection training setting, with a bias layer, where the supervision is either a projected label or label distribution (used for NULL aligned words).

to predict the POS tag y_t. Consider the training effect of the projected POS tags: when performing error backpropagation, the cross-entropy error signal must pass through the tag transformation linking $\tilde{o}$ with o, which can be seen as a debiasing step, after which the cleaned error signal can be further backpropagated to the rest of the model. Provided there are consistent patterns of errors in the projection output, this technique can readily model these sources of variation with a tiny handful of parameters, and thus greatly improve the utility of this form of distant supervision.

Directly training the whole deep neural network with random initialization is impractical, because without a good estimate for the A matrix, the errors from the projected tags may misdirect training result in a poor local optima. For this reason the training process contains two stages. In the first stage we use the clean annotated data to pre-train the network. In the second stage we jointly use both projected and annotated data to continue training the model.

4   Experiments

We evaluate our algorithm using two kinds of experimental setups, simulation experiments and real-world experiments. For the simulation experiments, we use the following eight European languages: Danish (da), Dutch (nl), German (de), Greek (el), Italian (it), Portuguese (pt), Spanish (es), Swedish (sv). These languages are obviously not low-resource languages, however we can use this data to simulate the low-resource setting by only using a small 1,000 tokens of the gold annotations for training. This evaluation technique is widely used in previous work, and allows us to compare our results with prior state-of-the-art algorithms. For the real-world experiments, we use the following two low-resource languages: Malagasy, an Austronesian language spoken in Madagascar, and Kinyarwanda, a Niger-Congo language spoken in Rwanda.

4.1   Evaluation Corpora

4.1.1   Parallel data

For the simulation experiments, we use the Europarl v7 corpus, with English as the source language and each of languages as the target language. There are an average of 1.85 million parallel sentences for each of the eight language pairs. For the real-world experiments, the parallel data is smaller and generally of a lower quality. For Malagasy, we use a web-sourced collection of parallel texts.[4] The parallel data of Malagasy has 100k sentences and 1,231k tokens. For Kinyarwanda, we obtained parallel texts from ARL MURI project.[5], constituting 11k sentences and

---

[4] http://www.cs.cmu.edu/~ark/global-voices

[5] The dataset was provided directly by Noah Smith.

	da	nl	de	el	it	pt	es	sv	Average
BiLSTM Annotated	89.3	87.4	89.5	88.1	85.9	89.5	90.6	84.7	88.1
BiLSTM Projected	64.4	81.9	81.3	78.9	80.1	81.9	81.2	74.9	78.0
BiLSTM Ann+Proj	85.4	88.9	90.2	84.2	86.1	88.2	91.3	83.6	87.2
MaxEnt Supervised	90.1	84.6	89.6	88.2	81.4	87.6	88.9	85.4	86.9
Duong et al. (2014)	92.1	91.1	92.5	92.1	89.9	92.5	91.6	88.7	91.3
BiLSTM Debias	92.3	91.7	92.5	92.8	90.2	92.9	92.4	89.1	91.7

Table 1: The POS tagging accuracy for various models in eight languages: Danish (da), Dutch (nl), German (de), Greek (el), Italian (it), Portuguese (pt), Spanish (es), Swedish (sv). The top results of the second part are taken from Duong et al. (2014), evaluated on the same data split.

52k tokens.

4.1.2 POS projection

We use GIZA++ to induce word alignments on the parallel data (Och and Ney, 2003), using IBM model 3 (Brown et al., 1993). Following prior work (Duong et al., 2014), we retain only one-to-one alignments. Using all alignments (i.e., many-to-one and one-to-many), would result in many more POS-tagged tokens, but also bring considerable additional noise. For example, the English *laws* (NNS) aligned to French *les* (DT) *lois* (NNS) would end up incorrectly tagging the French determiner *les* as a noun (NNS). We use the Stanford POS tagger (Toutanova et al., 2003) to tag the English side of the parallel data and then project the labels to the target side. As we show in the following section, and confirmed in many studies (Täckström et al., 2013; Das and Petrov, 2011), the directly projected labels have many errors and therefore it is unwise to use the tags directly. We further filter the corpus using the approach of Yarowsky and Ngai (2001) which selects sentences with the highest sentence alignment scores from IBM model 3. For the European languages, we retain 200k sentences for each language, while for the low-resource languages, we use all the parallel data.

4.1.3 Annotated data

Gold annotated data is expensive and difficult to obtain, and thus we assume that only a small annotated dataset is available. For the simulation experiments, annotated data is obtained from the CoNLL-X shared tasks (Buchholz and Marsi, 2006). To simulate the low-resource setting, we take the first 1,000 tagged tokens for training and the remaining data is split equally between development and testing sets, following Duong et al. (2014). For the real-world experiments, we use

the Malagasy and Kinyarwanda data from Garrette and Baldridge (2013), who showed that a small annotated dataset could be collected very cheaply, requiring less than 2 hours of non-expert time to tag 1,000 tokens. This constitutes a reasonable demand for cheap portability to other low-resource languages. We use the datasets from Garrette and Baldridge (2013), constituting annotated datasets of 383 sentences and 5,294 tokens in Malagasy and 196 sentences and 4,882 tokens for Kinyarwanda. We use 1,000 tokens as training set and the rest is used for testing for each language.

4.2 Setup and baselines

We compare our algorithm with several baselines, including the state-of-the-art algorithm from Duong et al. (2014), a two-output maxent model, their reported baseline method of a supervised maximum entropy model trained on the annotated data, and our BiLSTM POS tagger trained directly from the annotated and/or projected data (denoted BiLSTM Annotated, Projected and Ann+Proj for the model trained on the union of the two datasets). For the real low-resource languages, we also compare our algorithm with Garrette et al. (2013), who reported good results on the two low-resource languages. Our implementation is based on the `cnn` toolkit.[6] In all cases, the BiLSTM models use 128 dimensional word embeddings and 128 dimensional hidden layers. We set the learning rate to 1.0 and use stochastic gradient descent model to learn the parameters.

We evaluate all algorithms on the gold testing sets, evaluating in terms of tagging accuracy. Following standard practice in POS tagging, we report results using per-token accuracy (i.e., the fraction of predicted tags that exactly match the gold standard tags). Note that for all our experiments,

---

[6] `https://github.com/clab/cnn`

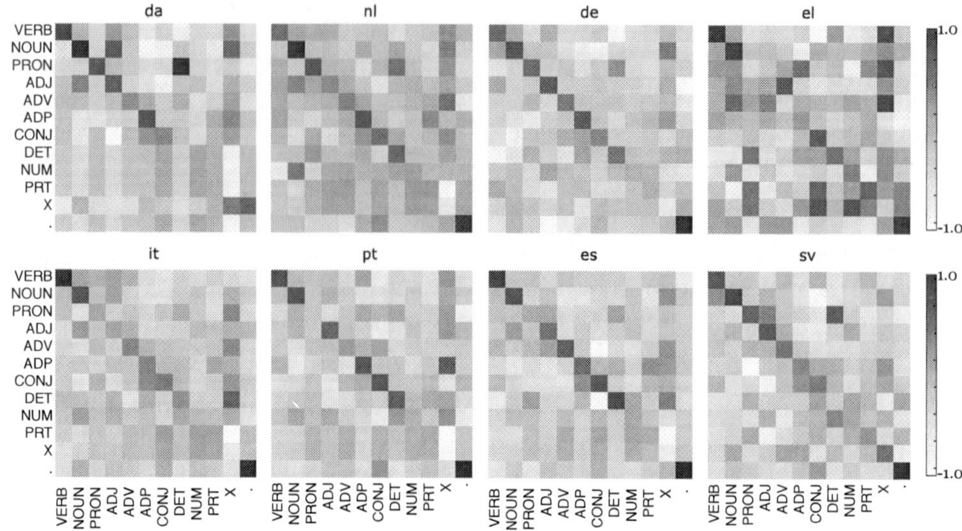

Figure 3: Bias transformation matrix A between POS tags and projection outputs, shown respectively as columns and rows for the eight languages.

we work with the universal POS tags and accordingly accuracy is measured against the gold tags after automatic mapping into the universal tagset.

4.3 Results

First, we present the results for the 8 simulation languages in Table 1. For most of the languages our method performs better than that of Duong et al. (2014) and the three naive BiLSTM baselines. Directly training on projected data hurts the performance, which can be seen by comparing BiLSTM Projected and BiLSTM Ann+Proj. BiLSTM Annotated mostly outperforms MaxEnt Supervised, but both methods are worse than Duong et al. and our BiLSTM Debias, which both use the projected data more effectively. The results show the debiasing layer makes more effective use of the projected data, improving the POS tagging accuracy.

We show the learned bias transformation matrices for the different languages in Figure 3. The blue (dark) cells in the grids denote values that are most highly weighted. Note the strong diagonal, showing that the tags are mostly trusted, although there is also evidence of significant mass in off-diagonal entries. The worst case is in Greek (el) with many weak values on the diagonal. In this case, PRON and X appear to be confused for one another. The light cells are also important, show-

Model	Accuracy	
	Malagasy	Kinyarwanda
BiLSTM Annotated	81.5	76.9
BiLSTM Projected	67.2	61.9
BiLSTM Ann+Proj	78.6	73.2
MaxEnt Supervised	80.0	76.4
Duong et al. (2014)	85.3	78.3
BiLSTM Debias	86.3	82.5
BiLSTM Debias (Penn)	86.7	82.6
Garrette et al. (2013)	81.2	81.9

Table 2: The POS tagging accuracy for various models in Malagasy and Kinyarwanda. The top results of the second part are taken from Duong et al. (2014), evaluated on the same data split.

[*] Penn indicates the Penn treebank tagset. The proposed BiLSTM Debias can use different tagsets for the source language.

ing tag combinations that the model learns to ignore, such as CONJ vs DET in Spanish (es) and PRON vs ADP in Swedish (sv). The tokens that are CONJ in Spanish (es) are seldom projected as DET. Overall, for most of languages the level of debiasing is modest, which might not come as a surprise given the large, clean parallel corpus for learning word alignments.

Now we present results for the two low-resource languages, Malagasy and Kinyarwanda, which

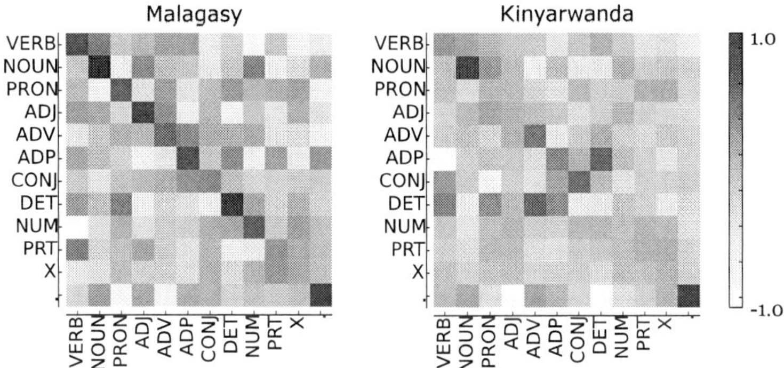

Figure 4: Bias transformation matrix A between POS tags and projected outputs, shown respectively as columns and rows for the two low-resource languages.

both have much smaller parallel corpora. The results in Table 2 show that our method works better than all others in both languages, with a similar pattern of results as for the European languages. We also used the original Penn treebank tagset for both two languages. The results of BiLSTM Debias (Penn) show a small improvement, presumably due to the information loss in the mapping to the universal tagset. Note that our method outperforms the state of the art on both languages (Duong et al., 2014; Garrette et al., 2013).

To better understand the effect of the bias layer, we present the learned transformation matrices A in Figure 4. Note the strong diagonal for Malagasy in Figure 4, showing that each tag is most likely to map to itself, however there are also many high magnitude off-diagonal elements. For instance nouns map to not just nouns, but also adjectives and numbers, but never pronouns (which are presumably well aligned). Comparing results of Malagasy and Kinyarwanda in Figure 4, we can see the divergence between the gold and projected tags is much greater in Kinyarwanda. This tallies with the performance results, in which we get stronger results and a greater improvement on Malagasy from using projection data where we had more parallel data.

5 Conclusion

In this paper we presented a technique for exploiting errorful cross-lingual projected annotations alongside a small amount of annotated data in the context of POS tagging. Projection on its own is unreliable and simple combination with gold is not sufficient to improve accuracy, even with only a tiny handful of gold annotations. To utilize both sources of data, we proposed a new model based on a bidirectional long short-term memory recurrent neural network, with a layer for explicitly handling projection labels. Over eight European and two real low-resource languages, our methods outperform other algorithms. Our technique is general, and is likely to prove useful for exploiting other noisy and biased annotations such as distant supervision and crowd-sourced annotations.

6 Acknowledgments

This work was sponsored by the Defense Advanced Research Projects Agency Information Innovation Office (I2O) under the Low Resource Languages for Emergent Incidents (LORELEI) program issued by DARPA/I2O under Contract No. HR0011-15-C-0114. The views expressed are those of the author and do not reflect the official policy or position of the Department of Defense or the U.S. Government. Trevor Cohn was supported by the Australian Research Council Future Fellowship (project number FT130101105).

References

Waleed Ammar, George Mulcaire, Miguel Ballesteros, Chris Dyer, and Noah A Smith. 2016. Many languages, one parser. *CoRR, abs/1602.01595*.

Michele Banko and Robert C Moore. 2004. Part of speech tagging in context. In *Proceedings of COLING*, page 556.

Peter F Brown, Vincent J Della Pietra, Stephen A Della Pietra, and Robert L Mercer. 1993. The mathematics of statistical machine translation: Parameter estimation. *Computational linguistics*, 19(2):263–311.

Sabine Buchholz and Erwin Marsi. 2006. Conll-x shared task on multilingual dependency parsing. In *Proceedings of CoNLL*, pages 149–164.

Dipanjan Das and Slav Petrov. 2011. Unsupervised part-of-speech tagging with bilingual graph-based projections. In *Proceedings of ACL*, pages 600–609.

Long Duong, Trevor Cohn, Karin Verspoor, Steven Bird, and Paul Cook. 2014. What can we get from 1000 tokens? a case study of multilingual pos tagging for resource-poor languages. In *Proceedings of EMNLP*.

Dan Garrette and Jason Baldridge. 2013. Learning a part-of-speech tagger from two hours of annotation. In *Proceedings of NAACL*, pages 138–147.

Dan Garrette, Jason Mielens, and Jason Baldridge. 2013. Real-world semi-supervised learning of pos-taggers for low-resource languages. In *Proceedings of ACL*, pages 583–592.

Yoav Goldberg, Meni Adler, and Michael Elhadad. 2008. EM can find pretty good HMM POS-taggers (when given a good start). In *Proceedings of ACL*, pages 746–754.

Alan Graves, Abdel-rahman Mohamed, and Geoffrey Hinton. 2013. Speech recognition with deep recurrent neural networks. In *Proceedings of ICASSP*, pages 6645–6649.

Jiang Guo, Wanxiang Che, David Yarowsky, Haifeng Wang, and Ting Liu. 2015. Cross-lingual dependency parsing based on distributed representations. In *Proceedings of ACL-CoNLL*, volume 1, pages 1234–1244.

Jiri Hana, Anna Feldman, and Chris Brew. 2004. A resource-light approach to russian morphology: Tagging russian using czech resources. In *Proceedings of EMNLP*, pages 222–229.

John Lafferty, Andrew McCallum, and Fernando Pereira. 2001. Conditional random fields: Probabilistic models for segmenting and labeling sequence data. In *Proceedings of ICML*, volume 1, pages 282–289.

Shen Li, Joao V Graça, and Ben Taskar. 2012. Wiki-ly supervised part-of-speech tagging. In *Proceedings of EMNLP-CoNLL*, pages 1389–1398.

Andrew McCallum, Dayne Freitag, and Fernando CN Pereira. 2000. Maximum entropy markov models for information extraction and segmentation. In *Proceedings of ICML*, volume 17, pages 591–598.

Ryan McDonald, Slav Petrov, and Keith Hall. 2011. Multi-source transfer of delexicalized dependency parsers. In *Proceedings of EMNLP*, pages 62–72.

Ryan T McDonald, Joakim Nivre, Yvonne Quirmbach-Brundage, Yoav Goldberg, Dipanjan Das, Kuzman Ganchev, Keith B Hall, Slav Petrov, Hao Zhang, Oscar Täckström, et al. 2013. Universal dependency annotation for multilingual parsing. In *Proceedings of ACL*, pages 92–97.

Mike Mintz, Steven Bills, Rion Snow, and Dan Jurafsky. 2009. Distant supervision for relation extraction without labeled data. In *Proceedings of ACL-IJCNLP*, pages 1003–1011.

Franz Josef Och and Hermann Ney. 2003. A systematic comparison of various statistical alignment models. *Computational linguistics*, 29(1):19–51.

Slav Petrov, Dipanjan Das, and Ryan McDonald. 2011. A universal part-of-speech tagset. In *Proceedings of ACL*.

Barbara Plank, Dirk Hovy, Ryan T McDonald, and Anders Søgaard. 2014. Adapting taggers to twitter with not-so-distant supervision. In *Proceedings of COLING*, pages 1783–1792.

Alan Ritter, Luke Zettlemoyer, Oren Etzioni, et al. 2013. Modeling missing data in distant supervision for information extraction. *Transactions of the Association for Computational Linguistics*, 1:367–378.

Oscar Täckström, Dipanjan Das, Slav Petrov, Ryan McDonald, and Joakim Nivre. 2013. Token and type constraints for cross-lingual part-of-speech tagging. *Transactions of the Association for Computational Linguistics*, 1:1–12.

Shingo Takamatsu, Issei Sato, and Hiroshi Nakagawa. 2012. Reducing wrong labels in distant supervision for relation extraction. In *Proceedings of ACL*, pages 721–729.

Kristina Toutanova, Dan Klein, Christopher D Manning, and Yoram Singer. 2003. Feature-rich part-of-speech tagging with a cyclic dependency network. In *Proceedings of NAACL*, pages 173–180.

Mengqiu Wang and Christopher D Manning. 2014. Cross-lingual pseudo-projected expectation regularization for weakly supervised learning. *Transactions of the Association of Computational Linguistics*, 2.

David Yarowsky and Grace Ngai. 2001. Inducing multilingual POS taggers and NP brackets via robust projection across aligned corpora. In *Proceedings of NAACL*.

Greedy, Joint Syntactic-Semantic Parsing with Stack LSTMs

Swabha Swayamdipta[♣]   Miguel Ballesteros[◇]   Chris Dyer[♠]   Noah A. Smith[♡]
[♣]School of Computer Science, Carnegie Mellon University, Pittsburgh, PA 15213, USA
[◇]Natural Language Processing Group, Universitat Pompeu Fabra, Barcelona, Spain
[♠]Google DeepMind, London, UK
[♡]Computer Science & Engineering, University of Washington, Seattle, WA 98195, USA
`swabha@cs.cmu.edu, miguel.ballesteros@upf.edu,`
`cdyer@cs.cmu.edu, nasmith@cs.washington.edu`

Abstract

We present a transition-based parser that jointly produces syntactic and semantic dependencies. It learns a representation of the entire algorithm state, using stack long short-term memories. Our greedy inference algorithm has linear time, including feature extraction. On the CoNLL 2008–9 English shared tasks, we obtain the best published parsing performance among models that jointly learn syntax and semantics.

1 Introduction

We introduce a new joint syntactic and semantic dependency parser. Our parser draws from the algorithmic insights of the incremental structure building approach of Henderson et al. (2008), with two key differences. First, it learns representations for the parser's entire algorithmic state, not just the top items on the stack or the most recent parser states; in fact, it uses no expert-crafted features at all. Second, it uses entirely greedy inference rather than beam search. We find that it outperforms all previous joint parsing models, including Henderson et al. (2008) and variants (Gesmundo et al., 2009; Titov et al., 2009; Henderson et al., 2013) on the CoNLL 2008 and 2009 (English) shared tasks. Our parser's multilingual results are comparable to the top systems at CoNLL 2009.

Joint models like ours have frequently been proposed as a way to avoid cascading errors in NLP pipelines; varying degrees of success have been attained for a range of joint syntactic-semantic analysis tasks (Sutton and McCallum, 2005; Henderson et al., 2008; Toutanova et al., 2008; Johansson, 2009; Lluís et al., 2013, *inter alia*).

One reason pipelines often dominate is that they make available the complete syntactic parse tree, and arbitrarily-scoped syntactic features—such as the "path" between predicate and argument, proposed by Gildea and Jurafsky (2002)—for semantic analysis. Such features are a mainstay of high-performance semantic role labeling (SRL) systems (Roth and Woodsend, 2014; Lei et al., 2015; FitzGerald et al., 2015; Foland and Martin, 2015), but they are expensive to extract (Johansson, 2009; He et al., 2013).

This study shows how recent advances in representation learning can bypass those expensive features, discovering cheap alternatives available during a greedy parsing procedure. The specific advance we employ is the stack LSTM (Dyer et al., 2015), a neural network that continuously summarizes the contents of the stack data structures in which a transition-based parser's state is conventionally encoded. Stack LSTMs were shown to obviate many features used in syntactic dependency parsing; here we find them to do the same for joint syntactic-semantic dependency parsing.

We believe this is an especially important finding for *greedy* models that cast parsing as a sequence of decisions made based on algorithmic state, where linguistic theory and researcher intuitions offer less guidance in feature design.

Our system's performance does not match that of the top expert-crafted feature-based systems (Zhao et al., 2009; Björkelund et al., 2010; Roth and Woodsend, 2014; Lei et al., 2015), systems which perform optimal decoding (Täckström et al., 2015), or of systems that exploit additional, differently-annotated datasets (FitzGerald et al., 2015). Many advances in those systems are orthogonal to our model, and we expect future work to achieve further gains by integrating them.

Because our system is very fast— with an end-to-end runtime of 177.6±18 seconds to parse the CoNLL 2009 English test data on a single core—we believe it will be useful in practical set-

Proceedings of the 20th SIGNLL Conference on Computational Natural Language Learning (CoNLL), pages 187–197,
Berlin, Germany, August 7-12, 2016. ©2016 Association for Computational Linguistics

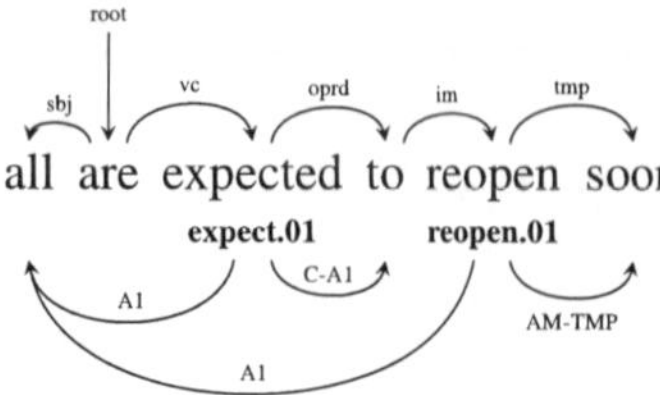

Figure 1: Example of a joint parse. Syntactic dependencies are shown by arcs above the sentence and semantic dependencies below; predicates are marked in boldface. C- denotes continuation of argument A1. Correspondences between dependencies might be close (between *expected* and *to*) or not (between *reopen* and *all*).

tings. Our open-source implementation has been released.[1]

2 Joint Syntactic and Semantic Dependency Parsing

We largely follow the transition-based, synchronized algorithm of Henderson et al. (2013) to predict joint parse structures. The input to the algorithm is a sentence annotated with part-of-speech tags. The output consists of a labeled syntactic dependency tree and a directed SRL graph, in which a subset of words in the sentence are selected as predicates, disambiguated to a sense, and linked by labeled, directed edges to their semantic arguments. Figure 1 shows an example.

2.1 Transition-Based Procedure

The two parses are constructed in a bottom-up fashion, incrementally processing words in the sentence from left to right. The state of the parsing algorithm at timestep t is represented by three stack data structures: a syntactic stack S_t, a semantic stack M_t—each containing partially built structures—and a buffer of input words B_t. Our algorithm also places partial syntactic and semantic parse structures onto the front of the buffer, so it is also implemented as a stack. Each arc in the output corresponds to a transition (or "action") chosen based on the current state; every transition modifies the state by updating S_t, M_t, and B_t to S_{t+1}, M_{t+1}, and B_{t+1}, respectively. While each state may license several valid actions, each action

has a deterministic effect on the state of the algorithm.

Initially, S_0 and M_0 are empty, and B_0 contains the input sentence with the first word at the front of B and a special root symbol at the end.[2] Execution ends on iteration t such that B_t is empty and S_t and M_t contain only a single structure headed by root.

2.2 Transitions for Joint Parsing

There are separate sets of syntactic and semantic transitions; the former manipulate S and B, the latter M and B. All are formally defined in Table 1. The syntactic transitions are from the "arc-eager" algorithm of Nivre (2008). They include:

- S-SHIFT, which copies[3] an item from the front of B and pushes it on S.
- S-REDUCE pops an item from S.
- S-RIGHT(ℓ) creates a syntactic dependency. Let u be the element at the top of S and v be the element at the front of B. The new dependency has u as head, v as dependent, and label ℓ. u is popped off S, and the resulting structure, rooted at u, is pushed on S. Finally, v is copied to the top of S.
- S-LEFT(ℓ) creates a syntactic dependency with label ℓ in the reverse direction as S-RIGHT. The top of S, u, is popped. The front of B, v, is replaced by the new structure, rooted at v.

The semantic transitions are similar, operating on the semantic stack.

- M-SHIFT removes an item from the front of B and pushes it on M.
- M-REDUCE pops an item from M.
- M-RIGHT(r) creates a semantic dependency. Let u be the element at the top of M and v, the front of B. The new dependency has u as head, v as dependent, and label r. u is popped off M, and the resulting structure, rooted at u, is pushed on M.
- M-LEFT(r) creates a semantic dependency with label r in the reverse direction as M-RIGHT. The buffer front, v, is replaced by the new v-rooted structure. M remains unchanged.

[2]This works better for the arc-eager algorithm (Ballesteros and Nivre, 2013), in contrast to Henderson et al. (2013), who initialized with root at the buffer front.

[3]Note that in the original arc-eager algorithm (Nivre, 2008), SHIFT and RIGHT-ARC actions *move* the item on the buffer front to the stack, whereas we only copy it (to allow the semantic operations to have access to it).

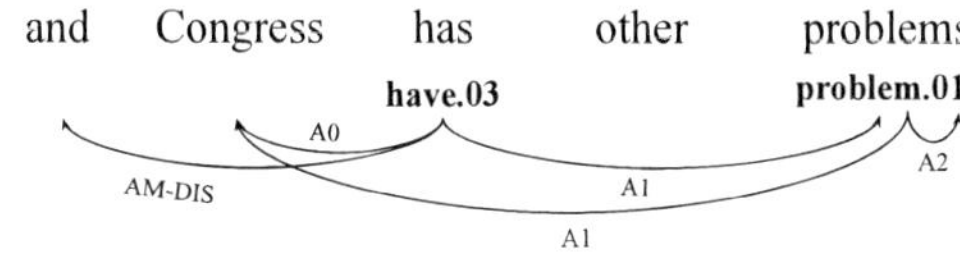

Figure 2: Example of an SRL graph with an arc from predicate **problem.01** to itself, filling the A2 role. Our SELF(A2) transition allows recovering this semantic dependency.

Because SRL graphs allow a node to be a semantic argument of two parents—like *all* in the example in Figure 1—M-LEFT and M-RIGHT do not remove the dependent from the semantic stack and buffer respectively, unlike their syntactic equivalents, S-LEFT and S-RIGHT. We use two other semantic transitions from Henderson et al. (2013) which have no syntactic analogues:

- M-SWAP swaps the top two items on M, to allow for crossing semantic arcs.
- M-PRED(p) marks the item at the front of B as a semantic predicate with the sense p, and replaces it with the disambiguated predicate.

The CoNLL 2009 corpus introduces semantic self-dependencies where many nominal predicates (from NomBank) are marked as their own arguments; these account for 6.68% of all semantic arcs in the English corpus. An example involving an eventive noun is shown in Figure 2. We introduce a new semantic transition, not in Henderson et al. (2013), to handle such cases:

- M-SELF(r) adds a dependency, with label r between the item at the front of B and itself. The result replaces the item at the front of B.

Note that the syntactic and semantic transitions both operate on the same buffer, though they independently specify the syntax and semantics, respectively. In order to ensure that both syntactic and semantic parses are produced, the syntactic and semantic transitions are interleaved. Only syntactic transitions are considered until a transition is chosen that copies an item from the buffer front to the syntactic stack (either S-SHIFT or S-RIGHT). The algorithm then switches to semantic transitions until a buffer-modifying transition is taken (M-SHIFT).[4] At this point, the buffer is modi-

fied and the algorithm returns to syntactic transitions. This implies that, for each word, its left-side syntactic dependencies are resolved before its left-side semantic dependencies. An example run of the algorithm is shown in Figure 3.

2.3 Constraints on Transitions

To ensure that the parser never enters an invalid state, the sequence of transitions is constrained, following Henderson et al. (2013). Actions that copy or move items from the buffer (S-SHIFT, S-RIGHT and M-SHIFT) are forbidden when the buffer is empty. Actions that pop from a stack (S-REDUCE and M-REDUCE) are forbidden when that stack is empty. We disallow actions corresponding to the same dependency, or the same predicate to be repeated in the sequence. Repetitive M-SWAP transitions are disallowed to avoid infinite swapping. Finally, as noted above, we restrict the parser to syntactic actions until it needs to shift an item from B to S, after which it can only execute semantic actions until it executes an M-SHIFT.

Asymptotic runtime complexity of this greedy algorithm is linear in the length of the input, following the analysis by Nivre (2009).[5]

3 Statistical Model

The transitions in §2 describe the execution paths our algorithm can take; like past work, we apply a statistical classifier to decide which transition to take at each timestep, given the current state. The novelty of our model is that it learns a finite-length vector representation of the entire joint parser's state (S, M, and B) in order to make this decision.

3.1 Stack Long Short-Term Memory (LSTM)

LSTMs are recurrent neural networks equipped with specialized memory components in addition to a hidden state (Hochreiter and Schmidhuber, 1997; Graves, 2013) to model sequences. Stack LSTMs (Dyer et al., 2015) are LSTMs that allow for stack operations: *query*, *push*, and *pop*. A "stack pointer" is maintained which determines which cell in the LSTM provides the memory and hidden units when computing the new memory cell contents. *Query* provides a summary of the stack in a single fixed-length vector. *Push* adds

---

[4]Had we *moved* the item at the buffer front during the syntactic transitions, it would have been unavailable for the semantic transitions, hence we only *copy* it.

[5]The analysis in (Nivre, 2009) does not consider SWAP actions. However, since we constrain the number of such actions, the linear time complexity of the algorithm stays intact.

S_t	M_t	B_t	Action	S_{t+1}	M_{t+1}	B_{t+1}	Dependency
S	M	$(\mathbf{v},v),B$	S-SHIFT	$(\mathbf{v},v),S$	M	$(\mathbf{v},v),B$	—
$(\mathbf{u},u),S$	M	B	S-REDUCE	S	M	B	—
$(\mathbf{u},u),S$	M	$(\mathbf{v},v),B$	S-RIGHT(ℓ)	$(\mathbf{v},v),(g_s(\mathbf{u},\mathbf{v},\mathbf{l}),u),S$	M	$(\mathbf{v},v),B$	$S\cup u\xrightarrow{\ell}v$
$(\mathbf{u},u),S$	M	$(\mathbf{v},v),B$	S-LEFT(ℓ)	S	M	$(g_s(\mathbf{v},\mathbf{u},\mathbf{l}),v),B$	$S\cup u\xleftarrow{\ell}v$
S	M	$(\mathbf{v},v),B$	M-SHIFT	S	$(\mathbf{v},v),M$	B	—
S	$(\mathbf{u},u),M$	B	M-REDUCE	S	M	B	—
S	$(\mathbf{u},u),M$	$(\mathbf{v},v),B$	M-RIGHT(r)	S	$(g_m(\mathbf{u},\mathbf{v},\mathbf{r}),u),M$	$(\mathbf{v},v),B$	$\mathcal{M}\cup u\xrightarrow{r}v$
S	$(\mathbf{u},u),M$	$(\mathbf{v},v),B$	M-LEFT(r)	S	$(\mathbf{u},u),M$	$(g_m(\mathbf{v},\mathbf{u},\mathbf{r}),v),B$	$\mathcal{M}\cup u\xleftarrow{r}v$
S	$(\mathbf{u},u),(\mathbf{v},v),M$	B	M-SWAP	S	$(\mathbf{v},v),(\mathbf{u},u),M$	B	—
S	M	$(\mathbf{v},v),B$	M-PRED(p)	S	M	$(g_d(\mathbf{v},\mathbf{p}),v),B$	—
S	M	$(\mathbf{v},v),B$	M-SELF(r)	S	M	$(g_m(\mathbf{v},\mathbf{v},\mathbf{r}),v),B$	$\mathcal{M}\cup v\xleftrightarrow{r}v$

Table 1: Parser transitions along with the modifications to the stacks and the buffer resulting from each. Syntactic transitions are shown above, semantic below. Italic symbols denote symbolic representations of words and relations, and bold symbols indicate (learned) embeddings (§3.5) of words and relations; each element in a stack or buffer includes both symbolic and vector representations, either atomic or recursive. S represents the set of syntactic transitions, and $\mathcal{M}$ the set of semantic transitions.

an element to the top of the stack, resulting in a new summary. *Pop*, which does not correspond to a conventional LSTM operation, moves the stack pointer to the preceding timestep, resulting in a stack summary as it was before the popped item was observed. Implementation details (Dyer et al., 2015; Goldberg, 2015) and code have been made publicly available.[6]

Using stack LSTMs, we construct a representation of the algorithm state by decomposing it into smaller pieces that are combined by recursive function evaluations (similar to the way a list is built by a *concatenate* operation that operates on a list and an element). This enables information that would be distant from the "top" of the stack to be carried forward, potentially helping the learner.

3.2 Stack LSTMs for Joint Parsing

Our algorithm employs four stack LSTMs, one each for the S, M, and B data structures. Like Dyer et al. (2015), we use a fourth stack LSTM, A, for the history of actions—A is never popped from, only pushed to. Figure 4 illustrates the architecture. The algorithm's state at timestep t is encoded by the four vectors summarizing the four stack LSTMs, and this is the input to the classifier that chooses among the allowable transitions at that timestep.

Let $\mathbf{s}_t$, $\mathbf{m}_t$, $\mathbf{b}_t$, and $\mathbf{a}_t$ denote the summaries of S_t, M_t, B_t, and A_t, respectively. Let $\mathcal{A}_t =$ Allowed(S_t, M_t, B_t, A_t) denote the allowed transitions given the current stacks and buffer. The parser state at time t is given by a rectified linear unit (Nair and Hinton, 2010) in vector $\mathbf{y}_t$:

$$\mathbf{y}_t = \text{elementwisemax}\left\{\mathbf{0}, \mathbf{d} + \mathbf{W}[\mathbf{s}_t;\mathbf{m}_t;\mathbf{b}_t;\mathbf{a}_t]\right\}$$

[6] https://github.com/clab/lstm-parser

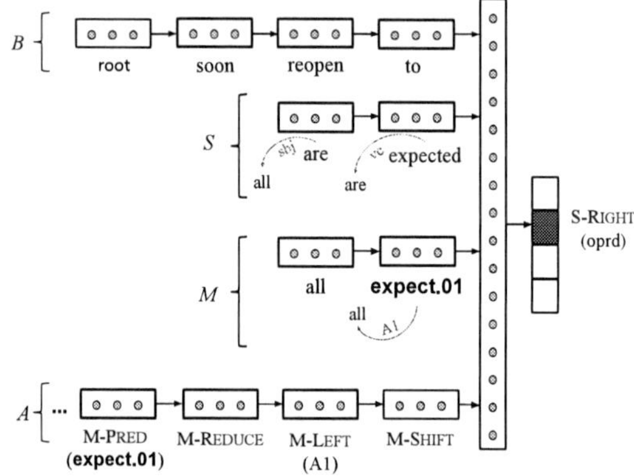

Figure 4: Stack LSTM for joint parsing. The state illustrated corresponds to the ***-marked row in the example transition sequence in Fig. 3.

where $\mathbf{W}$ and $\mathbf{d}$ are the parameters of the classifier. The transition selected at timestep t is

$$\arg\max_{\tau\in\mathcal{A}_t} q_\tau + \boldsymbol{\theta}_\tau \cdot \mathbf{y}_t \qquad (1)$$

$$\equiv \arg\max_{\tau\in\mathcal{A}_t} \text{score}(\tau; S_t, M_t, B_t, A_t)$$

where $\boldsymbol{\theta}_\tau$ and q_τ are parameters for each transition type τ. Note that only allowed transitions are considered in the decision rule (see §2.3).

3.3 Composition Functions

To use stack LSTMs, we require vector representations of the elements that are stored in the stacks. Specifically, we require vector representations of atoms (words, possibly with part-of-speech tags) and parse fragments. Word vectors can be pre-trained or learned directly; we consider a concatenation of both in our experiments; part-of-speech

Transition	S	M	B	Dependency
	[]	[]	[all, are, expected, to, reopen, soon, root]	—
S-SHIFT	[all]	[]	[all, are, expected, to, reopen, soon, root]	—
M-SHIFT	[all]	[all]	[are, expected, to, reopen, soon, root]	—
S-LEFT(*sbj*)	[]	[all]	[are, expected, to, reopen, soon, root]	all $\xleftarrow{\text{sbj}}$ are
S-SHIFT	[are]	[all]	[are, expected, to, reopen, soon, root]	—
M-SHIFT	[are]	[all, are]	[expected, to, reopen, soon, root]	—
S-RIGHT(*vc*)	[are, expected]	[all, are]	[expected, to, reopen, soon, root]	are $\xrightarrow{\text{vc}}$ expected
M-PRED(**expect.01**)	[are, expected]	[all, are]	[expected, to, reopen, soon, root]	—
M-REDUCE	[are, expected]	[all]	[expected, to, reopen, soon, root]	—
M-LEFT(*A1*)	[are, expected]	[all]	[expected, to, reopen, soon, root]	all $\xleftarrow{\text{A1}}$ expect.01
M-SHIFT	[are, expected]	[all, expected]	[to, reopen, soon, root]	—
***S-RIGHT(oprd)	[are, expected, to]	[all, expected]	[to, reopen, soon, root]	expected $\xrightarrow{\text{oprd}}$ to
M-RIGHT(*C-A1*)	[are, expected, to]	[all, expected]	[to, reopen, soon, root]	expect.01 $\xrightarrow{\text{C-A1}}$ to
M-REDUCE	[are, expected, to]	[all]	[to, reopen, soon, root]	—
M-SHIFT	[are, expected, to]	[all, to]	[reopen, soon, root]	—
S-RIGHT(*im*)	[are, expected, to, reopen]	[all, to]	[reopen, soon, root]	to $\xrightarrow{\text{im}}$ reopen
M-PRED(**reopen.01**)	[are, expected, to, reopen]	[all, to]	[reopen, soon, root]	—
M-REDUCE	[are, expected, to, reopen]	[all]	[reopen, soon, root]	—
M-LEFT(*A1*)	[are, expected, to, reopen]	[all]	[reopen, soon, root]	all $\xleftarrow{\text{A1}}$ reopen.01
M-REDUCE	[are, expected, to, reopen]	[]	[reopen, soon, root]	—
M-SHIFT	[are, expected, to, reopen]	[reopen]	[soon, root]	—
S-RIGHT(*tmp*)	[are, expected, to, reopen, soon]	[reopen]	[soon, root]	reopen $\xrightarrow{\text{tmp}}$ soon
M-RIGHT(*AM-TMP*)	[are, expected, to, reopen, soon]	[reopen]	[soon, root]	reopen.01 $\xrightarrow{\text{AM-TMP}}$ soon
M-REDUCE	[are, expected, to, reopen, soon]	[]	[soon, root]	—
M-SHIFT	[are, expected, to, reopen, soon]	[soon]	[root]	—
S-REDUCE	[are, expected, to, reopen]	[soon]	[root]	—
S-REDUCE	[are, expected, to]	[soon]	[root]	—
S-REDUCE	[are, expected]	[soon]	[root]	—
S-REDUCE	[are]	[soon]	[root]	—
S-LEFT(*root*)	[]	[soon]	[root]	are $\xleftarrow{\text{root}}$ root
S-SHIFT	[root]	[soon]	[root]	—
M-REDUCE	[root]	[]	[root]	—
M-SHIFT	[root]	[root]	[]	—

Figure 3: Joint parser transition sequence for the sentence in Figure 1, "*all are expected to reopen soon.*" Syntactic labels are in lower-case and semantic role labels are capitalized. *** marks the operation predicted in Figure 4.

vectors are learned and concatenated to the same.

To obtain vector representations of parse fragments, we use neural networks which recursively compute representations of the complex structured output (Dyer et al., 2015). The tree structures here are always ternary trees, with each internal node's three children including a head, a dependent, and a label. The vectors for leaves are word vectors and vectors corresponding to syntactic and semantic relation types.

The vector for an internal node is a squashed (tanh) affine transformation of its children's vectors. For syntactic and semantic attachments, re-

191

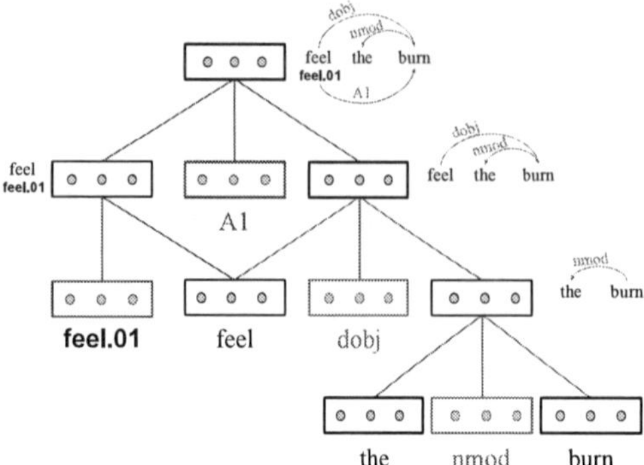

Figure 5: Example of a joint parse tree fragment with vector representations shown at each node. The vectors are obtained by recursive composition of representations of head, dependent, and label vectors. Syntactic dependencies and labels are in green, semantic in blue.

spectively, the composition function is:

$$g_s(\mathbf{v}, \mathbf{u}, \mathbf{l}) = \tanh(\mathbf{Z}_s[\mathbf{v}; \mathbf{u}; \mathbf{l}] + \mathbf{e}_s) \quad (2)$$

$$g_m(\mathbf{v}, \mathbf{u}, \mathbf{r}) = \tanh(\mathbf{Z}_m[\mathbf{v}; \mathbf{u}; \mathbf{r}] + \mathbf{e}_m) \quad (3)$$

where $\mathbf{v}$ and $\mathbf{u}$ are vectors corresponding to atomic words or composed parse fragments; $\mathbf{l}$ and $\mathbf{r}$ are learned vector representations for syntactic and semantic labels respectively. Syntactic and semantic parameters are separated ($\mathbf{Z}_s$, $\mathbf{e}_s$ and $\mathbf{Z}_m$, $\mathbf{e}_m$, respectively).

Finally, for predicates, we use another recursive function to compose the word representation, $\mathbf{v}$ with a learned representation for the dismabiguated sense of the predicate, $\mathbf{p}$:

$$g_d(\mathbf{v}, \mathbf{p}) = \tanh(\mathbf{Z}_d[\mathbf{v}; \mathbf{p}] + \mathbf{e}_d) \quad (4)$$

where $\mathbf{Z}_d$ and $\mathbf{e}_d$ are parameters of the model. Note that, because syntactic and semantic transitions are interleaved, the fragmented structures are a blend of syntactic and semantic compositions. Figure 5 shows an example.

3.4 Training

Training the classifier requires transforming each training instance (a joint parse) into a transition sequence, a deterministic operation under our transition set. Given a collection of algorithm states at time t and correct classification decisions τ_t, we minimize the sum of log-loss terms, given (for one timestep) by:

$$-\log \frac{\exp(\mathbf{q}_{\tau_t} + \boldsymbol{\theta}_{\tau_t} \cdot \mathbf{y}_t)}{\sum_{\tau' \in \mathcal{A}_t} \exp(\mathbf{q}_{\tau'} + \boldsymbol{\theta}_{\tau'} \cdot \mathbf{y}_t)} \quad (5)$$

with respect to the classifier and LSTM parameters. Note that the loss is differentiable with respect to the parameters; gradients are calculated using backpropagation. We apply stochastic gradient descent with dropout for all neural network parameters.

3.5 Pretrained Embeddings

Following Dyer et al. (2015), "structured skip-gram" embeddings (Ling et al., 2015) were used, trained on the English (AFP section), German, Spanish and Chinese Gigaword corpora, with a window of size 5; training was stopped after 5 epochs. For out-of-vocabulary words, a randomly initialized vector of the same dimension was used.

3.6 Predicate Sense Disambiguation

Predicate sense disambiguation is handled within the model (M-PRED transitions), but since senses are lexeme-specific, we need a way to handle unseen predicates at test time. When a predicate is encountered at test time that was not observed in training, our system constructs a predicate from the predicted lemma of the word at that position and defaults to the "01" sense, which is correct for 91.22% of predicates by type in the English CoNLL 2009 training data.

4 Experimental Setup

Our model is evaluated on the CoNLL shared tasks on joint syntactic and semantic dependency parsing in 2008 (Surdeanu et al., 2008) and 2009 (Hajič et al., 2009). The standard training, development and test splits of all datasets were used. Per the shared task guidelines, automatically predicted POS tags and lemmas provided in the datasets were used for all experiments. As a preprocessing step, pseudo-projectivization of the syntactic trees (Nivre et al., 2007) was used, which allowed an accurate conversion of even the non-projective syntactic trees into syntactic transitions. However, the oracle conversion of semantic parses into transitions is not perfect despite using the M-SWAP action, due to the presence of multiple crossing arcs.[7]

---

[7] For 1.5% of English sentences in the CoNLL 2009 English dataset, the transition sequence incorrectly encodes the gold-standard joint parse; details in Henderson et al. (2013).

The standard evaluation metrics include the syntactic labeled attachment score (LAS), the semantic F_1 score on both in-domain (WSJ) and out-of-domain (Brown corpus) data, and their macro average (Macro F_1) to score joint systems. Because the task was defined somewhat differently in each year, each dataset is considered in turn.

4.1 CoNLL 2008

The CoNLL 2008 dataset contains annotations from the Penn Treebank (Marcus et al., 1993), PropBank (Palmer et al., 2005) and Nom-Bank (Meyers et al., 2004). The shared task evaluated systems on predicate identification in addition to predicate sense disambiguation and SRL.

To identify predicates, we trained a zero-Markov order bidirectional LSTM two-class classifier. As input to the classifier, we use learned representations of word lemmas and POS tags. This model achieves an F_1 score of 91.43% on marking words as predicates (or not).

Hyperparameters The input representation for a word consists of pretrained embeddings (size 100 for English, 80 for Chinese, 64 for German and Spanish), concatenated with additional learned word and POS tag embeddings (size 32 and 12, respectively). Learned embeddings for syntactic and semantic arc labels are of size 20 and predicates 100. Two-layer LSTMs with hidden state dimension 100 were used for each of the four stacks. The parser state $\mathbf{y_t}$ and the composition function $\mathbf{g}$ are of dimension 100. A dropout rate of 0.2 (Zaremba et al., 2014) was used on all layers at training time, tuned on the development data from the set of values $\{0.1, 0.2, 0.3, 1.0\}$. The learned representations for actions are of size 100, similarly tuned from $\{10, 20, 30, 40, 100\}$. Other hyperparameters have been set intuitively; careful tuning is expected to yield improvements (Weiss et al., 2015).

An initial learning rate of 0.1 for stochastic gradient descent was used and updated in every training epoch with a decay rate of 0.1 (Dyer et al., 2015). Training is stopped when the development performance does not improve for approximately 6–7 hours of elapsed time. Experiments were run on a single thread on a CPU, with memory requirements of up to 512 MB.

4.2 CoNLL 2009

Relative to the CoNLL 2008 task (above), the main change in 2009 is that predicates are pre-identified, and systems are only evaluated on predicate sense disambiguation (not identification). Hence, the bidirectional LSTM classifier is not used here. The preprocessing for projectivity, and the hyperparameter selection is the same as in §4.1.

In addition to the joint approach described in the preceding sections, we experiment here with several variants:

Semantics-only: the set of syntactic transitions $\mathcal{S}$, the syntactic stack S, and the syntactic composition function g_s are discarded. As a result, the set of constraints on transitions is a subset of the full set of constraints in §2.3. Effectively, this model does not use any syntactic features, similar to Collobert et al. (2011) and Zhou and Xu (2015). It provides a controlled test of the benefit of explicit syntax in a semantic parser.

Syntax-only: all semantic transitions in $\mathcal{M}$, the semantic stack M, and the semantic composition function g_m are discarded. S-SHIFT and S-RIGHT now *move* the item from the front of the buffer to the syntactic stack, instead of copying. The set of constraints on the transitions is again a subset of the full set of constraints. This model is an arc-eager variant of Dyer et al. (2015), and serves to check whether semantic parsing degrades syntactic performance.

Hybrid: the semantics parameters are trained using automatically predicted syntax from the syntax-only model. At test time, only semantic parses are predicted. This setup bears similarity to other approaches which pipeline syntax and semantics, extracting features from the syntactic parse to help SRL. However, unlike other approaches, this model does not offer the entire syntactic tree for feature extraction, since only the partial syntactic structures present on the syntactic stack (and potentially the buffer) are visible at a given timestep. This model helps show the effect of joint prediction.

5   Results and Discussion

CoNLL 2008 (Table 2) Our joint model significantly outperforms the joint model of Henderson et al. (2008), from which our set of tran-

Model	LAS	Sem. F_1	Macro F_1
joint models:			
Lluís and Màrquez (2008)	85.8	70.3	78.1
Henderson et al. (2008)	87.6	73.1	80.5
Johansson (2009)	86.6	77.1	81.8
Titov et al. (2009)	87.5	76.1	81.8
CoNLL 2008 best:			
#3: Zhao and Kit (2008)	87.7	76.7	82.2
#2: Che et al. (2008)	86.7	78.5	82.7
#2: Ciaramita et al. (2008)	87.4	78.0	82.7
#1: J&N (2008)	89.3	81.6	85.5
Joint (this work)	89.1	80.5	84.9

Table 2: Joint parsers: comparison on the CoNLL 2008 test (WSJ+Brown) set.

sitions is derived, showing the benefit of learning a representation for the entire algorithmic state. Several other joint learning models have been proposed (Lluís and Màrquez, 2008; Johansson, 2009; Titov et al., 2009) for the same task; our joint model surpasses the performance of all these models. The best reported systems on the CoNLL 2008 task are due to Johansson and Nugues (2008), Che et al. (2008), Ciaramita et al. (2008) and Zhao and Kit (2008), all of which pipeline syntax and semantics; our system's semantic and overall performance is comparable to these. We fall behind only Johansson and Nugues (2008), whose success was attributed to carefully designed global SRL features integrated into a pipeline of classifiers, making them asymptotically slower.

CoNLL 2009 English (Table 3) All of our models (Syntax-only, Semantics-only, Hybrid and Joint) improve over Gesmundo et al. (2009) and Henderson et al. (2013), demonstrating the benefit of our entire-parser-state representation learner compared to the more locally scoped model.

Given that syntax has consistently proven useful in SRL, we expected our Semantics-only model to underperform Hybrid and Joint, and it did. In the training domain, syntax and semantics benefit each other (Joint outperforms Hybrid). Out-of-domain (the Brown test set), the Hybrid pulls ahead, a sign that Joint overfits to WSJ. As a syntactic parser, our Syntax-only model performs slightly better than Dyer et al. (2015), who achieve 89.56 LAS on this task. Joint parsing is very slightly better still.

The overall performance of Joint is on par with the other winning participants at the CoNLL 2009 shared task (Zhao et al., 2009; Che et al., 2009; Gesmundo et al., 2009), falling behind only Zhao et al. (2009), who carefully designed language-specific features and used a series of pipelines for the joint task, resulting in an accurate but computationally expensive system.

State-of-the-art SRL systems (shown in the last block of Table 3) which use advances orthogonal to the contributions in this paper, perform better than our models. Many of these systems use expert-crafted features derived from full syntactic parses in a pipeline of classifiers followed by a global reranker (Björkelund et al., 2009; Björkelund et al., 2010; Roth and Woodsend, 2014); we have not used these features or reranking. Lei et al. (2015) use syntactic parses to obtain interaction features between predicates and their arguments and then compress feature representations using a low-rank tensor. Täckström et al. (2015) present an exact inference algorithm for SRL based on dynamic programming and their local and structured models make use of many syntactic features from a pipeline; our search procedure is greedy. Their algorithm is adopted by FitzGerald et al. (2015) for inference in a model that jointly learns representations from a combination of PropBank and FrameNet annotations; we have not experimented with extra annotations.

Our system achieves an end-to-end runtime of 177.6 ± 18 seconds to parse the CoNLL 2009 English test set on a single core. This is almost 2.5 times faster than the pipeline model of Lei et al. (2015) (439.9 ± 42 seconds) on the same machine.[8]

CoNLL 2009 Multilingual (Table 4) We tested the joint model on the non-English CoNLL 2009 datasets, and the results demonstrate that it adapts easily—it is on par with the top three systems in most cases. We note that our Chinese parser relies on pretrained word embeddings for its superior performance; without them (not shown), it was on par with the others. Japanese is a small-data case (4,393 training examples), illustrating our model's dependence on reasonably large training datasets.

We have not extended our model to incorporate morphological features, which are used by the systems to which we compare. Future work might in-

---

[8]See `https://github.com/taolei87/SRLParser`; unlike other state-of-the-art systems, this one is publicly available.

Model	LAS	Sem. F_1 (WSJ)	Sem. F_1 (Brown)	Macro F_1
CoNLL'09 best:				
#3 G+ '09	88.79	83.24	70.65	86.03
#2 C+ '09	88.48	85.51	73.82	87.00
#1 Z+ '09a	89.19	86.15	74.58	87.69
this work:				
Syntax-only	89.83			
Sem.-only		84.39	73.87	
Hybrid	89.83	84.58	75.64	87.20
Joint	89.94	84.97	74.48	87.45
pipelines:				
R&W '14		86.34	75.90	
L+ '15		86.58	75.57	
T+ '15		87.30	75.50	
F+ '15		87.80	75.50	

Table 3: Comparison on the CoNLL 2009 English test set. The first block presents results of other models evaluated for both syntax and semantics on the CoNLL 2009 task. The second block presents our models. The third block presents the best published models, each using its own syntactic pre-processing.

corporate morphological features where available; this could potentially improve performance, especially in highly inflective languages like Czech. An alternative might be to infer word-internal representations using character-based word embeddings, which was found beneficial for syntactic parsing (Ballesteros et al., 2015).

Language	#1 C+'09	#2 Z+ '09a	#3 G+ '09	Joint
Catalan	81.84	**83.01**	82.66	82.40
Chinese	76.38	76.23	76.15	**79.27**
Czech	**83.27**	80.87	83.21	79.53
English	87.00	**87.69**	86.03	87.45
German	**82.44**	81.22	79.59	81.05
Japanese	**85.65**	85.28	84.91	80.91
Spanish	81.90	**83.31**	82.43	83.11
Average	82.64	82.52	82.14	81.96

Table 4: Comparison of macro F_1 scores on the multilingual CoNLL 2009 test set.

6 Related Work

Other approaches to joint modeling, not considered in our experiments, are notable. Lluís et al. (2013) propose a graph-based joint model using dual decomposition for agreement between syntax and semantics, but do not achieve competitive performance on the CoNLL 2009 task. Lewis et al. (2015) proposed an efficient joint model for CCG syntax and SRL, which performs better than a pipelined model. However, their training necessitates CCG annotation, ours does not. Moreover, their evaluation metric rewards semantic dependencies regardless of where they attach within the argument span given by a PropBank constituent, making direct comparison to our evaluation infeasible. Krishnamurthy and Mitchell (2014) propose a joint CCG parsing and relation extraction model which improves over pipelines, but their task is different from ours. Li et al. (2010) also perform joint syntactic and semantic dependency parsing for Chinese, but do not report results on the CoNLL 2009 dataset.

There has also been an increased interest in models which use neural networks for SRL. Collobert et al. (2011) proposed models which perform many NLP tasks without hand-crafted features. Though they did not achieve the best results on the constituent-based SRL task (Carreras and Màrquez, 2005), their approach inspired Zhou and Xu (2015), who achieved state-of-the-art results using deep bidirectional LSTMs. Our approach for dependency-based SRL is not directly comparable.

7 Conclusion

We presented an incremental, greedy parser for joint syntactic and semantic dependency parsing. Our model surpasses the performance of previous joint models on the CoNLL 2008 and 2009 English tasks, without using expert-crafted, expensive features of the full syntactic parse.

Acknowledgments

The authors thank Sam Thomson, Lingpeng Kong, Mark Yatskar, Eunsol Choi, George Mulcaire, and Luheng He, as well as the anonymous reviewers, for many useful comments. This research was supported in part by DARPA grant FA8750-12-2-0342 funded under the DEFT program and by the U.S. Army Research Office under grant number W911NF-10-1-0533. Any opinion, findings, and conclusions or recommendations expressed in this material are those of the author(s) and do not necessarily reflect the view of the U.S. Army Research Office or the U.S. Government. Miguel Ballesteros was supported by the European Commission under the contract numbers FP7-ICT-610411 (project MULTISENSOR) and H2020-RIA-645012 (project KRISTINA).

References

Miguel Ballesteros and Joakim Nivre. 2013. Going to the roots of dependency parsing. *Computational Linguistics*, 39(1):5–13.

Miguel Ballesteros, Chris Dyer, and Noah A. Smith. 2015. Improved transition-based parsing by modeling characters instead of words with LSTMs. In *Proc. of EMNLP*.

Anders Björkelund, Love Hafdell, and Pierre Nugues. 2009. Multilingual semantic role labeling. In *Proc. of CoNLL*.

Anders Björkelund, Bernd Bohnet, Love Hafdell, and Pierre Nugues. 2010. A high-performance syntactic and semantic dependency parser. In *Proc. of COLING*.

Xavier Carreras and Lluís Màrquez. 2005. Introduction to the CoNLL-2005 shared task: Semantic role labeling. In *Proc. of CoNLL*.

Wanxiang Che, Zhenghua Li, Yuxuan Hu, Yongqiang Li, Bing Qin, Ting Liu, and Sheng Li. 2008. A cascaded syntactic and semantic dependency parsing system. In *Proc. of CoNLL*.

Wanxiang Che, Zhenghua Li, Yongqiang Li, Yuhang Guo, Bing Qin, and Ting Liu. 2009. Multilingual dependency-based syntactic and semantic parsing. In *Proc. of CoNLL*.

Massimiliano Ciaramita, Giuseppe Attardi, Felice Dell'Orletta, and Mihai Surdeanu. 2008. DeSRL: A linear-time semantic role labeling system. In *Proc. of CoNLL*.

Ronan Collobert, Jason Weston, Léon Bottou, Michael Karlen, Koray Kavukcuoglu, and Pavel Kuksa. 2011. Natural language processing (almost) from scratch. *Journal of Machine Learning Research*, 12:2493–2537.

Chris Dyer, Miguel Ballesteros, Wang Ling, Austin Matthews, and Noah A. Smith. 2015. Transition-based dependency parsing with stack long short-term memory. In *Proc. of ACL*.

Nicholas FitzGerald, Oscar Täckström, Kuzman Ganchev, and Dipanjan Das. 2015. Semantic role labelling with neural network factors. In *Proc. of EMNLP*.

William R. Foland and James Martin. 2015. Dependencybased semantic role labeling using convolutional neural networks. In *Proc. of *SEM*.

Andrea Gesmundo, James Henderson, Paola Merlo, and Ivan Titov. 2009. A latent variable model of synchronous syntactic-semantic parsing for multiple languages. In *Proc. of CoNLL*.

Daniel Gildea and Daniel Jurafsky. 2002. Automatic labeling of semantic roles. *Computational Linguistics*, 28(3):245–288.

Yoav Goldberg. 2015. A primer on neural network models for natural language processing. arXiv:1510.00726.

Alex Graves. 2013. Generating sequences with recurrent neural networks. arXiv:1308.0850.

Jan Hajič, Massimiliano Ciaramita, Richard Johansson, Daisuke Kawahara, Maria Antònia Martí, Lluís Màrquez, Adam Meyers, Joakim Nivre, Sebastian Padó, Jan Štěpánek, Pavel Straňák, Mihai Surdeanu, Nianwen Xue, and Yi Zhang. 2009. The CoNLL-2009 shared task: Syntactic and semantic dependencies in multiple languages. In *Proc. of CoNLL*.

He He, Hal Daumé III, and Jason Eisner. 2013. Dynamic feature selection for dependency parsing. In *Proc. of EMNLP*.

James Henderson, Paola Merlo, Gabriele Musillo, and Ivan Titov. 2008. A latent variable model of synchronous parsing for syntactic and semantic dependencies. In *Proc. of CoNLL*.

James Henderson, Paola Merlo, Ivan Titov, and Gabriele Musillo. 2013. Multi-lingual joint parsing of syntactic and semantic dependencies with a latent variable model. *Computational Linguistics*, 39(4):949–998.

Sepp Hochreiter and Jürgen Schmidhuber. 1997. Long short-term memory. *Neural Computation*, 9(8):1735–1780.

Richard Johansson and Pierre Nugues. 2008. Dependency-based syntactic-semantic analysis with PropBank and NomBank. In *Proc. of CoNLL*.

Richard Johansson. 2009. Statistical bistratal dependency parsing. In *Proc. of EMNLP*.

Jayant Krishnamurthy and Tom M. Mitchell. 2014. Joint syntactic and semantic parsing with combinatory categorial grammar. In *Proc. of ACL*.

Tao Lei, Yuan Zhang, Lluís Màrquez i Villodre, Alessandro Moschitti, and Regina Barzilay. 2015. High-order low-rank tensors for semantic role labeling. In *Proc. of NAACL*.

Mike Lewis, Luheng He, and Luke Zettlemoyer. 2015. Joint A* CCG parsing and semantic role labelling. In *Proc. of EMNLP*.

Junhui Li, Guodong Zhou, and Hwee Tou Ng. 2010. Joint syntactic and semantic parsing of Chinese. In *Proc. of ACL*.

Wang Ling, Chris Dyer, Alan Black, and Isabel Trancoso. 2015. Two/too simple adaptations of word2vec for syntax problems. In *Proc. of NAACL*.

Xavier Lluís and Lluís Màrquez. 2008. A joint model for parsing syntactic and semantic dependencies. In *Proc. of CoNLL*.

Xavier Lluís, Xavier Carreras, and Lluís Màrquez. 2013. Joint arc-factored parsing of syntactic and semantic dependencies. *Transactions of the ACL*, 1:219–230.

Mitchell P. Marcus, Mary Ann Marcinkiewicz, and Beatrice Santorini. 1993. Building a large annotated corpus of English: The Penn treebank. *Computational Linguistics*, 19(2):313–330.

Adam Meyers, Ruth Reeves, Catherine Macleod, Rachel Szekely, Veronika Zielinska, Brian Young, and Ralph Grishman. 2004. The NomBank project: An interim report. In *Proc. of NAACL*.

Vinod Nair and Geoffrey E. Hinton. 2010. Rectified linear units improve restricted Boltzmann machines. In *Proc. of ICML*.

Joakim Nivre, Johan Hall, Jens Nilsson, Atanas Chanev, Gülsen Eryigit, Sandra Kübler, Svetoslav Marinov, and Erwin Marsi. 2007. MaltParser: A language-independent system for data-driven dependency parsing. *Natural Language Engineering*, 13:95–135.

Joakim Nivre. 2008. Algorithms for deterministic incremental dependency parsing. *Computational Linguistics*, 34(4):513–553.

Joakim Nivre. 2009. Non-projective dependency parsing in expected linear time. In *Proc. of ACL*.

Martha Palmer, Daniel Gildea, and Paul Kingsbury. 2005. The Proposition Bank: An annotated corpus of semantic roles. *Computational Linguistics*, 31(1):71–106.

Michael Roth and Kristian Woodsend. 2014. Composition of word representations improves semantic role labelling. In *Proc. of EMNLP*.

Mihai Surdeanu, Richard Johansson, Adam Meyers, Lluís Màrquez, and Joakim Nivre. 2008. The CoNLL-2008 shared task on joint parsing of syntactic and semantic dependencies. In *Proc. of CoNLL*.

Charles Sutton and Andrew McCallum. 2005. Joint parsing and semantic role labeling. In *Proc. of CoNLL*.

Oscar Täckström, Kuzman Ganchev, and Dipanjan Das. 2015. Efficient inference and structured learning for semantic role labeling. *Transactions of the ACL*, 3:29–41.

Ivan Titov, James Henderson, Paola Merlo, and Gabriele Musillo. 2009. Online graph planarisation for synchronous parsing of semantic and syntactic dependencies. In *Proc. of IJCAI*.

Kristina Toutanova, Aria Haghighi, and Christopher D. Manning. 2008. A global joint model for semantic role labeling. *Computational Linguistics*, 34(2):161–191.

David Weiss, Chris Alberti, Michael Collins, and Slav Petrov. 2015. Structured training for neural network transition-based parsing. In *Proc. of ACL*.

Wojciech Zaremba, Ilya Sutskever, and Oriol Vinyals. 2014. Recurrent neural network regularization. arXiv:1409.2329.

Hai Zhao and Chunyu Kit. 2008. Parsing syntactic and semantic dependencies with two single-stage maximum entropy models. In *Proc. of CoNLL*.

Hai Zhao, Wenliang Chen, Jun'ichi Kazama, Kiyotaka Uchimoto, and Kentaro Torisawa. 2009. Multilingual dependency learning: Exploiting rich features for tagging syntactic and semantic dependencies. In *Proc. of CoNLL*.

Jie Zhou and Wei Xu. 2015. End-to-end learning of semantic role labeling using recurrent neural networks. In *Proc. of ACL*.

Beyond Prefix-Based Interactive Translation Prediction

Jesús González-Rubio
Daniel Ortiz-Martínez
Webinterpret Inc.
{jesus.g,daniel.o}@webinterpret.com

José Miguel Benedí
Francisco Casacuberta
PRHLT Research Center
Univ. Politècnica de València
{jbenedi,fcn}@prhlt.upv.es

Abstract

Current automatic machine translation systems require heavy human proof-reading to produce high-quality translations. We present a new interactive machine translation approach aimed at providing a natural collaboration between humans and translation systems. As such, we grant the user complete freedom to validate and correct any part of the translations suggested by the system. Our approach is then designed according to the requirements placed by this unrestricted proof-reading protocol. In particular, the ability of the system to suggest new translations coherent with the set of potentially disjoint translation segments validated by the user.

We evaluate our approach in a user-simulated setting where reference translations are considered the output desired by a human expert. Results show important reductions in the number of edits in comparison to decoupled post-editing and conventional prefix-based interactive translation prediction. Additionally, we provide evidence that it can also reduce the cognitive overload reported for interactive translation systems in previous user studies.

1 Introduction

Research in the field of *machine translation* (MT) aims at developing computer systems that reduce the effort required to generate translations, whether by assisting human translators or by directly replacing them. However, most research in MT has focused on the development of fully automatic MT approaches. Despite that, except for a handful of very constrained domains, current automatic MT technology still only achieves results that are not satisfactory in practice; automatic MT still require heavy human proof-reading to produce human-quality translations.

We present a new computer-assisted translation approach that integrates human translators and automatic MT into a tight feedback loop. In our approach, the user[1] and the MT system collaborate to generate translations through a series of interactions. At each interaction, the system proposes its best translation for the given input sentence. If the user finds it correct, then it is accepted and the process goes on with the next input sentence. Otherwise, the user makes some corrections that the system takes into account to improve the proposed translation. The rationale behind this *interactive translation prediction* (ITP) approach is to combine the accuracy provided by the human expert with the efficiency of the MT system in contrast to decoupled *post-editing* (PE). Previous works, e.g. (Barrachina et al., 2009), have explored this paradigm; however their practical implementation limits this general proof-reading approach to a prefix-based interaction where the user is forced to correct the errors in the sentence strictly according to the reading order.

Our main contribution, described in Section 3, is a new proof-reading protocol focused on providing a more natural interaction between the user and the system. Specifically, we give complete freedom to the user to validate or to correct any part of the translation at any given interaction. As such, the user is no longer bound to correct the errors following the reading order as in previous prefix-based ITP works (Barrachina et al., 2009; González-Rubio et al., 2013; Green et al., 2014). Preffix-based interaction can be a frustrating and cognitively demanding limitation for the user, and may be a factor in the somehow disappointing

---

[1] We use the terms "human expert", "human translator", and 'user" indistinctly.

Proceedings of the 20th SIGNLL Conference on Computational Natural Language Learning (CoNLL), pages 198–207,
Berlin, Germany, August 7-12, 2016. ©2016 Association for Computational Linguistics

results of prefix-based ITP with users (Koehn, 2009; Underwood et al., 2014; Green et al., 2014; Sanchis-Trilles et al., 2014). We design our approach to meet the requirements placed by the unrestricted proof-reading protocol, not the opposite way. The most significant new feature is *conditioned decoding*, for translation generation coherently to a set of segments validated by the user.

An evaluation involving human users is most desirable to study the impact of any proof-reading protocol. However, such a study is expensive, time-consuming and it will require to take into account additional sources of variation, namely the human factor, that may obscure the comparison between different approaches. Therefore, we chose to follow previous works, for instance (Barrachina et al., 2009), and carry out our experiments on a simulated setting intended to provide a direct and, more importantly, objective comparison to previous approaches (Section 4). Regarding evaluation, we propose a new metric to automatically estimate the cognitive load of potential users working on the different ITP environments. To the best of our knowledge, this is the first proposal at this respect. Results in Section 5 confirm the soundness of the proposed ITP approach. Reported figures show important reductions in both the number of corrections typed by the user and her estimated cognitive load.

2 Related Work

Common proof-read MT protocols implement a decoupled PE process in which, first, the MT system returns a translation of a whole given document. Next, a human reads it correcting, in any order, the possible mistakes made by the system.

Interactive approaches (Isabelle and Church, 1998; Langlais and Lapalme, 2002; Tomás and Casacuberta, 2006) were proposed as a more sophisticate way of taking advantage of MT technology. Barrachina et al., (Barrachina et al., 2009) presented a prefix-based ITP approach in which the user is assumed to proof-read each automatic translation correcting each time the first error, if any, in the usual reading order. This can be a reasonable assumption in text or speech transcription (Toselli et al., 2007; Rodríguez et al., 2007) where the output sequence is generated monotonically respect to the input data. However, it has always be an important handicap for translation due to the intrinsic reordering involved in the process.

ITP is a fruitful research field with diverse contributions for multiple authors: (González-Rubio et al., 2010; Alabau et al., 2013; Koehn et al., 2014) among others. We share with (Sanchis-Trilles et al., 2008) the idea of making a more sophisticated use of the mouse actions performed by the user while interacting with the system, and with (González-Rubio et al., 2013) the common ITP formulation for both phrase-based and hierarchical MT models. In particular, we significantly modify the prefix-based ITP implementation presented in the latter work to support the proposed unrestricted proof-reading protocol.

User studies of prefix-based ITP versus PE have shown that while users tend to make less corrections, overall translation time tend to be higher (Koehn, 2009; Underwood et al., 2014; Green et al., 2014; Sanchis-Trilles et al., 2014). Coherently with these results, users also perceive prefix-based ITP as a more cognitive demanding task than PE. This is not surprising given that users are asked to proof-read one new translation (suffix) after each individual correction, which increases significantly the amount of text to be processed to generate a single translation. This is particularly frustrating when the user observes how a correct translation is rewritten with a wrong one by the next suffix suggested by the system. Given that PE do not suffer from this effect, it provides a comprehensive explanation of the somehow disappointing results reported for prefix-based ITP.

To the best of our knowledge, the only alternative to prefix-based proof-reading was proposed in the context of text recognition. Serrano et al., (2014) implement a constrained search procedure that profits from the monotonic alignment between input image, search states and user corrections, to limit the set of possible transcriptions to those coherent with a set of (disjoint) user corrections. We apply a similar idea in a translation context and provide solutions to cope with the nonmonotonicity inherent to the task.

3 Beyond Prefix-Based ITP

The goal of our approach is to give complete freedom to the user in her interaction with the system. The process starts when the MT system proposes a full translation of the source language sentence. Then, the user reads the translation and is allowed to validate -all or part of- the correct segments in it and corrects any of its potential errors. Then, the

source (s): No era el hombre más honesto ni el más piadoso , pero era un hombre valiente .
desired translation (t): He was not the most honest or pious of men , but he was courageous .

BEGIN { **MT** : It was not the most honest and the most pious man , but it was a brave man .

IT-1 { **User**: It was not the most honest and the most **pious** of man , **but** it **was** a brave man .
MT : He was not the most honest or pious of men , but it **was** a brave man .

IT-2 { **User**: He was not the most honest or pious of men , but it was courageous .
MT : He was not the most honest or pious of men , but he **was courageous** .

END { **User**: He was not the most honest or pious of men , but **he was courageous** .

Figure 1: Interactive translation of a Spanish sentence into English. First, the system suggests an initial translation. At iteration 1, the user validates the parts of the suggestions she considers to be right and introduces a correction by typing a word: "of". This defines a new user feedback with five segments: {"was not the most honest", "pious of", ", but", "was", "."}. Then, the system suggests a new translation that contains these segments in the given order. Iteration 2 is similar; the user validates words "He" and "or", and she types a new correction: "courageous". The process ends when the user accepts the translation suggested by the system in the last step. Only two edits are required. In comparison, PE would have needed 10 edits.

system takes into account this feedback to suggest a new translation that contains the segments validated by the user as well as the typed corrections. Such process is repeated until the user validates the whole suggested translation. An example of this process is shown in Figure 1.

The crucial MT feature is the generation of a new translation coherent to the segments already validated by the user. Formally, we represent such user feedback as a sequence of disjoint segments $\mathbf{f} = \tilde{f}_1, \ldots, \tilde{f}_k, \ldots, \tilde{f}_{|f|}$, where each $\tilde{f}_k$ is a sequence of consecutive target language words. For example, user feedback at iteration one in Figure 1 is composed of five disjoint segments: $\tilde{f}_1 =$ "was not the most honest", $\tilde{f}_2 =$ "pious of", $\tilde{f}_3 =$ ", but", $\tilde{f}_4 =$ "was" and $\tilde{f}_5 =$ ".". Segments in $\mathbf{f}$ do not overlap and do not necessarily cover the whole sentence. Prefix-based feedback in conventional ITP is a special case of this with only one segment starting at the beginning of the sentence.

Next, we describe the statistical formalization of our approach, the models actually used to implement such formalization, and the search procedures required to efficiently generate translations coherent with this generalized user feedback.

3.1 Statistical Framework

Our problem can be stated as follows: given a source sentence $\mathbf{s} = s_1 \ldots s_{|s|}$ and some user feedback $\mathbf{f}$, we must find the best target language trans-

lation $\mathbf{t} = t_1 \ldots t_{|\mathbf{t}|}$ of $\mathbf{s}$ coherent with $\mathbf{f}$:

$$\hat{\mathbf{t}} = \arg\max_{\mathbf{t}} \Pr(\mathbf{t} \mid \mathbf{s}, \mathbf{f})$$

We can make the naïve Bayes' assumption that $\mathbf{s}$ and $\mathbf{f}$ are statistically independent variables given $\mathbf{t}$. This results in the basic equation for ITP with error correction (Ortiz-Martínez, 2011):

$$\hat{\mathbf{t}} = \arg\max_{\mathbf{t}} \Pr(\mathbf{t} \mid \mathbf{s}) \cdot \Pr(\mathbf{f} \mid \mathbf{t}) \qquad (1)$$

where, as we will see in Section 3.2, distribution $\Pr(\mathbf{t} \mid \mathbf{s})$ can be approximated by a machine translation model, and $\Pr(\mathbf{f} \mid \mathbf{t})$ by an error correction model that measures the degree of compatibility between $\mathbf{f}$ and $\mathbf{t}$.

Note that by using a probability distribution $\Pr(\mathbf{f} \mid \mathbf{t})$, any translation is compatible with a given user feedback to some degree. As a consequence, the translation returned by Equation (1) may still not contain the segments validated by the user; we need to identify the sub-string of the returned sentence that corresponds to the each of the segments validated by the user. To solve this problem, we define an alignment $\mathbf{a} = a_1, \ldots, a_{|f|}$ between the user-validated segments $\mathbf{f} = \tilde{f}_1, \ldots, \tilde{f}_{|f|}$ and a list of segments $\tilde{\mathbf{t}} = \tilde{t}_1, \ldots, \tilde{t}_{|f|}$, where each $\tilde{t}_k = t_{k_i} \ldots t_{k_j}$ is a sub-sequence of words in $\mathbf{t}$. Each alignment link $a_k = \tilde{t}_k$ indicates the particular segment in $\mathbf{t}$ that should be replaced by the kth user-validated segment $\tilde{f}_k$ to make $\mathbf{t}$ coherent to $\mathbf{f}$. Unaligned words in $\mathbf{t}$ constitute the free text that completes the gaps in between the user-validated segments in $\mathbf{f}$ (González-Rubio et al., 2013). The alignment also must be monotonic to preserve the order of the user-validated segments. Formally, for every pair of alignment links: $a_k = \tilde{t}_k$ and $a_{k'} = \tilde{t}_{k'}, k < k' \iff k_j < k'_i$.

After including alignment in Equation (1) and following a maximum approximation, we arrive to our final formulation of ITP with error correction:

$$(\hat{\mathbf{t}}, \hat{\mathbf{a}}) = \arg\max_{\mathbf{t},\mathbf{a}} \Pr(\mathbf{t} \mid \mathbf{s}) \cdot \Pr(\mathbf{f}, \mathbf{a} \mid \mathbf{t}) \quad (2)$$

In practice, we combine the probability distributions in Equation (2) in a log-linear fashion as it is typically done in MT (Och and Ney, 2002).

3.2 Models

Equation (2) includes two probability distributions: $\Pr(\mathbf{t} \mid \mathbf{s})$ and $\Pr(\mathbf{f}, \mathbf{a} \mid \mathbf{t})$. The first one can be modeled by any of the multiple machine translation models that have been proposed in the literature; (Koehn, 2009) for example provide a good description of them. We will focus our exposition in the latter distribution, $\Pr(\mathbf{f}, \mathbf{a} \mid \mathbf{t})$, that evaluates the compatibility between a translation $\mathbf{t}$ and some user feedback $\mathbf{f}$ through alignment $\mathbf{a}$.

Following (González-Rubio et al., 2013), we model $\Pr(\mathbf{f}, \mathbf{a} \mid \mathbf{t})$ as an error correction model based on the edit distance (Levenshtein, 1966). Given a candidate string and the corresponding reference string, we model edit distance as a Bernoulli process where each word of the candidate has a probability p_e of being edited. Under this interpretation, the number of edits δ observed in a candidate of length n is a random variable that follows a binomial distribution, $\delta \sim \mathrm{B}(n, p_e)$. By assuming independence between each alignment link, we can model error-correction probability as:

$$\Pr(\mathbf{f}, \mathbf{a} \mid \mathbf{t}) \approx \prod_{k=1}^{|\mathbf{a}|} P_E(\tilde{f}_k, a_k)$$
$$= \prod_{k=1}^{|\mathbf{a}|} \binom{n_k}{\delta_k} p_e^{\delta_k} (1 - p_e)^{(n_k - \delta_k)}$$

where $P_E(\tilde{f}_k, a_k)$ is the error correction probability for the k-th alignment link whose value is given by the probability mass function of the binomial distribution, $n_k = |\tilde{f}_k|$ is the length in words of the k-th segment validated by the user ($\tilde{f}_k$), and δ_k is the edit distance between $\tilde{f}_k$ and the segment $a_k = \tilde{t}_k$ of $\mathbf{t}$ aligned to it according to $\mathbf{a}$.

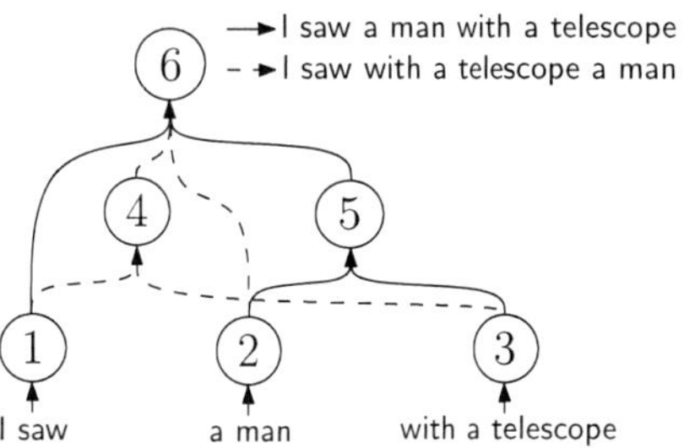

Figure 2: Example of a hypergraph encoding two different translations for the Spanish sentence: "Vi a un hombre con un telescopio".

The probability of editing p_e is the single free parameter of this model. Alternatively, we can use a model based on a multinomial distribution assigning different probabilities to different edit operations. Nevertheless, we adhere to the binomial approximation due to its simplicity.

3.3 Search

Next, we address the problem posed by the maximization in Equation (2). Following (Barrachina et al., 2009), we split search into a two step process. Given a source language sentence, we first generate a graph-based representation that contains its most probable translations. Then, we search for the optimal translation and alignment on it according to Equation (2). In particular, we use *hypergraphs* to represent such search space.

One important advantage of this approach, is that it separates the proof-read step from the MT engine used to generate the initial translations. As such it provides an unified framework that accepts both the use of phrase-based and hierarchical/syntax translation models.

3.3.1 Hypergraphs

A hypergraph (Gallo et al., 1993) is a generalization of the concept of graph where the edges (now called hyperedges) may connect several nodes (hypernodes) at the same time. Formally, a hypergraph is a weighted acyclic graph represented by a pair $\mathcal{H} = <\mathcal{V}, \mathcal{E}>$, where $\mathcal{V}$ is a set of hypernodes and $\mathcal{E}$ is a set of hyperedges. Each hyperedge $\varepsilon \in \mathcal{E}$ connects a set of tail hypernodes $\mathcal{T}(\varepsilon) = \{\tau_1 \ldots \tau_{|\mathcal{T}(\varepsilon)|}\}\ \tau_l \in \mathcal{V}$, to a head hypernode $\mathrm{H}(\varepsilon) \in \mathcal{V}$. A hypernode with no ingoing hyperedges is a leaf, while a hypernode with no outgoing hyperedges is a root. Each hypernode represents a partial translation generated during the MT decoding process. Each ingoing hyperedge ε

represents the rule applied to generate the partial solution in the head from the partial solutions in the tail hypernodes, as such it has an associated probability $P(\varepsilon)$. Figure 2 shows an example hypergraph[2]. Two alternative translations are constructed from the leaf hypernodes (1, 2 and 3) up to the root hypernode (6). Hypergraphs provide a compact representation of the translation space that allows us to derive efficient search algorithms.

Hypergraphs are the natural representation for hierarchical MT models (Chiang, 2005; Zollmann and Venugopal, 2006). Note, however, that wordgraphs (Ueffing et al., 2002), which are used to represent the search space for phrase-based models (Koehn et al., 2003), are a special case of hypergraphs in which hyperedges have at most one tail hypernode.

3.3.2 Search on hypergraphs

We formalize the maximization in Equation (2) as a bottom-up search problem. Starting from the leaf hypernodes, we keep track of the best solutions (partial translation and alignment) achievable at each hypernode. We define $Q(\nu, [m, n])$ as the probability of the most likely partial translation derivable from hypernode ν aligned to (accounting for) user-validated segments from m-th to n-th, we will refer to this interval as the coverage of the partial solution. Given a node ν and a coverage, we compute its score from its ingoing hyperedges. Specifically, $Q(\nu, [m, n])$ will be equal to the maximum score of the partial solutions computed from any ingoing hyperedge. Partial solutions from an ingoing hyperedge ε are defined as combinations of partial solutions on its tail hypernodes under the constrain that the concatenation of their coverages equals $[m, n]$. Formally, given an ingoing hyperedge ε, a combination $\mathbf{c} = \{Q(\tau_l, [m_l, n_l])\}_{l=1}^{|\mathcal{T}(\varepsilon)|}$ is valid if it holds the following four conditions:

1. $m_1 = m$

2. $n_{|\mathcal{T}(\varepsilon)|} = n$

3. $\forall l, \tau_l \in \mathcal{T}(\varepsilon)$

4. $\forall l : 1 < l \leq |\mathcal{T}(\varepsilon)|, m_l = n_{l-1} + 1$

$Q(\nu, [m, n])$ can be computed efficiently via the following dynamic programming recursion:

$$Q(\nu, [m, n]) = \max_{\substack{\varepsilon \in \mathcal{I}(\nu) \\ \mathbf{c} \in \mathcal{C}(\varepsilon, [m,n])}} P(\varepsilon) \prod_{Q(\tau_l, [m_l, n_l]) \in \mathbf{c}} Q(\tau_l, [m_l, n_l])$$

	EU corpus (Es/En)		
	train	tune	test
Sentences	214K	400	800
Tokens	5.9M / 5.2M	12K / 10K	23K / 20K
Vocabulary	97K / 84K	3K / 3K	5K / 4K

Table 1: Main figures of the EU corpus. K and M stand for thousands and millions of elements.

where $\mathcal{I}(\nu)$ are the ingoing hyperedges of ν, $P(\varepsilon)$ is the probability of hyperedge ε, $\mathcal{C}(\varepsilon, [m, n])$ is the set of valid combinations for hyperedge ε and coverage $[m, n]$, and $\mathbf{c} \in \mathcal{C}(\varepsilon, [m, n])$ is one of such valid combinations

Leaf hypernodes represent the base cases for this recursion. For simplicity, we restrict them to be fully-aligned to at most one user-validated segment[3]. That is, given a leaf hypernode $\lambda \in \mathcal{V}$:

$$Q(\lambda, [m, n]) = \begin{cases} P_{\mathrm{MT}}(\lambda) P_E(\mathrm{w}(\lambda), \tilde{\mathbf{f}}_m) & \text{if } m = n \\ 0 & \text{otherwise.} \end{cases}$$

where $P_{\mathrm{MT}}(\lambda)$ is the MT probability (language plus translation model) of λ, and $P_E(\mathrm{w}(\lambda), \tilde{\mathbf{f}}_m)$ is the error correction probability between the target text covered by the leaf hypernode, $\mathrm{w}(\lambda)$, and the m-th user-validated segment in $\mathbf{f}$.

The score of the optimal solution is given by $Q(\alpha, [1, |\mathbf{f}|])$, where $\alpha \in \mathcal{V}$ is the root hypernode. We can recover $(\hat{\mathbf{t}}, \hat{\mathbf{a}})$ through backtracking.

The process described above loops over all hyperedges and coverages (bounded by $|\mathcal{E}||\mathbf{f}|^2$), evaluating all valid combinations (bounded by the coverage partitions). It can be implemented by an algorithm with a complexity in $O(|\mathcal{E}||\mathbf{f}|^{2\tau})$, where τ is the average number of tail hypernodes per hyperedge (usually set to 2). In practice, our approach has a complexity in $O(|\mathcal{E}||\mathbf{f}|^4)$.

4 Experimental Setup

4.1 Corpus and MT systems

We tested the proposed methods in the Spanish-to-English (Es–En) partition of the *Bulletin of the European Union* (EU) corpus (Barrachina et al., 2009; González-Rubio et al., 2013). We tokenized the corpus keeping the real case of the sentences. Table 1 shows the main figures of the corpus.

We estimated a hierarchical MT model for the train partition with the standard configuration of

---

[2]For simplicity, we do not show hyperedge probabilities.

[3]Preliminary experiments did not show a difference in the final results when relaxing this restriction.

the Moses toolkit (Koehn et al., 2007). Log-linear weighs were estimated by minimum error-rate training (Och, 2003) on the tune partition. Then, we automatically translated tune and test partitions using the optimized model to obtain the corresponding hypergraphs. Next, we optimized the single free parameter p_e of the error correction model (see Section 3.2) on the tune partition. Finally, we interactively translated both partitions according to the unrestricted ITP approach proposed in Section 3.

4.2 User Simulation

ITP evaluation with human translators is simply to slow and expensive to be applied on a frequent and ongoing basis during system development. Instead, we carried out an automatic evaluation with simulated users which is faster and cheaper.

At each ITP iteration (see Figure 1), we have to decide which segments in the suggested translation should be validated, and which error should be corrected. To do that, we considered the reference translations in the corpus as the output that a human expert would want to obtain. Then, we align the suggested translation and the reference via edit distance: words aligned to itself are marked as valid, while edited words are potential corrections to be typed by the simulated user.

Without loss of generality, we introduced two restrictions: (1) we restrict users to validate segments only at the first iteration, and (2) the simulated user always corrected the first (in reading order) error in the suggested translation. We are aware that the results obtained with this user simulation will be pessimistic since it forbids behaviors that may improve user productivity, e.g. validating segments at each iteration or correcting more promising parts of the suggested translation. Our goal is not to match the behavior of a human translator, but to allow for a meaningful comparison against conventional ITP. Note that prefix-based proof-reading is a particular case of our user simulation with no segment validation.

4.3 Evaluation Metrics

ITP systems are evaluated according to the effort needed to generate the desired translations. This effort is usually estimated as the number of actions performed by the user while interacting with the system. In our user simulation, we describe two different actions: segment-validation, and word-correction. Each segment validation involves the

user to "click" on the initial and final words of the segment[4]. Each correction corresponds to an edit operation performed by the user. Specifically, we used the following measures in our experiments:

Word stroke ratio (WSR): Proposed in (Tomás and Casacuberta, 2006) as the quotient between the number of words edited by the user (word-strokes), and the number of words in the final translation. Word-strokes are considered as single actions with constant cost independently of the length of the edited word.

Mouse action ratio (MAR): Proposed in (Barrachina et al., 2009) as the quotient between the number of "clicks" made by the user (mouse-actions), and the number of words in the final translation. In addition to the "clicks" for segment validation, we count one more mouse action per sentence accounting for the final acceptance of the suggested translation.

Conceptually (Macklovitch et al., 2005), MAR can be seen as accounting for the cognitive part of the supervision process: undertanding the translation and identifying the errors in it, while WSR accounts for the actual physical effort required to type the corrections. As such, both metrics are complementary to express the total human effort involved in proof-reading a document.

We also evaluated the quality of the initial automatic translations generated by the system:

Bilingual evaluation understudy (BLEU): Proposed in (Papineni et al., 2002), it is based on the precision of n-grams between the suggested translation and the reference; it also includes a *brevity penalty* to penalize short translations. This score ranges between 0 and 100, with 100 denoting a perfect translation.

Translation edit rate (TER): Proposed in (Snover et al., 2006), it measures the number of edit operations (substitution, insertion and deletion of single words, and swap of word sequences) divided by the number of words in the reference.

In addition to be an MT quality metric, TER can also be seen as a human-effort measure in PE scenarios. Therefore, we can use TER and WSR to compare human effort between PE and ITP.

---

[4] One single "click" is enough for one-word segments.

	tune		test	
	BLEU [%]($\Uparrow$)	TER [%]($\Downarrow$)	BLEU [%]($\Uparrow$)	TER [%]($\Downarrow$)
	38.9±1.4	47.2±1.4	44.2±1.3	41.1±1.2

	TER [%]($\Downarrow$)		TER [%]($\Downarrow$)	
Post-editing	47.2±1.4		41.1±1.2	
	MAR [%]($\Downarrow$)	WSR [%]($\Downarrow$)	MAR [%]($\Downarrow$)	WSR [%]($\Downarrow$)
prefix-based ITP	11.2±0.4	45.8±2.0	10.3±0.3	54.5±1.4
Our approach	33.9±1.2	**30.5±1.6**	35.4±0.9	**35.1±1.1**

Table 2: Results of different approaches when interactively translating the tune and test partitions of the EU corpus. We compare decoupled PE, prefix-based ITP and the unrestricted ITP approach proposed in this work. Automatic translation results are shown to indicate the difficulty of the task. Results in bold indicate the lowest human effort (typing) achievable by the different scenarios.

Finally, in order to assess the statistical significance of the results, we also provide 95% confidence intervals for their values. These intervals were computed via pair-wise bootstrap resampling as proposed in (Zhang and Vogel, 2004).

5 Results

This section presents the results of the experiments performed to assess the unrestricted ITP approach proposed in Section 3. First, we compare our ITP approach to the prefix-based ITP scenario described in (Barrachina et al., 2009) and the decoupled PE approach. Then, we further study our approach investigating the relationship between segment-validation and typing effort. Finally, we provide evidence that the proposed unrestricted proof-reading protocol allows to reduce the cognitive overload produced by the changing translation completions of prefix-based ITP approaches.

Table 2 displays user-effort results for the proposed ITP approach against prefix-based ITP (Barrachina et al., 2009)[5] and a decoupled PE baseline approach. Automatic translation results are also displayed to give an idea of the difficulty of the task. We can observe how our approach clearly outperformed both prefix-based ITP and PE in terms of user typing effort as measured by WSR and TER respectively. According to these results, a human translator assisted by our ITP system would only need to correct only about one third of the words to generate the correct translations. In comparison, PE would require to type

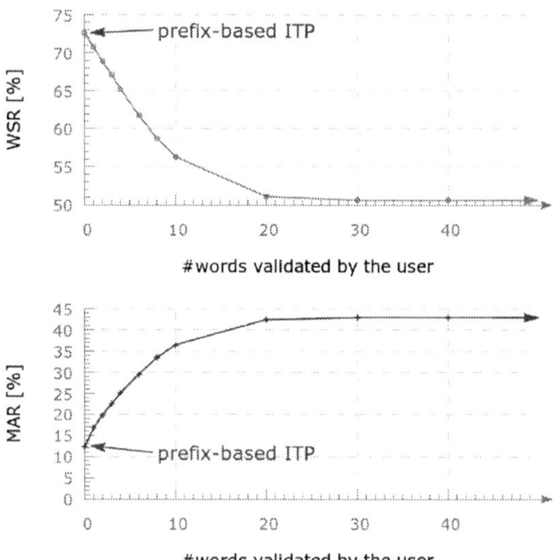

Figure 3: WSR and MAR as a function of the maximum number of words validated by the simulated user in our ITP approach. No changes were observed for more than 40 validated words.

$\sim 41\%$ of the words (17% more) while prefix-based ITP would require to correct more that half of them (55% more). Additionally, we can observe that prefix-based ITP was not better than the PE baseline in all cases. This result, coherent with previous works e.g. (González-Rubio et al., 2013; Green et al., 2014), exemplifies the potential limitations of prefix-based ITP.

The large reductions in typing effort observed for our ITP approach came together with an important increase in the number of mouse actions.

---

[5]For prefix-based ITP, MAR accounts for the prefixes validated by the user while proof-reading the translations.

Next, we focused on the differences between prefix-based and our approach. To do that, we carried out different experiments allowing the simulated user to validate an increasing number of words from zero to infinity (corresponding respectively to the results of prefix-based ITP and our approach in Table 2). Figure 3 shows WSR (top) and MAR (bottom) for the Test partition as a function of the maximum number or words allowed to be validated by the user.

As we allowed the simulated user to validate more words, the amount of words to be corrected (WSR) decreased dramatically. For example, we obtained a 10% relative reduction in WSR when we allowed the user to validate a maximum of 4 words. A similar trend (but in the opposite direction) can be observed for MAR: as we allowed the user to validate more words, the number of mouse actions increased until stabilization. In other words, our ITP approach allows to reduce user typing effort at the expense of an increase in the number of mouse actions. As we have said before, WSR and MAR account for different phenomena and thus have different cost from a human point of view (Macklovitch et al., 2005). It may seem that we have simply exchanged typing effort for cognitive effort. However, two considerations allow us to consider this a beneficial exchange. On the one hand, from a pure mechanistic point of view, typying a whole word usually requires more effort than "clicking" on it. On the other hand, from a cognitive point of view, the user has to read, understand, and evaluate the suggested translation in both prefix-based ITP and our approach. Hence, the difference in cognitive effort between these two approaches approaches is most probably negligible. Nevertheless, these considerations should be tested with actual human users before reaching categorical conclusions.

Average response time of our Python prototype was below 3 seconds[6]. Obviously, it does not qualify as real-time. However, we expect an important reduction in response time after implementing our approach in a more efficient language.

We performed a final analysis to evaluate to which extent our proposal alleviates the main annoying effect inherent to prefix-based ITP, namely correct words in a given suffix overwritten by the next suggested suffix. This common effect, observed in several user studies, make human users

---

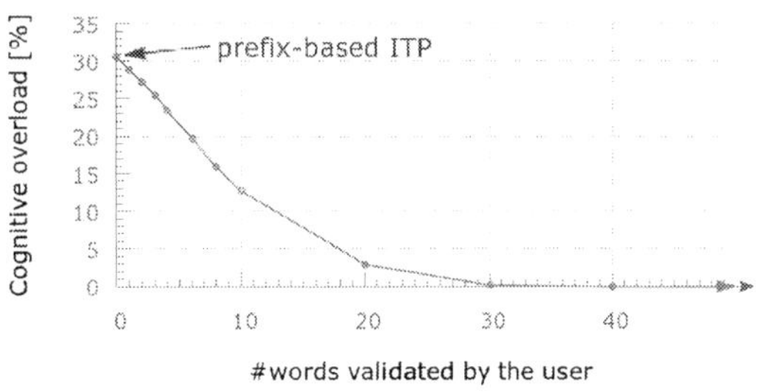

Figure 4: Percentage of words suggested by the system that were correct but overwritten in subsequent translation suggestions, as a function of the number of words validated by the simulated user. This ratio can be seen as a measure of the user cognitive overload.

feel that cognitive effort invested in evaluating each suggested translation was wasted.

To do that, we measured the number of correct words that were modified by subsequent translation suggestions, normalized by the total number of suggested words. Figure 4 displays this percentage as a function of the maximum number of words that can be validated by the simulated user. We can observe how for prefix-based ITP (zero value in the x-axis), this cognitive overload is a very important phenomena; more than 30% of the words suggested by the system were correct but modified by following suffix suggestions. As we allowed more words to be fixed, this percentage steadily decreased down to zero. This indicates that our ITP proposal actually provides a mechanism to overcome the cognitive overload inherent to prefix-based ITP.

6 Summary

We have presented a new ITP approach where the user is not longer bound to interact with the system in a prefix-based fashion (Barrachina et al., 2009). The proposed ITP approach gives the user complete freedom to validate and correct any part of the suggested translations thus providing a more natural working environment for human translators. We formalize the problem as a MT model with error correction which, in practice, is implemented as a constrained search on hypergraphs.

Simulated results showed that the proposed ITP approach drastically reduced the typing effort needed to generate translations, improving results of both decoupled PE and prefix-based ITP. This

---

[6]The test machine was an Intel i5 CPU at 3.4 GHz.

reduction in typing effort came at the expense of a larger amount of mouse actions required to validate correct segments of the suggested translations. However, since mouse actions are cheaper than typing full words, we can expect this exchange to reduce overall user effort. Nevertheless, this expectation should be confirmed in future experiments with actual human users. Finally, in addition to reduce user effort, we also provide evidence indicating that the proposed ITP approach can reduce the cognitive overload commonly reported by humans using prefix-based ITP systems.

Acknowledgments

Work supported by the Generalitat Valenciana under grant ALMAMATER (PrometeoII/2014/030).

References

Vicent Alabau, Jesús Gonzlez-Rubio, Luis A. Leiva, Daniel Ortiz-Martínez, Germán Sanchis-Trilles, Francisco Casacuberta, Bartolomé' Mesa-Lao, Ragnar Bonk, Michael Carl, and Mercedes García-Martínez. 2013. User evaluation of advanced interaction features for a computer-assisted translation workbench. In *Proceedings of the XIV Machine Translation Summit*, pages 361–368.

Sergio Barrachina, Oliver Bender, Francisco Casacuberta, Jorge Civera, Elsa Cubel, Shahram Khadivi, Antonio Lagarda, Hermann Ney, Jesús Tomás, Enrique Vidal, and Juan-Miguel Vilar. 2009. Statistical approaches to computer-assisted translation. *Computational Linguistics*, 35:3–28, March.

David Chiang. 2005. A hierarchical phrase-based model for statistical machine translation. In *Proceedings of the 43rd Annual Meeting of the Association for Computational Linguistics*, pages 263–270.

Giorgio Gallo, Giustino Longo, Stefano Pallottino, and Sang Nguyen. 1993. Directed hypergraphs and applications. *Discrete Applied Mathematics*, 42(2-3):177–201, April.

Jesús González-Rubio, Daniel Ortiz-Martínez, and Francisco Casacuberta. 2010. Balancing user effort and translation error in interactive machine translation via confidence measures. In *Proceedings of the 48th Annual Meeting of the Association for Computational Linguistics*, pages 173–177.

Jesús González-Rubio, Daniel Ortíz-Martinez, José-Miguel Benedí, and Francisco Casacuberta. 2013. Interactive machine translation using hierarchical translation models. In *Proceedings of the conference on Empirical Methods in Natural Language Processing*, pages 244–254.

Spence Green, Sida I. Wang, Jason Chuang, Jeffrey Heer, Sebastian Schuster, and Christopher D. Manning. 2014. Human effort and machine learnability in computer aided translation. In *Proceedings of the conference on Empirical Methods in Natural Language Processing*, pages 1225–1236.

Pierre Isabelle and Ken Church. 1998. *Special issue on: New tools for human translators*, volume 12. Kluwer Academic Publishers, January.

Philipp Koehn, Franz Josef Och, and Daniel Marcu. 2003. Statistical phrase-based translation. In *Proceedings of the the North American Chapter of the Association for Computational Linguistics on Human Language Technology*, pages 48–54.

Philipp Koehn, Hieu Hoang, Alexandra Birch, Chris Callison-Burch, Marcello Federico, Nicola Bertoldi, Brooke Cowan, Wade Shen, Christine Moran, Richard Zens, Chris Dyer, Ondrej Bojar, Alexandra Constantin, and Evan Herbst. 2007. Moses: Open Source Toolkit for Statistical Machine Translation. In *Proceedings of the 45th Annual Meeting of the Association for Computational Linguistics*.

Philipp Koehn, Chara Tsoukala, and Herve Saint-Amand. 2014. Refinements to interactive translation prediction based on search graphs. In *Proceedings of the 52nd Annual Meeting of the Association for Computational Linguistics*, pages 574–578.

Philipp Koehn. 2009. A process study of computer-aided translation. *Machine Translation*, 23(4):241–263.

Philippe Langlais and Guy Lapalme. 2002. TransType: development-evaluation cycles to boost translator's productivity. *Machine Translation*, 17(2):77–98, September.

Vladimir Levenshtein. 1966. Binary codes capable of correcting deletions, insertions and reversals. *Soviet Physics Doklady*, 10(8):707–710, February.

Elliot Macklovitch, Nam-Trung Nguyen, and Roberto Silva. 2005. User evaluation report. Technical report, Université de Montréal. TransType2 (IST-2001-32091).

Franz Josef Och and Hermann Ney. 2002. Discriminative training and maximum entropy models for statistical machine translation. In *Proceedings of the 40th Annual Meeting on Association for Computational Linguistics*, pages 295–302.

Franz Och. 2003. Minimum error rate training in statistical machine translation. In *Proceedings of the 41st Annual Meeting on Association for Computational Linguistics*, pages 160–167.

Daniel Ortiz-Martínez. 2011. *Advances in Fully-Automatic and Interactive Phrase-Based Statistical Machine Translation*. Ph.D. thesis, Universitat Politècnica de València.

Kishore Papineni, Salim Roukos, Todd Ward, and Wei-Jing Zhu. 2002. BLEU: a method for automatic evaluation of machine translation. In *Proceedings of the 40th Annual Meeting on Association for Computational Linguistics*, pages 311–318.

Luis Rodríguez, Francisco Casacuberta, and Enrique Vidal. 2007. Computer assisted transcription of speech. In *Proceedings of the 3rd Iberian Conference on Pattern Recognition and Image Analysis*, volume 4477 of *Lecture Notes in Computer Science*, pages 241–248.

Germán Sanchis-Trilles, Daniel Ortiz-Martínez, Jorge Civera, Francisco Casacuberta, Enrique Vidal, and Hieu Hoang. 2008. Improving Interactive Machine Translation via Mouse Actions. In *Proceedings of the Conference on Empirical Methods in Natural Language Processing*, pages 485–494.

Germán Sanchis-Trilles, Vicent Alabau, Christian Buck, Michael Carl, Francisco Casacuberta, Mercedes García-Martínez, Ulrich Germann, Jesús González-Rubio, Robin L. Hill, Philipp Koehn, Luis A. Leiva, Bartolomé Mesa-Lao, Daniel Ortiz-Martínez, Herve Saint-Amand, and Chara Tsoukala. 2014. Interactive translation prediction versus conventional post-editing in practice: a study with the casmacat workbench. *Machine Translation*, 28(3-4):217–235, December.

Nicols Serrano, Adri Gimnez, Jorge Civera, Alberto Sanchis, and Alfons Juan. 2014. Interactive handwriting recognition with limited user effort. *International Journal on Document Analysis and Recognition*, 17:47–59.

Matthew Snover, Bonnie Dorr, Richard Schwartz, Linnea Micciulla, and John Makhoul. 2006. A study of translation edit rate with targeted human annotation. In *Proceedings of Association for Machine Translation in the Americas*, pages 223–231.

Jesús Tomás and Francisco Casacuberta. 2006. Statistical phrase-based models for interactive computer-assisted translation. In *Proceedings of the 21st International Conference on Computational Linguistics and 44th Annual Meeting of the Association for Computational Linguistics*, pages 835–841.

Alejando H. Toselli, Verónica Romero, Luis Rodriguez, and Eenrique Vidal. 2007. Computer assisted transcription of handwritten text images. In *9th International Conference on Document Analysis and Recognition*, volume 2, pages 944–948.

Nicola Ueffing, Franz J. Och, and Hermann Ney. 2002. Generation of word graphs in statistical machine translation. In *Proceedings of the conference on Empirical Methods in Natural Language Processing*, pages 156–163.

Nancy Underwood, Bartolomé Mesa-Lao, Mercedes García Martinez, Michael Carl, Vicent Alabau, Jesús González-Rubio, Luis A. Leiva, Germán Sanchis-Trilles, Daniel Ortíz-Martinez, and Francisco Casacuberta. 2014. Evaluating the effects of interactivity in a post-editing workbench. In *Proceedings of the 9th International Conference on Language Resources and Evaluation*, pages 553–559.

Ying Zhang and Stephan Vogel. 2004. Measuring confidence intervals for the machine translation evaluation metrics. In *Proceedings of the 10th International Conference on Theoretical and Methodological Issues in Machine Translation*, pages 85–94.

Andreas Zollmann and Ashish Venugopal. 2006. Syntax augmented machine translation via chart parsing. In *Proceedings of the Workshop on Statistical Machine Translation*, pages 138–141.

Exploring Prediction Uncertainty in Machine Translation Quality Estimation

Daniel Beck[†]   **Lucia Specia**[†]   **Trevor Cohn**[‡]
[†]Department of Computer Science
University of Sheffield, United Kingdom
[‡]Computing and Information Systems
University of Melbourne, Australia
{debeck1,l.specia}@sheffield.ac.uk, t.cohn@unimelb.edu.au

Abstract

Machine Translation Quality Estimation is a notoriously difficult task, which lessens its usefulness in real-world translation environments. Such scenarios can be improved if quality predictions are accompanied by a measure of uncertainty. However, models in this task are traditionally evaluated only in terms of point estimate metrics, which do not take prediction uncertainty into account. We investigate probabilistic methods for Quality Estimation that can provide well-calibrated uncertainty estimates and evaluate them in terms of their full posterior predictive distributions. We also show how this posterior information can be useful in an asymmetric risk scenario, which aims to capture typical situations in translation workflows.

1 Introduction

Quality Estimation (QE) (Blatz et al., 2004; Specia et al., 2009) models aim at predicting the quality of automatically translated text segments. Traditionally, these models provide point estimates and are evaluated using metrics like Mean Absolute Error (MAE), Root-Mean-Square Error (RMSE) and Pearson's r correlation coefficient. However, in practice QE models are built for use in decision making in large workflows involving Machine Translation (MT). In these settings, relying on point estimates would mean that only very accurate prediction models can be useful in practice.

A way to improve decision making based on quality predictions is to explore uncertainty estimates. Consider for example a post-editing scenario where professional translators use MT in an effort to speed-up the translation process. A QE

model can be used to determine if an MT segment is good enough for post-editing or should be discarded and translated from scratch. But since QE models are not perfect they can end up allowing bad MT segments to go through for post-editing because of a prediction error. In such a scenario, having an uncertainty estimate for the prediction can provide additional information for the filtering decision. For instance, in order to ensure good user experience for the human translator and maximise translation productivity, an MT segment could be forwarded for post-editing only if a QE model assigns a high quality score with *low uncertainty* (high confidence). Such a decision process is not possible with point estimates only.

Good uncertainty estimates can be acquired from well-calibrated probability distributions over the quality predictions. In QE, arguably the most successful probabilistic models are Gaussian Processes (GPs) since they considered the state-of-the-art for regression (Cohn and Specia, 2013; Hensman et al., 2013), especially in the low-data regimes typical for this task. We focus our analysis in this paper on GPs since other common models used in QE can only provide point estimates as predictions. Another reason why we focus on probabilistic models is because this lets us employ the ideas proposed by Quiñonero-Candela et al. (2006), which defined new evaluation metrics that take into account probability distributions over predictions.

The remaining of this paper is organised as follows:

- In Section 2 we further motivate the use of GPs for uncertainty modelling in QE and revisit their underlying theory. We also propose some model extensions previously developed in the GP literature and argue they are more appropriate for the task.

Proceedings of the 20th SIGNLL Conference on Computational Natural Language Learning (CoNLL), pages 208–218,
Berlin, Germany, August 7-12, 2016. ©2016 Association for Computational Linguistics

- We intrinsically evaluate our proposed models in terms of their posterior distributions on training and test data in Section 3. Specifically, we show that differences in uncertainty modelling are not captured by the usual point estimate metrics commonly used for this task.

- As an example of an application for predicitive distributions, in Section 4 we show how they can be useful in scenarios with asymmetric risk and how the proposed models can provide better performance in this case.

We discuss related work in Section 5 and give conclusions and avenues for future work in Section 6.

While we focus on QE as application, the methods we explore in this paper can be applied to any text regression task where modelling predictive uncertainty is useful, either in human decision making or by propagating this information for further computational processing.

2 Probabilistic Models for QE

Traditionally, QE is treated as a regression task with hand-crafted features. Kernel methods are arguably the state-of-the-art in QE since they can easily model non-linearities in the data. Furthermore, the scalability issues that arise in kernel methods do not tend to affect QE in practice since the datasets are usually small, in the order of thousands of instances.

The most popular method for QE is Support Vector Regression (SVR), as shown in the multiple instances of the WMT QE shared tasks (Callison-burch et al., 2012; Bojar et al., 2013; Bojar et al., 2014; Bojar et al., 2015). While SVR models can generate competitive predictions for this task, they lack a probabilistic interpretation, which makes it hard to extract uncertainty estimates using them. Bootstrapping approaches like bagging (Abe and Mamitsuka, 1998) can be applied, but this requires setting and optimising hyperparameters like bag size and number of bootstraps. There is also no guarantee these estimates come from a well-calibrated probabilistic distribution.

Gaussian Processes (GPs) (Rasmussen and Williams, 2006) is an alternative kernel-based framework that gives competitive results for point estimates (Cohn and Specia, 2013; Shah et al., 2013; Beck et al., 2014b). Unlike SVR, they explicitly model uncertainty in the data and in the predictions. This makes GPs very applicable when well-calibrated uncertainty estimates are required. Furthermore, they are very flexible in terms of modelling decisions by allowing the use of a variety of kernels and likelihoods while providing efficient ways of doing model selection. Therefore, in this work we focus on GPs for probabilistic modelling of QE. In what follows we briefly describe the GPs framework for regression.

2.1 Gaussian Process Regression

Here we follow closely the definition of GPs given by Rasmussen and Williams (2006). Let $\mathcal{X} = \{(\mathbf{x}_1, y_1), (\mathbf{x}_2, y_2), \ldots, (\mathbf{x}_n, y_n)\}$ be our data, where each $\mathbf{x} \in \mathbb{R}^D$ is a D-dimensional input and y is its corresponding response variable. A GP is defined as a stochastic model over the latent function f that generates the data $\mathcal{X}$:

$$f(\mathbf{x}) \sim \mathcal{GP}(m(\mathbf{x}), k(\mathbf{x}, \mathbf{x}')),$$

where $m(\mathbf{x})$ is the *mean* function, which is usually the 0 constant, and $k(\mathbf{x}, \mathbf{x}')$ is the kernel or *covariance* function, which describes the covariance between values of f at the different locations of $\mathbf{x}$ and $\mathbf{x}'$.

The prior is combined with a likelihood via Bayes' rule to obtain a posterior over the latent function:

$$p(f|\mathcal{X}) = \frac{p(\mathbf{y}|\mathbf{X}, f)p(f)}{p(\mathbf{y}|\mathbf{X})},$$

where $\mathbf{X}$ and $\mathbf{y}$ are the training inputs and response variables, respectively. For regression, we assume that each $y_i = f(\mathbf{x}_i) + \eta$, where $\eta \sim \mathcal{N}(0, \sigma_n^2)$ is added white noise. Having a Gaussian likelihood results in a closed form solution for the posterior.

Training a GP involves the optimisation of model hyperparameters, which is done by maximising the marginal likelihood $p(\mathbf{y}|\mathbf{X})$ via gradient ascent. Predictive posteriors for unseen $\mathbf{x}_*$ are obtained by integrating over the latent function evaluations at $\mathbf{x}_*$.

GPs can be extended in many different ways by applying different kernels, likelihoods and modifying the posterior, for instance. In the next Sections, we explain in detail some sensible modelling choices in applying GPs for QE.

2.2 Matèrn Kernels

Choosing an appropriate kernel is a crucial step in defining a GP model (and any other kernel method). A common choice is to employ the exponentiated quadratic (EQ) kernel[1]:

$$k_{\text{EQ}}(\mathbf{x}, \mathbf{x}') = \sigma_v \exp\left(-\frac{r^2}{2}\right),$$

$$\text{where } r^2 = \sum_{i=1}^{D} \frac{(x_i - x_i')^2}{l_i^2}$$

is the scaled distance between the two inputs, σ_v is a scale hyperparameter and l is a vector of lengthscales. Most kernel methods tie all lengthscale to a single value, resulting in an isotropic kernel. However, since in GPs hyperparameter optimisation can be done efficiently, it is common to employ one lengthscale per feature, a method called Automatic Relevance Determination (ARD).

The EQ kernel allows the modelling of non-linearities between the inputs and the response variables but it makes a strong assumption: it generates smooth, infinitely differentiable functions. This assumption can be too strong for noisy data. An alternative is the Matèrn class of kernels, which relax the smoothness assumption by modelling functions which are ν-times differentiable only. Common values for ν are the half-integers $3/2$ and $5/2$, resulting in the following Matèrn kernels:

$$k_{\text{M32}} = \sigma_v(1 + \sqrt{3r^2}) \exp(-\sqrt{3r^2})$$

$$k_{\text{M52}} = \sigma_v\left(1 + \sqrt{5r^2} + \frac{5r^2}{3}\right) \exp(-\sqrt{5r^2}),$$

where we have omitted the dependence of k_{M32} and k_{M52} on the inputs $(\mathbf{x}, \mathbf{x}')$ for brevity. Higher values for ν are usually not very useful since the resulting behaviour is hard to distinguish from limit case $\nu \to \infty$, which retrieves the EQ kernel (Rasmussen and Williams, 2006, Sec. 4.2).

The relaxed smoothness assumptions from the Matèrn kernels makes them promising candidates for QE datasets, which tend to be very noisy. We expect that employing them will result in a better models for this application.

2.3 Warped Gaussian Processes

The Gaussian likelihood of standard GPs has support over the entire real number line. However, common quality scores are strictly positive values, which means that the Gaussian assumption

is not ideal. A usual way to deal with this problem is model the logarithm of the response variables, since this transformation maps strictly positive values to the real line. However, there is no reason to believe this is the best possible mapping: a better idea would be to learn it from the data.

Warped GPs (Snelson et al., 2004) are an extension of GPs that allows the learning of arbitrary mappings. It does that by placing a monotonic *warping function* over the observations and modelling the warped values inside a standard GP. The posterior distribution is obtained by applying a change of variables:

$$p(y_*|\mathbf{x}_*) = \frac{f'(y_*)}{\sqrt{2\pi\sigma_*^2}} \exp\left(\frac{f(y_*) - \mu_*}{2\sigma_*}\right),$$

where μ_* and σ_* are the mean and standard deviation of the latent (warped) response variable and f and f' are the warping function and its derivative.

Point predictions from this model depend on the loss function to be minimised. For absolute error, the median is the optimal value while for squared error it is the mean of the posterior. In standard GPs, since the posterior is Gaussian the median and mean coincide but this in general is not the case for a Warped GP posterior. The median can be easily obtained by applying the inverse warping function to the latent median:

$$y_*^{\text{med}} = f^{-1}(\mu_*).$$

While the inverse of the warping function is usually not available in closed form, we can use its gradient to have a numerical estimate.

The mean is obtained by integrating y^* over the latent density:

$$\mathbb{E}[y_*] = \int f^{-1}(z)\mathcal{N}_z(\mu_*, \sigma_*^2)dz,$$

where z is the latent variable. This can be easily approximated using Gauss-Hermite quadrature since it is a one dimensional integral over a Gaussian density.

The warping function should be flexible enough to allow the learning of complex mappings, but it needs to be monotonic. Snelson et al. (2004) proposes a parametric form composed of a sum of tanh functions, similar to a neural network layer:

$$f(y) = y + \sum_{i=1}^{I} a_i \tanh(b_i(y + c_i)),$$

---

where I is the number of tanh terms and $\mathbf{a}, \mathbf{b}$ and $\mathbf{c}$ are treated as model hyperparameters and optimised jointly with the kernel and likelihood hyperparameters. Large values for I allow more complex mappings to be learned but raise the risk of overfitting.

Warped GPs provide an easy and elegant way to model response variables with non-Gaussian behaviour within the GP framework. In our experiments we explore models employing warping functions with up to 3 terms, which is the value recommended by Snelson et al. (2004). We also report results using the $f(y) = \log(y)$ warping function.

3 Intrinsic Uncertainty Evaluation

Given a set of different probabilistic QE models, we are interested in evaluating the performance of these models, while also taking their uncertainty into account, particularly to distinguish among models with seemingly same or similar performance. A straightforward way to measure the performance of a probabilistic model is to inspect its negative (log) marginal likelihood. This measure, however, does not capture if a model overfit the training data.

We can have a better generalisation measure by calculating the likelihood on *test data* instead. This was proposed in previous work and it is called Negative Log Predictive Density (NLPD) (Quiñonero-Candela et al., 2006):

$$\text{NLPD}(\hat{\mathbf{y}}, \mathbf{y}) - -\frac{1}{n}\sum_{i=1}^{n}\log p(\hat{y}_i = y_i | \mathbf{x}_i).$$

where $\hat{\mathbf{y}}$ is a set of test predictions, $\mathbf{y}$ is the set of true labels and n is the test set size. This metric has since been largely adopted by the ML community when evaluating GPs and other probabilistic models for regression (see Section 5 for some examples).

As with other error metrics, lower values are better. Intuitively, if two models produce equally incorrect predictions but they have different uncertainty estimates, NLPD will penalise the overconfident model more than the underconfident one. On the other hand, if predictions are close to the true value then NLPD will penalise the underconfident model instead.

In our first set of experiments we evaluate models proposed in Section 2 according to their negative log likelihood (NLL) and the NLPD on test

data. We also report two point estimate metrics on test data: Mean Absolute Error (MAE), the most commonly used evaluation metric in QE, and Pearson's r, which has recently proposed by Graham (2015) as a more robust alternative.

3.1 Experimental Settings

Our experiments comprise datasets containing three different language pairs, where the label to predict is post-editing time:

English-Spanish (en-es) This dataset was used in the WMT14 QE shared task (Bojar et al., 2014). It contains 858 sentences translated by one MT system and post-edited by a professional translator.

French-English (fr-en) Described in (Specia, 2011), this dataset contains 2,525 sentences translated by one MT system and post-edited by a professional translator.

English-German (en-de) This dataset is part of the WMT16 QE shared task[2]. It was translated by one MT system for consistency we use a subset of 2,828 instances post-edited by a single professional translator.

As part of the process of creating these datasets, post-editing time was logged on an sentence basis for all datasets. Following common practice, we normalise the post-editing time by the length of the machine translated sentence to obtain post-editing *rates* and use these as our response variables.

Technically our approach could be used with any other numeric quality labels from the literature, including the commonly used Human Translation Error Rate (HTER) (Snover et al., 2006). Our decision to focus on post-editing time was based on the fact that time is a more complete measure of post-editing effort, capturing not only technical effort like HTER, but also cognitive effort (Koponen et al., 2012). Additionally, time is more directly applicable in real translation environments – where uncertainty estimates could be useful, as it relates directly to productivity measures.

For model building, we use a standard set of 17 features from the QuEst framework (Specia et al., 2015). These features are used in the strong baseline models provided by the WMT

---

[2] www.statmt.org/wmt16

QE shared tasks. While the best performing systems in the shared tasks use larger feature sets, these are mostly resource-intensive and language-dependent, and therefore not equally applicable to all our language pairs. Moreover, our goal is to compare probabilistic QE models through the predictive uncertainty perspective, rather than improving the state-of-the-art in terms of point predictions. We perform 10-fold cross validation instead of using a single train/test splits and report averaged metric scores.

The model hyperparameters were optimised by maximising the likelihood on the training data. We perform a two-pass procedure similar to that in (Cohn and Specia, 2013): first we employ an isotropic kernel and optimise all hyperparameters using 10 random restarts; then we move to an ARD equivalent kernel and perform a final optimisation step to fine tune feature *lengthscales*. Point predictions were fixed as the median of the distribution.

3.2 Results and Discussion

Table 1 shows the results obtained for all datasets. The first two columns shows an interesting finding in terms of model learning: using a warping function drastically decreases both NLL and NLPD. The main reason behind this is that standard GPs distribute probability mass over negative values, while the warped models do not. For the **fr-en** and **en-de** datasets, NLL and NLPD follow similar trends. This means that we can trust NLL as a measure of uncertainty for these datasets. However, this is not observed in the **en-es** dataset. Since this dataset is considerably smaller than the others, we believe this is evidence of overfitting, thus showing that NLL is not a reliable metric for small datasets.

In terms of different warping functions, using the parametric tanh function with 3 terms performs better than the log for the **fr-en** and **en-de** datasets. This is not the case of the **en-es** dataset, where the log function tends to perform better. We believe that this is again due to the smaller dataset size. The gains from using a Matèrn kernel over EQ are less conclusive. While they tend to perform better for **fr-en**, there does not seem to be any difference in the other datasets. Different kernels can be more appropriate depending on the language pair, but more experiments are needed to verify this, which we leave for future work.

English-Spanish - 858 instances			
	NLL	NLPD	MAE	r
EQ	1244.03	1.632	0.828	0.362
Mat32	1237.48	1.649	0.862	0.330
Mat52	1240.76	1.637	0.853	0.340
log EQ	986.14	1.277	0.798	0.368
log Mat32	982.71	1.271	0.793	0.380
log Mat52	982.31	1.272	0.794	0.376
tanh1 EQ	992.19	1.274	0.790	0.375
tanh1 Mat32	991.39	1.272	0.790	0.379
tanh1 Mat52	992.20	1.274	0.791	0.376
tanh2 EQ	982.43	1.275	0.792	0.376
tanh2 Mat32	982.40	1.281	0.791	0.382
tanh2 Mat52	981.86	1.282	0.792	0.278
tanh3 EQ	980.50	1.282	0.791	0.380
tanh3 Mat32	981.20	1.282	0.791	0.380
tanh3 Mat52	980.70	1.275	0.790	0.385

French-English - 2525 instances			
	NLL	NLPD	MAE	r
EQ	2334.17	1.039	0.491	0.322
Mat32	2335.81	1.040	0.491	0.320
Mat52	2344.86	1.037	0.490	0.320
log EQ	1935.71	0.855	0.493	0.314
log Mat32	1949.02	0.857	0.493	0.310
log Mat52	1937.31	0.855	0.493	0.313
tanh1 EQ	1884.82	0.840	0.482	0.322
tanh1 Mat32	1890.34	0.840	0.482	0.317
tanh1 Mat52	1887.41	0.834	0.482	0.320
tanh2 EQ	1762.33	0.775	0.483	0.323
tanh2 Mat32	1717.62	0.754	0.483	0.313
tanh2 Mat52	1748.62	0.768	0.486	0.306
tanh3 EQ	1814.99	0.803	0.484	0.314
tanh3 Mat32	1723.89	0.760	0.486	0.302
tanh3 Mat52	1706.28	0.751	0.482	0.320

English-German - 2828 instances			
	NLL	NLPD	MAE	r
EQ	4852.80	1.865	1.103	0.359
Mat32	4850.27	1.861	1.098	0.369
Mat52	4850.33	1.861	1.098	0.369
log EQ	4053.43	1.581	1.063	0.360
log Mat32	4054.51	1.580	1.063	0.363
log Mat52	4054.39	1.581	1.064	0.363
tanh1 EQ	4116.86	1.597	1.068	0.343
tanh1 Mat32	4113.74	1.593	1.064	0.351
tanh1 Mat52	4112.91	1.595	1.068	0.349
tanh2 EQ	4032.70	1.570	1.060	0.359
tanh2 Mat32	4031.42	1.570	1.060	0.362
tanh2 Mat52	4032.06	1.570	1.060	0.361
tanh3 EQ	4023.72	1.569	1.062	0.359
tanh3 Mat32	4024.64	1.567	1.058	0.364
tanh3 Mat52	4026.07	1.566	1.059	0.365

Table 1: Intrinsic evaluation results. The first three rows in each table correspond to standard GP models, while the remaining rows are Warped GP models with different warping functions. The number after the tanh models shows the number of terms in the warping function (see Equation 2.3). All r scores have $p < 0.05$.

The differences in uncertainty modelling are by and large not captured by the point estimate metrics. While MAE does show gains from standard to Warped GPs, it does not reflect the difference found between warping functions for **fr-en**. Pearson's r is also quite inconclusive in this sense, except for some observed gains for **en-es**. This shows that NLPD indeed should be preferred as a evaluation metric when proper prediction uncertainty estimates are required by a QE model.

3.3 Qualitative Analysis

To obtain more insights about the performance in uncertainty modelling we inspected the predictive distributions for two sentence pairs in the **fr-en** dataset. We show the distributions for a standard GP and a Warped GP with a $\mathrm{tanh}3$ function in Figure 1. In the first case, where both models give accurate predictions, we see that the Warped GP distribution is peaked around the predicted value, as it should be. It also gives more probability mass to positive values, showing that the model is able to learn that the label is non-negative. In the second case we analyse the distributions when both models make inaccurate predictions. We can see that the Warped GP is able to give a broader distribution in this case, while still keeping most of the mass outside the negative range.

We also report above each plot in Figure 1 the NLPD for each prediction. Comparing only the Warped GP predictions, we can see that their values reflect the fact that we prefer sharp distributions when predictions are accurate and broader ones when predictions are not accurate. However, it is interesting to see that the metric also penalises predictions when their distributions are too broad, as it is the case with the standard GPs since they can not discriminate between positive and negative values as well as the Warped GPs.

Inspecting the resulting warping functions can bring additional modelling insights. In Figure 2 we show instances of $\mathrm{tanh}3$ warping functions learned from the three datasets and compare them with the $\log$ warping function. We can see that the parametric $\mathrm{tanh}3$ model is able to learn non-trivial mappings. For instance, in the **en-es** case the learned function is roughly logarithmic in the low scales but it switches to a linear mapping after $y = 4$. Notice also the difference in the scales, which means that the optimal model uses a latent Gaussian with a larger variance.

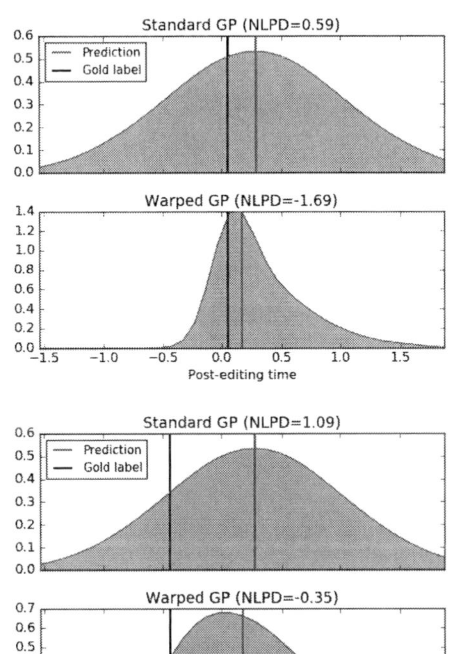

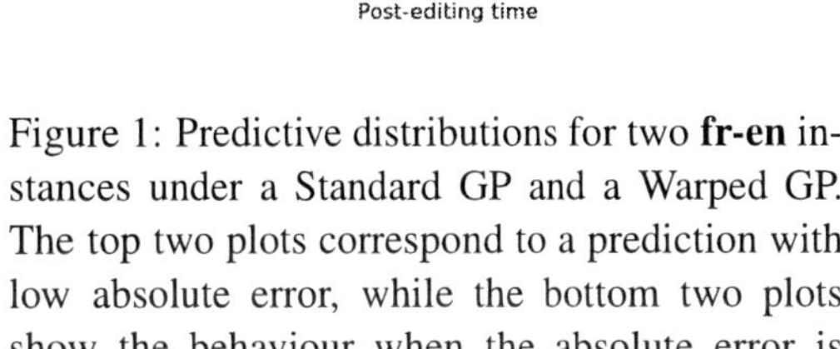

Figure 1: Predictive distributions for two **fr-en** instances under a Standard GP and a Warped GP. The top two plots correspond to a prediction with low absolute error, while the bottom two plots show the behaviour when the absolute error is high.

4 Asymmetric Risk Scenarios

Evaluation metrics for QE, including those used in the WMT QE shared tasks, are assumed to be symmetric, i.e., they penalise over and underestimates equally. This assumption is however too simplistic for many possible applications of QE. For example:

- In a *post-editing* scenario, a project manager may have translators with limited expertise in post-editing. In this case, automatic translations should not be provided to the translator unless they are highly likely to have very good quality. This can be enforced this by increasing the penalisation weight for underestimates. We call this the *pessimistic* scenario.

- In a *gisting* scenario, a company wants to automatically translate their product reviews so

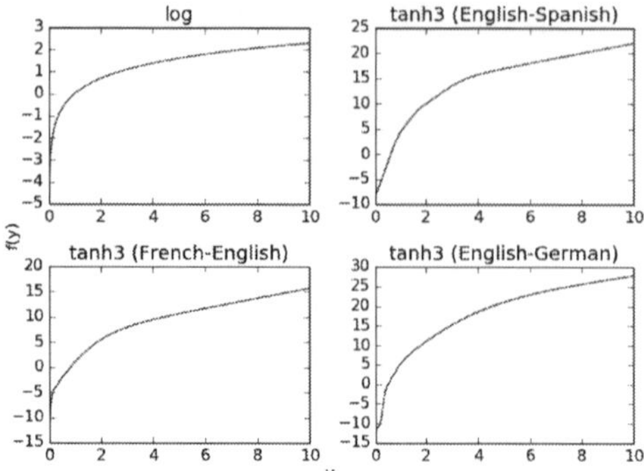

Figure 2: Warping function instances from the three datasets. The vertical axis correspond to the latent warped values. The horizontal axis show the observed response variables, which are always positive in our case since they are post-editing times.

that they can be published in a foreign language without human intervention. The company would prefer to publish only the reviews translated well enough, but having more reviews published will increase the chances of selling products. In this case, having better recall is more important and thus only reviews with very poor translation quality should be discarded. We can accomplish this by heavier penalisation on overestimates, a scenario we call *optimistic*.

In this Section we show how these scenarios can be addressed by well-calibrated predictive distributions and by employing *asymmetric* loss functions. An example of such a function is the asymmetric linear (henceforth, AL) loss, which is a generalisation of the absolute error:

$$L(\hat{y}, y) = \begin{cases} w(\hat{y} - y) & \text{if } \hat{y} > y \\ y - \hat{y} & \text{if } \hat{y} \leq y, \end{cases}$$

where $w > 0$ is the weight given to overestimates. If $w > 1$ we have the pessimistic scenario, and the optimistic one can be obtained using $0 < w < 1$. For $w = 1$ we retrieve the original absolute error loss.

Another asymmetric loss is the linear exponential or *linex* loss (Zellner, 1986):

$$L(\hat{y}, y) = \exp[w(\hat{y} - y)] - (\hat{y} - y) - 1$$

where $w \in \mathbb{R}$ is the weight. This loss attempts to keep a linear penalty in lesser risk regions, while imposing an exponential penalty in the higher risk ones. Negative values for w will result in a pessimistic setting, while positive values will result in the optimistic one. For $w = 0$, the loss approximates a squared error loss. Usual values for w tend to be close to 1 or -1 since for higher weights the loss can quickly reach very large scores. Both losses are shown on Figure 3.

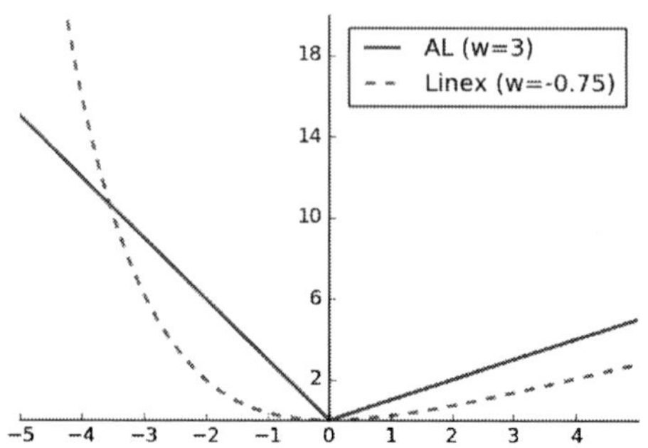

Figure 3: Asymmetric losses. These curves correspond to the pessimistic scenario since they impose larger penalties when the prediction is lower than the true label. In the optimistic scenario the curves would be reflected with respect to the vertical axis.

4.1 Bayes Risk for Asymmetric Losses

The losses introduced above can be incorporated directly into learning algorithms to obtain models for a given scenario. In the context of the AL loss this is called *quantile regression* (Koenker, 2005), since optimal estimators for this loss are posterior quantiles. However, in a production environment the loss can change over time. For instance, in the gisting scenario discussed above the parameter w could be changed based on feedback from indicators of sales revenue or user experience. If the loss is attached to the underlying learning algorithms, a change in w would require full model retraining, which can be costly.

Instead of retraining the model every time there is a different loss, we can train a single probabilistic model and derive Bayes risk estimators for the loss we are interested in. This allows estimates to be obtained without having to retrain models when the loss changes. Additionally, this allows different losses/scenarios to be employed at the same time using the same model.

Minimum Bayes risk estimators for asymmetric losses were proposed by Christoffersen and

Diebold (1997) and we follow their derivations in our experiments. The best estimator for the AL loss is equivalent to the $\frac{w}{w+1}$ quantile of the predictive distribution. Note that we retrieve the median when $w = 1$, as expected. The best estimator for the linex loss can be easily derived and results in:

$$\hat{y} = \mu_y - \frac{w\sigma_y^2}{2}$$

where μ_y and σ_y^2 are the mean and the variance of the predictive posterior.

4.2 Experimental Settings

Here we assess the models and datasets used in Section 3.1 in terms of their performance in the asymmetric setting. Following the explanation in the previous Section, we do not perform any re-training: we collect the predictions obtained using the 10-fold cross-validation protocol and apply different Bayes estimators corresponding to the asymmetric losses. Evaluation is performed using the same loss employed in the estimator (for instance, when using the linex estimator with $w = 0.75$ we report the results using the linex loss with same w) and averaged over the 10 folds.

To simulate both pessimistic and optimistic scenarios, we use $w \in \{3, 1/3\}$ for the AL loss and $w \in \{-0.75, 0.75\}$ for the linex loss. The only exception is the **en-de** dataset, where we report results for $w \in -0.25, 0.75$ for linex[3]. We also report results only for models using the Matèrn52 kernel. While we did experiment with different kernels and weighting schemes[4] our findings showed similar trends so we omit them for the sake of clarity.

4.3 Results and Discussion

Results are shown on Table 2. In the optimistic scenario the tanh-based warped GP models give consistently better results than standard GPs. The log-based models also gives good results for AL but for linex the results are mixed except for en-es. This is probably again related to the larger sizes of the fr-en and en-de datasets, which allows the tanh-based models to learn richer representations.

---

[3]Using $w = -0.75$ in this case resulted in loss values on the order of 10^7. In fact, as it will be discussed in the next Section, the results for the linex loss in the pessimistic scenario were inconclusive. However, we report results using a higher w in this case for completeness and to clarify the inconclusive trends we found.

[4]We also tried $w \in \{1/9, 1/7, 1/5, 5, 7, 9\}$ for the AL loss and $w \in \{-0.5, -0.25, 0.25, 0.5\}$ for the linex loss.

English-Spanish				
	Optimistic		**Pessimistic**	
	AL	Linex	AL	Linex
Std GP	1.187	0.447	1.633	3.009
log	1.060	0.299	1.534	3.327
tanh1	1.050	0.300	1.528	3.251
tanh2	1.054	0.300	1.543	3.335
tanh3	1.053	0.299	1.538	3.322

French-English				
	Optimistic		**Pessimistic**	
	AL	Linex	AL	Linex
Std GP	0.677	0.127	0.901	0.337
log	0.675	0.161	0.914	0.492
tanh1	0.677	0.124	0.901	0.341
tanh2	0.671	0.121	0.894	0.347
tanh3	0.666	0.120	0.886	0.349

English-German				
	Optimistic		**Pessimistic**	
	AL	Linex	AL	Linex
Std GP	1.528	0.610	2.120	0.217
log	1.457	0.537	2.049	0.222
tanh1	1.459	0.503	2.064	0.220
tanh2	1.455	0.504	2.045	0.220
tanh3	1.456	0.497	2.042	0.219

Table 2: Asymmetric loss experiments results. The first line in each table corresponds to a standard GP while the others are Warped GPs with different warping functions. All models use the Matèrn52 kernel. The optimistic setting corresponds to $w = 1/3$ for AL and $w = 0.75$ for linex. The pessimistic setting uses $w = 3$ for AL and $w = -0.75$ for linex, except for English-German, where $w = -0.25$.

The pessimistic scenario shows interesting trends. While the results for AL follow a similar pattern when compared to the optimistic setting, the results for linex are consistently worse than the standard GP baseline. A key difference between AL and linex is that the latter depends on the variance of the predictive distribution. Since the warped models tend to have less variance, we believe the estimator is not being "pushed" towards the positive tails as much as in the standard GPs. This turns the resulting predictions not conservative enough (i.e. the post-editing time predictions are lower) and this is heavily (exponentially) penalised by the loss. This might be a case where a standard GP is preferred but can also indicate that this loss is biased towards models with high variance, even if it does that by assigning probability mass to nonsensical values (like negative time). We leave further investigation of this phenomenon for future work.

5 Related Work

Quality Estimation is generally framed as text regression task, similarly to many other applications such as movie revenue forecasting based on reviews (Joshi et al., 2010; Bitvai and Cohn, 2015) and detection of emotion strength in news headlines (Strapparava and Mihalcea, 2008; Beck et al., 2014a) and song lyrics (Mihalcea and Strapparava, 2012). In general, these applications are evaluated in terms of their point estimate predictions, arguably because not all of them employ probabilistic models.

The NLPD is common and established metric used in the GP literature to evaluate new approaches. Examples include the original work on Warped GPs (Snelson et al., 2004), but also others like Lázaro-Gredilla (2012) and Chalupka et al. (2013). It has also been used to evaluate recent work on uncertainty propagation methods for neural networks (Hernández-Lobato and Adams, 2015).

Asymmetric loss functions are common in the econometrics literature and were studied by Zellner (1986) and Koenker (2005), among others. Besides the AL and the linex, another well studied loss is the asymmetric quadratic, which in turn relates to the concept of *expectiles* (Newey and Powell, 1987). This loss generalises the commonly used squared error loss. In terms of applications, Cain and Janssen (1995) gives an example in real estate assessment, where the consequences of under- and over-assessment are usually different depending on the specific scenario. An engineering example is given by Zellner (1986) in the context of dam construction, where an underestimate of peak water level is much more serious than an overestimate. Such real-world applications guided many developments in this field: we believe that translation and other language processing scenarios which rely on NLP technologies can heavily benefit from these advancements.

6 Conclusions

This work explored new probabilistic models for machine translation QE that allow better uncertainty estimates. We proposed the use of NLPD, which can capture information on the whole predictive distribution, unlike usual point estimate-based metrics. By assessing models using NLPD we can make better informed decisions about which model to employ for different settings. Furthermore, we showed how information in the predictive distribution can be used in asymmetric loss scenarios and how the proposed models can be beneficial in these settings.

Uncertainty estimates can be useful in many other settings beyond the ones explored in this work. Active Learning can benefit from variance information in their query methods and it has shown to be useful for QE (Beck et al., 2013). Exploratory analysis is another avenue for future work, where error bars can provide further insights about the task, as shown in recent work (Nguyen and O'Connor, 2015). This kind of analysis can be useful for tracking post-editor behaviour and assessing cost estimates for translation projects, for instance.

Our main goal in this paper was to raise awareness about how different modelling aspects should be taken into account when building QE models. Decision making can be risky using simple point estimates and we believe that uncertainty information can be beneficial in such scenarios by providing more informed solutions. These ideas are not restricted to QE and we hope to see similar studies in other natural language applications in the future.

Acknowledgements

Daniel Beck was supported by funding from CNPq/Brazil (No. 237999/2012-9). Lucia Specia was supported by the QT21 project (H2020 No. 645452). Trevor Cohn is the recipient of an Australian Research Council Future Fellowship (project number FT130101105). The authors would like to thank James Hensman for his advice on Warped GPs and the three anonymous reviewers for their comments.

References

Naoki Abe and Hiroshi Mamitsuka. 1998. Query learning strategies using boosting and bagging. In

Proceedings of the Fifteenth International Conference on Machine Learning, pages 1–9.

Daniel Beck, Lucia Specia, and Trevor Cohn. 2013. Reducing Annotation Effort for Quality Estimation via Active Learning. In *Proceedings of ACL*.

Daniel Beck, Trevor Cohn, and Lucia Specia. 2014a. Joint Emotion Analysis via Multi-task Gaussian Processes. In *Proceedings of EMNLP*, pages 1798–1803.

Daniel Beck, Kashif Shah, and Lucia Specia. 2014b. SHEF-Lite 2.0 : Sparse Multi-task Gaussian Processes for Translation Quality Estimation. In *Proceedings of WMT14*, pages 307–312.

Zsolt Bitvai and Trevor Cohn. 2015. Non-Linear Text Regression with a Deep Convolutional Neural Network. In *Proceedings of ACL*.

John Blatz, Erin Fitzgerald, and George Foster. 2004. Confidence estimation for machine translation. In *Proceedings of the 20th Conference on Computational Linguistics*, pages 315–321.

Ondej Bojar, Christian Buck, Chris Callison-Burch, Christian Federmann, Barry Haddow, Philipp Koehn, Christof Monz, Matt Post, Radu Soricut, and Lucia Specia. 2013. Findings of the 2013 Workshop on Statistical Machine Translation. In *Proceedings of WMT13*, pages 1–44.

Ondej Bojar, Christian Buck, Christian Federmann, Barry Haddow, Philipp Koehn, Johannes Leveling, Christof Monz, Pavel Pecina, Matt Post, Herve Saint-amand, Radu Soricut, Lucia Specia, and Aleš Tamchyna. 2014. Findings of the 2014 Workshop on Statistical Machine Translation. In *Proceedings of WMT14*, pages 12–58.

Ondej Bojar, Rajen Chatterjee, Christian Federmann, Barry Haddow, Matthias Huck, Chris Hokamp, Philipp Koehn, Varvara Logacheva, Christof Monz, Matteo Negri, Matt Post, Carolina Scarton, Lucia Specia, and Marco Turchi. 2015. Findings of the 2015 Workshop on Statistical Machine Translation. In *Proceedings of WMT15*, pages 22–64.

Michael Cain and Christian Janssen. 1995. Real Estate Price Prediction under Asymmetric Loss. *Annals of the Institute of Statististical Mathematics*, 47(3):401–414.

Chris Callison-burch, Philipp Koehn, Christof Monz, Matt Post, Radu Soricut, and Lucia Specia. 2012. Findings of the 2012 Workshop on Statistical Machine Translation. In *Proceedings of WMT12*.

Krzysztof Chalupka, Christopher K. I. Williams, and Iain Murray. 2013. A Framework for Evaluating Approximation Methods for Gaussian Process Regression. *Journal of Machine Learning Research*, 14:333–350.

Peter F. Christoffersen and Francis X. Diebold. 1997. Optimal Prediction Under Asymmetric Loss. *Econometric Theory*, 13(06):808–817.

Trevor Cohn and Lucia Specia. 2013. Modelling Annotator Bias with Multi-task Gaussian Processes: An Application to Machine Translation Quality Estimation. In *Proceedings of ACL*, pages 32–42.

Yvette Graham. 2015. Improving Evaluation of Machine Translation Quality Estimation. In *Proceedings of ACL*.

James Hensman, Nicolò Fusi, and Neil D. Lawrence. 2013. Gaussian Processes for Big Data. In *Proceedings of UAI*, pages 282–290.

José Miguel Hernández-Lobato and Ryan P. Adams. 2015. Probabilistic Backpropagation for Scalable Learning of Bayesian Neural Networks. In *Proceedings of ICML*.

Mahesh Joshi, Dipanjan Das, Kevin Gimpel, and Noah A. Smith. 2010. Movie Reviews and Revenues: An Experiment in Text Regression. In *Proceedings of NAACL*.

Roger Koenker. 2005. *Quantile Regression*. Cambridge University Press.

Maarit Koponen, Wilker Aziz, Luciana Ramos, and Lucia Specia. 2012. Post-editing time as a measure of cognitive effort. In *Proceedings of WPTP*.

Miguel Lázaro-Gredilla. 2012. Bayesian Warped Gaussian Processes. In *Proceedings of NIPS*, pages 1–9.

Rada Mihalcea and Carlo Strapparava. 2012. Lyrics, Music, and Emotions. In *Proceedings of the Joint Conference on Empirical Methods in Natural Language Processing and Computational Natural Language Learning*, pages 590–599.

Whitney K. Newey and James L. Powell. 1987. Asymmetric Least Squares Estimation and Testing. *Econometrica*, 55(4).

Khanh Nguyen and Brendan O'Connor. 2015. Posterior Calibration and Exploratory Analysis for Natural Language Processing Models. In *Proceedings of EMNLP*, number September, page 15.

Joaquin Quiñonero-Candela, Carl Edward Rasmussen, Fabian Sinz, Olivier Bousquet, and Bernhard Schölkopf. 2006. Evaluating Predictive Uncertainty Challenge. MLCW 2005, *Lecture Notes in Computer Science*, 3944:1–27.

Carl Edward Rasmussen and Christopher K. I. Williams. 2006. *Gaussian processes for machine learning*, volume 1. MIT Press Cambridge.

Kashif Shah, Trevor Cohn, and Lucia Specia. 2013. An Investigation on the Effectiveness of Features for Translation Quality Estimation. In *Proceedings of MT Summit XIV*.

Edward Snelson, Carl Edward Rasmussen, and Zoubin Ghahramani. 2004. Warped Gaussian Processes. In *Proceedings of NIPS*.

Matthew Snover, Bonnie Dorr, Richard Schwartz, Linnea Micciulla, and John Makhoul. 2006. A study of translation edit rate with targeted human annotation. In *Proceedings of AMTA*.

Lucia Specia, Nicola Cancedda, Marc Dymetman, Marco Turchi, and Nello Cristianini. 2009. Estimating the sentence-level quality of machine translation systems. In *Proceedings of EAMT*, pages 28–35.

Lucia Specia, Gustavo Henrique Paetzold, and Carolina Scarton. 2015. Multi-level Translation Quality Prediction with QUEST++. In *Proceedings of ACL Demo Session*, pages 850–850.

Lucia Specia. 2011. Exploiting Objective Annotations for Measuring Translation Post-editing Effort. In *Proceedings of EAMT*, pages 73–80.

Carlo Strapparava and Rada Mihalcea. 2008. Learning to identify emotions in text. In *Proceedings of the 2008 ACM Symposium on Applied Computing*, pages 1556–1560.

Arnold Zellner. 1986. Bayesian Estimation and Prediction Using Asymmetric Loss Functions. *Journal of the American Statistical Association*, 81(394):446–451.

Cross-Lingual Named Entity Recognition via Wikification

Chen-Tse Tsai, Stephen Mayhew, and **Dan Roth**
University of Illinois, Urbana-Champaign
201 N. Goodwin, Urbana, Illinois, 61801
{ctsai12, mayhew2, danr}@illinois.edu

Abstract

Named Entity Recognition (NER) models for language L are typically trained using annotated data in that language. We study *cross-lingual NER*, where a model for NER in L is trained on another, source, language (or multiple source languages). We introduce a language independent method for NER, building on cross-lingual wikification, a technique that grounds words and phrases in non-English text into English Wikipedia entries. Thus, mentions in any language can be described using a set of categories and FreeBase types, yielding, as we show, strong language-independent features. With this insight, we propose an NER model that can be applied to all languages in Wikipedia. When trained on English, our model outperforms comparable approaches on the standard CoNLL datasets (Spanish, German, and Dutch) and also performs very well on low-resource languages (e.g., Turkish, Tagalog, Yoruba, Bengali, and Tamil) that have significantly smaller Wikipedia. Moreover, our method allows us to train on multiple source languages, typically improving NER results on the target languages. Finally, we show that our language-independent features can be used also to enhance monolingual NER systems, yielding improved results for all 9 languages.

1 Introduction

Named Entity Recognition (NER) is the task of identifying and typing phrases that contain the names of persons, organizations, locations, and so on. It is an information extraction task that is im-portant for understanding large bodies of text and is considered an essential pre-processing stage in Natural Language Processing (NLP) and Information Retrieval systems.

NER is successful for languages which have a large amount of annotated data, but for languages with little to no annotated data, this task becomes very challenging. There are two common approaches to address the lack of training data problem. The first approach is to automatically generate annotated training data in the target language from Wikipedia articles or from parallel corpora. The performance of this method depends on the quality of the generated data and how well the language-specific features are explored. The second approach is to train a model on another language which has abundant training data, and then apply the model directly on test documents in the target language. This direct transfer technique relies on developing language-independent features. Note that these two approaches are orthogonal and can be used together.

In this paper, we focus on the second, direct transfer setting. We propose a cross-lingual NER model which is trained on annotated documents in one or multiple source languages, and can be applied to all languages in Wikipedia. The model depends on a cross-lingual wikifier, which only requires multilingual Wikipedia, no sentence-aligned or word-aligned parallel text is needed.

The key contribution of this paper is the development of a method that makes use of cross-lingual wikification and entity linking (Tsai and Roth, 2016; Ji et al., 2015; Ji et al., 2016; Moro et al., 2014) to generate language-independent features for NER, and showing how useful this can be for training NER models with no annotation in the target language. Given a mention (sub-string) from a document written in a foreign language, the goal of cross-lingual wikification is to find the cor-

219

Proceedings of the 20th SIGNLL Conference on Computational Natural Language Learning (CoNLL), pages 219–228,
Berlin, Germany, August 7-12, 2016. ©2016 Association for Computational Linguistics

NER Tags:			Person		Location	
Sentence:	Schwierigkeiten beim nachvollziehenden	Verstehen	Albrecht Lehmann	läßt	Flüchtlinge und Vertriebene in	Westdeutschland
Wikipedia titles:	Problem_solving	Understanding	Albert,_Duke_of_Prussia	Jens_Lehmann	Refugee	Western_Germany
FreeBase types:	hobby media_genre	media_common quotation_subject	person noble_person	person athlete	field_of_study literature_subject	location country

Figure 1: An example of a German sentence. We ground each word to the English Wikipedia using a cross-lingual wikifier. A word is not linked if it is a stop word or the wikifier returns NIL. We can see that the FreeBase types are strong signals to NER even with imperfect disambiguation.

responding title in the English Wikipedia. Traditionally, wikification has been considered a downstream task of NER. That is, a named entity recognizer is first applied to identify mentions of interest, and then a wikifier is used to ground the extracted mentions to Wikipedia entries. In contrast to this traditional pipeline, we show that the ability to ground and disambiguate words is very useful to NER. By grounding every n-gram to the English Wikipedia, we obtain useful clues to NER, regardless of the target language.

Figure 1 shows an example of a German sentence. We use a cross-lingual wikifier to ground each word to the English Wikipedia. We can see that even though the disambiguation is not perfect, the FreeBase types still provide valuable information. That is, although "Albrecht Lehmann" is not an entry in Wikipedia, the wikifier still links "Albrecht" and "Lehmann" to people. Since words in any language are grounded to the English Wikipedia, the corresponding Wikipedia categories and Freebase types can be used as language-independent features.

The proposed model significantly outperforms comparable direct transfer methods on the Spanish, Dutch, and German CoNLL data. We also evaluate the model on five low-resource languages: Turkish, Tagalog, Yoruba, Bengali, and Tamil. Due to small sizes of Wikipedia, the overall performance is not as good as the CoNLL experiments. Nevertheless, the wikifier features still give significant improvements, and the proposed direct transfer model outperforms the state of the art, which assumes parallel text and some interaction with a native speaker of the target language. In addition, we show that the proposed language-independent features not only perform well on the direct transfer scenario, but also improve monolingual models, which are trained on the target language. Another advantage of the proposed direct transfer model is that we can train on documents from multiple languages together, and further im-

prove the results.

2   Related Work

There are three main branches of work for extending NLP systems to many languages: projection across parallel data, Wikipedia-based approaches, and direct transfer. Projection and direct transfer take advantage of the success of NLP tools on high-resource languages. Wikipedia-based approaches exploit the fact that, by editing Wikipedia, thousands of people have made annotations in hundreds of languages.

2.1   Projection

Projection methods take a parallel corpus between source and target languages, annotate the source side, and push annotations across learned alignment edges. Assuming that source side annotations are of high quality, success depends largely on the quality of the alignments, which depends, in turn, on the size of the parallel data, and the difficulty of aligning with the target language.

There is work on projection for POS tagging (Yarowsky et al., 2001; Das and Petrov, 2011; Duong et al., 2014), NER (Wang and Manning, 2014; Kim et al., 2012; Ehrmann et al., 2011), and parsing (Hwa et al., 2005; McDonald et al., 2011).

Wang and Manning (2014) show that projecting expectations of labels instead of hard labels can improve results. They experiment in two different settings: weakly-supervised, where only parallel data is available, and semi-supervised, where annotated training data is available along with unlabeled parallel data.

2.2   Using Wikipedia

Wikipedia has been used for a large number of NLP tasks, from use as a semantic space (Gabrilovich and Markovitch, 2007; Chang et al., 2008; Song and Roth, 2014), to generating parallel data (Smith et al., 2010), to use in open information extraction (Wu and Weld, 2010). It has also been used to extract training data for NER, under the intuition that Wikipedia is already (partially) annotated with NER labels, in the form of links to pages. Nothman et al. (2012) generate *silver-standard* NER data from Wikipedia using link targets, and other heuristics. This can be gathered for any language in Wikipedia, but several of the heuristics depend on language-specific rules. Al-Rfou et al. (2015) generate training data from Wikipedia articles using a similar manner. The polyglot word embeddings (Al-Rfou et al., 2013) are used as features in their NER model. Although the features are delexicalized, the embeddings are unique to each language, and so the model cannot transfer.

Kim et al. (2012) use Wikipedia to generate parallel sentences with NE annotations. They propose a semi-CRF model for aligning entities in parallel sentences. Results are very strong on Wikipedia data. This is a hybrid approach in that it is supervised projection using Wikipedia.

Our work is most closely related to Kazama and Torisawa (2007). They do NER using Wikipedia category features for each mention. However, their method for wikifying text is not robust to ambiguity, and they only do monolingual NER.

Sil and Yates (2013) create a joint model for NER and entity linking in English. They avoid the traditional pipeline by overgenerating mentions in the first stage and using NER features to rank candidates. While the results are promising, the model is not scalable to other languages because it requires both a trained NER and a NP chunker.

2.3 Direct Transfer

In direct transfer once trains a model in a high-resource setting using delexicalized features, that is, features that do not depend on word forms, and then directly applies it to text in a new language.

Täckström et al. (2012) experimented with direct transfer of dependency parsing and NER, and showed that using word cluster features can help, especially if the clusters are forced to conform across languages. The cross-lingual word clusters were induced using large parallel corpora.

Building on this work, Täckström (2012) focuses solely on NER, and includes experiments on self-training and multi-source transfer for NER. Their experiments are orthogonal to ours, and could be combined nicely. This work is closest to ours in terms of method, and therefore we compare against it in our experiments.

Base features
Non-Lexical
    Previous Tags (t_{i-1}, t_{i-2})
    Tag Context (distr. for $[w_i, w_{i+1}, w_{i+2}]$)
Lexical
    Forms $(..., w_{i-1}, w_i, w_{i+1}, ...)$
    Affixes   (prefixes and suffixes of w_i)
    Capitalization   (w_i capitalized?)
    Prev. Tag Pattern (t_{i-2}, w_{i-1}, w_i)
    Word type   (capital? digits? letter?)
Gazetteers
    Multilingual Wikipedia titles
Cross-lingual Wikifier Features
    Freebase types of (w_{i-1}, w_i, w_{i+1})
    Wikipedia categories of (w_{i-1}, w_i, w_{i+1})

Table 1: Feature groups. Base features are the features used by Ratinov and Roth (2009), the state of the art English NER model. Gazetteers and cross-lingual wikifier features are described in detail in Section 3.

pare against it in our experiments.

Our work falls under the umbrella of direct transfer methods combined with the use of Wikipedia. We introduce wikifier features, which are truly delexicalized, and use Wikipedia as a source of information for each language.

3 Named Entity Recognition Model

We use the state of the art English NER model of Ratinov and Roth (2009) as the base model. This model approaches NER as a multiclass classification problem with greedy decoding, using the BIO labeling scheme. The underlying classifier is averaged perceptron.

Table 1 summarizes the features used in our model. These can be divided into a base set of standard features which are included in Ratinov and Roth (2009), a set of gazetteer features which are based on titles in multilingual Wikipedia, and our novel cross-lingual wikifier features. The base set of features can be further divided into non-lexical and lexical categories.

3.1 Base Features

Non-Lexical Features Ratinov and Roth (2009) uses a small number of non-lexical features. For example, the previous tag feature is useful in predicting I- tags, because the previous tag should never be an O. The tag context feature looks in a

1000 word history and gathers statistics over tags assigned to words $[w_i, w_{i+1}, w_{i+2}]$. These features are included in all experiments.

In contrast with (Täckström et al., 2012), we do not use POS tags as features. We could not get the universal POS tags for all languages in our experiments, and an earlier experiment indicated that adding POS tags does not improve the performance due to the accuracy of tagger.

Lexical Features Lexical features are very important for monolingual NER. In the direct transfer setting, lexical features are useful if the target language is close to the training language. We use a small number of simple features, including word forms, affixes, capitalization, and tag patterns. The latter feature considers a small window (at most 2 tokens) before the word in question. If there is a named entity in the window, it makes a feature out of NETag$+w_{i-2} + w_{i-1}$. Word type features simply indicate whether the word in question is all capitalized, is all digits, or is all letters.

3.2 Gazetteer Features

One of the larger performance improvements in Ratinov and Roth (2009) came from the use of (partial matches with) gazetteers. We include gazetteers also in our model, except we gather them in each language from Wikipedia. As in Ratinov and Roth (2009), we use the gazetteers as features. Specifically, we group them by topic, and use the name of the gazetteer file as the feature.

The method iteratively extends a short window to the right of the word in question. As the window increases in size, we search all gazetteers for occurrences of the phrase in the window. If we find a match, we add a feature to each word in the phrase according to its position in the phrase, either B for beginning, or I for inside.

This method generalizes gazetteers to unseen entities. For example, given the phrase "Bill and Melinda Gates Foundation", "Bill" is marked as both B-PersonNames and B-Organizations, while "Foundation" is marked as I-Organizations. Imagine encountering at test time a fictional organization called "Dave and Sue Harris Foundation." Although there is no gazetteer that contains this name, we have learned that "B-PersonName and B-PersonName B-PersonName Foundation" is a strong signal for an organization.

3.3 Cross-lingual Wikifier Features

As shown in Figure 1, disambiguating words to Wikipedia entries allows us to obtain useful information for NER from the corresponding Free-Base types and Wikipedia categories. A cross-lingual wikifier grounds words and phrases of non-English languages to the English Wikipedia, which provides language-independent features for transferring an NER model directly.

We use the system proposed in Tsai and Roth (2016), which grounds input strings to the intersection of (the title spaces of) the English and the target language Wikipedias. The only requirement is a multilingual Wikipedia dump and it can be applied to all languages in Wikipedia.

Since we want to ground every n-gram ($n \leq 4$) in the document, deviating from the normal usage that only considers a few mentions of interest, we modify the system in the following two ways:

- The original candidate generation process queries the index by both whole input string and the individual tokens of the string. For the n-grams where $n > 1$, we generate title candidates only according to the whole string, not individual tokens. If we allow generating title candidates based on individual tokens then, for instance, the bigram "in Germany" will be linked to the title Germany thus wrongly considered as a named entity.

- The original ranking model includes the embeddings of other mentions in the document as features. It is clear that if we know what other important entities exist in the document, they provide useful clues to disambiguate a mention. However, if we want to wikify all n-grams, it makes no sense to include all of them as features, since the ranking model has already included features from TF-IDF weighted context words.

After wikifying every n-gram [1], we set the types of each n-gram as the coarse- and fine-grained FreeBase types and Wikipedia categories from the top 2 title candidates returned by wikifier. For each word w_i, we use the types of w_i, w_{i+1}, and w_{i-1}, and the types of the n-grams which contain w_i as features. Moreover, we also include wikifier's ranking features from the top candidate as features. This could serve as a linker (Ratinov et

---

[1] We set n to 4 in all our experiments.

al., 2011), which rejects the top prediction if it has a low confidence.

4 Experiments and Analysis

In this section, we conduct experiments to validate and analyze the proposed NER model. First, we show that adding wikifier features improves results on monolingual NER. Second, we show that wikifier features are strong signals in direct transfer of a trained NER model across languages. Finally, we explore the importance of Wikipedia size to the quality of wikifier features and study the use of multiple source languages.

4.1 Datasets

We use data from CoNLL2002/2003 shared tasks (Tjong Kim Sang, 2002; Tjong Kim Sang and De Meulder, 2003). The 4 languages represented are English, German, Spanish, and Dutch, each annotated using the IOB1 labeling scheme, which we convert to the BIO labeling scheme. All training is on the train set, and testing is on the test set. The evaluation metric for all experiments is phrase level F1, as explained in (Tjong Kim Sang, 2002). In order to experiment on a broader range of languages, we also use data from the REFLEX (Simpson et al., 2008) and LORELEI projects. From LORELEI, we use Turkish,[2] From REFLEX, we use Bengali, Tagalog, Tamil, and Yoruba.[3] While Turkish, Tagalog, and Yoruba each has a few non-Latin characters, Bengali and Tamil are with an entirely non-Latin script. This is a major reason for inclusion in our experiments. We use the same set of test documents as used in Zhang et al. (2016). All other documents in the REFLEX and LORELEI packages are used as the training documents in our monolingual experiments. We refer to these five languages collectively as low-resource languages.

Besides PER, LOC, and ORG, some low-resource languages contain TIME tags and TTL tags, which represented titles in text, such as Secretary, President, or Minister. Since such words are not tagged in the CoNLL training data, we opted to simply remove these tags. On the other hand, there is no MISC tag in the low-resource languages. Instead, many MISC-tagged entities in the CoNLL datasets have LOC tags in the RE-FLEX and LORELEI packages, e.g., Italian and Chinese. We modify a MISC-tagged word to LOC tag if it is grounded to an entity with location as a FreeBase type, and remove all the other MISC tags in the training data. This process of changing MISC tags is only done when we train on CoNLL documents and test on low-resource languages.

The only requirement to build the cross-lingual wikifier model is a multilingual Wikipedia dump, and it can be trivially applied to all languages in Wikipedia. The top section of Table 2 lists Wikipedia sizes in terms of articles,[4] the number of titles linked to English titles, and the number of training and test mentions for each language.

Besides the English gazetteers used in Ratinov and Roth (2009), we collect gazetteers for each language using Wikipedia titles. A Wikipedia title is included in the list for person names if it contains FreeBase type person. Similarly, we also create a location list and an organization list for each language. The total number of names in the gazetteers of each language is listed in Table 2.

4.2 Monolingual Experiments

We begin by showing that wikifier features help when we train and test on the same language. The middle section of Table 2 shows these results.

In the 'Wikifier only' row, we use only wikifier features and previous tags features. This is intended to show the predictive power of wikifier features alone. Without using any lexical features, it gets good scores on the languages that have a large Wikipedia. These numbers represent the quality of the cross-lingual wikifier in that language, which in turn is correlated with the size of Wikipedia and size of the intersection with English Wikipedia.

The next row, 'Base features', shows that lexical features are always better than wikifier features only. This agrees with the common wisdom that lexical features are important for NER.

Adding gazetteers to the base features improves by more than 3 points for higher-resource languages. This is because the low-resource languages have much smaller gazetteers which have lower coverage than other languages' gazetteers.

Finally, the '+Wikifier' row shows that our proposed features are valuable even in combination with strong features. It improves upon base features and gazetteer features for all 9 languages.

---

[2]LDC2014E115
[3]LDC2015E13,LDC2015E90,LDC2015E83,LDC2015E91

[4]From https://en.wikipedia.org/wiki/List_of_Wikipedias, retrieved March 2016

| | Latin Script | | | | | | | Non-Latin Script | | |
APPROACH	EN	NL	DE	ES	TR	TL	YO	BN	TA	AVG
Wiki size	5.1M	1.9M	1.9M	1.3M	269K	64K	31K	42K	85K	-
En. intersection	-	755K	964K	757K	169K	49K	30K	34K	51K	-
Gazetteer size	8.5M	579K	1M	943K	168K	54K	20K	29K	10K	-
Entities (train)	23.5K	18.8K	11.9K	13.3K	5.1K	4.6K	4.1K	8.8K	7.0K	-
Entities (test)	5.6K	3.6K	3.7K	3.9K	2.2K	3.4K	3.4K	3.5K	4.6K	-
Monolingual Experiments										
Wikifier only	71.57	57.02	49.74	60.13	52.84	51.02	29.35	47.78	38.05	50.83
Base Features	85.50	76.64	65.88	80.66	64.98	75.03	55.26	69.26	55.93	69.90
+Gazetteers	89.49	82.41	69.31	83.62	70.41	76.71	57.12	69.51	57.10	72.89
+Wikifier	**89.92**	**84.49**	**73.13**	**83.87**	**73.86**	**77.64**	**57.60**	**71.15**	**60.02**	**74.72**
Direct Transfer Experiments										
Wikifier only		40.44	39.83	43.82	41.79	42.11	27.91	**43.27**	**29.64**	38.01
Base Features		43.38	24.93	42.85	29.21	49.85	32.57	2.53	1.74	28.06
+Gazetteers		50.26	34.47	54.59	30.21	64.06	34.37	3.25	0.30	33.83
+Wikifier		**61.56**	**48.12**	**60.55**	**47.12**	**65.44**	**36.65**	18.18	5.65	**41.41**
Täckström baseline		48.4	23.5	45.6	-	-	-	-	-	-
Täckström bitext clusters		58.4	40.4	59.3	-	-	-	-	-	-
Zhang et al. (2016)		-	-	-	43.6	51.3	36.0	34.8	26.0	38.3

Table 2: **Data sizes, monolingual experiments, and direct transfer experiments**. Wiki size is the number of articles in Wikipedia. For monolingual experiments, we train the proposed model on the training data of the target languages. 'Wikifier only' uses the previous tags features also. For direct transfer experiments, all models are trained on CoNLL English training set. The rows marked Täckström come from (Täckström et al., 2012), and are the baseline and clustering result. The plus signs (+) signify cumulative addition. EN: English, NL: Dutch, DE: German, ES: Spanish, TR: Turkish, TL: Tagalog, YO: Yoruba, BN: Bengali, TA: Tamil.

These numbers may be less than state of the art because the features we use are designed for English, and may not capture lexical subtleties in every language. Nevertheless, they show that wikifier features have a non-trivial signal that has not been captured by other features.

4.3 Direct Transfer Experiments

We evaluate our direct transfer experiments by training on English and testing on the target language. The results from these experiments are shown in the bottom section of Table 2.

The 'Wikifier only' row shows that the wikifier features alone preserve a signal across languages. Interestingly, for both Bengali and Tamil, this is the strongest signal, and gets the highest score. If the lexical features are included when we train the English model, the learning algorithm will give them too much emphasis, thus decreasing the importance of the wikifier features. Since Bengali and Tamil use non-Latin scripts, no lexical feature in English will fire at test time. Thus, approaches that include base features perform poorly.

The results of 'Base features' can be viewed as a sort of language similarity to English, which, in this case, is related to lexical overlap and similarity between the scripts. Comparing to monolingual experiments, we can see that the lexical features become weak in the cross-lingual setting.

The gazetteer features are again shown to be very useful for almost all languages except Bengali and Tamil due to the reason explained in the monolingual experiment and to the inclusion of lexical features. For all other languages, the gain from adding gazetteers is even larger than it is in the monolingual setting.

For nearly every language, wikifier features help dramatically, which indicates that they are very good delexicalized features. Wikifier features add more than 10 points on Dutch, German, and Turkish.

The trend in Table 2 suggests the following strategy when we want to extract named entities in a new foreign language: It is better to include all features if the foreign language uses Latin script, since the names are likely to be mentioned similarly to the English names. Otherwise, using wikifier features only could be the best setting.

Täckström et al. (2012) also directly transfer an English NER model using the same setting as ours: train on the CoNLL English training set and predict on the test set of other three languages. We compare our baseline transfer model (Base Features) to the row denoted by "Täckström baseline". Even though we do not use gold POS tags, we see that our results are comparable. The second Täckström row uses parallel text to induce multilingual word clustering. While this approach is orthogonal to ours, and could be used in tandem to get even better scores, we compare against it for lack of a more closely aligned scenario. We see that for each language, our approach significantly outperforms their approach.

We note that our numbers are comparable to those reported for WIKI-2 in Nothman et al. (2012) for the CoNLL languages (with the exception of German, where their result is higher). However, they require language-specific heuristics to generate *silver-standard* training data from Wikipedia articles. What they gain for single languages, they likely lose in generalization to other languages. This approach is orthogonal to ours; we, too, can use their silver-standard data in training.

For the low-resource languages, we compare our direct transfer model with the expectation learning model proposed in Zhang et al. (2016). This model is not a direct transfer model, but it does not use any training data in the target languages either. Instead, for each target language, it generates patterns from parallel documents between English and the target language, a large monolingual corpus in the target language, and one-hour interaction with a native speaker of the target language. Note that they also use a cross-lingual wikifier, but only for refining the entity types. On the other hand, in our model, the features from the wikifier are used both in detecting entity mention boundaries and entity types. We can see that our approach performs better than their model on all five languages even though we assume much fewer resources. The difference is most significant on Turkish, Tagalog, and Bengali.

4.4 Quality of Wikifier Features

One immediate question is, why are wikifier features less helpful on the low-resource languages results than on the CoNLL languages? In this experiment, we show that smaller Wikipedia sizes result in worse Wikipedia features, which is the

FEATURES	SPANISH		GERMAN	
	#inter.	F1	#inter.	F1
Wikifier only	757K	43.82	964K	39.83
W.−FB query	757K	34.69	964K	28.27
W.−FB−50% inter.	379K	30.32	482K	27.24
W.−FB−90% inter.	76K	29.44	96K	25.94

Table 3: The F1 scores of using only wikifier features with removing the support from FreeBase and varying the number of titles linked to the English Wikipedia. 'W.−FB query' removes the component of querying FreeBase by the target language title from 'Wikifier only'. '−X% inter.' indicates removing X% of the interlanguage links with English titles. The column #inter. shows the number of titles that intersect with English.

reason Yoruba has bad 'Wikifier only' results and then only small improvement from the wikifier features over base features.

The cross-lingual wikifier that we use in our system only grounds words to the intersection of the English and target language Wikipedia. Given a Wikipedia title in the target language, we first retrieve FreeBase IDs by querying the FreeBase API. If it fails, we find the corresponding English Wikipedia title via interlanguage links and then query the API with the English title. However, FreeBase does not contain entities in Yoruba, Bengali, and Tamil, so the first step will always fail for these three languages. We remove this step in the experiments of high-resource languages and the results are shown in the row 'W.−FB query ' of Table 3. We see that the performance drops significantly, because many words have no features from FreeBase types.

Next, we randomly remove 50% and 90% of the interlanguage links to English titles. This will not only reduce the number of fired features from Wikipedia categories, but also FreeBase types since English titles are used to query FreeBase IDs. When 90% of interlanguage links are removed, the scores of Spanish and German are closer to Yoruba's score (27.91).

4.5 Training Languages

In all previous experiments, the training language is always English. In order to test the efficacy of training with languages other than English, we create a train/test matrix with all combinations of languages, as seen in Figure 2.

The vertical axis represents training language,

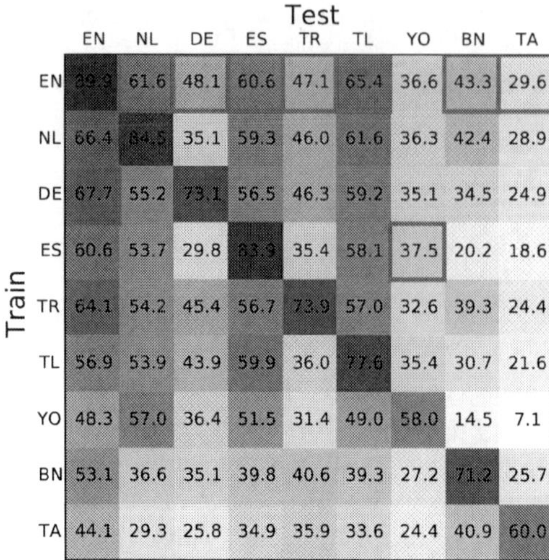

Figure 2: Different training/test language pairs. Scores shown are the F1 scores. The red boxes signify the best non-target training languages.

TRAINING LANG	TR	TL	YO	AVG
EN	47.12	65.44	36.65	49.74
EN+ES	44.85	66.61	37.57	49.68
EN+NL	48.34	66.09	36.87	50.43
EN+DE	49.47	64.10	35.14	49.57
EN+ES+NL+DE	49.00	66.37	**38.02**	51.13
ALL−Test Lang	**49.83**	**67.12**	37.56	**51.50**

Table 4: The F1 scores of the proposed direct transfer model on three low-resource languages using training data in multiple languages. The row "ALL−Test Lang" trains the model on all languages except the test language, Bengali, and Tamil. Bengali and Tamil are excluded since we use all features in this experiment.

and the horizontal axis represents test language. A darker color signifies a higher score. For example, if we train on Spanish (ES) and test on Yoruba (YO), we get an F1 of 37.5. When the training or test language is Bengali (BN) or Tamil (TA), we only use wikifier features. For other settings, all features are included. Note that when the test language is one of the CoNLL languages (EN, NL, DE, ES) and the training language is a non-CoNLL language, we ignore all MISC tags in evaluation, since there is no MISC tag in the low-resource languages. The diagonals represent the monolingual setting in which we use all features for all languages. Since we are interested in transferring a model, we ignore the diagonals, and identify the best training language for a given test language as the largest off-diagonal in each column. These are demarcated with red boxes.

English is the best for most languages, with the only exception of Spanish being the best for Yoruba. It makes sense that high-resource languages are better training languages because 1) there are more annotated training instances, 2) larger Wikipedia creates denser wikifier features, therefore providing better estimation of the weights to these features.

Table 4 shows the results of training on multiple languages. We use all features in this experiment. The row "EN" only trains the model on the English training documents, and the results are iden-

tical to those shown in Table 2. Using all CoNLL languages (EN+ES+NL+DE) adds more than 1 point F1 in average comparing to using English only. Finally, training on all but the test languages further improves the results.

This experiment shows that we can augment training data from other languages' annotated documents. Although the performance only increases a little, it does not hurt most of the time.

4.6 Domain Adaptation

To improve the results of the monolingual experiments, we consider the domain adaptation setting where there is annotated data for both source and target domains. The question is whether training data from the source domain can improve a model that is trained solely on the target-domain data. In this experiment, we use English as the source domain, and use Spanish, Dutch, Turkish, and Tagalog as four different target domains. We compare three approaches:

- **Target:** only uses the training data in the target domain. This is the setting of the monolingual experiments in Table 2.

- **Src+Tgt:** directly uses the training data from both source and target domains. This method is identical to the setting in our previous multi-source direct transfer experiments.

- **FrustEasy:** the "Frustratingly Easy" adaptation framework proposed by (Daumé, 2007).

All types of features are used in all settings. The results are shown in Table 5. We can see that although *Src+Tgt* is always the best approach, the improvement over the baseline, *Target*, is tiny.

APPROACH	ES	NL	TR	TL	AVG
Target	83.87	84.49	73.86	77.64	79.96
Src+Tgt	**84.17**	**84.81**	**74.52**	**77.80**	**80.33**
FrustEasy	83.89	84.08	73.73	77.04	79.69

Table 5: The domain adaptation experiments. The source domain (English) training examples are used to improve the monolingual baseline model (*Target*) which is only trained on the target domain (Spanish, Dutch, Turkish, and Tagalog) training data. The numbers are the phrase-level F1 scores.

Interestingly, the *FrustEasy* framework does not help for most languages. This result is consistent with the analysis and observation in Chang et al. (2010) that 1) when the source and target domains are very different, the baseline approach (*Target*) is very strong, and 2) when there are cross-domain clustering features (e.g., the wikifier features), *Src+Tgt* is better than *FrustEasy*. To further improve the monolingual baselines via adaptation from other languages, better cross-lingual or language-independent information may be needed.

5 Conclusion and Discussion

We propose a language-independent model for cross-lingual NER building on a cross-lingual wikifier. This model works on all languages in Wikipedia and the only requirement is a Wikipedia dump. We study a wide range of languages in both the monolingual and the cross-lingual settings, and show significant improvements over strong baselines. An analysis shows that the quality of the wikifier features depends on the Wikipedia size of the test language.

This work shows that if we can disambiguate words and phrases to the English Wikipedia, the typing information from Wikipedia categories and FreeBase are useful language-independent features for NER. However, there is additional information in Wikipedia that could be helpful and which we do not use, including words in the documents and relations between titles; this would require additional research.

In the future, we would like to experiment with combining our method with other techniques for multilingual NER (Section 2), including parallel projection and the automatic generation of training data from Wikipedia.

Acknowledgments

This research is supported by NIH grant U54-GM114838, a grant from the Allen Institute for Artificial Intelligence (allenai.org), and Contract HR0011-15-2-0025 with the US Defense Advanced Research Projects Agency (DARPA). Approved for Public Release, Distribution Unlimited. The views expressed are those of the authors and do not reflect the official policy or position of the Department of Defense or the U.S. Government.

References

Rami Al-Rfou, Bryan Perozzi, and Steven Skiena. 2013. Polyglot: Distributed word representations for multilingual NLP. In *Proceedings of the Seventeenth Conference on Computational Natural Language Learning*, pages 183–192, Sofia, Bulgaria, August. Association for Computational Linguistics.

Rami Al-Rfou, Vivek Kulkarni, Bryan Perozzi, and Steven Skiena. 2015. Polyglot-ner: Massive multilingual named entity recognition. In *Proceedings of the 2015 SIAM International Conference on Data Mining, Vancouver, British Columbia, Canada*. SIAM.

Ming-Wei Chang, Lev Ratinov, Dan Roth, and Vivek Srikumar. 2008. Importance of semantic representation: Dataless classification. In *Proceedings of the National Conference on Artificial Intelligence (AAAI)*, July.

Ming-Wei Chang, Michael Connor, and Dan Roth. 2010. The necessity of combining adaptation methods. In *Proceedings of the Conference on Empirical Methods for Natural Language Processing (EMNLP)*, Massachusetts, USA, 10.

D. Das and S. Petrov. 2011. Unsupervised part-of-speech tagging with bilingual graph-based projections. In *Proceedings of the Annual Meeting of the Association for Computational Linguistics (ACL)*, Portland, OR, June. Association for Computational Linguistics.

Hal Daumé. 2007. Frustratingly easy domain adaptation. In *Proceedings of the Annual Meeting of the Association for Computational Linguistics (ACL)*, pages 256–263, Prague, Czech Republic, June. Association for Computational Linguistics.

Long Duong, Trevor Cohn, Karin Verspoor, Steven Bird, and Paul Cook. 2014. What can we get from 1000 tokens? A case study of multilingual POS tagging for resource-poor languages. In *EMNLP*, pages 886–897. Citeseer.

Maud Ehrmann, Marco Turchi, and Ralf Steinberger. 2011. Building a multilingual named entity-annotated corpus using annotation projection. In *RANLP*.

Evgeniy Gabrilovich and Shaul Markovitch. 2007. Computing semantic relatedness using Wikipedia-based explicit semantic analysis. In *IJCAI*.

Rebecca Hwa, Philip Resnik, Amy Weinberg, Clara I. Cabezas, and Okan Kolak. 2005. Bootstrapping parsers via syntactic projection across parallel texts. *Natural Language Engineering*, 11:311–325.

H. Ji, J. Nothman, and B. Hachey. 2015. Overview of tac-kbp2014 entity discovery and linking tasks. In *Text Analysis Conference (TAC2014)*.

H. Ji, J. Nothman, B. Hachey, and R. Florian. 2016. Overview of tac-kbp2015 tri-lingual entity discovery and linking. In *Text Analysis Conference (TAC2015)*.

Jun'ichi Kazama and Kentaro Torisawa. 2007. Exploiting Wikipedia as external knowledge for named entity recognition. In *Proceedings of the 2007 Joint Conference of EMNLP-CoNLL*, pages 698–707.

Sungchul Kim, Kristina Toutanova, and Hwanjo Yu. 2012. Multilingual named entity recognition using parallel data and metadata from Wikipedia. In *ACL*.

R. McDonald, S. Petrov, and K. Hall. 2011. Multi-source transfer of delexicalized dependency parsers. In *Proceedings of the Conference on Empirical Methods for Natural Language Processing (EMNLP)*, pages 62–72, Edinburgh, Scotland, UK., July. Association for Computational Linguistics.

Andrea Moro, Alessandro Raganato, and Roberto Navigli. 2014. Entity linking meets word sense disambiguation: A unified approach. In *Transactions of the Association for Computational Linguistics*, volume 2, pages 231–244.

Joel Nothman, Nicky Ringland, Will Radford, Tara Murphy, and James R. Curran. 2012. Learning multilingual named entity recognition from Wikipedia. *Artificial Intelligence*, 194:151–175.

Lev Ratinov and Dan Roth. 2009. Design challenges and misconceptions in named entity recognition. In *Proc. of the Annual Conference on Computational Natural Language Learning (CoNLL)*, Jun.

Lev Ratinov, Doug Downey, Mike Anderson, and Dan Roth. 2011. Local and global algorithms for disambiguation to Wikipedia. In *Proceedings of the Annual Meeting of the Association for Computational Linguistics (ACL)*.

Avirup Sil and Alexander Yates. 2013. Re-ranking for joint named-entity recognition and linking. In *Proceedings of the 22nd ACM international conference on Conference on information & knowledge management*, pages 2369–2374. ACM.

Heather Simpson, Christopher Cieri, Kazuaki Maeda, Kathryn Baker, and Boyan Onyshkevych. 2008. Human language technology resources for less commonly taught languages: Lessons learned toward creation of basic language resources. *Collaboration: interoperability between people in the creation of language resources for less-resourced languages*, page 7.

Jason R Smith, Chris Quirk, and Kristina Toutanova. 2010. Extracting parallel sentences from comparable corpora using document level alignment. In *Human Language Technologies: The 2010 Annual Conference of the North American Chapter of the Association for Computational Linguistics*, pages 403–411. Association for Computational Linguistics.

Yangqiu Song and Dan Roth. 2014. On dataless hierarchical text classification. In *Proceedings of the National Conference on Artificial Intelligence (AAAI)*, 7.

Oscar Täckström, Ryan T. McDonald, and Jakob Uszkoreit. 2012. Cross-lingual word clusters for direct transfer of linguistic structure. In *NAACL*.

Oscar Täckström. 2012. Nudging the envelope of direct transfer methods for multilingual named entity recognition. In *Proceedings of the NAACL-HLT Workshop on the Induction of Linguistic Structure*, pages 55–63. Association for Computational Linguistics.

Erik F. Tjong Kim Sang and Fien De Meulder. 2003. Introduction to the conll-2003 shared task: Language-independent named entity recognition. In Walter Daelemans and Miles Osborne, editors, *Proceedings of CoNLL-2003*, pages 142–147. Edmonton, Canada.

Erik F. Tjong Kim Sang. 2002. Introduction to the CoNLL-2002 shared task: Language-independent named entity recognition. In *Proceedings of CoNLL-2002*, pages 155–158. Taipei, Taiwan.

Chen-Tse Tsai and Dan Roth. 2016. Cross-lingual wikification using multilingual embeddings. In *NAACL*.

Mengqiu Wang and Christopher D Manning. 2014. Cross-lingual projected expectation regularization for weakly supervised learning. In *TACL*.

Fei Wu and Daniel S. Weld. 2010. Open information extraction using Wikipedia. In *ACL*.

David Yarowsky, Grace Ngai, and Richard Wicentowski. 2001. Inducing multilingual text analysis tools via robust projection across aligned corpora. In *Proceedings of the first international conference on Human language technology research*, pages 1–8. Association for Computational Linguistics.

Boliang Zhang, Xiaoman Pan, Tianlu Wang, Ashish Vaswani, Heng Ji, Kevin Knight, and Daniel Marcu. 2016. Name tagging for low-resource incident languages based on expectation-driven learning. In *NAACL*.

Coreference in Wikipedia: Main Concept Resolution

Abbas Ghaddar
RALI-DIRO
Université de Montréal
Montréal, Canada
abbas.ghaddar@umontreal.ca

Philippe Langlais
RALI-DIRO
Université de Montréal
Montréal, Canada
felipe@iro.umontreal.ca

Abstract

Wikipedia is a resource of choice exploited in many NLP applications, yet we are not aware of recent attempts to adapt coreference resolution to this resource. In this work, we revisit a seldom studied task which consists in identifying in a Wikipedia article all the mentions of the main concept being described. We show that by exploiting the Wikipedia markup of a document, as well as links to external knowledge bases such as Freebase, we can acquire useful information on entities that helps to classify mentions as coreferent or not. We designed a classifier which drastically outperforms fair baselines built on top of state-of-the-art coreference resolution systems. We also measure the benefits of this classifier in a full coreference resolution pipeline applied to Wikipedia texts.

1 Introduction

Coreference Resolution (CR) is the task of identifying all mentions of entities in a document and grouping them into equivalence classes. CR is a prerequisite for many NLP tasks. For example, in Open Information Extraction (OIE) (Yates et al., 2007), one acquires subject-predicate-object relations, many of which (e.g., <the foundation stone, was laid by, the Queen s daughter>) are useless because the subject or the object contains material coreferring to other mentions in the text being mined.

Most CR systems, including state-of-the-art ones (Durrett and Klein, 2014; Martschat and Strube, 2015; Clark and Manning, 2015) are essentially adapted to news-like texts. This is basically imputable to the availability of large datasets where this text genre is dominant. This includes

resources developed within the Message Understanding Conferences (Hirshman and Chinchor, 1998) or the Automatic Content Extraction (ACE) program (Doddington et al., 2004), as well as resources developed within the collaborative annotation project OntoNotes (Pradhan et al., 2007).

It is now widely accepted that coreference resolution systems trained on newswire data performs poorly when tested on other text genres (Hendrickx and Hoste, 2009; Schäfer et al., 2012), including Wikipedia texts, as we shall see in our experiments.

Wikipedia is a large, multilingual, highly structured, multi-domain encyclopedia, providing an increasingly large wealth of knowledge. It is known to contain well-formed, grammatical and meaningful sentences, compared to say, ordinary internet documents. It is therefore a resource of choice in many NLP systems, see (Medelyan et al., 2009) for a review of some pioneering works.

While being a ubiquitous resource in the NLP community, we are not aware of much work conducted to adapt CR to this text genre. Two notable exceptions are (Nguyen et al., 2007) and (Nakayama, 2008), two studies dedicated to extract tuples from Wikipedia articles. Both studies demonstrate that the design of a dedicated rule-based CR system leads to improved extraction accuracy. The focus of those studies being information extraction, the authors did not spend much efforts in designing a fully-fledged CR designed for Wikipedia, neither did they evaluate it on a coreference resolution task.

Our main contribution in this work is to revisit the task initially discussed in (Nakayama, 2008) which consists in identifying in a Wikipedia article all the mentions of the concept being described by this article. We refer to this concept as the "main concept" (MC) henceforth. For instance, within the article Chilly_Gonzales, the task is to find

229

Proceedings of the 20th SIGNLL Conference on Computational Natural Language Learning (CoNLL), pages 229–238,
Berlin, Germany, August 7-12, 2016. ©2016 Association for Computational Linguistics

all proper (e.g. *Gonzales*, *Beck*), nominal (e.g. *the performer*) and pronominal (e.g. *he*) mentions that refer to the MC "Chilly Gonzales".

More specifically, we frame this task as a binary classification problem, where one has to decide whether a detected mention refers to the MC. Our classifier exploits carefully designed features extracted from Wikipedia markup and characteristics, as well as from Freebase; many of which we borrowed from the related literature.

We show that our approach outperforms state-of-the-art generic coreference resolution engines on this task. We further demonstrate that the integration of our classifier into the state-of-the-art rule-based coreference system of Lee et al. (2013) improves the detection of coreference chains in Wikipedia articles.

The paper is organized as follows. We discuss related works in Section 2. We describe in Section 3 the Wikipedia-based dataset we exploited in this study, and show the drop in performance of state-of-the-art coreference resolution systems when faced to this corpus. We describe in Section 4 the baselines we built on top of two state-of-the-art coreference resolution systems, and present our approach in Section 5. We report on experiments we conducted in section 6, and conclude in Section 7.

2   Related Works

Our approach is inspired by, and extends, previous works on coreference resolution which show that incorporating external knowledge into a CR system is beneficial. In particular, a variety of approaches (Ponzetto and Strube, 2006; Ng, 2007; Haghighi and Klein, 2009) have been shown to benefit from using external resources such as Wikipedia, WordNet (Miller, 1995), or YAGO (Suchanek et al., 2007). Ratinov and Roth (2012) and Hajishirzi et al. (2013) both investigate the integration of named-entity linking into machine learning and rule-based coreference resolution system respectively. They both use GLOW (Ratinov et al., 2011) a *wikification* system which associates detected mentions with their equivalent entity in Wikipedia. In addition, they assign to each mention a set of highly accurate knowledge attributes extracted from Wikipedia and Freebase (Bollacker et al., 2008), such as the Wikipedia categories, gender, nationality, aliases, and NER type (ORG, PER, LOC, FAC, MISC).

One issue with all the aforementioned studies is that inaccuracies often cause cascading errors in the pipeline (Zheng et al., 2013). Consequently, most authors concentrate on high-precision linking at the cost of low recall.

Dealing specifically with Wikipedia articles, we can directly exploit the wealth of markup available (redirects, internal links, links to Freebase) without resorting to named-entity linking, thus benefiting from much less ambiguous information on mentions.

3   Dataset

As our approach is dedicated to Wikipedia articles, we used the freely[1] available resource called WikiCoref (Ghaddar and Langlais, 2016). This ressource consists in 30 English Wikipedia articles manually coreference-annotated. It comprises 60k tokens annotated with the OntoNotes project guidelines (Pradhan et al., 2007). Each mention is annotated with three attributes: the mention type (named-entity, noun phrase, or pronominal), the coreference type (identity, attributive or copular) and the equivalent Freebase entity if it exists. The resource contains roughly 7 000 non singleton mentions, among which 1 800 refer to the main concept, which is to say that 30 chains out of 1 469 make up for 25% of the mentions annotated.

System	WikiCoref	OntoNotes
Dcoref	51.77	55.59
Durrett and Klein (2013)	51.01	61.41
Durrett and Klein (2014)	49.52	61.79
Cort	49.94	62.47
Scoref	46.39	63.61

Table 1: CoNLL F1 score of recent state-of-the-art systems on the WikiCoref dataset, and the 2012 OntoNotes test data for predicted mentions.

Since most coreference resolution systems for English are trained and tested on ACE (Doddington et al., 2004) or OntoNotes (Hovy et al., 2006) resources, it is interesting to measure how state-of-the art systems perform on the WikiCoref dataset. To this end, we ran a number of recent CR systems: the rule-based system of (Lee et al., 2013), hereafter named Dcoref; the Berkeley systems described in (Durrett and Klein, 2013; Durrett and Klein, 2014); the latent model of Martschat and

---

[1] http://rali.iro.umontreal.ca/rali/?q=
en/wikicoref

Strube (2015); and the system described in (Clark and Manning, 2015), hereafter named `Scoref`.

We evaluate the systems on the whole dataset, using the v8.01 of the CoNLL scorer[2] (Pradhan et al., 2014). The results are reported in Table 1 along with the performance of the systems on the CoNLL 2012 test data (Pradhan et al., 2012). Expectedly, the performance of all systems dramatically decrease on WikiCoref, which calls for further research on adapting the coreference resolution technology to new text genres.

Somehow more surprisingly, the rule-based system of (Lee et al., 2013) works better than the machine-learning based systems on the WikiCoref dataset. Nevertheless, statistical systems can be trained or adapted to the WikiCoref dataset, a point we leave for future investigations. Also, we observe that the ranking of the statistical systems on this dataset differs from the one obtained on the OntoNotes test set.

The WikiCoref dataset is far smaller than the OntoNotes one; still, the authors paid attention to sample Wikipedia articles of various characteristics: size, topic (people, organizations, locations, events, etc.) and internal link density. Therefore, we believe our results to be representative. Those results further confirm the conclusions in (Hendrickx and Hoste, 2009), which show that a CR system trained on news-paper significantly underperforms on data coming from users comments and blogs.

4   Baselines

Since there is no system readily available for our task, we devised four baselines on top of two available coreference resolution systems. Given the output of a CR system applied on a Wikipedia article, our goal here is to isolate the coreference chain that represents the main concept. We experimented with several heuristics, yielding the following baselines.

B1 picks the longest coreference chain identified and considers that its mentions are those that co-refer to the main concept. The underlying assumption is that the most mentioned concept in a Wikipedia article is the main concept itself.

B2 picks the longest coreference chain identified

if it contains a mention that exactly matches the MC title, otherwise it checks in decreasing order (longest to shortest) for a chain containing the title. We expect this baseline to be more precise than the previous one overall.

It turns out that, for CR systems, mentions of the MC often are spread over several coreference chains. Therefore we devised two more baselines that aggregate chains, with an expected increase in recall.

B3 conservatively aggregates chains containing a mention that exactly matches the MC title.

B4 more loosely aggregates all chains that contain at least one mention whose span is a substring of the title.[3] For instance, given the main concept *Barack Obama*, we concatenate all chains containing either *Obama* or *Barack* in their mentions. Obviously, this baseline should show a higher recall than the previous ones, but risks aggregating mentions that are not related to the MC. For instance, it will aggregate the coreference chain referring to *University of Sydney* concept with a chain containing the mention *Sydney*.

We observed that, for pronominal mentions, those baselines were not performing very well in terms of recall. With the aim of increasing recall, we added to the chain all the occurrences of pronouns found to refer to the MC (at least once) by the baseline. This heuristic was first proposed by Nguyen et al. (2007). For instance, if the pronoun *he* is found in the chain identified by the baseline, all pronouns *he* in the article are considered to be mentions of the MC *Barack Obama*. Obviously, there are cases where those pronouns do not co-refer to the MC, but this step significantly improves the performance on pronouns.

5   Approach

Our approach is composed of a preprocessor which computes a representation of each mention in an article as well as its main concept; and a feature extractor which compares both representations for inducing a set of features.

5.1   Preprocessing

We extract mentions using the same mention detection algorithm embedded in Lee et al. (2013)

---

[3] Grammatical words are not considered for matching.

and Clark and Manning (2015). This algorithm described in (Raghunathan et al., 2010) extracts all named-entities, noun phrases and pronouns, and then removes spurious mentions.

We leverage the hyperlink structure of the article in order to enrich the list of predicted mentions with shallow semantic attributes. For each link found within the article under consideration, we look through the list of predicted mentions for all mentions that match the surface string of the link. We assign to them the attributes (entity type, gender and number) extracted from the Freebase entry (if it exists) corresponding to the Wikipedia article the hyperlink points to. This module behaves as a substitute to the named-entity linking pipelines used in other works, such as (Ratinov and Roth, 2012; Hajishirzi et al., 2013). We expect it to be of high quality because it exploits human-made links.

We use the `WikipediaMiner` (Milne and Witten, 2008) API for easily accessing any piece of structure (clean text, labels, internal links, redirects, etc) in Wikipedia, and Jena[4] to index and query Freebase.

In the end, we represent a mention by three strings (actual mention span, head word, and span up to the head noun), as well as its coarse attributes (entity type, gender and number). Figure 1 shows the representation collected for the mention *San Fernando Valley region of the city of Los Angeles* found in the `Los_Angeles_Pierce_College` article.

---

string span	
	▷ *San Fernando Valley region*
	of the city of Los Angeles
head word span	
	▷ *region*
span up to the head noun	
	▷ *San Fernando Valley region*
coarse attribute	
	▷ *∅, neutral, singular*

Figure 1: Representation of a mention.

We represent the main concept of a Wikipedia article by its **title**, its **inferred type** (a common noun inferred from the first sentence of the article). Those attributes were used by Nguyen et al. (2007) to heuristically link a mention to the main concept of an article. We further extend this representation by the MC **name variants** extracted

---

[4]http://jena.apache.org

from the markup of Wikipedia (redirects, text anchored in links) as well as aliases from Freebase; the MC **entity types** we extracted from the Freebase `notable types` attribute, and its **coarse attributes** extracted from Freebase, such as its NER type, its gender and number. If the concept category is a person (PER), we import the `profession` attribute. Figure 2 illustrates the information we collect for the Wikipedia concept `Los_Angeles_Pierce_College`.

---

title	(W)
	▷ *Los Angeles Pierce College*
inferred type	(W)
Los Angeles Pierce College, also known as Pierce College and just Pierce, is a community college that serves …	
	▷ *college*
name variants	(W,F)
	▷ *Pierce Junior College, LAPC*
entity type	(F)
	▷ College/University
coarse attributes	(F)
	▷ ORG, neutral, singular

Figure 2: Representation of a Wikipedia concept. The source from which the information is extracted is indicated in parentheses: (W)ikipedia, (F)reebase.

5.2 Feature Extraction

We experimented with a few hundred features for characterizing each mention, focusing on the most promising ones that we found simple enough to compute. In part, our features are inspired by coreference systems that use Wikipedia and Freebase as feature sources (see Section 2). These features, along with others related to the characteristics of Wikipedia texts, allow us to recognize mentions of the MC more accurately than current CR systems. We make a distinction between features computed for pronominal mentions and features computed from the other mentions.

5.2.1 Non-pronominal Mentions

For each mention, we compute seven families of features we sketch below.

base Number of occurrences of the mention span and the mention head found in the list of candidate mentions. We also add a normalized version of those counts (frequency / total number of mentions).

title, inferred type, name variants, entity type
Most often, a concept is referred to by its name, one of its variants, or its type which are encoded in the four first fields of our MC representation. We define four families of comparison features, each corresponding to one of the first four fields of a MC representation (see Figure 2). For instance, for the title family, we compare the title text span with each of the text spans of the mention representation (see Figure 1). A comparison between a field of the MC representation and a mention text span yields 10 boolean features. These features encode string similarities (exact match, partial match, one being the substring of another, sharing of a number of words, etc.). An eleventh feature is the semantic relatedness score of Wu and Palmer (1994). For **title**, we therefore end up with 3 sets of 11 feature vectors.

tag Part-of-speech tags of the first and last words of the mention, as well as the tag of the words immediately before and after the mention in the article. We convert this into 34×4 binary features (presence/absence of a specific combination of tags).

main Boolean features encoding whether the MC and the mention **coarse attributes** matches; also we use conjunctions of all pairs of features in this family.

5.2.2 Pronominal Mentions

We characterize pronominal mentions by five families of features, which, with the exception of the first one, all capture information extracted from Wikipedia.

base The pronoun span itself, number, gender and person attributes, to which we add the number of occurrences of the pronoun, as well as its normalized count. The most frequently occurring pronoun in an article is likely to co-refer to the main concept, and we expect these features to capture this to some extent.

main MC coarse attributes, such as NER type, gender, number (see Figure 2).

tag Part-of-speech of the previous and following tokens, as well as the previous and the next POS bigrams (this is converted into 2380 binary features).

position Often, pronouns at the beginning of a new section or paragraph refer to the main concept. Therefore, we compute 5 (binary) features encoding the relative position (first, first tier, second tier, last tier, last) of a mention in the sentence, paragraph, section and article.

distance Within a sentence, we search before and after the mention for an entity that is compatible (according to Freebase information) with the pronominal mention of interest. If a match is found, one feature encodes the distance between the match and the mention; another feature encodes the number of other compatible pronouns in the same sentence. We expect that this family of features will help the model to capture the presence of local (within a sentence) co-references.

6   Experiments

In this section, we first describe the data preparation we conducted (section 6.1), and provide details on the classifier we trained (section 6.2). Then, we report experiments we carried out on the task of identifying the mentions co-referent (positive class) to the main concept of an article (section 6.3). We compare our approach to the baselines described in section 4, and analyze the impact of the families of features described in section 5. We also investigate a simple extension of `Dcoref` which takes advantage of our classifier for improving coreference resolution (section 6.4).

6.1   Data Preparation

Each article in WikiCoref was part-of-speech tagged, syntactically parsed and the named-entities were identified. This was done thanks to the `Stanford CoreNLP` toolkit (Manning et al., 2014). Since WikiCoref does not contain singleton mentions (in conformance to the OntoNotes guidelines), we automatically extract singleton mentions using the method described in (Raghunathan et al., 2010). Overall, we added about 13 400 automatically extracted mentions (singletons) to the 7 000 coreferent mentions annotated

	Pronominal			Non Pronominal			All		
	P	R	F1	P	R	F1	P	R	F1
Dcoref									
B1	64.51	76.55	70.02	70.33	63.09	66.51	67.92	67.77	67.85
B2	76.45	50.23	60.63	83.52	49.57	62.21	80.90	49.80	61.65
B3	76.39	65.55	70.55	83.67	56.20	67.24	80.72	59.45	68.47
B4	71.74	83.41	77.13	74.39	75.59	74.98	73.30	78.31	75.77
Scoref									
B1	76.59	78.30	77.44	54.66	39.37	45.77	64.11	52.91	57.97
B2	**89.59**	74.16	81.15	69.90	31.20	43.15	79.69	46.14	58.44
B3	83.91	77.35	80.49	73.17	55.44	63.08	77.39	63.06	69.49
B4	78.48	90.74	84.17	67.51	67.85	67.68	71.68	75.81	73.69
this work	85.46	**92.82**	**88.99**	**91.65**	**85.88**	**88.67**	**89.29**	**88.30**	**88.79**

Table 2: Performance of the baselines on the task of identifying all MC coreferent mentions.

in WikiCoref. In the end, our training set consists of 20 362 mentions: 1 334 pronominal ones (627 of them referring to the MC), and 19 028 non-pronominal ones (16% of them referring to the MC).

6.2 Classifier

We trained two Support Vector Machine classifiers (Cortes and Vapnik, 1995), one for pronominal mentions and one for non-pronominal ones, making use of the LIBSVM library (Chang and Lin, 2011) and the features described in Section 5.2. For both models, we selected[5] the C-support vector classification and used a linear kernel. Since our dataset is unbalanced (at least for non-pronominal mentions), we penalized the negative class with a weight of 2.0.

During training, we do not use gold mention attributes, but we automatically enrich mentions with the information extracted from Wikipedia and Freebase, as described in Section 5.

6.3 Main Concept Resolution Performance

We focus on the task of identifying all the mentions referring to the main concept of an article. We measure the performance of the systems we devised by average precision, recall and F1 rates computed by a 10-fold cross-validation procedure.

We generated baselines for all the systems discussed in Section 3, but found results derived from statistical approaches to be close enough that we

only include results of two systems in the sequel: Dcoref (Lee et al., 2013) and Scoref (Clark and Manning, 2015). We choose these two because they use the same pipeline (parser, mention detection, etc), while applying very different techniques (rules versus machine learning). The results of the baselines and our approach are reported in Table 2.

Clearly, our approach outperforms all baselines for both pronominal and non-pronominal mentions, and across all metrics. On all mentions, our best classifier yields an absolute F1 increase of 13 points over Dcoref, and 15 points over Scoref.

In order to understand the impact of each family of features we considered in this study, we trained various classifiers in a greedy fashion. We started with the simplest feature set (**base**) and gradually added one family of features at a time, keeping at each iteration the one leading to the highest increase in F1. The outcome of this process for the pronominal mentions is reported in Table 3.

	P	R	F1
always positive	46.70	100.00	63.70
base	70.34	78.31	74.11
+main	74.15	90.11	81.35
+position	80.43	89.15	84.57
+tag	82.12	90.11	85.93
+distance	85.46	92.82	88.99

Table 3: Performance of our approach on the pronominal mentions, as a function of the features.

A baseline that always considers that a pronom-

---

[5] We tried with less success other configurations on a held-out dataset.

inal mention is co-referent to the main concept results in an F1 measure of 63.7%. This naive baseline is outperformed by the simplest of our model (**base**) by a large margin (over 10 absolute points). We observe that recall significantly improves when those features are augmented with the MC coarse attributes (+**main**). In fact, this variant already outperforms all the `Dcoref`-based baselines in terms of F1 score. Each feature family added further improves the performance overall, leading to better precision and recall than any of the baselines tested. Inspection shows that most of the errors on pronominal mentions are introduced by the lack of information on noun phrase mentions surrounding the pronouns. In example (f) shown in Figure 3, the classifier associates the mention *it* with the MC instead of *the Johnston Atoll " Safeguard C " mission*.

	P	R	F1
base	60.89	62.24	61.56
+title	85.56	68.03	75.79
+inferred type	87.45	75.26	80.90
+name variants	86.49	81.12	83.72
+entity type	86.37	82.99	84.65
+tag	87.09	85.46	86.27
+main	91.65	85.88	88.67

Table 4: Performance of our approach on the non-pronominal mentions, as a function of the features.

Table 4 reports the results obtained for the non-pronominal mentions classifier. The simplest classifier is outperformed by most baselines in terms of F1. Still, this model is able to correctly match mentions in example (a) and (b) of Figure 3 simply because those mentions are frequent within their respective article. Of course, such a simple model is often wrong as in example (c), where all mentions *the United States* are associated to the MC, simply because this is a frequent mention.

The **title** feature family drastically increases precision, and the resulting classifier (+**title**) outperforms all the baselines in terms of F1 score. Adding the **inferred type** feature family gives a further boost in recall (7 absolute points) with no loss in precision (gain of almost 2 points). For instance, the resulting classifier can link the mention *the team* to the MC *Houston Texans* (see example (d)) because it correctly identifies the term *team* as a type. The family **name variants** also gives a nice boost in recall, in a slight expense of

precision. This drop is due to some noisy redirects in Wikipedia, misleading our classifier. For instance, *Johnston and Sand Islands* is a redirect of the `Johnston_Atoll` article.

The **entity type** family further improves performance, mainly because it plays a role similar to the **inferred type** features extracted from Freebase. This indicates that the noun type induced directly from the first sentence of a Wikipedia article is pertinent and can complement the types extracted from Freebase when available or serve as proxy when they are missing.

a MC= *Anatole France*
  France is also widely believed to be the model for narrator Marcel's literary idol Bergotte in Marcel Proust's In Search of Lost Time.
b MC= *Harry Potter and the Chamber of Secrets*
  Although Rowling found it difficult to finish *the book*, it won . . . .
c MC= *Barack Obama*
  On August 31, 2010, Obama announced that *the United States** combat mission in Iraq was over.
d MC= *Houston Texans*
  In 2002, *the team* wore a patch commemorating their inaugural season...
e MC= *Houston Texans*
  The name Houston Oilers was unavailable to *the expansion team*...
f MC= *Johnston Atoll*
  In 1993 , Congress appropriated no funds for the Johnston Atoll Safeguard C mission , bringing *it** to an end.
g MC= *Houston Texans*
  The Houston Texans are a professional American football team based in *Houston** , Texas.

Figure 3: Examples of mentions (underlined) associated with the MC. An asterisk indicates wrong decisions.

Finally, the **main** family significantly increases precision (over 4 absolute points) with no loss in recall. To illustrate a negative example, the resulting classifier wrongly recognizes mentions referring to the town *Houston* as coreferent to the football team in example (g). We handpicked a number of classification errors and found that most of these are difficult coreference cases. For instance, our best classifier fails to recognize that the mention *the expansion team* refers to the main concept *Houston Texans* in example (e).

System	MUC			B^3			CEAFϕ_4			CoNLL
	P	R	F1	P	R	F1	P	R	F1	F1
Dcoref	61.59	60.42	61.00	53.55	43.33	47.90	42.68	**50.86**	46.41	51.77
D&K (2013)	68.52	55.96	61.61	59.08	39.72	47.51	48.06	40.44	43.92	51.01
D&K (2014)	63.79	57.07	60.24	52.55	40.75	45.90	45.44	39.80	42.43	49.52
M&S (2015)	70.39	53.63	60.88	**60.81**	37.58	46.45	**47.88**	38.18	42.48	49.94
C&M (2015)	**69.45**	49.53	57.83	57.99	34.42	43.20	46.61	33.09	38.70	46.58
Dcoref++	66.06	**62.93**	**64.46**	57.73	**48.58**	**52.76**	46.76	49.54	**48.11**	**55.11**

Table 5: Performance of Dcoref++ on WikiCoref compared to the state-of-the-art systems: Lee et al. (2013); Durrett and Klein (2013) - Final; Durrett and Klein (2014) - Joint; Martschat and Strube (2015) - Ranking:Latent; Clark and Manning (2015) - Statistical mode with clustering.

6.4 Coreference Resolution Performance

While identifying all the mentions of the MC in a Wikipedia article is certainly useful in a number of NLP tasks (Nguyen et al., 2007; Nakayama, 2008), finding all coreference chains in a Wikipedia article is also worth studying. In the following, we describe an experiment where we introduced in Dcoref a new high-precision sieve which uses our classifier[6]. Sieves in Dcoref are ranked in decreasing order of precision, and we ranked this new sieve first. The aim of this sieve is to construct the coreference chain equivalent to the main concept. It merges two chains whenever they both contain mentions to the MC according to our classifier. We further prevent other sieves from appending new mentions to the MC coreference chain.

We ran this modified system (called Dcoref++) on the WikiCoref dataset, where mentions were automatically predicted. The results of this system are reported in Table 5, measured in terms of MUC (Vilain et al., 1995), B3 (Bagga and Baldwin, 1998), CEAFϕ_4 (Luo, 2005) and the average F1 CoNLL score (Denis and Baldridge, 2009).

We observe an improvement for Dcoref++ over the other systems, for all the metrics. In particular, Dcoref++ increases by 4 absolute points the CoNLL F1 score. This shows that early decisions taken by our classifier benefit other sieves as well. It must be noted, however, that the overall gain in precision is larger than the one in recall.

7 Conclusion

We developed a simple yet powerful approach that accurately identifies all the mentions that co-refer to the concept being described in a Wikipedia article. We tackle the problem with two (pronominal and non-pronominal) models based on well designed features. The resulting system is compared to baselines built on top of state-of-the-art systems adapted to this task. Despite being relatively simple, our model reaches 89 % in F1 score, an absolute gain of 13 F1 points over the best baseline. We further show that incorporating our system into the Stanford deterministic rule-based system (Lee et al., 2013) leads to an improvement of 4% in F1 score on a fully fledged coreference task. A natural extension of this work is to identify all coreference relations in a Wikipedia article, a task we are currently investigating.

The material used in this study, as well as a (huge) dump of all the mentions in English Wikipedia (version of April 2013) our classifier identified as referring to the main concept, along with information we extracted from Wikipedia and Freebase are available at http://rali.iro.umontreal.ca/rali/en/wikipedia-main-concept. We hope this ressource will foster further research on Wikipedia-based coreference resolution.

Acknowledgments

This work has been funded by Nuance Foundation. We are grateful to the reviewers for their helpful comments.

References

Amit Bagga and Breck Baldwin. 1998. Algorithms for scoring coreference chains. In *The first international conference on language resources and evaluation workshop on linguistics coreference*, volume 1, pages 563–566.

---

[6]We use predicted results from 10-fold cross validation.

Kurt Bollacker, Colin Evans, Praveen Paritosh, Tim Sturge, and Jamie Taylor. 2008. Freebase: a collaboratively created graph database for structuring human knowledge. In *Proceedings of the 2008 ACM SIGMOD international conference on Management of data*, pages 1247–1250.

Chih-Chung Chang and Chih-Jen Lin. 2011. LIBSVM: a library for support vector machines. *ACM Transactions on Intelligent Systems and Technology (TIST)*, 2(3):27.

Kevin Clark and Christopher D. Manning. 2015. Entity-centric coreference resolution with model stacking. In *Association of Computational Linguistics (ACL)*.

Corinna Cortes and Vladimir Vapnik. 1995. Support-vector networks. *Machine learning*, 20(3):273–297.

Pascal Denis and Jason Baldridge. 2009. Global joint models for coreference resolution and named entity classification. *Procesamiento del Lenguaje Natural*, 42(1):87–96.

George R. Doddington, Alexis Mitchell, Mark A. Przybocki, Lance A. Ramshaw, Stephanie Strassel, and Ralph M. Weischedel. 2004. The Automatic Content Extraction (ACE) Program-Tasks, Data, and Evaluation. In *LREC*, volume 2, page 1.

Greg Durrett and Dan Klein. 2013. Easy victories and uphill battles in coreference resolution. In *EMNLP*, pages 1971–1982.

Greg Durrett and Dan Klein. 2014. A joint model for entity analysis: Coreference, typing, and linking. *Transactions of the Association for Computational Linguistics*, 2:477–490.

Abbas Ghaddar and Phillippe Langlais. 2016. Wikicoref: An english coreference-annotated corpus of wikipedia articles. In *Proceedings of the Ninth International Conference on Language Resources and Evaluation (LREC 2016)*.

Aria Haghighi and Dan Klein. 2009. Simple coreference resolution with rich syntactic and semantic features. In *Proceedings of the 2009 Conference on Empirical Methods in Natural Language Processing: Volume 3-Volume 3*, pages 1152–1161.

Hannaneh Hajishirzi, Leila Zilles, Daniel S. Weld, and Luke S. Zettlemoyer. 2013. Joint Coreference Resolution and Named-Entity Linking with Multi-Pass Sieves. In *EMNLP*, pages 289–299.

Iris Hendrickx and Veronique Hoste. 2009. Coreference resolution on blogs and commented news. In *Anaphora Processing and Applications*, pages 43–53.

Lynette Hirshman and Nancy Chinchor. 1998. MUC-7 coreference task definition. version 3.0. In *Proceedings of the Seventh Message Understanding Conference (MUC-7)*.

Eduard Hovy, Mitchell Marcus, Martha Palmer, Lance Ramshaw, and Ralph Weischedel. 2006. OntoNotes: the 90% solution. In *Proceedings of the human language technology conference of the NAACL, Companion Volume: Short Papers*, pages 57–60.

Heeyoung Lee, Angel Chang, Yves Peirsman, Nathanael Chambers, Mihai Surdeanu, and Dan Jurafsky. 2013. Deterministic coreference resolution based on entity-centric, precision-ranked rules. *Computational Linguistics*, 39(4):885–916.

Xiaoqiang Luo. 2005. On coreference resolution performance metrics. In *Proceedings of the conference on Human Language Technology and Empirical Methods in Natural Language Processing*, pages 25–32.

Christopher D. Manning, Mihai Surdeanu, John Bauer, Jenny Rose Finkel, Steven Bethard, and David McClosky. 2014. The Stanford CoreNLP Natural Language Processing Toolkit. In *ACL (System Demonstrations)*, pages 55–60.

Sebastian Martschat and Michael Strube. 2015. Latent structures for coreference resolution. *Transactions of the Association for Computational Linguistics*, 3:405–418.

Olena Medelyan, David Milne, Catherine Legg, and Ian H. Witten. 2009. Mining meaning from wikipedia. *Int. J. Hum.-Comput. Stud.*, 67(9):716–754, September.

George A. Miller. 1995. WordNet: A Lexical Database for English. *Commun. ACM*, 38(11):39–41.

David Milne and Ian H. Witten. 2008. Learning to link with wikipedia. In *Proceedings of the 17th ACM conference on Information and knowledge management*, pages 509–518.

Kotaro Nakayama. 2008. Wikipedia mining for triple extraction enhanced by co-reference resolution. In *The 7th International Semantic Web Conference*, page 103.

Vincent Ng. 2007. Shallow Semantics for Coreference Resolution. In *IJcAI*, volume 2007, pages 1689–1694.

Dat PT Nguyen, Yutaka Matsuo, and Mitsuru Ishizuka. 2007. Relation extraction from wikipedia using subtree mining. In *Proceedings of the National Conference on Artificial Intelligence*, page 1414.

Simone Paolo Ponzetto and Michael Strube. 2006. Exploiting semantic role labeling, WordNet and Wikipedia for coreference resolution. In *Proceedings of the main conference on Human Language Technology Conference of the North American Chapter of the Association of Computational Linguistics*, pages 192–199.

Sameer S. Pradhan, Lance Ramshaw, Ralph Weischedel, Jessica MacBride, and Linnea Micciulla. 2007. Unrestricted coreference: Identifying entities and events in OntoNotes. In *First IEEE International Conference on Semantic Computing*, pages 446–453.

Sameer Pradhan, Alessandro Moschitti, Nianwen Xue, Olga Uryupina, and Yuchen Zhang. 2012. CoNLL-2012 shared task: Modeling multilingual unrestricted coreference in OntoNotes. In *Joint Conference on EMNLP and CoNLL-Shared Task*, pages 1–40.

Sameer Pradhan, Xiaoqiang Luo, Marta Recasens, Eduard Hovy, Vincent Ng, and Michael Strube. 2014. Scoring coreference partitions of predicted mentions: A reference implementation. In *Proceedings of the 52nd Annual Meeting of the Association for Computational Linguistics (Volume 2: Short Papers)*, pages 30–35, June.

Karthik Raghunathan, Heeyoung Lee, Sudarshan Rangarajan, Nathanael Chambers, Mihai Surdeanu, Dan Jurafsky, and Christopher Manning. 2010. A multipass sieve for coreference resolution. In *Proceedings of the 2010 Conference on Empirical Methods in Natural Language Processing*, pages 492–501.

Lev Ratinov and Dan Roth. 2012. Learning-based multi-sieve co-reference resolution with knowledge. In *Proceedings of the 2012 Joint Conference on Empirical Methods in Natural Language Processing and Computational Natural Language Learning*, pages 1234–1244.

Lev Ratinov, Dan Roth, Doug Downey, and Mike Anderson. 2011. Local and global algorithms for disambiguation to wikipedia. In *Proceedings of the 49th Annual Meeting of the Association for Computational Linguistics: Human Language Technologies-Volume 1*, pages 1375–1384.

Ulrich Schäfer, Christian Spurk, and Jörg Steffen. 2012. A fully coreference-annotated corpus of scholarly papers from the acl anthology. In *Proceedings of the 24th International Conference on Computational Linguistics (COLING-2012)*, pages 1059–1070.

Fabian M. Suchanek, Gjergji Kasneci, and Gerhard Weikum. 2007. Yago: a core of semantic knowledge. In *Proceedings of the 16th international conference on World Wide Web*, pages 697–706.

Marc Vilain, John Burger, John Aberdeen, Dennis Connolly, and Lynette Hirschman. 1995. A model-theoretic coreference scoring scheme. In *Proceedings of the 6th conference on Message understanding*, pages 45–52.

Alexander Yates, Michael Cafarella, Michele Banko, Oren Etzioni, Matthew Broadhead, and Stephen Soderland. 2007. Textrunner: open information extraction on the web. In *Proceedings of Human Language Technologies: The Annual Conference of the North American Chapter of the Association for Computational Linguistics: Demonstrations*, pages 25–26.

Jianping Zheng, Luke Vilnis, Sameer Singh, Jinho D. Choi, and Andrew McCallum. 2013. Dynamic knowledge-base alignment for coreference resolution. In *Conference on Computational Natural Language Learning (CoNLL)*.

Event Linking with Sentential Features from Convolutional Neural Networks

Sebastian Krause, Feiyu Xu, Hans Uszkoreit, Dirk Weissenborn
Language Technology Lab
German Research Center for Artificial Intelligence (DFKI)
Alt-Moabit 91c, 10559 Berlin, Germany
{skrause,feiyu,uszkoreit,diwe01}@dfki.de

Abstract

Coreference resolution for event mentions enables extraction systems to process document-level information. Current systems in this area base their decisions on rich semantic features from various knowledge bases, thus restricting them to domains where such external sources are available. We propose a model for this task which does not rely on such features but instead utilizes sentential features coming from convolutional neural networks. Two such networks first process coreference candidates and their respective context, thereby generating latent-feature representations which are tuned towards event aspects relevant for a linking decision. These representations are augmented with lexical-level and pairwise features, and serve as input to a trainable similarity function producing a coreference score. Our model achieves state-of-the-art performance on two datasets, one of which is publicly available. An error analysis points out directions for further research.

1 Introduction

Event extraction aims at detecting mentions of real-world events and their arguments in text documents of different domains, e.g., news articles. The subsequent task of *event linking* is concerned with resolving coreferences between recognized event mentions in a document, and is the focus of this paper.

Several studies investigate event linking and related problems such as relation mentions spanning multiple sentences. Swampillai and Stevenson (2010) find that 28.5 % of binary relation mentions in the MUC 6 dataset are affected, as are 9.4 % of

relation mentions in the ACE corpus from 2003. Ji and Grishman (2011) estimate that 15 % of slot fills in the training data for the "TAC 2010 KBP Slot Filling" task require cross-sentential inference. To confirm these numbers, we analyzed the event annotation of the ACE 2005 corpus and found that approximately 23 % of the event mentions lack arguments which are present in other mentions of the same event instance in the respective document. These numbers suggest that event linking is an important task.

Previous approaches for modeling event mentions in context of coreference resolution (Bejan and Harabagiu, 2010; Sangeetha and Arock, 2012; Liu et al., 2014) make either use of external feature sources with limited cross-domain availability like WordNet (Fellbaum, 1998) and FrameNet (Baker et al., 1998), or show low performance. At the same time, recent literature proposes a new kind of feature class for modeling events (and relations) in order to detect mentions and extract their arguments, i.e., *sentential features* from event-/relation-mention representations that have been created by taking the full extent and surrounding sentence of a mention into account (Zeng et al., 2014; Nguyen and Grishman, 2015; Chen et al., 2015; dos Santos et al., 2015; Zeng et al., 2015). Their promising results motivate our work. We propose to use such features for event coreference resolution, hoping to thereby remove the need for extensive external semantic features while preserving the current state-of-the-art performance level.

Our contributions in this paper are as follows: We design a neural approach to event linking which in a first step models intra-sentential event mentions via the use of convolutional neural networks for the integration of sentential features. In the next step, our model learns to make coreference decisions for pairs of event mentions based on the previously generated representations. This approach

Proceedings of the 20th SIGNLL Conference on Computational Natural Language Learning (CoNLL), pages 239–249,
Berlin, Germany, August 7-12, 2016. ©2016 Association for Computational Linguistics

does not rely on external semantic features, but rather employs a combination of local and sentential features to describe individual event mentions, and combines these intermediate event representations with standard pairwise features for the coreference decision. The model achieves state-of-the-art performance in our experiments on two datasets, one of which is publicly available. Furthermore, we present an analysis of the system errors to identify directions for further research.

2 Problem definition

We follow the notion of events from the ACE 2005 dataset (LDC, 2005; Walker et al., 2006). Consider the following example:

> British bank Barclays had agreed to **buy** Spanish rival Banco Zaragozano for 1.14 billion euros. The **combination** of the banking operations of Barclays Spain and Zaragozano will bring together two complementary businesses and will happen this year, in contrast to Barclays' postponed **merger** with Lloyds.[1]

Processing these sentences in a prototypical, ACE-style information extraction (IE) pipeline would involve (a) the recognition of entity mentions. In the example, mentions of entities are underlined. Next, (b) words in the text are processed as to whether they elicit an event reference, i.e., event *triggers* are identified and their semantic type is classified. The above sentences contain three event mentions with type *Business.Merge-Org*, shown in boldface. The task of event extraction further requires that (c) participants of recognized events are determined among the entity mentions in the same sentence, i.e., an event's *arguments* are identified and their semantic role wrt. the event is classified. The three recognized event mentions are:

E1: **buy**(British bank Barclays, Spanish rival Banco Zaragozano, 1.14 billion euros)
E2: **combination**(Barclays Spain, Zaragozano, this year)
E3: **merger**(Barclays, Lloyds)

Often, an IE system involves (d) a disambiguation step of the entity mentions against one another in the same document. This allows to identify the three mentions of "Barclays" in the text as referring to the same real-world entity. The analogous task on the level of event mentions is called (e) event linking (or: event coreference resolution) and is the focus of this paper. Specifically, the task is

to determine that E3 is a singleton reference in this example, while E1 and E2 are coreferential, with the consequence that a document-level event instance can be produced from E1 and E2, listing four arguments (two companies, buying price, and acquisition date).

3 Model design

This section first motivates the design decisions of our model for event linking, before going into details about its two-step architecture.

Event features from literature So far, a wide range of features has been used for the representation of events and relations for extraction (Zhou et al., 2005; Mintz et al., 2009; Sun et al., 2011; Krause et al., 2015) and coreference resolution (Bejan and Harabagiu, 2010; Lee et al., 2012; Liu et al., 2014; Araki and Mitamura, 2015; Cybulska and Vossen, 2015) purposes. The following is an attempt to list the most common classes among them, along with examples:

- **lexical:** surface string, lemma, word embeddings, context around trigger
- **syntactic:** depth of trigger in parse tree, dependency arcs from/to trigger
- **discourse:** distance between coreference candidates, absolute position in document
- **semantic (intrinsic):** comparison of event arguments (entity fillers, present roles), event type of coreference candidates
- **semantic (external):** coreference-candidates similarity in lexical-semantic resources (WordNet, FrameNet) and other datasets (VerbOcean corpus), enrichment of arguments with alternative names from external sources (DBpedia, Geonames)

While lexical, discourse, and intrinsic-semantic features are available in virtually all application scenarios of event extraction/linking, and even syntactic parsing is no longer considered an expensive feature source, semantic features from external knowledge sources pose a significant burden on the application of event processing systems, as these sources are created at high cost and come with limited domain coverage.

Fortunately, recent work has explored the use of a new feature class, *sentential features*, for tackling relation-/event-extraction related tasks with neural networks (Zeng et al., 2014; Nguyen and Grishman, 2015; Chen et al., 2015; dos Santos et al., 2015; Zeng et al., 2015). These approaches have shown that processing sentences with neural models yields representations suitable for IE, which motivates their use in our approach.

---

[1] Based on an example in (Araki and Mitamura, 2015).

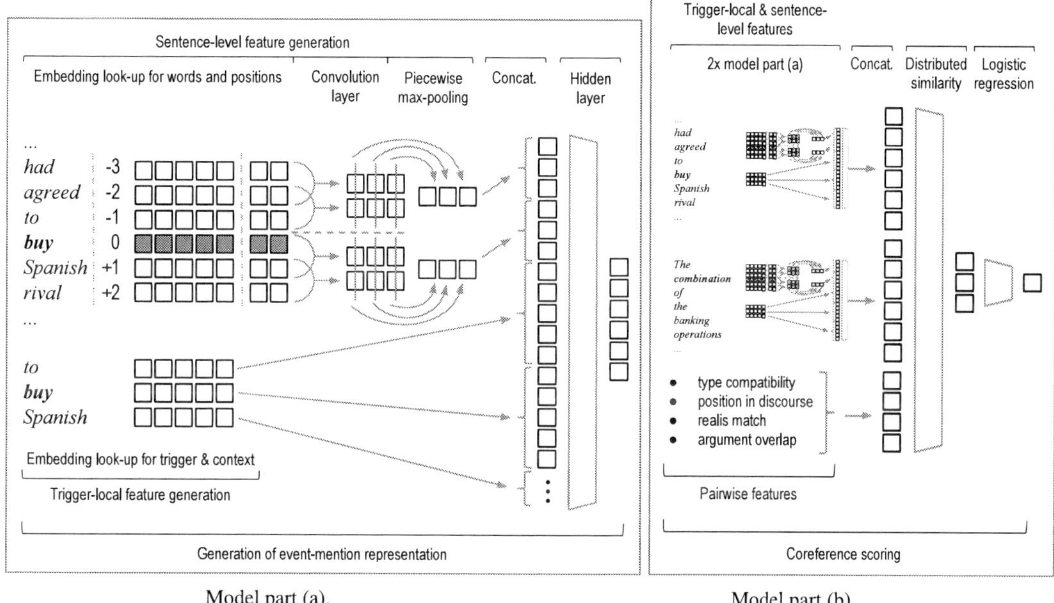

Figure 1: The two parts of the model. The first part computes a representation for a single event mention. The second part is fed with two such event-mention representations plus a number of pairwise features for the input event-mention pair, and calculates a coreference score.

Data properties A preliminary analysis of one dataset used in our experiments (ACE^{++}; see Section 5) further motivates the design of our model. We found that 50.97 % of coreferential event-mentions pairs share no arguments, either by mentioning distinct argument roles or because one/both mentions have no annotated arguments. Furthermore, 47.29 % of positive event-mention pairs have different trigger words. It is thus important to not solely rely on intrinsic event properties in order to model event mentions, but to additionally take the surrounding sentence's semantics into account. Another observation regards the distance of coreferential event mentions in a document. 55.42% are more than five sentences apart. This indicates that a locality-based heuristic would not perform well and also encourages the use of sentential features for making coreference decisions.

3.1 Learning event representations

The architecture of the model (Figure 1) is split into two parts. The first one aims at adequately representing individual event mentions. As is common in literature, words of the whole sentence of an input event mention are represented as real-valued vectors v_w^i of a fixed size d_w, with i being a word's position in the sentence. These *word embeddings* are updated during model training and are stored in a matrix $W_w \in \mathbb{R}^{d_w \times |V|}$; $|V|$ being the vocabulary size of the dataset.

Furthermore, we take the relative position of tokens with respect to the mention into account, as suggested by (Collobert et al., 2011; Zeng et al., 2014). The rationale is that while the absolute position of learned features in a sentence might not be relevant for an event-related decision, the position of them wrt. the event mention is. Embeddings v_p^i of size d_p for relative positions of words are generated in a way similar to word embeddings, i.e., by table lookup from a matrix $W_p \in \mathbb{R}^{d_p \times s_{\max}*2-1}$ of trainable parameters. Again i denotes the location of a word in a sentence; $s_{\max}$ is the maximum sentence length in the dataset. Embeddings for words and positions are concatenated into vectors v_t^i of size $d_t = d_w + d_p$, this means that now every word in the vocabulary has a different representation for each distinct distance with which it occurs to an event trigger.

A sentence with s words is represented by a matrix of dimensions $s \times d_t$. This matrix serves as input to a convolution layer. In order to compress the semantics of s words into a sentence-level feature vector with constant size, the convolution layer applies d_c filters to each window of n consecutive words, thereby calculating d_c features for each n-gram of a sentence. For a single filter $w_c \in \mathbb{R}^{n*d_t}$ and particular window of n words starting at position i, this operation is defined as

$$v_c^i = relu(w_c \cdot v_t^{i:i+n-1} + b_c), \qquad (1)$$

where $v_t^{i:i+n-1}$ is the flattened concatenation of vectors $v_t^{(\cdot)}$ for the words in the window, b_c is a bias, and $relu$ is the activation function of a rectified linear unit. In Figure 1, $d_c = 3$ and $n = 2$.

In order to identify the most indicative features in the sentence and to introduce invariance for the absolute position of these, we feed the n-gram representations to a max-pooling layer, which identifies the maximum value for each filter. We treat n-grams on each side of the trigger word separately during pooling, which allows the model to handle multiple event mentions per sentence, similar in spirit to (Chen et al., 2015; Zeng et al., 2015). The pooling step for a particular convolution filter $j \in [1, d_c]$ and sentence part $k \in \{\hookleftarrow, \hookrightarrow\}$ is defined as

$$v_m^{j,k} = max(v_c^i), \qquad (2)$$

where i runs through the convolution windows of k. The output of this step are sentential features $v_{\text{sent}} \in \mathbb{R}^{2*d_c}$ of the input event mention:

$$v_{\text{sent}} = (v_m^{1,\hookleftarrow}, \ldots, v_m^{d_c,\hookleftarrow}, v_m^{1,\hookrightarrow}, \ldots, v_m^{d_c,\hookrightarrow}) \quad (3)$$

Additionally, we provide the network with trigger-local, lexical-level features by concatenating v_{sent} with the word embeddings $v_w^{(\cdot)}$ of the trigger word and its left and right neighbor, resulting in $v_{\text{sent+lex}} \in \mathbb{R}^{2*d_c+3*d_w}$. This encourages the model to take the lexical semantics of the trigger into account, as these can be a strong indicator for coreference. The result is processed by an additional hidden layer, generating the final event-mention representation v_e with size d_e used for the subsequent event-linking decision:

$$v_e = tanh(W_e v_{\text{sent+lex}} + b_e). \qquad (4)$$

3.2 Learning coreference decisions

The second part of the model (Figure 1b) processes the representations for two event mentions v_e^1, v_e^2, and augments these with pairwise comparison features v_{pairw} to determine the compatibility of the event mentions. The following features are used, in parentheses we give the feature value for the pair E1, E2 from the example in Section 1:

- Coarse-grained and/or fine-grained event type agreement (*yes, yes*)
- Antecedent event is in first sentence (yes)
- Bagged distance between event mentions in #sentences/#intermediate event mentions (1, 0)
- Agreement in event modality (yes)
- Overlap in arguments (two shared arguments)

The concatenation of these vectors

$$v_{\text{sent+lex+pairw}} = (v_e^1, v_e^2, v_{\text{pairw}}) \qquad (5)$$

is processed by a single-layer neural network which calculates a distributed similarity of size d_{sim} for the two event mentions:

$$v_{\text{sim}} = square(W_{\text{sim}} v_{\text{sent+lex+pairw}} + b_{\text{sim}}). \quad (6)$$

The use of the square function as the network's non-linearity is backed by the intuition that for measuring similarity, an invariance under polarity changes is desirable. Having d_{sim} similarity dimensions allows the model to learn multiple similarity facets in parallel; in our experiments, this setup outperformed model variants with different activation functions as well as a cosine-similarity based comparison.

To calculate the final output of the model, v_{sim} is fed to a logistic regression classifier, whose output serves as the coreference score:

$$score = \sigma(W_{\text{out}} v_{\text{sim}} + b_{\text{out}}) \qquad (7)$$

We train the model parameters

$$\theta = \{W_w, W_p, \{w_c\}, \{b_c\}, W_e, b_e, W_{\text{sim}}, b_{\text{sim}}, W_{\text{out}}, b_{\text{out}}\} \quad (8)$$

by minimizing the logistic loss over shuffled mini-batches with gradient descent using Adam (Kingma and Ba, 2014).

3.3 Example generation and clustering

We investigated two alternatives for the generation of examples from documents with recognized event mentions. Figure 2 shows the strategy we found to perform best, which iterates over the event mentions of a document and pairs each mention (the "anaphors") with all preceding ones (the "antecedent" candidates). This strategy applies to both training and inference time. Soon et al. (2001) propose an alternative strategy, which during training creates positive examples only for the closest actual antecedent of an anaphoric event mention with intermediate event mentions serving as negative antecedent candidates. In our experiments, this

```
1: procedure GENERATEEXAMPLES($\mathcal{M}_d$):
2:     $\mathcal{M}_d = (m_1, \ldots, m_{|\mathcal{M}_d|})$
3:     $\mathcal{P}_d \leftarrow \varnothing$
4:     for $i = 2, \ldots, |\mathcal{M}_d|$ do
5:         for $j = 1, \ldots, i - 1$ do
6:             $\mathcal{P}_d \leftarrow \mathcal{P}_d \cup \{(m_i, m_j)\}$
7: return $\mathcal{P}_d$
```

Figure 2: Generation of examples $\mathcal{P}_d$ for a document d with a sequence of event mentions $\mathcal{M}_d$.

```
1: procedure GENERATECLUSTERS($\mathcal{P}_d$, score):
2:     $\mathcal{P}_d = \{(m_i, m_j)\}_{i,j}$
3:     score : $\mathcal{P}_d \mapsto [0, 1]$
4:     $\mathcal{C}_d \leftarrow \{(m_i, m_j) \in \mathcal{P}_d : score(m_i, m_j) > 0.5\}$
5:     while $\exists (m_i, m_k), (m_k, m_j) \in \mathcal{C}_d : (m_i, m_j) \notin \mathcal{C}_d$ do
6:         $\mathcal{C}_d \leftarrow \mathcal{C}_d \cup \{(m_i, m_j)\}$
7: return $\mathcal{C}_d$
```

Figure 3: Generation of event clusters $\mathcal{C}_d$ for a document d based on the coreference scores from the model. $\mathcal{P}_d$ is the set of all event-mention pairs from a document, as implemented in Figure 2.

strategy performed worse than the less elaborate algorithm in Figure 2.

The pairwise coreference decisions of our model induce a clustering of a document's event mentions. In order to force the model to output a consistent view on a given document, a strategy for resolving conflicting decisions is needed. We followed the strategy detailed in Figure 3, which builds the transitive closure of all positive links. Additionally, we experimented with Ng and Gardent (2002)'s "BestLink" strategy, which discards all but the highest-scoring antecedent of an anaphoric event mention. Liu et al. (2014) reported that for event linking, BestLink outperforms naive transitive closure, however, in our experiments (Section 5) we come to a different conclusion.

4 Experimental setting, model training

We implemented our model using the TensorFlow framework (Abadi et al., 2015, v0.6), and chose the ACE 2005 dataset (Walker et al., 2006, later: ACE) as our main testbed. The annotation of this corpus focuses on the event types *Conflict.Attack*, *Movement.Transport*, and *Life.Die* reporting about terrorist attacks, movement of goods and people, and deaths of people; but also contains many more related event types as well as mentions of business-relevant and judicial events. The corpus consists of merely 599 documents, which is why we create a second dataset that encompasses these documents and additionally contains 1351 more web

	ACE	ACE^{++}
# documents	599	1950
# event instances	3617	7520
# event mentions	4728	9956

Table 1: Dataset properties.

d_w	300	η	10^{-5}
d_p	8	β_1	0.2
d_c	256	β_2	0.999
d_e	50	ϵ	10^{-2}
d_{sim}	2	batch size	512
n	3	epochs	≤ 2000
Dropout	no	$\ell 2$ reg.	no

Table 2: Hyperparameter settings.

documents annotated in an analogous fashion with the same set of event types. We refer to this second dataset as ACE^{++}. Both datasets are split 9:1 into a development (*dev*) and *test* partition; we further split *dev* 9:1 into a training (*train*) and validation (*valid*) partition. Table 1 lists statistics for the datasets.

There are a number of architectural alternatives in the model as well as hyperparameters to optimize. Besides varying the size of intermediate representations in the model ($d_w, d_p, d_c, d_e, d_{sim}$), we experimented with different convolution window sizes n, activation functions for the similarity-function layer in model part (b), whether to use the dual pooling and final hidden layer in model part (a), whether to apply regularization with $\ell 2$ penalties or Dropout, and parameters to Adam ($\eta, \beta_1, \beta_2, \epsilon$). We started our exploration of this space of possibilities from previously reported hyperparameter values (Zhang and Wallace, 2015; Chen et al., 2015) and followed a combined strategy of random sampling from the hyperparameter space (180 points) and line search. Optimization was done by training on ACE$^{++}_{train}$ and evaluating on ACE$^{++}_{valid}$. The final settings we used for all following experiments are listed in Table 2. W_w is initialized with pre-trained embeddings of (Mikolov et al., 2013)[2], the embedding matrix for relative positions (W_p) and all other model parameters are randomly initialized. Model training is run for 2000 epochs, after which the best model on the respective *valid* partition is selected.

---

[2]https://code.google.com/archive/p/word2vec/

	BLANC			B-CUBED			MUC			Positive links		
	*4 * (Precision / Recall / F1 score) in %*											
This paper	**71.80**	**75.16**	**73.31**	**90.52**	86.12	88.26	**61.54**	45.16	**52.09**	47.89	**56.20**	**51.71**
(Liu et al., 2014)	70.88	70.01	70.43	89.90	**88.86**	**89.38**	53.42	**48.75**	50.98	**55.86**	40.52	46.97
(Bejan and Harabagiu, 2010)	—	—	—	83.4	84.2	83.8	—	—	—	43.3	47.1	45.1
(Sangeetha and Arock, 2012)	—	—	—	—	—	87.7	—	—	—	—	—	—

Table 3: Event-linking performance of our model & competitors on ACE. Best value per metric in bold.

5 Evaluation

This section elaborates on the conducted experiments. First, we compare our approach to state-of-art systems on dataset ACE, after which we report experiments on ACE^{++}, where we contrast variations of our model to gain insights about the impact of the utilized feature classes. We conclude this section with an error analysis.

5.1 Comparison to state-of-the-art on ACE

Table 3 depicts the performance of our model, trained on ACE$_{train}$, on ACE$_{test}$, along with the performance of state-of-the-art systems from the literature. From the wide range of proposed metrics for the evaluation of coreference resolution, we believe BLANC (Recasens and Hovy, 2011) has the highest validity, as it balances the impact of positive and negative event-mention links in a document. Negative links and consequently singleton event mentions are more common in this dataset (more than 90 % of links are negative). As Recasens and Hovy (2011) point out, the informativeness of metrics like MUC (Vilain et al., 1995), B-CUBED (Bagga and Baldwin, 1998), and the naive positive-link metric suffers from such imbalance. We still add these metrics for completeness, and because BLANC scores are not available for all systems.

Unfortunately, there are two caveats to this comparison. First, while a 9:1 train/test split is the commonly accepted way of using ACE, the exact documents in the partitions vary from system to system. We are not aware of any publicized split from previous work on event linking, which is why we create our own and announce the list of documents in ACE$_{valid}$/ACE$_{test}$ at https://git.io/vwEEP. Second, published methods follow different strategies regarding preprocessing components. While *all* systems in Table 3 use gold-annotated event-mention *triggers*, Bejan and Harabagiu (2010) and Liu et al. (2014) use a semantic-role labeler and other tools instead of gold-argument information. We argue that using full gold-annotated event mentions is reasonable in order to mitigate error propagation along the extraction pipeline and make performance values for the task at hand more informative.

We beat Liu et al. (2014)'s system in terms of F1 score on BLANC, MUC, and positive-links, while their system performs better in terms of B-CUBED. Even when taking into account the caveats mentioned above, it seems justified to assess that our model performs in general on-par with their state-of-the-art system. Their approach involves random-forest classification with best-link clustering and propagation of attributes between event mentions, and is grounded on a manifold of external feature sources, i.e., it uses a "rich set of 105 semantic features". Thus, their approach is strongly tied to domains where these semantic features are available and is potentially hard to port to other text kinds. In contrast, our approach does not depend on resources with restricted domain availability.

Bejan and Harabagiu (2010) propose a non-parametric Bayesian model with standard lexical-level features and WordNet-based similarity between event elements. We outperform their system in terms of B-CUBED and positive-links, which indicates that their system tends to over-merge event mentions, i.e., has a bias against singletons. They use a slightly bigger variant of ACE with 46 additional documents in their experiments.

Sangeetha and Arock (2012) hand-craft a similarity metric for event mentions based on the number of shared entities in the respective sentences, lexical terms, synsets in WordNet, which serves as input to a mincut-based cluster identification. Their system performs well in terms of B-CUBED F1, however their paper provides few details about the exact experimental setup.

Another approach with results on ACE was presented by Chen et al. (2009), who employ a maximum-entropy classifier with agglomerative clustering and lexical, discourse, and semantic features, e.g., also a WordNet-based similarity mea-

	Model	Dataset	BLANC (P/R/F1 in %)		
1)	Section 3	ACE	71.80	**75.16**	**73.31**
2)	Sec. 3 + BestLink	ACE	**75.68**	69.72	72.19
3)	Section 3	ACE^{++}	73.22	**83.21**	**76.90**
4)	Sec. 3 + BestLink	ACE^{++}	**74.24**	68.86	71.09

Table 4: Impact of data amount and clustering.

	Pw	Loc	Sen	Dataset	BLANC (P/R/F1 in %)		
1)	✓			ACE^{++}	57.45	68.16	56.69
2)	✓	✓		ACE^{++}	62.24	76.23	64.12
3)	✓	✓	✓	ACE^{++}	73.22	**83.21**	**76.90**
4)	✓		✓	ACE^{++}	**82.60**	70.71	74.97
5)		✓	✓	ACE^{++}	59.67	66.25	61.28
6)			✓	ACE^{++}	58.38	55.85	56.70

Table 5: Impact of feature classes; "Pw" is short for pairwise features, "Loc" refers to trigger-local lexical features, "Sen" corresponds to sentential features.

sure. However, they report performance using a threshold optimized on the test set, thus we decided to not include the performance here.

5.2 Further evaluation on ACE and ACE^{++}

We now look at several aspects of the model performance to gain further insights about it's behavior.

Impact of dataset size and clustering strategy Table 4 shows the impact of increasing the amount of training data (ACE → ACE^{++}). This increase (rows 1, 3) leads to a boost in recall, from 75.16% to 83.21%, at the cost of a small decrease in precision. This indicates that the model can generalize much better using this additional training data.

Looking into the use of the alternative clustering strategy BestLink recommended by Liu et al. (2014), we can make the expected observation of a precision improvement (row 1 vs. 2; row 3 vs. 4), due to fewer positive links being used before the transitive-closure clustering takes place. This is however outweighed by a large decline in recall, resulting in a lower F1 score (73.31 → 72.19; 76.90 → 71.09). The better performance of BestLink in Liu et al.'s model suggests that our model already weeds out many low confidence links in the classification step, which makes a downstream filtering unnecessary in terms of precision, and even counter-productive in terms of recall.

Model	Dataset	BLANC (P/R/F1 in %)		
Section 3	ACE^{++}	**73.22**	83.21	**76.90**
All singletons	ACE^{++}	45.29	50.00	47.53
One instance	ACE^{++}	4.71	50.00	8.60
Same type	ACE^{++}	62.73	**84.75**	61.35

Table 6: Event-linking performance of our model against naive baselines.

Impact of feature classes Table 5 shows our model's performance when particular feature classes are removed from the model (with re-training), with row 3 corresponding to the full model as described in Section 3. Unsurprisingly, classifying examples with just pairwise features (row 1) results in the worst performance, and adding first trigger-local lexical features (row 2), then sentential features (row 3) subsequently raises both precision and recall. Just using pairwise features and sentential ones (row 4), boosts precision, which is counter-intuitive at first, but may be explained by a different utilization of the sentential-feature part of the model during training. This part is then adapted to focus more on the trigger-word aspect, meaning the sentential features degrade to trigger-local features. While this allows to reach higher precision (recall that Section 3 finds that more than fifty percent of positive examples have trigger-word agreement), it substantially limits the model's ability to learn other coreference-relevant aspects of event-mention pairs, leading to low recall. Further considering rows 5 & 6, we can conclude that all feature classes indeed positively contribute to the overall model performance.

Baselines The result of applying three naive baselines to ACE^{++} is shown in Table 6. The *all singletons/one instance* baselines predict every input link to be negative/positive, respectively. In particular the all-singletons baseline performs well, due to the large fraction of singleton event mentions in the dataset. The third baseline, *same type*, predicts a positive link whenever there is agreement on the event type, namely, it ignores the possibility that there could be multiple event mentions of the same type in a document which do not refer to the same real-world event, e.g., referring to different terrorist attacks. This baseline also performs quite well, in particular in terms of recall, but shows low precision.

Error analysis We manually investigated a sample of 100 false positives and 100 false negatives from ACE^{++} in order to get an understanding of system errors.

It turns out that a significant portion of the false negatives would involve the resolution of a pronoun to a previous event mention, a very hard and yet unsolved problem. Consider the following examples:

- *"It's crazy that we're **bombing** Iraq. **It** sickens me."*
- *"Some of the slogans sought to rebut **war** supporters' arguments that the protests are unpatriotic. [...] Nobody questions whether **this** is right or not.*

In both examples, the event mentions (trigger words in bold font) are gold-annotated as coreferential, but our model failed to recognize this.

Another observation is that for 17 false negatives, we found analogous cases among the sampled false positives where annotators made a different annotation decision. Consider these examples:

- *The 1860 Presidential **Election**. [...] Lincoln **won** a plurality with about 40% of the vote.*
- *She **lost** her seat in the 1997 **election**.*

Each bullet point has two event mentions (in bold font) taken from the same document and referring to the same event type, i.e., *Personnel.Elect*. While in the first example, the annotators identified the mentions as coreferential, the second pair of mentions is not annotated as such. Analogously, 22 out of the 100 analyzed false positives were cases where the misclassification of the system was plausible to a human rater. This exemplifies that this task has many boundary cases were a positive/negative decision is hard to make even for expert annotators, thus putting the overall performance of all models in Table 3 in perspective.

6   Related work

We briefly point out other relevant approaches and efforts from the vast amount of literature.

Event coreference In addition to the competitors mentioned in Section 5, approaches for event linking were presented, e.g., by Chen and Ji (2009), who determine link scores with hand-crafted compatibility metrics for event mention pairs and a maximum-entropy model, and feed these to a spectral clustering algorithm. A variation of the event-coreference resolution task extends the scope to cross-document relations. Cybulska and Vossen (2015) approach this task with various classification models and propose to use a type-specific

granularity hierarchy for feature values. Lee et al. (2012) further extend the task definition by jointly resolving entity and event coreference, through several iterations of mention-cluster merge operations. Sachan et al. (2015) describe an active-learning based method for the same problem, where they derive a clustering of entities/events by incorporating bits of human judgment as constraints into the objective function. Araki and Mitamura (2015) simultaneously identify event triggers and disambiguate them wrt. one another with a structured-perceptron algorithm.

Resources Besides the ACE 2005 corpus, a number of other datasets with event-coreference annotation have been presented. Hovy et al. (2013) reports on the annotation process of two corpora from the domains of "violent events" and biographic texts; to our knowledge neither of them is publicly available. OntoNotes (Weischedel et al., 2013) comprises different annotation layers including coreference (Pradhan et al., 2012), however intermingles entity and event coreference. A series of releases of the EventCorefBank corpus (Bejan and Harabagiu, 2010; Lee et al., 2012; Cybulska and Vossen, 2014) combine linking of event mentions within and across documents, for which Liu et al. (2014) report a lack of completeness on the within-document aspect. The ProcessBank dataset (Berant et al., 2014) provides texts with event links from the difficult biological domain.

Other A few approaches to the upstream task of event extraction, while not considering within-document event linking, still utilize discourse-level information or even cross-document inference. For example, Liao and Grishman (2010) showed how the output of sentence-based classifiers can be filtered wrt. discourse-level consistency. Yao et al. (2010) resolved coreferences between events from different documents in order to make a global extraction decision, similar to (Ji and Grishman, 2008) and (Li et al., 2011).

In addition to convolutional neural networks, more types of neural architectures lend themselves to the generation of sentential features. Recently many recursive networks and recurrent ones have been proposed for the task of relation classification, with state-of-the-art results (Socher et al., 2012; Hashimoto et al., 2013; Ebrahimi and Dou, 2015; Xu et al., 2015; Li et al., 2015).

7 Conclusion

Our proposed model for the task of event linking achieves state-of-the-art results without relying on external feature sources. We have thus shown that low linking performance, coming from a lack of semantic knowledge about a domain, is evitable. In addition, our experiments give further empirical evidence for the usefulness of neural models for generating latent-feature representations for sentences.

There are several areas for potential future work. As next steps, we plan to test the model on more datasets and task variations, i.e., in a cross-document setting or for joint trigger identification and coreference resolution. On the other hand, separating anaphoricity detection from antecedent scoring, as is often done for the task of entity coreference resolution (e.g., by Wiseman et al. (2015)), might result in performance gains; also the generation of sentential features from recurrent neural networks seems promising. Regarding our medium-term research agenda, we would like to investigate if the model can benefit from more fine-grained information about the discourse structure underlying a text. This could guide the model when encountering the problematic case of pronoun resolution, described in the error analysis.

Acknowledgments

This research was supported by the German Federal Ministry of Education and Research (BMBF) through the projects ALL SIDES (contract 01IW14002) and BBDC (contract 01IS14013E), and by a Google Focused Research Award granted in July 2013.

References

Abadi et al. 2015. TensorFlow: Large-scale machine learning on heterogeneous systems. Software available from tensorflow.org.

Jun Araki and Teruko Mitamura. 2015. Joint event trigger identification and event coreference resolution with structured perceptron. In *EMNLP*, pages 2074–2080. The Association for Computational Linguistics.

Amit Bagga and Breck Baldwin. 1998. Algorithms for scoring coreference chains. In *Proceedings of the LREC 1998 Workshop on Linguistic Coreference*, pages 563—-566.

Collin F. Baker, Charles J. Fillmore, and John B. Lowe. 1998. The Berkeley FrameNet Project. In *COLING-ACL*, pages 86–90. Morgan Kaufmann Publishers / ACL.

Cosmin Adrian Bejan and Sanda M. Harabagiu. 2010. Unsupervised event coreference resolution with rich linguistic features. In *ACL*, pages 1412–1422. The Association for Computational Linguistics.

Jonathan Berant, Vivek Srikumar, Pei-Chun Chen, Abby Vander Linden, Brittany Harding, Brad Huang, Peter Clark, and Christopher D. Manning. 2014. Modeling biological processes for reading comprehension. In *EMNLP*. The Association for Computational Linguistics.

Zheng Chen and Heng Ji. 2009. Graph-based event coreference resolution. In *Proceedings of the 2009 Workshop on Graph-based Methods for Natural Language Processing*, pages 54–57. The Association for Computational Linguistics.

Zheng Chen, Heng Ji, and Robert Haralick. 2009. A pairwise event coreference model, feature impact and evaluation for event coreference resolution. In *Proceedings of the Workshop on Events in Emerging Text Types*, pages 17–22, Borovets, Bulgaria, September. Association for Computational Linguistics.

Yubo Chen, Liheng Xu, Kang Liu, Daojian Zeng, and Jun Zhao. 2015. Event extraction via dynamic multi-pooling convolutional neural networks. In *ACL (1)*, pages 167–176. The Association for Computational Linguistics.

Ronan Collobert, Jason Weston, Léon Bottou, Michael Karlen, Koray Kavukcuoglu, and Pavel P. Kuksa. 2011. Natural language processing (almost) from scratch. *Journal of Machine Learning Research*, 12:2493–2537.

Agata Cybulska and Piek Vossen. 2014. Using a sledgehammer to crack a nut? Lexical diversity and event coreference resolution. In *LREC*, pages 4545–4552. European Language Resources Association (ELRA).

Agata Cybulska and Piek Vossen. 2015. Translating granularity of event slots into features for event coreference resolution. In *Proceedings of the The 3rd Workshop on EVENTS: Definition, Detection, Coreference, and Representation*, pages 1–10, Denver, Colorado, June. Association for Computational Linguistics.

Cícero Nogueira dos Santos, Bing Xiang, and Bowen Zhou. 2015. Classifying relations by ranking with convolutional neural networks. In *ACL (1)*, pages 626–634. The Association for Computational Linguistics.

Javid Ebrahimi and Dejing Dou. 2015. Chain based RNN for relation classification. In *HLT-NAACL*, pages 1244–1249. The Association for Computational Linguistics.

Christiane Fellbaum, editor. 1998. *WordNet: an electronic lexical database*. Christiane Fellbaum.

Kazuma Hashimoto, Makoto Miwa, Yoshimasa Tsuruoka, and Takashi Chikayama. 2013. Simple customization of recursive neural networks for semantic relation classification. In *EMNLP*, pages 1372–1376. The Association for Computational Linguistics.

Eduard Hovy, Teruko Mitamura, Felisa Verdejo, Jun Araki, and Andrew Philpot. 2013. Events are not simple: Identity, non-identity, and quasi-identity. In *Workshop on Events: Definition, Detection, Coreference, and Representation*, pages 21–28, Atlanta, Georgia, June. Association for Computational Linguistics.

Heng Ji and Ralph Grishman. 2008. Refining event extraction through cross-document inference. In *ACL*, pages 254–262. The Association for Computational Linguistics.

Heng Ji and Ralph Grishman. 2011. Knowledge base population: Successful approaches and challenges. In *ACL*, pages 1148–1158. The Association for Computational Linguistics.

Diederik P. Kingma and Jimmy Ba. 2014. Adam: A method for stochastic optimization. *CoRR*, abs/1412.6980.

Sebastian Krause, Enrique Alfonseca, Katja Filippova, and Daniele Pighin. 2015. Idest: Learning a distributed representation for event patterns. In *NAACL-HLT*, pages 1140–1149. Association for Computational Linguistics.

LDC. 2005. ACE (Automatic Content Extraction) English annotation guidelines for events. Linguistic Data Consortium. Version 5.4.3 2005.07.01. https://www.ldc.upenn.edu/sites/www.ldc.upenn.edu/files/english-events-guidelines-v5.4.3.pdf.

Heeyoung Lee, Marta Recasens, Angel X. Chang, Mihai Surdeanu, and Dan Jurafsky. 2012. Joint entity and event coreference resolution across documents. In *EMNLP-CoNLL*, pages 489–500. The Association for Computational Linguistics.

Qi Li, Sam Anzaroot, Wen-Pin Lin, Xiang Li, and Heng Ji. 2011. Joint inference for cross-document information extraction. In *CIKM*, pages 2225–2228. ACM.

Jiwei Li, Thang Luong, Dan Jurafsky, and Eduard H. Hovy. 2015. When are tree structures necessary for deep learning of representations? In *EMNLP*, pages 2304–2314. The Association for Computational Linguistics.

Shasha Liao and Ralph Grishman. 2010. Using document level cross-event inference to improve event extraction. In *ACL*, pages 789–797. The Association for Computational Linguistics.

Zhengzhong Liu, Jun Araki, Eduard H. Hovy, and Teruko Mitamura. 2014. Supervised within-document event coreference using information propagation. In *LREC*, pages 4539–4544. European Language Resources Association (ELRA).

Tomas Mikolov, Ilya Sutskever, Kai Chen, Gregory S. Corrado, and Jeffrey Dean. 2013. Distributed representations of words and phrases and their compositionality. In *NIPS*, pages 3111–3119.

Mike Mintz, Steven Bills, Rion Snow, and Daniel Jurafsky. 2009. Distant supervision for relation extraction without labeled data. In *ACL/IJCNLP*, pages 1003–1011. The Association for Computational Linguistics.

Vincent Ng and Claire Gardent. 2002. Improving machine learning approaches to coreference resolution. In *ACL*, pages 104–111. The Association for Computational Linguistics.

Thien Huu Nguyen and Ralph Grishman. 2015. Event detection and domain adaptation with convolutional neural networks. In *ACL (2)*, pages 365–371. The Association for Computational Linguistics.

Sameer Pradhan, Alessandro Moschitti, Nianwen Xue, Olga Uryupina, and Yuchen Zhang. 2012. CoNLL-2012 shared task: Modeling multilingual unrestricted coreference in OntoNotes. In *Joint Conference on EMNLP and CoNLL - Shared Task*, pages 1–40. The Association for Computational Linguistics.

Marta Recasens and Eduard H. Hovy. 2011. BLANC: implementing the rand index for coreference evaluation. *Natural Language Engineering*, 17(4):485–510.

Mrinmaya Sachan, Eduard H. Hovy, and Eric P. Xing. 2015. An active learning approach to coreference resolution. In *IJCAI*, pages 1312–1318. AAAI Press.

S. Sangeetha and Michael Arock. 2012. Event coreference resolution using mincut based graph clustering. In *The Fourth International Workshop on Computer Networks & Communications*, pages 253–260.

Richard Socher, Brody Huval, Christopher D. Manning, and Andrew Y. Ng. 2012. Semantic compositionality through recursive matrix-vector spaces. In *EMNLP-CoNLL*, pages 1201–1211. The Association for Computational Linguistics.

Wee Meng Soon, Hwee Tou Ng, and Chung Yong Lim. 2001. A machine learning approach to coreference resolution of noun phrases. *Computational Linguistics*, 27(4):521–544.

Ang Sun, Ralph Grishman, and Satoshi Sekine. 2011. Semi-supervised relation extraction with large-scale word clustering. In *ACL*, pages 521–529. The Association for Computational Linguistics.

Kumutha Swampillai and Mark Stevenson. 2010. Inter-sentential relations in information extraction corpora. In *LREC*. European Language Resources Association.

Marc B. Vilain, John D. Burger, John S. Aberdeen, Dennis Connolly, and Lynette Hirschman. 1995. A model-theoretic coreference scoring scheme. In *MUC*, pages 45–52.

Christopher Walker, Stephanie Strassel, Julie Medero, and Kazuaki Maeda. 2006. ACE 2005 multilingual training corpus. Catalog number LDC2006T06. Linguistic Data Consortium. Philadelphia.

Ralph Weischedel, Martha Palmer, Mitchell Marcus, Eduard Hovy, Sameer Pradhan, Lance Ramshaw, Nianwen Xue, Ann Taylor, Jeff Kaufman, Michelle Franchini, Mohammed El-Bachouti, Robert Belvin, and Ann Houston. 2013. OntoNotes release 5.0. Catalog number LDC2013T19. Linguistic Data Consortium. Philadelphia.

Sam Wiseman, Alexander M. Rush, Stuart Shieber, and Jason Weston. 2015. Learning anaphoricity and antecedent ranking features for coreference resolution. In *ACL (1)*, pages 1416–1426. Association for Computational Linguistics.

Yan Xu, Lili Mou, Ge Li, Yunchuan Chen, Hao Peng, and Zhi Jin. 2015. Classifying relations via long short term memory networks along shortest dependency paths. In *EMNLP*, pages 1785–1794. The Association for Computational Linguistics.

Limin Yao, Sebastian Riedel, and Andrew McCallum. 2010. Collective cross-document relation extraction without labelled data. In *EMNLP*. The Association for Computational Linguistics.

Daojian Zeng, Kang Liu, Siwei Lai, Guangyou Zhou, and Jun Zhao. 2014. Relation classification via convolutional deep neural network. In *COLING*, pages 2335–2344. The Association for Computational Linguistics.

Daojian Zeng, Kang Liu, Yubo Chen, and Jun Zhao. 2015. Distant supervision for relation extraction via piecewise convolutional neural networks. In *EMNLP*, pages 1753–1762. The Association for Computational Linguistics.

Ye Zhang and Byron Wallace. 2015. A sensitivity analysis of (and practitioners' guide to) convolutional neural networks for sentence classification. *CoRR*, abs/1510.03820.

Guodong Zhou, Jian Su, Jie Zhang, and Min Zhang. 2005. Exploring various knowledge in relation extraction. In *ACL*. The Association for Computational Linguistics.

Joint Learning of the Embedding of Words and Entities for Named Entity Disambiguation

Ikuya Yamada[1,4]   **Hiroyuki Shindo**[2]   **Hideaki Takeda**[3]   **Yoshiyasu Takefuji**[4]

ikuya@ousia.jp   shindo@is.naist.jp   takeda@nii.ac.jp   takefuji@sfc.keio.ac.jp

[1]Studio Ousia, 4489-105-221 Endo, Fujisawa, Kanagawa, Japan
[2]Nara Institute of Science and Technology, 8916-5 Takayama, Ikoma, Nara, Japan
[3]National Institute of Informatics, 2-1-2 Hitotsubashi, Chiyoda, Tokyo, Japan
[4]Keio University, 5322 Endo, Fujisawa, Kanagawa, Japan

Abstract

Named Entity Disambiguation (NED) refers to the task of resolving multiple named entity mentions in a document to their correct references in a knowledge base (KB) (e.g., Wikipedia). In this paper, we propose a novel embedding method specifically designed for NED. The proposed method *jointly* maps words and entities into the same continuous vector space. We extend the *skip-gram* model by using two models. The *KB graph model* learns the relatedness of entities using the link structure of the KB, whereas the *anchor context model* aims to align vectors such that similar words and entities occur close to one another in the vector space by leveraging KB anchors and their context words. By combining contexts based on the proposed embedding with standard NED features, we achieved state-of-the-art accuracy of 93.1% on the standard CoNLL dataset and 85.2% on the TAC 2010 dataset.

1 Introduction

Named Entity Disambiguation (NED) is the task of resolving ambiguous mentions of entities to their referent entities in a knowledge base (KB) (e.g., Wikipedia). NED has lately been extensively studied (Cucerzan, 2007; Mihalcea and Csomai, 2007; Milne and Witten, 2008b; Ratinov et al., 2011) and used as a fundamental component in numerous tasks, such as information extraction, knowledge base population (McNamee and Dang, 2009; Ji et al., 2010), and semantic search (Blanco et al., 2015). We use Wikipedia as KB in this paper.

The main difficulty in NED is ambiguity in the meaning of entity mentions. For example, the mention "Washington" in a document can refer to various entities, such as the state, or the capital of the US, the actor Denzel Washington, the first US president George Washington, and so on. In order to resolve these ambiguous mentions into references to the correct entities, early approaches focused on modeling *textual* context, such as the similarity between contextual words and encyclopedic descriptions of a candidate entity (Bunescu and Pasca, 2006; Mihalcea and Csomai, 2007). Most state-of-the-art methods use more sophisticated *global* approaches, where all mentions in a document are simultaneously disambiguated based on global *coherence* among disambiguation decisions.

Word embedding methods are also becoming increasingly popular (Mikolov et al., 2013a; Mikolov et al., 2013b; Pennington et al., 2014). These involve learning continuous vector representations of words from large, unstructured text corpora. The vectors are designed to capture the semantic similarity of words when similar words are placed near one another in a relatively low-dimensional vector space.

In this paper, we propose a method to construct a novel embedding that *jointly* maps words and entities into the same continuous vector space. In this model, similar words and entities are placed close to one another in a vector space. Hence, we can measure the similarity between any pair of items (i.e., words, entities, and a word and an entity) by simply computing their cosine similarity. This enables us to easily measure the contextual information for NED, such as the similarity between a context word and a candidate entity, and the relatedness of entities required to model coherence.

Our model is based on the skip-gram model (Mikolov et al., 2013a; Mikolov et al., 2013b), a

Proceedings of the 20th SIGNLL Conference on Computational Natural Language Learning (CoNLL), pages 250–259,
Berlin, Germany, August 7-12, 2016. ©2016 Association for Computational Linguistics

recently proposed embedding model that learns to predict each context word given the target word. Our model consists of the following three models based on the skip-gram model: 1) the conventional skip-gram model that learns to predict neighboring words given the target word in text corpora, 2) the *KB graph model* that learns to estimate neighboring entities given the target entity in the link graph of the KB, and 3) the *anchor context model* that learns to predict neighboring words given the target entity using anchors and their context words in the KB. By jointly optimizing these models, our method simultaneously learns the embedding of words and entities.

Based on our proposed embedding, we also develop a straightforward NED method that computes two contexts using the proposed embedding: textual context similarity, and coherence. Textual context similarity is measured according to vector similarity between an entity and words in a document. Coherence is measured based on the relatedness between the target entity and other entities in a document. Our NED method combines these contexts with several standard features (e.g., prior probability) using supervised machine learning.

We tested the proposed method using two standard NED datasets: the CoNLL dataset and the TAC 2010 dataset. Experimental results revealed that our method outperforms state-of-the-art methods on both datasets by significant margins. Moreover, we conducted experiments to separately assess the quality of the vector representation of entities using an entity relatedness dataset, and discovered that our method successfully learns the quality representations of entities.

2 Joint Embedding of Words and Entities

In this section, we first describe the conventional skip-gram model for learning word embedding. We then explain our method to construct an embedding that jointly maps words and entities into the same continuous d-dimensional vector space. We extend the skip-gram model by adding the *KB graph model* and the *anchor context model*.

2.1 Skip-gram Model for Word Similarity

The training objective of the skip-gram model is to find word representations that are useful to predict context words given the target word. Formally, given a sequence of T words $w_1, w_2, ..., w_T$, the model aims to maximize the following objective function:

$$\mathcal{L}_w = \sum_{t=1}^{T} \sum_{-c \le j \le c, j \ne 0} \log P(w_{t+j}|w_t) \quad (1)$$

where c is the size of the context window, w_t denotes the target word, and w_{t+j} is its context word. The conditional probability $P(w_{t+j}|w_t)$ is computed using the following softmax function:

$$P(w_{t+j}|w_t) = \frac{\exp(\mathbf{V}_{w_t}{}^\top \mathbf{U}_{w_{t+j}})}{\sum_{w \in W} \exp(\mathbf{V}_{w_t}{}^\top \mathbf{U}_w)} \quad (2)$$

where W is a set containing all words in the vocabulary, and $\mathbf{V}_w \in \mathbb{R}^d$ and $\mathbf{U}_w \in \mathbb{R}^d$ denote the vectors of word w in matrices $\mathbf{V}$ and $\mathbf{U}$, respectively.

The skip-gram model is trained to optimize the above function $\mathcal{L}_w$, and $\mathbf{V}$ are used as the resulting vector representations of words.

2.2 Extending the Skip-gram Model

We extend the skip-gram model to learn the vector representations of entities. We expand matrices $\mathbf{V}$ and $\mathbf{U}$ to include the vectors of entities $\mathbf{V}_e \in \mathbb{R}^d$ and $\mathbf{U}_e \in \mathbb{R}^d$ in addition to the vectors for words.

2.2.1 KB Graph Model

We use an internal link structure in KB to enable the model to learn the relatedness between pairs of entities. Wikipedia Link-based Measure (WLM) (Milne and Witten, 2008a) is a method to measure entity relatedness based on its link structure. It has been used as a standard method to compute the relatedness of entities for modeling coherence in past NED studies. The relatedness between two entities is computed using the following function:

$$WLM(e_1, e_2) = 1 - \frac{\log \max(|C_{e_1}|, |C_{e_2}|) - \log |C_{e_1} \cap C_{e_2}|}{\log |E| - \log \min(|C_{e_1}|, |C_{e_2}|)} \quad (3)$$

where E is the set of all entities in KB and C_e is the set of entities with a link to an entity e. Intuitively, WLM assumes that entities with similar incoming links are related. Despite its simplicity, WLM yields state-of-the art performance (Hoffart et al., 2012).

Inspired by WLM, the KB graph model simply learns to place entities with similar incoming links near one another in the vector space. We formalize this as the following objective function:

$$\mathcal{L}_e = \sum_{e_i \in E} \sum_{e_o \in C_{e_i}, e_i \ne e_o} \log P(e_o|e_i) \quad (4)$$

We compute the conditional probability $P(e_o|e_i)$ using the following softmax function:

$$P(e_o|e_i) = \frac{\exp(\mathbf{V}_{e_i}{}^\top \mathbf{U}_{e_o})}{\sum_{e \in E} \exp(\mathbf{V}_{e_i}{}^\top \mathbf{U}_e)} \quad (5)$$

We train the model to predict the incoming links C_e given an entity e. Therefore, C_e plays a similar role to context words in the skip-gram model.

2.2.2 Anchor Context Model

If we add only the KB graph model to the skip-gram model, the vectors of words and entities do not interact, and can be placed in different subspaces of the vector space. To address this issue, we introduce the anchor context model to place similar words and entities near one another in the vector space.

The idea underlying this model is to leverage KB anchors and their context words to train the model. As mentioned in Section 1, we use Wikipedia as a KB. It contains many internal anchors that can be safely treated as unambiguous occurrences of referent KB entities. By using these anchors, we can easily obtain many occurrences of entities and their corresponding context words directly from the KB.

As in the skip-gram model, we simply train the model to predict the context words of an entity pointed to by the target anchor. The objective function is as follows:

$$\mathcal{L}_a = \sum_{(e_i, Q) \in A} \sum_{w_o \in Q} \log P(w_o|e_i) \quad (6)$$

where A denotes a set of anchors in the KB, each of which contains a pair of a referent entity e_i and a set of its context words Q. Here, Q contains the previous c words and the next c words. Note that $|A|$ equals the number of internal anchors in the KB. As in past models, the conditional probability $P(w_o|e_i)$ is computed using the softmax function:

$$P(w_o|e_i) = \frac{\exp(\mathbf{V}_{e_i}{}^\top \mathbf{U}_{w_o})}{\sum_{w \in W} \exp(\mathbf{V}_{e_i}{}^\top \mathbf{U}_w)} \quad (7)$$

Using the proposed model, we align the vector representations of words and entities by placing words and entities with similar context words close to one another in the vector space.

2.3 Training

Considering the three model components mentioned above, we propose the following objective function by linearly combining the above objective functions:

$$\mathcal{L} = \mathcal{L}_w + \mathcal{L}_e + \mathcal{L}_a \quad (8)$$

The training of the model is intended to maximize the above function, and the resulting matrix $\mathbf{V}$ is used to embed words and entities.

One of the problems in training our model is that the normalizers contained in the softmax functions $P(w_{t+j}|w_t)$, $P(e_o|e_i)$, and $P(w_o|e_i)$ are computationally very expensive because they involve summation over all words W or entities E. To address this problem, we use *negative sampling (NEG)* (Mikolov et al., 2013b) to convert original objective functions into computationally feasible ones. NEG is defined by the following objective function:

$$\log \sigma(\mathbf{V}_{w_t}{}^\top \mathbf{U}_{w_{t+j}}) + \sum_{i=1}^{g} \mathbb{E}_{w_i \sim P_{neg}(w)} \left[\log \sigma(-\mathbf{V}_{w_t}{}^\top \mathbf{U}_{w_i}) \right] \quad (9)$$

where $\sigma(x) = 1/(1 + \exp(-x))$ and g is the number of negative samples. We replace the $\log P(w_{t+j}|w_t)$ term in Eq. (1) with the above objective function. Consequently, the objective function is transformed from that in Eq. (1) to a simple objective function of the binary classification to distinguish the observed word w_t from words drawn from noise distribution $P_{neg}(w)$. We also replace $\log P(e_o|e_i)$ in Eq. (4) and $\log P(w_o|e_i)$ in Eq. (6) in the same manner.

Note that NEG takes a negative distribution $P_{neg}(w)$ as a free parameter. Following (Mikolov et al., 2013b), we use the unigram distribution of words ($U(w)$) raised to the $3/4^{th}$ power (i.e., $U(w)^{3/4}/Z$, where Z is a normalization constant) in the skip-gram model and the anchor context model. In the KB graph model, we use a uniform distribution over KB entities E as the negative distribution.

We use Wikipedia to train all the above models. Optimization is carried out simultaneously to maximize the transformed objective function by iterating over Wikipedia pages several times. We use stochastic gradient descent (SGD) for the optimization. The optimization is performed using a multiprocess-based implementation of our model using Python, Cython, and NumPy configured with OpenBLAS with storing matrices $\mathbf{V}$ and $\mathbf{U}$ in the shared memory. To improve speed, we decide not to introduce locks to the shared matrices.

3 Named Entity Disambiguation Using Embedding

In this section, we explain our NED method using our proposed embedding. Let us formally define the task. Given a set of entity mentions $M = \{m_1, m_2, ..., m_N\}$ in a document d with an entity set $E = \{e_1, e_2, ..., e_K\}$ in the KB, the task is defined as resolving mentions (e.g., "Washington") into their referent entities (e.g., Washington D.C.).

We introduce two measures that have been frequently observed in past NED studies: *entity prior* $P(e)$ and *prior probability* $P(e|m)$. We define entity prior $P(e) = |A_{e,*}|/|A_{*,*}|$ where $A_{*,*}$ denotes all anchors in the KB and $A_{e,*}$ is the set of anchors that point to entity e. Prior probability is defined as $P(e|m) = |A_{e,m}|/|A_{*,m}|$ where $A_{*,m}$ represents all anchors with the same surface as mention m in KB and $A_{e,m}$ is a subset of $A_{*,m}$ that points to entity e.

We separate the NED task into two sub-tasks: *candidate generation* and *mention disambiguation*. In candidate generation, candidates of referent entities are generated for each mention. Details of candidate generation are provided in Section 4.3.1.

3.1 Mention Disambiguation

Given a document d and mention m with its candidate referent entities $\{e_1, e_2, ..., e_k\}$ generated in the candidate generation step, the task is to disambiguate mention m by selecting the most relevant entity from the candidate entities.

The key to improving the performance of this task is to effectively model the context. We propose two novel methods to model the context using the proposed embedding. Further, we combine these two models with several standard NED features using supervised machine learning described in 3.1.3.

3.1.1 Modeling Textual Context

Textual context is designed based on the assumption that an entity is more likely to appear if the context of a given mention is similar to that of the entity.

We propose a method to measure the similarity between textual context and entity using the proposed embedding by first deriving the vector representation of the context and then computing the similarity between the context and the entity using cosine similarity. To derive the vector of context, we average the vectors of context words:

$$\vec{v_{c_w}} = \frac{1}{|W_{c_m}|} \sum_{w \in W_{c_m}} \vec{v_w} \tag{10}$$

where W_{c_m} is a set of the context words of mention m and $\vec{v_w} \in \mathbf{V}$ denotes the vector representation of word w. We use all noun words in document d as context words.[1] Moreover, we ignore a context word if the surface of mention m contains it.

We then measure the similarity between candidate entity and the derived textual context by using cosine similarity between $\vec{v_{c_w}}$ and the vector of entity $\vec{v_e}$.

3.1.2 Modeling Coherence

It has been revealed that effectively modeling coherence in the assignment of entities to mentions is important for NED. However, this is a chicken-and-egg problem because the assignment of entities to mentions, which is required to measure coherence, is not possible prior to performing NED.

Similar to past work (Ratinov et al., 2011), we address this problem by employing a simple *two-step* approach: we first train the machine learning model using the coherence score among unambiguous mentions[2], in addition to other features, and then retrain the model using the coherence score among the predicted entity assignments instead.

To estimate coherence, we first calculate the vector representation of the context entities and measure the similarity between the vector of the context entities and that of the target entity e. Note that context entities are unambiguous entities in the first step, and predicted entities are used instead in the second step.

To derive the vector representation of context entities, we average their vector representations:

$$\vec{v_{c_e}} = \frac{1}{|E_{c_m}|} \sum_{e^* \in E_{c_m}} \vec{v_{e^*}} \tag{11}$$

where E_{c_m} denotes the set of context entities described above.

To estimate the coherence score, we again use cosine similarity between the vector of entity $\vec{v_e}$ and that of context entities $\vec{v_{c_e}}$.

3.1.3 Learning to Rank

To combine the proposed contextual information described above with standard NED features, we employ a method of supervised machine learning to rank the candidate entities given mention m and document d.

In particular, we use Gradient Boosted Regression Trees (GBRT) (Friedman, 2001), a state-of-the-art point-wise learning-to-rank algorithm widely used for various tasks, which has been recently adopted for the sort of tasks for which we employ it here (Meij et al., 2012). GBRT consists of an ensemble of regression trees, and predicts a relevance score given an instance. We use the GBRT implementation in *scikit-learn*[3] and the logistic loss is used as the loss function. The main parameters of GBRT are the number of iterations η, the learning rate β, and the maximum depth of the decision trees ξ.

With regard to the features of machine learning, we first use prior probability ($P(e|m)$) and entity prior ($P(e)$). Further, we include a feature representing the maximum prior probability of the candidate entity e of all mentions in the document. We also add the number of entity candidates for mention m as a feature. The above set of four features is called *base* features in the rest of the paper.

We also use several *string similarity* features used in past work on NED (Meij et al., 2012). These features aim to capture the similarity between the title of entity e and the surface of mention m, and consist of the edit distance, whether the title of entity e exactly equals or contains the surface of mention m, and whether the title of entity e starts or ends with the surface of mention m.

Finally, we include contextual features measured using the proposed embedding. We use cosine similarity between the candidate entity and the textual context (see Section 3.1.1), and similarity between an entity and contextual entities (see Section 3.1.2). Furthermore, we include the rank of entity e among candidate entities of mention m, sorted according to these two similarity scores in descending order.

4 Experiments

In this section, we describe the setup and results of our experiments. In addition to experiments on the NED task, we separately assessed the quality of pairwise *entity relatedness* in order to test the

	NDCG@1	NDCG@5	NDCG@10	MAP
Our Method	**0.59**	**0.56**	**0.59**	**0.52**
WLM	0.54	0.52	0.55	0.48

Table 1: Results of the entity relatedness task.

effectiveness of our method in capturing pairwise similarity between pairs of entities. We first describe the details of the training of the embedding and then present the experimental results.

4.1 Training for the Proposed Embedding

To train the proposed embedding, we used the December 2014 version of the Wikipedia dump[4]. We first removed the pages for navigation, maintenance, and discussion, and used the remaining 4.9 million pages. We parsed the Wikipedia pages and extracted text and anchors from each page. We further tokenized the text using the *Apache OpenNLP* tokenizer. We also filtered out rare words that appeared fewer than five times in the corpus. We thus obtained approximately 2 billion tokens and 73 million anchors. The total number of words and entities in the embedding were approximately 2.1 million and 5 million, respectively. Consequently, the number of rows of matrices $\mathbf{V}$ and $\mathbf{U}$ were 7.1 million.

The number of dimensions d of the embedding was set to 500. Following (Mikolov et al., 2013b), we also used learning rate $\alpha = 0.025$ which linearly decreased with the iterations of the Wikipedia dump. Regarding the other parameters, we set the size of the context window $c = 10$ and the negative samples $g = 30$. The model was trained online by iterating over pages in the Wikipedia dump 10 times. The training lasted approximately five days using a server with a 40-core CPU on Amazon EC2.

4.2 Entity Relatedness

To test the quality of the vector representation of entities, we conducted an experiment using a dataset for entity relatedness created by Ceccarelli et al. (Ceccarelli et al., 2013). The dataset consists of training, test, and validation sets, and we only use the test set for this experiment. The test set contains 3,314 entities, where each entity has 91 candidate entities with *gold-standard* labels indicating whether the two entities are related.

---

[3] http://scikit learn.org/

[4] The dump was retrieved from Wikimedia Downloads. http://dumps.wikimedia.org/

Following (Huang et al., 2015), we obtained the ranked order of the candidate entities using cosine similarity between the target entity and each of the candidate entities, and computed the two standard measures: normalized discounted cumulative gain (NDCG) (Järvelin and Kekäläinen, 2002) and mean average precision (MAP) (Manning et al., 2008). We adopted WLM as baseline.

Table 1 shows the results. The score for WLM was obtained from Huang et al. (Huang et al., 2015). Our method clearly outperformed WLM. The results show that our method accurately captures pairwise entity relatedness.

4.3 Named Entity Disambiguation

4.3.1 Setup

We now explain our experimental setup for the NED task. We tested the performance of our proposed method on two standard NED datasets: the *CoNLL* dataset and the *TAC 2010* dataset. The details of these datasets are provided below. Moreover, as with the corpus used in the embedding, we used the December 2014 version of the Wikipedia dump as the referent KB, and to derive the prior probability as well as the entity prior.

To find the best parameters for our machine learning model, we ran a parameter search on the CoNLL development set. We used $\eta = 10,000$ trees, and tested all combinations of the learning rate $\beta = \{0.01, 0.02, 0.03, 0.05\}$ and the maximum depth of the decision trees $\xi = \{3, 4, 5\}$. We computed their accuracy on the dataset, and found that the parameters did not significantly affect performance (1.0% at most). We used $\beta = 0.02$ and $\xi = 4$ which yielded the best performance.

CoNLL The CoNLL dataset is a popular NED dataset constructed by Hoffart et al. (Hoffart et al., 2011). The dataset is based on NER data from the CoNLL 2003 shared task, and consists of training, development, and test sets, containing 946, 216, and 231 documents, respectively. We trained our machine learning model using the training set and reported its performance using the test set. We also used the development set for the parameter tuning described above. Following (Hoffart et al., 2011), we only used 27,816 mentions with valid entries in the KB and reported the standard micro- (aggregates over all mentions) and macro- (aggregates over all documents) accuracies of the top-ranked candidate entities to assess disambiguation performance. For candidate generation, we use the fol-

lowing two resources: 1) a public dataset recently built by Pershina et al. (Pershina et al., 2015) (denoted by *PPRforNED*) for the sake of compatibility with their state-of-the-art results, and 2) a dictionary built using a standard YAGO means relation dataset (Hoffart et al., 2011) (denoted by *YAGO*). Moreover, we used PPRforNED for the parameter tuning of the machine learning model and for error analysis.

TAC 2010 The TAC 2010 dataset is another popular NED dataset constructed for the Text Analysis Conference (TAC)[5] (Ji et al., 2010). The dataset is based on news articles from various agencies and Web log data, and consists of a training and a test set containing 1,043 and 1,013 documents, respectively. Following past work (He et al., 2013; Chisholm and Hachey, 2015), we used mentions only with a valid entry in the KB, and reported the micro-accuracy score of the top-ranked candidate entities. We trained our model using the training set and assessed its performance using the test set. Consequently, we evaluated our model on 1,020 mentions contained in the test set. For candidate generation, we used a dictionary that was directly built from the Wikipedia dump mentioned previously. Similar to past work, we retrieved possible mention surfaces of an entity from (1) the title of the entity, (2) the title of another entity redirecting to the entity, and (3) the names of anchors that point to the entity. We retained the top 50 candidates through their entity priors for computational efficiency.

4.3.2 Comparison with State-of-the-art Methods

We compared our method with the following recently proposed state-of-the-art methods:

- Hoffart et al. (Hoffart et al., 2011) is a graph-based approach that finds a dense subgraph of entities in a document to address NED.

- He et al. (He et al., 2013) uses deep neural networks to derive the representations of entities and mention contexts and applies them to NED.

- Chisholm and Hachey (Chisholm and Hachey, 2015) uses a Wikilinks dataset (Singh et al., 2012) to improve the performance of NED.

---

[5]http://www.nist.gov/tac/

	Micro accuracy	Macro accuracy
CoNLL (PPRforNED)	93.1	92.6
CoNLL (YAGO)	91.5	90.9
TAC 2010	85.2	-

Table 2: Experimental results of our proposed NED method.

	CoNLL (Micro)	CoNLL (Macro)	TAC10 (Micro)
Our Method	**93.1**	**92.6**	**85.2**
Hoffart et al., 2011	82.5	81.7	-
He et al., 2013	85.6	84.0	81.0
Chisholm & Hachey, 2015	88.7	-	80.7
Pershina et al., 2015	91.8	89.9	-

Table 3: Accuracy scores of the proposed method and the state-of-the-art methods.

- Pershina et al. (Pershina et al., 2015) improved NED by modeling coherence using the personalized page rank algorithm, and achieved the best-known accuracy on the CoNLL dataset.

4.3.3 Results

Table 2 shows the experimental results of our proposed method. Our method successfully achieved enhanced performance on both the CoNLL and the TAC 2010 datasets. Moreover, we found that the choice of candidate generation method considerably affected performance on the CoNLL dataset.

Further, Table 3 shows the experimental results of our proposed method as well as those of state-of-the-art methods. Our method outperformed all the state-of-the-art methods on both datasets.

4.3.4 Feature Study

We conducted a feature study on our method. We began with base features, added various features to our system incrementally, and reported their impact on performance. We then introduced our two-step approach to achieve the final results.

Table 4 shows the results. Surprisingly, we attained results comparable with those of some state-of-the-art methods on the both datasets by only using base features. Adding string similarity features slightly further improved performance.

We observed significant improvement when adding textual context features based on our proposed embedding. Our method outperformed

	Micro accuracy	Macro accuracy
CoNLL (PPRforNED):		
Base	85.4	87.4
+String similarity	85.8	87.8
+Textual context	90.9	92.4
+Coherence	91.4	92.1
Two-step	**93.1**	**92.6**
CoNLL (YAGO):		
Base	81.1	83.6
+String similarity	81.3	84.2
+Textual context	87.2	89.6
+Coherence	90.3	90.8
Two-step	**91.5**	**90.9**
TAC 2010:		
Base	80.1	-
+String similarity	81.7	-
+Textual context	84.6	-
+Coherence	**85.5**	-
Two-step	85.2	-

Table 4: The results of our feature study.

some state-of-the-art methods without using coherence.

Further, coherence based on unambiguous entity mentions and our two-step approach significantly improved performance on the CoNLL dataset. However, it did not contribute to performance on the TAC 2010 dataset. This was because of the significant difference in the density of entity mentions between the datasets. The CoNLL dataset contains approximately 20 entity mentions per document, but the TAC 2010 only contains approximately one mention per document which is unarguably insufficient to model coherence.

4.3.5 Error Analysis

We also conducted an error analysis on the CoNLL test set with candidate generation using PPRforNED dataset. We observed that approximately 48.6% errors were caused by *metonymy* mentions (Ling et al., 2015) (i.e., mentions with more than one plausible annotation). In particular, our NED method often erred when an incorrect entity was highly popular and exactly matched the mention surface (e.g., "South Africa" referring to the entity South Africa national rugby union team rather than the entity South Africa). This makes sense because our machine learning model uses the popularity statistics of the KB (i.e., prior probability and entity prior), and the string similarity between the title of the entity and the mention surface. This problem is discussed further in (Ling et al., 2015).

Furthermore, because our method depends on the presence of KB anchors in order to learn entity representation, it arguably fails to learn satisfactory representations of tail entities (i.e., entities rarely referred to by anchors), thus resulting in disambiguation errors. We discovered that nearly 9.6% errors were due to referent entities with less than 10 inbound KB anchors, and 4.5% involved entities with no inbound KB anchor. These errors might be addressed using KB data other than KB anchors, such as the description of the entities and the KB categories in order to avoid dependence on the KB anchors. This remains part of our future work.

5 Related Work

Early NED methods addressed the problem as a well-studied *word sense disambiguation* problem (Mihalcea and Csomai, 2007). These methods primarily focused on modeling the similarity of *textual* (*local*) context. Most recent state-of-the-art methods focus on modeling *coherence* among disambiguated entities in the same document (Cucerzan, 2007; Milne and Witten, 2008b; Hoffart et al., 2011; Ratinov et al., 2011). These approaches have also been called *collective* or *global* approaches in the literature.

Learning the representations of entities for NED has been addressed in past literature. Guo and Barbosa (Guo and Barbosa, 2014) used random walks on KB graphs to construct vector representations of entities and documents to address NED. Blanco et al. (Blanco et al., 2015) proposed a method to map entities into the word embedding (i.e., Word2vec (Mikolov et al., 2013b)) space using entity descriptions in the KB and applied it for NED. He et al. (He et al., 2013) used deep neural networks to compute representations of entities and contexts of mentions directly from the KB. Similarly, Sun et al. (Sun et al., 2015) proposed a method based on deep neural networks to model representations of mentions, contexts of mentions, and entities. Huang et al. (Huang et al., 2015) also leveraged deep neural networks to learn entity representations such that the consequent pairwise entity relatedness was more suitable than of a standard method (i.e., WLM) for NED. Further, Hu et

al. (Hu et al., 2015) used hierarchical information in the KB to build entity embedding and applied it to model coherence. Unlike these methods, our proposed approach involves jointly learning vector representations of entities as well as words, hence enabling the accurate computation of the semantic similarity among its items to model both the textual context and coherence.

Moreover, Yaghoobzadeh and Schutze (Yaghoobzadeh and Schütze, 2015) addressed an entity typing task by building an embedding of words and entities on a corpus with annotated entities (i.e., FACC1 (Gabrilovich et al., 2013)) using the skip-gram model. Compared to our method, in addition to the significant difference between their task and NED, their embedding does not incorporate the link graph data of KB, which is known to be highly important for NED.

Furthermore, in the context of *knowledge graph embedding*, another tenor of recent works has been published (Bordes et al., 2011; Socher et al., 2013; Lin et al., 2015). These methods focus on learning vector representations of entities to primarily address the *link prediction* task that aims to predict a new fact based on existing facts in KB. Particularly, Wang et al. (Wang et al., 2014) have recently revealed that the joint modeling of the embedding of words and entities can improve performance in several tasks including the link prediction task, which is somewhat analogous to our experimental results.

6 Conclusions

In this paper, we proposed an embedding method to jointly map words and entities into the same continuous vector space. Our method enables us to effectively model both *textual* and *global* contexts. Further, armed with these context models, our NED method outperforms state-of-the-art NED methods.

In future work, we intend to improve our model by leveraging relevant knowledge, such as relations in a knowledge graph (e.g., Freebase).

References

Roi Blanco, Giuseppe Ottaviano, and Edgar Meij. 2015. Fast and Space-Efficient Entity Linking for Queries. In *Proceedings of the Eighth ACM International Conference on Web Search and Data Mining (WSDM)*, pages 179–188.

Antoine Bordes, Jason Weston, Ronan Collobert, and Yoshua Bengio. 2011. Learning Structured Embeddings of Knowledge Bases. In *Proceedings of the 25th Conference on Artificial Intelligence (AAAI)*, pages 301–306.

Razvan Bunescu and Marius Pasca. 2006. Using Encyclopedic Knowledge for Named Entity Disambiguation. In *Proceedings of the 11th Conference of the European Chapter of the Association for Computational Linguistics (EACL)*, pages 9–16.

Diego Ceccarelli, Claudio Lucchese, Salvatore Orlando, Raffaele Perego, and Salvatore Trani. 2013. Learning Relatedness Measures for Entity Linking. In *Proceedings of the 22nd ACM International Conference on Information and Knowledge Management (CIKM)*, pages 139–148.

Andrew Chisholm and Ben Hachey. 2015. Entity Disambiguation with Web Links. *Transactions of the Association for Computational Linguistics*, 3:145–156.

Silviu Cucerzan. 2007. Large-Scale Named Entity Disambiguation Based on Wikipedia Data. In *Proceedings of the 2007 Joint Conference on Empirical Methods in Natural Language Processing and Computational Natural Language Learning (EMNLP-CoNLL)*, pages 708–716.

Jerome H. Friedman. 2001. Greedy Function Approximation: A Gradient Boosting Machine. *The Annals of Statistics*, 29(5):1189–1232.

Evgeniy Gabrilovich, Michael Ringgaard, and Amarnag Subramanya. 2013. FACC1: Freebase annotation of ClueWeb corpora, Version 1 (Release date 2013-06-26, Format version 1, Correction level 0).

Zhaochen Guo and Denilson Barbosa. 2014. Entity Linking with a Unified Semantic Representation. In *Proceedings of the 23rd International Conference on World Wide Web (WWW)*, pages 1305–1310.

Zhengyan He, Shujie Liu, Mu Li, Ming Zhou, Longkai Zhang, and Houfeng Wang. 2013. Learning Entity Representation for Entity Disambiguation. In *Proceedings of the 51st Annual Meeting of the Association for Computational Linguistics (ACL) (Volume 2: Short Papers)*, pages 30–34.

Johannes Hoffart, Mohamed Amir Yosef, Ilaria Bordino, Hagen Fürstenau, Manfred Pinkal, Marc Spaniol, Bilyana Taneva, Stefan Thater, and Gerhard Weikum. 2011. Robust Disambiguation of Named Entities in Text. In *Proceedings of the Conference on Empirical Methods in Natural Language Processing (EMNLP)*, pages 782–792.

Johannes Hoffart, Stephan Seufert, Dat Ba Nguyen, Martin Theobald, and Gerhard Weikum. 2012. KORE: Keyphrase Overlap Relatedness for Entity Disambiguation. In *Proceedings of the 21st ACM International Conference on Information and Knowledge Management (CIKM)*, pages 545–554.

Zhiting Hu, Poyao Huang, Yuntian Deng, Yingkai Gao, and Eric Xing. 2015. Entity Hierarchy Embedding. In *Proceedings of the 53rd Annual Meeting of the Association for Computational Linguistics and the 7th International Joint Conference on Natural Language Processing (ACL-IJCNLP) (Volume 1: Long Papers)*, pages 1292–1300.

Hongzhao Huang, Larry Heck, and Heng Ji. 2015. Leveraging Deep Neural Networks and Knowledge Graphs for Entity Disambiguation. *CoRR*, abs/1504.0.

Kalervo Järvelin and Jaana Kekäläinen. 2002. Cumulated gain-based evaluation of IR techniques. *ACM Transactions on Information Systems*, 20(4):422–446.

Heng Ji, Ralph Grishman, Hoa Trang Dang, Kira Griffitt, and Joe Ellis. 2010. Overview of the TAC 2010 Knowledge Base Population Track. In *Proceeding of Text Analytics Conference (TAC)*.

Yankai Lin, Zhiyuan Liu, Maosong Sun, Yang Liu, and Xuan Zhu. 2015. Learning Entity and Relation Embeddings for Knowledge Graph Completion. In *Proceedings of the 29th AAAI Conference on Artificial Intelligence (AAAI)*.

Xiao Ling, Sameer Singh, and Daniel S. Weld. 2015. Design Challenges for Entity Linking. *Transactions of the Association for Computational Linguistics*, 3:315–328.

Christopher D. Manning, Prabhakar Raghavan, and Hinrich Schütze. 2008. *Introduction to Information Retrieval*. Cambridge University Press.

P McNamee and HT Dang. 2009. Overview of the TAC 2009 Knowledge Base Population Track. In *Proceeding of Text Analysis Conference (TAC)*.

Edgar Meij, Wouter Weerkamp, and Maarten de Rijke. 2012. Adding Semantics to Microblog Posts. In *Proceedings of the Fifth ACM International Conference on Web Search and Data Mining (WSDM)*, pages 563–572.

Rada Mihalcea and Andras Csomai. 2007. Wikify!: Linking Documents to Encyclopedic Knowledge. In *Proceedings of the Sixteenth ACM Conference on Information and Knowledge Management (CIKM)*, pages 233–242.

Tomas Mikolov, Greg Corrado, Kai Chen, and Jeffrey Dean. 2013a. Efficient Estimation of Word Representations in Vector Space. In *Proceedings of the International Conference on Learning Representations (ICLR)*, pages 1–12.

Tomas Mikolov, Ilya Sutskever, Kai Chen, Greg S. Corrado, and Jeff Dean. 2013b. Distributed Representations of Words and Phrases and their Compositionality. In *Advances in Neural Information Processing Systems (NIPS)*, pages 3111–3119.

David Milne and Ian H. Witten. 2008a. An Effective, Low-Cost Measure of Semantic Relatedness Obtained from Wikipedia Links. In *Proceedings of the First AAAI Workshop on Wikipedia and Artificial Intelligence (WIKIAI)*.

David Milne and Ian H. Witten. 2008b. Learning to Link with Wikipedia. In *Proceeding of the 17th ACM Conference on Information and Knowledge Management (CIKM)*, pages 509–518.

Jeffrey Pennington, Richard Socher, and Christopher D Manning. 2014. GloVe: Global Vectors for Word Representation. In *Proceedings of the 2014 Conference on Empirical Methods in Natural Language Processing (EMNLP)*, pages 1532–1543.

Maria Pershina, Yifan He, and Ralph Grishman. 2015. Personalized Page Rank for Named Entity Disambiguation. In *Proceedings of the 2015 Conference of the North American Chapter of the Association for Computational Linguistics: Human Language Technologies (NAACL-HLT)*, pages 238–243.

Lev Ratinov, Dan Roth, Doug Downey, and Mike Anderson. 2011. Local and Global Algorithms for Disambiguation to Wikipedia. In *Proceedings of the 49th Annual Meeting of the Association for Computational Linguistics: Human Language Technologies*, volume 1, pages 1375–1384.

Sameer Singh, Amarnag Subramanya, Fernando Pereira, and Andrew McCallum. 2012. Wikilinks: A Large-scale Cross-Document Coreference Corpus Labeled via Links to Wikipedia. Technical Report UM-CS-2012-015.

Richard Socher, Danqi Chen, Christopher D Manning, and Andrew Ng. 2013. Reasoning With Neural Tensor Networks for Knowledge Base Completion. In *Advances in Neural Information Processing Systems (NIPS)*, pages 926–934.

Yaming Sun, Lei Lin, Duyu Tang, Nan Yang, Zhenzhou Ji, and Xiaolong Wang. 2015. Modeling Mention, Context and Entity with Neural Networks for Entity Disambiguation. In *Proceedings of the Twenty-Fourth International Joint Conference on Artificial Intelligence (IJCAI)*, pages 1333–1339.

Zhen Wang, Jianwen Zhang, Jianlin Feng, and Zheng Chen. 2014. Knowledge Graph and Text Jointly Embedding. In *Proceedings of the 2014 Conference on Empirical Methods in Natural Language Processing (EMNLP)*, pages 1591–1601.

Yadollah Yaghoobzadeh and Hinrich Schütze. 2015. Corpus-level fine-grained entity typing using contextual information. In *Proceedings of the 2015 Conference on Empirical Methods in Natural Language Processing*, pages 715–725.

Entity Disambiguation by Knowledge and Text Jointly Embedding

Wei Fang[1,2], Jianwen Zhang[3], Dilin Wang[4], Zheng Chen[3], Ming Li[1,2]
[1]SYSU-CMU Joint Institute of Engineering,
School of Electronics and Information Technology, Sun Yat-Sen University
[2]SYSU-CMU Shunde International Joint Research Institute
{fangwei7@mail2, liming46@mail}.sysu.edu.cn
[3]Microsoft, Redmond, WA
{jiazhan, zhengc}@microsoft.com
[4]Computer Science, Dartmouth College
dilin.wang.gr@dartmouth.edu

Abstract

For most entity disambiguation systems, the secret recipes are feature representations for mentions and entities, most of which are based on Bag-of-Words (BoW) representations. Commonly, BoW has several drawbacks: (1) It ignores the intrinsic meaning of words/entities; (2) It often results in high-dimension vector spaces and expensive computation; (3) For different applications, methods of designing handcrafted representations may be quite different, lacking of a general guideline. In this paper, we propose a different approach named EDKate. We first learn low-dimensional continuous vector representations for entities and words by jointly embedding knowledge base and text in the same vector space. Then we utilize these embeddings to design simple but effective features and build a two-layer disambiguation model. Extensive experiments on real-world data sets show that (1) The embedding-based features are very effective. Even a single one embedding-based feature can beat the combination of several BoW-based features. (2) The superiority is even more promising in a difficult set where the mention-entity prior cannot work well. (3) The proposed embedding method is much better than trivial implementations of some off-the-shelf embedding algorithms. (4) We compared our EDKate with existing methods/systems and the results are also positive.

1 Introduction

Entity disambiguation is the task of linking entity mentions in unstructured text to the corresponding entities in a knowledge base. For example, in the sentence *"Michael Jordan is newly elected as AAAI fellow"*, the mention *"Michael Jordan"* should be linked to *"Michael I. Jordan"* (Berkeley Professor) rather than *"Michael Jordan"* (NBA Player). Formally, given a set of mentions $M = \{m_1, m_2, ..., m_k\}$ (specified or detected automatically) in a document d, for each mention $m_i \in M$, the task is to find the correct entity e_i in the knowledge base (KB) $\mathcal{K}$ to which the mention m_i refers.

There are various methods proposed for the problem in the past decades. But generally speaking, an entity disambiguation method is commonly composed of three stages/components. (1) Constructing representations for mentions/entities from raw data, often as the form of sparse vectors. (2) Extracting features for disambiguation models based on the representations of mentions and entities constructed in stage (1). (3) Optimizing the disambiguation model by empirically setting or learning weights on the extracted features, e.g., by training a classifier/ranker. There exist few features directly defined by heuristics, skipping the first stage. For example, string similarity or edit distance between a mention surface and an entity's canonical form (Cucerzan, 2011; Cassidy et al., 2011), and the prior probability of a mention surface being some entity, etc. However, they are the minority as it is difficult for human to design such features.

Almost all the existing methods focus on the second or the third stages while the importance of the first stage is often overlooked. The common practice to deal with the first stage of representa-

Proceedings of the 20th SIGNLL Conference on Computational Natural Language Learning (CoNLL), pages 260–269,
Berlin, Germany, August 7-12, 2016. ©2016 Association for Computational Linguistics

tions is defining handcrafted BoW representations. For example, an entity is often represented by a sparse vector of weights on the n-grams contained in the description text of the entity, i.e., the standard Bag-of-Words (BoW) representation. TF-IDF is often used to set the weights. There are several variants for this way, e.g., using selected key phrases or Wikipedia in-links/out-links instead of all n-grams as the dimensions of the vectors (Ratinov et al., 2011). The problem is more challenging when representing a mention. The common choice is using the n-gram vector of the surrounding text. Obviously the information of the local text window is too limited to well represent a mention. In practice, there is another constraint, the representations of entities and mentions should be in the same space, i.e., the dimensions of the vectors should be shared. This constraint makes the representation design more difficult. How to define such representations and the features based on them almost become the secret sauce of a disambiguation system. For example, Cucerzan (2007) uses Wikipedia anchor surfaces and "Category" values as dimensions and designed complex mechanisms to represent words, mentions and entities as sparse vectors on those dimensions.

BoW representations have several intrinsic drawbacks: First, the semantic meaning of a dimension is largely ignored. For example, "cat", "cats" and "tree" are equally distant under one-hot BoW representations. Second, BoW representations often introduce high dimension vector spaces and lead to expensive computation. Third, for different applications, methods of designing handcrafted representations may be quite different, lacking of a general guideline. The intuitive questions like "why using n-grams, Wikipedia links or category values as dimensions" and "why using TF-IDF as weights" are hinting us it is very likely these handcrafted representations are not the best and there should be some better representations.

In this paper we focus on the first stage, the problem of representations. Inspired by the recent works on word embedding (Bengio et al., 2003; Collobert et al., 2011; Mikolov et al., 2013a; Mikolov et al., 2013b), knowledge embedding (Bordes et al., 2011; Bordes et al., 2013; Socher et al., 2013; Wang et al., 2014b) and joint embedding KBs and texts (Wang et al., 2014a; Zhong and Zhang, 2015), we propose to learn representations

for entity disambiguation. Specifically, from KBs and texts, we jointly embed entities and words into the same low-dimensional continuous vector space. The embeddings are obtained by optimizing a global objective considering all the information in the KBs and texts thus the intrinsic semantics of words and entities are believed to be preserved during the embedding. Then we design simple but effective features based on embeddings and build a two-layer disambiguation model. We conduct extensive experiments on real-word data sets and exhibit the effectiveness of our words and entities' representation.

2 Related Work

Entity Disambiguation Entity disambiguation methods roughly fall into two categories: local approaches and collective approaches. Local approaches disambiguate each mention in a document separately. For example, Bunescu and Pasca (2006) compare the context of each mention with the Wikipedia categories of an entity candidate; Milne and Witten (2008) come up with the concept "unambiguous link" and make it convenient to compute entity relatedness. Differently, collective approaches require all entities in a document "coherent" in semantic, measured by some objective functions. Cucerzan (2007) proposes a topic representation for document by aggregating topic vectors of all entity candidates in the document. Kulkarni et al. (2009) model pair-wise coherence of entity candidates for two different mentions and use hill-climbing algorithm to get a proximate solution. Hoffart et al. (2011) treat entity disambiguation as the task of finding a dense subgraph which contain all mention nodes and exactly one mention-entity edge for each mention from a large graph.

Most methods above design various representations for mentions and entities. For example, based on Wikipedia, Cucerzan (2007) uses anchor surfaces to represent entities in "context space" and use items in the category boxes to represent entities in "topic space". For mentions, he takes context words among a fixed-size window around the mention as the context vector. Kulkarni et al. (2009) exploit sets of words, sets of word counts and sets of TF-IDFs to represent entities. Ratinov et al. (2011) express entities with extensive in-links and out-links in Wikipedia.

In recent years, some works are considering

how to apply neural network to disambiguate entities from context. For example, He et al. (2013) use feed-forward network to represent context based on BoW input while Sun et al. (2015) turn to convolution network directly based on the original word2vec (Mikolov et al., 2013a). However, they pay little attention to design effective word and entity representations. In this paper, we focus on learning representative word and entity vectors for disambiguation.

Embedding Word embedding aims to learn continuous vector representation for words. Word embeddings are usually learned from unlabeled text corpus by predicting context words surrounded or predicting the current word given context words (Bengio et al., 2003; Collobert et al., 2011; Mikolov et al., 2013a; Mikolov et al., 2013b). These embeddings can usually catch syntactic and semantic relations between words.

Recently knowledge embedding also becomes popular. The goal is to embed entities and relations of knowledge graphs into a low-dimension continuous vector space while certain properties in the graph are preserved (Bordes et al., 2011; Bordes et al., 2013; Socher et al., 2013; Wang et al., 2014a; Wang et al., 2014b). To connect word embedding and knowledge embedding, (Wang et al., 2014a) propose to align these two spaces by Wikipedia anchors and names of entities. (Zhong and Zhang, 2015) conduct alignment by entities' description.

3 Disambiguation by Embedding

In this part, we first refine current joint embedding techniques to train word and entity embeddings from Freebase and Wikipedia texts for disambiguation tasks. Then in section 3.2, we design simple features based on embeddings. Finally in section 3.3, we propose a two-layer disambiguation model to balance mention-entity prior and other features.

3.1 Embeddings Jointly Learning

We mainly base the joint learning framework on (Wang et al., 2014a)'s joint model and also utilize the alignment technique from (Zhong and Zhang, 2015) to better align word and entity embeddings into a same space. Furthermore, we optimize the embedding for disambiguation from two aspects. First, we add url-anchor (entity-entity) co-occurrence from Wikipedia. Second, we refine

the traditional negative sampling part to have entities in candidate list more probable to be sampled, which aims to discriminate entity candidates from each other.

3.1.1 Knowledge Model

A knowledge base $\mathcal{K}$ is usually composed of a set of triplets (h, r, t), where $h, t \in \mathcal{E}$ (the set of entities) and $r \in \mathcal{R}$ (the set of relations). Here, we follow (Wang et al., 2014a) to use $\mathbf{h}, \mathbf{r}, \mathbf{t}$ to denote the embeddings of h, r, t respectively. And score a triplet in this way:

$$z(h, r, t) = b - \frac{1}{2} \|\mathbf{h} + \mathbf{r} - \mathbf{t}\|^2 \qquad (1)$$

where b is a constant for numerical stability in the approximate optimization stage described in 3.1.5. Then normalize z and define:

$$\Pr(h|r, t) = \frac{\exp\{z(h, r, t)\}}{\sum_{\tilde{h} \in \mathcal{E}} \exp\{z(\tilde{h}, r, t)\}} \qquad (2)$$

$\Pr(r|h, t)$ and $\Pr(t|h, r)$ are also defined in a similar way. And the likelihood of observing a triplet is:

$$\mathcal{L}_{triplet}(h, r, t) = \log \Pr(h|r, t) + \log \Pr(r|h, t) \\ + \log \Pr(t|h, r) \qquad (3)$$

Then the goal is to maximize the likelihood of all triplets in the whole knowledge graph:

$$\mathcal{L}_K = \sum_{(h, r, t) \in \mathcal{K}} \mathcal{L}_{triplet}(h, r, t) \qquad (4)$$

3.1.2 Text Model

In text model, to be compatible with the knowledge model, a pair of co-occurrence words is scored in this way:

$$z(w, v) = b - \frac{1}{2} \|\mathbf{w} - \mathbf{v}\|^2 \qquad (5)$$

where w and v represent co-occurrence of two words in a context window; $\mathbf{w}$ and $\mathbf{v}$ represent the corresponding embeddings for w and v. Then normalize $z(w, v)$ and give a probability representation:

$$\Pr(w|v) = \frac{\exp\{z(w, v)\}}{\sum_{\tilde{w} \in \mathcal{V}} \exp\{z(\tilde{w}, v)\}} \qquad (6)$$

where $\mathcal{V}$ is our vocabulary. Then the goal of the text model is to maximize the likelihood of all word co-occurrence pairs:

$$\mathcal{L}_T = \sum_{(w, v)} [\log \Pr(w|v) + \log \Pr(v|w)] \qquad (7)$$

3.1.3 Alignment Model

Alignment model guarantees the vectors of entities and words are in the same space, i.e., the similarity/distance between an entity vector and an word vector is meaningful. We combine all the three alignment models proposed in (Wang et al., 2014a) and (Zhong and Zhang, 2015).

Alignment by Wikipedia Anchors (Wang et al., 2014a). Mentions are replaced with the entities they link to and word-word co-occurrence becomes word-entity co-occurrence.

$$\mathcal{L}_{AA} = \sum_{(w,a),a \in \mathcal{A}} [\log \Pr(w|e_a) + \log \Pr(e_a|w)]$$
$$(8)$$

where $\mathcal{A}$ denotes the set of anchors and e_a denotes the entity behind the anchor a.

Alignment by Names of Entities (Wang et al., 2014a). For each triplet (h, r, t), h or t are replaced with their corresponding names, so we get (w_h, r, t), (h, r, w_t) and (w_h, r, w_t), where w_h denotes the name of h and w_t denotes the name of t.

$$\mathcal{L}_{AN} = \sum_{(h,r,t)} [\mathcal{L}_{triplet}(w_h, r, t) + \mathcal{L}_{triplet}(h, r, w_t)$$
$$+ \mathcal{L}_{triplet}(w_h, r, w_t)]$$
$$(9)$$

Alignment by Entities' Description (Zhong and Zhang, 2015). This alignment utilizes the co-occurrence of Wikipedia url and words in the description of that url page, which is similar to the PV DBOW model in (Le and Mikolov, 2014).

$$\mathcal{L}_{AD} = \sum_{e \in \mathcal{E}} \sum_{w \in \mathcal{D}_e} [\log \Pr(e|w) + \log \Pr(w|e)]$$
$$(10)$$

where $\mathcal{D}_e$ denotes the description of an entity e. To clarify again, "url" is equivalent with "entity" in this paper. Combine these three kinds of alignment techniques, we get the whole alignment model:

$$\mathcal{L}_A = \mathcal{L}_{AA} + \mathcal{L}_{AN} + \mathcal{L}_{AD} \qquad (11)$$

3.1.4 Url-Anchor Co-occurrence

For entity disambiguation, the entity relatedness graph is useful to capture the "topics" of an entity in Wikipedia. Thus we also hope to encode such information into our embedding. Specifically we further incorporate "url-anchor" co-occurrence to the training objective. "url" stands for the url of a Wikipedia page and "anchor" stands for the hyperlinks of anchor fields in that page.

$$\mathcal{L}_U = \sum_{e \in \mathcal{E}} \sum_{a \in \mathcal{A}_{\mathcal{D}_e}} [\Pr(e|e_a) + \Pr(e_a|e)] \qquad (12)$$

where $\mathcal{A}_{\mathcal{D}_e}$ stands for all anchors in Wikpedia page $\mathcal{D}_e$. $\Pr(e|e_a)$ and $\Pr(e_a|e)$ are defined similarly as equation 6.

Considering knowledge model, text model, alignment model and url-anchor co-occurrence all together, we get the overall objective (likelihood) to maximize:

$$\mathcal{L} = \mathcal{L}_K + \mathcal{L}_T + \mathcal{L}_A + \mathcal{L}_U \qquad (13)$$

3.1.5 Negative Sampling Refinement

In training phase, to avoid the computation of the normalizer in equation (2) and (6), we follow (Mikolov et al., 2013b) to transform the origin softmax-like objective to a simpler binary classification objective, which aims to distinguish observed data from noise.

To optimize for entity disambiguation, when using the context words to predict an anchor (entity), i.e., optimizing $\Pr(e_a|w)$, rather than uniformly sampling negatives from the vocabulary as (Mikolov et al., 2013b), we conduct our sampling according to the candidates' prior distribution.

3.2 Disambiguation Features Design

With the embeddings we train above, many entity disambiguation methods can directly take them as the words and entities' representation and redefine their features. In this section, we only design some simple features to illustrate the capability of the embeddings in disambiguation. In the section of experiment, we can observe that even a single embedding-based feature can beat the combination of several BoW-based features.

3.2.1 Mention-Entity Prior

This feature is directly counted from Wikipedia's anchor fields and measures the link probability of an entity e given a mention m. Prior is a strong indicator (Fader et al., 2009) to select the correct entity. However, it is unwise to take prior as a feature all the time because prior usually get a very large weight, which overfits the training data. Later in this paper, we will propose a classifier to tell when to use the prior or not.

3.2.2 Global Context Relatedness (E-GCR)

This feature comes from the hypothesis that the true entity of a mention will coincide with the meaning of most of the other words in the same document. So this feature sums up all idf-weighted relatedness scores between an entity candidate and each context word, then average them:

$$\forall e \in \Gamma(m), E - GCR(e, d|m) =$$
$$\frac{1}{|d|} \sum_{w \in d} \mathrm{idf}(w) \cdot \Omega(e, w) \quad (14)$$

where $\Gamma(m)$ denotes the entity candidate set of mention m; d denotes the document containing m; $\Omega(e, w)$ denotes a distance-based relatedness $b - \frac{1}{2} \|\mathbf{e} - \mathbf{w}\|^2$, which is compatible with the embedding model.

3.2.3 Local Context Relatedness (E-LCR)

E-GCR can only coarsely rank topic-related candidates to one of the top positions. But sometimes there is nearly no relation between the true entity and the topic of the document:

Ex.1 *"Stefani, a DJ at The Zone 101.5 FM in Phoenix, AZ, sent me an awesome MP3 of the interview..."*

In this example, E-GCR will link *AZ* to *AZ (rapper)* because the context is all about music although *Phoenix* should be a strong hint to link *AZ* to *Arizona*.

To avoid this kind of errors, we design a feature to describe the relatedness between an entity candidate and some important words around the mention. To identify these words, we turn to dependency parser provided by Stanford CoreNLP (Manning et al., 2014). Formulate this feature:

$$\forall e \in \Gamma(m), E - LCR(e, d|m) =$$
$$\frac{1}{|S_{depend}|} \sum_{w \in S_{depend}} \Omega(e, w) \quad (15)$$

where S_{depend} is the set consisting all adjacent words of m in the dependency graph of the document d.

3.2.4 Local Entity Coherence (E-LEC)

In practice, there are usually many casual mentions linked to an entity, such as *w v* for *West Virginia*.

Ex.2 *"We would like to welcome you to the official*

website for the city of Chester, w v. "

In this case, "*w v*" should be a strong hint for the disambiguation of "*Chester*". However, "*w*", "*v*" or "*w v*" is too casual to catch useful information if we only take their lexical expression. So we should not only take the relative surface forms but also their entity candidates into consideration. Then the entity "*West Virginia*" will be quite helpful to link "*Chester*" to "*Chester, West Virginia*" This feature is similar to the previous collective or topic-coherence methods. And our local entity coherence is more accurate because we only consider relative mentions/entities around rather than all entities in a document. Formulate this feature:

$$\forall e \in \Gamma(m), E - LEC(e, d|m) =$$
$$\frac{1}{|S_{depend}|} \sum_{w \in S_{depend}} \max_{e' \in \Gamma(w), e' \neq e} \Omega(e, e') \,(16)$$

3.3 Two-layer Disambiguation Model

To balance the usage of prior and other features, we propose a two-layer disambiguation model. It includes two steps: (1) Build a binary classifier to give a probability p_{conf} denoting the confidence to use prior only. Features used to construct this classifier are E-GCR, mention word itself and context words in a window sized 4 around the mention. (2) If p_{conf} achieve a designated threshold ξ, we only adopt prior to select the best candidate, otherwise we only consider other embedding-based features described in section 3.2. Formulate this model:

$$\forall m, e^* = \begin{cases} \arg\max_{e \in \Gamma(m)} prior(e|m), & p_{conf} \geq \xi \\ \arg\max_{e \in \Gamma(m)} \sum_i^{|F|} w_i \cdot f_i, & p_{conf} < \xi \end{cases}$$
$$(17)$$

where e^* is the entity we choose for the mention m.

4 Experiments

In the experiments, we first compare our embedding-based features with some traditional BoW-based features. Then we illustrate the capability of the two-layer disambiguation model. After that we compare our embedding technique EDKate in entity disambiguation tasks with some other straightforward work-arounds. Finally we incorporate mention detection and construct a disambiguation system to compare with other existing systems.

4.1 Data

We take Freebase as the KB, full Wikipedia corpus as text corpus. For comparison, we also use some small benchmark corpus for testing purpose.

4.1.1 Wikipedia

We adopt the Wikipedia dumped from Feb. 13th, 2015. With the raw htmls, we first filter out non-English and non-entity pages. Then we extract text and anchors information according to the html templates. After the preprocessing procedures, we get 4,532,397 pages with 93,299,855 anchors. Furthermore, we split the remained pages into training, developing and testing sets with proportion 8:1:1. In some experiments, only "valid entities" will be considered and a "(filtered)" tag will be added to the name of the dataset. For statistical summary, please refer to Table 1.

4.1.2 Valid Entities

In some experiments, we limit our KB entities to the Wikipedia training set and remove entities which are mentioned less than 3 times in Wikipedia training set for efficiency. We call the remaining entities "valid entities".

4.1.3 Knowledge Base

We use Freebase dumped from Feb. 13th, 2015 as our knowledge base. We only want to link mentions to Wikipedia entities so we filter out triplets whose head or tail entity isn't covered by Wikipedia. Finally we get 99,980,159 triplets. If we only consider valid entities, there are 37,606,158.

4.1.4 Small Benchmark Corpus

Besides Wikipedia, we also evaluate our embedding-based method in some small benchmark datasets. KBP 2010 comes from the KBP's annual tracks held by TAC and contains only one mention in one document. AQUAINT is originally collected by (Milne and Witten, 2008) and mimics the structure of Wikipedia. MSNBC is taken from (Cucerzan, 2007) and focuses on news wire text; ACE is collected by (Ratinov et al., 2011) from the ACE co-reference dataset. For statistics in detail, see Table 1.

4.1.5 Difficult Set

We find that in all the data sets, large part of the examples can be simply well solved by the mention-entity prior without considering any contexts. But there indeed exist some examples the

Dataset	# documents	# mentions
Wiki:all	4,532,397	93,299,855
Wiki:all (filtered)	2,476,438	52,422,949
Wiki:train (filtered)	1,567,080	37,956,309
Wiki:develop (filtered)	454,906	7,248,850
Wiki:test (filtered)	454,452	7,217,790
Wiki:test (filtered, difficult)	454,452	1,069,428
KBP 2010	1020	1020
KBP 2010 (filtered)	780	780
KBP 2010 (filtered, difficult)	780	183
AQUAINT	50	727
ACE	35	257
MSNBC	20	747

Table 1: Statistics for each corpus

prior cannot work well. We think disambiguation should pay more attention to this part of examples rather than the part where prior already works well. Thus from the testing sets "Wikipedia:test (filtered)" and "KBP 2010 (filtered)", we collect the cases where prior cannot rank the correct entity to top 1 and construct the separate "difficult" set.

4.2 Embedding Training

We use stochastic gradient descent (SGD) to optimize the objective (see equation (13)). We set the dimension of word and entity embeddings to 150 and initialize each element of an embedding with a random number near 0. For the constant b, we empirically set it to 7.

In knowledge model, we use Freebase as our knowledge base. We don't set a fix epoch number and the knowledge training thread will not terminate until the text training thread stop. Furthermore, we also adapt the learning rate in knowledge training to that in text training. When a triplet (h, r, t) is considered, the numbers of negative samples to construct $(\tilde{h}, r, t)$, $(h, \tilde{r}, t)$ and $(h, r, \tilde{t})$ are all 10, in which $\tilde{h}$ and $\tilde{t}$ are uniformly sampled from $\mathcal{E}$ while $\tilde{r}$ is uniformly sampled from $\mathcal{R}$.

In text model, we use the filtered Wikipedia training set as our text corpus. We set the number of epoch to 6 and set initial learning rate to 0.025, which will decreases linearly with the training process. When a word is encountered, we take words inside a 5-word-window as co-occurred words. For each co-occurred word, we sample 30 negatives from the unigram distribution raised to the 3/4rd power.

In alignment model, "alignment by Wikipedia anchors" and "alignment by entity names" can be absorbed into text model and knowledge model respectively. For "alignment by entity's description," we sample 10 negatives in $\Pr(e|w)$ and 30 negatives in $\Pr(w|e)$.

For $\Pr(e_a|w)$ in "url-anchor co-occurrence", we sample 20 negatives from the candidate list of the anchor mention and 10 negatives from the whole entity set.

To balance the training process, we give knowledge model 10 threads and text model 20 threads. We adopt the share-memory scheme like (Bordes et al., 2013) and don't apply locks.

4.3 Comparison between Embedding-based and BoW-based Feature

We set up this experiment to exhibit the expressiveness of our embeddings. We compare E-GCR (global context relatedness) with some traditional BoW-based features. Moreover, in this experiment, we report the results on "difficult set" where the mention-entity prior fails. Following the same metric used in (Cucerzan, 2011), we take accuracy to evaluate the disambiguation performance, that is, the fraction of all mentions for which the correct entity is ranked to top 1.

4.3.1 Implementation

For embedding-based features, we only consider the E-GCR, which is more comparable with the BoW-based features B-CS and B-TS we use here because they all consider the whole document as context. These BoW-based features include: (1)Mention-Entity Prior; (2)BoW Context Similarity (B-CS). This feature is proposed by (Cucerzan, 2011). First, for each entity in Wikipedia, take all surface forms of anchors in that page as its representation vector. Then compute scalar product between this representation vector and the context word vector of a given mention; (3)BoW Topic Similarity (B-TS). First construct the topic vector for each entity from category boxes like (Cucerzan, 2011). Then compute scalar product between topic vector and context word vector of a given mention.

4.3.2 Results

From Table 2, we get (1) E-GCR can beat the combination of several BoW-based features. This is mainly because, embeddings training owns a inner optimizaiton objective and embraces the information of these BoW-based representations. (2) Embedding-based feature appear robust and significantly outperform BoW-based features in diffi-

Feature	Wiki:test (filtered)		KBP 2010 (filtered)	
	overall	difficult	overall	difficult
Prior	0.8488	0	0.7645	0
Prior+B-CS	0.8545	0.0587	0.7645	0.0308
Prior+B-CS+B-TS	0.8680	0.1609	0.7907	0.1437
B-CS	0.6375	0.3159	0.3648	0.3210
B-CS+B-TS	0.6793	0.3943	0.5422	0.4491
E-GCR	**0.8738**	**0.5183**	**0.8445**	**0.6358**

Table 2: Comparison between Embedding-based Feature and BoW-based Feature

Model Type	Wiki:test (filtered)		KBP 2010 (filtered)	
	overall	difficult	overall	difficult
Linear	0.8671	0.1310	0.7791	0.0617
Two-layer	**0.8931**	**0.4795**	**0.8474**	**0.5140**

Table 3: Comparison between Linear Disambiguation Model and Two-layer Model

cult set, which indicate that these BoW representation cannot well catch the information in these cases while embeddings are still expressive . (3) Unlike the situation in difficult set, the gap between "E-GCR" and "Prior+B-CS+B-TS" is not so large mainly because "difficult set" only occupy a small proportion and prior would cover the drawbacks of BoW-based features.

This experiment hints us to pay more attention to the difficult set, which is helpful to improve the overall performance.

4.4 Comparison between Linear and Two-layer Disambiguation Model

In this section we evaluate the quality of the two-layer disambiguation model and compare it with the linear disambiguation model (Cucerzan, 2011). Moreover, we also report results in the "difficult set" defined above to see whether our two-layer model could balance prior and other features or not. The features we use here are prior and E-GCR. Accuracy is used as the evaluation metric.

4.4.1 Implementation

We use logistic regression for both models. For the two-layer model, we first apply the prior classification and get p_{conf}. Here we set the threshold ξ to 0.95 according to experiments in development set.

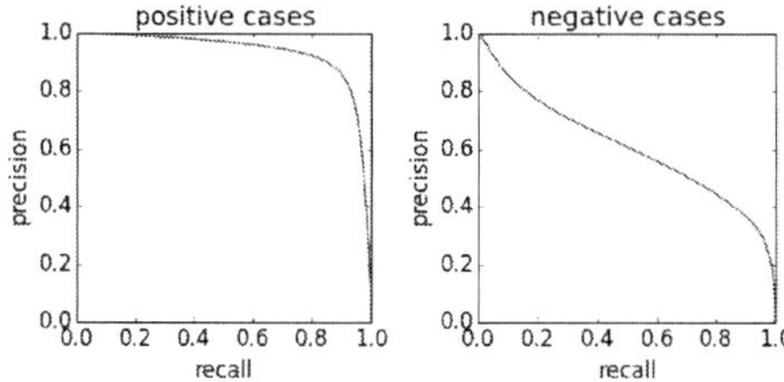

Figure 1: Precision-Recall Curves for Prior Classification

4.4.2 Results

From Figure 1, we see that the classifier is quite good at classifying positive cases to the correct class. From Table 3, we observe that our two-layer model receive a promising result in overall and difficult set against the linear model. This evidence indicates the prior classifier works and the two-layer model can balance the usage of prior and other features.

4.5 Comparison between Different Embeddings

This experiment compares our embeddings technique (EDKate) with some other methods: (Mikolov et al., 2013b), (Wang et al., 2014a) and (Zhong and Zhang, 2015). Here, We only consider the cases given mentions and take accuracy as the evaluation metric.

4.5.1 Implementation

For (Mikolov et al., 2013b), we directly take their word2vec model and replace anchor surface with the entity symbol in the training corpus. In this way, we get embeddings for words and entities. For (Wang et al., 2014a) and (Zhong and Zhang, 2015), we completely follow the model in the original paper. For our method. We use the knowledge model and text model described in (Wang et al., 2014a) and combine the alignment techniques in both of (Wang et al., 2014a) and (Zhong and Zhang, 2015). Moreover, we add "url-anchor" co-occurence to the training objective and refine the negative sampling method by having entities in candidates list more probable to be sampled. In this experiment, we only use E-GCR as our feature for simplicity.

4.5.2 Results

From Table 4, we observe that (Wang et al., 2014a) outperform (Mikolov et al., 2013b), which indicates the introduction of some structure informa-

Embedding Version	Wiki: test (filtered)	KBP 2010 (filtered)
(Mikolov et al., 2013b)	0.8062	0.7311
(Wang et al., 2014a)	0.8283	0.7922
(Zhong and Zhang, 2015)	0.8355	0.7965
EDKate	**0.8738**	**0.8445**

Table 4: Comparison between Different Embeddings

Method	Accuracy on KBP 2010
(Lehmann et al., 2010)	0.806
(He et al., 2013)	0.809
(Sun et al., 2015)	0.839
(Cucerzan, 2011)	0.873
EDKate	**0.889**

Table 5: Comparison with other reported results on KBP 2010

tion like knowledge base is quite beneficial. And the utilization of description message for entities improve the performance as well. For our method EDKate, we further take advantages of "url-anchor" co-occurrence and special sampling method, which make embeddings more expressive and guarantee the performance.

4.6 Comparison with Reported Results on KBP 2010

In this section, we will compare our result on KBP 2010 with other existing reported results, in which Cucerzan (2011) holds the best record in KBP 2010 so far; Lehmann et al. (2010) rank first in the 2010 competition while He et al. (2013) and Sun et al. (2015) adopt neural-network-based methods. We still use accuracy as the evaluation metric because KBP 2010 specifies the input mentions. Because some papers only report the accuracy with 3 decimal places, we unify all results to 3 decimal places.

4.6.1 Implementation

We take the dataset "Wikipedia:all" to train embeddings here and use all features we defined in section 3.2. In this experiment, we adopt the unfiltered version of KBP 2010 as the test corpus.

4.6.2 Results

Table 5 shows that EDKate outperforms the current best record (Cucerzan, 2011) in KBP 2010 dataset. Sun et al. (2015) apply convolution neural network and take advantages of (Mikolov et al., 2013a)'s word2vec as input but it seems not so ef-

System	AQUAINT	ACE	MSNBC
WikipediaMiner	0.8361	0.7276	0.6849
Wikifier_v1	0.8394	0.7725	0.7488
EDKate	0.8515	0.8079	0.7550
Wikifier_v2	**0.8888**	**0.8530**	**0.8120**

Table 6: Comparison with other Wikification systems in BoT F1 metric

fective as ours, which shows the importance of the embedding quality in this disambiguation task.

4.7 Comparison with Other Wikification Systems

In this section, we equip EDKate with mention detection and compare our system with WikipediaMiner (Milne and Witten, 2008), Wikifier_v1 (Ratinov et al., 2011) and Wikifier_v2 (Cheng and Roth, 2013). For the evaluation metric, we adopt the Bag-of-Title (BoT) F1 evaluation metric which is used in all other systems we choose here.

4.7.1 Implementation

We first make use of all mentions in the mention-entity table to construct a Trie-tree, which is used to detect mentions in input text. To remove noise, we simply retain mentions which contain at least one noun and filter mentions that completely consist of stop words. Then we apply our disambiguation technique to the mentions detected. The same as experiment 4.6, we make use of all features described in section 3.2 here.

4.7.2 Results

Table 6 shows that our embedding-based method EDKate is better than two popular systems but cannot outperform Wikifier_v2 in these three datasets. It should be mentioned that Wikifier_v2 is largely based on Wikifier_v1 and its magic is to add relational inference with some handcrafted rules. Actually, the embedding methods can performs well to model relations (Wang et al., 2014a), so the idea to introduce relational information into our current framework is promising and will be the future work.

5 Conclusion

In this paper, we propose to refine a knowledge and text joint learning framework for entity disambiguation tasks and learn semantics-rich embeddings for words and entities. Then we design some simple embedding-based features and build a two-layer disambiguation model. Extensive experiments show that our embeddings are very expressive and is quite helpful in the entity disambiguation tasks.

References

Yoshua Bengio, Réjean Ducharme, Pascal Vincent, and Christian Janvin. 2003. A neural probabilistic language model. *The Journal of Machine Learning Research*, 3:1137–1155.

Antoine Bordes, Jason Weston, Ronan Collobert, and Yoshua Bengio. 2011. Learning structured embeddings of knowledge bases. In *Conference on Artificial Intelligence*, number EPFL-CONF-192344.

Antoine Bordes, Nicolas Usunier, Alberto Garcia-Duran, Jason Weston, and Oksana Yakhnenko. 2013. Translating embeddings for modeling multi-relational data. In *Advances in Neural Information Processing Systems*, pages 2787–2795.

Razvan C Bunescu and Marius Pasca. 2006. Using encyclopedic knowledge for named entity disambiguation. In *Proceedings of European Chapter of the Association for Computational Linguistics*, volume 6, pages 9–16.

Taylor Cassidy, Zheng Chen, Javier Artiles, Heng Ji, Hongbo Deng, Lev-Arie Ratinov, Jing Zheng, Jiawei Han, and Dan Roth. 2011. Cuny-uiuc-sri tac-kbp2011 entity linking system description. In *Proceedings of Text Analysis Conference*.

Xiao Cheng and Dan Roth. 2013. Relational inference for wikification. In *Proceedings of Conference on Empirical Methods in Natural Language Processing*.

Ronan Collobert, Jason Weston, Léon Bottou, Michael Karlen, Koray Kavukcuoglu, and Pavel Kuksa. 2011. Natural language processing (almost) from scratch. *The Journal of Machine Learning Research*, 12:2493–2537.

Silviu Cucerzan. 2007. Large-scale named entity disambiguation based on wikipedia data. In *Proceedings of the Conference on Empirical Methods in Natural Language Processing*, volume 7, pages 708–716.

Silviu Cucerzan. 2011. Tac entity linking by performing full-document entity extraction and disambiguation. In *Proceedings of Text Analysis Conference*, volume 2011.

Anthony Fader, Stephen Soderland, Oren Etzioni, and Turing Center. 2009. Scaling wikipedia-based named entity disambiguation to arbitrary web text. In *Proceedings of the International Joint Conferences on Artificial Intelligence Workshop on User-contributed Knowledge and Artificial Intelligence: An Evolving Synergy, Pasadena, CA, USA*, pages 21–26.

Zhengyan He, Shujie Liu, Mu Li, Ming Zhou, Longkai Zhang, and Houfeng Wang. 2013. Learning entity representation for entity disambiguation. In *ACL (2)*, pages 30–34.

Johannes Hoffart, Mohamed Amir Yosef, Ilaria Bordino, Hagen Fürstenau, Manfred Pinkal, Marc Spaniol, Bilyana Taneva, Stefan Thater, and Gerhard Weikum. 2011. Robust disambiguation of named entities in text. In *Proceedings of the Conference on Empirical Methods in Natural Language Processing*, pages 782–792.

Sayali Kulkarni, Amit Singh, Ganesh Ramakrishnan, and Soumen Chakrabarti. 2009. Collective annotation of wikipedia entities in web text. In *Proceedings of Special Interest Group on Knowledge Discovery and data Mining*, pages 457–466.

Quoc V Le and Tomas Mikolov. 2014. Distributed representations of sentences and documents. *arXiv preprint arXiv:1405.4053*.

John Lehmann, Sean Monahan, Luke Nezda, Arnold Jung, and Ying Shi. 2010. Lcc approaches to knowledge base population at tac 2010. In *Proceedings of Text Analysis Conference*.

Christopher D Manning, Mihai Surdeanu, John Bauer, Jenny Finkel, Steven J Bethard, and David McClosky. 2014. The stanford corenlp natural language processing toolkit. In *Proceedings of Association for Computational Linguistics*, pages 55–60.

Tomas Mikolov, Kai Chen, Greg Corrado, and Jeffrey Dean. 2013a. Efficient estimation of word representations in vector space. *arXiv preprint arXiv:1301.3781*.

Tomas Mikolov, Ilya Sutskever, Kai Chen, Greg S Corrado, and Jeff Dean. 2013b. Distributed representations of words and phrases and their compositionality. In *Advances in neural information processing systems*, pages 3111–3119.

David Milne and Ian H Witten. 2008. Learning to link with wikipedia. In *Proceedings of Information and knowledge management*, pages 509–518.

Lev Ratinov, Dan Roth, Doug Downey, and Mike Anderson. 2011. Local and global algorithms for disambiguation to wikipedia. In *Proceedings of Association for Computational Linguistics*, pages 1375–1384.

Richard Socher, Danqi Chen, Christopher D Manning, and Andrew Ng. 2013. Reasoning with neural tensor networks for knowledge base completion. In *Advances in Neural Information Processing Systems*, pages 926–934.

Yaming Sun, Lei Lin, Duyu Tang, Nan Yang, Zhenzhou Ji, and Xiaolong Wang. 2015. Modeling mention, context and entity with neural networks for entity disambiguation. In *Proceedings of the Twenty-Fourth International Joint Conference on Artificial Intelligence (IJCAI)*, pages 1333–1339.

Zhen Wang, Jianwen Zhang, Jianlin Feng, and Zheng Chen. 2014a. Knowledge graph and text jointly embedding. In *Proceedings of the 2014 Conference on Empirical Methods in Natural Language Processing. Association for Computational Linguistics*, pages 1591–1601.

Zhen Wang, Jianwen Zhang, Jianlin Feng, and Zheng Chen. 2014b. Knowledge graph embedding by translating on hyperplanes. In *Proceedings of Association for the Advancement of Artificial Intelligence*, pages 1112–1119.

Huaping Zhong and Jianwen Zhang. 2015. Aligning knowledge and text embeddings by entity descriptions. In *Proceedings of Conference on Empirical Methods in Natural Language Processing*.

Substring-based unsupervised transliteration with phonetic and contextual knowledge

Anoop Kunchukuttan[1], Pushpak Bhattacharyya[1], Mitesh M. Khapra[2]
[1] Department of Computer Science & Engineering,
Indian Institute of Technology Bombay.
{anoopk,pb}@cse.iitb.ac.in
[2] IBM Research India.
mikhapra@in.ibm.com

Abstract

We propose an unsupervised approach for *substring-based* transliteration which incorporates two new sources of knowledge in the learning process: (i) context by learning substring mappings, as opposed to single character mappings, and (ii) phonetic features which capture cross-lingual character similarity via prior distributions.

Our approach is a *two-stage iterative, boot-strapping solution*, which vastly outperforms Ravi and Knight (2009)'s state-of-the-art unsupervised transliteration method and outperforms a rule-based baseline by up to 50% for top-1 accuracy on multiple language pairs. We show that substring-based models are superior to character-based models, and observe that their top-10 accuracy is comparable to the top-1 accuracy of supervised systems.

Our method only requires a phonemic representation of the words. This is possible for many language-script combinations which have a high grapheme-to-phoneme correspondence *e.g.* scripts of Indian languages derived from the Brahmi script. Hence, Indian languages were the focus of our experiments. For other languages, a grapheme-to-phoneme converter would be required.

1 Introduction

Transliteration is a key building block for multilingual and cross-lingual NLP since it is useful for user-friendly input methods and applications like machine translation and cross-lingual information retrieval. The best performing solutions are supervised, discriminative learning methods which learn transliteration models from parallel transliteration corpora. However, such corpora are available only for some language pairs. It is also expensive and time-consuming to build a parallel corpus.

This limitation can be addressed in three ways: **(i)** train a transliteration model on mined parallel transliterations. The transliterations can be mined from monolingual comparable corpora (Jagarlamudi and Daumé III, 2012) or parallel translation corpora (Sajjad et al., 2012). However, it may not be possible to mine enough transliteration pairs to train a system for most languages (Irvine et al., 2010). **(ii)** transliterate via a bridge language (Khapra et al., 2010) when transliteration corpora involving bridge languages is available. **(iii)** learn transliteration models in an unsupervised setting using only monolingual word lists. *Unsupervised transliteration* can be defined as: Learn a transliteration model ($\mathcal{TX}$) from the source language (F) to the target (E) language given their respective monolingual word lists, W_F and W_E respectively. We explore this direction in the present work, addressing shortcomings in the previous work (Ravi and Knight, 2009; Chinnakotla et al., 2010).

Our work addresses two major limitations in existing unsupervised transliteration approaches: (i) lack of linguistic signals to drive the learning, and (ii) limited use of context since their model is character-based. Due to this knowledge-lite approach, these model performs poorly. Our **primary contributions** are novel methods to incorporate two knowledge sources, phonetic and contextual, in the training process. These knowledge sources are critical since statistical co-occurrence signals used in supervised learning are not available for unsupervised learning. Unlike transliteration mining, our approach can learn effectively even if the source and target corpus do not have any transliteration pairs in common.

We propose a *two-stage* iterative, bootstrapping

Proceedings of the 20th SIGNLL Conference on Computational Natural Language Learning (CoNLL), pages 270–279,
Berlin, Germany, August 7-12, 2016. ©2016 Association for Computational Linguistics

approach for learning unsupervised transliteration models. In the first stage, a character-based model is learnt which is used to bootstrap and learn a series of improved substring-based models in the second stage.

The first stage incorporates two linguistic signals to drive the learning process: **phonemic correspondence** and **phonetic similarity**. This means we make the model aware that two characters represent either the same phoneme (क in Hindi and ক in Bengali [IPA: k]) or similar phonemes (क [IPA: k] in Hindi and খ [IPA: k^h] in Bengali - which differ only in aspiration). We achieve this by incorporating phonetic information as **prior distributions** in our EM-MAP approach to character-based unsupervised learning. We show that these linguistic signals can improve top-1 accuracy by 20%-100% over a baseline rule-based system. It is also vastly superior to knowledge-lite unsupervised methods.

The second stage incorporates **contextual knowledge** by unsupervised learning of a substring-based transliteration model *viz.* learning mappings from substring in one language to another, as opposed to learning single character mappings. In other words, along with learning mappings of the form ($k_{hindi} \rightarrow k_{bengali}$), we also try to learn mappings of the form ($kaa_{hindi} \rightarrow kaa_{bengali}$). It is known that substring-based transliteration outperforms character-based transliteration in a supervised setting due to the additional context information (Sherif and Kondrak, 2007). To the best of our knowledge, ours is the **first unsupervised approach for substring-based transliteration**. It outperforms a character-based model by up to 11% in terms of top-1 accuracy and 27% in terms of top-10 accuracy.

The top-10 accuracy of our unsupervised system is comparable to the top-1 accuracy of a supervised system. Hence, the unsupervised system may be a reasonable substitute for supervised systems in applications which require transliteration (*e.g.* handling untranslated words in MT) and can disambiguate from the top-k transliterations with information available to the application (*e.g.* LM in MT systems).

The focus of our work was Indian languages using scripts descended from the ancient Brahmi script. We show that our methods can be applied to these languages **without requiring phoneme dic-tionaries or grapheme-to-phoneme converters**. We achieve this by using **scriptural properties and similarity across scripts** to capture phonemic correspondence and phonetic similarity, and show results on 4 languages using 4 different scripts. At least 19 of the Indian subcontinent's top 30 and 9 of the top 10 most spoken languages use Brahmi-derived scripts. Each of these languages have more than a million speakers with an aggregate speaker population of about 900 million, so our method is widely applicable.

2   Related Work

Unsupervised transliteration has not been widely explored. Chinnakotla et al. (2010) generate transliteration candidates using manually developed character mapping rules and rerank them with a character language model. The major limitations are: (i) character transliteration probability is not learnt, so there is undue reliance on the language model to handle ambiguity, and (ii) significant manual effort for good coverage of mapping rules.

Ravi and Knight (2009) propose a decipherment framework based approach (Knight et al., 2006) to learn phoneme mappings for transliteration without parallel data. In theory, it should be able to learn transliteration probabilities and is a generalization of Chinnakotla et al. (2010)'s approach. But its performance is very poor due to lack of linguistic knowledge and has a reasonable performance only when a unigram word-level LM is used. This signal essentially reduces the approach to a lookup for the generated transliterations in a target language word list; the method resembles transliteration mining. It will perform well only if the unigram LM has a good coverage of all named entities in the source word list. For morphologically rich target languages, it may be difficult to find the exact surface words in the unigram LM.

Our character level model approach is a further generalization of Ravi and Knight (2009)'s work since it also allows modelling of prior linguistic knowledge in the learning process. This overcomes the most significant gap in their work.

Some approaches to transliteration mining are also relevant to the present work. Tao et al. (2006) show improvement in transliteration mining performance using phonetic feature vectors resembling the ones we have used. Jagarlamudi and Daumé III (2012) use phonemic representa-

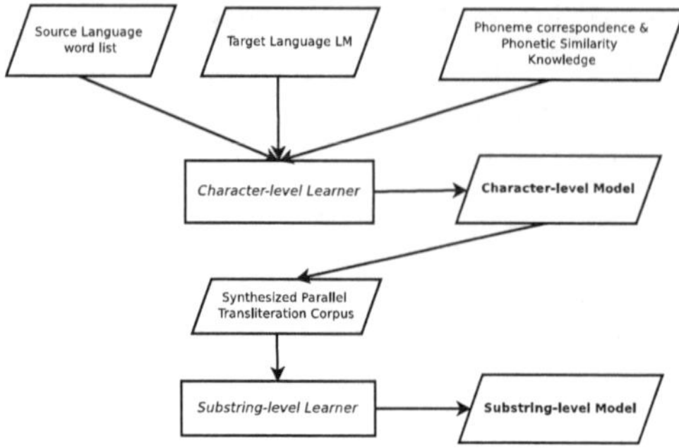

Figure 1: Overview of Proposed Approach

tion based interlingual projection for multilingual transliteration mining. To the best of our knowledge, ours is the first work to use phonetic feature vectors for transliteration as opposed to transliteration mining.

We use a substring-based log-linear model in our second stage. There are some parallels to this approach in the transliteration mining litereature. Some transliteration mining approaches have used a log-linear classifier to incorporate features to distinguish transliterations from non-transliterations (Klementiev and Roth, 2006; Chang et al., 2009). Sajjad et al. (2011) use a substring-based log-linear model trained on a noisy, intermediate transliteration corpus to iteratively remove *bad* (low-scoring) transliteration pairs found in the discovery process.

3 Unsupervised Substring-based Transliteration

In this section, we give a high-level overview of our approach for learning a substring-based transliteration model in an unsupervised setting (depicted in Figure 1). The inputs are monolingual lists of words, W_F and W_E, for the source (F) and target (E) languages respectively. Note that these are neither parallel nor comparable lists. We need a **phonemic representation** of the words.

For Indic scripts, which are used in our experiments, we use the orthographic representation itself as the phonemic representation since there is high grapheme to phoneme correspondence. Hence, we use the terms *character* and *phoneme* interchangeably.

The training is a two-stage process as described below. First, character mappings are learnt followed by learning of substring mappings by bootstrapping the character-based model. This process

is analogous to phrase-based statistical machine translation, where phrase pairs are extracted from word aligned sentence pairs.

Stage One: In the first stage, character transliteration probabilities are learnt from the monolingual word lists.

In a supervised setting, an EM algorithm using maximum likelihood estimation (EM-MLE) (Knight and Graehl, 1998) exploits co-occurrence of characters to learn model parameters. But, prior linguistic knowledge has to be incorporated for effective learning in an unsupervised setting. Hence, we propose an unsupervised Expectation Maximization with Maximum Aposteriori estimation framework (EM-MAP) for learning the character-level transliteration model. Linguistic knowledge is incorporated in the form of prior distributions on the model parameters in this framework. The details of the model and choice of prior distributions are described in Section 4.

We considered two linguistic signals for designing the prior distributions. The first is **phonemic correspondence** *i.e.* characters in the two languages representing the same phoneme. *e.g.* The characters क (ka) in Hindi and ক (ka) Bengali represent the same phoneme (IPA: k). But phonemic correspondence cannot account for phonemes which differ only by some phonetic features. *e.g.* vowel length (short इ [i] in Hindi, long ঈ [I] in Bengali), aspiration (unaspirated क in Hindi [IPA: k], aspirated খ in Bengali [IPA: k^h]). Such transformations are common during transliteration, so we use **phonetic similarity** as our second linguistic signal.

Stage Two: In the second stage, we learn a discriminative, log-linear model with **arbitrary substrings as the unit of transliteration**. For learning the substring based model, a **pseudo-parallel** transliteration corpus is first synthesized using the character-level model. We discuss Stage 2 in detail in Section 5.

We illustrate the need for substring level models with an example. In Indic scripts, the *anusvaara* (nasalization diacritic) can map to any of the 5 nasal consonants depending on the consonant following the *ansuvaara* in the source word. So, in the hi-bn pair (चंबल [ca.mbala], চম্বল [cambala]), the *anusvaara* (.m) maps to the nasal consonant (m) since the next character is the labial consonant *ba*. This shows the need for contextual information to resolve transliteration ambiguities. Substring-

272

Algorithm 1 Train character-level model

1: **procedure** UNSUP-CHAR(W_F, LM_E)
      ▷ LM_E: char-level language model for E
2:     $\Theta \leftarrow$ initialize-params()
3:     $i \leftarrow 0$
4:     **while** $i \leq N$ **do** ▷ N: Number of iterations
5:         $W_{E'} \leftarrow$ c-decode(W_F, Θ, LM_E)
6:         $A \leftarrow$ gen-alignments($W_F, W_{E'}$)
7:         $\Theta \leftarrow \arg\max_\Theta \mathcal{Q}'_{W_F}(\Theta)$ ▷ m-step
8:         **if** converged(Θ) **then**
9:             **break**
10:         $\sigma \leftarrow$ e-step(A, Θ)
11:     **return** Θ

---

based models, which learn substring mappings like *.mba* → *mba*, are one way to incorporate contextual information and have been shown to perform better in a supervised setting (Sherif and Kondrak, 2007). Contextual information is especially important in an unsupervised setting.

4 Character-based Unsupervised Transliteration

In the first stage, we **learn character transliteration probabilities** from monolingual word lists. The generative story for the training data (the source language corpus, W_F) is explained below using a noisy channel model.

An unknown target language word **e** is selected using a language model $P(\mathbf{e})$. The target word is transformed to a source language word **f** by a channel whose properties are represented by the transliteration probability distribution (Θ). *The target language word **e** is a latent variable in the unsupervised setting*, so we need to compute the expectation over all possible values of **e**.

$$P(\mathbf{f}) = \sum_{\mathbf{e}} P(\mathbf{f}|\mathbf{e})P(\mathbf{e}) \tag{1}$$

We use Knight and Graehl (1998)'s transliteration model where, the word pair $(\mathbf{f}, \mathbf{e})$ is generated by successively selecting one or more source characters f for each target character e as per a latent alignment **a** with probability $P(f|e) = \theta_{f,e}$. We restrict our model to 1-1 and 1-2 character mappings from target to source characters. The **likelihood of a single training instance** is given by:

$$L(\Theta) = \sum_{\mathbf{e}} P(\mathbf{e}) \sum_{\mathbf{a}} \prod_{i=1}^{|\mathbf{e}|} \theta_{f_{a_i}, e_i} \tag{2}$$

In the supervised framework of Knight and Graehl (1998), parameters are learnt using the EM algorithm where the alignment structure **a** is the latent variable. The discovery of hidden alignments helps compute the transliteration probabilities based on co-occurrence of characters. In the absence of parallel corpora, co-occurrence is no longer a learning signal and it is not possible to learn the character transliteration probabilities reliably. To compensate for this, we define **Dirichlet priors** (D_e) over each character transliteration probability distributions (Θ_e), which can be used to encode linguistic knowledge. This leads to our proposed **EM-MAP training objective** for the M-step over the entire training set (W_F).

$$\mathcal{Q}_{W_F}(\Theta) = \sum_{\mathbf{f} \in W_F} \left\{ \sum_{\mathbf{e}} \left\{ \delta_{\mathbf{e},\mathbf{f}} \sum_{\mathbf{a}} \left[\sigma_{\mathbf{a},\mathbf{f},\mathbf{e}} \right. \right. \right.$$

$$\left. \left. \sum_{f,e} n_{f,e,\mathbf{a}} \log \theta_{f,e} \right] + \log P(\mathbf{e}) \right\} \right\}$$

$$+ \sum_{e \in C_E} \log D_e(\alpha_{f_1,e}...\alpha_{f_{|C_F|},e}) \tag{3}$$

s.t

$$\forall e \in C_E, \sum_{j=1}^{j=|C_F|} \theta_{f_j,e} = 1$$

where,
$\delta_{\mathbf{e},\mathbf{f}} = P(\mathbf{e}|\mathbf{f})$, $\sigma_{\mathbf{a},\mathbf{f},\mathbf{e}} = P(\mathbf{a}|\mathbf{e},\mathbf{f})$ are conditional probabilities of the latent variables computed in the E-step. These are computed using the previous iteration's parameter values, whose values are fixed in the current iteration.
$n_{f,e,\mathbf{a}}$ is the number of times characters e and f are aligned in the alignment structure **a**.
C_F and C_E are the character sets of the source and target languages respectively.

In the unsupervised setting, the target word (**e**) is also an latent variable. As seen in Equation 3, the M-step requires computing an expectation over all latent variables (target word and alignments). Given the target word, it is possible to enumerate all alignments of the word pairs, but it is not possible to enumerate all possible strings (**e**). *Hence, we approximate the expectation over e by a **max** operation* (the so-called Viterbi approximation).

The modified objective ($\mathcal{Q}'_{W_F}$) for the M-step effectively means: With the current set of parameter values, we decode the source words to generate the target words, creating a synthetic parallel transliteration corpus. Then, the M-step updates can be done using Knight and Graehl (1998)'s supervised framework. The resulting update equation for the transliteration probabilities in the **M-step** is:

$$\theta_{f,e} = \frac{1}{\lambda_e}\left\{\alpha_{f,e} - 1 + \sum_{f \in W_F} \sum_{\mathbf{a}} \sigma_{\mathbf{a,f,e}} n_{f,e,\mathbf{a}}\right\} \quad (4)$$

where, λ_e is a normalizing factor and $\mathbf{e}$ is the best transliteration of $\mathbf{f}$ as per the previous iteration's parameters. Note that $\delta_{\mathbf{e,f}}$ plays no role in $(\mathcal{Q}'_{W_F})$.

The **E-step** update to compute the conditional probabilities of the latent alignment variables is given by:

$$\sigma_{\mathbf{a,f,e}} = \frac{1}{Z} \times \prod_{i=1}^{|\mathbf{e}|} \theta_{f_{a_i}, e_i} \quad (5)$$

where, Z is a normalizing factor.

The training procedure can thus be understood to follow a *decode-train-iterate* paradigm. Algorithm 1 shows the procedure for character level training. In each iteration, a pseudo-parallel corpus by decoding W_F using the current set of parameters (Line 5, Viterbi approximation) from which updated parameters are learnt (Line 7) and alignment probabilities recomputed (Line 10).

4.1 Linguistically Informed Priors:

In this section, the different prior distributions we designed to encode phonetic knowledge about characters is described. These are instantiations of Dirichlet priors (D_e), which serve as a conjugate prior to the multinomial distribution ($\theta_{f,e}$). The hyperparameters ($\alpha_{f,e}$) of D_e determine the nature of the prior distribution. They can be interpreted as additional, virtual alignment counts of the character pair (f, e) for maximum likelihood estimation of $\theta_{f,e}$.

Phoneme Correspondence (PC) Prior: This simply establishes a one-one correspondence (denoted by $\hat{=}$) between the same phonemes (or characters representing the same phonemes). It does not capture the notion of similarity between characters.

$$\alpha_{f,e} = \beta \quad \text{if} f \hat{=} e \quad (6)$$
$$= 0.01 \quad \text{elsewhere} \quad (7)$$

Phonemic correspondence is also used to initialize the transliteration probabilities for the EM algorithm (*PC Init*):

Basic Character Type:
vowel, consonant, anusvaara, nukta, halanta, others

Vowel Features
Length: short, long
Strength: weak, medium, strong
Status: Independent, Dependent
Horizontal position: Front, Back
Vertical position: Close, Close-Mid, Open-Mid, Open
Lip roundedness: Close, Open

Consonant Features
Place of Articulation:
velar, palatal, retroflex, dental, labial
Manner of Articulation:
plosive, fricative, flap, approximant (central or lateral)
Aspiration, Voicing, Nasal: True, False

Table 1: Phonetic features for Indic scripts

$$\theta_{f,e}^{\text{init}} = \frac{\alpha_{f,e}}{\sum_{x \in C_F} \alpha_{x,e}} \quad (8)$$

Phonetic Similarity Priors This prior captures similarity between two phonemes based on their phonetic properties. The phonetic properties of a phoneme can be encoded as a bit vector (v) as explained in Section 4.2. We experimented with two priors based on phonetic properties.

- Cosine Prior: It is based on the cosine similarity between the two bit vectors.

$$\alpha_{f,e} = \gamma_c \cos(v_f, v_e) \quad (9)$$

- Sim1 Prior: Cosine similarity tends to produce very diffused transliteration probability distributions. We propose a modified prior (called *sim1*) which tries to alleviate this problem by making the phonemic differences sharper.

$$\alpha_{f,e} = \gamma_s \frac{5^{v_f \cdot v_e}}{\sum_{x \in C_F} 5^{v_x \cdot v_e}} \quad (10)$$

β, γ_c and γ_s are scale factors for the Dirichlet distribution.

4.2 Extracting Phonetic Features for Indic scripts

We now describe a method for deriving phonetic correspondences and constructing phonetic feature vectors for Indic scripts. Indic scripts generally have a one-one correspondence from characters to phonemes in the scripts. Hence, each character is represented by a feature vector representing its phonetic properties as described in Table

1. The feature vector is represented as a bit vector with a bit for each value of every property.

The logical character set is roughly the same across all Indic scripts, though the visual glyph varies to a great extent. So phonemic correspondence can be easily determined for Unicode text since the first 85 characters of all Indic scripts are aligned to each other by virtue of having the same offset from the start of the script's code-page. These cover all commonly used characters. There are a few exceptions to this simple mapping scheme, most of which can be handled using simple rules.

Notable among these is the Tamil script, which does not have characters for aspirated as well as voiced plosives, so the corresponding unvoiced, unaspirated plosive characters are used to represent these sounds too. In the phonetic feature representation of such characters for Tamil, both the voiced as well as unvoiced bits and aspirated/unaspirated bits are set on, reflecting the ambiguity in the grapheme-to-phoneme mapping.

5 Bootstrapping substring-based models

In the second stage, we train a **discriminative, log-linear transliteration model which learns substring mappings**. We use the log-linear model proposed by Och and Ney (2002) for statistical machine translation and analogous transliteration features. The features are: substring transliteration probabilities, weighted average character transliteration probabilities and character language model score. The conditional probability of the target word $\mathbf{e}$ given the source word $\mathbf{f}$ is:

$$P(\mathbf{e}|\mathbf{f}) = \prod_{i=1}^{NP} P(\bar{e}_i|\bar{f}_i) = \prod_{i=1}^{NP} \exp \sum_{j=0}^{NF} \lambda_j g_j(\bar{f}_i, \bar{e}_i)$$

$$(11)$$

where, $\bar{f}_i$ and $\bar{e}_i$ are source and target substrings respectively, λ_j and g_j are feature weight and feature function respectively for feature j, NP number of substrings and NF is number of features.

We synthesize a **pseudo-parallel transliteration corpus** $(W_F, W_{E'})$ for training the discriminative model by transliterating the source language words (W_F) using the character level model from the first stage. Since the top-1 transliteration may be incorrect, we consider the top-k transliterations to improve the odds that the pseudo-parallel corpus contains the correct transliteration. For **train-**

ing, the pseudo-parallel corpus contains k transliteration pairs for every source language word. For **tuning** the feature weights, we use a small held-out set of top-1 transliteration pairs from the pseudo-parallel corpus, since it likely to be the most accurate one.

We run **multiple iterations** of the discriminative training process, with each being trained on the pseudo-parallel corpus synthesized using the previous iteration's models. The models in subsequent iterations are **bootstrapped** from the earlier models. The training continues for a fixed number of iterations although other convergence methods can also be explored. Like the MAP-EM solution for the first stage, the second stage also uses a *decode - train - iterate* paradigm for learning a substring-based model.

6 Experiments

Data: We experimented on the following Indian language pairs representing two language families: Bengali→Hindi, Kannada→Hindi, Hindi→Kannada and Tamil→Kannada. Bengali (bn) and Hindi (hi) are Indo-Aryan languages, while Kannada (kn) and Tamil (ta) are Dravidian languages. We used 10k source language names as training corpus, which were collected from various sources.

We evaluated our systems on the NEWS 2015 Indic dataset. We created this set from the English to Indian language training corpora of the NEWS 2015 shared task (Banchs et al., 2015) by mining name pairs which have English names in common. 1500 words were selected at random to create the testset. The remaining pairs are used to train and tune a skyline supervised transliteration system for comparison. The training sets are small, the number of name pairs being: 2556 (bn-hi), 4022 (kn-hi), 3586 (hi-kn) and 3230 (ta-kn).

Experimental Setup: We trained the character level unsupervised transliteration systems with source language word lists using a custom implementation [1]. We set the the value of the scaling factors $(\beta, \gamma_c, \gamma_s)$ to 100. Viterbi decoding was done with a bigram character language model, followed by re-ranking with a 5-gram character language model.

We trained the substring level discriminative transliteration models as well as a skyline su-

---

[1] https://github.com/anoopkunchukuttan/transliterator

Method	bn-hi			hi-kn			kn-hi			ta-kn		
	A_1	F_1	A_{10}	A_1	F_1	A_{10}	A_1	F_1	A_{10}	A_1	F_1	A_{10}
PC_Init	12.72	68.95	18.94	0.00	44.76	0.07	0.20	48.84	0.54	0.00	44.46	0.27
Rule	16.13	74.60	16.13	**13.75**	**79.67**	13.75	12.90	79.29	12.90	10.25	68.49	10.25
Initialization: PC_Init+												
PC_Prior	**18.27**	**75.50**	27.04	12.53	77.32	17.89	**27.69**	**81.06**	**43.55**	13.49	**69.85**	**29.06**
Cosine Prior	17.74	75.09	26.57	11.38	75.08	18.09	17.54	77.69	32.86	13.21	69.44	26.64
Sim1 Prior	18.07	75.25	**29.05**	11.72	75.61	**20.26**	19.69	78.18	37.84	**13.55**	69.74	28.19
Supervised	32.06	83.03	63.32	30.01	85.93	69.37	54.23	90.05	80.04	30.74	81.62	64.33

Table 2: Results for character-based model (% scores)

pervised transliteration system using the *Moses* (Koehn et al., 2007) machine translation system with default parameters. Batch MIRA (Cherry and Foster, 2012) was used to tune the Stage 2 systems with 1000 name pairs and supervised systems with 500 name pairs. The tuning set for the Stage 2 systems were drawn from the the top-1 transliterations in the synthesized, pseudo-parallel corpus; no true parallel corpus is used. Monotone decoding was performed. We used a 5-gram character language model trained with Witten-Bell smoothing on 40k names for all target languages. We ran Stage 2 for 5 iterations.

For a rule-based baseline, we used the script conversion method implemented in the *Indic NLP Library*[2] (Kunchukuttan et al., 2015) which is based on phonemic correspondences.

Evaluation: We used top-1 accuracy based on exact match (A_1) and Mean F-score (F_1) at the character level as defined in the NEWS shared tasks as our evaluation metrics (Banchs et al., 2015). We also used top-10 accuracy as an evaluation metric (A_{10}), since applications like MT and IR can further disambiguate with context information available to these applications.

7 Results and Discussion

Table 2 shows the results for the rule-based system and various character-based unsupervised models. Table 3 shows results for substring-level models bootstrapped from different character-based models. Results of supervised transliteration on a small training set are also shown in both tables.

Baseline models: Parameter initialization with phoneme correspondence mappings and add-one smoothing prior (*PC_Init*) is comparable to Ravi and Knight (2009)'s method and performs very

[2]http://anoopkunchukuttan.github.io/indic_nlp_library

poorly as reported in their work too. We also experimented with re-ranking the results using a unigram word based LM - our approximation to Ravi and Knight (2009)'s use of a word based LM - and its accuracy is comparable to *PC_Init*. The unigram LM was trained on a corpus of 185 million and 42 million tokens for *hi* and *kn* respectively. Thus, this knowledge-lite approach cannot learn a transliteration model effectively.

Rule-based transliteration (*Rule*) performs significantly better than *PC_Init*. The phonetic nature of Indic scripts makes the rule-based system a stronger baseline, yet this simple approach does not ensure high accuracy transliteration. Phonetic changes like changes in manner/place of articulation, voicing, *etc.* make transliteration non-trivial and phonetic correspondence is not sufficient to ensure good transliteration.

Effect of linguistic priors: The addition of linguistically motivated priors (*PC_Prior, Cosine_Prior, Sim1_Prior*) significantly improves the transliteration accuracy over the *PC_Init* approach. There is a significant improvement in top-1 accuracy over the *Rule* approach too for 2 language pairs (12%, 31% and 133% increase for bn-hi, ta-kn and kn-hi pairs respectively), but a drop of 9% for the hi-kn pair. A major reason for lower accuracy of hi→kn pair is an important difference between Kannada and Hindi writing conventions. Unlike Hindi, Kannada assumes an implicit vowel 'A' at the end of a word unless another vowel or nasal character terminates the word. Therefore, the vowel suppressor character (*halanta*) must be generated during hi→kn transliteration. Our method is poor at this generation, but conversely it does better at deletion of *halanta* for kn→hi transliteration. There is substantial improvement for the ta-kn pair also, even though there are some grapheme-to-phoneme ambiguities in the Tamil script.

In general, the phonemic correspondence prior results in better top-1 accuracy, whereas priors us-

Stage1 Model	Iterations	bn-hi		hi-kn		kn-hi		ta-kn	
		A_1	A_{10}	A_1	A_{10}	A_1	A_{10}	A_1	A_{10}
PC_Init	1	14.12	22.89	0.00	0.06	0.53	4.50	0.07	1.35
	5	15.26	25.43	0.00	0.47	1.01	8.53	0.40	2.76
PC_Init+PC_Prior	1	18.74	29.38	13.21	19.31	**28.43**	44.96	15.31	32.23
	5	19.34	32.73	13.21	20.39	21.10	45.03	**19.29**	37.15
PC_Init+Cosine prior	1	18.86	29.65	12.40	20.94	17.94	39.92	15.71	32.91
	5	18.94	31.33	12.94	23.92	16.73	44.76	18.88	36.08
PC_Init+Sim1 prior	1	19.28	34.34	12.6	23.85	19.62	47.98	16.99	34.86
	5	**20.54**	**37.61**	**13.82**	**25.88**	18.55	**50.27**	18.95	**38.50**
Supervised		32.06	63.32	30.01	69.37	54.23	80.04	30.74	64.33
Mined Pairs		26.97	51.34	-	-	-	-	-	-
Bridge Languages		25.97	58.23	18.22	52.85	33.60	67.88	13.01	42.28

Table 3: Results for substring-based model (% scores)

ing phonetic similarity give better top-10 accuracy. The phonetic similarity based priors are smoother compared to the sparse *PC_Prior* since they capture character similarity. This allows them to discover more character mappings, resulting in better top-10 accuracy at the cost of a drop in top-1 accuracy. The sparse *sim1* prior outperforms the smoother cosine similarity prior.

Effect of learning substring mappings: Substring-based transliteration improves the top-1 as well as top-10 accuracy significantly over the underlying character-based models. Across languages, the best substring-based models improve top-1 accuracy by upto 11% and top-10 accuracy by upto 25% over the best character-based models. Therefore, it is clear that contextual information can be harnessed in an unsupervised setting to substantially improve transliteration accuracy.

The iterative procedure is beneficial and transliteration accuracy increases as improved models are built in successive iterations. Large gains are particularly observed in top-10 accuracy.

While *PC_Prior* gives best top-1 accuracy results at the character-level, substring-based models bootstrapped from the *Sim1* prior give better results for both top-1 and top-10 accuracy metrics. Since the *Sim1* prior based character model has better top-10 accuracy, the pseudo-parallel corpus created using this mode is likely to be better than one created using *PC_Prior*. We also observe that substring-based models built without using phonetic priors cannot improve over much over the baseline transliteration.

Illustrative Examples:

- Phonetic similarity based priors were able to discover mappings between similar phonemes. *e.g.* The Bengali word উয়েস্ট (keolAdeo) was correctly transliterated to the Hindi word केवलादेव (kevalAdeva), due to discovery of similarity between the labial sounds (v) and (o).
- Substring-based models made use of the context to learn the correct transliteration. *e.g.* The Bengali word কেওলাদেও (oyaesTa) was correctly transliterated to the Hindi word वेस्ट (vesta), since the model learnt the substring mapping *oya→ve*.
- Substring-based models could make the right choice between short and long vowels (a major source of errors in character-based models).

Comparison with supervised system and some resource-constrained approaches: We compared our best substring-based model (based on *sim1* prior) with a supervised system and the following resource-constrained transliteration systems built using: **(i) Mined pairs** from a translation corpus: We experimented with *bn-hi* on the *Brahminet* mined pairs corpus (Kunchukuttan et al., 2015). Mined corpora involving *kn* were not available. **(ii) Bridge languages:** We used the NEWS 2015 corpus for our experiments with English as the bridge language. (Results in Table 3).

The accuracies of this substring-based system are less than the accuracies of the other methods. This is not unexpected since these methods use more parallel resources than the substring-based approach. But, note that the top-10 accuracy of the substring-based model is comparable to the top-1 accuracies of other approaches. Hence, the substring-based model may be sufficient for an application, like MT or cross-lingual IR, which uses the output of a transliteration system. In MT, untranslated words are replaced by their top-k transliterations. A language model can choose among the transliterations based on context while re-ranking resulting candidate sentences.

Applicability to different languages and scripts:
Our experiments span 4 widely-spoken languages
from the two major language families in the Indian subcontinent (Indo-Aryan [IA] and Dravidian [DR]). All languages use different Brahmi-
descended scripts. We show improvements in
IA→IA, DR→DR, DR→IA and IA→DR transliteration.

The first stage leverages the phonetic nature
of Indic scripts to obtain phonetic representations
from orthographic representations. There are at
least 19 languages in India where this condition
holds, so at least 171 language pairs can use
this approach without grapheme to phoneme converters. Many other script/language pairs also
show high grapheme-phoneme correspondence[3].
Our method, though, can also be applied to non-
phonetic scripts also by representing the training
data at the phonemic level using grapheme-to-
phoneme converters.

The second stage makes no assumptions about
language or script.

8 Conclusion and Future work

We show that *unsupervised transliteration can
substantially benefit from contextual and rich phonetic knowledge*. Phonetic knowledge is incorporated through a novel design of prior distributions
for character-level learning, while context is incorporated via substring-based learning. The top-10
accuracy of our systems is comparable with top-1
accuracy of supervised systems, but *requires only
monolingual resources*: word lists for Indic languages using Brahmi-derived scripts or phoneme
dictionaries for other languages.

In future, we plan to evaluate our method for
non-Indic languages and for languages that are less
related than the ones studied in this work. Possibilities for improvement include incorporation
of phonetic knowledge while learning substring
mappings (Stage 2) and better handling of noisy
transliterations in the bootstrapping process. It
would also be interesting to compare our method
with other unsupervised log-linear learning methods like contrastive estimation (Smith and Eisner,
2005).

We would like to note the potential for harnessing similarities among languages for statistical NLP, especially in an unsupervised setting, as

demonstrated by our use of similarity among Indic
scripts. Finally, the iterative, bootstrapping framework may be useful for unsupervised translation.

References

Rafael E. Banchs, Min Zhang, Xiangyu Duan, Haizhou
Li, and A Kumaran. 2015. Report of news
2015 machine transliteration shared task. In *The
ACL/IJCNLP 2015's Named Entity Workshop*.

Ming-Wei Chang, Dan Goldwasser, Dan Roth, and
Yuancheng Tu. 2009. Unsupervised constraint
driven learning for transliteration discovery. In *Proceedings of Human Language Technologies: The
2009 Annual Conference of the North American
Chapter of the Association for Computational Linguistics*.

Colin Cherry and George Foster. 2012. Batch tuning
strategies for statistical machine translation. In *Proceedings of the 2012 Conference of the North American Chapter of the Association for Computational
Linguistics: Human Language Technologies*.

Manoj K Chinnakotla, Om P Damani, and Avijit
Satoskar. 2010. Transliteration for resource-scarce
languages. *ACM Transactions on Asian Language
Information Processing (TALIP)*.

Ann Irvine, Chris Callison-Burch, and Alexandre Klementiev. 2010. Transliterating from all languages.
In *Proceedings of the Conference of the Association
for Machine Translation in the Americas (AMTA)*.

Jagadeesh Jagarlamudi and Hal Daumé III. 2012. Reg-
ularized interlingual projections: evaluation on mul-
tilingual transliteration. In *Proceedings of the 2012
Joint Conference on Empirical Methods in Natural
Language Processing and Computational Natural
Language Learning*. Association for Computational
Linguistics.

Mitesh M. Khapra, A. Kumaran, and Pushpak Bhattacharyya. 2010. Everybody loves a rich cousin:
An empirical study of transliteration through bridge
languages. In *Human Language Technologies: The
2010 Annual Conference of the North American
Chapter of the Association for Computational Linguistics*.

Alexandre Klementiev and Dan Roth. 2006. Weakly
supervised named entity transliteration and discovery from multilingual comparable corpora. In
*Proceedings of the 21st International Conference
on Computational Linguistics and the 44th annual
meeting of the Association for Computational Linguistics*.

Kevin Knight and Jonathan Graehl. 1998. Machine
transliteration. *Computational Linguistics*.

Kevin Knight, Anish Nair, Nishit Rathod, and Kenji
Yamada. 2006. Unsupervised analysis for decipherment problems. In *Proceedings of the COLING/ACL*

---

[3]`http://www.omniglot.com` lists grapheme-phoneme
correspondences for many language/script combinations

on Main conference poster sessions. Association for Computational Linguistics.

Philipp Koehn, Hieu Hoang, Alexandra Birch, Chris Callison-Burch, Marcello Federico, Nicola Bertoldi, Brooke Cowan, Wade Shen, Christine Moran, Richard Zens, et al. 2007. Moses: Open source toolkit for statistical machine translation. In *Proceedings of the 45th Annual Meeting of the ACL on Interactive Poster and Demonstration Sessions*.

Anoop Kunchukuttan, Ratish Puduppully, and Pushpak Bhattacharyya. 2015. Brahmi-net: A transliteration and script conversion system for languages of the indian subcontinent.

Franz Josef Och and Hermann Ney. 2002. Discriminative training and maximum entropy models for statistical machine translation. In *Proceedings of the 40th Annual Meeting on Association for Computational Linguistics*.

Sujith Ravi and Kevin Knight. 2009. Learning phoneme mappings for transliteration without parallel data. In *Proceedings of Human Language Technologies: The 2009 Annual Conference of the North American Chapter of the Association for Computational Linguistics*.

Hassan Sajjad, Alexander Fraser, and Helmut Schmid. 2011. An algorithm for unsupervised transliteration mining with an application to word alignment. In *Proceedings of the 49th Annual Meeting of the Association for Computational Linguistics: Human Language Technologies-Volume 1*.

Hassan Sajjad, Alexander Fraser, and Helmut Schmid. 2012. A statistical model for unsupervised and semi-supervised transliteration mining. In *Proceedings of the 50th Annual Meeting of the Association for Computational Linguistics*.

Tarek Sherif and Grzegorz Kondrak. 2007. Substring-based transliteration. In *Proceedings of the 45th Annual Meeting of the Association of Computational Linguistics*.

Noah A Smith and Jason Eisner. 2005. Contrastive estimation: Training log-linear models on unlabeled data. In *Proceedings of the 43rd Annual Meeting on Association for Computational Linguistics*.

Tao Tao, Su-Youn Yoon, Andrew Fister, Richard Sproat, and ChengXiang Zhai. 2006. Unsupervised named entity transliteration using temporal and phonetic correlation. In *Proceedings of the 2006 Conference on Empirical Methods in Natural Language Processing*.

Abstractive Text Summarization using Sequence-to-sequence RNNs and Beyond

Ramesh Nallapati
IBM Watson
`nallapati@us.ibm.com`

Bowen Zhou
IBM Watson
`zhou@us.ibm.com`

Cicero dos Santos
IBM Watson
`cicerons@us.ibm.com`

Çağlar Gülçehre
Université de Montréal
`gulcehrc@iro.umontreal.ca`

Bing Xiang
IBM Watson
`bingxia@us.ibm.com`

Abstract

In this work, we model abstractive text summarization using Attentional Encoder-Decoder Recurrent Neural Networks, and show that they achieve state-of-the-art performance on two different corpora. We propose several novel models that address critical problems in summarization that are not adequately modeled by the basic architecture, such as modeling key-words, capturing the hierarchy of sentence-to-word structure, and emitting words that are rare or unseen at training time. Our work shows that many of our proposed models contribute to further improvement in performance. We also propose a new dataset consisting of multi-sentence summaries, and establish performance benchmarks for further research.

1 Introduction

Abstractive text summarization is the task of generating a headline or a short summary consisting of a few sentences that captures the salient ideas of an article or a passage. We use the adjective 'abstractive' to denote a summary that is not a mere selection of a few existing passages or sentences extracted from the source, but a compressed paraphrasing of the main contents of the document, potentially using vocabulary unseen in the source document.

This task can also be naturally cast as mapping an input sequence of words in a source document to a target sequence of words called summary. In the recent past, deep-learning based models that map an input sequence into another output sequence, called sequence-to-sequence models, have been successful in many problems such as machine translation (Bahdanau et al., 2014),

speech recognition (Bahdanau et al., 2015) and video captioning (Venugopalan et al., 2015). In the framework of sequence-to-sequence models, a very relevant model to our task is the attentional Recurrent Neural Network (RNN) encoder-decoder model proposed in Bahdanau et al. (2014), which has produced state-of-the-art performance in machine translation (MT), which is also a natural language task.

Despite the similarities, abstractive summarization is a very different problem from MT. Unlike in MT, the target (summary) is typically very short and does not depend very much on the length of the source (document) in summarization. Additionally, a key challenge in summarization is to optimally compress the original document in a *lossy manner* such that the key concepts in the original document are preserved, whereas in MT, the translation is expected to be loss-less. In translation, there is a strong notion of almost one-to-one word-level alignment between source and target, but in summarization, it is less obvious.

We make the following main contributions in this work: (i) We apply the off-the-shelf attentional encoder-decoder RNN that was originally developed for machine translation to summarization, and show that it already outperforms state-of-the-art systems on two different English corpora. (ii) Motivated by concrete problems in summarization that are not sufficiently addressed by the machine translation based model, we propose novel models and show that they provide additional improvement in performance. (iii) We propose a new dataset for the task of abstractive summarization of a document into multiple sentences and establish benchmarks.

The rest of the paper is organized as follows. In Section 2, we describe each specific problem in abstractive summarization that we aim to solve, and present a novel model that addresses it. Sec-

Proceedings of the 20th SIGNLL Conference on Computational Natural Language Learning (CoNLL), pages 280–290,
Berlin, Germany, August 7-12, 2016. ©2016 Association for Computational Linguistics

tion 3 contextualizes our models with respect to closely related work on the topic of abstractive text summarization. We present the results of our experiments on three different data sets in Section 4. We also present some qualitative analysis of the output from our models in Section 5 before concluding the paper with remarks on our future direction in Section 6.

2 Models

In this section, we first describe the basic encoder-decoder RNN that serves as our baseline and then propose several novel models for summarization, each addressing a specific weakness in the baseline.

2.1 Encoder-Decoder RNN with Attention and Large Vocabulary Trick

Our baseline model corresponds to the neural machine translation model used in Bahdanau et al. (2014). The encoder consists of a bidirectional GRU-RNN (Chung et al., 2014), while the decoder consists of a uni-directional GRU-RNN with the same hidden-state size as that of the encoder, and an attention mechanism over the source-hidden states and a soft-max layer over target vocabulary to generate words. In the interest of space, we refer the reader to the original paper for a detailed treatment of this model. In addition to the basic model, we also adapted to the summarization problem, the large vocabulary 'trick' (LVT) described in Jean et al. (2014). In our approach, the decoder-vocabulary of each mini-batch is restricted to words in the source documents of that batch. In addition, the most frequent words in the target dictionary are added until the vocabulary reaches a fixed size. The aim of this technique is to reduce the size of the soft-max layer of the decoder which is the main computational bottleneck. In addition, this technique also speeds up convergence by focusing the modeling effort only on the words that are essential to a given example. This technique is particularly well suited to summarization since a large proportion of the words in the summary come from the source document in any case.

2.2 Capturing Keywords using Feature-rich Encoder

In summarization, one of the key challenges is to identify the key concepts and key entities in the document, around which the story revolves. In order to accomplish this goal, we may need to go beyond the word-embeddings-based representation of the input document and capture additional linguistic features such as parts-of-speech tags, named-entity tags, and TF and IDF statistics of the words. We therefore create additional look-up based embedding matrices for the vocabulary of each tag-type, similar to the embeddings for words. For continuous features such as TF and IDF, we convert them into categorical values by discretizing them into a fixed number of bins, and use one-hot representations to indicate the bin number they fall into. This allows us to map them into an embeddings matrix like any other tag-type. Finally, for each word in the source document, we simply look-up its embeddings from all of its associated tags and concatenate them into a single long vector, as shown in Fig. 1. On the target side, we continue to use only word-based embeddings as the representation.

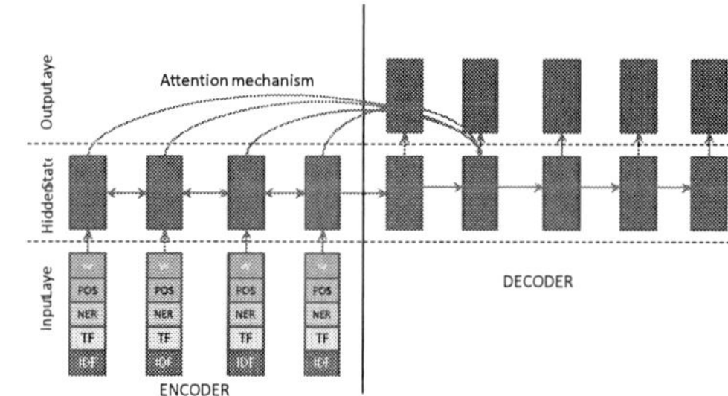

Figure 1: Feature-rich-encoder: We use one embedding vector each for POS, NER tags and discretized TF and IDF values, which are concatenated together with word-based embeddings as input to the encoder.

2.3 Modeling Rare/Unseen Words using Switching Generator-Pointer

Often-times in summarization, the keywords or named-entities in a test document that are central to the summary may actually be unseen or rare with respect to training data. Since the vocabulary of the decoder is fixed at training time, it cannot emit these unseen words. Instead, a most common way of handling these out-of-vocabulary (OOV) words is to emit an 'UNK' token as a placeholder. However this does not result in legible summaries. In summarization, an intuitive way to handle such OOV words is to simply point to their location in the source document instead. We model this notion using our novel switching decoder/pointer architecture which is graphically represented in Figure 2. In this model, the decoder is equipped with a 'switch' that decides between using the generator or a pointer at every time-step. If the switch is turned on, the decoder produces a word from its target vocabulary in the normal fashion. However, if the switch is turned off, the decoder instead generates a pointer to one of the word-positions in the source. The word at the pointer-location is then copied into the summary. The switch is modeled as a sigmoid activation function over a linear layer based on the entire available context at each time-step as shown below.

$$P(s_i = 1) = \sigma(\mathbf{v}^s \cdot (\mathbf{W}_h^s \mathbf{h}_i + \mathbf{W}_e^s \mathbf{E}[o_{i-1}]$$
$$+ \mathbf{W}_c^s \mathbf{c}_i + \mathbf{b}^s)),$$

where $P(s_i = 1)$ is the probability of the switch turning on at the ith time-step of the decoder, $\mathbf{h}_i$ is the hidden state, $\mathbf{E}[o_{i-1}]$ is the embedding vector of the emission from the previous time step, $\mathbf{c_i}$ is the attention-weighted context vector, and $\mathbf{W}_h^s, \mathbf{W}_e^s, \mathbf{W}_c^s, \mathbf{b}^s$ and $\mathbf{v}^s$ are the switch parameters. We use attention distribution over word positions in the document as the distribution to sample the pointer from.

$$P_i^a(j) \propto \exp(\mathbf{v}^a \cdot (\mathbf{W}_h^a \mathbf{h}_{i-1} + \mathbf{W}_e^a \mathbf{E}[o_{i-1}]$$
$$+ \mathbf{W}_c^a \mathbf{h}_j^d + \mathbf{b}^a)),$$
$$p_i = \arg\max_j (P_i^a(j)) \text{ for } j \in \{1, \ldots, N_d\}.$$

In the above equation, p_i is the pointer value at i^{th} word-position in the summary, sampled from the attention distribution $\mathbf{P}_i^a$ over the document word-positions $j \in \{1, \ldots, N_d\}$, where $P_i^a(j)$ is the probability of the ith time-step in the decoder pointing to the jth position in the document, and $\mathbf{h}_j^d$ is the encoder's hidden state at position j.

At training time, we provide the model with explicit pointer information whenever the summary word does not exist in the target vocabulary. When the OOV word in summary occurs in multiple document positions, we break the tie in favor of its first occurrence. At training time, we optimize the conditional log-likelihood shown below, with additional regularization penalties.

$$\log P(\mathbf{y}|\mathbf{x}) = \sum_i (g_i \log\{P(y_i|\mathbf{y}_{-i}, \mathbf{x})P(s_i)\}$$
$$+(1 - g_i) \log\{P(p(i)|\mathbf{y}_{-i}, \mathbf{x})(1 - P(s_i))\})$$

where $\mathbf{y}$ and $\mathbf{x}$ are the summary and document words respectively, g_i is an indicator function that

is set to 0 whenever the word at position i in the summary is OOV with respect to the decoder vocabulary. At test time, the model decides automatically at each time-step whether to generate or to point, based on the estimated switch probability $P(s_i)$. We simply use the $\arg\max$ of the posterior probability of generation or pointing to generate the best output at each time step.

The pointer mechanism may be more robust in handling rare words because it uses the encoder's hidden-state representation of rare words to decide which word from the document to point to. Since the hidden state depends on the entire context of the word, the model is able to accurately point to unseen words although they do not appear in the target vocabulary.[1]

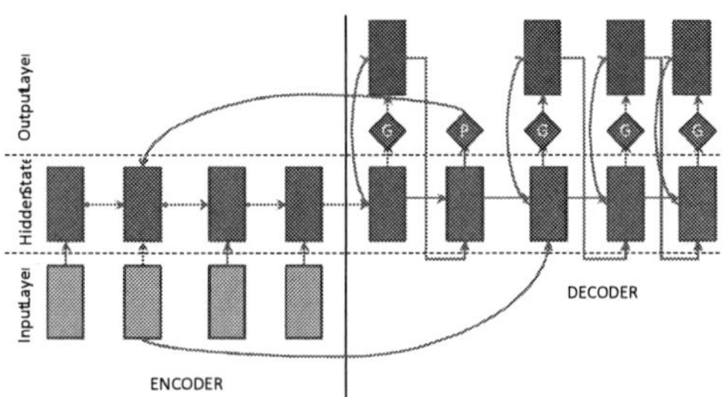

Figure 2: Switching generator/pointer model: When the switch shows 'G', the traditional generator consisting of the softmax layer is used to produce a word, and when it shows 'P', the pointer network is activated to copy the word from one of the source document positions. When the pointer is activated, the embedding from the source is used as input for the next time-step as shown by the arrow from the encoder to the decoder at the bottom.

2.4 Capturing Hierarchical Document Structure with Hierarchical Attention

In datasets where the source document is very long, in addition to identifying the keywords in the document, it is also important to identify the key sentences from which the summary can be drawn. This model aims to capture this notion of two levels of importance using two bi-directional

---

[1] Even when the word does not exist in the source vocabulary, the pointer model may still be able to identify the correct position of the word in the source since it takes into account the contextual representation of the corresponding 'UNK' token encoded by the RNN. Once the position is known, the corresponding token from the source document can be displayed in the summary even when it is not part of the training vocabulary either on the source side or the target side.

RNNs on the source side, one at the word level and the other at the sentence level. The attention mechanism operates at both levels simultaneously. The word-level attention is further re-weighted by the corresponding sentence-level attention and re-normalized as shown below:

$$P^a(j) \; = \; \frac{P_w^a(j)P_s^a(s(j))}{\sum_{k=1}^{N_d} P_w^a(k)P_s^a(s(k))},$$

where $P_w^a(j)$ is the word-level attention weight at j^{th} position of the source document, and $s(j)$ is the ID of the sentence at j^{th} word position, $P_s^a(l)$ is the sentence-level attention weight for the lth sentence in the source, N_d is the number of words in the source document, and $P^a(j)$ is the re-scaled attention at the jth word position. The re-scaled attention is then used to compute the attention-weighted context vector that goes as input to the hidden state of the decoder. Further, we also concatenate additional positional embeddings to the hidden state of the sentence-level RNN to model positional importance of sentences in the document. This architecture therefore models key sentences as well as keywords within those sentences jointly. A graphical representation of this model is displayed in Figure 3.

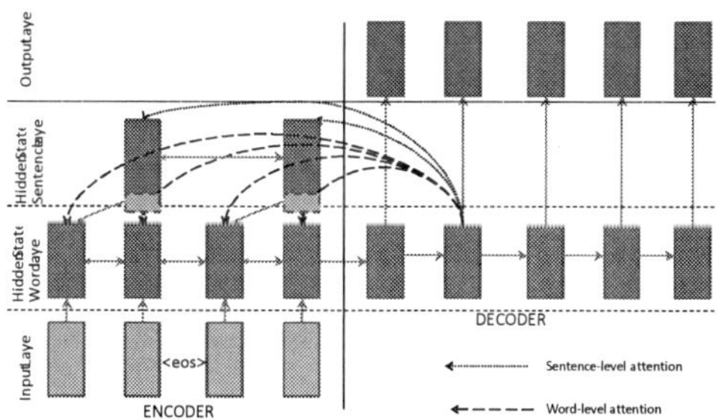

Figure 3: Hierarchical encoder with hierarchical attention: the attention weights at the word level, represented by the dashed arrows are re-scaled by the corresponding sentence-level attention weights, represented by the dotted arrows. The dashed boxes at the bottom of the top layer RNN represent sentence-level positional embeddings concatenated to the corresponding hidden states.

3   Related Work

A vast majority of past work in summarization has been extractive, which consists of identifying key sentences or passages in the source document and reproducing them as summary (Neto et al., 2002; Erkan and Radev, 2004; Wong et al., 2008a; Filippova and Altun, 2013; Colmenares et al., 2015; Litvak and Last, 2008; K. Riedhammer and Hakkani-Tur, 2010; Ricardo Ribeiro, 2013).

Humans on the other hand, tend to paraphrase the original story in their own words. As such, human summaries are abstractive in nature and seldom consist of reproduction of original sentences from the document. The task of abstractive summarization has been standardized using the DUC-2003 and DUC-2004 competitions.[2] The data for these tasks consists of news stories from various topics with multiple reference summaries per story generated by humans. The best performing system on the DUC-2004 task, called TOPIARY (Zajic et al., 2004), used a combination of linguistically motivated compression techniques, and an unsupervised topic detection algorithm that appends keywords extracted from the article onto the compressed output. Some of the other notable work in the task of abstractive summarization includes using traditional phrase-table based machine translation approaches (Banko et al., 2000), compression using weighted tree-transformation rules (Cohn and Lapata, 2008) and quasi-synchronous grammar approaches (Woodsend et al., 2010).

With the emergence of deep learning as a viable alternative for many NLP tasks (Collobert et al., 2011), researchers have started considering this framework as an attractive, fully data-driven alternative to abstractive summarization. In Rush et al. (2015), the authors use convolutional models to encode the source, and a context-sensitive attentional feed-forward neural network to generate the summary, producing state-of-the-art results on Gigaword and DUC datasets. In an extension to this work, Chopra et al. (2016) used a similar convolutional model for the encoder, but replaced the decoder with an RNN, producing further improvement in performance on both datasets. In another paper that is closely related to our work, Hu et al. (2015) introduce a large dataset for Chinese short text summarization. They show promising results on their Chinese dataset using an encoder-decoder RNN, but do not report experiments on English corpora. In another very recent work, Cheng and Lapata (2016) used RNN based encoder-decoder for extractive summarization of documents.

Our work starts with the same framework as (Hu et al., 2015), but we go beyond the stan-

---

[2] http://duc.nist.gov/

dard architecture and propose novel models that address critical problems in summarization. We analyze the similarities and differences of our proposed models with related work on abstractive summarization below.

Feature-rich encoder (Sec. 2.2): Linguistic features such as POS tags, and named-entities as well as TF and IDF information were used in many extractive approaches to summarization (Wong et al., 2008b), but they are novel in the context of deep learning approaches for abstractive summarization, to the best of our knowledge.

Switching generator-pointer model (Sec. 2.3): This model combines extractive and abstractive approaches to summarization in a single end-to-end framework. Rush et al. (2015) also used a combination of extractive and abstractive approaches, but their extractive model is a separate log-linear classifier with handcrafted features. Pointer networks (Vinyals et al., 2015) have also been used earlier for the problem of rare words in the context of machine translation (Luong et al., 2015), but the novel addition of switch in our model allows it to strike a balance between when to be faithful to the original source (e.g., for named entities and OOV) and when it is allowed to be creative. We believe such a process arguably mimics how human produces summaries. For a more detailed treatment of this model, and experiments on multiple tasks, please refer to the parallel work published by some of the authors of this work (Gulcehre et al., 2016).

Hierarchical attention model (Sec. 2.4): Previously proposed hierarchical encoder-decoder models use attention only at sentence-level (Li et al., 2015). The novelty of our approach lies in joint modeling of attention at both sentence and word levels, where the word-level attention is further influenced by sentence-level attention, thus capturing the notion of important sentences and important words within those sentences. Concatenation of positional embeddings with the hidden state at sentence-level is also new.

4 Experiments and Results

4.1 Gigaword Corpus

In this series of experiments[3], we used the annotated Gigaword corpus as described in Rush et al.

(2015). We used the scripts made available by the authors of this work[4] to preprocess the data, which resulted in about 3.8M training examples. The script also produces about 400K validation and test examples, but we created a randomly sampled subset of 2000 examples each for validation and testing purposes, on which we report our performance. Further, we also acquired the exact test sample used in Rush et al. (2015) to make precise comparison of our models with theirs. We also made small modifications to the script to extract not only the tokenized words, but also system-generated parts-of-speech and named-entity tags.

Training: For all the models we discuss below, we used 200 dimensional word2vec vectors (Mikolov et al., 2013) trained on the same corpus to initialize the model embeddings, but we allowed them to be updated during training. The hidden state dimension of the encoder and decoder was fixed at 400 in all our experiments. When we used only the first sentence of the document as the source, as done in Rush et al. (2015), the encoder vocabulary size was 119,505 and that of the decoder stood at 68,885. We used Adadelta (Zeiler, 2012) for training, with an initial learning rate of 0.001. We used a batch-size of 50 and randomly shuffled the training data at every epoch, while sorting every 10 batches according to their lengths to speed up training. We did not use any dropout or regularization, but applied gradient clipping. We used early stopping based on the validation set and used the best model on the validation set to report all test performance numbers. For all our models, we employ the large-vocabulary trick, where we restrict the decoder vocabulary size to 2,000[5], because it cuts down the training time per epoch by nearly three times, and helps this and all subsequent models converge in only 50%-75% of the epochs needed for the model based on full vocabulary.

Decoding: At decode-time, we used beam search of size 5 to generate the summary, and limited the size of summary to a maximum of 30 words, since this is the maximum size we noticed in the sampled validation set. We found that the average system summary length from all our models (7.8 to 8.3) agrees very closely with that of the ground truth on the validation set (about 8.7 words), without any specific tuning.

---

[4]https://github.com/facebook/NAMAS

[5]Larger values improved performance only marginally, but at the cost of much slower training.

Computational costs: We trained all our models on a single *Tesla K40* GPU. Most models took about 10 hours per epoch on an average except the hierarchical attention model, which took 12 hours per epoch. All models typically converged within 15 epochs using our early stopping criterion based on the validation cost. The wall-clock training time until convergence therefore varies between 6-8 days depending on the model. Generating summaries at test time is reasonably fast with a throughput of about 20 summaries per second on a single GPU, using a batch size of 1.

Evaluation metrics: In Rush et al. (2015), the authors used full-length version of Rouge recall[6] to evaluate their systems on the Gigaword corpus[7]. However, full-length recall favors longer summaries, so it may not be fair to use this metric to compare two systems that differ in summary lengths. Full-length F1 solves this problem since it can penalize longer summaries. Therefore, we use full-length F1 scores from 1, 2 and L variants of Rouge using the official script to evaluate our systems. However, in the interest of fair comparison with previous work, we also report full-length recall scores where necessary. In addition, we also report the percentage of tokens in the system summary that occur in the source (which we call 'src. copy rate' in Table 1).

We describe all our experiments and results on the Gigaword corpus below.

words-lvt2k-1sent: This is the baseline attentional encoder-decoder model with the large vocabulary trick. This model is trained only on the first sentence from the source document, as done in Rush et al. (2015).

words-lvt2k-2sent: This model is identical to the model above except for the fact that it is trained on the first two sentences from the source. On this corpus, adding the additional sentence in the source does seem to aid performance, as shown in Table 1. We also tried adding more sentences, but the performance dropped, which is probably because the latter sentences in this corpus are not pertinent to the summary.

words-lvt2k-2sent-hieratt: Since we used two sentences from source document, we trained the hierarchical attention model proposed in Sec 2.4. As shown in Table 1, this model improves perfor-

mance compared to its flatter counterpart by learning the relative importance of the first two sentences automatically.

feats-lvt2k-2sent: Here, we still train on the first two sentences, but we exploit the parts-of-speech and named-entity tags in the annotated gigaword corpus as well as TF, IDF values, to augment the input embeddings on the source side as described in Sec 2.2. In total, our embedding vector grew from the original 100 to 155, and produced incremental gains compared to its counterpart *words-lvt2k-2sent* as shown in Table 1, demonstrating the utility of syntax based features in this task.

feats-lvt2k-2sent-ptr: This is the switching generator/pointer model described in Sec. 2.3, but in addition, we also use feature-rich embeddings on the document side as in the above model. Our experiments indicate that the new model is able to achieve the best performance on our test set by all three Rouge variants as shown in Table 1.

Comparison with state-of-the-art: (Rush et al., 2015) reported *recall-only* from *full-length* version of Rouge, but the authors kindly provided us with their F1 numbers, as well as their test sample. We compared the performance of our model *words-lvt2k-1sent* with their best system on their sample, on both Recall as well as F1, as displayed in Table 1. The reason we did not evaluate our best models here is that this test set consisted of only 1 sentence from the source document, and did not include NLP annotations, which are needed in our best models. The table shows that, despite this fact, our model outperforms the state of the art model of Rush et al. (2015), on both recall and F1, with statistical significance. In addition, our models exhibit better abstractive ability as shown by the *src. copy rate* metric in the last column of the table.

We believe the bidirectional RNN we used to model the source captures richer contextual information of every word than the bag-of-embeddings representation used by Rush et al. (2015) in their convolutional and attentional encoders, which might explain our superior performance. Further, explicit modeling of important information such as multiple source sentences, word-level linguistic features, using the switch mechanism to point to source words when needed, and hierarchical attention, solve specific problems in summarization, each boosting performance incrementally.

---

[6]http://www.berouge.com/Pages/default.aspx

[7]confirmed from personal communication with the first-author of the paper.

#	Model name	Rouge-1	Rouge-2	Rouge-L	Src. copy rate (%)
Full length F1 on our internal test set					
1	words-lvt2k-1sent	34.97	17.17	32.70	75.85
2	words-lvt2k-2sent	35.73	17.38	33.25	79.54
3	words-lvt2k-2sent-hieratt	36.05	18.17	33.52	78.52
4	feats-lvt2k-2sent	35.90	17.57	33.38	78.92
5	feats-lvt2k-2sent-ptr	*36.40	17.77	*33.71	78.70
Full length Recall on the test set used by (Rush et al., 2015)					
6	ABS+ (Rush et al., 2015)	31.47	12.73	28.54	91.50
7	words-lvt2k-1sent	*34.19	*16.29	*32.13	74.57
Full length F1 on the test set used by (Rush et al., 2015)					
8	ABS+ (Rush et al., 2015)	29.78	11.89	26.97	91.50
9	words-lvt2k-1sent	*32.67	*15.59	*30.64	74.57

Table 1: Performance comparison of various models. '*' indicates statistical significance of the corresponding model with respect to the baseline model on its dataset as given by the 95% confidence interval in the official Rouge script. We report statistical significance only for the best performing models. 'src. copy rate' for the reference data on our validation sample is 45%. Please refer to Section 4 for explanation of notation.

4.2 DUC Corpus

The DUC corpus[8] comes in two parts: the 2003 corpus consisting of 624 document, summary pairs and the 2004 corpus consisting of 500 pairs. Since these corpora are too small to train large neural networks on, Rush et al. (2015) trained their models on the Gigaword corpus, but combined it with an additional log-linear extractive summarization model with handcrafted features, that is trained on the DUC 2003 corpus. They call the original neural attention model the ABS model, and the combined model ABS+. The latter model is current state-of-the-art since it outperforms all previously published baselines including non-neural network based extractive and abstractive systems, as measured by the official DUC metric of limited-length recall. In these experiments, we use the same metric to evaluate our models too, but we omit reporting numbers from other systems in the interest of space.

In our work, we simply run the model trained on Gigaword corpus as it is, without tuning it on the DUC validation set. The only change we made to the decoder is to suppress the model from emitting the end-of-summary tag, and force it to emit exactly 30 words for every summary, since the official evaluation on this corpus is based on limited-length Rouge recall. On this corpus too, since we have only a single sentence from source and no NLP annotations, we ran just the model *words-lvt2k-1sent*.

The performance of this model on the test set is compared with ABS and ABS+ models, as well as TOPIARY, the top performing system on DUC-2004 in Table 2. We note that although our model consistently outperforms ABS+ on all three variants of Rouge, the differences are not statistically significant. However, when the comparison is made with ABS model, which is really the true un-tuned counterpart of our model, the results are indeed statistically significant.

Model	Rouge-1	Rouge-2	Rouge-L
TOPIARY	25.12	6.46	20.12
ABS	26.55	7.06	22.05
ABS+	28.18	8.49	23.81
words-lvt2k-1sent	28.35	9.46	24.59

Table 2: Evaluation of our models using the limited-length Rouge Recall on DUC validation and test sets. Our best model, although trained exclusively on the Gigaword corpus, consistently outperforms the ABS+ model which is tuned on the DUC-2003 validation corpus in addition to being trained on the Gigaword corpus.

We would also like to bring the reader's attention to the concurrently published work of Chopra et al. (2016) where they also used an RNN based decoder for summary generation. While their numbers on Gigaword corpus are slightly better than our best performance on all three Rouge F1 metrics, our performance is marginally higher on DUC-2004 corpus on Rouge-2 and Rouge-L. We believe their work also confirms the effectiveness of RNN-based models for abstractive text summarization.

4.3 CNN/Daily Mail Corpus

The existing abstractive text summarization corpora including Gigaword and DUC consist of only one sentence in each summary. In this section, we present a new corpus that comprises multi-sentence summaries. To produce this corpus, we modify an existing corpus that has been used

---

[8] *http://duc.nist.gov/duc2004/tasks.html*

Model	Rouge-1	Rouge-2	Rouge-L
words-lvt2k	**32.49**	**11.84**	**29.47**
words-lvt2k-ptr	32.12	11.72	29.16
words-lvt2k-hieratt	31.78	11.56	28.73

Table 3: Performance of various models on CNN/Daily Mail test set using full-length Rouge-F1 metric. Bold faced numbers indicate best performing system.

for the task of passage-based question answering (Hermann et al., 2015). In this work, the authors used the human generated abstractive summary bullets from new-stories in *CNN* and *Daily Mail* websites as questions (with one of the entities hidden), and stories as the corresponding passages from which the system is expected to answer the fill-in-the-blank question. The authors released the scripts that crawl, extract and generate pairs of passages and questions from these websites. With a simple modification of the script, we restored all the summary bullets of each story in the original order to obtain a multi-sentence summary, where each bullet is treated as a sentence. In all, this corpus has 286,817 training pairs, 13,368 validation pairs and 11,487 test pairs, as defined by their scripts. The source documents in the training set have 766 words spanning 29.74 sentences on an average while the summaries consist of 53 words and 3.72 sentences. The unique characteristics of this dataset such as long documents, and ordered multi-sentence summaries present interesting challenges, and we hope will attract future researchers to build and test novel models on it.

The dataset is released in two versions: one consisting of actual entity names, and the other, in which entity occurrences are replaced with document-specific integer-ids beginning from 0. Since the vocabulary size is smaller in the anonymized version, we used it in all our experiments below. We limited the source vocabulary size to 150K, and the target vocabulary to 60K, the source and target lengths to at most 800 and 100 words respectively. We used 100-dimensional word2vec embeddings trained on this dataset as input, and we fixed the model hidden state size at 200. We also created explicit pointers in the training data by matching only the anonymized entity-ids between source and target on similar lines as we did for the OOV words in Gigaword corpus.

Computational costs: We used a single Tesla K-40 GPU to train our models on this dataset as well. While the flat models (*words-lvt2k* and *words-lvt2k-ptr*) took under 5 hours per epoch, the hier-archical attention model was very expensive, consuming nearly 12.5 hours per epoch. Convergence of all models is also slower on this dataset compared to Gigaword, taking nearly 35 epochs for all models. Thus, the wall-clock time for training until convergence is about 7 days for the flat models, but nearly 18 days for the hierarchical attention model. Decoding is also slower as well, with a throughput of 2 examples per second for flat models and 1.5 examples per second for the hierarchical attention model, when run on a single GPU with a batch size of 1.

Evaluation: We evaluated our models using the full-length Rouge F1 metric that we employed for the Gigaword corpus, but with one notable difference: in both system and gold summaries, we considered each highlight to be a separate sentence.[9]

Results: Results from three models we ran on this corpus are displayed in Table 3. Although this dataset is smaller and more complex than the Gigaword corpus, it is interesting to note that the Rouge numbers are in the same range. However, our switching pointer/generator model as well as the hierarchical attention model described in Sec. 2.4 fail to outperform the baseline attentional decoder, indicating that further research and experimentation needs to be done on this dataset. These results, although preliminary, should serve as a good baseline for future researchers to compare their models against.

5 Qualitative Analysis

Table 4 presents a few high quality and poor quality output on the validation set from *feats-lvt2k-2sent*, one of our best performing models. Even when the model differs from the target summary, its summaries tend to be very meaningful and relevant, a phenomenon not captured by word/phrase matching evaluation metrics such as Rouge. On the other hand, the model sometimes 'misinterprets' the semantics of the text and generates a summary with a comical interpretation as shown in the poor quality examples in the table. Clearly, capturing the 'meaning' of complex sentences remains a weakness of these models.

Our next example output, presented in Figure 4, displays the sample output from the switching generator/pointer model on the Gigaword corpus.

---

[9]This was done by modifying the pre-processing script such that each highlight gets its own "<a>" tag in the xml file that goes as input to the evaluation script.

Figure 4: Sample output from switching generator/pointer networks. An arrow indicates that a pointer to the source position was used to generate the corresponding summary word.

It is apparent from the examples that the model learns to use pointers very accurately not only for named entities, but also for multi-word phrases. Despite its accuracy, the performance improvement of the overall model is not significant. We believe the impact of this model may be more pronounced in other settings with a heavier tail distribution of rare words. We intend to carry out more experiments with this model in the future.

On CNN/Daily Mail data, although our models are able to produce good quality multi-sentence summaries, we notice that the same sentence or phrase often gets repeated in the summary. We believe models that incorporate intra-attention such as Cheng et al. (2016) can fix this problem by encouraging the model to 'remember' the words it has already produced in the past.

6 Conclusion

In this work, we apply the attentional encoder-decoder for the task of abstractive summarization with very promising results, outperforming state-of-the-art results significantly on two different datasets. Each of our proposed novel models addresses a specific problem in abstractive summarization, yielding further improvement in performance. We also propose a new dataset for multi-sentence summarization and establish benchmark numbers on it. As part of our future work, we plan to focus our efforts on this data and build more robust models for summaries consisting of multiple sentences.

Good quality summary output
S: a man charged with the murder last year of a british backpacker confessed to the slaying on the night he was charged with her killing , according to police evidence presented at a court hearing tuesday . ian douglas previte , ## , is charged with murdering caroline stuttle , ## , of yorkshire , england **T**: man charged with british backpacker 's death confessed to crime police officer claims **O**: man charged with murdering british backpacker confessed to murder
S: following are the leading scorers in the english premier league after saturday 's matches : ## - alan shearer -lrb- newcastle united -rrb- , james beattie . **T**: leading scorers in english premier league **O**: english premier league leading scorers
S: volume of transactions at the nigerian stock exchange has continued its decline since last week , a nse official said thursday . the latest statistics showed that a total of ##.### million shares valued at ###.### million naira -lrb- about #.### million us dollars -rrb- were traded on wednesday in , deals . **T**: transactions dip at nigerian stock exchange **O**: transactions at nigerian stock exchange down
Poor quality summary output
S: broccoli and broccoli sprouts contain a chemical that kills the bacteria responsible for most stomach cancer , say researchers , confirming the dietary advice that moms have been handing out for years . in laboratory tests the chemical , <unk> , killed helicobacter pylori , a bacteria that causes stomach ulcers and often fatal stomach cancers . **T**: for release at #### <unk> mom was right broccoli is good for you say cancer researchers **O**: broccoli sprouts contain deadly bacteria
S: norway delivered a diplomatic protest to russia on monday after three norwegian fisheries research expeditions were barred from russian waters . the norwegian research ships were to continue an annual program of charting fish resources shared by the two countries in the barents sea region . **T**: norway protests russia barring fisheries research ships **O**: norway grants diplomatic protest to russia
S: j.p. morgan chase 's ability to recover from a slew of recent losses rests largely in the hands of two men , who are both looking to restore tarnished reputations and may be considered for the top job someday . geoffrey <unk> , now the co-head of j.p. morgan 's investment bank , left goldman , sachs & co. more than a decade ago after executives say he lost out in a bid to lead that firm . **T**: # executives to lead j.p. morgan chase on road to recovery **O**: j.p. morgan chase may be considered for top job

Table 4: Examples of generated summaries from our best model on the validation set of Gigaword corpus. **S**: source document, **T**: target summary, **O**: system output. Although we displayed equal number of good quality and poor quality summaries in the table, the good ones are far more prevalent than the poor ones.

References

Dzmitry Bahdanau, Kyunghyun Cho, and Yoshua Bengio. 2014. Neural machine translation by jointly learning to align and translate. *CoRR*, abs/1409.0473.

Dzmitry Bahdanau, Jan Chorowski, Dmitriy Serdyuk, Philemon Brakel, and Yoshua Bengio. 2015. End-to-end attention-based large vocabulary speech recognition. *CoRR*, abs/1508.04395.

Michele Banko, Vibhu O. Mittal, and Michael J Witbrock. 2000. Headline generation based on statistical translation. *In Proceedings of the 38th Annual Meeting on Association for Computational Linguistics*, 22:318–325.

Jianpeng Cheng and Mirella Lapata. 2016. Neural summarization by extracting sentences and words. In *Proceedings of the 54th Annual Meeting of the Association for Computational Linguistics*.

Jianpeng Cheng, Li Dong, and Mirella Lapata. 2016. Long short-term memory-networks for machine reading. *CoRR*, abs/1601.06733.

Sumit Chopra, Michael Auli, and Alexander M. Rush. 2016. Abstractive sentence summarization with attentive recurrent neural networks. In *HLT-NAACL*.

Junyoung Chung, Çaglar Gülçehre, KyungHyun Cho, and Yoshua Bengio. 2014. Empirical evaluation of gated recurrent neural networks on sequence modeling. *CoRR*, abs/1412.3555.

Trevor Cohn and Mirella Lapata. 2008. Sentence compression beyond word deletion. In *Proceedings of the 22Nd International Conference on Computational Linguistics - Volume 1*, pages 137–144.

Ronan Collobert, Jason Weston, Léon Bottou, Michael Karlen, Koray Kavukcuoglu, and Pavel P. Kuksa. 2011. Natural language processing (almost) from scratch. *CoRR*, abs/1103.0398.

Carlos A. Colmenares, Marina Litvak, Amin Mantrach, and Fabrizio Silvestri. 2015. Heads: Headline generation as sequence prediction using an abstract feature-rich space. In *Proceedings of the 2015 Conference of the North American Chapter of the Association for Computational Linguistics: Human Language Technologies*, pages 133–142.

G. Erkan and D. R. Radev. 2004. Lexrank: Graph-based lexical centrality as salience in text summarization. *Journal of Artificial Intelligence Research*, 22:457–479.

Katja Filippova and Yasemin Altun. 2013. Overcoming the lack of parallel data in sentence compression. In *Proceedings of the 2013 Conference on Empirical Methods in Natural Language Processing*, pages 1481–1491.

Caglar Gulcehre, Sungjin Ahn, Ramesh Nallapati, Bowen Zhou, and Yoshua Bengio. 2016. Pointing the unknown words. In *Proceedings of the 54th Annual Meeting of the Association for Computational Linguistics*.

Karl Moritz Hermann, Tomás Kociský, Edward Grefenstette, Lasse Espeholt, Will Kay, Mustafa Suleyman, and Phil Blunsom. 2015. Teaching machines to read and comprehend. *CoRR*, abs/1506.03340.

Baotian Hu, Qingcai Chen, and Fangze Zhu. 2015. Lcsts: A large scale chinese short text summarization dataset. In *Proceedings of the 2015 Conference on Empirical Methods in Natural Language Processing*, pages 1967–1972, Lisbon, Portugal, September. Association for Computational Linguistics.

Sébastien Jean, Kyunghyun Cho, Roland Memisevic, and Yoshua Bengio. 2014. On using very large target vocabulary for neural machine translation. *CoRR*, abs/1412.2007.

B. Favre K. Riedhammer and D. Hakkani-Tur. 2010. Long story short âĂŞ global unsupervised models for keyphrase based meeting summarization. In *Speech Communication*, pages 801–815.

Jiwei Li, Minh-Thang Luong, and Dan Jurafsky. 2015. A hierarchical neural autoencoder for paragraphs and documents. *CoRR*, abs/1506.01057.

M. Litvak and M. Last. 2008. Graph-based keyword extraction for single-document summarization. In *Coling 2008*, pages 17–24.

Thang Luong, Ilya Sutskever, Quoc V. Le, Oriol Vinyals, and Wojciech Zaremba. 2015. Addressing the rare word problem in neural machine translation. In *Proceedings of the 53rd Annual Meeting of the Association for Computational Linguistics and the 7th International Joint Conference on Natural Language Processing of the Asian Federation of Natural Language Processing*, pages 11–19.

Tomas Mikolov, Ilya Sutskever, Kai Chen, Greg Corrado, and Jeffrey Dean. 2013. Distributed representations of words and phrases and their compositionality. *CoRR*, abs/1310.4546.

Joel Larocca Neto, Alex Alves Freitas, and Celso A. A. Kaestner. 2002. Automatic text summarization using a machine learning approach. In *Proceedings of the 16th Brazilian Symposium on Artificial Intelligence: Advances in Artificial Intelligence*, pages 205–215.

David Martins de Matos JoÃčo P. Neto Anatole Gershman Jaime Carbonell Ricardo Ribeiro, LuÃ■s Marujo. 2013. Self reinforcement for important passage retrieval. In *36th international ACM SIGIR conference on Research and development in information retrieval*, pages 845–848.

Alexander M. Rush, Sumit Chopra, and Jason Weston. 2015. A neural attention model for abstractive sentence summarization. *CoRR*, abs/1509.00685.

Subhashini Venugopalan, Marcus Rohrbach, Jeff Donahue, Raymond J. Mooney, Trevor Darrell, and Kate Saenko. 2015. Sequence to sequence - video to text. *CoRR*, abs/1505.00487.

O. Vinyals, M. Fortunato, and N. Jaitly. 2015. Pointer Networks. *ArXiv e-prints*, June.

Kam-Fai Wong, Mingli Wu, and Wenjie Li. 2008a. Extractive summarization using supervised and semi-supervised learning. In *Proceedings of the 22Nd International Conference on Computational Linguistics - Volume 1*, pages 985–992.

Kam-Fai Wong, Mingli Wu, and Wenjie Li. 2008b. Extractive summarization using supervised and semi-supervised learning. In *Proceedings of the 22nd Annual Meeting of the Association for Computational Linguistics*, pages 985–992.

Kristian Woodsend, Yansong Feng, and Mirella Lapata. 2010. Title generation with quasi-synchronous grammar. In *Proceedings of the 2010 Conference on Empirical Methods in Natural Language Processing*, EMNLP '10, pages 513–523, Stroudsburg, PA, USA. Association for Computational Linguistics.

David Zajic, Bonnie J. Dorr, and Richard Schwartz. 2004. Bbn/umd at duc-2004: Topiary. In *Proceedings of the North American Chapter of the Association for Computational Linguistics Workshop on Document Understanding*, pages 112–119.

Matthew D. Zeiler. 2012. ADADELTA: an adaptive learning rate method. *CoRR*, abs/1212.5701.

Compression of Neural Machine Translation Models via Pruning

Abigail See*   **Minh-Thang Luong***   **Christopher D. Manning**
Computer Science Department, Stanford University, Stanford, CA 94305
`{abisee,lmthang,manning}@stanford.edu`

Abstract

Neural Machine Translation (NMT), like many other deep learning domains, typically suffers from over-parameterization, resulting in large storage sizes. This paper examines three simple magnitude-based pruning schemes to compress NMT models, namely *class-blind*, *class-uniform*, and *class-distribution*, which differ in terms of how pruning thresholds are computed for the different classes of weights in the NMT architecture. We demonstrate the efficacy of weight pruning as a compression technique for a state-of-the-art NMT system. We show that an NMT model with over 200 million parameters can be pruned by 40% with very little performance loss as measured on the WMT'14 English-German translation task. This sheds light on the distribution of redundancy in the NMT architecture. Our main result is that with *retraining*, we can recover and even surpass the original performance with an 80%-pruned model.

1 Introduction

Neural Machine Translation (NMT) is a simple new architecture for translating texts from one language into another (Sutskever et al., 2014; Cho et al., 2014). NMT is a single deep neural network that is trained end-to-end, holding several advantages such as the ability to capture long-range dependencies in sentences, and generalization to unseen texts. Despite being relatively new, NMT has already achieved state-of-the-art translation results for several language pairs including English-French (Luong et al., 2015b), English-German (Jean et al., 2015a; Luong et al., 2015a; Luong and

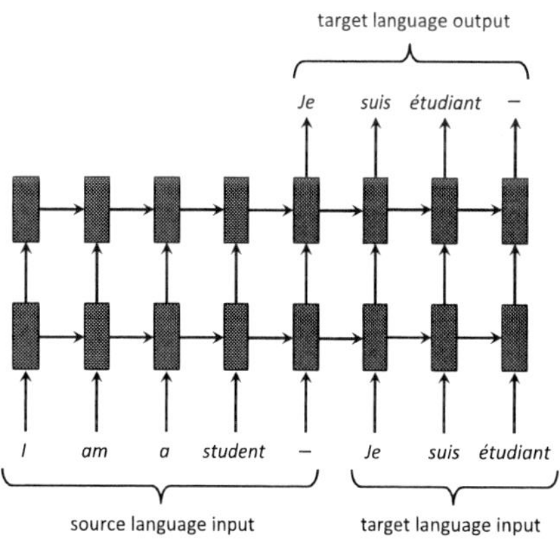

Figure 1: A simplified diagram of NMT.

Manning, 2015; Sennrich et al., 2016), English-Turkish (Sennrich et al., 2016), and English-Czech (Jean et al., 2015b; Luong and Manning, 2016). Figure 1 gives an example of an NMT system.

While NMT has a significantly smaller memory footprint than traditional phrase-based approaches (which need to store gigantic phrase-tables and language models), the model size of NMT is still prohibitively large for mobile devices. For example, a recent state-of-the-art NMT system requires over 200 million parameters, resulting in a storage size of hundreds of megabytes (Luong et al., 2015a). Though the trend for bigger and deeper neural networks has brought great progress, it has also introduced over-parameterization, resulting in long running times, overfitting, and the storage size issue discussed above. A solution to the over-parameterization problem could potentially aid all three issues, though the first (long running times) is outside the scope of this paper.

Our contribution. In this paper we investigate the efficacy of weight pruning for NMT as a means of compression. We show that despite

---

*Both authors contributed equally.

291

Proceedings of the 20th SIGNLL Conference on Computational Natural Language Learning (CoNLL), pages 291–301,
Berlin, Germany, August 7-12, 2016. ©2016 Association for Computational Linguistics

its simplicity, magnitude-based pruning with retraining is highly effective, and we compare three magnitude-based pruning schemes — *class-blind*, *class-uniform* and *class-distribution*. Though recent work has chosen to use the latter two, we find the first and simplest scheme — *class-blind* — the most successful. We are able to prune 40% of the weights of a state-of-the-art NMT system with negligible performance loss, and by adding a retraining phase after pruning, we can prune 80% with no performance loss. Our pruning experiments also reveal some patterns in the distribution of redundancy in NMT. In particular we find that higher layers, attention and softmax weights are the most important, while lower layers and the embedding weights hold a lot of redundancy. For the Long Short-Term Memory (LSTM) architecture, we find that at lower layers the parameters for the input are most crucial, but at higher layers the parameters for the gates also become important.

2   Related Work

Pruning the parameters from a neural network, referred to as *weight pruning* or *network pruning*, is a well-established idea though it can be implemented in many ways. Among the most popular are the Optimal Brain Damage (OBD) (Le Cun et al., 1989) and Optimal Brain Surgeon (OBS) (Hassibi and Stork, 1993) techniques, which involve computing the Hessian matrix of the loss function with respect to the parameters, in order to assess the *saliency* of each parameter. Parameters with low saliency are then pruned from the network and the remaining sparse network is retrained. Both OBD and OBS were shown to perform better than the so-called 'naive magnitude-based approach', which prunes parameters according to their magnitude (deleting parameters close to zero). However, the high computational complexity of OBD and OBS compare unfavorably to the computational simplicity of the magnitude-based approach, especially for large networks (Augasta and Kathirvalavakumar, 2013).

In recent years, the deep learning renaissance has prompted a re-investigation of network pruning for modern models and tasks. Magnitude-based pruning with iterative retraining has yielded strong results for Convolutional Neural Networks (CNN) performing visual tasks. (Collins and Kohli, 2014) prune 75% of AlexNet parameters with small accuracy loss on the ImageNet task, while (Han et al., 2015b) prune 89% of AlexNet parameters with no accuracy loss on the ImageNet task.

Other approaches focus on pruning neurons rather than parameters, via sparsity-inducing regularizers (Murray and Chiang, 2015) or 'wiring together' pairs of neurons with similar input weights (Srinivas and Babu, 2015). These approaches are much more constrained than weight-pruning schemes; they necessitate finding entire zero rows of weight matrices, or near-identical pairs of rows, in order to prune a single neuron. By contrast weight-pruning approaches allow weights to be pruned freely and independently of each other. The neuron-pruning approach of (Srinivas and Babu, 2015) was shown to perform poorly (it suffered performance loss after removing only 35% of AlexNet parameters) compared to the weight-pruning approach of (Han et al., 2015b). Though (Murray and Chiang, 2015) demonstrates neuron-pruning for language modeling as part of a (non-neural) Machine Translation pipeline, their approach is more geared towards architecture selection than compression.

There are many other compression techniques for neural networks, including approaches based on on low-rank approximations for weight matrices (Jaderberg et al., 2014; Denton et al., 2014), or weight sharing via hash functions (Chen et al., 2015). Several methods involve reducing the precision of the weights or activations (Courbariaux et al., 2015), sometimes in conjunction with specialized hardware (Gupta et al., 2015), or even using binary weights (Lin et al., 2016). The 'knowledge distillation' technique of (Hinton et al., 2015) involves training a small 'student' network on the soft outputs of a large 'teacher' network. Some approaches use a sophisticated pipeline of several techniques to achieve impressive feats of compression (Han et al., 2015a; Iandola et al., 2016).

Most of the above work has focused on compressing CNNs for vision tasks. We extend the magnitude-based pruning approach of (Han et al., 2015b) to recurrent neural networks (RNN), in particular LSTM architectures for NMT, and to our knowledge we are the first to do so. There has been some recent work on compression for RNNs (Lu et al., 2016; Prabhavalkar et al., 2016), but it focuses on other, non-pruning compression techniques. Nonetheless, our general observations on the distribution of redundancy in a LSTM, de-

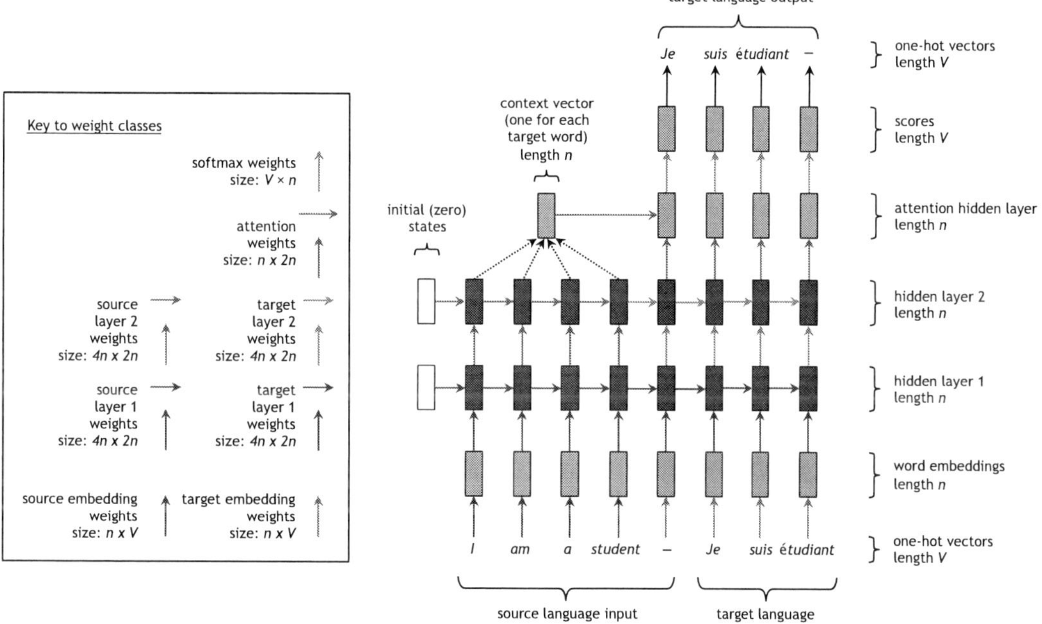

Figure 2: NMT architecture. This example has two layers, but our system has four. The different weight classes are indicated by arrows of different color (the black arrows in the top right represent simply choosing the highest-scoring word, and thus require no parameters). Best viewed in color.

tailed in Section 4.5, are corroborated by (Lu et al., 2016).

3 Our Approach

We first give a brief overview of Neural Machine Translation before describing the model architecture of interest, the deep multi-layer recurrent model with LSTM. We then explain the different types of NMT weights together with our approaches to pruning and retraining.

3.1 Neural Machine Translation

Neural machine translation aims to directly model the conditional probability $p(y|x)$ of translating a source sentence, $x_1, \ldots, x_n$, to a target sentence, $y_1, \ldots, y_m$. It accomplishes this goal through an *encoder-decoder* framework (Kalchbrenner and Blunsom, 2013; Sutskever et al., 2014; Cho et al., 2014). The *encoder* computes a representation s for each source sentence. Based on that source representation, the *decoder* generates a translation, one target word at a time, and hence, decomposes the log conditional probability as:

$$\log p(y|x) = \sum_{t=1}^{m} \log p\left(y_t | y_{<t}, s\right) \quad (1)$$

Most NMT work uses RNNs, but approaches differ in terms of: (a) architecture, which can

be unidirectional, bidirectional, or deep multilayer RNN; and (b) RNN type, which can be Long Short-Term Memory (LSTM) (Hochreiter and Schmidhuber, 1997) or the Gated Recurrent Unit (Cho et al., 2014).

In this work, we specifically consider the *deep multi-layer recurrent* architecture with *LSTM* as the hidden unit type. Figure 1 illustrates an instance of that architecture during training in which the source and target sentence pair are input for supervised learning. During testing, the target sentence is not known in advance; instead, the most probable target words predicted by the model are fed as inputs into the next timestep. The network stops when it emits the end-of-sentence symbol — a special 'word' in the vocabulary, represented by a dash in Figure 1.

3.2 Understanding NMT Weights

Figure 2 shows the same system in more detail, highlighting the different types of parameters, or weights, in the model. We will go through the architecture from bottom to top. First, a vocabulary is chosen for each language, assuming that the top V frequent words are selected. Thus, every word in the source or target vocabulary can be represented by a one-hot vector of length V.

293

The source input sentence and target input sentence, represented as a sequence of one-hot vectors, are transformed into a sequence of word embeddings by the *embedding* weights. These embedding weights, which are learned during training, are different for the source words and the target words. The word embeddings and all hidden layers are vectors of length n (a chosen hyperparameter).

The word embeddings are then fed as input into the main network, which consists of two multilayer RNNs 'stuck together' — an encoder for the source language and a decoder for the target language, each with their own weights. The *feed-forward* (vertical) weights connect the hidden unit from the layer below to the upper RNN block, and the *recurrent* (horizontal) weights connect the hidden unit from the previous time-step RNN block to the current time-step RNN block.

The hidden state at the top layer of the decoder is fed through an *attention* layer, which guides the translation by 'paying attention' to relevant parts of the source sentence; for more information see (Bahdanau et al., 2015) or Section 3 of (Luong et al., 2015a). Finally, for each target word, the top layer hidden unit is transformed by the *softmax* weights into a score vector of length V. The target word with the highest score is selected as the output translation.

Weight Subgroups in LSTM – For the aforementioned RNN block, we choose to use LSTM as the hidden unit type. To facilitate our later discussion on the different subgroups of weights within LSTM, we first review the details of LSTM as formulated by Zaremba et al. (2014) as follows:

$$\begin{pmatrix} i \\ f \\ o \\ \hat{h} \end{pmatrix} = \begin{pmatrix} \text{sigm} \\ \text{sigm} \\ \text{sigm} \\ \text{tanh} \end{pmatrix} T_{4n,2n} \begin{pmatrix} h_t^{l-1} \\ h_{t-1}^{l} \end{pmatrix} \tag{2}$$

$$c_t^l = f \circ c_{t-1}^l + i \circ \hat{h} \tag{3}$$

$$h_t^l = o \circ \tanh(c_t^l) \tag{4}$$

Here, each LSTM block at time t and layer l computes as output a pair of hidden and memory vectors (h_t^l, c_t^l) given the previous pair (h_{t-1}^l, c_{t-1}^l) and an input vector h_t^{l-1} (either from the LSTM block below or the embedding weights if $l = 1$). All of these vectors have length n.

The core of a LSTM block is the weight matrix $T_{4n,2n}$ of size $4n \times 2n$. This matrix can be decomposed into 8 subgroups that are responsible for the

interactions between $\{$input gate i, forget gate f, output gate o, input signal $\hat{h}\} \times \{$feed-forward input h_t^{l-1}, recurrent input $h_{t-1}^l\}$.

3.3 Pruning Schemes

We follow the general magnitude-based approach of (Han et al., 2015b), which consists of pruning weights with smallest absolute value. However, we question the authors' pruning scheme with respect to the different weight classes, and experiment with three pruning schemes. Suppose we wish to prune $x\%$ of the total parameters in the model. How do we distribute the pruning over the different weight classes (illustrated in Figure 2) of our model? We propose to examine three different pruning schemes:

1. *Class-blind*: Take all parameters, sort them by magnitude and prune the $x\%$ with smallest magnitude, regardless of weight class. (So some classes are pruned proportionally more than others).

2. *Class-uniform*: Within each class, sort the weights by magnitude and prune the $x\%$ with smallest magnitude. (So all classes have exactly $x\%$ of their parameters pruned).

3. *Class-distribution*: For each class c, weights with magnitude less than $\lambda \sigma_c$ are pruned. Here, σ_c is the standard deviation of that class and λ is a universal parameter chosen such that in total, $x\%$ of all parameters are pruned. This is used by (Han et al., 2015b).

All these schemes have their seeming advantages. Class-blind pruning is the simplest and adheres to the principle that pruning weights (or equivalently, setting them to zero) is least damaging when those weights are small, regardless of their locations in the architecture. Class-uniform pruning and class-distribution pruning both seek to prune proportionally within each weight class, either absolutely, or relative to the standard deviation of that class. We find that class-blind pruning outperforms both other schemes (see Section 4.1).

3.4 Retraining

In order to prune NMT models aggressively without performance loss, we retrain our pruned networks. That is, we continue to train the remaining weights, but maintain the sparse structure introduced by pruning. In our implementation, pruned

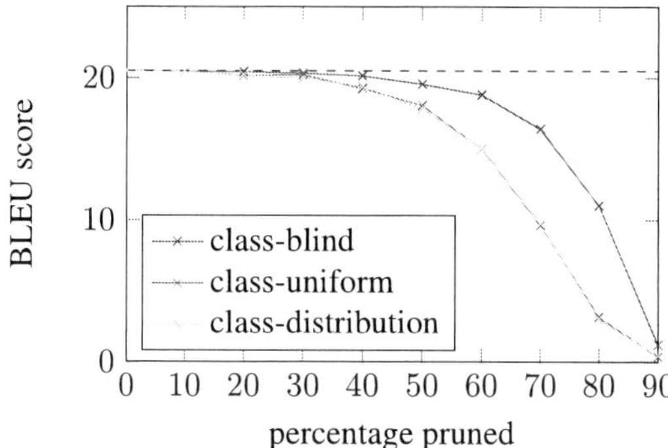

Figure 3: Effects of different pruning schemes.

weights are represented by zeros in the weight matrices, and we use binary 'mask' matrices, which represent the sparse structure of a network, to ignore updates to weights at pruned locations. This implementation has the advantage of simplicity as it requires minimal changes to the training and deployment code, but we note that a more complex implementation utilizing sparse matrices and sparse matrix multiplication could potentially yield speed improvements. However, such an implementation is beyond the scope of this paper.

4 Experiments

We evaluate the effectiveness of our pruning approaches on a state-of-the-art NMT model.[1] Specifically, an attention-based English-German NMT system from (Luong et al., 2015a) is considered. Training data was obtained from WMT'14 consisting of 4.5M sentence pairs (116M English words, 110M German words). For more details on training hyperparameters, we refer readers to Section 4.1 of (Luong et al., 2015a). All models are tested on newstest2014 (2737 sentences). The model achieves a perplexity of 6.1 and a BLEU score of 20.5 (after unknown word replacement).[2]

When *retraining* pruned NMT systems, we use the following settings: (a) we start with a smaller learning rate of 0.5 (the original model uses a learning rate of 1.0), (b) we train for fewer epochs, 4 instead of 12, using plain SGD, (c) a simple learning rate schedule is employed; after 2 epochs, we begin to halve the learning rate every half an epoch, and (d) all other hyperparameters are the

same, such as mini-batch size 128, maximum gradient norm 5, and dropout with probability 0.2.

4.1 Comparing pruning schemes

Despite its simplicity, we observe in Figure 3 that *class-blind* pruning outperforms both other schemes in terms of translation quality at all pruning percentages. In order to understand this result, for each of the three pruning schemes, we pruned each class separately and recorded the effect on performance (as measured by perplexity). Figure 4 shows that with class-uniform pruning, the overall performance loss is caused disproportionately by a few classes: target layer 4, attention and softmax weights. Looking at Figure 5, we see that the most damaging classes to prune also tend to be those with weights of greater magnitude — these classes have much larger weights than others at the same percentile, so pruning them under the class-uniform pruning scheme is more damaging. The situation is similar for class-distribution pruning.

By contrast, Figure 4 shows that under class-blind pruning, the damage caused by pruning softmax, attention and target layer 4 weights is greatly decreased, and the contribution of each class towards the performance loss is overall more uniform. In fact, the distribution begins to reflect the number of parameters in each class — for example, the source and target embedding classes have larger contributions because they have more weights. We use only class-blind pruning for the rest of the experiments.

Figure 4 also reveals some interesting information about the distribution of redundancy in NMT architectures — namely it seems that higher layers are more important than lower layers, and that attention and softmax weights are crucial. We will explore the distribution of redundancy further in Section 4.5.

4.2 Pruning and retraining

Pruning has an immediate negative impact on performance (as measured by BLEU) that is exponential in pruning percentage; this is demonstrated by the blue line in Figure 6. However we find that up to about 40% pruning, performance is mostly unaffected, indicating a large amount of redundancy and over-parameterization in NMT.

We now consider the effect of retraining pruned models. The orange line in Figure 6 shows that after retraining the pruned models, baseline performance (20.48 BLEU) is both recovered and im-

---

¹We thank the authors of (Luong et al., 2015a) for providing their trained models and assistance in using the codebase at `https://github.com/lmthang/nmt.matlab`.

²The performance of this model is reported under row *global (dot)* in Table 4 of (Luong et al., 2015a).

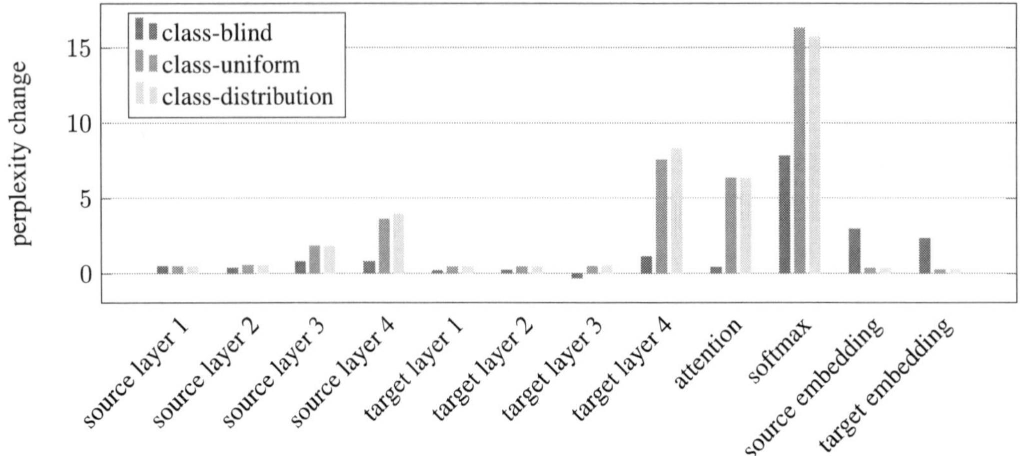

Figure 4: 'Breakdown' of performance loss (i.e., perplexity increase) by weight class, when pruning 90% of weights using each of the three pruning schemes. Each of the first eight classes have 8 million weights, attention has 2 million, and the last three have 50 million weights each.

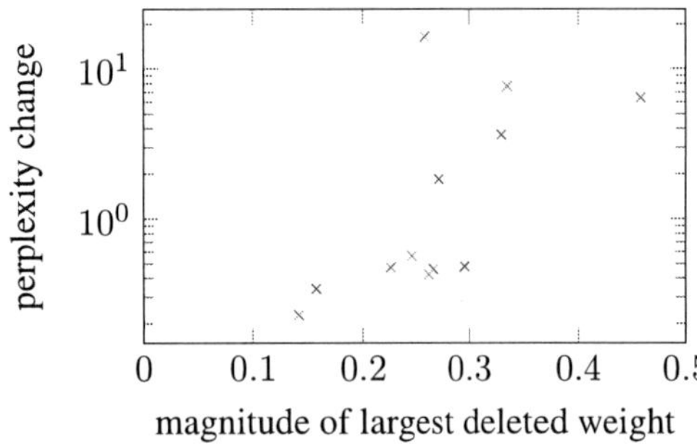

Figure 5: Magnitude of largest deleted weight vs. perplexity change, for the 12 different weight classes when pruning 90% of parameters by class-uniform pruning.

Figure 6: Performance of pruned models (a) after pruning, (b) after pruning and retraining, and (c) when trained with sparsity structure from the outset (see Section 4.3).

proved upon, up to 80% pruning (20.91 BLEU), with only a small performance loss at 90% pruning (20.13 BLEU). This may seem surprising, as we might not expect a sparse model to significantly out-perform a model with five times as many parameters. There are several possible explanations, two of which are given below.

Firstly, we found that the less-pruned models perform better on the training set than the validation set, whereas the more-pruned models have closer performance on the two sets. This indicates that pruning has a regularizing effect on the retraining phase, though clearly more is not always better, as the 50% pruned and retrained model has better validation set performance than the 90%

pruned and retrained model. Nonetheless, this regularization effect may explain why the pruned and retrained models outperform the baseline.

Alternatively, pruning may serve as a means to escape a local optimum. Figure 7 shows the loss function over time during the training, pruning and retraining process. During the original training process, the loss curve flattens out and seems to converge (note that we use early stopping to obtain our baseline model, so the original model was trained for longer than shown in Figure 7). Pruning causes an immediate increase in the loss function, but enables further gradient descent, allowing the retraining process to find a new, better local optimum. It seems that the disruption caused by

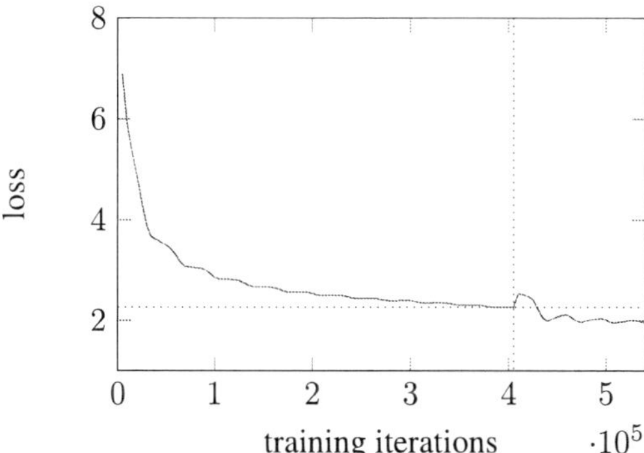

Figure 7: The validation set loss during training, pruning and retraining. The vertical dotted line marks the point when 80% of the parameters are pruned. The horizontal dotted line marks the best performance of the unpruned baseline.

pruning is beneficial in the long-run.

4.3 Starting with sparse models

The favorable performance of the pruned and retrained models raises the question: can we get a shortcut to this performance by *starting* with sparse models? That is, rather than train, prune, and retrain, what if we simply prune then train? To test this, we took the sparsity structure of our 50%–90% pruned models, and trained completely new models with the same sparsity structure. The purple line in Figure 6 shows that the 'sparse from the beginning' models do not perform as well as the pruned and retrained models, but they do come close to the baseline performance. This shows that while the sparsity structure alone contains useful information about redundancy and can therefore produce a competitive compressed model, it is important to interleave pruning with training.

Though our method involves just one pruning stage, other pruning methods interleave pruning with training more closely by including several iterations (Collins and Kohli, 2014; Han et al., 2015b). We expect that implementing this for NMT would likely result in further compression and performance improvements.

4.4 Storage size

The original unpruned model (a MATLAB file) has size 782MB. The 80% pruned and retrained model is 272MB, which is a 65.2% reduction. In this work we focus on compression in terms of number of parameters rather than storage size, be-

cause it is invariant across implementations.

4.5 Distribution of redundancy in NMT

We visualize in Figure 8 the redundancy structure of our NMT baseline model. *Black* pixels represent weights near to zero (those that can be pruned); *white* pixels represent larger ones. First we consider the embedding weight matrices, whose columns correspond to words in the vocabulary. Unsurprisingly, in Figure 8, we see that the parameters corresponding to the less common words are more dispensable. In fact, at the 80% pruning rate, for 100 uncommon source words and 1194 uncommon target words, we delete *all* parameters corresponding to that word. This is not quite the same as removing the word from the vocabulary — true out-of-vocabulary words are mapped to the embedding for the 'unknown word' symbol, whereas these 'pruned-out' words are mapped to a zero embedding. However in the original unpruned model these uncommon words already had near-zero embeddings, indicating that the model was unable to learn sufficiently distinctive representations.

Returning to Figure 8, now look at the eight weight matrices for the source and target connections at each of the four layers. Each matrix corresponds to the $4n \times 2n$ matrix $T_{4n,2n}$ in Equation (2). In all eight matrices, we observe — as does (Lu et al., 2016) — that the weights connecting to the input $\hat{h}$ are most crucial, followed by the input gate i, then the output gate o, then the forget gate f. This is particularly true of the lower layers, which focus primarily on the input $\hat{h}$. However for higher layers, especially on the target side, weights connecting to the gates are as important as those connecting to the input $\hat{h}$. The gates represent the LSTM's ability to add to, delete from or retrieve information from the memory cell. Figure 8 therefore shows that these sophisticated memory cell abilities are most important at the *end* of the NMT pipeline (the top layer of the decoder). This is reasonable, as we expect higher-level features to be learned later in a deep learning pipeline.

We also observe that for lower layers, the feed-forward input is much more important than the recurrent input, whereas for higher layers the recurrent input becomes more important. This makes sense: lower layers concentrate on the low-level information from the current word embedding (the feed-forward input), whereas higher layers make

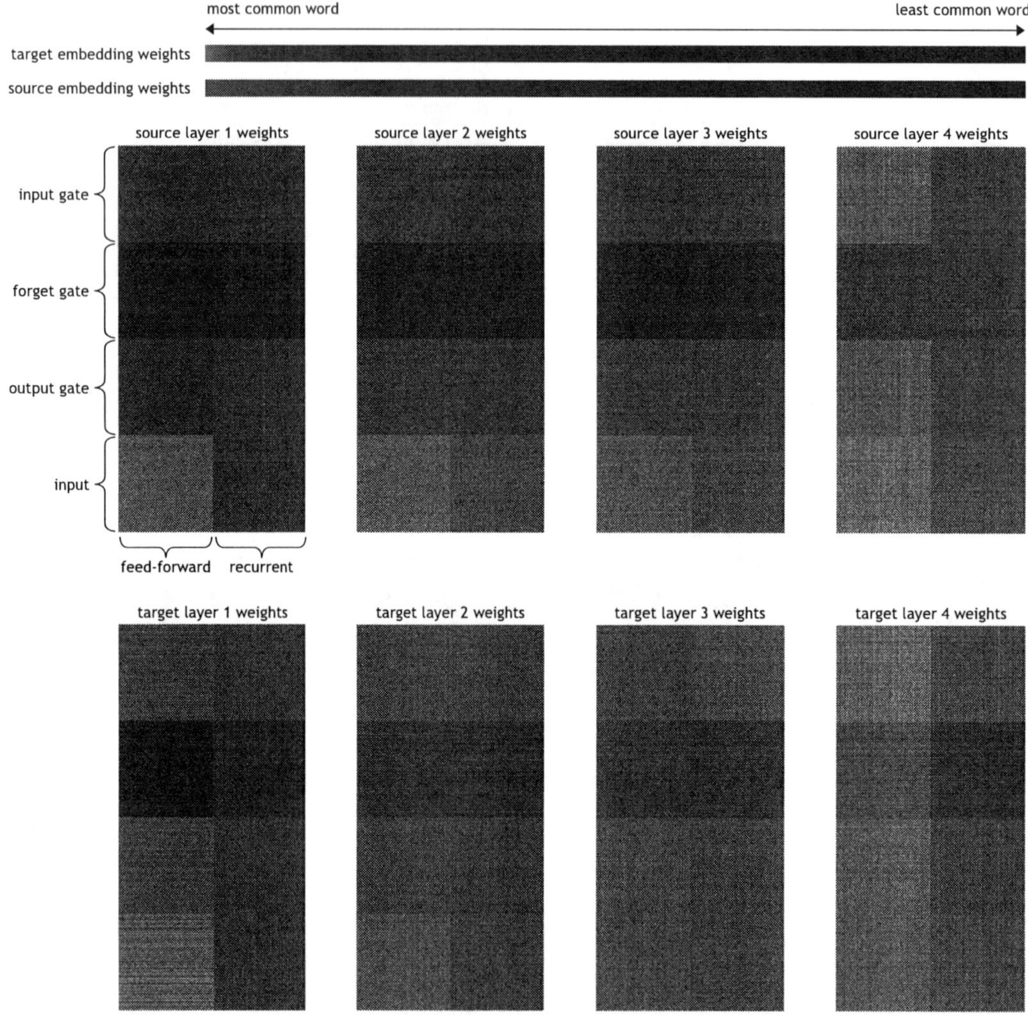

Figure 8: Graphical representation of the location of small weights in various parts of the model. Black pixels represent weights with absolute size in the bottom 80%; white pixels represent those with absolute size in the top 20%. Equivalently, these pictures illustrate which parameters remain after pruning 80% using our class-blind pruning scheme.

use of the higher-level representation of the sentence so far (the recurrent input).

Lastly, on close inspection, we notice several white diagonals emerging within some subsquares of the matrices in Figure 8, indicating that even without initializing the weights to identity matrices (as is sometimes done (Le et al., 2015)), an identity-like weight matrix is learned. At higher pruning percentages, these diagonals become more pronounced.

5 Generalizability of our results

To test the generalizability of our results, we also test our pruning approach on a smaller, non-state-of-the-art NMT model trained on the WIT3 Vietnamese-English dataset (Cettolo et al., 2012), which consists of 133,000 sentence pairs. This model is effectively a scaled-down version of the state-of-the-art model in (Luong et al., 2015a), with fewer layers, smaller vocabulary size, smaller hidden layer size, no attention mechanism, and about 11% as many parameters in total. It achieves a BLEU score of 9.61 on the validation set.

Although this model and its training set are on a different scale to our main model, and the language pair is different, we found very similar results. For this model, it is possible to prune 60% of parameters with no immediate performance loss, and with retraining it is possible to prune 90%, and regain original performance. Our main observations from Sections 4.1 to 4.5 are also replicated; in particular, class-blind pruning is most successful, 'sparse from the beginning' models are less successful than pruned and retrained models, and we observe the same patterns as seen in Figure 8.

6 Future Work

As noted in Section 4.3, including *several* iterations of pruning and retraining would likely improve the compression and performance of our pruning method. If possible it would be highly valuable to exploit the sparsity of the pruned models to speed up training and runtime, perhaps through sparse matrix representations and multiplications (see Section 3.4). Though we have found magnitude-based pruning to perform very well, it would be instructive to revisit the original claim that other pruning methods (for example Optimal Brain Damage and Optimal Brain Surgery) are more principled, and perform a comparative study.

7 Conclusion

We have shown that weight pruning with retraining is a highly effective method of compression and regularization on a state-of-the-art NMT system, compressing the model to 20% of its size with no loss of performance. Though we are the first to apply compression techniques to NMT, we obtain a similar degree of compression to other current work on compressing state-of-the-art deep neural networks, with an approach that is simpler than most. We have found that the absolute size of parameters is of primary importance when choosing which to prune, leading to an approach that is extremely simple to implement, and can be applied to any neural network. Lastly, we have gained insight into the distribution of redundancy in the NMT architecture.

8 Acknowledgment

This work was partially supported by NSF Award IIS-1514268 and partially supported by a gift from Bloomberg L.P. We gratefully acknowledge the support of the Defense Advanced Research Projects Agency (DARPA) Communicating with Computers (CwC) program under ARO prime contract no. W911NF-15-1-0462. Lastly, we acknowledge NVIDIA Corporation for the donation of Tesla K40 GPUs.

References

M Gethsiyal Augasta and T Kathirvalavakumar. 2013. Pruning algorithms of neural networks - a comparative study. *Central European Journal of Computer Science*, 3(3):105–115.

Dzmitry Bahdanau, Kyunghyun Cho, and Yoshua Bengio. 2015. Neural machine translation by jointly learning to align and translate. In *ICLR*.

Mauro Cettolo, Christian Girardi, and Marcello Federico. 2012. Wit^3: Web inventory of transcribed and translated talks. In *EAMT*.

Wenlin Chen, James T Wilson, Stephen Tyree, Kilian Q Weinberger, and Yixin Chen. 2015. Compressing neural networks with the hashing trick. In *ICML*.

Kyunghyun Cho, Bart van Merrienboer, Caglar Gulcehre, Fethi Bougares, Holger Schwenk, and Yoshua Bengio. 2014. Learning phrase representations using RNN encoder-decoder for statistical machine translation. In *EMNLP*.

Maxwell D Collins and Pushmeet Kohli. 2014. Memory bounded deep convolutional networks. *arXiv preprint arXiv:1412.1442*.

Matthieu Courbariaux, Yoshua Bengio, and Jean-Pierre David. 2015. Low precision arithmetic for deep learning. In *ICLR workshop*.

Emily L Denton, Wojciech Zaremba, Joan Bruna, Yann LeCun, and Rob Fergus. 2014. Exploiting linear structure within convolutional networks for efficient evaluation. In *NIPS*.

Suyog Gupta, Ankur Agrawal, Kailash Gopalakrishnan, and Pritish Narayanan. 2015. Deep learning with limited numerical precision. In *ICML*.

Song Han, Huizi Mao, and William J Dally. 2015a. Deep compression: Compressing deep neural networks with pruning, trained quantization and huffman coding. In *ICLR*.

Song Han, Jeff Pool, John Tran, and William Dally. 2015b. Learning both weights and connections for efficient neural network. In *NIPS*.

Babak Hassibi and David G Stork. 1993. *Second order derivatives for network pruning: Optimal brain surgeon*. Morgan Kaufmann.

Geoffrey Hinton, Oriol Vinyals, and Jeff Dean. 2015. Distilling the knowledge in a neural network. In *NIPS Deep Learning Workshop*.

Sepp Hochreiter and Jürgen Schmidhuber. 1997. Long short-term memory. *Neural computation*, 9(8):1735–1780.

Forrest N Iandola, Matthew W Moskewicz, Khalid Ashraf, Song Han, William J Dally, and Kurt Keutzer. 2016. Squeezenet: Alexnet-level accuracy with 50x fewer parameters and < 1mb model size. *arXiv preprint arXiv:1602.07360*.

Max Jaderberg, Andrea Vedaldi, and Andrew Zisserman. 2014. Speeding up convolutional neural networks with low rank expansions. In *NIPS*.

Sébastien Jean, Kyunghyun Cho, Roland Memisevic, and Yoshua Bengio. 2015a. On using very large target vocabulary for neural machine translation. In *ACL*.

Sébastien Jean, Orhan Firat, Kyunghyun Cho, Roland Memisevic, and Yoshua Bengio. 2015b. Montreal neural machine translation systems for WMT'15. In *WMT*.

Nal Kalchbrenner and Phil Blunsom. 2013. Recurrent continuous translation models. In *EMNLP*.

Quoc V Le, Navdeep Jaitly, and Geoffrey E Hinton. 2015. A simple way to initialize recurrent networks of rectified linear units. *arXiv preprint arXiv:1504.00941*.

Yann Le Cun, John S Denker, and Sara A Solla. 1989. Optimal brain damage. In *NIPS*.

Zhouhan Lin, Matthieu Courbariaux, Roland Memisevic, and Yoshua Bengio. 2016. Neural networks with few multiplications. In *ICLR*.

Zhiyun Lu, Vikas Sindhwani, and Tara N Sainath. 2016. Learning compact recurrent neural networks. In *ICASSP*.

Minh-Thang Luong and Christopher D. Manning. 2015. Stanford neural machine translation systems for spoken language domain. In *IWSLT*.

Minh-Thang Luong and Christopher D. Manning. 2016. Achieving open vocabulary neural machine translation with hybrid word-character models. In *ACL*.

Minh-Thang Luong, Hieu Pham, and Christopher D Manning. 2015a. Effective approaches to attention-based neural machine translation. In *EMNLP*.

Minh-Thang Luong, Ilya Sutskever, Quoc V Le, Oriol Vinyals, and Wojciech Zaremba. 2015b. Addressing the rare word problem in neural machine translation. In *ACL*.

Kenton Murray and David Chiang. 2015. Auto-sizing neural networks: With applications to n-gram language models. In *EMNLP*.

Rohit Prabhavalkar, Ouais Alsharif, Antoine Bruguier, and Ian McGraw. 2016. On the compression of recurrent neural networks with an application to lvcsr acoustic modeling for embedded speech recognition. In *ICASSP*.

Rico Sennrich, Barry Haddow, and Alexandra Birch. 2016. Improving neural machine translation models with monolingual data. In *ACL*.

Suraj Srinivas and R Venkatesh Babu. 2015. Data-free parameter pruning for deep neural networks. In *BMVC*.

Ilya Sutskever, Oriol Vinyals, and Quoc V. Le. 2014. Sequence to sequence learning with neural networks. In *NIPS*.

Wojciech Zaremba, Ilya Sutskever, and Oriol Vinyals. 2014. Recurrent neural network regularization. *arXiv preprint arXiv:1409.2329*.

Modeling the Usage of Discourse Connectives as Rational Speech Acts

Frances Yung
Nara Institute of Science and Technology
8916-5 Takayama, Ikoma,
Nara, 630-0192, Japan
pikyufrances-y@is.naist.jp

Kevin Duh
John Hopkins University
810 Wyman Park Drive,
Baltimore, MD 21211-2840, USA
kevinduh@cs.jhu.edu

Taku Komura
University of Edinburgh
10 Crichton Street,
Edinburgh, EH8 9AB, United Kingdom
tkomura@inf.ed.ac.uk

Yuji Matsumoto
Nara Institute of Science and Technology
8916-5 Takayama, Ikoma,
Nara, 630-0192, Japan
matsu@is.naist.jp

Abstract

Discourse relations can either be implicit or explicitly expressed by markers, such as *'therefore'* and *'but'*. How a speaker makes this choice is a question that is not well understood. We propose a psycholinguistic model that predicts whether a speaker will produce an explicit marker given the discourse relation s/he wishes to express. Based on the framework of the Rational Speech Acts model, we quantify the utility of producing a marker based on the information-theoretic measure of surprisal, the cost of production, and a bias to maintain uniform information density throughout the utterance. Experiments based on the Penn Discourse Treebank show that our approach outperforms state-of-the-art approaches, while giving an explanatory account of the speaker's choice.

1 Introduction

Speakers or authors[1] produce informative utterances, such that the listeners or readers can understand his/her message. Grice's *Maxim of Quantity* states that human speakers communicate by being as informative as required, but no more (Grice, 1975). If a speaker always tries to provide as much information as possible, the resulting utterance could become excessively long and tedious. Such utterance is not only effort consuming for the speaker to produce, but also contains redundant information that is not necessary for the listener.

In this work, we model how speakers plan the presentation of discourse structure optimally in terms of informativeness. Specifically, we propose a model that predicts whether the speaker will use or omit a discourse connective, given the sense of discourse relation s/he wants to convey.

Discourse relations are relations between unit of texts (known as *arguments*) that make a document coherent. These relations can be marked in the surface text or inferred by the readers, as shown in the below examples.

1. It was a great movie, **but** I did not like it.

2. It was a great movie, **therefore** I liked it.

3. It was a great movie. I liked it.

The word *'but'* indicates a *Concession* relation in Example (1), and *'therefore'* indicates a *Result* relation in Example (2). We call 'but' and 'therefore' *explicit* discourse connectives (DCs). In Example (3), DCs are absent but a *Result* relation can be inferred. We say the DC is implicit in this case.

Explicit DCs are highly informative cues to identify discourse relations (Pitler et al., 2008) while implicit DCs are more ambiguous. For example, *'I liked it'* can also be read as a *Justification* for the first sentence in Example (3).

Marking a discourse relation or not is subject to ambiguity and redundancy. On one hand, using an explicit DC avoids ambiguity. For example, if the DC 'but' is omitted in Example (1), readers may have problems in inferring the *Concession* sense. On the other hand, if the intended discourse sense is highly predictable, it is verbose or redundant to insert an explicit DC in the utterance, such as the DC *'therefore'* in Example (2).

---

[1] *'Speakers'* and *'listeners'* are interchangeably used with *'authors'* and *'readers'* in this article

Proceedings of the 20th SIGNLL Conference on Computational Natural Language Learning (CoNLL), pages 302–313,
Berlin, Germany, August 7-12, 2016. ©2016 Association for Computational Linguistics

A model that predicts the markedness of discourse relations not only contributes to a better understanding of the human language production mechanism, but is also important in generating natural, humanlike texts and dialogues. In particular, the degree of markedness in discourse relations differs cross-lingually. Yung et al. (2015) analyze the manual alignments of explicit and implicit DCs in a Chinese-English translation corpus and find that 30% of implicit DCs in Chinese are translated to explicit DCs in English. It remains a challenge for machine translation systems to explicitate or implicitate discourse relations in the source texts as human translators do (Becher, 2011; Meyer and Webber, 2013; Zuffery and Cartoni, 2014; Hoek and Zufferey, 2015; Hoek et al., 2015), since the markedness of the translation is subject to the discourse planning of the target text.

In order to explain how human speakers choose the optimal level of markedness in his utterance, we model how speakers rationally balance between ambiguity and redundancy. In particular, we use the Rational Speech Acts (RSA) model (Frank and Goodman, 2012) to predict how speakers reason about the ambiguity of an utterance. In addition, we model how speakers adjust the redundancy of the utterance following the Uniform Information Density (UID) principle (Levy and Jaeger, 2006).

We apply the framework to predict whether an explicit or implicit DC is used in corpus data, given the two arguments of the discourse relations and the discourse sense to be conveyed. Our model not only achieves higher accuracy comparing with previous work (Patterson and Kehler, 2013), but also provides an interpretable account of various cognitive factors behind the predicted decision.

We start by a review of related work in Section 2, followed by the descriptions of our model in Section 3 and experiments in Section 4.

2 Related work

We first provide background information on RSA and UID, which are used in our proposed method. It is followed by introduction of previous work about prediction of DC markedness in corpus data.

2.1 Rational Speech Acts model

The RSA model (Frank and Goodman, 2012) is a variation of the game-theoretic approach in prag-matics (Jäger, 2012). It explains the communicative reasoning of a speaker and a listener in terms of Bayesian probabilities.

A rational listener assumes the utterance s/he hears contains the optimal amount of information. S/he predicts the intended message of a speaker by Bayesian inference (Equation 1).

$$P_{listener}(s|w, C) \propto P_{speaker}(w|s, C)P(s) \quad (1)$$

where w is the *utterance* produced by the speaker; s is the *message* of an utterance; and C is the *context*. $P_{speaker}(w|s, C)$ represents the *listener's predicted* speaker's model, and $P(s)$ represents the *salience* of the message, which is shared knowledge between the speaker and listener.

A rational speaker chooses an utterance by soft-max optimizing the expected *utility* ($U(w; s, C)$) of the utterance (Equation 2).

$$P_{speaker}(w|s, C) \propto e^{\alpha \cdot U(w;s,C)} \quad (2)$$

α is the decision noise parameter, which is set to 1 to represent a rational speaker [2]. S/He emulates the listener's interpretation and chooses an utterance s/he believes to be informative. Also, an utterance that is easy to produce is preferred.

Utility is thus defined as the *informativeness* ($I(s; w, C)$) of the utterance, deducted by the cost ($D(w)$) to produce it (Equation 3).

$$U(w; s, C) = I(s; w, C) - D(w) \quad (3)$$

Since utterances that are unconventional and surprising are less useful, *Informativeness* is quantified as the *negative surprisal* of the utterance with respect to the message to be conveyed (Equation 4).

$$I(s; w, C) = \ln P(s|w, C) \quad (4)$$

The RSA model has successfully simulated results of psycholinguistic experiments concerning different aspects of human communication, such as scalar implicature, referential expressions and language acquisition (Frank and Goodman, 2012; Goodman and Stuhlmüller, 2013; Smith et al., 2013; Bergen et al., 2014; Kao et al., 2014; Potts et al., 2015). Besides experimental data, Orita et al.(2015) applies RSA model to predict the choice of referring expressions in corpus data and Monroe and Potts (2015) optimizes a classifier based

---

[2] $\alpha = 0$ means the decision is totally unrelated to pragmatic reasoning. $\alpha = 1$ represents the Luce's choice axiom (Frank and Goodman, 2012), i.e. a rational decision without bias. $\alpha > 1$ suggests biased choices.

on RSA by inducing the semantic lexicon from a training corpus. These works focus on the pragmatic use of language, where the informativeness and lexicon of an utterance largely depends on the context (e.g. *'Red'* is not *valid* to be used to refer to a *blue* ball).

In this work, we apply RSA to predict the usage of DCs, which is more universal across different contexts (i.e. A DC can be used or dropped given various discourse senses and contexts). Our model is built upon the *speaker's model* of RSA to predict speaker's choice of explicit or implicit DCs.

2.2 Uniform Information Density

The UID principle views language communication as a form of information transmission through a noisy channel and a constant rate of information flow is optimal according to Shannon's Information Theory (Levy and Jaeger, 2006; Genzel and Charniak, 2002; Shannon, 1948). It states that speakers structure utterances by optimizing *information density*, which is the quantity of information (measured by *surprisal*[3]) transmitted per unit of utterance, such as word.

Information density rises when the utterance is 'surprising' and drops when an utterance is highly predictable. To smooth the peaks and troughs, speakers adjust the ambiguity of an utterance by including or reducing linguistic markers.

Following the UID principle, linguistic choices made by speakers are predicted more accurately by incorporating an *information density predictor* on top of other constraints. The predictor measures how easily a candidate utterance can be predicted and the speaker adjusts information density based on the expected predictability.

UID is applied to explain a variety of speaker's options, such as phonetic (Aylett and Turk, 2004), morphological (Frank and Jaeger, 2008) and syntactic (Jaeger, 2010) reductions, and also referring expressions (Tily and Piantadosi, 2009).

2.3 Explicit vs. Implicit DCs

The choice of discourse marking strategies has been studied in earlier works as a subtask for natural language generation (Scott and de Souza, 1990; Moser and Moore, 1995; Grote and Stede, 1998; Soria and Ferrari, 1998; Allbritton and Moore, 1999). In the absence of large-scale resources, investigations are based on manually derived rules

and lexicons or psycholinguistic experiments.

More recently, Asr and Demberg (2012) presents an analysis of the PDTB, showing that 'causal' and 'continuous' senses are more often implicit, or marked by less specific DCs. Indeed these senses are presupposed by listeners according to linguistics theories (Segal et al., 1991; Murray, 1997; Levinson, 2000; Sanders, 2005; Kuperberg et al., 2011). On the other hand, Asr and Demberg (2015) finds that DCs are more often dropped for the discourse relation *Chosen Alternative* (the relation typically signalled by the DC 'instead'), if the context contains negation words, which are identified cues for this relation. Similarly, contextual difference in explicit and implicit discourse relations are reported in attempts to train implicit DC classifiers based on explicit DC instances (Sporleder and Lascarides, 2008; Webber, 2009).

Asr and Demberg (2012; 2015) attribute the corpus statistics to the UID hypothesis, which explains that expected, predictable relations are more likely to be conveyed implicitly, and thus more ambiguously, to maintain steady information flow. However, there are explicit 'causal' and 'continuous' relations and some *Chosen Alternative* are marked even *argument 1* is negated. Although markedness measures are proposed to rate the implicitness of a relation sense (Asr and Demberg, 2013; Jin and de Marneffe, 2015), these measures only quantify the general markedness of the sense in the data, but not the speaker's choice for each particular instance. In contrast, this work specifically measures the predictability of a given relation; generalizes the approach to all discourse senses instead of particular senses or cues; and combines the markedness preference with other language production factors, in order to model each instance of relation.

Patterson and Kehler (2013) is the only study we are aware of that predicts the choice of explicit or implicit DCs of each instance of relation. They argue that while the decision is related to the ease to infer the relation, it may also depend on other stylistic or textual factors. A classifier is trained to predict whether a *candidate DC* (i.e. the DC that actually occurs in the text as an explicit DC, or annotated as an implicit DC) is actually present, given the sense of the discourse relation and the arguments. Relatively shallow linguistic features are used, such as whether the relations are em-

---

[3]This is opposite to *'informativeness'* in RSA, which is defined by *negative surprisal* (Equation 4).

304

bedded or shared, the previous discourse relation, argument lengths, and content word ratios. The classifier is trained and tested on a subset of relations from the PDTB, after screening away infrequent senses and DCs. An overall high classification accuracy is achieved. Relation-level and discourse-level features are found to be more useful than argument-level features.

However, this work does not target at explaining why an utterance is preferred by the speaker. The focus is a data-driven approach that replicates the occurrence of DCs in the corpus data. Our work differs in that we model the option of markedness from the viewpoint of human language production, explaining the factors behind the speaker's choice. For example, we do not make use of the *candidate DC* as a feature, since it is the result of the speaker's choice, if an explicit DC is preferred. Nonetheless, our model achieves higher accuracy when evaluated on the same test set.

3 The markedness model

Our model is based on the speaker's model of RSA. We first explain how we adapt the RSA model to discourse presentation, followed by the details of each component.

3.1 RSA for discourse relation presentation

According to Equation (2), the probability for a speaker to use utterance w to convey his intended message s in context C is:

$$P(w|s,C) = \frac{e^{U(w;s,C)}}{\sum_{w'\in W} e^{U(w';s,C)}} \quad (5)$$

In the case of discourse connectives, the utterance w comes from the set $W = \{(\text{exp})\text{licit}, (\text{imp})\text{licit}\}$, if both explicit and implicit DCs are grammatically valid to convey s, the sense of discourse relation. Our model thus predicts speaker's choice of DCs based on the following two probabilities:

$$P(exp|s,C) = \frac{e^{U(exp;s,C)}}{e^{U(exp;s,C)} + e^{U(imp;s,C)}}$$
$$P(imp|s,C) = \frac{e^{U(imp;s,C)}}{e^{U(exp;s,C)} + e^{U(imp;s,C)}} \quad (6)$$

According to Equation (3), the *utility* U of an explicit DC equals to its *informativeness* I deducted by production cost D.

$$U(exp;s,C) = I(s;exp,C) - D(exp) \quad (7)$$

$I(s;exp,C)$ is the informativeness of using an explicit DC to present the sense s in discourse-level context C. Each discourse sense has its salience within the discourse context. It means C is also informative, but we want to quantify the informativeness of the DC only. Therefore, we define $I(s;exp,C)$ by the difference between the informativess of 'the explicit DC in context C' and the informativeness of 'context C', which are quantified by negative *surprisal*.

$$I(s;exp,C) = \ln P(s|exp,C) - \ln P(s|C) \quad (8)$$

High $I(s;exp,C)$ means it is informative and not surprising to use an explicit DC for this sense. $P(s|exp,C)$ and $P(s|C)$ are extracted from corpus data. Details are explained in Subsection 3.2.

The principle of UID is incorporated into the RSA model as a bias on the utility of the DCs. A discourse relation is presented not only by the DCs but also the arguments, and the amount of discourse information of the whole utterance (DC + arguments) is fixed. According to UID, information should be transmitted uniformly across the utterance. If the arguments has much information about the sense, the sense is predictable from the arguments and thus the surprisal is small. The information density drops and has to be smoothed by using a more ambiguous, less predictable utterance, which can be achieved by reduction of a DC (Asr and Demberg, 2015).

Therefore, according to UID, an implicit DC is preferred if the arguments are informative. We thus raise the utility of an implicit DC by defining the probability for a speaker to choose an implicit DC to be proportional to the *sum of the the utilities* of a *null* DC and the arguments $(args)$[4].

$$e^{U(imp;s,C)} = e^{U(null;s,C)} + e^{U(args;s,C)} \quad (9)$$

$$U(null;s,C) = I(s;null,C) - D(null) \quad (10)$$

$$U(args;s,C) = I(s;arg,C) - D(args) \quad (11)$$

The amount of information that the null DC provides for the discourse relation is defined similarly as in Equation (8):

$$I(s;null,C) = \ln P(s|null,C) - \ln P(s|C) \quad (12)$$

---

[4]In turn, an explicit DC is preferred if the arguments are not informative. We could also penalize the utility of an explicit DC by the argument utility, but the result will be the same since the decision is based on Equation 13.

On the other hand, the informativeness of arguments, $I(s; arg, C)$ is quantified by *negative surprisal* in RSA. However, arguments are clauses and sentences. It is not applicable to extract $P(s|args, C)$ from the corpus. We thus approximate $I(s; arg, C)$ by *the confidence of a discourse parser in predicting discourse senses from the arguments*. Details will be explained in Section 3.3.

Lastly, various psycholinguistically motivated measures are explored to approximate the production cost $D(exp)$ in Subsection 3.4. In contrast, no effort is required to produce a *null* DC. Also, we assume that the arguments have been produced to convey other information irrespective of their discourse informativeness, so no extra effort is needed. Therefore, $D(null)$ and $D(args)$ both equal 0.

To summarize, the model predicts that the speaker will use an explicit DC if:

$$e^{U(exp;s,C)} > e^{U(null;s,C)} + e^{U(args;s,C)} \quad (13)$$

and that s/he will use an implicit DC otherwise.

3.2 Informativeness of DCs

This section explains how we estimate the informativeness in Equations (8) and (12). In discourse production, the utterance lexicon, $W = \{exp, imp\}$ in Equation (5), and the set of speaker's intended messages (all possible discourse relation senses) are always *valid*[5]. Thus $P(s|C)$, $P(s|exp, C)$, and $P(s|null, C)$ are universal distributions and can be extracted from corpus data based on the co-occurrences of senses, DCs, and contexts. We extract these empirical distributions from the training portion of the corpus.

We define context C as the surrounding discourse relations. Specifically, the discourse contexts (and their abbreviation in Table 2) are: the full discourse sense annotated in PDTB (S), the 4-way top level sense (TS), the form of discourse presentation (F) such as 'explicit' or 'implicit'[6], and the pair of sense and form (SF or TSF). The contexts are taken from window sizes of 1 to 2: previous one (10) , next one (01), previous two (20), next two (02), previous one paired with next one (11). We hypothesize that the speaker also

thinks ahead the coming discourse structures when planning the current ones. Various discourse contexts are compared in the experiment.

3.3 Informativeness of arguments

$I(s; arg, C)$ in Equation (11) refers to the amount of information in the arguments that contributes to the interpretation of the discourse sense. According to UID, information density drops when the discourse sense is predictable from the arguments alone, and an implicit DC is preferred.

Presence of features in the arguments that signal a particular sense makes the sense more predictable, and thus promote the reduction of a DC. For example, the DC *'instead'* is less used to present the *Chosen Alternative* sense if the first argument is negated (Asr and Demberg, 2015).

Generalizing this idea to capture various cues in the arguments for various senses, we approximate $I(s; arg, C)$ by the confidence of an automatic discourse parser in predicting the discourse sense. An implicit relation parser uses various features in the arguments to identify the implicit relation sense (Pitler et al., 2009; Lin et al., 2009; Park and Cardi, 2012; Rutherford and Xue, 2014). If the arguments contain much informative features, the parser will predict the sense more confidently.

We propose two methods, for comparison, to measure the confidence of the parser prediction. A confident prediction means the parser will assign a high probability to the one output sense. Therefore, we use the *negative surprisal* of the estimated probability P_p of the parser output sense s_{output} (Equation 14) to approximate $I(s; arg, C)$.

$$I(s; arg, C) \approx w_a \cdot \ln P_p(s_{output}) \quad (14)$$

At the same time, the probability distribution of all senses is less uniform if one sense is assigned a high probability. We thus alternatively approximate $I(s; arg, C)$ by the *negative entropy* of the probability distribution estimated by the parser (Equation 15)[7].

$$I(s; arg, C) \approx w_a \sum_{s_p \in O} P_p(s_p) \log P_p(s_p) \quad (15)$$

where O is the set of senses defined in the parser and w_a is a positive weight tuned on the dev set.

---

[5]In case of referring expressions, for example, the lists of referents and grammatically correct pronouns differ case by case, e.g. *'she'* is not a *valid* pronoun for a male.

[6]We use the 5 forms of discourse presentation defined in the PDTB: explicit DC, implicit DC, alternative lexicalization, entity relation and 'no relation'.

[7]Note that we use information-theoretic measures to approximate $I(s; arg, C)$, but these approximations are not related to the formulation of RSA nor UID.

We measure the *general informativeness* of the arguments to imply *any* discourse senses, so s_{output} does not necessarily equal s.

We employ the implicit sense classifier from the winning parser of shared task 2015 (Wang and Lan, 2015), which is designed to identify a subset of 14 implicit senses plus the *entity relation*. The two arguments of a relation instance, which can actually be explicit or implicit, are passed to the implicit DC classifier and $I(s; arg, C)$ is approximated based on the output probabilities [8]. Although the performance of this state-of-the-art implicit DC classifier is still unsatisfactory (34.45% on PDTB Section 23[9]) , our method only makes use of the probability estimation of the prediction[10].

Our motivation of using the implicit DC classifier is based on the hypothesis that the classifier can better predict the sense of relations that are actually implicit, than those that are actually explicit, since more features in the arguments are identifiable. In fact, it is the case. The classification accuracy of the originally explicit relations is significantly lower. This supports our motivation to use the parser estimation as an information density predictor.

3.4   Cost function

The cost function $D(exp)$ models speaker's effort required to produce an explicit DC for the intended discourse sense. We propose 5 versions of the cost function that are inspired by existing psycholinguistic findings.

Mean DC length: Production cost intuitively increases with word length. We define the mean DC length of a discourse relation as the mean word length of all valid DCs for that sense, normalized by the average word length of all DCs. A lexicon of possible DC per each discourse sense is derived from the whole corpus. For multi-word DCs, a white space is simply counted as one character. We do not use the length of the *candidate DC* (refer to Section 2.3), because we view that speakers first decide to use an explicit DC or not, then decide which DC best expresses the relation.

DC/arg2 ratio: Similarly, we use the mean word count normalized by the word count of *argument 2* as another version of cost function.

Prime frequency: Structural priming refers to the tendency for human to process a linguistic construction (the target) more easily if the construction is used before. In terms of language production, a speaker tends to repeat a previous construction (the prime) since it consumes less effort than to generate an alternative construction. We use the reciprocal of the count of primes (any explicit DC occurring before the current position) as the production cost, since the strength of priming effect is known to be increasing with the frequency of the primes (Levelt and Kelter, 1982; Bock, 1986; Smith and Wheeldon, 2001).

Prime distance: We also use the prime-target distance, normalized by the length of the article, as another version of the production cost. Psycholinguistic findings suggest that the priming effect is more subtly affected by the prime-target distance (Gries, 2005; Bock et al., 2007; Jaeger and Snider, 2008).

Distance from start: We use the relative position of the relation within the article as the production cost. We hypothesize that more effort is needed as the production proceeds.

The range of values of the cost function depends on the cost definition. We thus adjust the values with a constant weight w_c that is tuned on the dev set in the experiments:

$$D(exp) = w_c \cdot cost(exp) \qquad (16)$$

4   Experiment

We apply the model to simulate speaker's choice of explicit or implicit DC for discourse relations in the PDTB corpus. The aim of the experiment is to answer two questions: (1) Does the model explain the factors affecting speaker's choice of DC markedness? If the hypotheses of the model is appropriate, each component in the model should

---

[8]The implicit DC classifier is trained by Naïve Bayes based on features including syntactic features, polarity, immediately preceding DC, and Brown cluster pairs. Syntactic features are based on automatic parsing using Stanford CoreNLP (Manning et al., 2014). The parser is trained on the same sections of the PDTB as the training set used in our experiment.

[9]http://www.cs.brandeis.edu/~clp/conll15st/results.html

[10]We use the parser's probability estimates as is; conceivably it may be improved by an additional probabilistic calibration step (Nguyen and O'Connor, 2015).

contribute to the prediction accuracy. (2) How does the prediction performance compare with the state-of-the-art, i.e. Patterson and Kelher (2013)?

We first describe the details of the data we use in the experiments.

4.1 Data: The Penn Discourse Treebank

The Penn Discourse Treebank (PDTB) is the largest available discourse-annotated corpus in English (Prasad et al., 2008). The text are news articles collected from the Wall Street Journals. Below are 3 examples of the annotation.

1. The OTC market has only a handful of takeover-related stocks. **But** (Explicit;*Comparison-Contrast*) they fell sharply. *(WSJ2379)*

2. Japan's Finance Ministry had set up mechanisms ... to give market operators the authority to suspend trading in futures at any time. (Implicit: **but**; *Comparison*) Maybe it wasn't enough. *(WSJ0097)*

3. **Before** (Explicit; *Temporal-Asynchronous-Precedence*) becoming a consultant in 1974, Mr. Achenbaum was a senior executive at J. Walter Thompson Co..*(WSJ0295)*

Explicit DCs are labelled with relation senses (Example 1). If an explicit DC is absent *between two sentences* within the same paragraph and an implicit relation can be inferred, a candidate DC and the relation sense are annotated (Example 2).

Our model is based on the assumption that $W = \{explicit, implicit\}$ for all relations, yet it is notable that *intra-sentential implicit* DCs are **not** annotated in the PDTB (Prasad et al., 2014). We thus exclude intra-sentential samples, such that $W = \{explicit, implicit\}$ is always true and free of grammatical constraints. Also, as a result of the annotation procedure, implicit DCs always occur *in between 2 arguments* in their original order, i.e. Arg1-DC-Arg2. To preserve the original order of the discourse arguments, which is also part of the communicative structure intended by the speaker but out of the scope of this model, we only use samples in the Arg1-DC-Arg2 order. For example, Example (3) is excluded from our training data. Finally, annotations of other forms of discourse relations, such as entity relations and attributions, are also excluded.

The screened data set contains 5,201 explicit and 16,049 implicit relations[11]. Sections 2-22 are used as the training set, from which probability distributions are extracted. For easier comparison with previous work, we select the dev set (sections 0-1) and test set (sections 23-24) in the same way as in Patterson and Kehler (2013), where only relations of infrequent DCs and senses are removed. The resulting dev and test sets contain 1720 and 1878 relations respectively. Samples not included in our screened dataset are classified as *explicit* by default.

	sense	exp	imp
1	Expansion.Conjunction	1,380	3,314
2	Comparison.Contrast	1,283	1,200
3	Expansion.Restatement. Specification	75	2,406
4	Contingency.Cause. Reason	28	2,295
5	Contingency.Cause. Result	269	1,649
6	Expansion.Instantiation	119	1,383
7	Comparison.Contrast. Juxtaposition	507	672
8	Comparison.Concession. Contra-expectation	475	179
9	Temporal.Asynchronous. Precedence	117	479
10	Expansion.List	84	374
...	...	...	...
17	Expansion.Conjunction. –Temporal.Synchrony	74	114
...	...	...	...
50	Contingency.Pragmatic cause.Justification #Expansion.Instantiation	0	6
...	...	...	...
122	Contingency	0	1
Total		**5,201**	**16,049**

Table 1: Sense distribution of explicit and implicit DCs in screened data set.

Senses in the PDTB are defined in a hierarchy of 2 to 3 levels. Some relations have multiple senses. Up to 2 DCs can be annotated to an implicit relation and in turn each (implicit or explicit) DC can be labelled with up to 2 senses. Most existing works split a multi-sense sample into separated

---

[11]4 cases of intra-sentential implicit relations, due to sentence splitting errors of the PTB (single sentences wrongly splitted into two), are removed.

	discourse context C	arg. info. $e^{U(args;s,C)}$	cost function $D(exp)$	Dev: Sections 0-1			Test: Sections 23-24		
				accuracy	$F1_{exp}$	$F1_{imp}$	accuracy	$F1_{exp}$	$F1_{imp}$
BL	constant	0	0	.849	.872	.817	.854	.875	.823
SOA (Patterson and Kehler, 2013)				–	–	–	.866	–	–
(a)	F10	0	0	.855	.876	.826	.855	.876	.826
	SF10	0	0	.859	.877	.835	.855	.874	.829
	F20	0	0	.854	.875	.825	.854	.875	.825
	F11	0	0	.851	.872	.822	.854	.875	.825
	TS10	0	0	.852	.872	.822	.854	.875	.824
(b)	constant	surprisal	0	.895[++]	.901	.887	.870	.881	.857
	constant	entropy	0	.895[++]	.902	.888	.870	.881	.856
(c)	constant	0	mean DC length	.894[++]	.897	.890	.876[+]	.886	.865
	constant	0	DC/arg2 ratio	.895[++]	.900	.889	.873	.882	.863
	constant	0	prime frequency	.886[+]	.888	.885	.873	.882	.862
	constant	0	prime distance	.892[++]	.902	.881	.875	.886	.862
	constant	0	distance from start	.893[++]	.894	.892	.877[+]	.879	.875
(d)	F10	entropy	DC/arg2 ratio	**.902[++]**	**.903**	**.901**	.882[+]	.883	.881
	TSF01	surprisal	prime frequency	.895[++]	.898	.892	.889[++*]	**.893**	.885
	TS01	entropy	prime distance	.895[++]	.900	.889	**.890[++*]**	.892	**.888**

Table 2: Accuracies and F1 scores of predicted DC markedness. The best values are bolded.
[+]/[++]:significant improvement over baseline (**BL**) accuracy at $p < 0.05$ and $p < 0.001$ respectively;
[*]:significant improvement over state-of-the-art (**SOA**) accuracy at $p < 0.03$ (by Pearson's χ^2 test)
(refer to Section 3.2 for abbreviations of discourse context C.)

samples, each labelled with one of the senses. However, it is notable that the individual senses of a multi-sense relation are not disjoint[12] and *having multiple senses is part of the sense* (Asr and Demberg, 2013; Prasad et al., 2014). Multi-sense is an important factor of our DC production model: a speaker could have chosen an explicit DC for each sense, but if s/he has to express two senses at the same time, an implicit DC could be more usable. Therefore, we treat all combination of senses as *individual senses*, each containing 1 to 3 joint sense labels[13] This results in a total of 122 senses.

Table 1 is a summary of the distribution in descending order of frequency. In fact, joint multi-senses are not rare: the most frequent multi-sense is the 17th most frequent sense.

4.2 Results

We apply the *markedness* model to predict the speaker's choice of DC markedness on the dev and test sets. Table 2 shows the results under various settings, evaluated by accuracy and the harmonic mean of precision and recall for explicit and implicit relations respectively.

Row **BL** shows the results of the *markedness* model without the cost function and argument informativeness component, and with constant context C. We consider this setting as the baseline, in which the prediction is solely based on the distributions of $P(s|exp)$ and $P(s|imp)$. Considerably high accuracy is achieved, suggesting that the speaker's choice of markedness is strongly related to the intended discourse sense.

Row (a) shows the prediction results based on the distributions of $P(s|exp, C)$ and $P(s|imp, C)$, where C is the discourse context. The 5 best combinations of contexts and window sizes are shown. Refining the utility of DCs by these contextual constraints, in particular previous contexts, improves the classification accuracy, but the improvement is not significant. This suggests that speaker's choice of markedness not only depends on surrounding discourse relations but also other contextual factors.

Row (b) shows the contribution of the *argument informativeness* component, under constant dis-

---

[12]Similarly, certain level 2 senses, as in Example (2), are backoffed from level 3 senses due to annotator disagreement. This is also a kind of multi-sense.

[13]There is only 1 sample of 3 joint labels in our screened dataset.

course context and production cost. Classification accuracy increases (significantly for the dev set) when the usability of explicit DC is deducted by the estimated informativeness of the arguments, supporting the UID principle. Predictions based on the surprisal of the parser output sense and the entropy of the parser output distribution are similar. We also experiment by adjusting with the estimated *argument informativeness* only if the parser output sense is correct (matching at the top level sense). Similar improvement is observed.

Row (c) shows the contribution of the cost function, when discourse context is set as constant and argument informativeness is not considered. Adjusting the utility of explicit DCs by their production cost increases the classification accuracy most significantly. Among the various features to model production cost, 'DC length' and 'distance from start' features give the best results.

Row (d) shows the performance of predictions based on the 3 best combinations of components. The highest accuracies and F_1 scores are achieved for both explicit and implicit relations.

These results answer the first question of the experiment purpose: the proposed model explains the speaker's choice of DC markedness in terms of DC and argument informativeness, and production cost, while contextual discourse structure is a moderate constraint to the choice.

The answer to the second question is also positive. Significant improvement above the state-of-the-art (Row **SOA**) is achieved by the 2 best combinations (89.0%, 88.9% vs. 86.6%).

Lastly, we compare the results with a linear classifier trained on the *features* specified in the model, i.e. the discrete values of the intended sense and various discourse context definitions, and real values of various cost functions and argument informativeness estimates. Note that in the proposed model, the training data is used to derive the $P(s|exp, C)$ and $P(s|null, C)$ distributions only, while the linear classifier learns from the features and DC markedness of the training set[14]. The classifier achieves accuracy of 88.3% on the test set, which does not significantly outperform previous work. This suggests the advantage of the

information-theoretic configuration of our model.

5   Conclusion

We present a language production model that predicts a speaker's choice of using an explicit DC or not given the discourse relation s/he wants to express. Our model gives an cognitive account of the speaker's choice and also outperforms previous work on the same task.

Our study shows that a speaker organizes the discourse structure by balancing the pro (informativeness) and con (production cost and redundancy) of using an explicit marker, although the option is a subtle preference in the absence of other grammatical constraints. Using an information-theoretic approach, our model tackles the option as a rational preference by the speaker, who wants to contribute to an informative speech act. Furthermore, we take a logical step forward to formalize the idea of the UID theory, that redundant explicit markers are avoided if the discourse relation is clear enough from the context.

As future work, we plan to improve the *markedness* model by making fuller use of the training data, such as learning a more expressive formulation of the context governing the choice of explicit or implicit DCs. We also plan to evaluate the effectiveness of the model in applications, such as natural language generation or machine translation tasks. On the other hand, as discourse presentation differs across genres (Webber, 2009) and mediums (Tonelli et al., 2010), the model can be applied to predict the explicitation of discourse relations from, for example, news articles to spoken dialogues. Another direction is to apply the RSA framework in the opposite direction - to build a *listener's model* that simulates a listener's recognition of a discourse sense given an utterance, as proposed in Yung et al.(2016).

Acknowledgments

We thank the anonymous reviewers for their valuable feedback on the previous versions of this paper.

References

David Allbritton and Johanna Moore. 1999. Discourse cues in narrative text: Using production to predict comprehension. In *AAAI Fall Symposium on Psychological Models of Communication in Collaborative Systems*.

---

[14] When extracting the argument informativeness features from the training set, using the automatic discourse parser, we penalize the parser estimates of the *implicit* samples by a constant ratio, since the discourse parser is also trained on these samples. We use LIBLINEAR (Fan et al., 2008) to build the classifiers.

Fatemeh Torabi Asr and Vera Demberg. 2012. Implicitness of discourse relations. In *COLING*, pages 2669–2684. Citeseer.

Fatemeh Torabi Asr and Vera Demberg. 2013. On the information conveyed by discourse markers. In *Proceedings of the Fourth Annual Workshop on Cognitive Modeling and Computational Linguistics*, pages 84–93.

Fatemeh Torabi Asr and Vera Demberg. 2015. Uniform information density at the level of discourse relations: Negation markers and discourse connective omission. *Proceedings of the International Conference on Computation Semantics*, pages 118–128.

Matthew Aylett and Alice Turk. 2004. The smooth signal redundancy hypothesis: A functional explanation for relationships between redundancy, prosodic prominence, and duration in spontaneous speech. *Language and Speech*, 47(1):31–56.

Viktor Becher. 2011. When and why do translators add connectives? a corpus-based study. *Target*, 23(1).

Leon Bergen, Roger Levy, and Noah D. Goodman. 2014. Pragmatic reasoning through semantic inference.

Kathryn Bock, Gary S Dell, Franklin Chang, and Kristine H Onishi. 2007. Persistent structural priming from language comprehension to language production. *Cognition*, 104(3):437–458.

J Kathryn Bock. 1986. Syntactic persistence in language production. *Cognitive psychology*, 18(3):355–387.

Rong-En Fan, Kai-Wei Chang, Cho-Jui Hsieh, Xiang-Rui Wang, and Chih-Jen Lin. 2008. Liblinear: A library for large linear classification. *The Journal of Machine Learning Research*, 9:1871–1874.

Michael C. Frank and Noah D. Goodman. 2012. Predicting pragmatic reasoning in lanugage games. *Science*, 336(6084):998.

Austin Frank and T Florian Jaeger. 2008. Speaking rationally: Uniform information density as an optimal strategy for language production. *Proceedings of the Annual Meeting of the Cognitive Science Society*, pages 933–938.

Dmitriy Genzel and Eugene Charniak. 2002. Entropy rage constancy in text. *Proceedings of the Annual Meeting of the Association for Computational Linguistics*, pages 199–206.

Noah D Goodman and Andreas Stuhlmüller. 2013. Knowledge and implicature: modeling language understanding as social cognition. *Topics in cognitive science*, 5(1):173–184.

H Paul Grice. 1975. Logic and conversation. *Syntax and Semantics*, 3:41–58.

Stefan Th Gries. 2005. Syntactic priming: A corpus-based approach. *Journal of psycholinguistic research*, 34(4):365–399.

Brigitte Grote and Manfred Stede. 1998. Discourse marker choice in sentence planning. In *Proceedings of the Ninth International Workshop on Natural Language Generation*, pages 128–137.

Jet Hoek and Sandrine Zufferey. 2015. Factors influencing the implicitation of discourse relations across languages. In *Proceedings 11th Joint ACL-ISO Workshop on Interoperable Semantic Annotation (isa-11)*, pages 39–45. TiCC, Tilburg center for Cognition and Communication.

Jet Hoek, Jacqueline Evers-Vermeul, and Ted JM Sanders. 2015. The role of expectedness in the implicitation and explicitation of discourse relations. In *Proceedings of the Second Workshop on Discourse in Machine Translation (DiscoMT)*, pages 41–46. Association for Computational Linguistics.

T Florian Jaeger and Neal Snider. 2008. Implicit learning and syntactic persistence: Surprisal and cumulativity. In *The 30th Annual Meeting of the Cognitive Science Society (CogSci08)*, page 827.

T Florian Jaeger. 2010. Redundancy and reduction: Speakers manage syntactic information density. *Cognitive psychology*, 61(1):23–62.

Gerhard Jäger. 2012. Game theory in semantics and pragmatics. In Claudia Maienborn, Klaus von Heusinger, and Paul Portner, editors, *Semantics: An International Handbook of Natural Language Meaning*, volume 3, pages 2487–2425. Mouton de Gruyter.

Lifeng Jin and Marie-Catherine de Marneffe. 2015. The overall markedness of discourse relations. *Proceedings of the Conference on Empirical Methods on Natural Language Processing*.

Justine T Kao, Jean Y Wu, Leon Bergen, and Noah D Goodman. 2014. Nonliteral understanding of number words. *Proceedings of the National Academy of Sciences*, 111(33):12002–12007.

Gina R Kuperberg, Martin Paczynski, and Tali Ditman. 2011. Establishing causal coherence across sentences: An erp study. *Journal of Cognitive Neuroscience*, 23(5):1230–1246.

Willem JM Levelt and Stephanie Kelter. 1982. Surface form and memory in question answering. *Cognitive psychology*, 14(1):78–106.

Stephen C Levinson. 2000. *Presumptive meanings: The theory of generalized conversational implicature*. MIT Press.

Roger Levy and T. Florian Jaeger. 2006. Speakers optimize information density through syntactic reduction. *Advances in neural information processing systems*, (849-856).

Ziheng Lin, Minyen Kan, and Hwee Tou Ng. 2009. Recognizing implicit discourse relations in the penn discourse treebank. *Proceedings of the Conference on Empirical Methods on Natural Language Processing.*

Christopher Manning, Mihai Surdeanu, John Bauer, Jenny Finkey, Steven J. Bethard, and David McClosky. 2014. The standord corenlp natural language processing toolkit. *Proceedings of the Annual Meeting of the Association for Computational Linguistics: System Demonstrations*, pages 55–60.

Thomas Meyer and Bonnie Webber. 2013. Implicitation of discourse connectives in (machine) translation. In *Proceedings of the 1st DiscoMT Workshop at ACL 2013 (51st Annual Meeting of the Association for Computational Linguistics)*, number EPFL-CONF-192528.

Will Monroe and Christopher Potts. 2015. Learning in the rational speech acts model. *arXiv preprint arXiv:1510.06807.*

Megan Moser and Johanna D Moore. 1995. Investigating cue selection and placement in tutorial discourse. In *Proceedings of the 33rd annual meeting on Association for Computational Linguistics*, pages 130–135. Association for Computational Linguistics.

John D Murray. 1997. Connectives and narrative text: The role of continuity. *Memory & Cognition*, 25(2):227–236.

Khanh Nguyen and Brendan O'Connor. 2015. Posterior calibration and exploratory analysis for natural language processing models. In *Proceedings of Conference on Empirical Methods in Natural Language Processing.*

Naho Orita, Eliana Vornov, Naomi H. Feldman, and Hal Daumé III. 2015. Why discourse affects speakers' choice of referring expressions. *Proceedings of the Annual Meeting of the Association for Computational Linguistics.*

Joonsuk Park and Claire Cardi. 2012. Improving implicit discourse relation recognition through feature set optimization. *Proceedings of Annual Meeting on Discourse and Dialogue.*

Gary Patterson and Andrew Kehler. 2013. Predicting the presence of discourse connectives. In *Proceedings of Conference on Empirical Methods in Natural Language Processing*, pages 914–923.

Emily Pitler, Mridhula Raghupathy, Hena Mehta, Ani Nenkova, Alan Lee, and Aravind Joshi. 2008. Easily identifiable discourse relations. Technical report, University of Pennsylvania.

Emily Pitler, Annie Louis, and Ani Nenkova. 2009. Automatic sense prediction for implicit discourse relations in text. *Proceedings of the Annual Meeting of the Association for Computational Linguistics and the International Joint Conference on Natural Language Processing.*

Christopher Potts, Daniel Lassiter, Roger Levy, and Michael C. Frank. 2015. Embedded implicatures as pragmatic inferences under compositional lexical uncertainty. Manuscript.

Rashmi Prasad, Nikhit Dinesh, Alan Lee, Eleni Miltsakaki, Livio Robaldo, Aravind Joshi, and Bonnie Webber. 2008. The penn discourse treebank 2.0. *Proceedings of the Language Resource and Evaluation Conference.*

Rashmi Prasad, Bonnie Webber, and Aravind Joshi. 2014. Reflections on the penn discourse treebank, comparable corpora, and complementary annotation. *Computational Linguistics.*

Attapol Rutherford and Nianwen Xue. 2014. Discovering implicit discourse relations through brown cluster pair representation and coreference patterns. *Proceedings of the Conference of the European Chapter of the Association for Computational Linguistics.*

Ted Sanders. 2005. Coherence, causality and cognitive complexity in discourse. In *Proceedings of the Symposium on the Exploration and Modelling of Meaning.*

Donia Scott and Clarisse Sieckenius de Souza. 1990. Getting the message across in rst-based text generation. *Current research in natural language generation*, 4:47–73.

Erwin M Segal, Judith F Duchan, and Paula J Scott. 1991. The role of interclausal connectives in narrative structuring: Evidence from adults' interpretations of simple stories. *Discourse processes*, 14(1):27–54.

C.E. Shannon. 1948. A mathematical theory of communication. *The Bell System Technical Journal*, 27(379-423; 623-656).

Mark Smith and Linda Wheeldon. 2001. Syntactic priming in spoken sentence production–an online study. *Cognition*, 78(2):123–164.

Nathaniel J Smith, Noah Goodman, and Michael Frank. 2013. Learning and using language via recursive pragmatic reasoning about other agents. In *Advances in neural information processing systems*, pages 3039–3047.

Claudia Soria and Giacomo Ferrari. 1998. Lexical marking of discourse relations-some experimental findings. In *Proceedings of the ACL-98 Workshop on Discourse Relations and Discourse Markers.*

Caroline Sporleder and Alex Lascarides. 2008. Using automatically labelled examples to classify rhetorical relations: An assessment. *Natural Language Engineering*, 14(3):369–416.

Harry Tily and Steven Piantadosi. 2009. Refer efficiently: Use less informative expressions for more predictable meanings. *Proceedings of the workshop on the production of referring expressions.*

Sara Tonelli, Giuseppe Riccardi, Rashmi Prasad, and Aravind K Joshi. 2010. Annotation of discourse relations for conversational spoken dialogs. In *Proceedings of the Language Resource and Evaluation Conference*.

Jianxiang Wang and Man Lan. 2015. A refined end-to-end discourse parser. *CoNLL 2015*, page 17.

Bonnie Webber. 2009. Genre distinctions for discourse in the penn treebank. In *Proceedings of the Joint Conference of the 47th Annual Meeting of the ACL and the 4th International Joint Conference on Natural Language Processing of the AFNLP: Volume 2-Volume 2*, pages 674–682. Association for Computational Linguistics.

Frances Yung, Kevin Duh, and Yuji Matsumoto. 2015. Crosslingual annotation and analysis of implicit discourse connectives for machine translation. In *Workshop of Discourse in machine translation, EMNLP*, page 142.

Frances Yung, Taku Komura, Kevin Duh, and Yuji Matsumoto. 2016. Modeling the interpretation of discourse connectives by bayesian pragmatics. In *Proceedings of the Annual Meeting of the Association for Computational Linguistics*.

Sandrine Zuffery and Bruno Cartoni. 2014. A multifactorial analysis of explicitation in translation. *Target*, 26(3).

Semi-supervised Convolutional Networks for Translation Adaptation with Tiny Amount of In-domain Data

Boxing Chen
National Research Council Canada
1200 Montreal Road
Ottawa, ON, Canada
`Boxing.Chen@nrc-cnrc.gc.ca`

Fei Huang
Facebook
770 Broadway
New York, NY, USA
`feihuang@fb.com`

Abstract

In this paper, we propose a method which uses semi-supervised convolutional neural networks (CNNs) to select in-domain training data for statistical machine translation. This approach is particularly effective when only tiny amounts of in-domain data are available. The in-domain data and randomly sampled general-domain data are used to train a data selection model with semi-supervised CNN, then this model computes domain relevance scores for all the sentences in the general-domain data set. The sentence pairs with top scores are selected to train the system. We carry out experiments on 4 language directions with three test domains. Compared with strong baseline systems trained with large amount of data, this method can improve the performance up to 3.1 BLEU. Its performances are significant better than three state-of-the-art language model based data selection methods. We also show that the in-domain data used to train the selection model could be as few as 100 sentences, which makes fine-grained topic-dependent translation adaptation possible.

1 Introduction

Statistical machine translation (SMT) systems are trained on bilingual parallel and monolingual data. The training corpora typically come from different sources, and vary across topics, genres, dialects, authors' written styles, etc., which are usually referred as "general domain" training data. Here the word "domain" is often used to indicate some combination of all above and other possible hidden factors (Chen et al., 2013). At run time, the content to be translated may come from a different domain. Due to the mismatch in "domains", it is possible to achieve better performance by adapting the SMT system to the test domain (in-domain).

However, manually creating training data to match the test domain is not a preferred solution, because 1) sometimes the test domain is not known when training the model, and it could change from sentence to sentence; 2) even if the test domain is pre-determined, the resources required and slow turnaround in data collection process will still delay the system development process.

Therefore, training data selection is widely used for domain adaptation in statistical machine translation (Zhao et al., 2004; Lü et al., 2007; Yasuda et al., 2008; Moore and Lewis, 2010; Axelrod et al., 2011; Duh et al., 2013; Axelrod et al., 2015). Data selection techniques select monolingual or bilingual data that are similar to the in-domain seed data based on some criteria, which are incorporated into the training data. The most successful data selection approaches (Moore and Lewis, 2010; Axelrod et al., 2011) train n-gram language models on in-domain text to select similar sentences from the large general-domain corpora according to the cross entropy. Furthermore, (Duh et al., 2013) obtained some gains by extending these approaches from n-gram models to recurrent neural network language models (Mikolov et al., 2010). To train the in-domain language model, a reasonable size in-domain data set, which typically includes several thousands of sentences, is required. In (Axelrod et al., 2011; Duh et al., 2013), the sizes of the in-domain data sets are 30K and over 100K sentences respectively.

However, we do not always have access to large or even medium amounts of in-domain data. With the growth of social media, new domains have emerged which need machine translation but

314

Proceedings of the 20th SIGNLL Conference on Computational Natural Language Learning (CoNLL), pages 314–323,
Berlin, Germany, August 7-12, 2016. ©2016 Association for Computational Linguistics

which have very limited in-domain data, maybe just a few hundred sentence pairs. What's more, if one wishes to build a large scale topic-specific MT system with hundreds of topics, it is prohibitively expensive to collect tens of thousands of in-domain sentences for each topic.

In this paper, we try to address this challenge, i.e., domain adaptation with very limited amounts of in-domain data. Inspired by the success of convolutional neural networks applied to image and text classification (Krizhevsky et al., 2012; Kim, 2014; Johnson and Zhang, 2015a; Johnson and Zhang, 2015b), we propose to use CNN to classify training sentence pairs as in-domain or out-of-domain sentences. To overcome the problem of limited in-domain data, we propose to augment the original model with semi-supervised convolutional neural networks for domain classification.

Convolutional neural networks (LeCun and Bengio, 1998) are feed-forward neural networks that exploit the internal structure of data through convolution layers; each computation unit processes a small region of the input data. CNN has been very successful on image classification. When applying it to text input, the convolution layers process small regions of a document, i.e., a sequence of sentences or words. CNN has been gaining attention, and is now used in many text classification tasks (Kalchbrenner et al., 2014; Zeng et al., 2014; Johnson and Zhang, 2015b; Yin and Schütze, 2015; Wang et al., 2015).

In many of these studies, the first layer of the network converts words to word embeddings using table lookup. The word embeddings are either trained as part of CNN training, or pre-trained (thus fixed during model training time) on an additional unlabled corpus. The later is termed semi-supervised CNN. Given tiny amounts of in-domain data, the information learned in these pre-trained word embeddings is very helpful.

We use a small amount of in-domain data, such as the development set, as the positive sample and randomly select the same number of sentences from the general-domain training data as the negative sample to form the training sample for training the CNN classification model. This is a typical supervised learning setting. To compensate the limit of in-domain data size, we use *word2vec* (Mikolov et al., 2013) to learn the word embedding from a large amount of general-domain data. Together with the labeled data, these word embed-

dings are fed to the convolution layer as additional input to train the final classification model. This is a semi-supervised framework. The learned models are then used to classify each sentence in the general-domain training data based on their domain relevance score. The top N sentence pairs are selected to train the SMT system. We carry out experiments on 4 different language directions with 9-15M sentence pairs in each direction. The test domains include short message (sms), tweets, and Facebook posts. The experimental results show that our method is able to select a small amount of training data that is used to create a system which outperforms baseline systems trained with all the general-domain data. For example, we obtain over 3.1 BLEU improvement on the Chinese-to-English sms task with around 3% of the whole training data. Experiments also show that we can reduce the size of the in-domain sample to around 100 sentences and still obtain a 2.1 BLEU improvement.

2 Related Work

2.1 SMT adaptation techniques

Domain adaptation to SMT systems has recently received considerable attention. Based on the availability of in-domain bilingual or monolingual training data, there are several adaptation scenarios. Different domain adaptation techniques, including self-training, data selection, data weighting, etc., have been developed for different scenarios.

Self-training (Ueffing and Ney, 2007; Schwenk, 2008; Bertoldi and Federico, 2009) uses general-domain bilingual parallel data and in-domain monolingual data. An MT system is first trained on bilingual general-domain data, then it is used to translate in-domain monolingual data. The resulting target sentences or bilingual sentence pairs are then used as additional training data for language model or translation model training.

Some early data selection approaches (Zhao et al., 2004; Lü et al., 2007; Moore and Lewis, 2010) use in-domain monolingual data to select monolingual or bilingual data that are similar to the in-domain data according to some criterion. The state-of-the-art data selection approaches (Axelrod et al., 2011; Duh et al., 2013; Axelrod et al., 2015) search for bilingual parallel sentences using the difference in language model perplexity between two language models trained on in-domain and out-domain data, respectively.

Data weighting approaches weight each data item according to its relevance to the in-domain data. Mixture model adaptation (Foster and Kuhn, 2007; Foster et al., 2010; Sennrich, 2012; Foster et al., 2013) assumes that the general-domain data can be clustered to several sub-corpora, with some parts that are not too far from test domain. It combines sub-models trained on different sub-corpus data sets linearly or log-linearly with different weights. Vector space model adaptation (Chen et al., 2013) has the same assumption, and it weights each phrase pair based on vector space model (VSM). (Chen et al., 2014) improved the VSM adaptation by extending it to distributed VSM and grouped VSM. Instance weighting adopts a rich set of features to compute weights for each instance in the training data; it can be applied to sentence pairs (Matsoukas et al., 2009) or phrase pairs (Foster et al., 2010).

If in-domain comparable data are available, (Daume III and Jagarlamudi, 2011; Irvine et al., 2013) propose mining translations from the comparable data to translate out-of-vocabulary (OOV) words and capture new senses for the new test domains. (Dou and Knight, 2012; Zhang and Zong, 2013) learn bilingual lexical or phrase tables from in-domain monolingual data with a decipherment method, then incorporate them into the SMT system.

All the above approaches assume that either there is an in-domain (mono-lingual, parallel, or comparable) data set with a reasonable size available, or that some sub-corpora are closer to the test domain than others. There is no previous work considering the scenario where only a tiny amount of in-domain data is available: this is the scenario we address in this paper.

2.2 CNNs for text classification

In a text classification task, key phrases (or n-grams) can help in determining the class of the text, regardless of their locations in the text. For example, the word "desktop" in a sentence may indicate this sentence has computers as its topic; the phrase "not satisfactory" may indicate that the sentiment of the entire sentence is negative. This kind of strong local information about the class of a text can appear in different regions in the input. Convolutional neural networks are useful for text classification because convolutional and pooling layers allow the model to find such local indicators, wherever they are in the text.

Recently, CNNs have shown promising results on many text classification tasks, such as sentiment analysis (Kalchbrenner et al., 2014; Kim, 2014), topic and sentiment classification (Johnson and Zhang, 2015a; Johnson and Zhang, 2015b), paraphrase identification (Yin and Schütze, 2015), entity relation type classification (Zeng et al., 2014; dos Santos et al., 2015), short-text classification (Wang et al., 2015), event extraction and detection (Chen et al., 2015; Nguyen and Grishman, 2015), question understanding and answering (Dong et al., 2015), and box-office prediction based on reviews (Bitvai and Cohn, 2015).

Within the CNN architecture, people also use word embeddings for text classification. (Kalchbrenner et al., 2014) proposes a CNN framework with multiple convolution layers, with latent, dense and low-dimensional word embeddings as inputs. (Kim, 2014) defines a one-layer CNN architecture with comparable performance to (Kalchbrenner et al., 2014). The word embeddings input to the CNN can be pre-trained, and treated as fixed input, or tuned for a specific task. (Johnson and Zhang, 2015b) extends their "one-hot" CNN in (Johnson and Zhang, 2015a) to take region embeddings trained on unlabeled data as CNN input. CNNs that input word embeddings trained on unlabeled data are considered to be semi-supervised CNNs.

3 Semi-supervised CNN

A CNN is a feed-forward network consisting of convolutional and pooling layers. Each neuron in the convolutional layer of a CNN processes a segment of input signals, which could be a region in an image or a window of words in a sentence. The convolution layer consists of a set of kernels that compute the dot product between different segments of the input. The kernel associated with the l-th segment of the input x computes:

$$\sigma(\mathbf{W} \cdot \mathbf{w}_l(\mathbf{x}) + \mathbf{b}), \qquad (1)$$

where $\mathbf{w}_l(\mathbf{x}) \in \mathbf{R}^q$ is the input window vector that represents the l-th segment of data. Weight matrix $\mathbf{W} \in \mathbf{R}^{m \times q}$ and bias vector $\mathbf{b} \in \mathbf{R}^m$ are shared by all the kernels in the same layer, and are learned during the training process.

Because the convolution kernel allows interaction between different parts of the input, it reduces the requirement to select features by hand. Important features in a sentence are automatically selected with pooling, which is a form of non-linear down-sampling. It takes the maximum or the average value observed in each of the d dimension vectors over different windows. As a result, information from multiple d dimension vectors is kept in a single d dimensional vector. At training time, both the weight vectors and the bias vectors are learned with stochastic gradient ascent.

3.1 One-hot CNN

When applying CNN to NLP tasks, the first layer of the network takes word embeddings as input. Word embeddings can be pre-trained using tools such as $word2vec$ (Mikolov et al., 2013) or $GloVe$ (Pennington et al., 2014), in which case a table lookup is enough. Alternatively, these vectors can be learned from scratch as a step in the network training process. When there are enough in-domain data, training in-domain word embeddings is meaningful. However, when the in-domain data are limited, the word embeddings learned from these data are unreliable. In this case, the input sentence x can be represented with one-hot vectors where each vector's length is the vocabulary size, value 1 at index i indicates word i appears in the sentence, and 0 indicates its absence. A CNN with one-hot vector input is called "one-hot CNN" (Johnson and Zhang, 2015a). $w_l(x)$ can be either a concatenation of one-hot vectors, in which the order of concatenation is the same as the word order in the sentence, or it can be a bag-of-word/n-gram vector. The bag-of-word (BOW) representation loses word order information but is more robust to data sparsity. In (Johnson and Zhang, 2015a), a CNN whose input being BOW representation is called bow-CNN while input with concatenation of vectors is called seq-CNN. The window size and stride (distance between the window centers) are meta-parameters. σ in Equation 1 is a component-wise non-linear function such as ReLU. Thus, each kernel generates an m-dimensional vector where m is the number of weight vectors or neurons. These vectors from all the windows of each sentence are aggregated by the pooling layer, by either component-wise maximum (max pooling) or average (average pooling), then used by the top layer as features for classification.

3.2 Semi-supervised CNN

Although the size of the in-domain data is normally small, the unlabeled data from general domains are much larger and easier to obtain. To exploit large amounts of unlabeled data, we adopt a semi-supervised learning framework similar to (Johnson and Zhang, 2015b). It first learns word embedding from unlabeled data, then generates the text segment embedding based on these unsupervised word embeddings. Both the one-hot vectors from the labeled data and the segment embeddings from unlabeled data are combined to train the CNN classifier.

The word embeddings map each word to a real-valued, dense vector (Bengio et al., 2003). Word embeddings are often learned with an unsupervised learning paradigm: each dimension of the continuous word embeddings aims at capturing a latent feature, reflecting certain syntactic and semantic meanings of the word. A widely used approach for generating useful word embeddings was proposed in (Mikolov et al., 2013). This method learns the word embeddings such that the likelihood of generating a word based on its contexts (or generating the context of a given word, aka "skip-gram" model) is maximized. It speeds up the training with the hierarchical softmax strategy and a simplified learning objective, which scales very well to very large training corpora. We adopt the skip-gram model, which intuitively learns a classifier that predicts words conditioned on the central word's vector representation. An advantage of such distributed representations is that words that have similar contexts, and therefore similar syntactic and semantic properties, will tend to be near one another in the low-dimensional vector space.

Given the word embeddings trained from unlabeled data, a sentence is represented as a sequence of d-dimensional vectors, which is the input to a convolution network that generates feature vectors for each text segment. The segment vectors and one-hot vectors are fed into another convolution layer, which outputs the classification labels. The second network is trained with the labeled in-domain/out-domain data. Therefore, Equation 1 is replaced with:

$$\sigma(\mathbf{W} \cdot \mathbf{w}_l(x) + \mathbf{V} \cdot \mathbf{u}_l(x) + \mathbf{b}), \qquad (2)$$

where $\mathbf{w}_l(x)$ is the one-hot vector obtained from segment l in a sentence, and $\mathbf{u}_l(x)$ is the embedding learned from the unlabeled data (general domain training data), applied to the same segment. We train this model with the labeled data. We update the weights W, V, bias b, and the top-layer parameters so that the loss function is minimized on the labeled training data.

4   Adaptation based on data selection

We use the in-domain data from the translation task as positive samples, and randomly select the same number of sentences from the general domain data as negative samples. We train the CNN model on the positive and negative samples with the one-hot CNN or semi-supervised CNN described previously. The trained CNN model is then used to classify the sentence pairs in the general domain data. The sentence pairs with high in-domain scores are selected to train the machine translation system.

We classify the source sentence and target sentences separately. The CNN model computes two scores for each sentence pair. The sentence pairs are selected based on the source scores, target scores or the sum of source and target scores (Moore and Lewis, 2010). Experiments show that selection based on the sum of the source and target scores achieves the best performance. We empirically determine the number of selected in-domain sentences for each MT system based on experimental results on a separate validation set.

When selecting the negative samples, we either randomly sample from the whole data pool, or select from the sentences which have been labeled as negative in the first round classification. Additional experiments show that the results from these two methods are very similar, so we sample the negative samples from the whole general domain for simplicity.

5   Experiments

Our goal is to adapt the MT system when only a tiny amount of in-domain data is available. So in our experiments, we did not consider any domain information about the training data, such as the source of each corpus. What we have is a small development set (dev) and one or more test sets (test) which are in the same domain.

5.1   Data setting

We carried out experiments in four different data settings. All four have large amounts of bilingual training data: 9-15M sentences. The first two involve translation into English (en) from Chinese (zh) and Arabic (ar), while the last two involve translation from English to Spanish (es) and Chinese. The training data are all publicly available, either from LDC,[1] and transcriptions of TED talks[2] where the data are the mixture of newswire, web crawl, UN proceedings and TED talks, etc., or from WMT,[3] where the data are the mixture of Europarl, web crawl, news-commentary, UN proceedings, etc. The dev and test sets are "short messages (sms)" for the first task, which are also available from LDC; "tweets" for the second task; publicly available "Facebook post" for the remaining two tasks. The last three tasks are from social media - an intriguing new area of application for MT - where in-domain parallel training data are seldom publicly available. Table 1 summarizes the statistics of the training, dev, and test data for all the test sets.

5.2   Experiment setup

We experiment with two CNN-based data selection strategies:

1. ohcnn: Data selection by supervised one-hot CNN (Section 3.1)

2. sscnn: Data selection by semi-supervised CNN (Section 3.2)

We employ the dev set as in-domain data. All the supervised CNN models are trained with the in-domain dev data as positive examples and an equal number of randomly selected general-domain sentences as negative examples. All the meta-parameters of the CNN are tuned on held-out data; we generate both *bow*-regions and *seq*-regions and input them to the CNN. We set the region size to 5 and stride size to 1. The non-linear function we chose is "ReLU", the number of weight vectors or neurons is 500. The pooling method is component-wise maximum (max pooling). We use the online available CNN toolkit *conText*.[4] To train the general domain word embedding, we used *word2vec*.[5] The size of the vector was set to 300. We also generate word-embedding-based *bow*-regions and *seq*-regions as additional input to the CNN.

---

[1] https://catalog.ldc.upenn.edu/
[2] https://wit3.fbk.eu/
[3] http://statmt.org/wmt15/
[4] http://riejohnson.com/cnn_download.html
[5] https://code.google.com/archive/p/word2vec/

language	zh2en	ar2en	en2es	en2zh
test domain	sms	tweets	facebook	facebook
train origin	LDC&TED	LDC&TED	WMT	LDC&TED
train size	12.20M	8.97M	15.23M	12.20M
dev size	6,016	1,000	800	650
test size	3,282	1,500	3,378	3,343

Table 1: Summary of the data. "sms" means "short message". "facebook" means "Facebook post". Data is given as the number of sentence pairs, "M" represents "million". The tasks "zh2en" and "en2zh" use the same training data.

We compared with four baselines for each task. The first baseline SMT system is trained using all general-domain data. The other three systems are trained with data selected with different LM-based data selection methods as same as in (Duh et al., 2013).[6] The four baselines are:

1. alldata: All general-domain data.

2. ngram: Data selection by 3-gram LMs with Witten-Bell [7] smoothing (Axelrod et al., 2011)

3. rnnlm: Data selection by recurrent neural network LM, with the RNNLM Toolkit (Duh et al., 2013)

4. comblm: Data selection by the combined LM using ngram & rnnlm (equal weight) (Duh et al., 2013).

All systems are trained with a standard phrase-based SMT system with standard settings, i.e., GIZA++ alignment, phrase table Kneser-Ney smoothing, hierarchical reordering models, target side 4-gram language model, "gigaword" 5-gram language model for systems with English as the target language, etc.

5.3 Experimental results

We evaluated the system using BLEU (Papineni et al., 2002) score on the test set. Following (Koehn, 2004), we use the bootstrap resampling test to do significance testing. Table 2 summarizes the results and numbers of the selected sentences for each task. First, we can see that all the data selection methods improved the performance over the baseline "alldata" with much less

training data (only around 2.5% to 10% of the whole training data). Consistent with (Duh et al., 2013), the three LM based data selection all got improvements, where "rnnlm" obtained better performance than the "ngram" on average. It is not clear that combining the two language model methods ("comblm") yields further improvement. While the one-hot CNN method "ohcnn" obtained similar improvement as the three LM-based methods on average. The semi-supervised CNN (sscnn) achieved the best performance for all the tasks: its improvements over the "alldata" baseline are 3.1, 1.4, 0.7 and 1.4 BLEU score respectively. It beats "ohcnn" by about 0.5 BLEU point on average.

There are two results worth noticing. First, task 1 (zh2en sms task) obtained very high BLEU improvement through data selection. This is because in this task, there is a 120K in-domain subset within the general-domain data. If we train a system on this in-domain data set, we get 25.7 BLEU on the test set. The LM-based methods did not beat this "in-domain data only (indata)" baseline, while the semi-supervised CNN method performed significantly better than this baseline at $p < 0.05$ level. In the top 300K selected sentence pairs, LM-based methods can select around 90K out of 120K in-domain sentence pairs, while both "ohcnn" and "sscnn" can select around 105K in-domain sentence pairs. This demonstrates the effectiveness of the proposed approach. Second, for the other three tasks, there is no in-domain data component in the general-domain data (that we know of). Even in this case, we achieved up to 1.4 BLEU improvement, which also demonstrates the effectiveness of our method: it can select highly suitable in-domain sentences, even when the in-domain data is very limited.

In our second experiment, we examine how many labeled samples are needed to train a strong CNN classifier to select the MT training in-domain

---

[6]The code and scripts for the three baselines are available at http://cl.naist.jp/ kevinduh/a/acl2013/.

[7]For small amounts of data, Witten-Bell smoothing had performed better than Kneser-Ney smoothing in our experiments.

	zh2en		ar2en		en2es		en2zh	
	#sent	BLEU	#sent	BLEU	#sent	BLEU	#sent	BLEU
alldata	12.2M	22.9	8.9M	17.6	15.2M	26.8	12.2M	10.0
ngram	300K	25.3**	800K	18.2**	1600K	26.9	400K	10.5*
rnnlm	300K	25.6**	800K	18.4**	1600K	27.0	400K	10.5*
comblm	400K	25.7**	800K	18.4**	1400K	27.0	500K	10.4*
ohcnn	300K	25.3**	700K	18.2*	1200K	27.1*	400K	11.0**+
sscnn	300K	26.0**+	700K	19.0**++	1300K	27.5**++	300K	11.4**++

Table 2: Summary of the results. Data size is given as number of sentence pairs. The number of selected in-domain sentences is determined by the performance on held-out data. "M" represents million, "K" represents thousand. */** means result is significantly better than the "alldata" baseline at $p < 0.05$ or $p < 0.01$ level, respectively. +/++ means result is significantly better than the best LM-based method at $p < 0.05$ or $p < 0.01$ level, respectively.

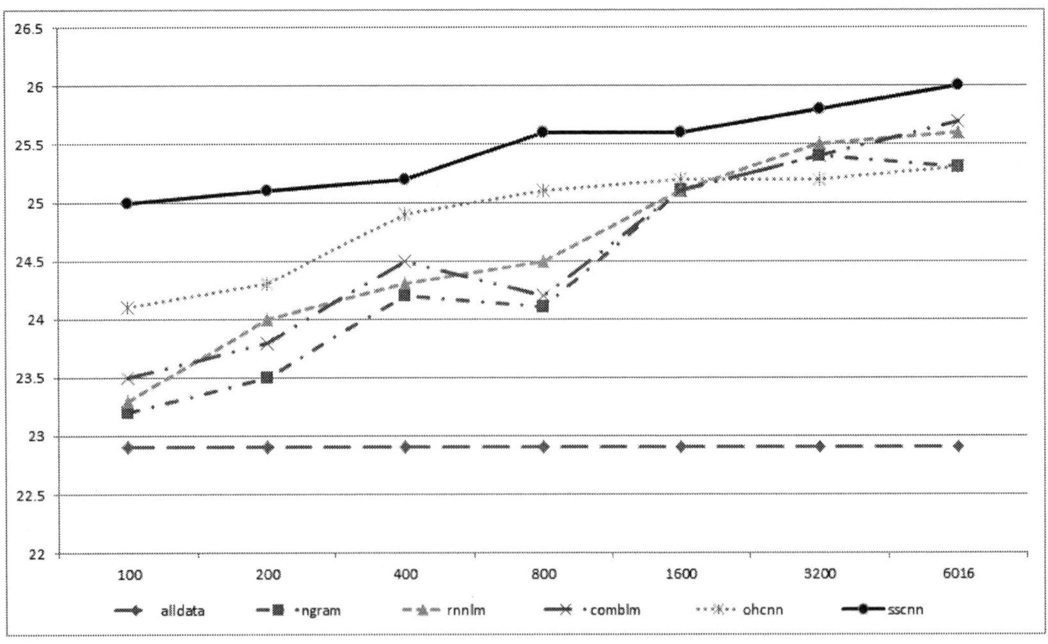

Figure 1: The performance on zh2en sms task with different numbers of in-domain sentences to train LM-based vs. CNN-based classifiers, which are then used to select 300K sentence pairs for MT system training. X-axis is the number of in-domain sentences, Y-axis is BLEU score.

data. Fixing the number of MT training sentence pairs to 300K that will be selected by the CNN, we reduce the CNN training data from 6,000 down to 100 sentence pairs in steps. The performance of the resulting MT systems for all five data selection methods is shown in Figure 1.

From Figure 1, we can see that all the data selection methods obtained improvement compared to the "alldata" baseline. When the in-domain training sample is more than 1600 sentence pairs, all the data selection methods obtain reasonable and comparable improvement, while "sscnn" is better than the best LM-based method by 0.3-0.5 BLEU. However, when the in-domain training sample is less than 800 sentence pairs, the difference between the "sscnn" and other methods gets bigger, and CNN-based methods get more stable results than the LM-based methods get. For instance, when the in-domain set increases from 400 to 800, the LM-based methods did not get an improvement; "ngram" and "comblm" even got a small loss on BLEU score. When the in-domain sample is reduced to 100 sentence pairs, the LM-based methods only get a small improvement over the baseline, while the "ohcnn" got a 1.2 BLEU score improvement over the baseline and "sscnn" got a 2.1 BLEU improvement over the baseline. Thus, even if we have no domain knowledge about the training data, when we have only 100 sentences in the test domain, the semi-supervised CNN classifier can still select a good in-domain subset and achieve good performance.

We obtained 2.1 BLEU improvement even when we randomly select only 100 in-domain sentence pairs to train the classification model. Is this just because we luckily sampled a good part of the in-domain data? We repeated the "100 in-domain sentence pairs experiment" three times for our most effective method - "sscnn" - by sampling three different in-domain sets from the whole 6,016-sentence dev set. The average BLEU score we got is 25.03, and the standard deviation is 0.12. This means that our algorithm is quite stable even when the in-domain set is very small.

5.4 Discussion

Why do semi-supervised convolutional neural networks perform so well for data selection? We think there are two main reasons. The first one is that convolution captures the important domain information of the words in the window, and

the max-pooling operation combines the vectors which, as a result, focuses on the most important "features" in the sentence. Even a highly domain-specific sentence normally contains both domain-specific words and general-domain words. For example, in *"I have a Dell desktop and a Macbook laptop"*, the words *"Dell, laptop, Macbook, laptop"* are from the computer domain, while the words *"I, have, a, and"* are general. However, the topic of this sentence is decided by the domain specific words, not the general-domain words. If the properties of the words *"Dell, laptop, Macbook, laptop"* are kept and highlighted, classification will be more accurate for this sentence. The second reason is the use of word embedding learned from the whole general-domain data. A very important advantage of word embedding is that words that have similar meaning will tend to be grouped together in the vector space. If the word *"Lenovo"* in the test sentence is not seen in the labeled data, it would be difficult for LM-based models to classify sentences like *"I prefer choosing a Lenovo machine"* as computer-domain sentence. However, the word embeddings learned from much larger unlabeled data ensure that the word embedding of *"Lenovo"* is close to that of *"Dell"*. According to the domain of its neighbor words, the CNN model can still label this sentence as belonging to the computer domain. This property is particularly useful for fast or fine grained adaptation, where obtaining large amount of in-domain samples may be slow or too expensive.

6 Conclusions and future work

Domain adaptation with only a tiny amount of in-domain data is a hard problem. In this paper, we proposed to use a semi-supervised CNN to train the domain classification model, then use the CNN to select the data which is most similar to the test domain. Experiments on large data condition SMT tasks showed that this outperforms state-of-the-art language-model-based data selection methods significantly. Particularly when the size of the in-domain data is small, semi-supervised CNN classifier can still select in-domain bilingual sentences to train an adapted SMT system. In future work, we plan to 1) apply this approach to select the data from large size target language corpus for language model training; 2) use the source sentences of the test set to select the data for online dynamic adaptation.

References

Amittai Axelrod, Xiaodong He, and Jianfeng Gao. 2011. Domain adaptation via pseudo in-domain data selection. In *EMNLP 2011*.

Amittai Axelrod, Philip Resnik, Xiaodong He, and Mari Ostendorf. 2015. Data selection with fewer words. In *Proceedings of the Tenth Workshop on Statistical Machine Translation*, pages 58–65, Lisbon, Portugal, September.

Yoshua Bengio, Réjean Ducharme, Pascal Vincent, and Christian Janvin. 2003. A neural probabilistic language model. *J. Mach. Learn. Res.*, 3:1137–1155, March.

Nicola Bertoldi and Marcello Federico. 2009. Domain adaptation for statistical machine translation with monolingual resources. In *Proceedings of the 4th Workshop on Statistical Machine Translation*, Athens, March. WMT.

Zsolt Bitvai and Trevor Cohn. 2015. Non-linear text regression with a deep convolutional neural network. In *Proceedings of the 53rd Annual Meeting of the Association for Computational Linguistics and the 7th International Joint Conference on Natural Language Processing (Volume 2: Short Papers)*, pages 180–185, Beijing, China, July.

Boxing Chen, Roland Kuhn, and George Foster. 2013. Vector space model for adaptation in statistical machine translation. In *Proceedings of the 51st Annual Meeting of the Association for Computational Linguistics (Volume 1: Long Papers)*, pages 1285–1293, Sofia, Bulgaria, August.

Boxing Chen, Roland Kuhn, and George Foster. 2014. A comparison of mixture and vector space techniques for translation model adaptation. In *Proceedings of AMTA*, Vancouver, Canada, Oct.

Yubo Chen, Liheng Xu, Kang Liu, Daojian Zeng, and Jun Zhao. 2015. Event extraction via dynamic multi-pooling convolutional neural networks. In *Proceedings of the 53rd Annual Meeting of the Association for Computational Linguistics and the 7th International Joint Conference on Natural Language Processing (Volume 1: Long Papers)*, pages 167–176, Beijing, China, July.

Hal Daume III and Jagadeesh Jagarlamudi. 2011. Domain adaptation for machine translation by mining unseen words. In *ACL 2011*.

Li Dong, Furu Wei, Ming Zhou, and Ke Xu. 2015. Question answering over freebase with multicolumn convolutional neural networks. In *Proceedings of the 53rd Annual Meeting of the Association for Computational Linguistics and the 7th International Joint Conference on Natural Language Processing (Volume 1: Long Papers)*, pages 260–269, Beijing, China, July.

Cicero dos Santos, Bing Xiang, and Bowen Zhou. 2015. Classifying relations by ranking with convolutional neural networks. In *Proceedings of the 53rd Annual Meeting of the Association for Computational Linguistics and the 7th International Joint Conference on Natural Language Processing (Volume 1: Long Papers)*, pages 626–634, Beijing, China, July.

Qing Dou and Kevin Knight. 2012. Large scale decipherment for out-of-domain machine translation. In *Proceedings of the 2012 Joint Conference on Empirical Methods in Natural Language Processing and Computational Natural Language Learning*, pages 266–275, Jeju Island, Korea, July.

Kevin Duh, Graham Neubig, Katsuhito Sudoh, and Hajime Tsukada. 2013. Adaptation data selection using neural language models: Experiments in machine translation. In *Proceedings of the 51st Annual Meeting of the Association for Computational Linguistics (Volume 2: Short Papers)*, pages 678–683, Sofia, Bulgaria, August.

George Foster and Roland Kuhn. 2007. Mixture-model adaptation for SMT. In *Proceedings of the ACL Workshop on Statistical Machine Translation*, Prague, June. WMT.

George Foster, Cyril Goutte, and Roland Kuhn. 2010. Discriminative instance weighting for domain adaptation in statistical machine translation. In *Proceedings of the 2010 Conference on Empirical Methods in Natural Language Processing (EMNLP)*, Boston.

George Foster, Boxing Chen, and Roland Kuhn. 2013. Simulating discriminative training for linear mixture adaptation in statistical machine translation. In *MT Summit*, Nice, France.

Ann Irvine, Chris Quirk, and Hal Daumé III. 2013. Monolingual marginal matching for translation model adaptation. In *Proceedings of the 2013 Conference on Empirical Methods in Natural Language Processing*, pages 1077–1088, Seattle, Washington, USA, October.

Rie Johnson and Tong Zhang. 2015a. Effective use of word order for text categorization with convolutional neural networks. In *Proceedings of the 2015 Conference of the North American Chapter of the Association for Computational Linguistics: Human Language Technologies*, pages 103–112, Denver, Colorado, May–June.

Rie Johnson and Tong Zhang. 2015b. Semi-supervised convolutional neural networks for text categorization via region embedding. In C. Cortes, N. D. Lawrence, D. D. Lee, M. Sugiyama, and R. Garnett, editors, *Advances in Neural Information Processing Systems 28*, pages 919–927. Curran Associates, Inc.

Nal Kalchbrenner, Edward Grefenstette, and Phil Blunsom. 2014. A convolutional neural network for modelling sentences. In *Proceedings of the 52nd*

Annual Meeting of the Association for Computational Linguistics (Volume 1: Long Papers), pages 655–665, Baltimore, Maryland, June.

Yoon Kim. 2014. Convolutional neural networks for sentence classification. *CoRR*, abs/1408.5882.

Philipp Koehn. 2004. Statistical significance tests for machine translation evaluation. In *Proceedings of the 2004 Conference on Empirical Methods in Natural Language Processing (EMNLP)*, Barcelona, Spain.

Alex Krizhevsky, Ilya Sutskever, and Geoffrey E. Hinton. 2012. Imagenet classification with deep convolutional neural networks. In F. Pereira, C. J. C. Burges, L. Bottou, and K. Q. Weinberger, editors, *Advances in Neural Information Processing Systems 25*, pages 1097–1105. Curran Associates, Inc.

Yann LeCun and Yoshua Bengio. 1998. Convolutional networks for images, speech, and time series. In Michael A. Arbib, editor, *The Handbook of Brain Theory and Neural Networks*, pages 255–258. MIT Press, Cambridge, MA, USA.

Yajuan Lü, Jin Huang, and Qun Liu. 2007. Improving Statistical Machine Translation Performance by Training Data Selection and Optimization. In *Proceedings of the 2007 Conference on Empirical Methods in Natural Language Processing (EMNLP)*, Prague, Czech Republic.

Spyros Matsoukas, Antti-Veikko I. Rosti, and Bing Zhang. 2009. Discriminative corpus weight estimation for machine translation. In *Proceedings of the 2009 Conference on Empirical Methods in Natural Language Processing (EMNLP)*, Singapore.

Tomáš Mikolov, Martin Karafiát, Lukáš Burget, Jan Černocký, and Sanjeev Khudanpur. 2010. Recurrent neural network based language model. In *Proceedings of the 11th Annual Conference of the International Speech Communication Association (INTERSPEECH2010)*, pages 1045–1048. International Speech Communication Association.

Tomas Mikolov, Kai Chen, Greg Corrado, and Jeffrey Dean. 2013. Efficient estimation of word representations in vector space. *CoRR*, abs/1301.3781.

Robert C. Moore and William Lewis. 2010. Intelligent selection of language model training data. In *ACL 2010*.

Thien Huu Nguyen and Ralph Grishman. 2015. Event detection and domain adaptation with convolutional neural networks. In *Proceedings of the 53rd Annual Meeting of the Association for Computational Linguistics and the 7th International Joint Conference on Natural Language Processing (Volume 2: Short Papers)*, pages 365–371, Beijing, China, July.

Kishore Papineni, Salim Roukos, Todd Ward, and Wei-Jing Zhu. 2002. BLEU: A method for automatic evaluation of Machine Translation. In *Proceedings of the 40th Annual Meeting of the Association for Computational Linguistics (ACL)*, pages 311–318, Philadelphia, July. ACL.

Jeffrey Pennington, Richard Socher, and Christopher D. Manning. 2014. Glove: Global vectors for word representation. In *Empirical Methods in Natural Language Processing (EMNLP)*, pages 1532–1543.

Holger Schwenk. 2008. Investigations on large-scale lightly-supervised training for statistical machine translation. In *IWSLT 2008*.

Rico Sennrich. 2012. Perplexity minimization for translation model domain adaptation in statistical machine translation. In *EACL 2012*.

Nicola Ueffing and Hermann Ney. 2007. Word-level confidence estimation for machine translation. *Computational Linguistics*, 33(1):9–40.

Peng Wang, Jiaming Xu, Bo Xu, Chenglin Liu, Heng Zhang, Fangyuan Wang, and Hongwei Hao. 2015. Semantic clustering and convolutional neural network for short text categorization. In *Proceedings of the 53rd Annual Meeting of the Association for Computational Linguistics and the 7th International Joint Conference on Natural Language Processing (Volume 2: Short Papers)*, pages 352–357, Beijing, China, July.

Keiji Yasuda, Ruiqiang Zhang, Hirofumi Yamamoto, and Eiichiro Sumita. 2008. Method of selecting training data to build a compact and ef?cient translation model. In *International Joint Conference on Natural Language Processing*.

Wenpeng Yin and Hinrich Schütze. 2015. Convolutional neural network for paraphrase identification. In *Proceedings of the 2015 Conference of the North American Chapter of the Association for Computational Linguistics: Human Language Technologies*, pages 901–911, Denver, Colorado, May–June.

Daojian Zeng, Kang Liu, Siwei Lai, Guangyou Zhou, and Jun Zhao. 2014. Relation classification via convolutional deep neural network. In *Proceedings of COLING 2014, the 25th International Conference on Computational Linguistics: Technical Papers*, pages 2335–2344, Dublin, Ireland, August. Dublin City University and Association for Computational Linguistics.

Jiajun Zhang and Chengqing Zong. 2013. Learning a phrase-based translation model from monolingual data with application to domain adaptation. In *Proceedings of the 51st Annual Meeting of the Association for Computational Linguistics (Volume 1: Long Papers)*, pages 1425–1434, Sofia, Bulgaria, August.

Bing Zhao, Matthias Eck, and Stephan Vogel. 2004. Language model adaptation for statistical machine translation with structured query models. In *Proceedings of the International Conference on Computational Linguistics (COLING) 2004*, Geneva, August.

Author Index

Association for Computational Linguistics
209 N. Eighth Street
Stroudsburg, Pennsylvania 18360

ISBN 978-1-5108-2756-1